Delaware & Hudson

Delaware & Hudson

"The D&H" *The history of an important railroad whose antecedent was a canal network to transport coal*

by **JIM SHAUGHNESSY**

SYRACUSE UNIVERSITY PRESS

> **FRONTISPIECE**
> Sleek locomotives in the English style with capped stacks, smooth boilers and "elephant ear" smoke lifters typified steam power on the D&H. Manville B. Wakefield has painted Pacific No. 605 speeding the *Laurentian* through West Waterford, New York.

Copyright© 1997 Syracuse University Press
Syracuse, New York 13244-5290

All Rights Reserved

First Syracuse University Press Edition 1997

24 25 26   7 6 5

Originally published in 1982 by Howell-North Books.

ISBN: 978-0-8156-0455-6 (paperback)

For a listing of books published and distributed by Syracuse University Press, visit https://press.syr.edu.

Library of Congress Cataloging-in-Publication Data

Shaughnessy, Jim.
    Delaware & Hudson : the history of an important railroad whose antecedent was a canal network to transport coal / by Jim Shaughnessy.
        p. cm.
    Originally published: San Diego, Calif. : Howell-North Books, 1982.
    Includes bibliographical references and index.
        ISBN 0-8156-0468-8 (cloth : alk. paper). - ISBN 0-8156-0455-6 (pbk. alk. paper)
    1. Delaware and Hudson Railroad Corporation. 2. Railroads-United States. I. Title.
TF25.D4S45 1997
385'. 0974--dc21   96-51168

To
MY MOTHER AND FATHER
MR. AND MRS. JAMES A. SHAUGHNESSY

Headed by a Northern type locomotive with "elephant ears", the Delaware & Hudson's southbound *Laurentian* roars through West Waterford, New York, on a crisp December day in 1952. *(Jim Shaughnessy)*

ACKNOWLEDGMENTS

Probably my greatest single regret after doing this book is that it couldn't be bigger. It is certainly impossible to tell all about an enterprise as long established as the Delaware & Hudson, so diverse, so rich in romance, history and accomplishment. Each day of its existence has been marked by at least something worth telling, whether it was a boatman overimbibing and falling into the canal, or a 10,000-ton coal train breaking in two on Ararat, and being started again with the aid of 10,800 roaring Diesel horsepower. A railroad, or any other institution for that matter, is more than wood and steel. It is people, each with a story to make or to tell. Unfortunately, it has been necessary to stick with the historical progression of events and the incidents associated with them in order to encompass the story in anything short of an encyclopedia.

The task of assembling this information, especially the illustrations, was not easy and never could have been accomplished at all without the generous help of many people. The illustrations give life to a work like this and without them it would be sterile indeed. I am most indebted to these friends for their interest and participation.

Manville B. Wakefield, artist, historian and author of the definitive history of the D&H Canal, *Coal Boats to Tidewater,* produced the original oil painting for the cover and a number of maps and pen-and-ink sketches. His knowledge and enthusiasm were contagious.

Miss Mildred Foley, head of the D&H printing and reproduction department, patiently sought innumerable original negatives from the D&H archives for the author to print, ranging in content from copies of early originals to marvelous builders' photos and details of Loree's famous locomotives. To her goes credit for the wealth of historical illustration contained herein.

Other D&H officials were most helpful and cooperative in obtaining various facts and data: Alan Dustin, assistant to the President; Walter Travis, motive power superintendent and his assistant, Robert Jenkins. Joe Mullin and Gerry Winters of the motive power department also helped greatly.

Gerald M. Best, dean of all railroad historians, made available his vast collection of illustrations and his store of fact and detail, for the enrichment of this project.

Maitland C. DeSormo has fortunately rescued from oblivion a portion of the work of S. R. Stoddard, the early photographer of the Adirondacks, and made it available to convey glimpses of early railroad and steamboat activity in northern New York.

Richard E. Cooper, a D&H fireman and spare engineer by vocation, is a tireless researcher of locomotive facts by avocation. He has spent many hours in the dusty file room at Colonie, preparing the comprehensive roster of D&H locomotives appearing in this volume.

David W. Messer provided valuable editorial assistance.

Mrs. James A. Shaughnessy, my mother, handled all the transcription, and my wife, Carol, was most encouraging and tolerant.

Photographers Robert F. Collins, Donald W. Furler and Dr. Philip R. Hastings were especially helpful in contributing many of their wonderful creations which added immeasurably to the recollection of the D&H during its glory days of steam.

All the following photographers, collectors and owners of rare prints have contributed greatly to this record as well. Without them it would be lean indeed:

Wallace W. Abbey; Adirondack Museum; John P. Ahrens; Association of American Railroads; Jean Banta; Gene Baxter; Francis Bayle; Beach collection, Oneonta Public Library; Arthur Bibb; Ed Bond; Roger Borrup; Hal Carstens; Edward O. Clark; Charles Clegg; Charles Clingman; Glyndon Cole, State University College at Plattsburgh.

Ladislav Dejnozska; Frank C. Dodge, Jr.; John Frisbee; John Gardiner; Al Gayer; Glens Falls Historical Society, Ralph Lapham; H. F. Haight; Warren Hamm; Dave Herbert; William Howell, Witherill Hotel, Plattsburgh; Industrial Photo Service; George King; Lake George Park Commission; Library of Congress, Detroit Photographic Corporation collection.

Morton MacDonald; Robert R. Malinoski; Mrs. Donald McCrea; James R. McFarlane; Don McLaughlin; Bill Middleton; H. Irving Moore; New York State Museum; A. M. Payne; John E. Pickett; Penfield Foundation, Eugene Barker; William P. Price; Rail Photo Service; Rensselaer County Historical Society; The Research Foundation of the State University of New York; Donald S. Robinson.

Fred Sankoff; Leonard Seton; Sherman Free Library at Port Henry, Mrs. Mary Clements; Silver Bay Association; Ned Spaulding; Perry Storm; Fred Thatcher; Allen Toohey, Canadian Railroad Historical Association collection; *Trains Magazine*, David P. Morgan, editor; Edwin R. Van Wormer; Don Wallworth; Howard Warren; Washington County Historian; Carl Wooley; S. S. Worthen; and J. J. Young, Jr.

My sincere gratitude and appreciation to all.

JIM SHAUGHNESSY

Troy, New York

November, 1967

CONTENTS

Chapter   Page

1. TOWPATH TO TIDEWATER 1

    The beginnings in anthracite . . . . The Wurts brothers . . . . Mr. Hone, the first president . . . . Canal construction . . . . Irish whisky on the rocks . . . . The grand opening . . . . Increasing traffic . . . . The first enlargement . . . . The second . . . . And finally the third . . . . Roebling's aqueducts . . . . The drop-gate . . . . Handwriting on the wall . . . . Trials and tribulations . . . . Life along the canal.

2. HORATIO AND THE LION 31

    The Gravity is born . . . . The first locomotive . . . . Horatio and the LION . . . . A fateful journey . . . . A sad ending . . . . The Gravity completed . . . . And extended . . . . And improved . . . . And extended again . . . . Passenger service . . . . The Gravity twins . . . . "The Old Gravity."

3. THE GREAT RAILROAD EXPANSION 59

    The D&H tries "flat" railroading again—now with success . . . . Mr. Olyphant takes the throttle . . . . Additional coal lands . . . . An arrangement with the Erie . . . . Rails to the north . . . . Connection to the Albany & Susquehanna . . . . Thomas Dickson assumes control . . . . Problems on the A&S . . . . The A&S becomes a partner . . . . Improvement and expansion . . . . Mr. Olyphant's report . . . . The Rensselaer & Saratoga joins the fold . . . . Passengers and prosperity . . . . The Adirondack Railroad . . . . A look to the future.

4. CHECKMATE MR. GOULD (The Albany & Susquehanna) 71

    Incorporation . . . . First construction . . . . Financial troubles . . . . Ramsey to the rescue . . . . The first train to Oneonta . . . . And finally Binghamton . . . . Enter the villains: Fisk and Gould . . . . Financial maneuvering . . . . Not-so-financial maneuvering . . . . The war is on! . . . . The Fisk forces retreat . . . . Back again . . . . The Ramsey cause upheld . . . . Exit Fisk and Gould . . . . The D&H takes over.

5. AN EMPIRE IN THE NORTH (The Rensselaer & Saratoga) 89

> The "Big Ditch" and the Mohawk & Hudson show the way . . . .
> The Saratoga & Schenectady . . . . The Davy Crockett . . . . Passengers and prosperity . . . . The Trojans' "Iron Horse" . . . . The Rensselaer & Saratoga . . . . Across the Hudson . . . . To Saratoga . . . . The R&S assumes control . . . . The Albany Northern . . . . Vermont soup . . . . Winner takes all . . . . *Fire!* . . . . More Vermont acquisitions . . . . And still more . . . . Expansion on to the lakes . . . . The D&H takes this one too . . . . The Saratoga & Whitehall . . . . The Rutland & Washington.

6. THROUGH THE MOUNTAINS—NOT AROUND THEM! 115
(The Adirondac Company)

> Iron! . . . . The Adirondac Iron & Steel Company . . . . Attempt at a railroad . . . . Enter Dr. Curant . . . . The Adirondac Company finally chartered . . . . Construction, and add the "k" . . . . The first train . . . . Money troubles . . . . New faces . . . . Forward . . . . To North Creek . . . . Item: repairs to locomotives, $3,477.21 . . . . More money troubles . . . . Tourists to the rescue . . . . The Doctor's son takes over . . . . The D&H makes another purchase.

7. NORTH TO CANADA (The New York & Canada Railroad) 135

> Headlines! . . . . Trackage in the north . . . . The Plattsburgh & Montreal . . . . The Montreal & Plattsburgh . . . . and the Whitehall & Plattsburgh . . . . Enter the Rutland . . . . Then the Vermont Central . . . . And finally the D&H . . . . Construction at last . . . . A notable journey . . . . "All aboard!" . . . . A dream fulfilled . . . . The Chateaugay & Lake Placid Railway.

8. A TIME TO BREAK DOWN AND A TIME TO BUILD UP 169

> Coal . . . . And connections . . . . A proposal . . . . Prosperity . . . . A death in the family . . . . A distinguished patron . . . . The nation mourns . . . . Saratoga the glorious . . . . A burden in Vermont . . . . A reluctant stockholder makes a sale . . . . A breaking down . . . . and a building up . . . . The end of an era.

9. BRANCHING OUT 197

> A famous passenger . . . . An urgent message . . . . Acquisition of the Chateaugay Ore & Iron Co. . . . . Branching out . . . . The Champlain Transportation Co. . . . . President Willcox and the electric lines . . . . Improvements . . . . The *Saratoga Limited* . . . . More branching out . . . . Into Canada . . . . More improvements . . . . A tight budget . . . . Enter Mr. Loree . . . . Out of the 19th century . . . into the 20th.

10. A SIDEWHEEL SAGA 231

  The white man discovers the lakes . . . . A scene of battle . . . . Early trade . . . . The *Vermont* — pioneer of a proud tradition . . . . The Champlain Transportation Co. . . . . The *Burlington* . . . . Epoch of the *Francis Saltus* . . . . The Lake George boats . . . . Sold to the Rutland & Burlington . . . . And repurchase . . . . The Champlain Company moves on to Lake George . . . . Enter the Rensselaer & Saratoga . . . . The North-South through route . . . . And finally the D&H . . . . Rail connections . . . . The *Ticonderoga* . . . . Steam goes down on the lakes . . . . Voyage to posterity.

11. THE REIGN OF L. F. LOREE 273

  The "Old Man" comes to the D&H . . . . New locomotives . . . . Longer trains . . . . New shops . . . . Labor troubles . . . . The D&H gets a new home . . . . The War . . . . And the U.S.R.A. . . . . More labor troubles . . . . The 100th anniversary . . . . Caboose No. 10 . . . . The HORATIO ALLEN . . . . End of the line for the electric railways . . . . Loree and "big mergers" . . . . Automatic train control . . . . The L. F. LOREE . . . . The "Monthly Plan" . . . . Red Edges . . . . Patriarch of the rails . . . . Remembered by all.

12. LOREE'S LOCOMOTIVES 317

  Heavier trains and more power . . . . The Consolidation, first of a long impressive line . . . . Upgrading the property . . . . Enter the Mallet . . . . Still more Consols . . . . The rebuilding program . . . . The tender booster . . . . Continuous innovation . . . . Stylish Pacifics . . . . The high pressure quartet: The HORATIO ALLEN . . . . The JOHN B. JERVIS . . . . The JAMES ARCHBALD . . . . and finally the L. F. LOREE . . . . Symbols of an era.

13. THE NEW ERA 347

  Nuelle and the new era . . . . Super power . . . . Increased bridge traffic . . . . More super power . . . . The "Old Man" finally succumbs . . . . The war brings a surge of traffic . . . . And passengers . . . . And titanium . . . . The first Diesel . . . . More Diesels . . . . Improvements . . . . The Diesel takes over . . . The last run for steam . . . . More improvements . . . . Mr. Nuelle retires . . . . The passenger decline . . . . Out of the coal business . . . . Second generation Diesels . . . . CTC . . . . Some comparisons . . . Increased efficiency through technology . . . . Merger possibilities . . . . Always remembered.

ALBUM 374

ROSTER 444

BIBLIOGRAPHY 471

INDEX 472

New York's Wall Street looked like this in the early 1800s. The Tontine Coffee House was in the building on the left with the balcony.

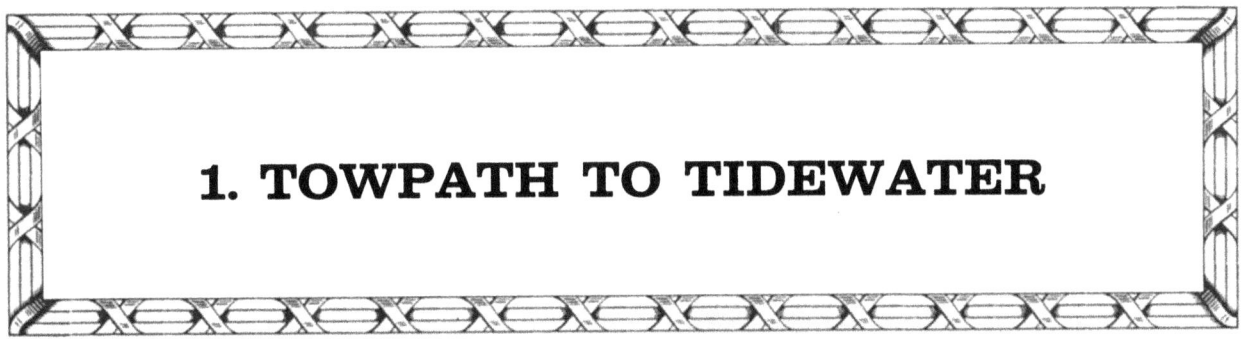

1. TOWPATH TO TIDEWATER

The glow of the Pennsylvania anthracite, burning with a blue flame in the huge fireplace of the Tontine Coffee House in New York, drove out the winter chill that blew in from the harbor outside. The congenial atmosphere of the establishment at the northwest corner of Wall and Water Streets, was enjoyed by a group of consequential gentlemen of finance and business who had gathered there on a bleak January day in 1825. They were duly impressed with the performance of this steadily burning, clean material.

Maurice and William Wurts, dry goods merchants from Philadelphia, had the coal shipped to New York for more than heating purposes. It was their hope to raise money for a canal to carry this coal cheaply out of the mine area of northern Pennsylvania to the Hudson River and New York. The glowing hearth must have warmed the hearts of the Wall Street barons, as well as their bodies, for by early afternoon they had oversubscribed the stock of the Delaware & Hudson Canal Co.

The Wurts brothers had often enjoyed the hunting and fishing of Wayne County in northeast Pennsylvania. In their travels through the woods they would frequently come upon outcroppings of black rock. This material, called stone coal by the local inhabitants, was in fact a rich anthracite coal. Over the years, beginning in 1814, they had acquired title to considerable properties which contained deposits of this hard coal at prices ranging from fifty cents to three dollars an acre, and were now interested in developing their investment.

Naturally, their first thought for a market was their home town of Philadelphia, and in the fall of 1822 they mined about a thousand tons of coal at Carbondale. During the following winter they hauled about 100 tons over the Moosic Mountains on sleds to the Lackawaxen River near Paupack Eddy, then on a raft to the Delaware River and eventually to Philadelphia. The selling price of coal was about ten dollars a ton but they found the Philadelphia market already adequately supplied with coal from the Lehigh coal fields through the Schuylkill Canal.

Another fact became readily apparent with respect to the rafting operation. For years raftloads of lumber, some containing as much as 20,000 board feet, were floated down the Lackawaxen and Delaware rivers, but in such cases the whole raft, cargo and all, would float. With a raftload of coal it was quite another story, and if they were ever going to do more than line the bottom of the Delaware River with coal they would have to find another method of transporting their product.

Maurice Wurts, during his many trips through the Delaware valley, became aware of the possibility of a canal being built to carry the product of their mines in both volume and safety. He explored the Lackawaxen and Delaware valleys and the valley of the Neversink, north of what is now Port Jervis. This was joined by a flat marshy area to the valley of Rondout Creek flowing to the Hudson at Kingston, and in total would provide a possible route for a canal that could open up the New York City market where the growing competition of the Lehigh coal fields would be eliminated.

Maurice made a rough survey of the valleys to satisfy both himself and his brothers that the route was feasible and in 1823 called Benjamin Wright to make a detailed appraisal of the route. Wright was then the principal engineer building

1

Maurice Wurts, a founder of the D&H.

After studying the route, Wright suggested digging a canal from Kingston to Carpenters Point, now called Port Jervis, then constructing nine dams on the Delaware and 17 more on the Lackawaxen to provide slack-water navigation on these rivers to a point near the mines. For awhile there was some consideration of a proposal to route the canal directly to New York from the Port Jervis area via a tunnel through the Shawangunk Mountains and then across northern New Jersey. This plan, although providing a more direct route, was without doubt financially unworkable.

In January, 1824, Wright and his associates completed their surveys and evaluations and proposed a canal four feet deep and 32 feet wide. This could be dug, they said, for $1,208,632.95, including a 5% cushion for unforeseen expenses.

The idea of putting dams across the Delaware and Lackawaxen rivers met vigorous opposition by

William Wurts, a founder of the D&H.

the famous Erie Canal and stood as high in the public esteem as any engineer in the United States.

Even before Wright's map was completed, the Pennsylvania Legislature on March 13, 1823, passed an act authorizing the Wurts brothers to canalize the Lackawaxen River. Six weeks later, on April 23, the New York lawmakers passed an act to incorporate an organization with the unusual name of "The President, Managers and Company of the Delaware & Hudson Canal Co." This legislation empowered the new enterprise to open water communication between the Delaware and Hudson rivers and conferred the right to purchase lands and transport "stone coal." Now things were beginning to move, because in those days before railroads, the popularity of canal building precipitated a spate of economic vigor that could rightfully be diagnosed as "canal fever."

the raftsmen who for decades had floated their lumber-laden rafts downstream without obstruction. If these dams were built, the burly whitewater sailors promised to blast every last one of them out of the valley. So, late in 1825, the dam idea was given up in favor of an independent canal system along the banks of each river.

It was now apparent that the Wurts brothers would need outside capital if they were to build this inland waterway, and they began to circulate copies of Wright's map in likely financial circles. Since New York City was the center of finance as well as the destination of their coal, it was logical that a possible source of funds might lie there.

A load of coal was therefore rafted down to Philadelphia late in 1824 where it was transshipped to New York aboard the sloop *Tripler*. On January 7, 1825 it burned brightly in a Tontine Coffee House hearth while the quill pens feverishly scratched the names of investors into the company's stock books. By two o'clock that afternoon all the shares available had been sold while at about the same time similar scenes were taking place at the Middle District Branch Bank in Kingston and the Orange County Bank in Goshen.

Nine weeks later, on March 8, at a meeting in the same establishment, the board of managers was chosen and they in turn designated 44-year-old Philip Hone the first president of the company three days later. Hone was one of the city's most prominent citizens, an astute businessman of considerable success and was soon to be Mayor of New York. His name lent substantial prestige to the company and the public's confidence in the enterprise was appreciably strengthened through his association with it.

In June the Lackawaxen Coal Mine and Navigation Co., the official name of the Wurts brothers' enterprise in the coal business thus far, was merged with the Delaware and Hudson Canal Co., allowing the whole operation from mine to market to be gathered into a single endeavor.

Now with the receipts from the stock sales, the real work of building a canal could begin. John B. Jervis, an associate of Benjamin Wright, took over the job early in 1825 and was soon officially appointed chief engineer. Jervis had gained vast experience under Wright during the building of the Erie Canal and would soon make an impressive

Philip Hone, first president of the D&H, 1825-1826, left that position when he was elected mayor of New York, but remained on the Board of Managers until 1851.

reputation for himself in both the canal and railroad fields.

By July 13, plans were developed to such a point that actual work could begin. On that day a large party gathered at a place midway between Wurtsboro and Ellenville near the little hamlet popularly known as Summitville but then officially called Beatysburg. Here, under sunny skies and to the roar of the cheering crowd, Philip Hone turned the first shovel of earth and the Delaware and Hudson Canal was under way.

The first section, formally contracted for a few weeks after Hone's groundbreaking act, was the 17-mile lock-free stretch later to be known as the Summit Level. Other sections were contracted for as the detailed surveys were completed and by December 6, the stretch from Eddy's Factory, now Eddyville, on the Rondout at tidewater to Mon-

John Bolton, second president of the D&H, 1826-1831.

gaup on the Delaware, over 60 miles, was under construction. Work continued through the winter and in the spring of 1826 construction was moving rapidly with 2500 men and 200 teams engaged in the Rondout and Summit sections alone. During the winter heavy frosts caused the cessation of earthwork operations but there was enough rock to keep almost everyone that was on the job in the fall busy through the winter.

It is difficult today to appreciate the problems of construction in bygone days, what with the fantastic machinery of the present. Earth-moving was done with pick and shovel; wagons and horse-drawn scrapers were used in places but rock work was the real problem. Holes were drilled by hand, black powder used as the explosive and the fuses were nightmares. A twisted piece of brown paper saturated with saltpeter and then dried was anything but dependable and many a "blower" lost a limb, or his life, when he crept back to a fuse that had fizzled.

The building of the canal through the wide, flat Rondout and Neversink valleys was relatively easy compared to the stretches along the rocky banks of the Delaware and Lackawaxen rivers. Here the mountains dropped abruptly to the solid rock banks in many places and blasting was necessary to carve out a niche for the canal bed.

These blasting operations, in addition to being slow, dangerous and costly, resulted in frequent and militant encounters between the Irish construction workers and the raftsmen on the Delaware, who resented the whole idea of the canal. To add to their irritation, the canal people were building a low dam across their river just below the mouth of the Lackawaxen. The raftsmen feared that the canal would rob water from the river and make rafting more difficult and possibly even replace their calling in time. There was no love lost between them and the "wild Irish" construction men.

The Irishmen, naturally, had a reputation for drinking and fully lived up to it. Whiskey cost fifty cents a gallon and most of the workers preferred it to water. When they saw a raft lobbing down the river they would set off a blast, if at all possible, just to aggravate the opposition. Rocks and dirt would shower down on the raftsmen and a battle was sure to ensue. The Irishmen fought with other laborers, lumbermen and even themselves, so it was a special treat when they took on the likes of the raftsmen.

On January 7, 1826, Philip Hone regretfully informed the Board of Managers that his recent election as Mayor of New York would require his resignation as president of the company. His fondness for public service made his new duties seem challenging but no more so than the post he was relinquishing. On January 21 when Hone submitted his resignation, John Bolton, treasurer of the company, was elected as the second president of the Delaware and Hudson Canal Co.

Work on the Delaware section was hindered during 1826 by wet weather and many items had to be deferred until the following season. In November of 1826 the last stone was placed in the tidewater lock at Eddyville with a colorful Masonic rite. On the summit level, water was let into the canal from the Neversink feeder but a light gravelly soil caused the canal bed to leak in many places. Aside from flooding adjacent fields it was difficult to keep a depth of water suitable for navigation, so a stiff clay, called puddle, had to be spread in the canal bed to render it watertight.

The most significant event of 1826 was the authorization by the Pennsylvania Legislature, on April 5th, to build a railroad from the coal beds at Carbondale over the Moosic Mountains to Honesdale. Originally the canal was to go all the way to the mines but further studies revealed it to be excessively costly and therefore impractical to build the canal over this 1200-foot natural barrier.

By midsummer in 1827, the canal was navigable from the Hudson to the Delaware and work on the remaining sections was progressing rapidly. Earlier in the year the company petitioned the State of New York for financial aid and with the urging of Governor DeWitt Clinton, a vigorous canal proponent himself, the legislature granted $500,000 in the form of State stock. A great amount of costly stone masonry work was required in both the Delaware and Lackawaxen valleys in order to build the canal bed along the edge of the rivers but up away from the usual ravages of spring floods.

On April 22, 1828 the canal actually began revenue operation when the company's toll collector at Eddyville issued a certificate showing the arrival of 15 boats and one raft. These shipments, probably cement and lumber, must have originated in the New York section of the waterway as the construction had not been completed on the upper end as yet. By early September, however, it became apparent that the canal could soon be opened throughout its entire length and on the 27th a celebration committee of three was appointed, consisting of President Bolton, former President Hone and Engineer R. F. Lord.

On October 16 the managers and their party cast off the lines of the *Orange Packet* and departed Rondout, bound for Honesdale, on what would be the first historic trip through the complete length of the canal. A great celebration was touched off with their arrival in Honesdale and the speeches foretold of the great promise the whole enterprise held for everyone. Actually, the future was exceptionally bright—far brighter than the most flowery orators even dreamed it could or would be.

The waterway was 108 miles long, contained 109 locks and held four feet of water between banks 36 feet apart at the water line—20 feet at the bottom—and could accommodate boats with up to 30 tons of cargo. It was carried across streams by stone or wooden aqueducts, but at the Delaware River crossing a dam provided a slackwater pool across which the boats were floated. It reached an elevation of 972.5 feet above tidewater at Honesdale with an average upward lift of 10 feet in all the 9x76-foot locks, excepting those descending from the summit level down to Port Jervis. The whole undertaking was completed in just about three years, not bad time for a project of such magnitude in the early 1800s.

Now that the speeches had been endured, the real work of the canal, moving coal to tidewater, could begin. Work was feverishly under way on the gravity railroad from the head of the canal at Honesdale over the Moosic Mountains to the mines but was far from completed. Enough coal had been laboriously hauled from the mines over a hastily built, rough and tortuous wagon road through Rix's Gap by late November to provide ten canal boats with a load of ten tons each. The history-making voyage to tidewater was led by a boat named *Superior* commanded by a Captain Hickson. As the little squadron moved through the canal a separate celebration would occur at almost every lock where toasts were drunk by boatmen and local residents. The trouble was, the boatmen had 109 locks to go through and a like number of celebrations to endure, where the lock tenders had only one each and by the time the flotilla neared Rondout the helmsmen were lucky if they could keep their boats in the canal at all. If it weren't for the temperance of the mules they might never have made it.

On December 5, 1828, the boats reached Rondout amid great celebration, musket fire and of course, more toasting. The Kingston band went up to Eddyville, boarded the *Superior* and rode down Rondout Creek with the fleet, playing all the way. At Rondout more speeches and predictions were heard while ten tons of the coal were hastily transferred to the sloop *Toleration*, destined for New York City to add fuel, in fact, to the wild-

John Wurts, third president of the D&H, 1831-1858.

fire expansion of the market for this new source of energy.

Honesdale was the scene of great activity throughout the winter of 1828 and on through most of 1829. Work was feverishly under way on the gravity railroad and hundreds of men and teams were hauling coal over the Rix's Gap wagon road from the mines at Carbondale. Work on the gravity line had not proceeded as rapidly as hoped and as a result only 7,000 tons of coal, that had been hauled over by wagon, were shipped through the canal in 1829. On October 8, however, the gravity line became operational and the first load of coal rolled down the hill into Honesdale. From that day on there was an ever-increasing amount of coal rolling over the hill and floating down through the valleys to tidewater.

In April of 1831, President Bolton submitted his resignation to the Board and John Wurts, brother of Maurice and William, founders of the company, was elected on the 13th to succeed him. There had been differences of opinion on questions of policy and expense between Bolton and the Wurts brothers and the health reasons given by the retiring president may have been more emotional than physical.

At 38 years of age, John Wurts was well prepared for his new job, although he had served as manager for only a month before his election as president. A Princeton graduate, he had served in the Pennsylvania Legislature and in Congress, and had always had a deep interest in his brothers' endeavors.

By 1841 it became apparent that the capacity of the canal would have to be expanded to meet the growing demand for coal. For several years the 30-ton capacity boats had been able to handle little more than ten tons, because it had been impossible to maintain the full four-foot depth of water in the canal's relatively new and porous earthwork. Gradually, however, the head could be increased to and maintained at the full four feet, so that the boats could carry their full 30 tons. Thus, for a time the coal-carrying capacity of the canal was able to keep up with the increasing demand, but now the limit had been reached and a change in design was necessary if it were to be increased further. Competition was beginning to increase somewhat and enlargement would permit movement of more coal at a lower cost and result in a more competitive price to the consumer.

The effects of the 1837 money panic were not felt by the canallers until the 1838 season and although severe, fortunately were short-lived. Only 76,321 tons of coal moved to tidewater compared to over 115,000 the previous year, but by the end of the 1839 boating season the total had reached a comfortable 122,300. Two years later with the quantity required for new applications of the fuel to iron-making and in the boilers of steamboats, an astounding 192,200 tons moved to market. With this staggering increase, along with the competitive advantage that would result, it was more than apparent that expansion of the canal's capacity was needed.

In September 1842 word went out from the managers and President Wurts to enlarge the canal. This was done by raising the sides with material removed from the bottom thereby allowing a depth of five feet of water in the channel,

On the steps of the company office at Honesdale in this 1884 scene, the gentleman sporting the top hat, left, is General Manager Coe F. Young; Canal Superintendent L. O. Rose, with the bowler, stands at the right. This building is now the museum of the Wayne County Historical Society. *(D&H collection)*

enough to support a boat carrying forty tons. The work was started as soon as the boating season of 1842 ended in November and continued through the winter until the opening of the 1843 season. It was not until the 1844 season that the job was finished, for navigation could not be held up in the process; moreover, the full five feet of water could not be let in immediately. By being disrupted during the reconstruction, the embankments and bottom of the canal required time to stabilize themselves again, so the additional foot of water had to be introduced gradually. The full benefit of the project therefore was not felt until the latter part of the 1845 season, at which time water enough could be maintained to allow loads of forty tons in the boats. The vast savings were so obvious at this point that the managers immediately started thinking about further improvements.

At the close of the 1845 season another project was initiated to increase the channel depth to 5½ feet, thereby allowing a load of 50 tons to be carried in each boat. This would be accomplished in the same manner as the previous deepening and took the same length of time—three seasons.

In their report of 1847 the managers noted that the enlargements had cost $232,000 and savings came to $300,000 already. More important, the seasonal capacity of the canal had been increased to 500,000 tons.

Coal sales had kept pace with the enlargement of the canal and with the prospect of other coal producers using the canal to forward their coal to market, it was decided in the fall of 1847 to enlarge the canal still further.

This next expansion would be on a colossal dimension as compared to the previous projects, involving a depth of six feet and widening the waterway to accommodate boats carrying 130 tons. This would necessitate rebuilding all the locks and aqueducts at an estimated cost of $1,105,000. After

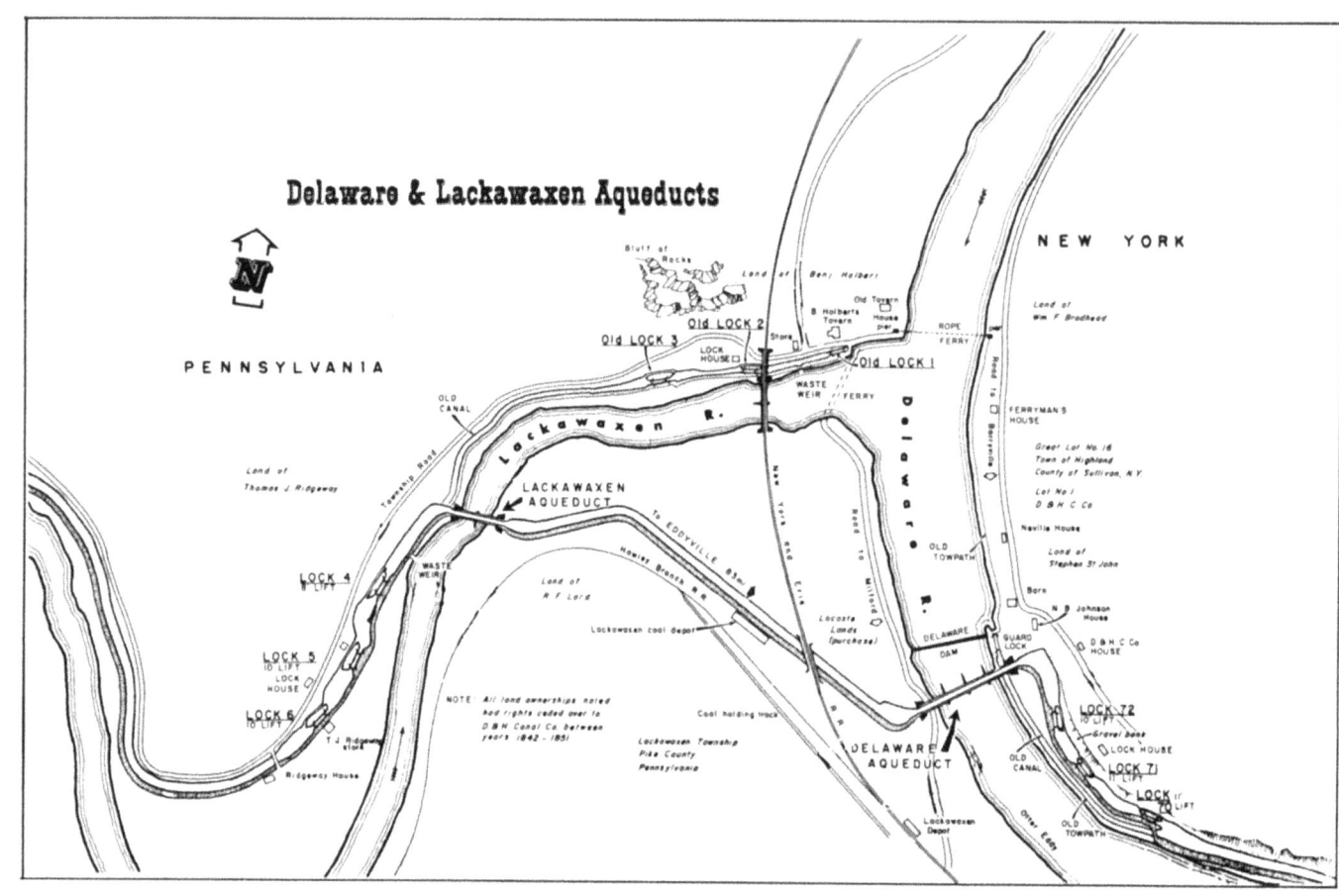

Map from *Coal Boats to Tidewater* by Manville B. Wakefield.

seeing the results of previous enlargements the managers authorized the project despite its cost, and suggested that it be started immediately so it could be substantially completed by the spring of 1850. Another advantage, in addition to expanding the annual capacity to one million tons, would be that the larger boats could be moved down the Hudson directly from the canal to New York City without requiring the time-consuming and costly handling at Rondout. By this over-all improvement it was estimated that freight costs could be reduced to 50 cents a ton.

Work got under way immediately. The sides of the canal were cut back considerably and laid up with dry stone walls to retain the soil and protect them from washing. Many of these walls are still to be found today. The locks were enlarged to 15x90 feet and two changes in the alignment were undertaken, one in the High Falls area and the other at the confluence of the Lackawaxen and Delaware rivers.

The High Falls change straightened out quite a winding section and allowed a better approach to the new aqueduct across Rondout Creek at that point. The Lackawaxen relocation was more extensive. Here the boats were floated across the Delaware in the slack-water pool formed by the low dam downstream from the mouth of the Lackawaxen. The boats would come out of the last lock on the Lackawaxen and would cross to the New York side on their momentum while the mules rode across the Delaware on a rope-operated ferryboat. On the opposite side they would re-enter the canal through a guard gate located downstream near the dam that formed the pool.

This operation was slow and uncertain at best and in times of high water was almost impossible. In addition to these natural problems there were the raftsmen who had disliked the canal from the beginning. Boats and rafts would collide, fights ensued, and damage to boats, rafts and men resulted. As the volume of traffic on the canal in-

The aqueduct over the Delaware River was serving the D&H Canal for its fiftieth season when this 1898 view was made, from the upstream New York end, looking toward Lackawaxen, Pennsylvania. John Roebling's ingenious suspension construction is clearly apparent. (D&H collection)

creased the whole operation at this point resulted in a bottleneck and lost time.

A change had been proposed at this point for some time even before it was finally decided to enlarge the whole canal in 1847. Two plans had been suggested, one for a wooden aqueduct bridge of conventional design and one using a wire rope suspension principle submitted by a young engineer of vision, John Roebling, who had built such an aqueduct over the Allegheny River, and more recently the Monongahela suspension bridge. Chief Engineer Lord went to Pittsburgh to see these, and reported favorably to the managers on this rather new concept in bridges. On January 6, 1847, a committee of the managers decided to accept Roebling's aqueduct proposal and he was ordered to start the project and to accomplish it as rapidly as possible. The main advantage of the suspended structure was its greater span, requiring only three piers rather than five with a normal bridge, thus providing economy and allowing more clearance in the river for ice floes and flood waters.

The canal alignment was changed to accommodate the new aqueduct but for some reason required building of another structure across the Lackawaxen River just upstream from the Delaware. Perhaps the grade or foundation conditions adjacent to the latter stream dictated this location rather than a single structure directly opposite the point where the Lackawaxen entered the Delaware.

Roebling began the work of stringing the 2,150 strands of wire over the saddles on top of the masonry piers that would make up the two 8½"-diameter supporting cables late in the fall of 1847. From these main cables which could hold 1,900 tons each, smaller wire rope hangers, attached at intervals along the length of the main cable, supported the wooden trunk in which the water would be contained. This trunk, or trough, measured 20 feet wide at the top and tapered slightly in its 8-foot depth to a 17.5-foot width at the bottom and contained a little over 6 feet of water. The whole structure was 600 feet long, made up of four spans varying in length from 132 feet to 142 feet each.

By the end of 1848 both the Delaware and the 228-foot, two-span, Lackawaxen aqueducts were completed and ready for use when the 1849 season opened. There was some degree of apprehension amid the crowd that watched the first boat approach the Delaware structure. They figured there was a tremendous weight of water suspended there already, almost 500 tons in fact, on the 142-foot span, and with the added weight of the boat and its 50-ton cargo, the whole works, boat and

9

These two views of the Delaware River and its aqueduct at Lackawaxen are from opposite directions. The photographer is taking the upper picture, looking downstream, under the watchful eye of a well dressed lad who stands on the front lawn of the Delaware House. Before the aqueduct was built, canal boats drifted across the Delaware in the slack water formed by a dam just upstream from the aqueduct, floating off the Lackawaxen River, which enters from the right, onto the placid pool enjoyed by canoeists, above. Meanwhile, mules were taken across the river on a rope ferry to the towpath on the far side, where they were rehitched to pull the boats into the guard lock located under the left end of the aqueduct to resume their journey on the canal. The lower picture looks downstream from the hillside above the village of Lackawaxen and shows the aqueduct the year after the D&H Canal was abandoned. In the center of the town are the tracks and station of the Erie Railroad. Its Hawley branch swings off to the left beyond the station. The distant three-story hotel at the mouth of the Lackawaxen River is the Delaware House, from which the upper picture was taken. Across the river is the house where Zane Grey wrote *Riders of the Purple Sage* and many other best-selling Western novels. *(D&H collection, two pictures)*

Half a mile west of the canal's big aqueduct was this smaller one over the Lackawaxen River. The canal was closed for more than a week in June 1862, when the center pier of the span was washed out by a cloudburst. (G. M. Best collection)

all, would go crashing down into the swirling waters of the Delaware below. But it didn't!

What the sidewalk superintendents failed to realize was, the boat displaced its exact weight of water when it was in the trunk of the aqueduct and the total weight didn't change a pound. Only the mules on the plank towpath walk added anything at all and they presented no problem. Great cheers went up when the boat reached the New York side to pass on down through newly-built Locks 72, 71 and 70, respectively. The dam across the river, now just upstream from the aqueduct, was maintained as the water it backed up entered the canal and supplied most of the water needed for navigating through the whole Delaware section of the canal, which was purposely built above the river level all the way to Port Jervis.

In April of 1849, now that the work at Lackawaxen was completed, Roebling began work on two more aqueducts, one across the Neversink River near Cuddebackville and the other over Rondout Creek at High Falls, both in New York State. These two structures were essentially the same as the others but the Neversink span was 170 feet long and the 9½-inch cables required for this longer span each contained 3,024 wrought iron wires. These were completed in the winter of 1850 and were ready for service when the canal opened for the 1851 season.

Roebling went on to fame as the builder of the famous Brooklyn Bridge but his efforts on the D&H aqueducts, although not as spectacular, were of no smaller consequence. The concept was advanced for its day and proved to be more than

Soon after the abandonment of the canal, the aqueduct was drained and used as a bridge for wagons and foot traffic. The sides of the trunk have since been removed and now on the automobile toll bridge one can examine the details of Roebling's pioneer cable suspension system that has well supported the structure for over a century. Both views are toward the New York side. *(D&H collection, above; Jim Shaughnessy)*

Lock No. 24 was at Middleport, now Kerhonkson, New York. In this drawing from *Coal Boats to Tidewater*, Manville B. Wakefield has depicted a loaded boat snubbed in, waiting for the upper gate to be raised. After abandonment this became the site of a station on the Kingston branch of the New York, Ontario & Western Railway.

---

adequate in both service and longevity. The Delaware aqueduct is in service to this day, as a toll bridge, and for 25 cents you can drive across the oldest suspension bridge still in use, which has endured well over a century now. This in itself is a testimonial to Roebling, his work and his bridge.

In the meantime, work on widening the canal and its locks had been progressing. The new locks, known as composite locks, were made mostly of dry stone masonry with a wood lining placed over the rough stonework in the lock chamber itself. Thirteen of the new locks were erected with cut stone masonry, smooth enough in themselves not to require the plank lining. The relocation of the canal in the High Falls area eliminated the need for one of the locks, thus reducing the total number in the canal to 108.

Discrepancies in the total number of locks reported in the canal are due to different ways of counting them. There was one double lock, with two chambers for the same lift, at the outlet of the boat basin at Honesdale; all the others were singles. There were also two weighlocks with a scale mechanism to determine the load carried on each boat. The total you came up with, therefore, depended on just what you called a lock. Oldtimers universally and unquestioningly described it: "108 locks in 108 miles."

In 1847 the Delaware and Hudson people made an agreement with the Wyoming Coal Association to transport their coal to market through the canal. This latter organization soon grew into the Pennsylvania Coal Co., and a gravity railroad similar to the D&H's in design was started in March of 1848. This line, much longer than the 16-mile D&H road, had 22 planes and extended from Port Griffith on the Susquehanna 47 miles to Hawley on the D&H Canal. Construction was completed in the spring of 1850 and the first coal from this new and potentially large source went down the canal to Rondout in May. In the following season 316,017 tons were shipped, making a grand total of 919,600 in-

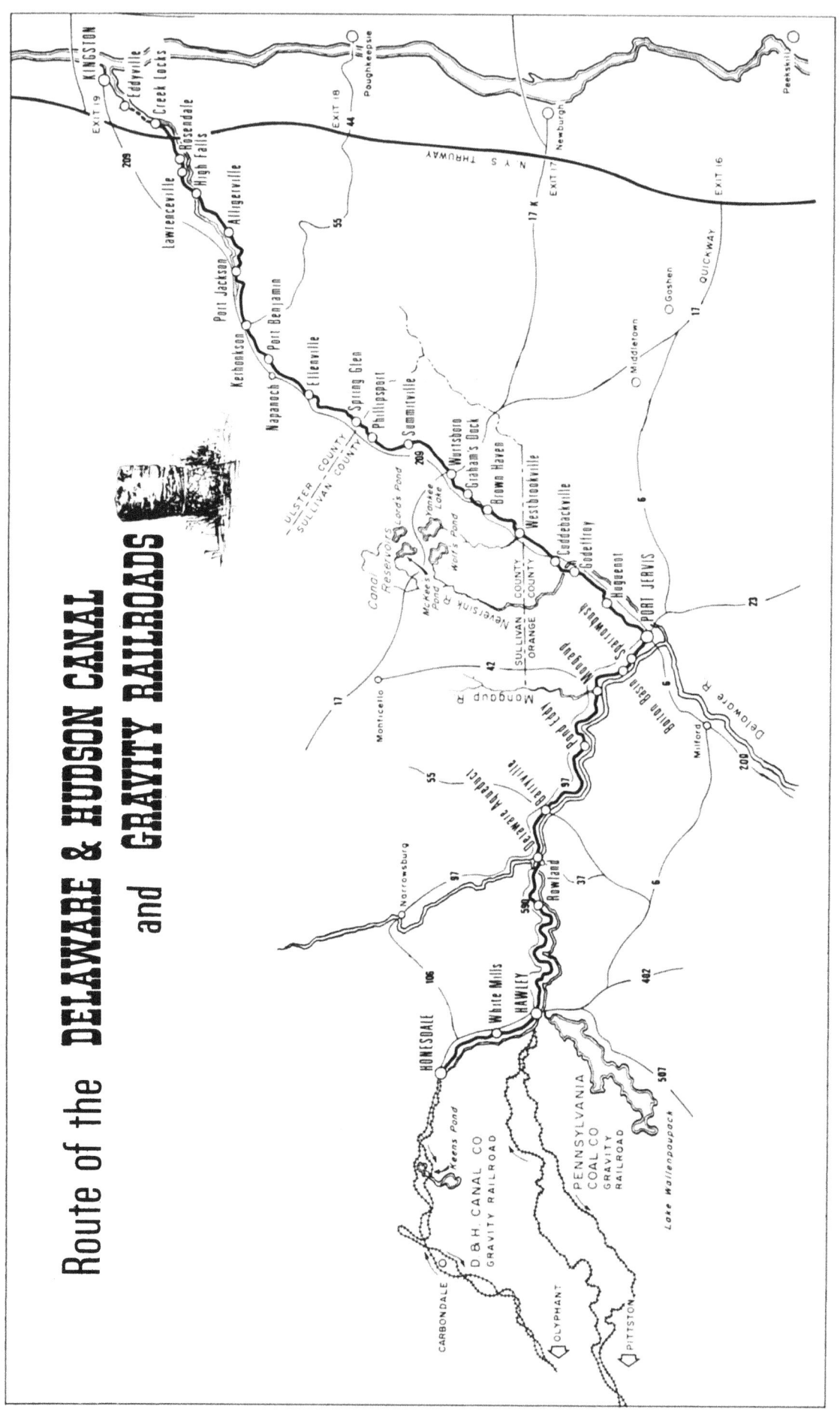

Map from *Coal Boats to Tidewater*, by Manville B. Wakefield.

A boat, probably carrying picnickers up from Port Jervis, waits just below Butler's Lock, adjacent to the Delaware near Hawk's Nest cliffs. The stone wall stretched most of the way along the river to support the towpath bank of the canal. A loaded boat moves on down the waterway in the distance. Below, an empty southbound boat approaches the lock at Godefroid, while a loaded boat is at the lower level in the plank-lined chamber. The dropgate can be seen at the upstream end of the lock. (*M. B. Wakefield collection, above; G. M. Best collection*)

Some of the tranquility of life on the old waterway is evoked in two paintings by the period painter, Edward L. Henry. Passengers relax contentedly atop a typical passenger packet going down the canal near Ellenville, New York. The barefoot girl below is probably the daughter of the boat's captain. She counts the petals of a daisy while the mules enjoy a repast of oats. *(D&H collection, above; New York State Museum)*

Mongaup Lock, No. 58, had been abandoned by the time of this picture, but its working parts are apparent. The little building spanning the lower gates housed machinery. Wooden planks lined the chamber. The drop-gate at the upper end is open to allow excess water to flow through the canal. Wagon tracks and weeds have now replaced the mule hoofprints on the old towpath. (*G. M. Best collection*)

cluding the D&H's own coal, giving more than graphic justification for the canal enlargement which came into full use just in time for the increase.

The year 1847 also saw the installation of the first telegraph line of any commercial importance or significance. Ezra Cornell ran the line along the public roads from New York City through Harlem, White Plains, Peekskill, across the river to Newburgh and to Goshen where a key was set up in the bar of the old Occidental Hotel for its first public display and immediately became a source of amazement. In 1848 the line was extended west along the newly completed New York, Lake Erie and Western Railway tracks to Lackawaxen, then up along the D&H Canal towpath to Honesdale and on to Carbondale along the Gravity right-of-way; finally, on to Buffalo through Binghamton, Owego and Fredonia. The Erie people watched the experiment closely and soon put this telegraph device in service dispatching trains, thus being the first railroad in the nation to do so. The D&H quickly saw the advantage in such a rapid means of communication and put the invention into operation at a number of offices along the line all the way to Eddyville. Out of this whole endeavor was to grow the Western Union Telegraph Co.

A new collector's office and weighlock was built at Hawley to handle the tonnage of coal being shipped through the canal by the Pennsylvania Coal Co., which amounted to about half a million tons annually when their operations got into full swing after 1851. This quantity represented just about the same tonnage the D&H moved themselves but the added tolls, although certainly welcome, were not what had originally been hoped for. There were several complicated agreements on the fee for moving the coal to tidewater and each company interpreted them differently. As a result the Pennsylvania Coal Co. refused to pay what the D&H wanted and the whole thing ended up in the courts of New York and Pennsylvania in 1856.

In both 1855 and 1856 over a million tons of coal went through the canal with about half of this amount originating at Hawley. The capacity

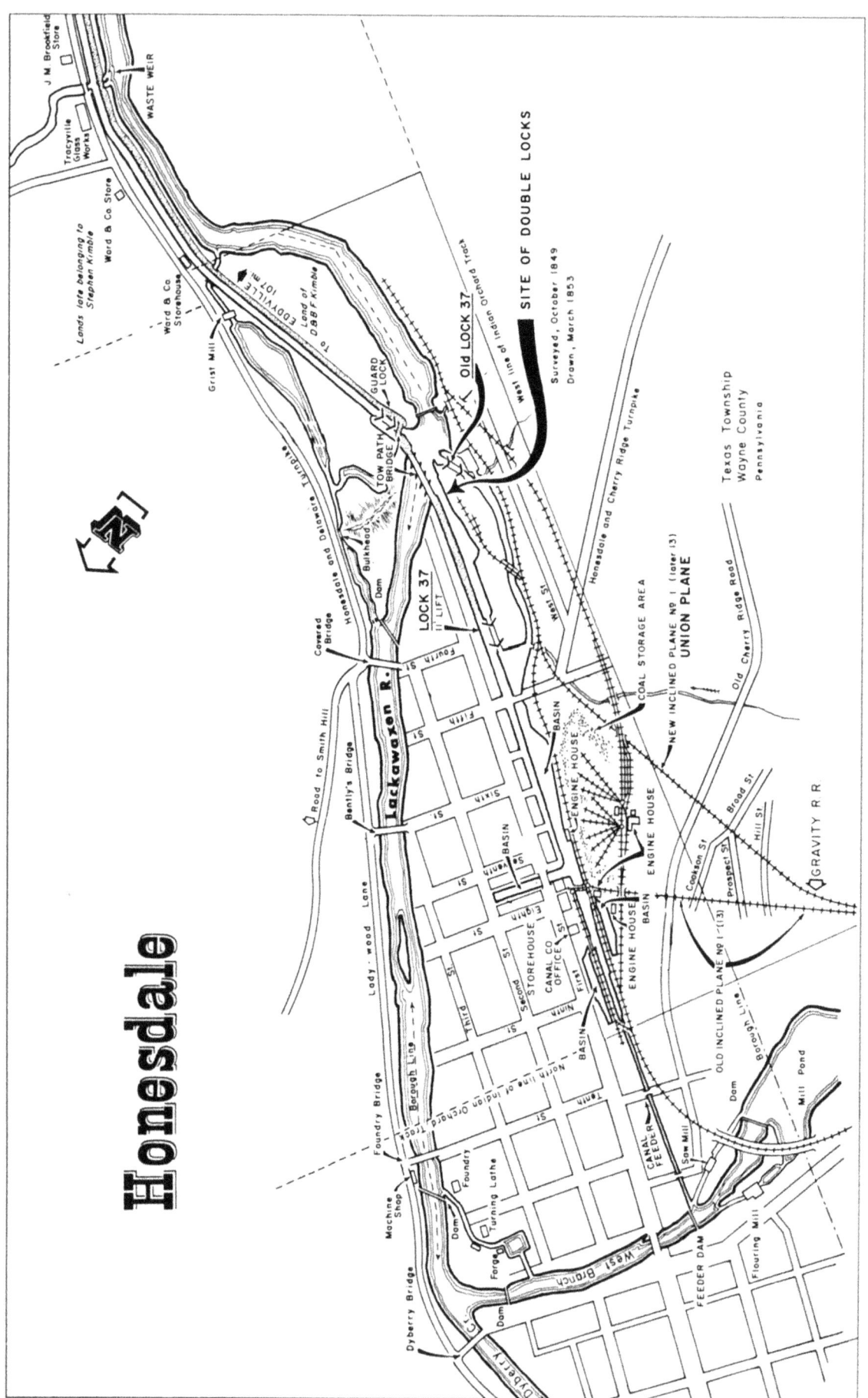

Map from *Coal Boats to Tidewater* by Manville B. Wakefield.

The general view of Honesdale above can be oriented by reference to the map on the other page. This picture was taken from a hill across the Lackawaxen River, while Fifth Street extends to the south along the left. The huge piles of coal stored along the canal obscure the engine house and yard and, at the right, the inclined plane is apparent, going straight up the hill. Nearby are the D&H station and offices. Below is an early view of the upper boat basin, showing several of the older and smaller boats "hipped" with boards to build up the sides and increase capacity after one of the canal deepening projects. At the left are slips and unloading tracks. *(D&H collection, below)*

The only power vessel to operate on the canal was the paymaster's launch *Minnie,* shown in this drawing from *Coal Boats to Tidewater* by Manville B. Wakefield. Here she steams south past S. A. Van Wagner's canal store in Ellenville. The Table of Distances, opposite, was arranged for the Telegraph Department. The advertisement for boatmen is from the *Pike County Democrat* of Milford, Pennsylvania. *(Jean Banta collection, far opposite)*

of the D&H's Gravity road was quite a bit below that of the canal and the only way they could keep coal enough in Honesdale for the boats was to operate the railroad all winter. While the canal was frozen over, coal would be routed over the Gravity at the same rate and stockpiled by the boat basin in Honesdale ready for the reopening of the canal. By mid-May there would be a huge stockpile, probably 100,000 tons there awaiting the warm weather and canal navigation once again. To offset this lack of capacity the managers authorized expansion of the railroad and work on the project was started early in 1856 and continued over a two-year period. This involved double tracking all the existing planes, constructing two more up the mountain out of Carbondale and changing and improving the grade at many points.

In 1855 a new type of lock gate, called a dropgate, was tried and proved to be a practical and timesaving invention. This one-piece affair was hinged across the bottom and installed at the upstream end of the lock chamber. It was weighted so it could swing out to the bottom of the channel above the lock and allow the boat to enter the lock on top of it. As soon as the boat was snubbed up, butterfly valves on the downstream gates would be opened to release some of the water from the chamber; the surge of water from upstream to

TABLE OF DISTANCES ON THE DELAWARE & HUDSON CANAL,

showing its Divisions and Sections, Counties, Telegraph Calls, Numbers of Locks, &c., and the Location of Aqueducts, Feeders, Stop-Gates, Waste-Weirs, &c.

ARRANGED FOR THE INFORMATION OF THE TELEGRAPH DEPARTMENT. BY CHARLES PETERSEN, SUPERINTENDENT.

Names of Places	Tel. Call	Miles from Honesdale	Miles from Eddyville	No. of Locks	County	Remarks
HONESDALE	H		108	27		R.R. Main Battery. Feeder.
Leonardsville		1	107	25		
Holbert's Basin		2	106			
Beardslee's Basin		3	105			Aqueduct
Beach Flat		4	104	24		
WHITE MILLS	CD	5	103	23	Wayne	R.R.
Brink's Dam		6	102	22		Feeder
Daniels'		7	101	21		
Newcastle		8	100			
HAWLEY	HY			20 20		R.R.
Tumbledam Rock						Feeder
Poolpit		11	97	25 26		
Punch Camp		12	96	24		
Narrows		13	95	21 22 23		R.R.
Snyder's Eddy		14	94	19 20		Feeder
Shimer's Eddy		15	93	18		
Blue Eddy		16	92	17		
Mouth of Blooming Grove		17	91	16		R.R.
Blooming Grove Island		18	90	15	Pike	
GRISWOLD	GD	19	89	13 14		
Westfall's		20	88	11 12		R.R. Aqueduct
Bowlands		21	87	10		R.R.
Port Howard		21	87	7 8		
Little Narrows		22	86	6		
Ridgway		23	85	4 5		
LACKAWAXEN	XN	24	84			R.R. Aqueduct
Delaware Aqueduct		25	83	70 72		Delaware Feeder
Stop Lock		26	82			
Beaver Brook		27	81			Four Mile Level
Panther Brook		28	80			Aqueduct
BARRYVILLE	B	30	78	68 69		Stop Gate. Hanging Rock
Mitchel		31	77	67		
Handsome Eddy		32	76			Waste Weir
Buttermilk Falls		33	75	65 66		
Craigsville		34	74			
Van Tuyle's Basin		35	73	64	Sullivan	
Van Tuyle's Brook		36	72	63		
POND EDDY	RM	37	71			
Decker's Dock		38	70	62		Shad Fishing
Fish Cabin		39	69	61		
Van Auken's Bridge		40	68	60		
Stairway Brook		41	67			
Dickerson's Eddy						
MONGAUP	MP	42	66	58 59		Feeder. Aqueduct.
Barton's Falls		43	65	57		
Bolton Basin		44	64			
Honesville		45	63			
Sparrowbush		46	62			
Westfall's Basin		47	61			
PORT JERVIS	SD	48	60		Orange	
Ben Cuddeback's		49	59			Twelve Mile Level
Pine Woods		50	58			Stop Gate
Bird-Nest Rock		51	57			
Hornbeck's Culvert		52	56			
Huguenot		53	55			Waste Weirs
Van Etten's Bridge		54	54			
Port Clinton		55	53			
NEVERSINK AQ.	Q	56	52	51 55		Neversink Feeder
Cuddebackville		57	51			Stop Gate
Van Inwegen's Basin		58	50			
Staunton's Basin		59	49			
WESTBROOKVILLE	WB	60	48			Stop Gate
Tussel Hill		61	47			Aq't Yankee Pd Feeder
Indian Spring		62	46			Stop Gate
Oak Brook		63	45			Aqueduct
Drop's Haven		64	44			Summit Level
Mineral Smith's		65	43			
Graham's Dock		66	42			
Snell's Basin		67	41			Stop Gate
WURTSBORO	WS	68	40		Sullivan	Aqueduct, Stop Gate.
Gumaer's Brook		69	39			Waste Weir. Stop Gate.
Swamp Bridge		70	38			
Log House		71	37			
Beattysburg		72	36			
Davis		73	35			
PHILLIPSPORT	SG	74	34	43 48		Summit. Waste Weir
County Line		75	33	42 46		Topping's Bas. Feeder
Fenny's Basin		76	32	38 41		Aqueduct. Change Bridge
Jared B. Tuttle's		77	31	37		Feeder
Brodhead's Brick-Kiln		78	30			
Cutler's Basin		79	29			
ELLENVILLE	RF	80	28	30 35		Mountain Brook Aqueduct
Terwilliger's		81	27	28 29	Ulster	
Decker's		82	26	27		
Napanoch		83	25			Enderly's Basin
Fort Benjamin		84	24			Aqueduct
Port Hyxson		85	23			Rondout Creek Feeder
Bruyan's Basin		86	22			Two Mile Level
MIDDLEP'T (Kerhonkson)	MI	87	21	24		Dewsond's Aq. Stony Kill
Mountain Brook		88	20			Mountain Brook Aq.
C. F. Hornbeck's		89	19			
David Vernooy's		90	18			Four Mile Level
Port Jackson		91	17			
Stony Kill		92	16	23		Aqueduct
Freeland's		93	15			
John S. Depuy's		94	14	23		Basin
ALLIGERVILLE	VI	95	13	21		Peterskill Feeder & Aq't
Andrewville		96	12	16		
Clove Church		97	11			Four Mile Level
Harbrook's		98	10			
HIGH FALLS	HF	99	9	12 20		Main Battery. Feeder
Cole's Basin		100	8	10 11		
Lawrenceville		101	7	8		
ROSENDALE	RA	102	6	7		
Le Fever's Falls		103	5			Basin
Hardenburgh		104	4			
CREEK LOCKS	CK	105	3	5 6		
Hornbeck's Bridge		106	2			
Greenkill						
EDDYVILLE	DE	107	1	1		Guard & Weigh Lock
RONDOUT D. & H. Co.'s Private Office	RN / RD	108				

Collector's Office. †Suspension Aqueduct. ‡Double Tow-path from Lock 12 to Lock 20. ‖Junction of Wallkill and Rondout Creeks. § Boats pass three miles through Rondout Creek.

Herald Job Printing Establishment, Honesdale, Pa.

---

replace it would automatically swing the drop-gate into place and the upstream head of water against it would hold it securely in position. This device saved considerable time and allowed a boat to be locked through more quickly, thus increasing the canal's efficiency and capacity. During the following winter drop-gates were installed on all the locks and they were operational for the 1856 season.

BOATMEN WANTED
ON THE
Delaware and Hudson Canal
FOR 1850.

The Company are now building several hundred Boats, which they will sell to temperate, industrious men, on favorable terms; to be employed in freighting coal from Honesdale to Rondout. The boats are built to carry 125 tons: the cargo for this year, however, will be only about 95 tons.

The terms will be $1400 purchase money for the Boat—$50 of which must be paid in cash, or good security given for its payment on or before the 1st day of August next. The balance of the purchase money will be received by installments of $18 per trip out of the freight of the boat.

The rate of freight for the present year will be as follows: For a trip made in 10 days, at the rate of 85 cents per ton. For 11 days trips 82 cents per ton; and if over 11 days at the rate of 80 cents per ton. Out of each cargo $3 will be retained until the end of the season. The balance of the freight will be paid in cash at the end of each trip. The expenses of unloading will not exceed 5 cents per ton.

The Canal is 108 miles long—the Locks are tended both day and night—and trips can be made in ten days without a change of horses.

The company engage to supply the freight and full employment for the Boats from the opening of Canal to the close of navigation. When boats are required to discharge at New York, the Company's Steamboats will tow them without charge, and an additional rate of freight will be paid, fully equal to the above rates.

The Company are also building a number of *Scows*, which they will sell at $700 each, on the same terms of payment as the boats, except that the installments will be only $13 per trip.

Apply at the Delaware & Hudson Canal office 31 Wall street, New York; at the Rondout and Honesdale offices; or at any of the Collectors' offices on the Canal; or Wm. Hathaway, Exchange Hotel, Syracuse.

MAURICE WURTS
Prest. Pro. Tem.

Delaware and Hudson Canal Office,
New York, Jan. 18th, 1850. } [26-3m

At the same time the downstream gates in all the locks received a set of gears and arms which allowed both of the conventional gates to be moved simultaneously. This mechanism, operated by a crank wheel, was installed in a little enclosure

Canal boats were left in this predicament after the disastrous embankment break in 1885. In the background is the Erie Railroad bridge built to replace the one destroyed by the walnut logs in the 1882 train wreck. This scene is at Bolton Basin, a few miles up the Delaware River from Port Jervis. *(Manville B. Wakefield collection)*

located directly over the entrance to the chamber at the downstream gates. The drop-gate was operated by a cable and winch from this point as well. These innovations, in addition to considerably speeding up movements allowed one-man operation of the locks where two were previously required. As early as 1856, technological displacement of labor was occurring.

The mid-1850s were by far the best years thus far for the company and the canal. A dividend of 18% a share was paid in 1855 and 16% the following year. However, 1857 was a depression year and in 1858 business activity reached bottom. Not only was the D&H's own business off sharply but the Pennsylvania Coal Co. had now defaulted to the tune of over $600,000 on tolls as a result of the disagreement over rates in the original contract.

By 1863 a settlement of the debt, now $1,100,000, was dictated by the courts but only a quarter of the outstanding amount was recovered. In the meantime an atmosphere of unpleasant relations existed between the two companies and the Pennsylvania Co. actively sought another outlet to market for its coal. In this connection, they concluded an agreement with the Erie Railroad to build a branch from the main line at Lackawaxen, up the valley of the same name to Hawley.

The building of this line was contingent on favorable public hearings and for several years the D&H people were able to offer enough opposition to prevent the project's approval. By 1860, however, the Pennsylvania Co. was successful in obtaining the franchise to construct a 16-mile 6-foot gauge line down to connect with the Erie main.

During 1862 and the following year, construction of the branch was eagerly pushed through the winding valley to a completion in December of 1863, and before Christmas the first coal train left Hawley. The D&H employees who stood on the banks of their frozen canal and watched that train puff out must have realized that a new era was dawning in the movement of coal. No longer was the Pennsylvania Coal Co. dependent on the D&H, or even more important, limited by the winter weather and its icy grip on the canal, to ship its product. The fact that a railroad could operate all year long and deliver coal directly to its destination must have been driven home in no uncertain terms to the D&H managers and no doubt similar thoughts crossed their own minds. The end was already in sight, although the canal still had almost a half century of productive life ahead of it. The canal remained essentially the same physically from the installation of the new gates in 1856 until it ceased operations in 1899.

The Civil War brought a flood of prosperity to the canal, moving coal to fire the furnaces of the industrial North. Other commodities also moved through the canal from the beginning. General freight and finished products as well as such raw materials as tanner's bark, stone, brick, lumber and especially cement all represented substantial tonnage each year.

Maintenance on a canal had its peculiar problems quite different from those on a railroad. A wreck on the railroad had its counterpart on the canal—a break in the banks! It is one thing to dig a ditch but it is quite another to keep water in it.

It was forbidden to use poles to push the boats as this would punch holes in the bottom and in places like the Neversink valley where the bottom was lined with clay to render it watertight, leaks would develop. These leaks would soon enlarge from the washing effect of the water and it was like pulling the plug in the bathtub. The boatmen were not the only culprits; eels, catfish, moles and especially muskrats found the canal an ideal home. They would often burrow into the banks only to find themselves riding out into a farmer's cornfield on the crest of a wall of muddy water.

To guard against such disasters a watchman or towpath walker was assigned a section of canal to patrol, repairing small leaks when he came upon them. This could usually be accomplished by plugging the hole with stones and straw then tamping sod or clay over it with his feet. If a leak could not be stopped in this manner and threatened to develop into a full fledged washout, the emergency crew would be summoned by telegraph.

This crew had the right-of-way over everything, much as a fire department, and its scow was loaded with timbers and planking along with wheelbarrows, shovels and other necessary equipment. A temporary dam would be built at the washout with the timber and planks, then the embankment filled in again behind it. This temporary structure soon soaked up, becoming watertight, and would remain in place until the new fill settled. Spring floods and summer cloudbursts would cause the most problems, mostly as a result of small outlets, called waste weirs, becoming plugged with debris and allowing the water level in the canal to rise above the prescribed level. A number of washouts and breaks occurred on the D&H but probably the most spectacular took place on the night of August 5, 1885, at Bolton Basin.

Map from *Coal Boats to Tidewater* by Manville B. Wakefield.

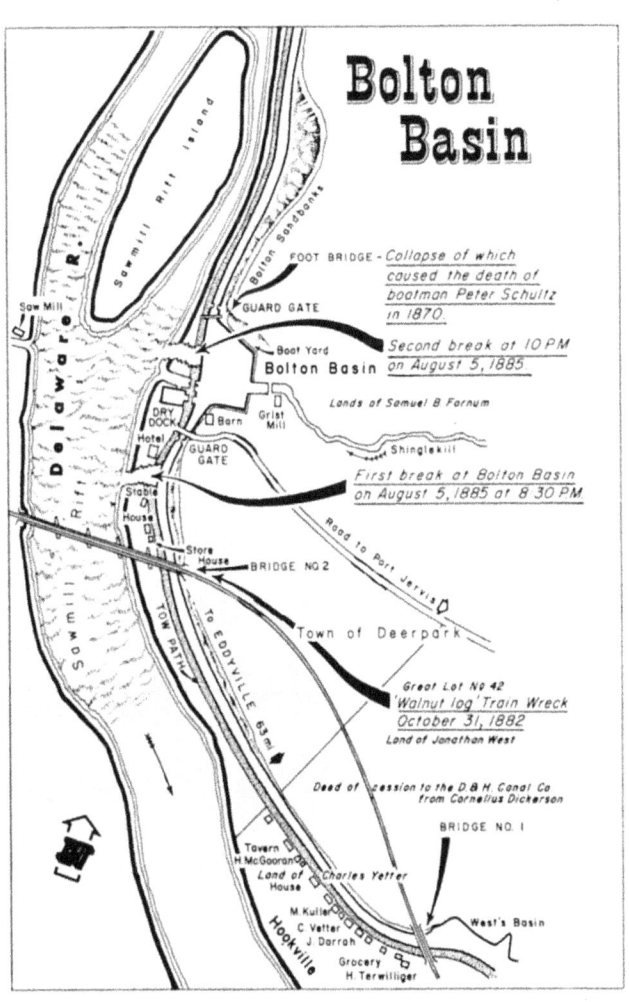

An island dock provided facilities for transfer and storage of coal at the Rondout Creek terminal of the D&H canal. Here larger vessels, like the one at left center, were loaded with coal for Boston, Providence and other coastal ports. Coal often moved to New York City and Hudson River points in the same boats that brought it from Honesdale.

On the opposite page the towboat *Austin* waits out the winter with canal boats that will be pushed in flotillas of twenty or more to New York during the boating season, thus bringing coal form Honesdale without intermediate handling. The waterway passed through the cement works at Rosendale, below. (*D&H collection, three pictures*)

A cloudburst turned Shinglekill Creek, which fed into the basin at that point, into a raging, frothing torrent of brown water. The force of the current surged across the basin to the towpath bank and easily cut through it. A large number of boats had moored at the basin for the night to ride out the storm. As the water rushed toward the breach the boats crashed together with sickening thuds as they too headed for the gap. Several of them wedged together, kept the others from going out into the Delaware and at the same time formed a haphazard dam at the break. An hour and a half later, at 10 p.m., the still-rising water found another way out, a thousand feet up from the first, now through a gap 200 feet long and 25 feet deep. This time a boat loaded with coal went out through the gap while a dozen others lay hopelessly twisted on the rocky basin floor.

In the morning Bolton Basin was a chaotic scene of broken and twisted boats. It took about two weeks to repair the banks and clean up the mess before the canal could be reopened.

Bolton Basin, named for the second president of the company, had more than its share of bad luck. In October 1882, three years before the big break, another unusual accident had occurred there, this time involving the Erie railroad. As a train from the west was approaching the bridge over the canal just south of the basin, a load of walnut logs, which had broken loose from their bindings, swung out over the edge of the flatcar carrying them. They hit and wiped out several main members of the truss bridge, plunging the whole structure along with 15 other cars into the canal. All the water had to be drained out to clean up the debris. Luckily, no boat was under the span at the time. This was usually the case anyway for when a boatman heard a train coming here, or at the Lackawaxen bridge, he would hold back on the team as frequently the whistle, or just the noise, would spook the animals and cause them to run away or injure themselves trying.

Life along the canal was congenial for the canallers and for their children, many of whom spent their entire lives on the old waterway. Their home was a cramped 12-foot square cabin, but their backyard was 108 miles long and 40 feet wide. There was a keen sense of rivalry between

25

The idyllic canal scenes at the tops of these pages depict "light"—unloaded—boats headed south out of Wurtsboro. The line was attached to the middle of the boat, allowing the tillerman to keep it properly guided down the narrow waterway. The bottom pictures show different views of the canal where it parallels the north shore of the Delaware River. A light boat, commanded by Captain Horace B. Schoonmaker, waits to enter lock No. 71, one of three needed to raise the boats to the level of the Delaware Aqueduct. Lock No. 72 is in the distance. The high view is from Hawk's Nest Cliff, an outcropping upstream from Port Jervis, looking down on the canal with its towpath following the north bank of the river, atop a stone wall. Boats passing each other had a tight squeeze, as can be seen just this side of Butler's Lock, No. 57, in the distance. The westbound Erie train on the left bank is blurred, because of its movement during the slow exposure of the original glass plate negative. *(Al Gayer collection, upper pictures; D&H collection, lower left; G. M. Best collection, lower right)*

During the golden years of the D&H Canal this scene was repeated many times over: several boats slowly moving down the waterway with animals and men plodding steadily along, always walking. *(Manville B. Wakefield collection)*

the boatmen, but they were all a part of the one big family whose lives were governed by the price of coal at Rondout and the first flakes of snow that flew in December. The slightest film of ice would make it impossible for the mules to pull the boat and navigation would be over for another season.

Mules were almost the exclusive motive power on the canal from the beginning. They were tougher than horses, cheaper to maintain and even had the virtue of dying quickly if they fell ill. Their ability to keep moving was graphically exhibited when a boatman would be pushing hard, day and night, to make Eddyville before a sudden freeze at the end of a season. The long-eared animals would plod steadily along with their eyes closed, literally asleep on their feet, while they chawed on hay carried along for them by one of the boatmen's children.

If a boat out on the canal got stuck in the ice for the winter, the captain could count himself lucky if he still had a boat the next spring, to say nothing of its cargo. Many a local farm family was able to arise comfortably on cold winter mornings in houses warmed by stoves stoked with anthracite from stranded canal boats.

Days on the canal were long, beginning at five in the morning when the locks opened and ending at sunset when operations ceased for the night. A boat starting right out and driving steadily until ten at night could cover about twenty miles. With a good team of mules that would "go by themselves," the driver could board the boat to eat while the long-eared critters plodded off the miles. Thus, by departing Honesdale on Monday morning, a boat could reach tidewater by Saturday afternoon. If one were caught somewhere along the line on Sunday, the trip would take a full seven days, for nothing moved on the Sabbath.

Sunday was truly a day of rest for man and mule. During the canal's seven decades of operation, it was always closed on that day. At one time in the 1840s the company provided Bibles for each boat in an effort to protect the morals of the boatmen. This would have probably taken more than a Bible, especially if they were in Rondout—a place that could conservatively be described as "wild." Some men would rather drink than pray while other family groups gave the Sabbath all the reverence accorded to it in those days. There were all kinds on the old canal.

There was a store and a tavern at almost every lock and you could get food or drink at your pleasure. Eggs sold for 80 cents a hundred, ham 8 cents a pound, bread 5 cents a loaf, butter was 13 cents a pound, and buttermilk was free. Each port had its specialties. Take for example Moses Van Inwegen's store adjacent to Lock 51 near the Neversink aqueduct. Here Mary Casey made bread that would melt in your mouth and the canallers waited in line to buy it. For the children she made little pies that they relished each time they came to the lock, not surprisingly called "the pie lock."

The Delaware and Hudson Canal was a world unto itself—historically, technically, economically and socially. It left more than a weed-filled scar across the land when its era passed. Maurice Wurts, who died on December 29, 1854, had seen over a million tons of coal in one season go down the valley to market from his beloved Pennsylvania hills—for him a dream of great magnitude had come true.

A New York State historical marker stands beside a weed-filled depression by the side of U. S. Highway 209 near Westbrookville. (*Jim Shaughnessy*)

Plane 13 of the gravity railroad rose from the canal basin at Honesdale. *(D&H collection)*

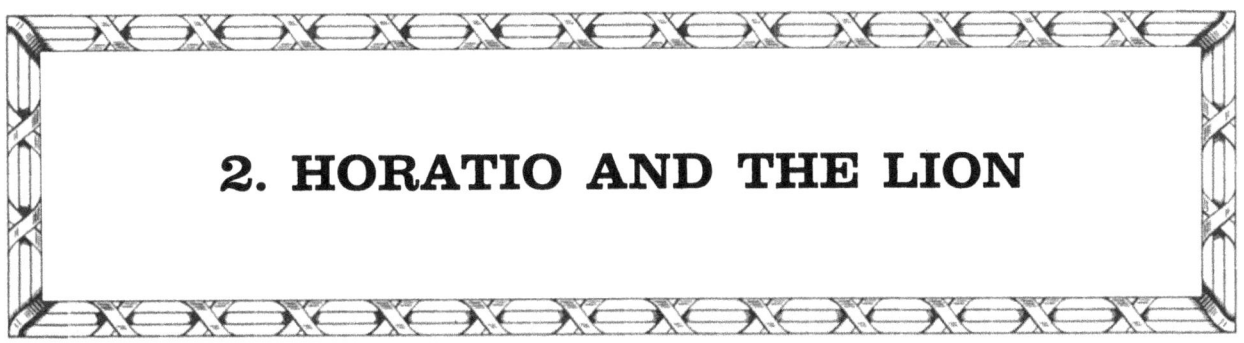

2. HORATIO AND THE LION

The Moosic Mountains are not in themselves an impressive range of hills and the original plan for the Delaware & Hudson Canal proposed crossing the range to bring the boats directly to the mines at Carbondale. This would have avoided the necessity of reloading the coal, but investigation soon proved it impracticable. Keens Pond, on the eastern slope of the ridge, was considered as the upper terminus for the canal from tidewater, but the site finally decided on was seven miles to the east, where the community that was named Honesdale was laid out. Beyond here it was evident that the number of locks required to scale the Moosic barrier was too great.

Colonel John L. Sullivan, an associate of Benjamin Wright, had a pair of daring and imaginative plans in which reloading might be avoided. A boat would be floated into a watertight chamber on a "transit." The chamber would then be drained, reducing the combined weight of transit and boat so that the unit could be raised, either vertically on a chain or up an incline on rails, by a counterweight. At the top, brakes would hold the transit in place while the chamber was again filled and the boat floated out. On the down trip the transit would remain filled with more water than actually needed to float the boat, so that the whole unit was heavy enough to move down and correspondingly raise the counterweight. The plan certainly was ingenious and involved some of the principles used in modern elevators.

Colonel Sullivan's alternative plan was also daring enough by 1826 standards, but less startling to one in the mid-twentieth century: The boats would be brought to the mines over a railroad.

The managers decided that the best and most practical answer lay in a proposal by John B. Jervis that a railroad be built over the mountains to carry coal to the boats. This was conservative to the extent that it accepted the necessity of reloading the coal, but in 1826 the very idea of a railroad was daring. This was the year the first railroad went into operation in the United States, the six-mile, horse-powered line at Quincy, Massachusetts, that moved granite from a quarry to the Neponset River, where it was loaded into barges to be hauled to Charlestown for construction of the Bunker Hill Monument. It was proving workable on a year-round basis, but people generally were far from convinced that a railroad had much value at all and the merits of a single- or double-rail roadway were widely debated.

The route east from Carbondale required an ascent of 950 feet within the first four miles in order to reach the crest of the Moosic Mountains at Rix's Gap and then a descent on the far side of the ridge to the canal basin in Honesdale, 20 feet lower than the elevation of the mines at Carbondale. The rolling nature of the landscape between the two terminals required considerable engineering judgment of an original nature since there were no other installations of its type for comparison or guidance. Since the canal was expected to handle 100,000 tons of coal each season, a similar capacity was required of the 16⅞-mile railroad line.

Jervis began his surveys in April of 1827 and presented his report to the managers on October 24, after a full summer of hacking through the forest on several possible routes. Since there was an abundance of native timber throughout the area he proposed the use of trestles rather than costly embankments. Excavation was kept to a minimum by selective location to maintain the grade without excessive curves or heavy earthwork. Where

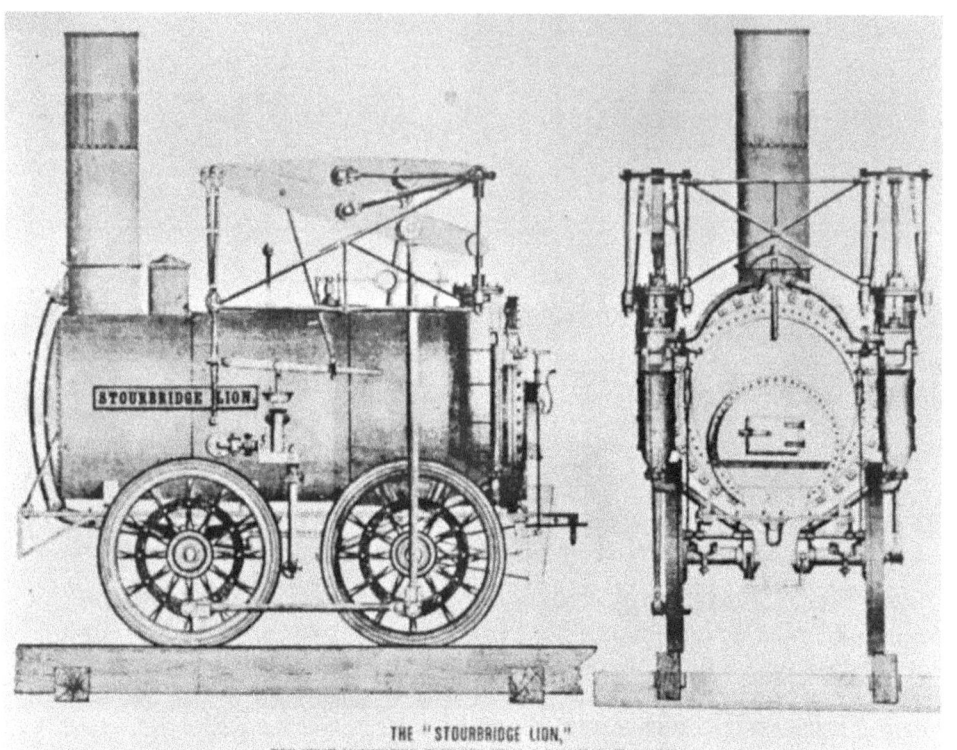

The STOURBRIDGE LION cost $3000, had 49-inch wheels and weighed 7 tons. The sketch at the left shows details of the engine and the track she rode. In the painting below, Horatio Allen talks with company officials before beginning his historic journey in which steam turned the wheels of an engine for the first time in America, August 8, 1829.

This exact replica of the STOURBRIDGE LION was built by shopmen at the D&H Colonie shops in 1933 and placed on this flatcar to go to the Century of Progress Exposition at Chicago. (*D&H collection, above, and lower opposite*)

the track was more than four feet above the ground trestlework was employed, a condition which prevailed over about one-third of the line. On the rest of the road the track was laid on 6x9-inch hemlock crossties embedded in the ground or supported on short vertical posts. The ties were placed ten feet apart, quite far by today's standards, and the 6x12-inch wooden rails spanned the whole distance between ties with no intermediate support. The rails were set into a slot cut in the ties and wedges were provided in these slots to allow lateral adjustment to the 4 ft. 3 in. gauge chosen for the line. These rails were alternately 20 feet and 30 feet in length so both joints would not fall on the same crosstie and thus tend to give somewhat better structural continuity but as would be proven later, this was not as functional as had been hoped. Iron strap rails 2¼ in. wide and ½ in. thick, imported from England, were fastened with countersunk screws to the inside edges of the wooden rails to serve as a wearing surface.

Jervis' plan was without precedent and a bold step forward, but the managers liked it and authorized him to start construction in the fall of 1827 to complete the job as soon as possible.

The route would consist of five inclined planes up the west side of the mountain and three descending inclines connected by three slightly sloping stretches, called levels, between the summit and the canal basin on the east side of the divide. Stationary steam engines would haul the cars up each of the ascending planes and a mechanical breaking mechanism would lower the cars down the descending planes. On the relatively level stretches between the descending planes Jervis proposed using steam locomotives as the motive power. He figured four such machines could operate for $41.30 a day, while enough horses to do the same work would require $71.87 a day to keep; best of all, the locomotives could work without rest.

A young associate of Jervis, 25-year-old Horatio Allen, was chosen to go to England, there to contract for the building of the locomotive engines and to secure the strap iron rails. Six days after his arrival in England on February 15, 1828, he met George Stephenson, builder of the first successful steam locomotive, the ROCKET, and recognized as the father of the steam locomotive. By July 19 he wrote home to the managers saying that he had contracted for one locomotive to be built on the same plan as the ROCKET by Robert Stephenson & Co. of Newcastle and for three from Foster, Rastrick & Co. of Stourbridge designed on a somewhat different plan. In the meantime he had arranged for a large quantity of strap rail to be made and rolled by Messrs. W. & I. Sparrow of Wolverhampton and a quantity was already on its way.

It was quite a responsibility for the young man to shoulder, especially in those days when you consider the difficulty of communication between him and his employers. The design and performance was left entirely up to his judgment. In order to reach sound conclusions on the specifications, especially the boilers, he visited the Liverpool & Manchester and the Stockton & Darlington railways to observe their equipment in use since 1814 and see how well it functioned.

The locomotive Stephenson built was named AMERICA while the DELAWARE and the HUDSON along with the famed STOURBRIDGE LION were fabricated by Foster & Rastrick. A painter in the latter's shop at Stourbridge is said to have detected in the rounded boiler head of the little machine a resemblance to the king of beasts and painted a brilliant likeness on the front of the iron monster. Whatever was the painter's motivation, true inspiration or a pint of ale at lunch, he stroked in a page of American history that day in 1829.

The AMERICA arrived in New York aboard the clipper ship *Columbia* on January 15, 1829 and cost $3663.30 delivered. It was unloaded and set up on blocks in the yard of Abeel & Dunscomb's foundry at 375 Water Street, there on May 27 to turn her wheels under steam for a number of demonstrations.

The STOURBRIDGE LION arrived in Gotham on May 13, costing $2914.90 delivered and was set on blocks at a different point and showed her stuff on May 28, a day after the AMERICA's first trial. Both made a number of stationary runs demonstrating the wonders of the dawning age of steam locomotion to the awe and astonishment of hundreds, many of whom might be encouraged to invest in the company after what they had witnessed.

On July 3rd, after a month in New York both locomotives were loaded aboard the steamer *Congress* and shipped up the Hudson to Rondout. From there canal boats would transfer them to the eastern end of the gravity line at Honesdale but there is no record of the AMERICA ever reaching its destination. Its whereabouts remained a mystery from the time it reached Rondout until a cylinder found in the Smithsonian Institution in 1823 and thought to be from the STOURBRIDGE LION was actually confirmed by the Stephenson company in England as belonging to the AMERICA. Apparently the little engine was unloaded at Rondout and left there or possibly even made the trip to Honesdale where it lay unused and eventually was dismantled and its boiler and cylinders used for other purposes. Years later the cylinder found its way to the Smithsonian from a Carbondale foundry proprietor who thought he was preserving a piece of the first locomotive to run in America and in fact was doing just that, although he had the wrong engine in mind. The AMERICA actually ran a day before the LION in the demonstrations in New York.

When the LION arrived in Honesdale, July 24, Horatio Allen was there to greet the little engine he had ordered in England and to place her on the rails. Several days later, on August 8, after all was in readiness Horatio climbed on the LION and opened the throttle to make his historic journey down the track and into the Pennsylvania woods. The epoch-making trip took him down along the canal basin, across Lackawaxen Creek on a 30-foot high curving trestle and on through the forest toward Seeleyville three miles away before reversing direction.

After the trip he frankly admitted he had some concern as to whether the roadbed would hold the seven-ton locomotive and if it would negotiate the curved stretch over the creek without plunging off the trestle into the water, but he had come too far with the project to falter now. The run was indeed historic, as this was the first locomotive to run on rails in America and antedated by a full two months the famous Rainhill trials of Stephenson's own Rocket on the Liverpool & Manchester Railway that established the practicability of steam railroad transportation.

The trial was a failure, unfortunately, despite the fact that the Lion performed beautifully. The roadbed was too light and inadequately braced to sustain both the weight and the thrust of the little engine. The hemlock rails and trestle structure groaned and shook under the Lion's seven-ton weight and it was obvious to those present—and certainly to Allen—that the roadbed was unsafe. It had been designed to sustain a load of about 1¼ tons per wheel, but as the engine was constructed, the load was nearer two tons. When the news was out that the new track could not adequately bear the weight of the locomotives, the company's stock weakened, dropping from 82 to 74 dollars a share in a single day, but this depression was short-lived.

A second trial was made with the Lion on September 9 and its operation and effect on the road were closely observed. It was painfully clear that the road as it stood was not up to the job and before the Lion, or any of its sisters, could be put to work considerable effort and expense would have to go into track work to make the whole thing safe and practical.

With sadness and disappointment, the Lion was rolled off the track there in Honesdale by the canal and stored. The little black engine with her grasshopper-type connecting rods and tall stack suffered some of the indignities that are the lot of the discarded for a time, but as winter approached it was given rough protection with a makeshift wooden enclosure. There it remained for about twenty years after which it was taken to Carbondale. The boiler was put to use in the company's shops and remained in service there until about 1870. It was a sad end indeed for an engine whose puffs were heard around the world.

The other two engines built by Foster & Rastrick, the Delaware and the Hudson, cost $2944.40 and $2992.90 respectively. They arrived in New York in late summer of 1829 and went up to Rondout where all traces of them were lost to the ages.

The Gravity Railroad. In the meantime the gravity line was nearing completion. Planking was now placed between the rails on the sections of the levels elevated on trestlework and earth put between them on those sections at ground level so horses could pull the cars where the locomotives were originally slated to work. It was also found that the hemlock rails were too soft to support the strap rail directly, and irregularities developed in the running rails where soft spots were encountered. To remedy this the strap rails were removed and hard oak strips 1⅛"x4" were spiked to the top of the hemlock rails. The strap rails were then replaced and spiked to the hardwood strips thus allowing the load to be distributed over a larger area and eliminating the unevenness. In appearance they resembled a heavy wagon-wheel tire. The first load of coal rolled down the hill to the canal basin at Honesdale on October 9, 1829, opening what was to be seven decades of service.

Beginning at the mines in Carbondale the cars climbed a short incline and then rolled to the foot of Plane 1, 2000 feet away. This first little incline, like a modern day hump yard, required one horse to pull a single car with 2½ tons of coal, weighing 3½ tons in all, up the incline. Once the cars reached the steam-powered planes it was easier going all the way to Honesdale.

There were five planes, climbing a total of 950 feet up the west side of the mountain out of Carbondale. Each was a single track, with a section of double track for passing, about 150 feet long, midway. A long chain extended the full length of the plane, attached to a stationary steam engine which, with its boiler house, stood at the top of the plane. Five loaded cars would be hooked to the lower end of the chain and five empties to the upper end. With power from the steam engine, the chain pulled the loaded cars up the plane, assisted by the weight of the descending empties. At the turnout, spring-operated switches guided the two strings of cars onto the passing tracks at the middle of the plane.

The three planes descending toward Honesdale on the east side of the mountain operated by gravity alone, for the descending loaded cars were heavy enough to raise the empties at the other end of the chain. Again the two cuts of cars would pass on spring-operated passing tracks in the middle

35

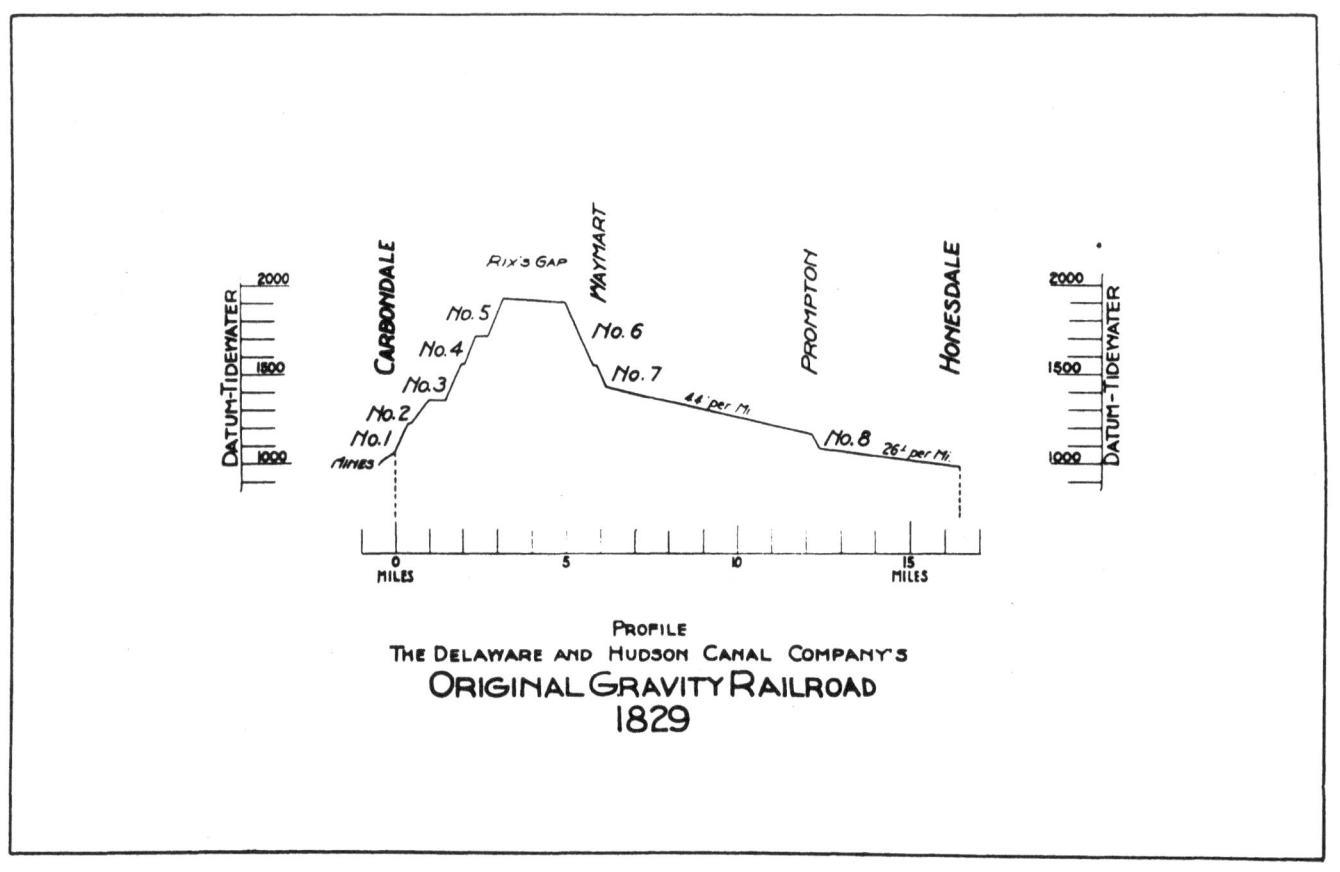

PROFILE
THE DELAWARE AND HUDSON CANAL COMPANY'S
ORIGINAL GRAVITY RAILROAD
1829

of the incline. The chain passed over a drum and brake bands were attached to the shaft of the drum to stop the cars at the end of the move. Even more imaginative, was the mechanism used to control the rate of descent during the trip down the plane. A large fan wheel, like a giant windmill, was geared to the drum and the resistance of the air on the blades of this big fan dissipated the energy created and controlled the velocity of the cars on the incline.

If for any reason there was an interruption in loaded car movements a tank car full of water was used as a counterbalance to pull the empties up the plane. At the foot of the plane the tank was emptied and the counterbalance car was returned to the top with the next trip of empties.

There were three relatively long stretches called levels between the summit and Honesdale. These stretches were not actually level but graded in favor of the loaded cars. The summit level, 9,250 feet long, descended only 14 feet from the top of Plane 5 at the crest of the ridge, 945 above the canal basin, to the head of Plane 6, the first descending plane. It was on this stretch that Jervis had proposed using one of the four steam locomotives. A horse could only pull two loaded cars on this level but fortunately it was short. From the east end of the summit level at Farview two descending planes connected by a 400-foot flat stretch brought the cars down to Waymart.

On the six-mile level between Waymart and Prompton a grade of 44 feet per mile allowed the cars to roll all the way by themselves and old Dobbin rode down in a car at the rear of the loaded train. Several horses would ride down on each descending train as they could only pull four empty cars each in the reverse direction.

The four-mile level ran from the last descending plane at Prompton to the canal basin and had a grade of 26½ feet per mile, allowing one horse to draw five loads down to Honesdale and the same number of empties back. Each of the two long levels had passing sidings near the middle.

Before long it became apparent that the chains were less than satisfactory as a means of raising and lowering the cars on the planes. Each string of cars was liable to be wrecked by the failure of any one of the more than 150,000 links comprising the chains securing them on the planes and as the chains began to wear accidents became more and more frequent. A portable blacksmith's forge was kept at each plane so it could be taken to the scene of a break and a new link immediately put in. Repairing the chain was nuisance enough but when it broke, the train attached to it at the time would careen down the incline usually wrecking itself and any cars waiting at the foot of the plane as well. To remedy this problem large hemp ropes were substituted for the chains and the accident rate dropped almost to nothing. Wear on the ropes could be easily seen and replacement made well in advance of failure. In later years wire rope, invented by John Roebling, replaced the hemp lines.

Until the bugs had been worked out of the whole operation, including both the mine and canal as well as the gravity road, the projected 100,000 tons annually was not achieved. The operational season was only 200 days, corresponding roughly to the boating season on the canal, but by 1834 the full capacity was reached. Improvements in both operational technique and hardware, such as the replacement of the chains with ropes, enabled this goal to be attained and soon passed. In 1837, another step toward greater production was the replacement of the steep incline leading from the mines at Carbondale to the foot of Plane 1, with a water-powered plane 1000 feet long. The cars were raised 80 feet and from the head of this new plane rolled 1500 feet to the foot of the steam-powered plane, considerably increasing efficiency and cutting the cost of moving the cars on that section by at least two cents a ton.

Once the railroad and canal were operating smoothly, the D&H got down to the serious business of moving coal, with the quantity increasing yearly as the market and the company's experience grew. The gravity line remained essentially the same until 1841, by which time annual volumes of almost 200,000 tons began to strain the existing facilities and it was clear that substantial expansion was necessary.

James Archbald, an astute Scotsman, was an associate of John B. Jervis and had been employed by the D&H almost from the beginning. He was the engineer in charge of the railroad and mines at the time and made a number of recommendations to the managers concerning changes on the railroad. He was authorized to execute these improvements and enlargements as soon as possible.

Archbald began his work at the end of the 1841 season and built a new set of planes up the hill out of Carbondale. They were all double tracked, as were Plane 1, which remained in its original location but was slightly lengthened, and Plane 7 which was otherwise virtually unchanged. The changes in location were made to equalize the lengths of the inclined planes and to give the levels between adjacent planes a greater slope in favor of the loaded cars. A half mile was saved between Plane 1 and the summit, and the five new steam hoisting engines were much more powerful than the old ones. All these changes were intended to increase the system's operating capacity.

The summit level was shortened somewhat so the cars would roll east on a steeper descending grade, and Plane 6 on the east side of the ridge was cut into two separate planes. Because of its great length, almost three-quarters of a mile, it was difficult to move more than 350,000 tons over it annually. Shorter planes would permit faster operation. The two halves of old Plane 6 were fitted with improved machinery as was Plane 7.

From the foot of Plane 7, at Waymart, on to Honesdale now was made one single descending grade for the whole ten miles. The six-mile level had a downgrade of 44 feet per mile and this was continued on past Plane 8, eliminating it completely, allowing the loads to go all the way into Honesdale on their own. Originally the six-mile and four-mile levels were single track with passing tracks in the middle but now they were both double tracked.

The most significant change Archbald made was to construct a "light track," an independent route from the basin at Honesdale back to Plane 7 at Waymart for the empty cars. This completely separated the routes of the empty and loaded cars. Due to the rolling nature of the country along this new route five planes were necessary to give the empty cars enough elevation to allow their run by gravity to the foot of the next plane. At first, four of these planes were powered by steam and one by water power. By 1847 another was powered with water and two more were scheduled for changeover too. The first plane up out of Honesdale was the steepest on the line, rising on a grade of one foot in five, and because of the location

The first locomotive used on the gravity line, the MAJOR SYKES, was originally built as an 0-4-0. After a wreck in 1872 she was rebuilt, emerging as an 0-6-0. Below, a cut of five cars ascends Plane 23 at Olyphant, from Valley Junction. *(G. M. Best collection, above; D&H collection)*

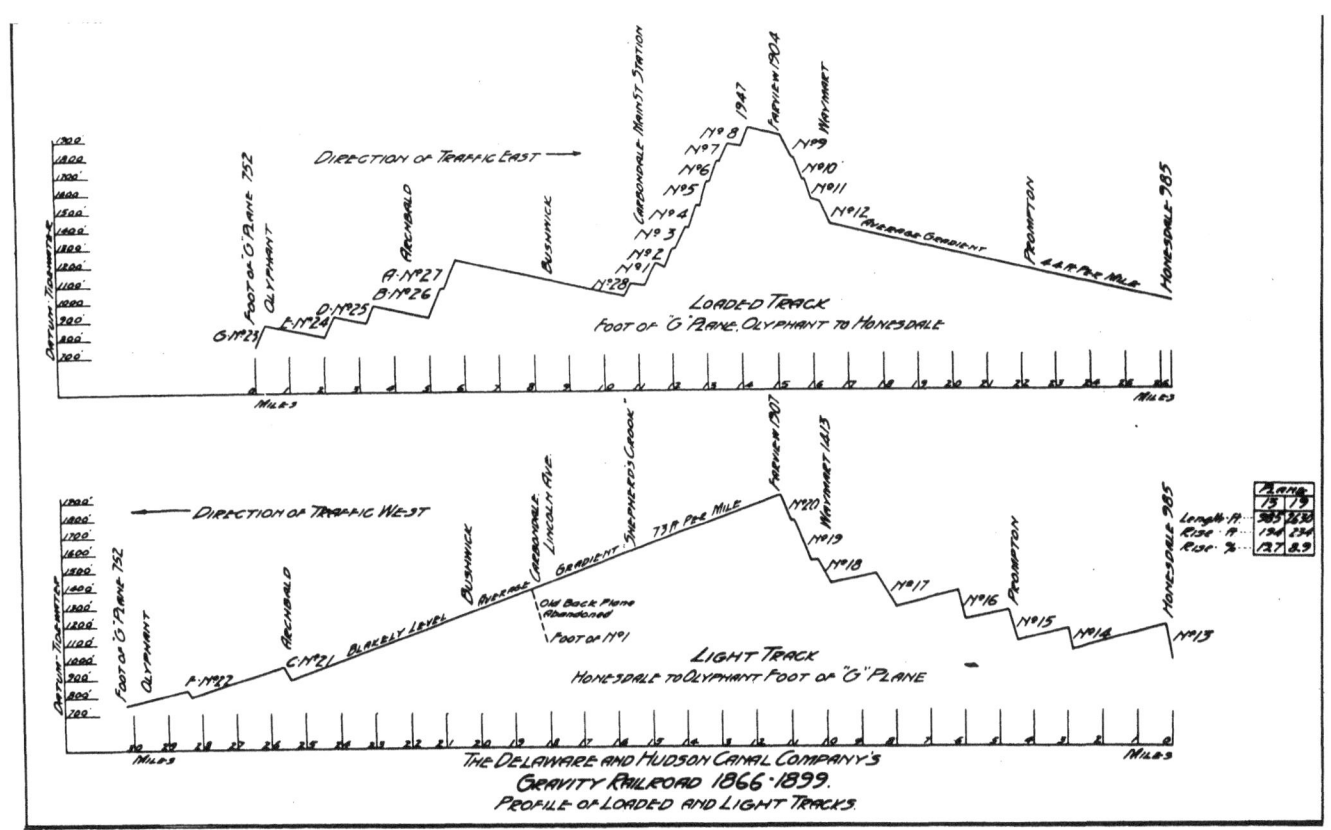

of the summit as well as the steepness of the grade, had to be powered by a steam engine. Several years later the others were changed to steam as well, due to the uncertainty of a steady supply of water all year.

South of Carbondale in the Lackawanna valley the company had owned coal lands for some time and during the general rebuilding program new mines were being opened at White Oak Run, now the borough named in honor of engineer Archbald. In 1843 when the other work was planned, the company decided to include a seven-mile extension of the gravity road, south from Carbondale to this point. Archbald used the same principle here that he employed on the light-track run from Honesdale into Waymart. Two steam-powered planes were built up the east side of the valley at the south end of the extension from which the loaded cars rolled all the way to Carbondale by gravity alone. At Carbondale a single incline, called the Back Plane, was built to give the empty cars enough elevation to start them on their seven-mile run down the valley to the new mines.

As the volume of coal steadily continued to increase further modifications were required on the gravity line and in 1856 it was necessary to rebuild the entire line from Carbondale to Waymart. New planes and connecting levels were installed adjacent to the existing ones between Carbondale and the summit and two more were added making eight, each double-tracked. The most important change at this time was the installation of iron "T" rail and regular crossties over the entire line replacing the strap rail and generally bringing the line up to the latest railroad standards of the day. The hemp hoisting ropes were replaced with wire rope at the same time.

Two years later, in 1858, the line was extended six more miles down the Lackawanna valley below Archbald through the town of Olyphant to a terminal called Valley Junction. This extension involved the use of two southbound and three northbound steam-powered planes.

The valley line was pushed four miles further down the valley in 1860 to new mines near Providence, now a suburb of Scranton, but this time the gravity principle was not employed. Locomotive power was used for the first time since the ill-fated trials of the STOURBRIDGE LION in 1829 to move the cars over this new section. This opera-

Engine No. 3, the HONESDALE, was built in 1861 by W. Cook & Co. The trim ISAAC N. SEYMOUR, an 1866 product of the New Jersey Locomotive & Machine Co., exploded at Carbondale in 1879. Although built to haul passenger trains, she appears in the view of Valley Junction, below, pushing a cut of coal cars to the foot of plane 23 to be pulled north toward Carbondale. (*D&H collection, middle; G. M. Best collection, two pictures*)

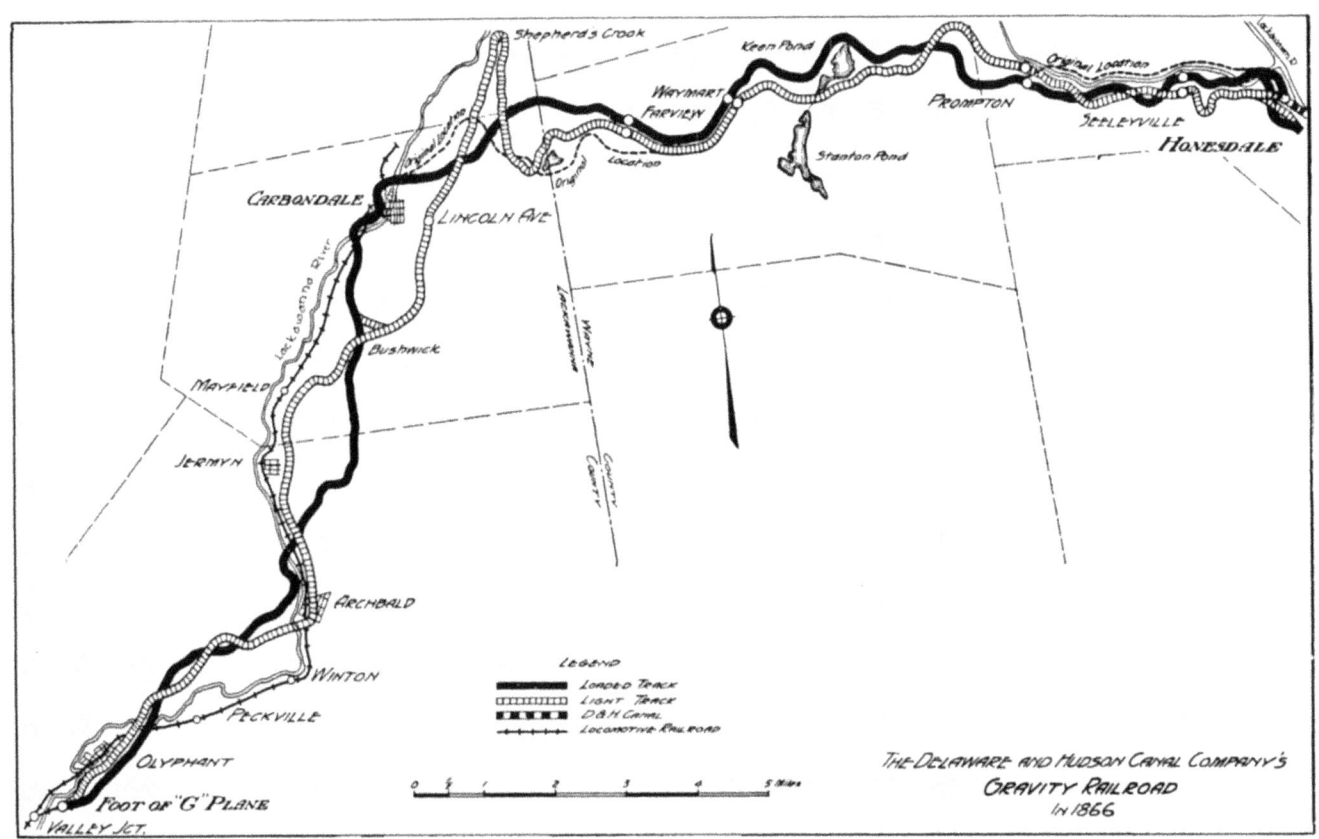

tion constituted the beginning of locomotive operations on what was eventually to become the Delaware & Hudson Railroad.

Two 4'3"-gauge engines were built for this operation by W. Cook & Co. of Scranton, an 0-4-0 called the MAJOR SYKES and a little 4-4-0 named C. P. WURTS. Passenger service was inaugurated that summer with two small cars having a single bench on each side, and within a couple of years developed into scheduled service up and down the valley from Carbondale to Providence via the gravity line and the locomotive road.

The Dickson Machine Co. of Scranton built and repaired mining machinery and in 1862 tried their hand at building a steam locomotive at the request of the D&H for their expanding flat railroad operation. This little 0-6-0 was named LACKAWANNA and turned out to be the first of a long line of locomotives built at their works not only for the D&H but for many other major roads in the east.

The last changes to the gravity road were made in 1866 and involved alterations to the planes on the eastern slope of Moosic Mountain between Farview and Waymart. This work provided independent movement of light and loaded cars which had been dependent on each other at this section and required the building of three new planes for the light track. The most significant change, however, was on the western slope where a new light car track was built from Farview down to the head of the Back Plane near Carbondale. The Back Plane was the beginning of the gravity line down the valley south of Carbondale, but was now abandoned in favor of the new line six miles long on which the cars moved by gravity alone. This new route thus eliminated the need for two ascending and eight descending planes.

The new section opened on April 21, 1868 and for the greater part of its length followed the contour of the ravines descending at a steady slope of 73 ft. per mile. From Farview it ran southwesterly and roughly paralleled the original gravity line for a distance but then swung to the north and crossed the loaded track near the head of Plane 5. Continuing north for about a mile the line then looped around a spectacular horseshoe curve known as Shepherd's Crook and headed south toward Archbald down the western slope of the ridge on the

41

original route of the extension from Carbondale south in the valley. From Farview to Archbald, a distance of 14 miles, the empty cars could roll in long trains without a single delay, thereby materially increasing the coal-carrying capacity of the road.

With the completion of these last changes the gravity railroad remained essentially the same until its abandonment in 1899 when the canal was shut down.

Passenger service was expanded to the entire gravity line in 1877, extending the movements already in operation down the valley south of Carbondale now to Honesdale as well. A connection was built between the light car track and the loaded car track at Bushwick, just south of Carbondale, so westbound passenger trains could roll down into Carbondale to a point called Lookout Junction. From there a standard gauge steam locomotive would haul the train up into town over three-rail trackage.

During the period after the last alterations the original coal cars were gradually replaced with larger cars having a five-ton capacity and at the peak nearly 5000 cars were carried on the gravity railroad roster. These were all eight-wheeled and had link and pin couplers. The loaded cars were hauled up the eastbound planes in groups of five at a speed of 15 to 20 mph. After reaching Waymart they were assembled into trains of 80 cars for the non-stop run all the way to the Canal Basin in Honesdale at a speed of 20 mph. For the long trip between Farview and Archbald westbound, the empty cars were made up into 75-car trains and with a three-man crew rolled at 20 mph around Shepherd's Crook back to the mines. Freight train crews consisted of three men, the head man, middle man and boss runner.

To protect the line against runaways in which cars became detached from the cable or from each other while being hauled up the planes, spring latches were spaced at intervals along the inclines. These derails were normally open for any downward moving cars but would be pushed closed by the ascending cars when they approached the point in normal operation.

Passenger trains were allowed speeds up to 35 mph and were run with a three-man crew, a conductor and two brakemen. Here the brakeman was exactly that and controlled the speed and opera-

The Carbondale yard was busy during this bright day in Civil War times. Cars laden with various sizes of anthracite wait their turn for the trip up the planes and over the mountain to the canal basin at Honesdale. The yard switchers are big white draft horses. *(D&H collection)*

Three official-looking gentlemen gaze at the big curve at Shepherd's Crook, right. In the foreground is an open observation car of a type used in summer. The gravity coal cars, below, carried five tons each. Engine No. 4, the LACKAWANNA, was the first of many fine steam locomotives built by the Dickson Machine Works of Scranton. (D&H collection, two pictures; G. M. Best collection, bottom)

The view of the Moosic mountain country must have been inspiring indeed from the wicker easy chairs on the open platforms of summer observation car No. 80. Gravity coach No. 9, the *Eclipse*, appears with standard gauge trucks, a number of years after abandonment of the gravity road, as a preserved memento of the old days on the hill. (*D&H collection*)

tion of the train. The head brakeman rode the front platform and operated a bell by pushing a foot button on the platform much like a trolley car, for signalling purposes and as a warning when approaching crossings or stations. When the train required braking the head man would apply the hand brake, bunching the slack in the cars and indicating to the rear man that he should do likewise. No doubt the crews were so thoroughly familiar with the route that they would automatically apply the brakes at the right time and with the proper force anyway. Running as they did long before the invention of multiple unit electric interurban trains, it must have been a strange sight indeed for an outsider to see a string of cars rolling through the countryside without a locomotive on the front.

The country encountered by the gravity road, especially the section from Waymart to Carbondale was of notable scenic beauty and was visited by large numbers of travelers after inauguration of service in 1877. At first the service was purely local but later the company developed a picnic park at Farview, which in the summer months attracted thousands of excursionists daily. There were few more popular trips than the ride up the planes from Carbondale to Farview and returning by way of Shepherd's Crook. On a record day in September 1898, nearly 15,000 passengers were transported to Farview in special trains.

The first passenger coaches were built with an enclosed section in the middle with an open section at each end having seats running lengthwise in both the open and closed sections. Later a standard type of coach with a slightly rounded roof but not as wide as a regular railroad coach, permitted double seats on one side but only a row of single seats on the opposite side of the aisles. A combination coach usually made up the front or rear of each train and handled the baggage and other items of a bulky nature. During the summer open cars, resembling open streetcars, were used. A regular consist for the scheduled runs was a baggage car on the head end, a closed coach and two open coaches. Special moves to the Farview picnic area usually were made up entirely of opens. At the height of passenger operations, the road had 36 open excursion cars and 12 regular passenger cars.

The scheduled running time for passenger trains from Carbondale to Honesdale was one hour and fifteen minutes and the return trip took ten minutes longer. Year around operation was a necessity, for the passenger service at least, and winter movements were seriously interrupted by a snowfall. Starting the trains was difficult and snowsheds were built at points where drifting was prevalent. At one point they were considering enclosing all the planes but this never came about. It was not unusual to see the front end brakeman clearing the rail with a broom as the train moved slowly along or to see the crew jumping on the chain that linked the cars together to obtain a little motion to get the train moving after a station stop. In addition to the passenger service some coal was moved in the winter and stored at Honesdale for spring shipment.

One day in 1869, Abraham Richards, a miner who came to this country from Wales that summer was waiting at the Lookout Junction station for his wife and five children to arrive from the old country. They had arrived in New York on September 6 and came by Delaware, Lackawanna & Western train to Scranton, then known as Slocum Hollow. The trip up the valley to Carbondale was made on the D&H's gravity line.

Trainman Elliott (Pop) Skeels and conductor A. W. Daly greeted the happy party that was looking forward to the reunion that was to take place shortly in Carbondale. As the train neared Jermyn, however, a passenger, Mrs. William Wilber, noticed that the mother was in distress and asked the conductor to have the car vacated and the train stopped. Mrs. Wilber recognized the problem immediately; the woman was expecting and her hour had arrived.

A doctor was summoned from the town and the car turned into a temporary maternity ward. Later, when the mother and the twin girls were made as comfortable as possible under the conditions, the train continued on up to the Lookout station just below Carbondale. There Mr. Richards was waiting for his wife and five children but to his utter astonishment there were seven children, all his, that got off the train that day. The only transportation he brought was a wagon and the Richards family went home—all 8 of them—in the back with a visibly shaken man holding the reins.

Farview station at Rix's Gap on the crest of the Moosic Mountains was destination for many picnic groups in the decades after 1866. The private car *Passaic*, along with what appears to be a work car, is stopped on the big curve at Shepherd's Crook. (*D&H collection*)

The twins, Dinah Delaware and Catherine Hudson, with their mother, Mrs. Abraham Richards.

Out of deference to the kindness of the trainmen and apparently always to remind the girls that they literally arrived in this world aboard a train, they were named Catherine Hudson and Dinah Delaware Richards. The superintendent of the railroad, Thomas Dickson, presented the little girls with a gift of $20 and two silver medallions made from a 50-cent piece with the inscription "Catherine H. Richards - Dinah D. Richards, twins, born in Delaware and Hudson R. R. cars, between Scranton and Carbondale, September 7, 1869."

Of all the incidents that took place on the old gravity lines over the years, and there were many both good and bad, none was more endearing than the birth of the two little girls as it was one of the happiest and to say the least, one of the most unexpected.

THE OLD GRAVITY
(By An Old Gravity Veteran)

Great stacks of reddish brick
  Rising like obelisks
Above sheds of sombre brown,
  On each hilltop conspicuous;
Your noisy groans heard afar
  Stretching your ropes and
Struggling hard to make
  Industry's wheels go round.
Born in a wilderness
  Of courage and brawn,
Over mountains and valleys
  And under great difficulties
Your course went on.
  But you were the Victor,
Your purpose well done,
  Old Gravity, your course is run.

I sat before the grate last night
  And watched the fire's gleam,
Before me passed the olden times,
  It seemed just like a dream.
Faces and forms of my younger days,
  Scenes long past and gone,
Came trooping by in an endless stream
  To the tune of an endless song.
It was the song of the gravity wheels,
  Of pulleys and ropes and gear,
A song that came softly as from afar,
  Though the touch to my heart was near.

The whistle blew at Number Eight,
  It was five o'clock in the morn,
And it was repeated along the line
  As another work-day was born.
Another day for effort and toil
  Every man taking his part,
And the coal went on over the hills
  To reach industry's mart.
A giant had awakened from his sleep
  And his sinews and muscles strong
Were drawn tense for another day
  To move black diamonds along.

Hark to the clank of the iron links,
  It's the sling detached from the cone,
And hark to the screech of the brakes on the wheels
  As over the head they have gone.
Five loads at a time go up the plane,
  And drop to their place in the train,
It's the tune of the wheels as forward they go,
  That comes in clattering refrain.
A refrain of the past, half joyful, half sad,
  Filled with memories of those gone away,
A longing for the days and the scenes that are past
  The old and the young and the gay.

The whistle blew at Number Eight,
  It was six o'clock at night,
It was repeated along the line,
  For the day had taken flight.
Since the morning blast the giant awoke,
  And aroused him from his sleep
The wheels had sung a continuous tune
  Like the wind and murmuring deep.
It was the song of the gravity wheels,
  Of the pulleys and ropes and gear,
A song that came softly as from afar,
  Though the touch to my heart was near.

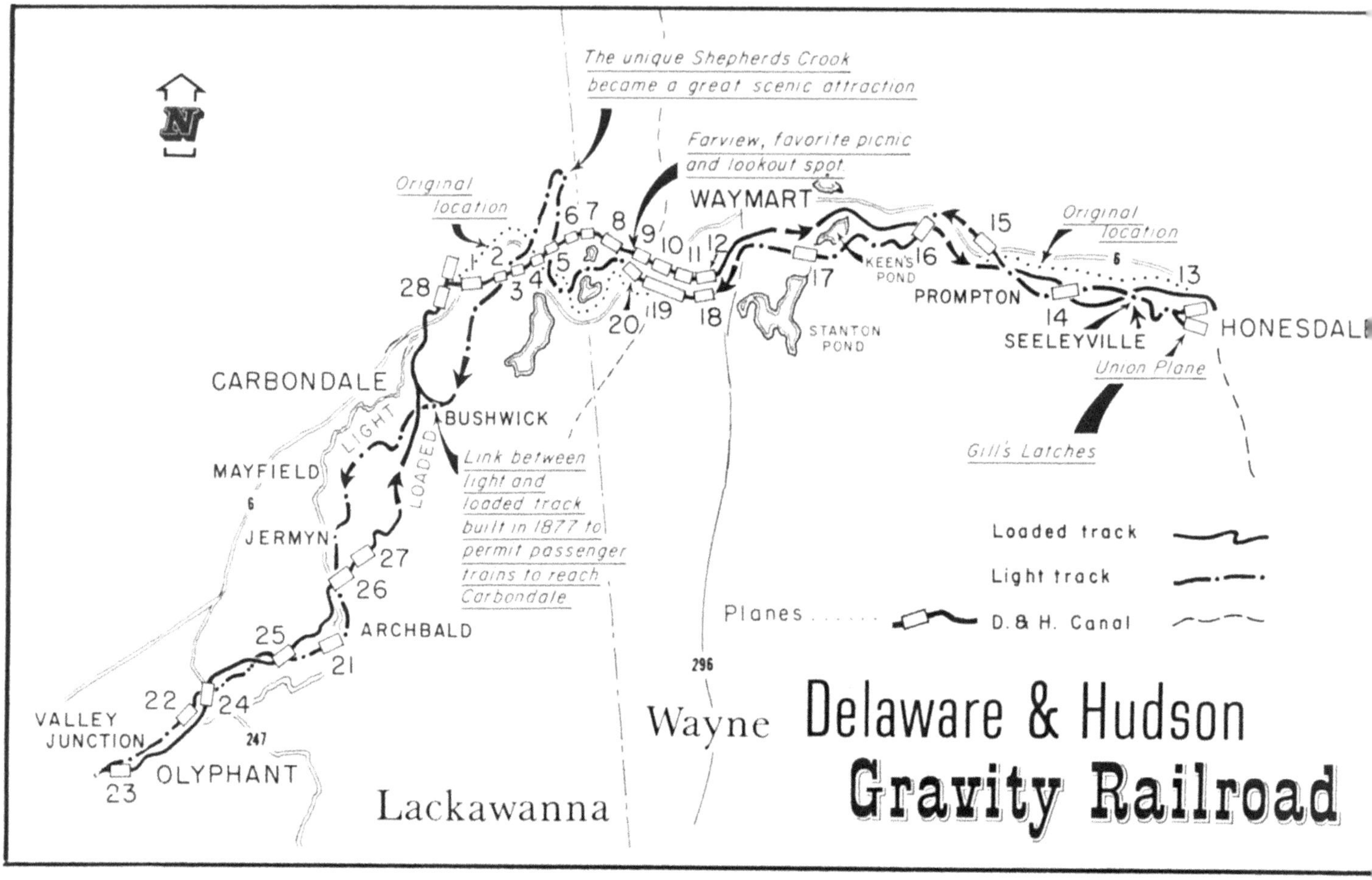

Delaware & Hudson Gravity Railroad

The map from *Coal Boats to Tidewater* shows the system as it was from 1866 to 1899. The private car *Passaic* is behind a coal train at the right, below, passing over the "high works" trestle in Carbondale on its way to the foot of Plane 1, for forwarding to Honesdale. The same plane appears in another Carbondale view, opposite. *(Manville B. Wakefield, above; G. M. Best collection, below; D&H collection, opposite)*

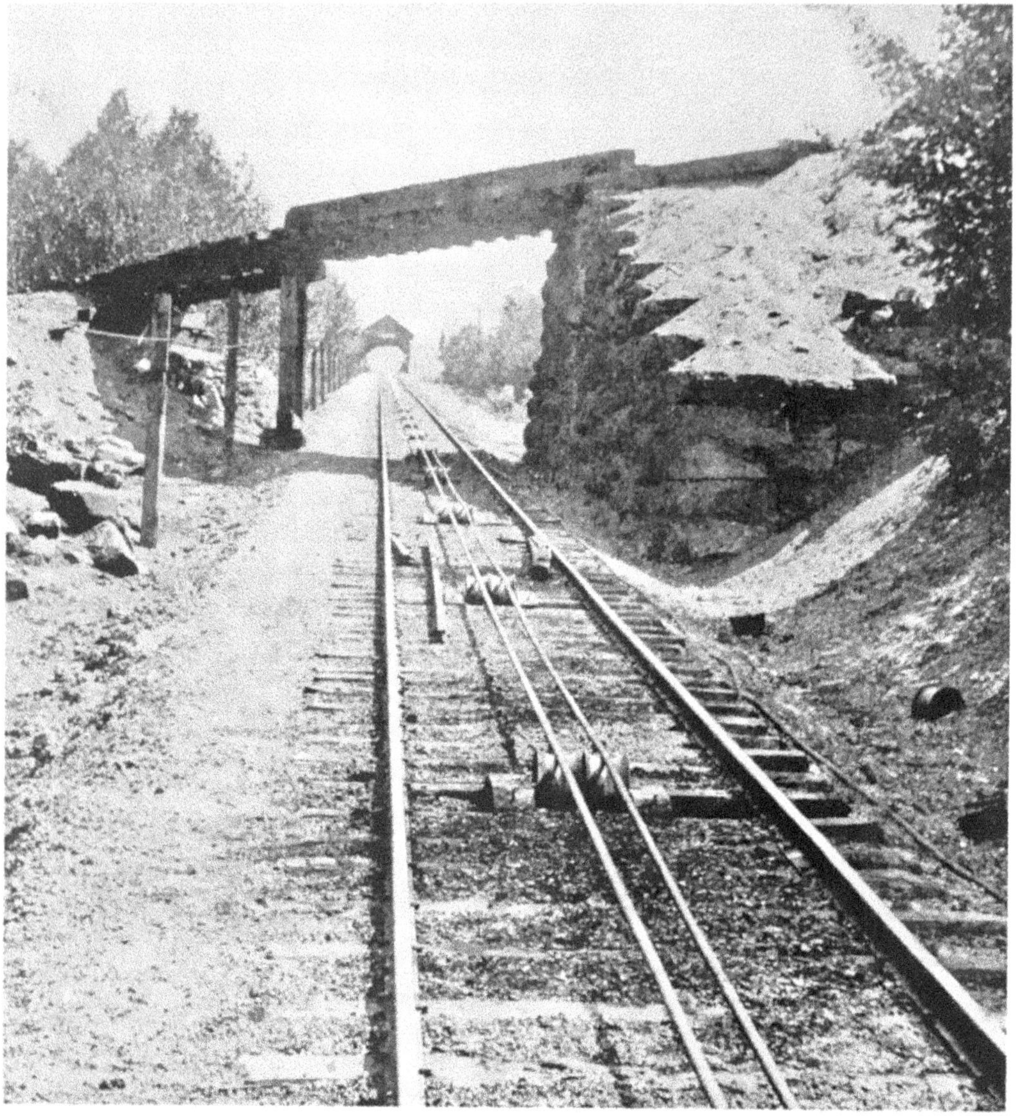

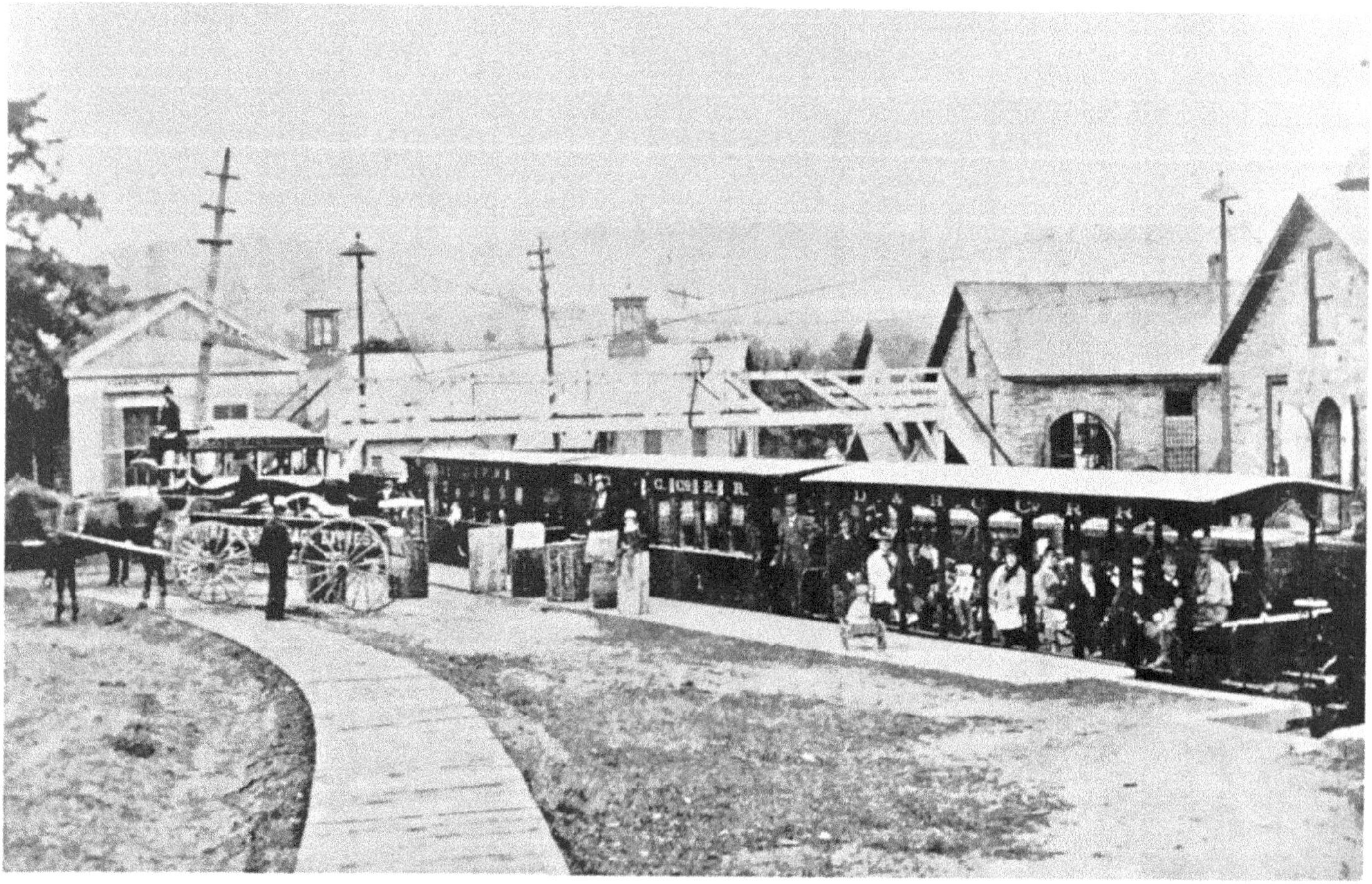

Details of the cable and idler pulleys can be seen, opposite, in the view of Plane 2, above Carbondale. The overpass carries the light car tracks toward the mines. Below that is a passenger train at Carbondale; the machine shops appear in the background. On this page are views of Racket Brook Breaker and Plane 4. At the right a group of workers push coal cars into the loading tracks, while a string of loads waits to go up the plane. (G. M. Best collection, below; D&H collection, three pictures)

Summer picnic traffic at Farview was so great as to warrant the overpass across Plane 9 to provide passengers with access to Plane 20, opposite above. Below that is a view of the passenger station at Honesdale with Plane 13 rising directly up the hill, with the chimney of its boiler house visible at the top. Other views of the boat basin and gravity tracks there appear on this page, with passenger cars starting up Plane 13. Loaded cars moved down the sloping track coming in above it. The white horse, below, moved cars to the foot of the plane. *(D&H collection)*

The westbound train in the wintry view above begins its ascent of Plane 18 toward the summit of the Moosic range at Farview. The counterbalance in the foreground, below, kept the cable taut on light-car Plane 20 that leads to Farview and the summit at Rix's Gap. Plane 9, at the right of the picture, brings loaded cars down from there. On the opposite page, a similar counterbalance appears in the upper picture, with a safety derail in the foreground. Plane 11, with loaded cars on it, and Plane 10, up the hill beyond it, are each about half the length of Plane 19, at the left. Gravity cars were hauled by steam locomotives between the Scranton terminal, below, and Carbondale. (*G. M. Best collection, above; D&H collection, three pictures*)

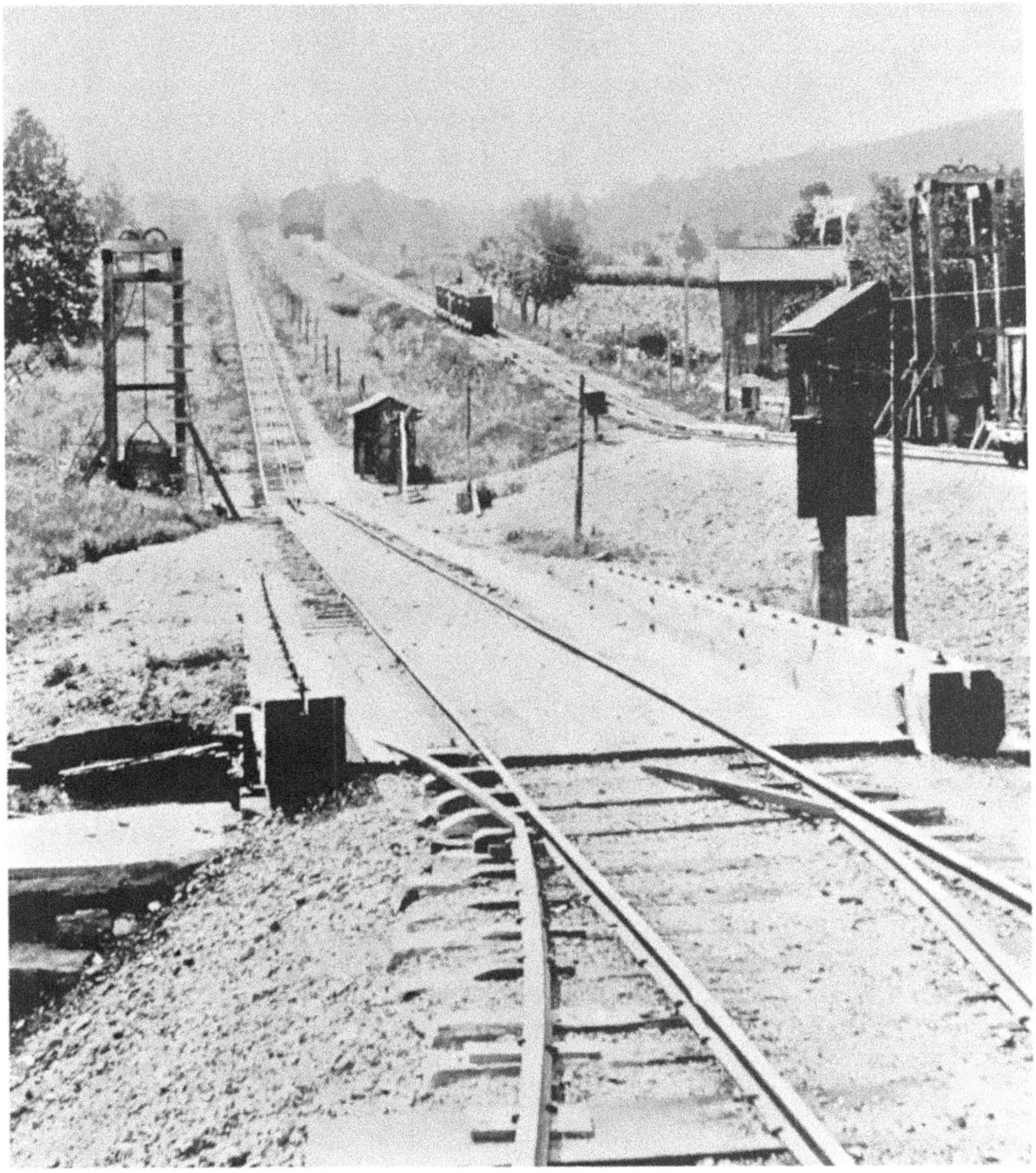

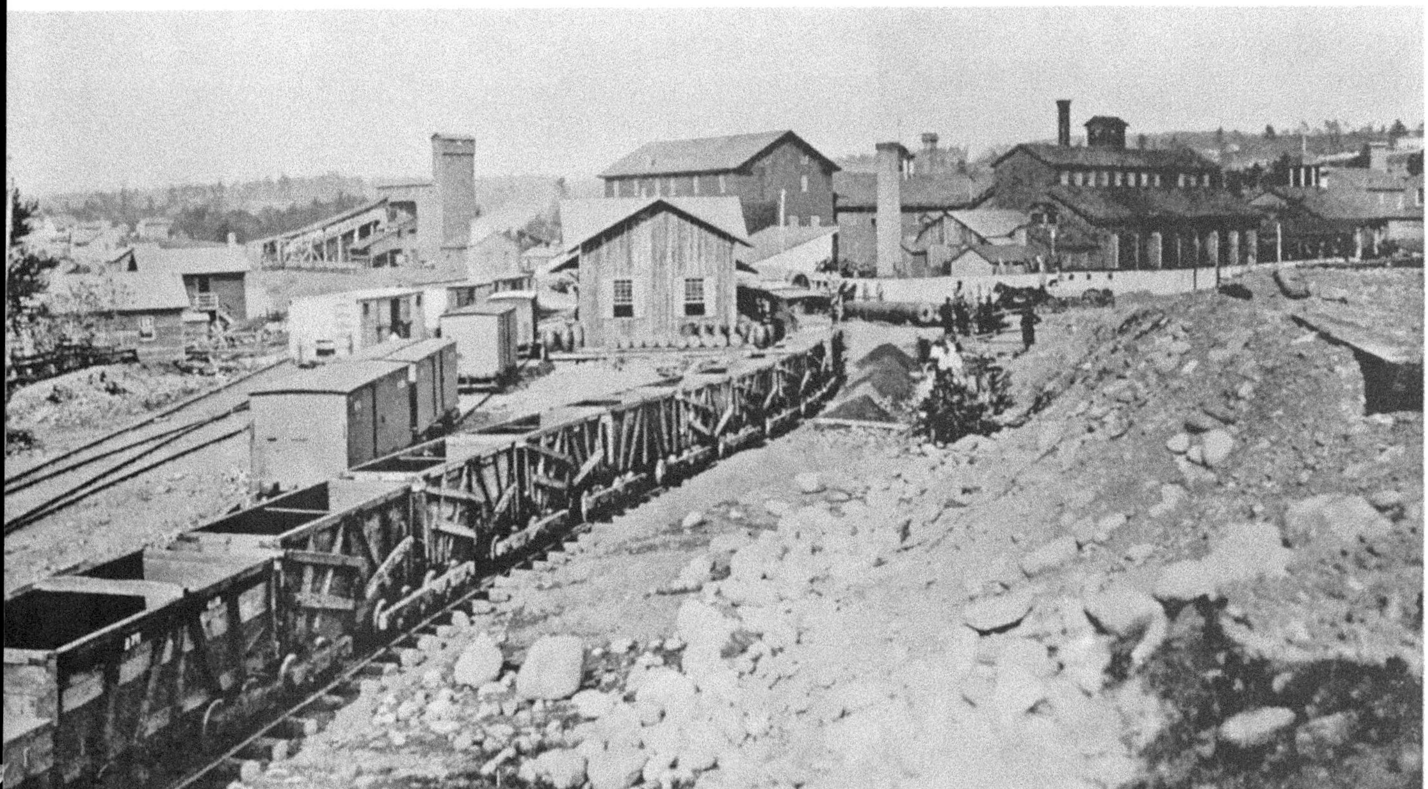

The curve of Shepherd's Crook had a diameter of 400 feet, a grade of 110 feet to the mile and returned to within 82 feet of itself, but 37 feet below the level of the rails in the foreground of the two pictures on this page. A 75-car train of empties rolls back to the mines, above, and a three-car passenger train is at the same point, below, on the 14-mile uninterrupted descent from Farview to Archbald. The gravity cars were hoisted up the planes by engines like the two-cylinder beauty, opposite, at the top of Plane 13. Below it is a view of the boiler and engine house at the head of Plane 22 between Carbondale and Olyphant, as it appeared in 1860. (*G. M. Best collection, two top pictures; D&H collection, below*)

This little 0-6-0 mine engine, the PORTO RICO, wasn't very impressive, even as compared with the D&H's early road power, but she made her contribution hauling big chunks of coal from the mines to the breaker. *(Al Gayer collection)*

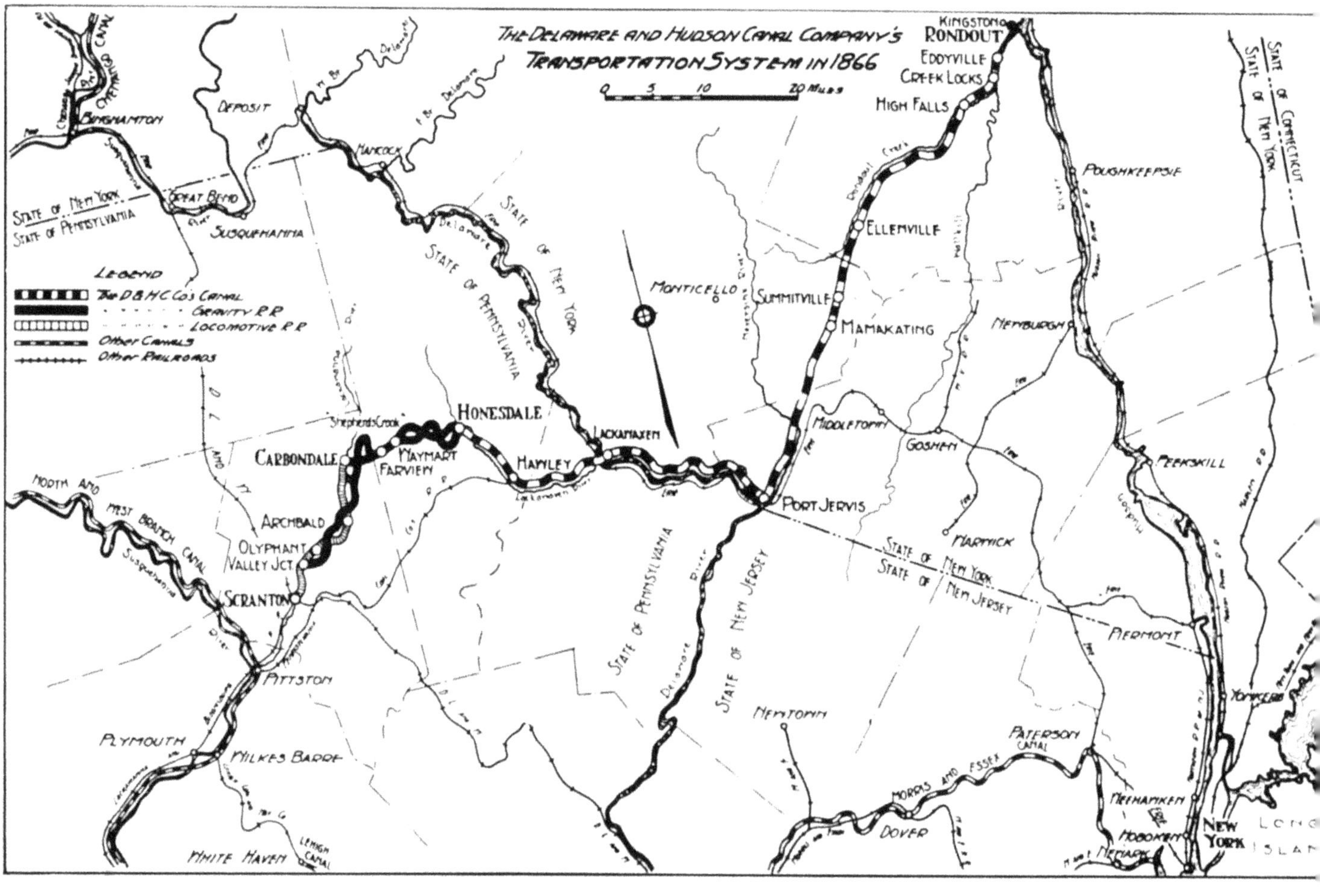

3. THE GREAT RAILROAD EXPANSION

The Delaware & Hudson's 16-mile gravity railroad constituted most of the railroad mileage in the United States in 1830, a meager total of 23 miles. By 1840 the total had grown to 2,818; a decade later it was 9,021 and then a railroad-building boom resulted in 30,635 miles being in operation by 1860.

Strangely enough, the D&H, which in 1829 operated the first steam locomotive in America, the STOURBRIDGE LION, had run none since the trial trips. The little pioneer engine had worked quite well, but was defeated, ironically, by the inadequate roadbed. Meanwhile, locomotives came into wide use on other railroads as their dependability and power increased. Probably even more important, in view of the LION's sad experience, was improvement in track design construction and hardware to the point that the railroad was technologically a sound and practical instrument of transportation.

The managers had for some time been aware of the advantages that the railroad could offer the company. It could permit year-around movement of coal, independent of the effects of winter on the canal. Even more important was the fact that vast new markets, free of competition, could be reached as an outlet for the company's ever-increasing production of anthracite. In 1860 the D&H embarked on its own career of flat railroading when it extended the gravity line down to Providence, three miles below Valley Junction, and elected to use locomotives on this section rather than building additional stationary-powered planes. Two little 4′3″ gauge locomotives were obtained from W. Cook & Co. to operate the new extension.

George Talbot Olyphant was elected president of the company on March 15, 1858, after having actually served in that capacity for three years since the spring of 1855 when President John Wurts' health prevented his full and effective leadership of the growing enterprise. Olyphant was the first D&H president who hadn't been identified with the company's formative years. He was from a new and different generation and closely in touch with most of the commercial and technical trends of his time.

Progress and expansion, he knew, would be necessary if the company were to maintain the leadership and success it had thus far enjoyed. Accordingly he followed a policy of acquiring additional coal-bearing lands and sought to expand the company's market. He was well aware of the potential advantages of moving coal by rail and began to explore all the available possibilities.

The Civil War greatly increased the demand for coal, and the mines in the Lackawanna valley were more active than ever, considerably increasing the income of the D&H Canal Co. This added income was doubly welcome in view of the unfavorable outcome of the suit that had been pending since 1856 against the Pennsylvania Coal Co. It will be recalled that the litigation concerned the canal tolls to be paid by that company for movement of coal from Hawley to tidewater, and that the final settlement in 1863 awarded the D&H only a quarter of the outstanding amount it claimed. This setback was eased by the flood of business activity brought by the war. In 1863 the demand for coal was even greater than the company's production or transportation facilities could handle, and the price was forced up. As a result,

59

George Talbot Olyphant, fourth president of the D&H, 1859-1869.

earnings that year were almost double those of 1862.

Late in 1863 the managers decided to investigate the possibility of shipping coal over the Erie Railroad from a point near Susquehanna, Pennsylvania—actually, the smaller nearby community of Lanesboro—37 miles north of Carbondale, to the Buffalo area and the Great Lakes basin to the west, when that line was completed all the way. The talks with the Erie went well enough to encourage the managers, early in 1864, to seek a rail connection between Carbondale and Lanesboro. At that time it was necessary to take coal on the gravity line to Honesdale, then on canal boats to Lackawaxen, where at last it could be loaded on cars of the Erie a full 81 miles to the southeast of Lanesboro. The 37-mile link therefore would replace a roundabout trip of about 120 miles involving two costly reloadings. The managers held conferences with the Jefferson Railroad, a company already chartered, to consider building a line from Carbondale to Lanesboro. The Civil War was still in progress and several years were to elapse before anything came of these discussions.

After the Civil War ended, the company easily made the transition from war to peacetime conditions, gradually returning to a somewhat lower level of production and income without noticeable effects. During and following the war the company greatly increased its coal holdings in the Lackawanna and Wyoming valleys, from Carbondale to Wilkes-Barre. By gaining control of such companies as the Plymouth & Wilkes-Barre Railroad & Bridge Co., the Howard Coal & Iron Co., the Union Coal Co. and the Northern Coal & Iron Co., it gained access to thousands of acres of additional coal-bearing lands, many mine openings, company houses and stores, breakers and processing plants, a first-class railroad bridge across the Susquehanna River from Wilkes-Barre to Plymouth, and miles of railroad which were then tied together to form a network of feeder rail lines. Because of franchise limitations in its own charter, the D&H came to use the Northern Coal & Iron Co. as the instrument through which it acquired these vast properties and railroads.

To Vice President Thomas Dickson was given the task of coordinating all these facilities into a smoothly-operating system that was soon sending a flood of anthracite north in the Lackawanna valley to Valley Junction above Scranton, and on over the gravity lines to Honesdale. Before long these railroad operations were moving nearly 5000 passengers a month as well as the huge tonnage of coal. In 1865 the D&H began the final expansion of its gravity lines east of Carbondale to match its coal-handling capacity to the increase in production facilities.

Meanwhile, in New York State, there was a development of interest to the D&H people, for it offered a prospect of expanding the company's market in that direction. The Albany & Susquehanna Railroad had been chartered in 1851 to build a six-foot gauge line south from Albany through the fertile Susquehanna valley to Binghamton. Through the 1850s and early 1860s there was often serious doubt that the project would ever be carried out, because of financial difficulties and ensuing delays, but in 1866 the line was completed to Unadilla. As it became apparent that the A&S was finally going to be completed, the managers of the D&H recognized this route as a means of reaching the towns in the valley, and the Albany area as well, on a year-round basis. They negotiated a contract with the A&S in July, 1866, providing for completion of the road to Nineveh, New York, within a year and for moving D&H anthracite over it in A&S cars from any point where tendered for loading. This somewhat peculiar provision was probably due to the fact that both the A&S and the Erie—as well as the proposed line north out of Carbondale—were six-foot gauge and the D&H had no equipment of this gauge in which it could move its coal. Under the agreement, the D&H bought $500,000 worth of A&S second-mortgage bonds to help keep the whole project moving. This agreement was reached some thirty months before the contract was finally made to build the line north from Carbondale; evidently the managers had already made the decision to seek a northern outlet and the only question still unresolved was whether the proposed line was to be built by the Erie or by the D&H's subsidiary, the Northern Coal & Iron Co., which had surveyed the route several years earlier.

The Delaware & Hudson Canal Co., as chartered in 1823, had no general railroad rights in New York State. As a prelude to the general expansion program in the railroad field, the managers petitioned and received these rights from the State Legislature in May of 1867. The act endowed the D&H with all the powers and privileges enjoyed by railroad companies incorporated under the general railroad act of 1850. In time this legislation would prove to be of far greater value than the managers ever could have foreseen in 1867.

By additional construction work in 1867 and 1868 the Albany & Susquehanna was completed down the valley to Nineveh and over Belden Hill to Binghamton. The line was finally opened throughout its entire length on January 14, 1869, to the jubilation of its own managers and with a sigh of relief by those of the D&H.

The previous May, with completion of the A&S in prospect, President Olyphant of the D&H remarked that it would be necessary "at no distant day" to make important changes in the railroad by widening its gauge and substituting a locomotive road for the existing gravity system below

Thomas Dickson, fifth president of the D&H, 1869-1884.

Carbondale. He also said that the company was already sending coal down the Susquehanna to Baltimore and along the railroad lines connecting Wilkes-Barre with Jersey City, and he expected to have facilities for putting coal into western markets "on a most favorable footing" next year. By this statement he referred to the projected arrangements made earlier with the Erie. The additional supply of anthracite obtained through the various acquisitions recently completed made it more pressing than ever that the company obtain new and broader outlets for its product.

On September 2, 1868, the managers of the D&H entered into a contract with the Erie Railroad to build a line north from Carbondale to connect with the Erie main line at Lanesboro Junction, just east of Susquehanna, Pennsylvania. While this line would be built under the existing charter of the Jefferson Railroad Co., labor and capital

61

A northbound passenger train moves on multigauge trackage near Dickson, on the line between Carbondale and Scranton that opened July 4, 1871. The running rail common to all gauges is at the right, while at the extreme left is the rail for the six-foot Erie equipment. Next is the standard gauge rail, while the 4'3" gauge gravity cars used the inner rail. In the background is one of the coal breakers and right, gravity cars. (*G. M. Best collection*)

would be furnished by the Erie. The D&H was granted trackage rights over the route to Lanesboro, from which the Erie could easily furnish transportation to connect with the A&S at Binghamton, and also, under the previous agreement, to Rochester and Buffalo when the line was completed to those points. The 1868 agreement also provided for moving D&H coal to Weehauken, New Jersey, and the New York City area in the winter months when the canal was closed, as soon as the Erie could extend its line from Hawley, ten miles up to the canal basin at Honesdale.

To finance the proposed line north out of Carbondale, the D&H agreed to buy at par $1,500,000 worth of Boston, Hartford & Erie Railroad bonds from the Erie; these bonds were of somewhat doubtful value and the Erie agreed to guarantee them. Their proceeds were to be made available as fast as equivalent funds were spent on actual construction.

The great railroad expansion program of the D&H can certainly be considered as having commenced in 1869 with the first shovel of earth on this line. The Erie followed, under the Jefferson Railroad franchise, the same alignment that had been surveyed some years earlier by the D&H's railroad front organization, the Northern Coal & Iron Co. It went north out of the Lackawanna valley over Ararat Summit to connect with the Erie tracks at Lanesboro Junction. (President Olyphant habitually referred to this place as Susquehanna, although that community was actually a mile or so to the west of the junction.) This was the first link in the chain of railroad acquisitions that would give the Delaware & Hudson an all-weather distribution system reaching vast new markets.

Already the D&H managers were considering an "easy line" of their own running from Lanesboro to Nineveh, where it would meet the Albany & Susquehanna. This would eliminate the need for going west over the Erie and through Binghamton to reach A&S iron. A direct connection up the Susquehanna valley to Nineveh would cut 27 miles off the route and eliminate the heavy grade on the A&S north out of Binghamton over Belden Hill.

Thomas Dickson was elected president of the D&H on May 13, 1869. He had been vice president during the previous several years while George

Talbot Olyphant was vigorously acquiring vast new coal lands and laying the groundwork for distribution of this coal by rail. The new president was well versed in the overall situation of the company and its future direction. Mr. Olyphant was suffering from failing health, but remained as chairman of the executive committee. President Dickson was able to pick up the ball and run with it—and he did just that. He became the motivating force behind the great railroad expansion of the company, driving it to levels far beyond anticipation.

During 1869 and well into 1870 work progressed on the Jefferson Railroad and by October 28 it was complete and open to traffic. In the meantime, however, ominous developments were imperiling the future value of the Albany & Susquehanna to the D&H. Jay Gould and Jim Fisk were trying to wrest control of the A&S from its President Joseph Ramsey, and a vicious proxy battle was raging. The D&H managers were gravely concerned, for they desperately depended on the A&S as the means of reaching Albany and the north. With this outlet blocked, the D&H would be literally up to its corporate ears in coal.

Gould and Fisk well knew this and tried to put the squeeze on Pennsylvania coal producers who would use the A&S to move their product north.

Fortunately for both the A&S and the D&H, the two managements were on friendly and congenial terms, and on February 24, 1870, the two companies entered into an agreement for a perpetual lease of the A&S by the D&H at $490,000 a year. No arrangement other than a lease in perpetuity could insure the future role the A&S would play in the D&H expansion plans. Both parties breathed a collective sigh of relief as the ink dried on the document.

On October 28, 1870, the first loads of coal rolled north out of Carbondale on the newly-completed Jefferson Railroad and on to Binghamton where they were switched to the Albany & Susquehanna, now under lease to the D&H. This was the fulfillment of plans conceived back in 1865, and it was a welcome sight indeed to see those six-foot gauge cars rolling off to new markets just when the canal was about to close for the season.

The managers were not entirely satisfied, however, with the route through Binghamton, which was subject to delays in transfer to A&S iron, and

The D&H gravel train at Wells Bridge on the A&S line, in 1873, is on track with three rails to enable standard gauge equipment to use the six-foot A&S road. This many laborers would make a general manager's blood run cold today, but modern machinery could do more in an hour than they could accomplish in a day. (*D&H collection*)

The Oneonta yards, shown in the 1875 view below, dominated by two roundhouses and lined with hundreds of cords of fuel wood for the locomotives, was the hub of A&S operations and became the main D&H overhaul base when A&S equipment was being converted from six-foot to standard gauge, and for many years thereafter during the heyday of anthracite movement to the north. Above is a "service interruption"—more bluntly a wreck—just north of Oneonta in 1874. Many spectators, including the bonneted lasses at the right, turned out to watch the cleanup. *(Jean Banta collection, above; D&H collection)*

The "easy line" reached A&S iron at Nineveh station on the tracks visible to the right of the new camelback 2-6-0 No. 70. The tracks in the foreground are on the original A&S location. The train with 2-6-0 No. 57 at the head end is just in from Oneonta and the three other Dickson engines are pushers waiting to help trains up Belden Hill to the tunnel on the Binghamton line. The year is 1880. *(John J. Young, Jr. collection)*

---

27 miles longer than a direct connection up the Susquehanna valley to Nineveh. That same month, therefore, a contract was made with General Andrew S. Diven for the building of the Lackawanna & Susquehanna Railroad, the so-called "easy line" from Lanesboro to Nineveh, that had been discussed two years before. The new line would branch off the Jefferson line at Jefferson Junction, about a mile east of Lanesboro Junction, and run up along the Susequehanna River 20 miles or so to Nineveh on the A&S. It was projected to be completed October 1, 1871, at a cost of $635,000.

As was frequently the case in the early days of railroad building, however, the work involved in building this line was somewhat underestimated, as was probably the cost, and the date of completion had to be postponed. Despite this delay, some trains were run over the line early in December, 1871, but the formal opening was not until June 17, 1872. The track was laid with three rails, as was the Jefferson line, so that equipment of both standard and six-foot gauge could be accommodated.

President Dickson, now in full command of the railroad expansion program, must have sat back and looked at the situation pretty closely. All the work accomplished, money spent and problems encountered thus far were expended on reaching Albany. The outlet to the west over the Erie was of unquestionable value, but Albany was not the jewel on the horizon it had first appeared to be. The city and the surrounding towns were not large centers of population or industry at that time. From the very beginning, Albany had been one of the points reached by water transportation of the coal through the canal and via the Hudson River from Rondout. It was nice to be able to send coal to Albany all winter long, but with adequate storage facilities there, this was no great advantage. There still remained unachieved the object of reaching, by rail, markets hitherto untouched by the D&H, and more important still, untouched by the competition. It was really this desire and its obvious necessity that led Thomas Dickson and the managers to look still further.

The Rensselaer & Saratoga Railroad, in 1870, was a line consisting of 181 miles of first-class trackage embracing the entire upper Hudson valley and extending from Albany to the head of Lake Champlain at Whitehall—a virtual empire in the north! The company had been chartered in 1852 to build a line from Troy to Ballston Spa, and connect with Saratoga Springs—a great watering place even then—via the Saratoga & Schenectady Railroad. The R&S, under aggressive and intelligent leadership, had absorbed various other lines over the years, and even included interests in the steamboat lines on Lakes George and Cham-

Big 54-inch-drivered No. 41, the RUTLAND, was ordered by the R&S from the Schenectady Locomotive Works just before the line was leased to the D&H. When delivered in 1872 she had the R&S number, but gold D&H lettering on her tank. With her greenish-gray boiler jacket, raised gold letters on a green background above maple inlay work on her cab, polished brass and shining black paint, she made a gorgeous picture on the turntable outside the R&S shops at Green Island. On the opposite page, above, No. 130, the GEORGE H. CRAMER had been R&S No. 35 before the D&H leased that line. She is shown with the pay car at West Troy in 1875. Below her is Dickson-built D&H No. 203 at Albany station in 1876, awaiting departure time for Binghamton. *(D&H collection, all)*

---

plain. The company enjoyed a good volume of both passenger and freight business, and the return on these endeavors was entirely satisfactory, perhaps even handsome.

President Dickson proposed that the D&H lease the Rensselaer & Saratoga system as a means of reaching new markets—a rather daring plan considering the new responsibilities and financial burdens imposed on the company by the A&S lease, and the extensive new coal properties recently acquired. In December, 1870, a letter went to the R&S directors inquiring whether they might be interested in a lease to the D&H. The following month the managers studied the matter and a group which included George Talbot Olyphant, former D&H president, and the Kingston steamboat magnate, Thomas Cornell, studied the proposal and recommended the lease. Mr. Olyphant was still actively urging the expansion he had promoted as president and had always considered vital to the continued growth and prosperity of the company. He and his colleagues pointed out that the lease would increase facilities and capacity for the movement of coal, and also increase non-coal revenues. It would increase earnings on the newly-acquired A&S and provide by that line an outlet to the west in direct competition with Commodore Vanderbilt's New York Central. Fi-

67

The Rutland & Washington branch train, stopped at West Rupert, Vermont, was headed by this high-drivered D&H engine in 1871, shortly after the lease of the R&S system. (*G. M. Best collection*)

nally, the Rensselaer & Saratoga's own traffic was "sufficient to yield an income greater than we propose to offer for its lease." This being the case, it seems odd that the R&S would even consider a lease, but lease they did and the D&H Canal Co.'s railroad now ran from the mines at Carbondale to the head of Lake Champlain at Whitehall.

The managers offered the R&S a rental of $650,000 for the current year, $700,000 for the next and $750,000 a year thereafter. The deal was made immediately but the perpetual lease was not formalized until May, 1871.

Now with all this railroad on hand, the next requirement would be to get it all into a unified, smooth-running network. On June 8, President Dickson pointed out to the managers that the laying of a third rail on the A&S to permit the handling of standard gauge equipment was of the greatest importance. This, he said, would place the railroad "in direct and close communication with the whole railroad system of the country." This was especially pressing now with the R&S as part of the family despite the fact the Erie was still broad gauge. It was Dickson's intention to have a uniform gauge of 4'8½" as soon as practicable and $985,000 was immediately appropriated and the work begun. By December 14, 1871, the third rail had been placed and brought into service from Albany to Nineveh, 120 miles, and mixed gauge traffic began rolling on the A&S. During the remainder of 1871 and in 1872 a substantial improvement was made by replacing the old iron rails with heavy steel on the R&S between Troy and Saratoga and on part of the Jefferson Railroad in Pennsylvania.

In the meantime in 1870, a locomotive-operated road was built between Carbondale and Olyphant, near Scranton, and a second track was added to the original flat stretch from Valley Junction near Olyphant to Green Ridge, adjoining Scranton. Strangely enough, a third rail was laid on this line too, only this one was at a 4'-3" gauge to accommodate gravity equipment. On many stretches of the lines below Carbondale four rails were used: one common running rail, a 4'-3" gravity rail, a standard gauge rail and a six-foot rail for Erie equipment

During the flurry of activity associated with the railroad expansion several names connected with the formative years of the enterprise were added to the growing list of the company's distinguished dead. Canal engineer R. F. Lord died in July 1867; gravity railroad builder James Archbald passed on in August of 1870, and railroad expansionist and ex-president George Talbot Olyphant succumbed in April, 1873.

With the acquisition of the Rensselaer & Saratoga system, the D&H acquired a new commodity to transport—passengers! The company already had some service, of course, on the gravity line south of Carbondale and then on the Albany & Susquehanna when it was taken over, but none to the extent—or of the quality—of that existing on the R&S. Because of Saratoga Springs' popularity as a summer watering place, the R&S moved large numbers of passengers between Albany, Troy and Schenectady, to and from the spa. The Saratoga & Schenectady Railroad, now part of the R&S, had originally carried nothing but passengers, and travel to the resort remained heavy from the time the place received its first great impetus in the 1830s.

It is hard to pin down an exact date when Saratoga Springs reached its highest point as a fashionable resort of the wealthy, but it is safe to say that from some time prior to 1840 until the turn of the century it stood easily pre-eminent in its field. According to generally accepted standards, most of the visitors who then traveled to the Springs occupied, for one reason or another, a high position in the society of their time. During a busy summer season as many as 1000 passengers were frequently carried on a single train, and thousands of Wagner Palace cars as well as the sumptuous private cars of the elite rolled north into town.

In October of 1871 the D&H subscribed to $25,000 worth of bonds in the new United States Hotel as a gesture in the support of bettering the accommodations at the Springs and attracting even more summer travelers to R&S rails. This, of course, was farsighted good business.

That same month, the company also indulged in an act of benevolence. It pledged $5000 for the relief of those who had suffered from the destructive Chicago fire. From its very inception, the Delaware & Hudson Canal Co. had from time to time donated money or land to such causes as this, or to churches and other worthy community activities.

It was in 1871 too that the Adirondack Railroad was completed and opened as far as North Creek, a mountain village west of Lake George and nearly at the head of the Hudson valley. This brought new traffic to the R&S at Saratoga Springs and provided access to central Adirondack resort regions, such as Blue Mountain Lake and Schroon Lake, bringing the line into the summer vacation market itself. Soon long trains of Wagners out of New York, with private mansions on wheels bringing up the rear, were rolling off the Hudson River Railroad at Albany and on to R&S rails bound for the Adirondack's line north out of Saratoga Springs.

The brisk traffic north of Albany called for improvement of the R&S tracks. In 1873, 2564 tons of steel rail were laid between Albany and Whitehall, and double tracking of the section between Ballston Spa and Saratoga Springs was ordered completed whenever traffic warranted it—and that was almost immediately.

The glamorous business of transporting fashionable passengers to holiday resorts did not distract the managers of the Delaware & Hudson Canal Co. from other, more prosaic aspects of their growing concern. In January of 1873 President Dickson reported to the managers that the 2,000,-000 tons of coal brought through the canal to tidewater had not paid costs and expenses, because of price-cutting by other producers in the markets reached this way. Coal sold on the rail lines, on the other hand, had netted handsome profits. The president said that this vindicated his efforts and the financial burden required to reach markets inaccessible to the competition, by means of railroads running north. With these facts starkly before them, President Dickson and the managers cast their eyes to the west shore of Lake Champlain and the cold countryside of Canada beyond.

SUSQUEHANNAH AND ALBANY RAIL ROAD.

The undersigned Central Corresponding Commttiee for the promotion of a plan to build a Rail Road from Albany to the New York and Erie Rail Road, through the valleys of the Cobleskill, Schenevas and Susquehannah, beg leave to call your attention and that of the public generally, to the annexed proceedings—and to advise that public meetings be speedily called in the several towns interested in said road, for the appointment of Town Committees, and also of Delegates to represent said several towns in Convention to be held at Oneonta, Otsego county, *on the second day of April next:* and that we be early advised of the names of those composing said committee.

Samuel B. Beach,	Daniel Waters,
William W. Snow,	George W. Chase,
Woodbury K. Cooke,	Hamilton Waterman,
Samuel H. Case,	Oliver Birdsall,
Samuel J. Cooke,	Franklin Wheeler,

Oneonta, February 25, 1851.

At a meeting of citizens favorable to the construction of the *Susquehannah and Albany Rail Road*, hed in pursuance of notice at the Inn of *J. M. Wakins*, in Oneonta, on the 25th day of Feb. 1851; *Elijah E. Ferry Esq.*, Chairman, and *Alfred Jones* and *DeWitt Ford*, Secretaries:

Resolved unanimously. That this meeting regards with deep interest and unqualified approbation the project of constructing a Rail Road, commencing on the line of the New York and Erie Rail Road, at some point between or in the village of Binghamton and Lanesborough, and running thence, by the most direct and feasible route, to the city of Albany; and is fully persuaded that such a road would not only be of incalculable advantage to the populous and productive region adjacent to it, but be of vastly more importance to New England, to our own Commercial Emporium and to the great and growing West, than any other Rail Road within this State, which is not already commenced or completed.

Resolved: That, in the opinion of this meeting, the only thing necessary to insure the speedy construction of said Road, is concert of action and cordial co-operation, on the part of those who, in reality, have a deep personal and pecuniary interest in having it built.

Resolved: That as the recent heavy rain and the almost impassable condition of the roads have prevented the attendance, at this time, of great numbers who are known to feel a deep interest in the subject; it is expedient, with the view to secure a more general and extended concert of action, to adjourn this meeting until 11 o'clock A. M. of Wednesday the 2d day of April next, at the same place.

Resolved: That Samuel B. Beech, William W. Snow, Woodbury K Cook, Samuel H Case, and Samuel J. Cooke, of Oneonta; Daniel Waters, of Worcester; George W. Chase, of Maryland; Hamilton Waterman, of Decatur; Oliver Birdsall, of Otego and Franklin Wheeler, of Windsor, be a Central Corresponding Committee; to correspond with the various Town Committees; to cause these resolutions to be printed and widely circulated among those interested in, or friendly to the projected Rail Road; all of whom are hereby cordially invited and earnestly requested to give their attendance at said adjourned meeting; and to take such further steps as may be deemed needful preparatory to organizing a Company for constructing said road.

Resolved: That this meeting do stand adjourned, to the tyme and place aforesaid.

ELIJAH E. FERRY, Chairman.
ALFRED JONES,
DeWITT FORD, } Secretaries,

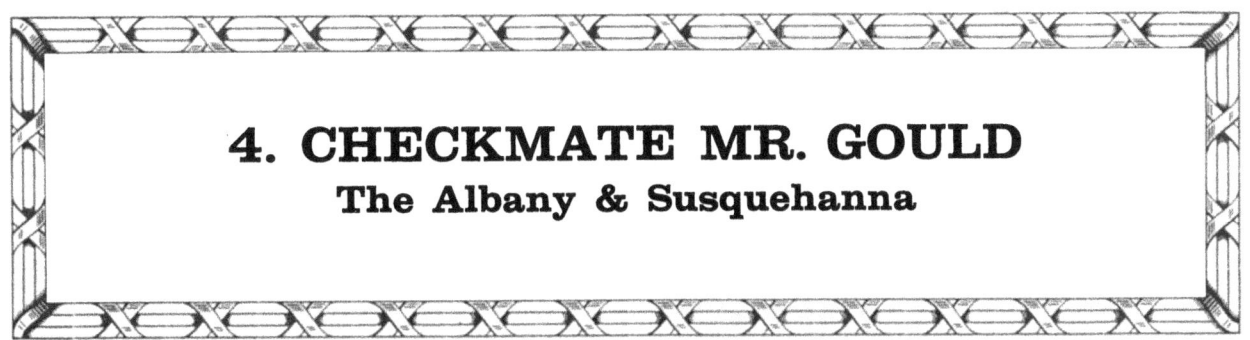

4. CHECKMATE MR. GOULD
The Albany & Susquehanna

By the middle of the 19th century, the farmers of the upper Susquehanna valley, observing the surging progress of the world outside their peaceful valley, were beginning to fear that it would pass them by. They were not particularly interested in the relative hustle and bustle of this new approach to life, but they would have liked to get their hands on some of its monetary rewards.

For example, a farmer in Cobleskill would have to spend three days jogging along dirt roads, sleeping under the wagon for two nights, to bring a load of cabbage, or anything else, to market in Albany. His wife would prepare provisions for the trip while he was busy in the barn packing a huge bundle of hay, binding it with bands of rope made by twisting rye straw, to keep it all on the wagon. This was done to avoid buying feed for the horses or himself during the trip, thus netting the maximum return of cash for the endeavor.

Meanwhile trains of the Erie Railroad swept past Binghamton on the west, and those of the New York Central rolled through Albany on the east. With the shrill blasts of locomotives resounding up the valley from each end, it seemed as if the days of the stagecoach and wagon were numbered.

One of the earliest advocates of a railroad through the valley between Albany and Binghampton was a Mr. Keyes of Bainbridge, New York. He proposed such a line in a letter dated December 31, 1844, to the Binghamton *Courier*. This was published as an effort to stimulate interest and in the hope that some action might follow but nothing developed for another seven years.

In 1851 interest was revived again. This time one of the promoters was Edward C. Delevan, hotel owner and businessman of Albany. The projectors of the line pointed out the advantages such an enterprise offered the district by the direct communication between Albany and the railroads terminating there, and the Erie Railroad at Binghampton. Even more important was the direct connection of Albany and eastern New York with the coal fields of Pennsylvania. A public meeting to promote this project was held in Oneonta on April 2, 1851 and was attended by nearly 2000 eager participants, including delegates from more than twenty towns in Albany, Schoharie, Otsego, Delaware, Chenango and Broome Counties. At the meeting, articles of association were drawn up, Edward C. Delevan was elected president, other officers were chosen and numerous subscriptions were made for the stock.

The articles of association incorporating the Albany & Susquehanna Rail Road Co. were filed on April 19, 1851, and on that day the directors met in Albany officially to elect Mr. Delevan president. The company's engineer was Martin B. Inches, a man with a name unusually appropriate to his profession. He began a preliminary survey in May of the 142-mile line that was to be built to a gauge of six feet, the same as that of the Erie Railroad, with which it would connect at Binghamton. Mr. Inches' survey was completed on January 28, 1852 and published in the hope of creating public interest and attracting financial support.

In March the New York State Legislature authorized the village of Binghamton to subscribe to $50,000 worth of stock and to offer more than double that amount in other forms of financial assistance. Later that month, Albany's Common Council authorized a million-dollar loan to the new company, but with strings attached that were to prove entangling.

A six-foot gauge A&S locomotive stops on one of the many trestles near Richmondville during the line's construction in 1865. Below, the original A&S station at Oneonta is hosting a group of D&H boys and a standard gauge locomotive, converted from the A&S wide gauge on a local freight. *(D&H collection)*

The twenty-year 6% bonds could not be issued until all the right of way had been obtained and at least $10,000 per mile expended on construction, a set of conditions which time would prove difficult to attain.

By November of 1852 the final alignment was established and proposals for bids were published. On May 30, 1853, a contract was let for the complete building of the line at a cost of $6.3 million. The combine of Morris, Miller, Baker & Co. was to receive the sum of $703,000 in cash, $700,000 in company stock and the rest in bonds. They sublet sections of the over-all job to seven subcontractors and work began in July. The 4th of July celebration in Oneonta was specially vigorous that year, for the large assemblage of citizens felt that their isolation from the outside world was soon to end. They might have been better off had they put their firecrackers under some of the rocks on Richmondville hill.

During 1853 many stockholders failed to pay the installments on their accounts when called and others repudiated their subscriptions completely. This did nothing to stabilize an already shaky situation and the management was forced into proceedings aimed at compelling the delinquents to meet their obligations. Although the courts ruled in the company's favor, the publicity aroused dissension among the stockholders and led an influential Albany group to propose, early in 1854, that all contracts be annulled and the entire enterprise abandoned.

This request was promptly refused, but such lack of confidence by the shareholders had a depressing effect on forthcoming capital. As a result it became necessary to ask the contractors to accept part of July's payment in the form of the now not-so-secure securities. The burly construction men could buy neither whiskey nor women with fancy-looking stock certificates and on August 4th they put down their picks and stabled the mules.

After this, collection of stock subscriptions was discontinued and the Legislature granted a number of extensions of time for completion of the road.

Several years the work lay idle and many friends of the enterprise who lived along the proposed route petitioned the Legislature to allow

Harvey Baker, Esq.

Dear Sir:

A section of the Albany and Susquehanna Railroad being about to be opened to the business of the community, the Directors solicit the favor of your company, in making a trip over it, on the 15th inst. The cars will leave the Station, corner of Church and Lydius streets, at 9 o'clock, A. M., and return about 5 o'clock, P. M.

Please present the enclosed Ticket upon entering the Cars.

By direction of the Board,

E. P. PRENTICE, President.

Albany, September, 1863.

Invitation to the official opening of the line to Central Bridge. *(Jean Banta collection)*

FARES.

ALBANY AND SUSQUEHANNA RAILROAD.

Adopted July, 1864.

Albany.	20	25	30	45	55	70	75	85	100	110
	Adamsville.	5	15	25	35	50	55	70	80	90
		Slingerlands.	10	25	30	50	55	65	75	90
			New Scotland	15	25	40	45	55	65	80
				Guilderland.	10	25	35	40	55	65
					Knowersville.	20	25	35	45	60
						Knox.	10	15	30	40
							Duanesburgh.	10	20	35
								Quaker Street.	15	25
									Esperance.	15
										Schoharie.

This panorama of Albany from the Hudson River was taken in 1865. Completion of the line to Oneonta that year was cause for celebration and President Ramsey invited a trainload of officials and friends to join in it. Such celebrations were still going on two years later, as the poster on the opposite page attests. *(Jean Banta collection, below; New York State Library, opposite)*

Albany & Susquehanna R. R. Co.'s Office,

Albany, August 17, 1865.

Dear Sir:

There will be a Special Train over the Albany and Susquehanna Railroad, on Tuesday the 20th inst., upon the opening of the road to Oneonta.

The Train will leave Albany at 7 o'clock 45 minutes, A. M., and return the same day.

You are cordially invited to join in the Excursion.

[Please present the enclosed Ticket upon entering the Cars.]

I am, very truly yours,

J. H. RAMSEY,
President.

---

the towns traversed to purchase its stock. After much agitation the lawmakers, in 1857, granted this permission to all the towns in the counties through which the A&S was proposed to run. Many objections to town subscriptions were raised and even the constitutionality of the law was contested, but the courts upheld the bill.

Joseph H. Ramsey of Cobleskill was elected vice-president on November 17, 1857 and immediately became a leading spirit in pushing construction. He was to loom large in the history of the A&S.

Late in 1857, stock subscriptions had been secured from twenty towns and, with Binghamton's contribution, almost a million dollars were on hand, enough to resume construction. By October of the next year, after some relocations and changes, hundreds of shovels were again swinging on the stretch from Albany to East Worcester.

In 1859 application was made to the State for financial aid, but it was turned down, as were similar requests during the next three years. In 1863, however, the Legislature granted $500,000 in aid. Half was to be paid only after $1,000,000 had been expended on construction and forty miles of line to Cobleskill had been put into operation, the balance upon reaching Oneonta. With this as collateral, the company went to the Erie magnate Daniel Drew and steamboat capitalist Alfred Van Santvoord, for a mortgage of $1,000,000.

These funds enabled the construction to be pressed forward and the line was opened from Albany to Central Bridge on September 16, 1863. By January 2, 1865, it was completed and opened

as far as Cobleskill, bringing the first quarter million in State aid. On August 26 the first train rolled triumphantly into Oneonta, bringing with it a jubilant crowd of officials and access to the balance of the State aid.

With the first 82 miles of the line in operation, from Albany to Oneonta, and only 60 miles to go, there was good cause to expect the project to be completed, and investors were more willing to furnish additional funds. With this new confidence and with still more State aid, construction pushed steadily down the flat Susquehanna valley, reaching Sidney October 22, 1866, and Harpursville on Christmas Day, 1867.

Rugged conditions, the need for boring a 2260-foot tunnel under Belden Hill and a scarcity of labor delayed completion of the final 22 miles, from Harpursville to Binghamton, but the last rail was finally laid, appropriately, on the last day of 1868. Twelve days later a gala excursion rolled from Albany to Binghamton for the customary ceremonies and banquet. The Rip Van Winkle spell had been broken in the Susquehanna valley.

Laid with 60-pound iron, the road was substantially built, and its six-foot gauge enabled it to connect freely with the Erie at Binghamton. At the time, this fact seemed to be to its advantage, but soon it was to become a source of some consternation.

Now that the A&S was finally completed — after almost twenty years — the management hoped to settle down to normal operation, under the guidance of Joseph Ramsey who became president in 1864. By agreement with the Cherry Valley & Mohawk Railroad Co., for construction and operation by the A&S, work began on a 23-mile branch from Cobleskill to Cherry Valley in mid-1868.

Ramsey's hopes for normal operations of the new railroad were soon threatened by the machi-

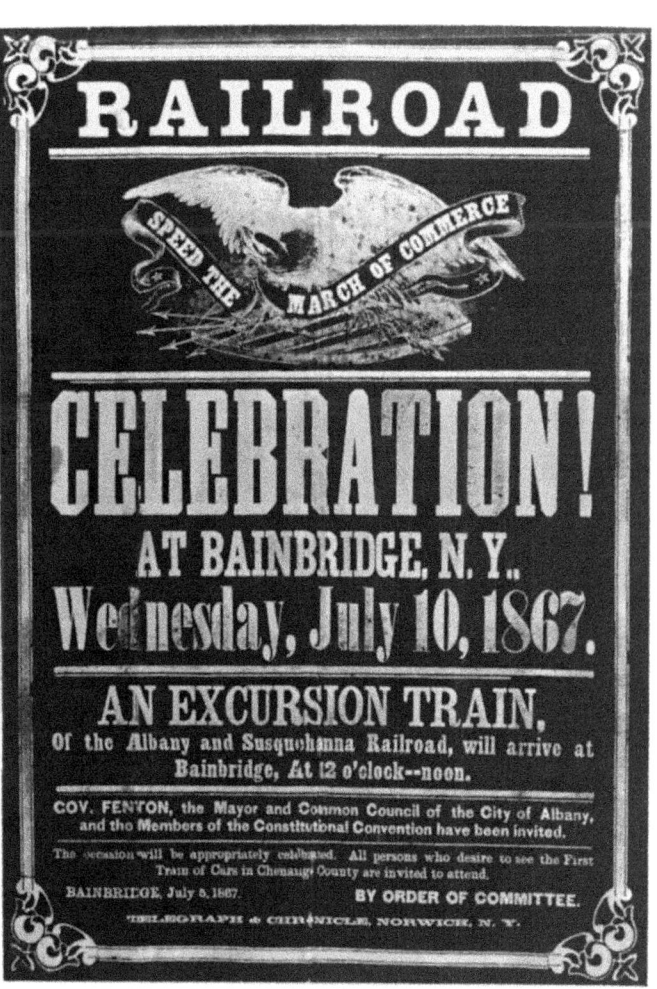

nations of the terrors of Wall Street, Jay Gould and James Fisk. The line's affairs were in a chaotic condition as the result of the election in 1868 of a Board of Directors evenly divided in its loyalties between the Ramsey management and the interests of Gould and Fisk.

These aggressive capitalists had secured control of the Erie by driving out Daniel Drew as treasurer and by compelling Commodore Vanderbilt to abandon his effort to control its management. Now they cast covetous eyes on the Albany & Susquehanna as an important element in their plan. Disappointed in their hopes of competing with the New York Central for western traffic, they turned to the movement of coal, contracting for the products of numerous coal companies in the rich anthracite fields of Pennsylvania, a short distance south of the Erie's main line. Wishing to extend their operations and to put the coal companies at their mercy, they sought control of the A&S, which would enable them to reach Albany and, via the lines extending north and east of there, all of New England.

Through their supporters on the divided Board of Directors, Gould and Fisk in June of 1869 laid their plans for a takeover. The stock, quoted at $25 a share and enjoying practically no sale, was held by three classes of owners: directors, municipalities along the line, and individuals and capitalists. Only $2.8 million of the $4 million authorized capital had been subscribed, and of this amount $800,000 had been forfeited for non-payment. Within three weeks the stock was selling for $65 a share, as its demand for control purposes became apparent.

It was obvious that a proxy fight for control of the line was at hand. President Ramsey quickly issued 12,000 shares of treasury stock to his friends at 10% down, thus insuring their proxies for his side. All the stock legitimately purchased by Gould

Two six-foot gauge locomotives built for the A&S by Danforth & Cooke, were the CHARLES COURTER, No. 5, dating from 1864, and the JOHN WESTOVER, No. 11, 1866. The No. 5 stands at the A&S station in Albany, just off Broadway, in the 1869 scene below. The company headquarters were in the building at 256 Broadway. The northern railroad department office of the D&H remained here until 1883. (*D&H collection, opposite*)

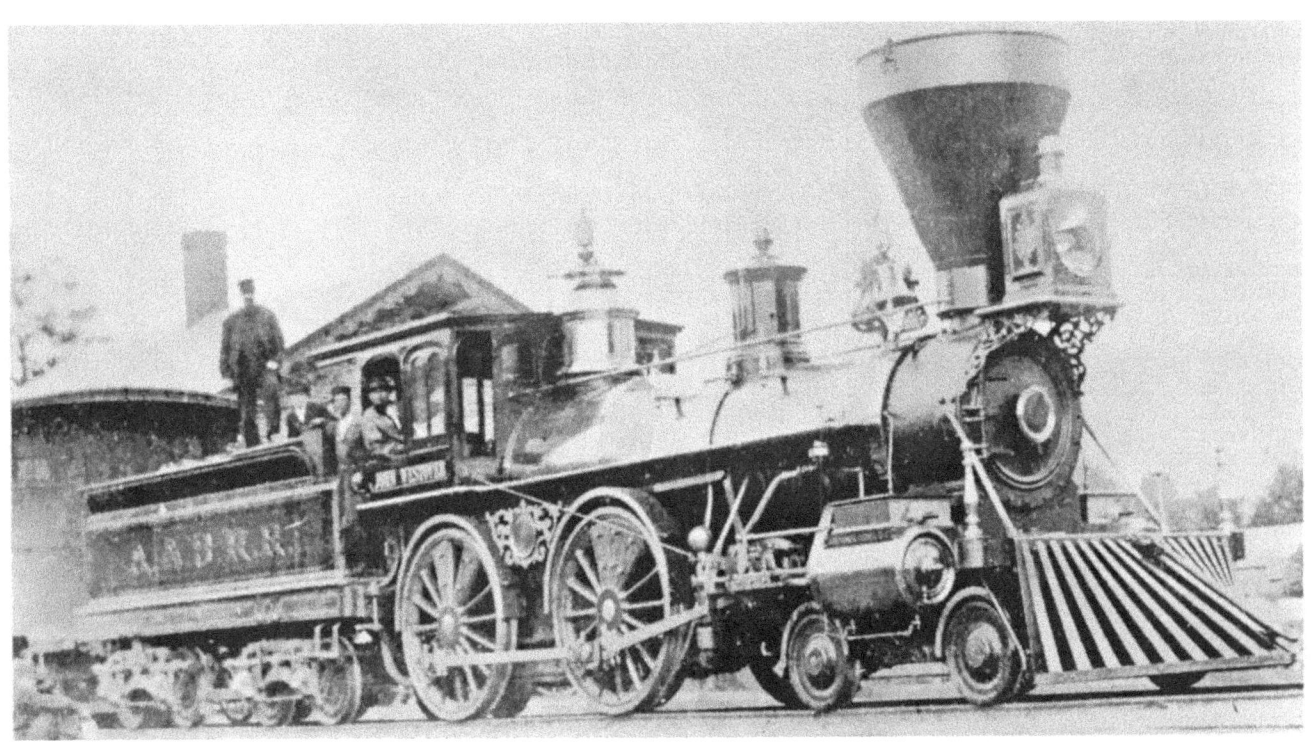

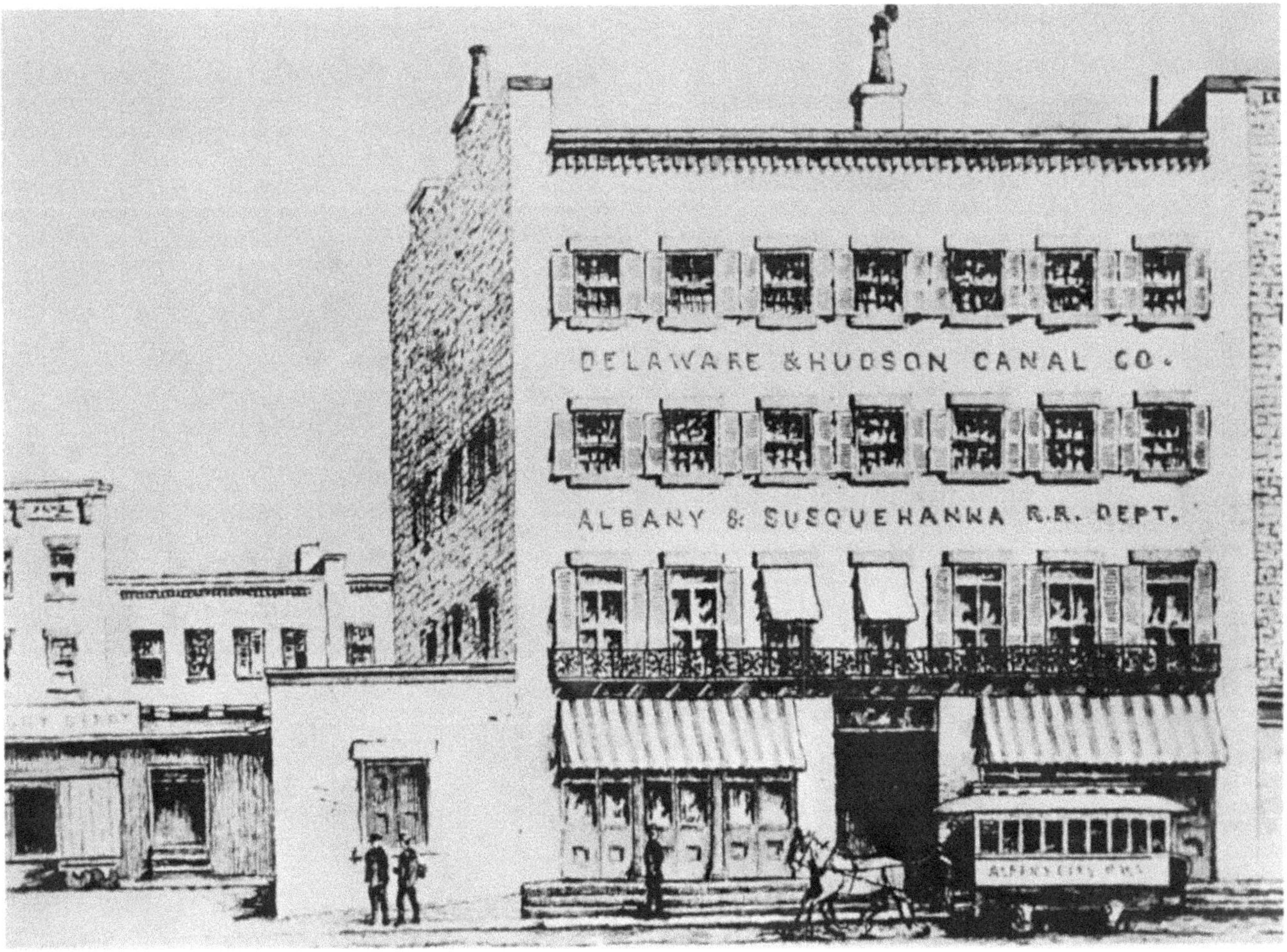
DELAWARE & HUDSON CANAL CO.
ALBANY & SUSQUEHANNA R.R. DEPT.

ALBANY & SUSQUEHANNA R. R.

CHANGE OF TIME.

On and after Tuesday, May 12th, 1868, Trains will run until further notice (Sundays excepted), as follows:

TRAINS EASTWARD.

STATIONS.	Miles	No. 1 F.& P.	No. 2 F.& P.	No. 3 Exp.	No 4. S Ex.
		A. M.	A. M.	A. M.	P. M
Harpersville			5 00	9 00	12 00
Afton	6		5 30	9 18	2 18
Bainbridge	12		6 00	9 35	2 35
Sidney	17		6 30	9 49	2 49
Unadilla	21		6 50	10 00	3 00
Wells Bridge	25		7 15	†10 12	†3 12
Otego	30		7 40	10 27	3 27
Oneonta	38	4 45	8 25	10 55	3 55
Emmons	41	4 54	8 38	11 02	4 02
Colliers	44	5 04	8 51	11 15	4 10
Maryland	50	**5 23**	9 20	11 31	**4 32**
Schenevus	53	5 33	9 35	11 39	4 43
Worcester	58	5 48	10 00	11 53	**5 00**
E. Worcester	63	6 04	**10 30**	12 07	5 15
Carylville	67	†6 16	*10 50	*12 18	*5 27
Richmondville	70	6 26	11 03	12 26	5 36
Cobleskill	75	6 42	11 29	12 41	5 51
Howe's Cave	81	†7 00	11 54	†12 58	†6 09
Schoharie	84	**7 21**	**12 18**	**1 20**	6 18
Esperance	89	7 36	**12 43**	1 34	6 34
Quaker Street	93	7 48	1 04	1 45	6 48
Duanesburgh	96	7 57	1 19	*1 54	†6 55
Knox	98	†8 01	*1 29	*1 59	*7 00
Knowersville	103	**8.17**	**2 20**	**2 13**	**7 13**
Guilderland	106	8 24	2 37	*2 21	7 22
New Scotland	109	8 32	2 52	**2 29**	7 31
Slingerlands	113	8 42	3 12	*2 41	7 42
Adamsville	114	8 45	3 17	*2 44	†7.47
Albany	120	**9 00**	**3.45**	**3 00**	**8 00**

TRAINS WESTWARD.

STATIONS.	Miles	No. 1 S. Ex	No. 2 F.& P.	No 3 Exp.	No. 4 F.&P
		A. M.	A. M.	P.M.	P. M
Albany		**7 30**	**10 00**	**2 00**	**6 00**
Adamsville	6	†7 47	10 29	*2 17	6 23
Slingerlands	7	7 51	10 34	†2 20	6 27
New Scotland	11	8 01	10 54	**2 29**	6 41
Guilderland	14	8 09	11 09	**2 37**	6 52
Knowersville	17	**8 25**	**11 35**	**12 50**	**7 13**
Knox	22	*8 39	*12 00	*3 05	†7 31
Duanesburgh	24	†8 44	12 10	†3 10	7 38
Quaker Street	27	8 51	12 24	3 17	7 49
Esperance	31	9 03	**12 43**	3 28	8 03
Schoharie	36	**9 23**	**1 30**	3 42	8 21
Howe's Cave	39	†9 32	1 43	†3 51	†8 32
Cobleskill	45	9 50	2 11	4 09	8 53
Richmondville	50	10 05	2 36	4 24	9 11
Carylville	53	*10 15	*2 49	*4 32	†9 22
E. Worcester	57	**10 26**	3 17	4 45	9 36
Worcester	62	10 38	3 42	**5 00**	9 54
Schenevus	67	10 50	4 07	5 14	10 12
Maryland	70	**10 58**	**4 32**	5 22	10 23
Colliers	76	**11 18**	4 57	5 40	10 44
Emmons	79	11 25	5 09	5 49	10 55
Oneonta	82	11 32	5 20	6 03	11 05
Otego	90	11 55	5 55	6 26	
Wells Bridge	95	†12 10	6 16	†6 41	
Unadilla	99	12 22	6 35	6 53	
Sidney	103	12 33	**7 10**	**7 05**	
Bainbridge	108	12 46	7 35	7 20	
Afton	114	1 02	8 04	7 38	
Harpersville	120	1 20	8 35	7 55	

Heavy Figures denote Meetings. *Trains do not stop. †Stop on Signal only.

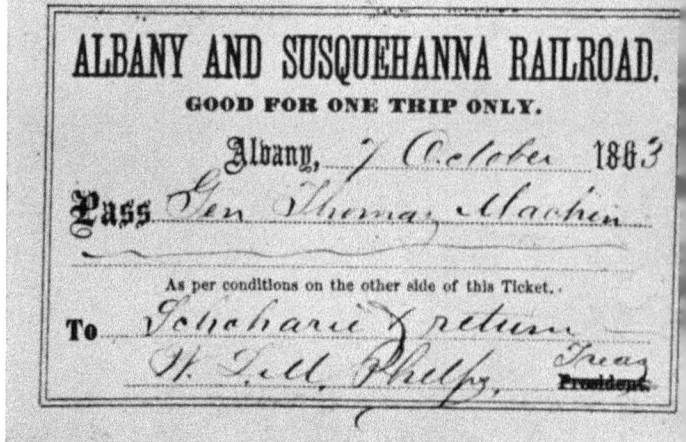

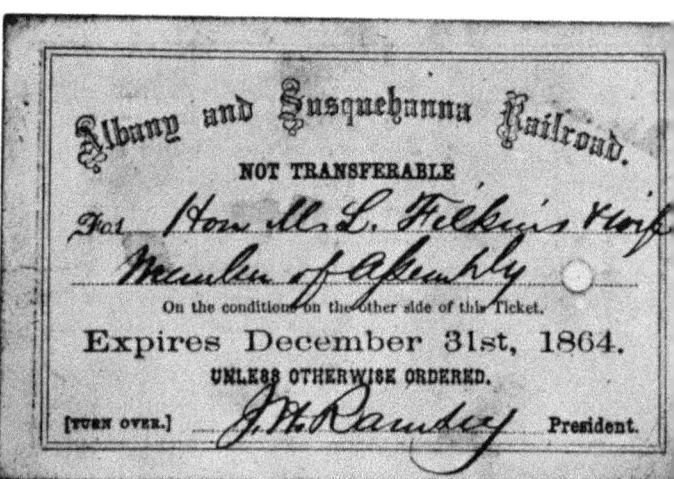

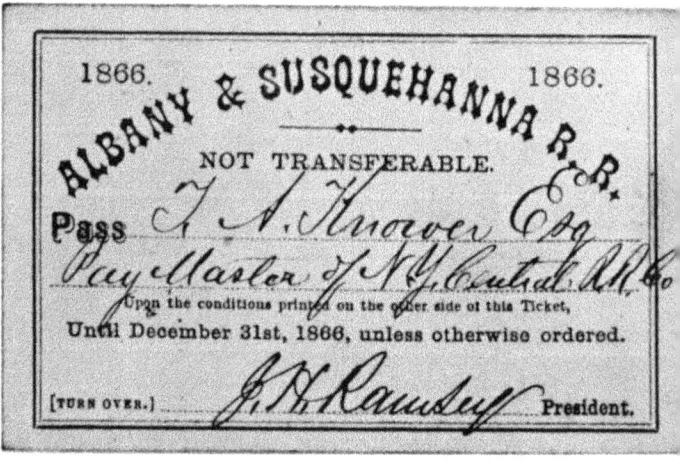

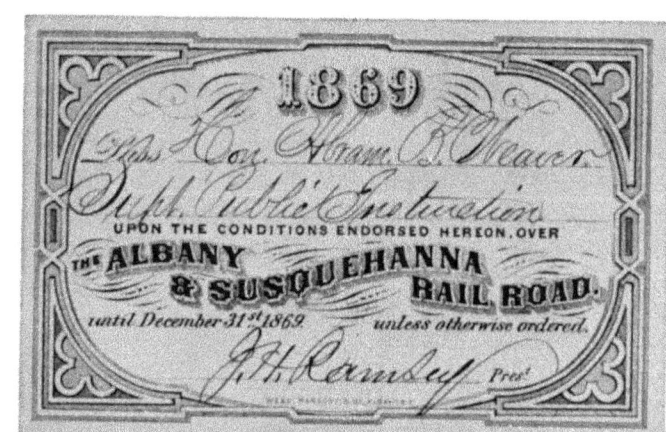

had to be lawfully transferred to him, and was. Now a great legal battle ensued with court orders, writs and injunctions as ammunition. Legal missiles issued by judges on either side flew back and forth, one ousting Ramsey as president, one appointing Fisk and Gould as receivers — it was judicial mayhem!

A meeting of the board was called at the company offices in Albany for Thursday, August 5 and the suspended President Ramsey was informed that his presence was not desired. The plan was to have Vice-President J. R. Herrick, a Gould man, preside and secure control of the books, after which the election would be a mere formality. This caused a wrangle that led to a call for the police. That night the company books were spirited out of the building by counsel for the Ramsey side.

The next day, before any business could be transacted, four of the directors, all Gould men, were served with judicial orders restraining them from acting in or interfering with company affairs. The Gould party, now without a quorum, took the first train to New York to regroup.

That night in New York, an order was drawn in Gould's counsel's office at the Grand Opera House appointing Jim Fisk and Charles Courter receivers and was immediately signed by Judge Barnard, a jurist Gould had in his pocket. Within an hour, the receivers were on their way back to Albany armed with the court order and accompanied by a bodyguard of directors, to take possession.

As a result the following order went out:

> To the officers and employees of the Albany & Susquehanna Railroad:
>
> *Take Notice* — By an order of Supreme Court, made August 6, 1869, we are duly appointed receivers of the property, franchises and effects of the said road, and by the same are authorized to take possession of, and run the said road. On and after this date you will make all reports and remittances to James Fisk, Jr. and Charles Courter, office of the Albany & Susquehanna Railroad.
>
> James Fisk, Jr. } Receivers
> Charles Courter }
>
> Albany, August 6th, 1869

Meanwhile in Albany the Ramsey interests were at work. That same evening they secured an order from Judge Peckham of Albany, obviously a Ramsey man, appointing Robert H. Pruyn as receiver. Pruyn immediately put Superintendent J. W. Van Valkenburgh in charge of the office. This man of determination then dispatched the following message:

> To the officers and employees of the Albany & Susquehanna Railroad:
>
> *Take Notice* — Robert H. Pruyn was first appointed receiver by Judge Peckham and has possession of the office, books and property of the company. He has continued me as superintendent and all transactions of the Company must be with him and my orders obeyed.
>
> J. W. Van Valkenburgh, Superintendent

The next morning, Saturday, August 7, Van Valkenburgh went to the offices and found they had been opened by the deposed vice-president. He immediately posted men at the entrances with orders to admit no one. Fisk soon appeared, demanding admission to take possession and when refused produced legal-looking papers purporting to show that he had been appointed receiver by Judge Barnard. Van Valkenburgh informed him that Pruyn had been appointed to that position, but Fisk refused to recognize any appointment but his own and became a bit nasty about it all. He was thereupon thrown off the property along with his cronies by the superintendent and a complement of huskies. Upon hitting the street Fisk was arrested but was later released. More orders were issued by Judge Barnard, Fisk returned to the office later in the day, was arrested again and released on bail. The next day, Sunday, everybody rested.

Fisk was off to a fresh start Monday morning, returning to Albany only to find himself opposed on all sides. On a train heading for Binghamton were Judge Peckham's orders retaining the Ramsey interests as operators of the A&S; the train stopped at each station along the way to serve these orders. Jim Fisk immediately telegraphed Judge Barnard's order of Saturday to Binghamton, demanding that immediate possession be given to his representatives. Accordingly, just before two o'clock, Sheriff Browne of Broome County appeared at the station, telegram in hand, to take possession of the line, including the station and the passenger train there that was awaiting departure.

There were three A&S locomotives in Binghamton at that time. The Sheriff was able to grab two, but one of the A&S men saw what was happening in time to flee with the third. No other resistance was available or offered, for Binghamton was definitely Erie territory and reinforcements were easy for the Fisk faction to obtain.

Now two sets of receivers were in possession of and operating the opposite ends of the road. The regular A&S crew of the confiscated passenger train was quickly removed and an Erie crew installed in the cab. This militant special then blasted north out of Binghamton, armed with Sheriff Browne's writs and a number of burly, club-wielding, impromptu commandos from the Erie shops in Binghamton. The two trains carrying conflicting court orders were bearing down on each other. As the sheriff's train rolled into a station, a horde of Erie men would spill off, rush into the depot, dispose of the A&S agent and replace him with one of their own.

The train that had left Albany in the morning was now at Harpursville and was ordered by Pruyn to stop there. In Albany, when Van Valkenburgh heard of the coup, he decided that the time for conciliation had passed and decided to clear the home office of all but friends of the Ramsey faction. He therefore requested Charles Courter to retire and, being refused, had him summarily ejected into the street, thus removing the last of the Fisk men from the railroad's principal office.

Later that afternoon, Van Valkenburgh telegraphed instructions to all trains to stop where they were. His message ended with, "Have all the men you can find to the station, so as to defend your station and the road."

An extra train was called and about 150 men, hastily gathered from the company's Albany shops under the command of Master Mechanic R. C. Blackall, were herded aboard. As the train scorched the rails toward Harpursville the following message checked through the paralleling telegraph lines:

> Superintendent's office, August 9, 1869
> Train No. 7 will go through to the front. Have all the men you can get to go with it. Drum them up!
>
> J. W. Van Valkenburgh, Superintendent

The Blackall special arrived in Bainbridge, 34 miles from Binghamton, late in the evening and took a sidetrack to ambush the oncoming Erie train, which soon sneaked into town. Suddenly the sheriff's 40 or so men found themselves on the ground, for under the cover of the darkness, Blackall had put a rerailing frog on the track to serve, in this case, as a derailing frog. In an instant his men were on the Erie crew, and the invaders meekly surrendered in face of the overwhelming odds. Sheriff Browne was picked up out of the cinders, brushed off and served with Judge Peckham's order.

Daylight soon dawned and Blackall moved cautiously to the southwest, through Afton, Nineveh and on to Harpursville, replacing the deposed

Picture of the "Erie War" at the tunnel, August 10, 1869, as depicted in *Harper's Weekly*.

A&S agents as he went. There he dispatched the following message:

> Harpursville, August 10, 1869
> To J. W. Van Valkenburgh, Superintendent:
> The Erie folks are preparing to move upon us. They have the militia with them encouraged by the Sheriff. Our retreat is cut off. We must resort to desperation if they attack us today or tonight. What are we to do? We must have reinforcements immediately. I will burn the high bridge if they move on us tonight. We have scouting parties now watching them. J. M. Bailey will return soon. He is now out reconnoitering.
> R. C. B.

Obviously Blackall was getting nervous, but he eased his train on up the hill toward the tunnel without incident. There he found an entirely different situation.

That afternoon the Erie forces were further strengthened when about 850 men had come out on a special train from Binghamton to the west end of the tunnel. At about seven that evening, the Erie army decided to move and started the train through the tunnel. Blackall's forces, now numbering about 400, realized that the opponents were coming and started their train toward the enemy.

The two locomotives met with a sickening thud on a curve just east of the tunnel and the Donnybrook was on, with hordes of shouting, cursing men spilling off the trains and lunging at each other. Shots were fired in the ensuing melee, clubs were swung, noses bloodied in the general pandemonium. The Fisk crowd, despite its size, was anything but well organized. It had counted on no such opposition and was soon in retreat toward Binghamton. As the Fisk men stumbled through the smoke-filled tunnel or took to the hills, the Erie

81

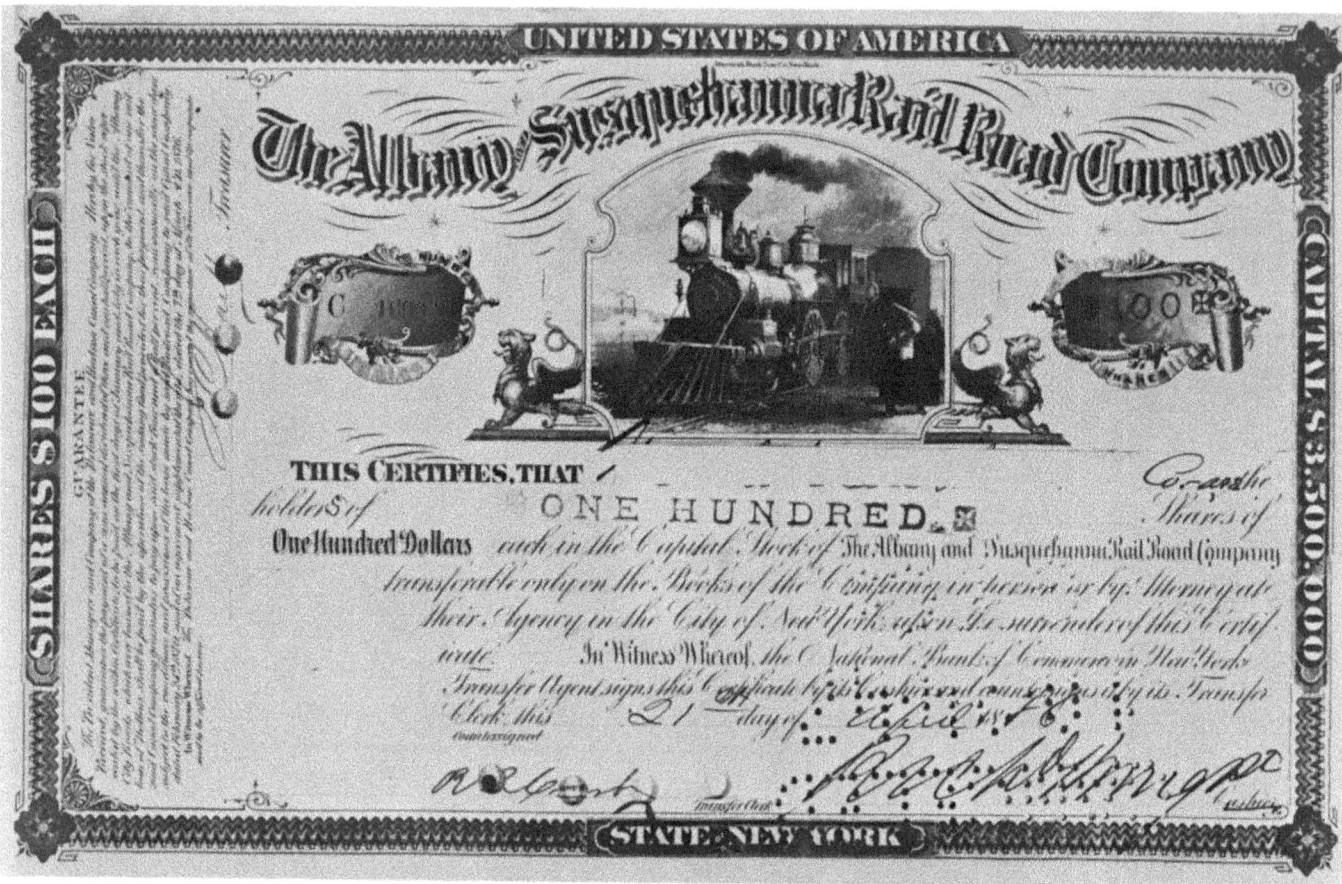

engineer moved his engine out of the mob scene and back through the tunnel.

Damage to the engines from the collision was minor: a broken headlight, a smashed pilot and a few dents, but the Blackall party's engine was also derailed. The victorious A&S men put it back on the track and pressed on through the tunnel after the Fisk commandos. At the south end of the bore the Erie men had rallied and as darkness fell on the field of battle the two parties again faced each other. This time the combat was limited to caustic exchanges, threats and loud shouting. How far it might have gone, had either side regained any great amount of courage and lunged at the other, is hard to say, for before the battle could resume in earnest the 44th Regiment of the State Militia rode in to the tune of blaring bugles.

The Broome County officials had called out the troops to try and restore some semblance of law and order. Fisk's adherents held possession on the field and the miniature army from Albany withdrew through the tunnel, blocking it with a freight car, and returned to Harpursville. Back in the station there, the master-mechanic-turned-conqueror received word from the war office in Albany:

Albany, August 10, 1869, 8:30 p.m.
To R. C. Blackall:
General James McQuade will leave here tonight to stop further disturbances. The Governor has charge of the road, and orders from James McQuade must be obeyed and regarded.

J. W. Van Valkenburgh, Superintendent

The state was in an uproar over the lawless acts; feeling almost everywhere was strongly in sympathy with Ramsey. The violence had stopped all through travel and the contest had now reached the point where it appeared that if the authorities did not interfere, the people would take matters into their own hands. On the very next night after the struggle at the tunnel, Fisk and Courter made yet another attempt to gain possession of the Albany office. This led to another altercation that brought the cops and arrests once again.

Governor John T. Hoffman thereupon stated that he was compelled to declare the district in a state of insurrection, take possession of the line as a matter of military necessity and run it as a military road. On August 11 he appointed Colonel Robert L. Banks executive agent and treasurer, while General James McQuade was made superintendent.

Both factions now began to gather strength for the election of directors on September 7, an event with the potential of becoming a legal battle comparable to the physical caper at the tunnel. Fisk with his army of heelers, prepared with proxies to vote, came up the river from their sanctuary in the Grand Opera House on a chartered Hudson River steamer. Landing at Albany, they immediately took possession of the board room where the election was to be held.

Now with quite a reputation going for him, Blackall and a contingent of muscle from his shop were on hand to see that there was "fair play" in the event any scrimmage developed. Van Valkenburgh strode through the hall, a veritable king among men, ready for any strategy, or even to fight for the good of the road, if need be. The two factions were there and it can be conservatively said that between them there was no more affinity than between oil and water.

A legal battle of wits raged, with the result that each party organized and elected a separate board of directors, each claiming authority to control the road. The election was indeed over but nothing had been decided. Fortunately, agents of Governor Hoffman were still in possession. He now instituted proceedings through the Attorney General to determine which board had been legally elected. The trial of this action took place at Rochester in November, before Judge E. Darwin Smith. The following January his decision sustained the Ramsey board on every point and finally crushed the scheme of Gould and Fisk.

Foiled in their attempt to gain possession of the road "by force," they now attempted to secure control by negotiating for a 99-year lease, but again were unsuccessful.

On February 24, 1870 a tired President Ramsey and his weary board leased the Albany & Susquehanna Railroad, in perpetuity, to the Delaware & Hudson Canal Co.

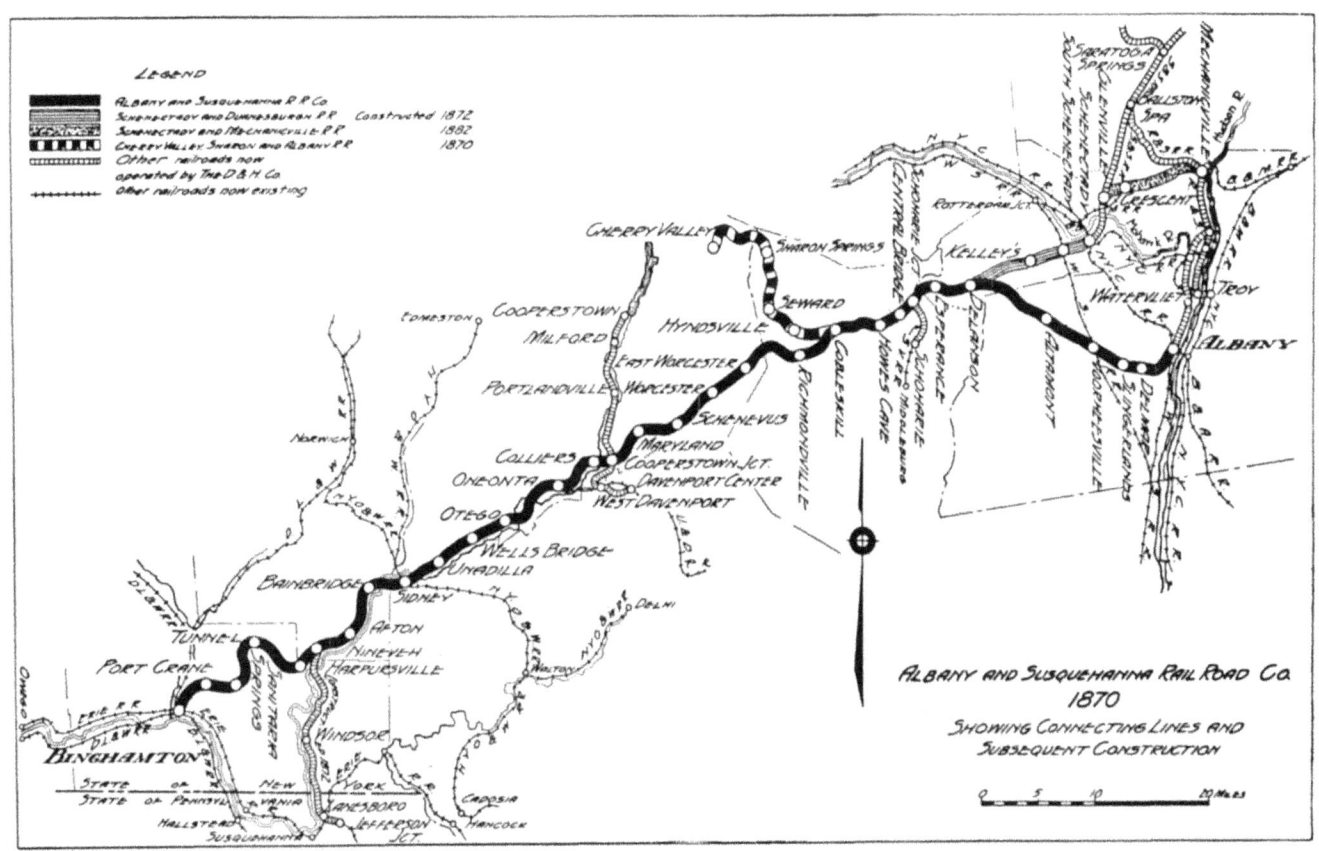

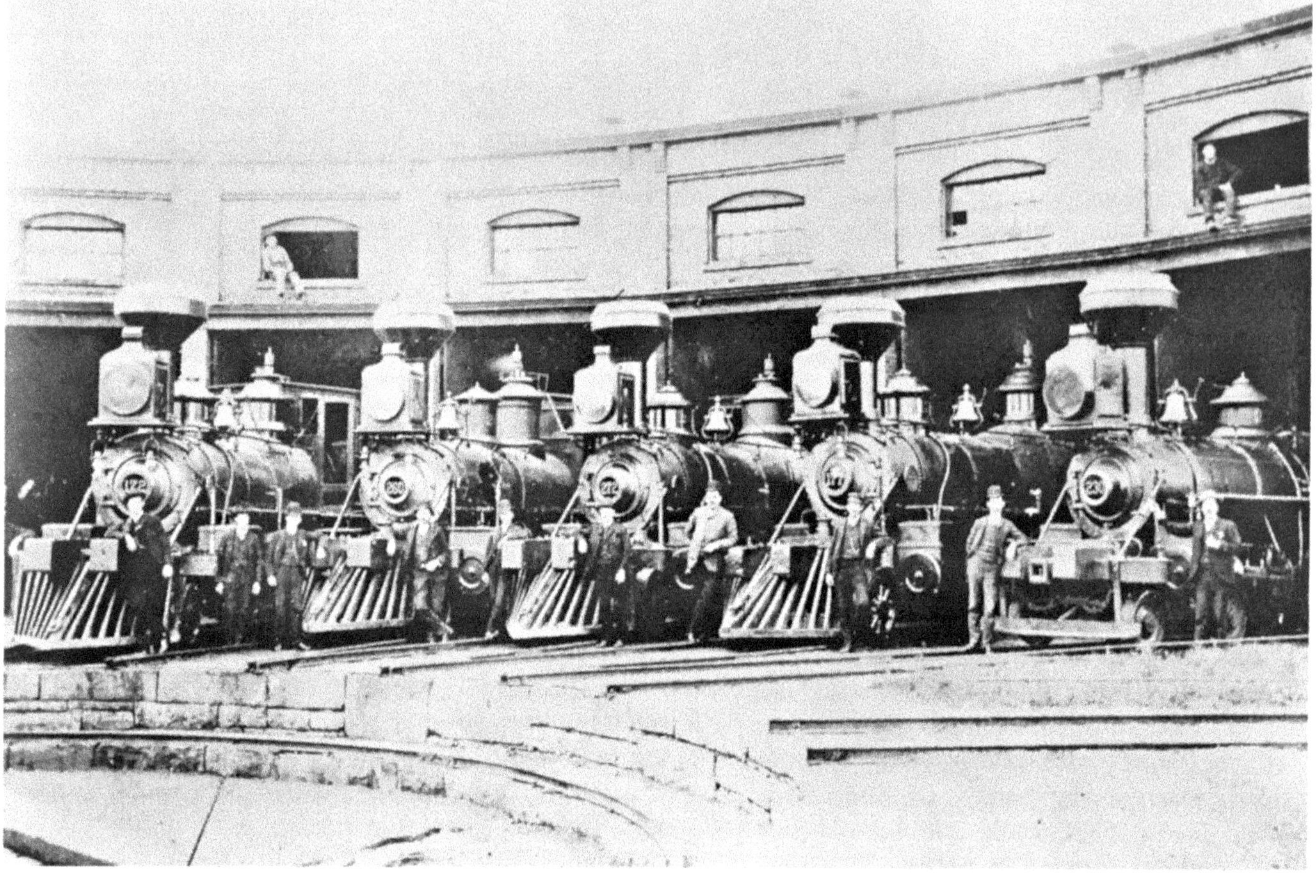

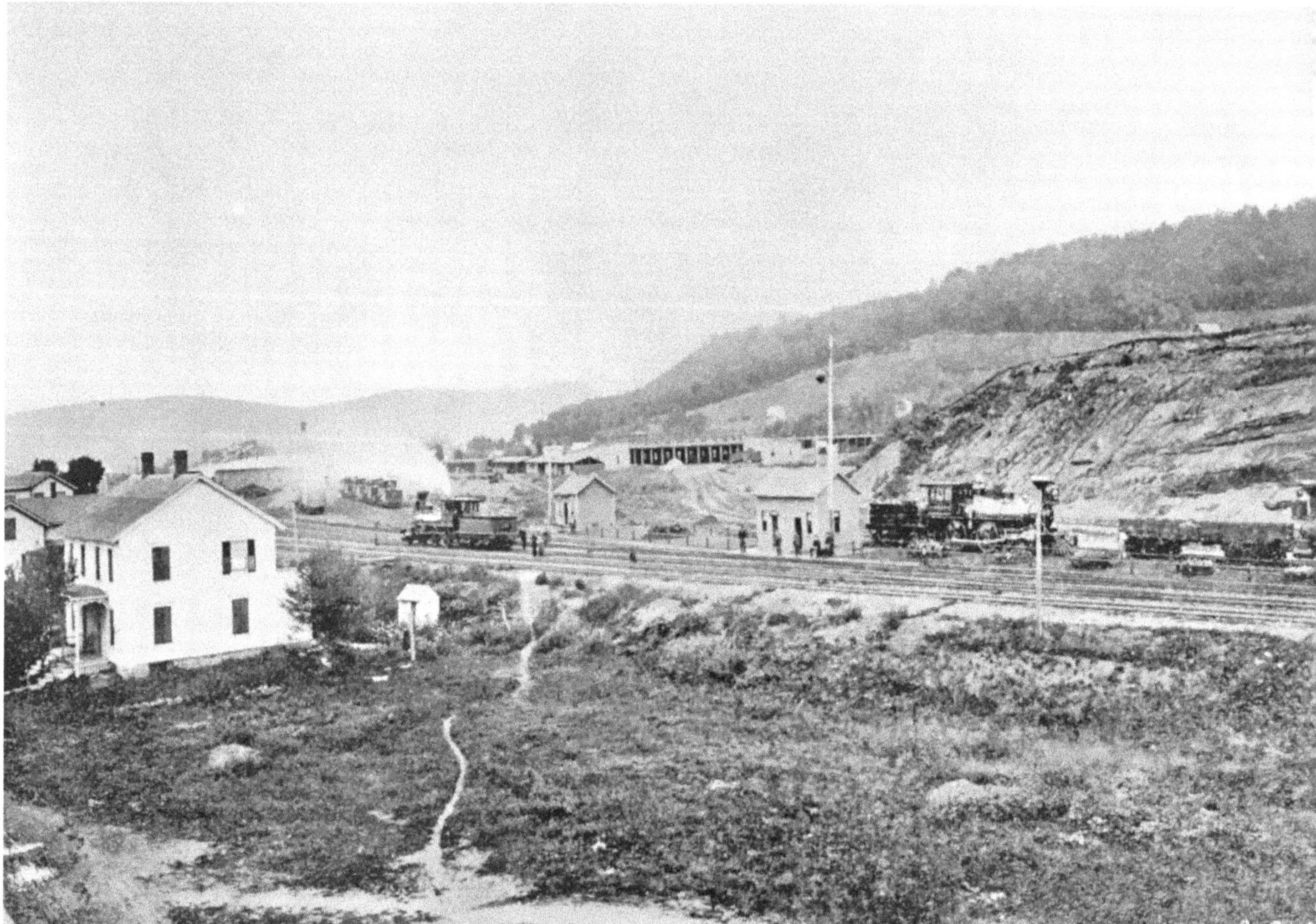
20814

Some of the local boys put on their Sunday best to be photographed with the impressive array of D&H Canal Co. power at the Delanson roundhouse in 1889, opposite above. In the 1875 view of the north end of the Oneonta yards, left, the original A&S shops and roundhouse can be seen in the left distance, while at the right a new roundhouse is being erected to accommodate new power for the increased traffic on the line under D&H operation. In the center foreground, with the aid of a ball signal, a switchman manages movements in and out of the Albany end of the yards. Two years later the Oneonta A&S shops were photographed from the office window of the master mechanic, with the shopmen appropriately lined up in front of the old A&S locomotive ONEONTA, now converted from its original six-foot gauge. The caboose on the three-rail track at the left has not yet been converted from the wide gauge. *(G. M. Best collection, opposite above; D&H collection, two pictures)*

The trim little Mogul No. 97, the R. A. HENRY, the 175th engine from the Dickson works at Scranton, is conveniently parked before the Severson House in Altamont. Apparently the fellow at the right straggled out of the bar and into the picture. The afternoon train from Cobleskill to Cherry Valley stands at the Seward, New York, station in the 1875 scene opposite. This branch was started by the Albany & Susquehanna and completed after the D&H took over in 1870. The snowplow pilot of No. 53 testifies to the winter problems experienced in this little country branch. (*D&H collection, two pictures; James R. McFarlane collection, map*)

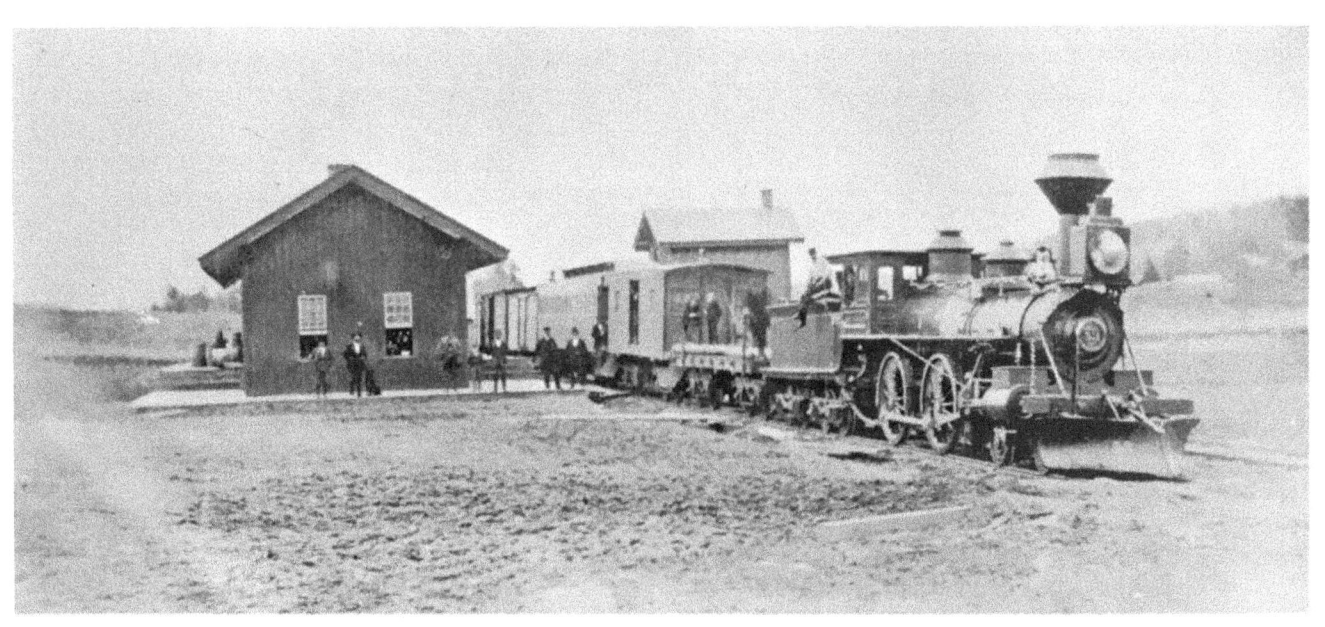

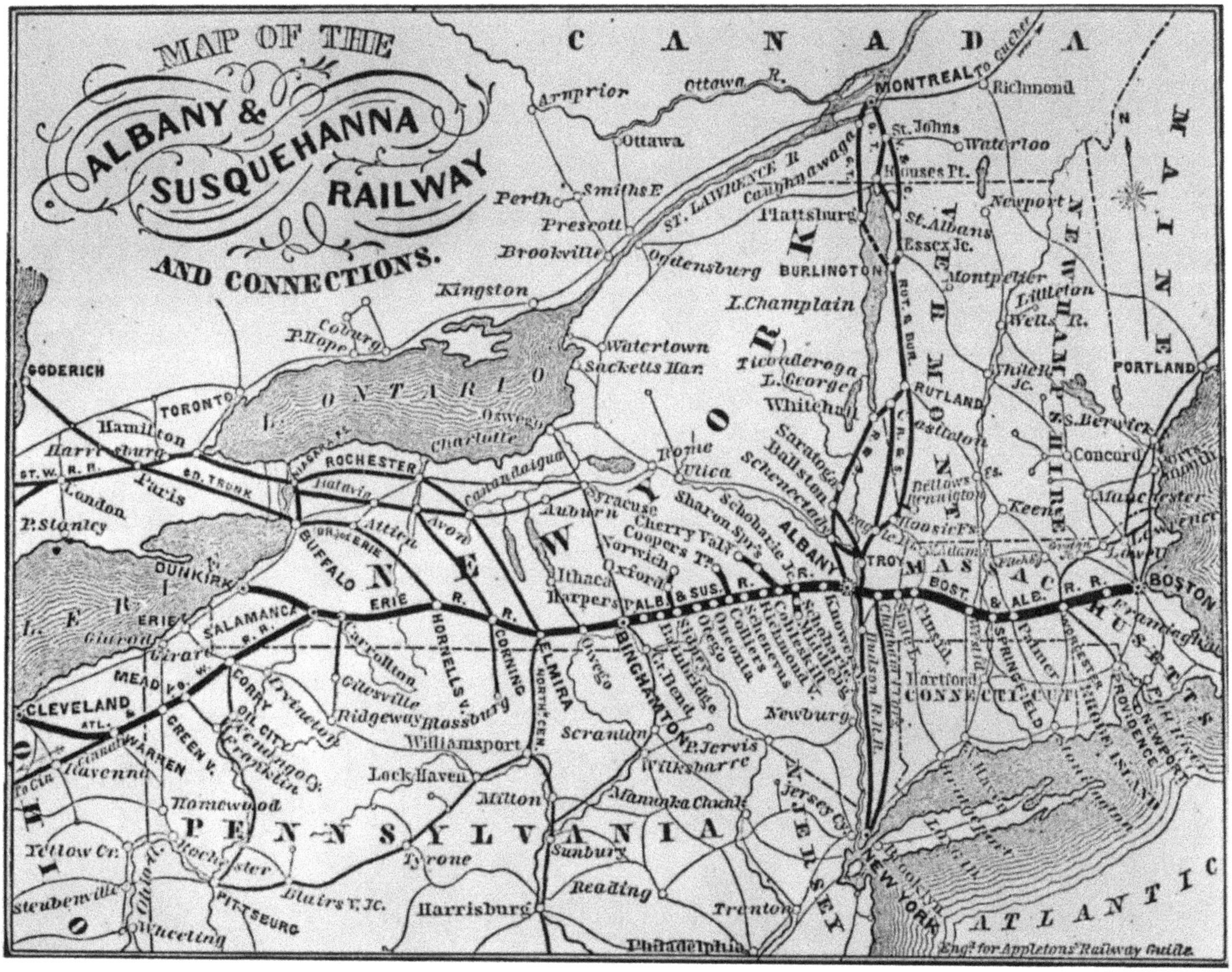

MAP OF THE
ALBANY & SUSQUEHANNA RAILWAY
AND CONNECTIONS.
CANADA
NEW YORK
PENNSYLVANIA
ONTARIO
ATLANTIC
MONTREAL
ALBANY
TROY
BINGHAMTON
ELMIRA
BUFFALO
ROCHESTER
BOSTON
NEW YORK
CLEVELAND
Engd for Appletons' Railway Guide.

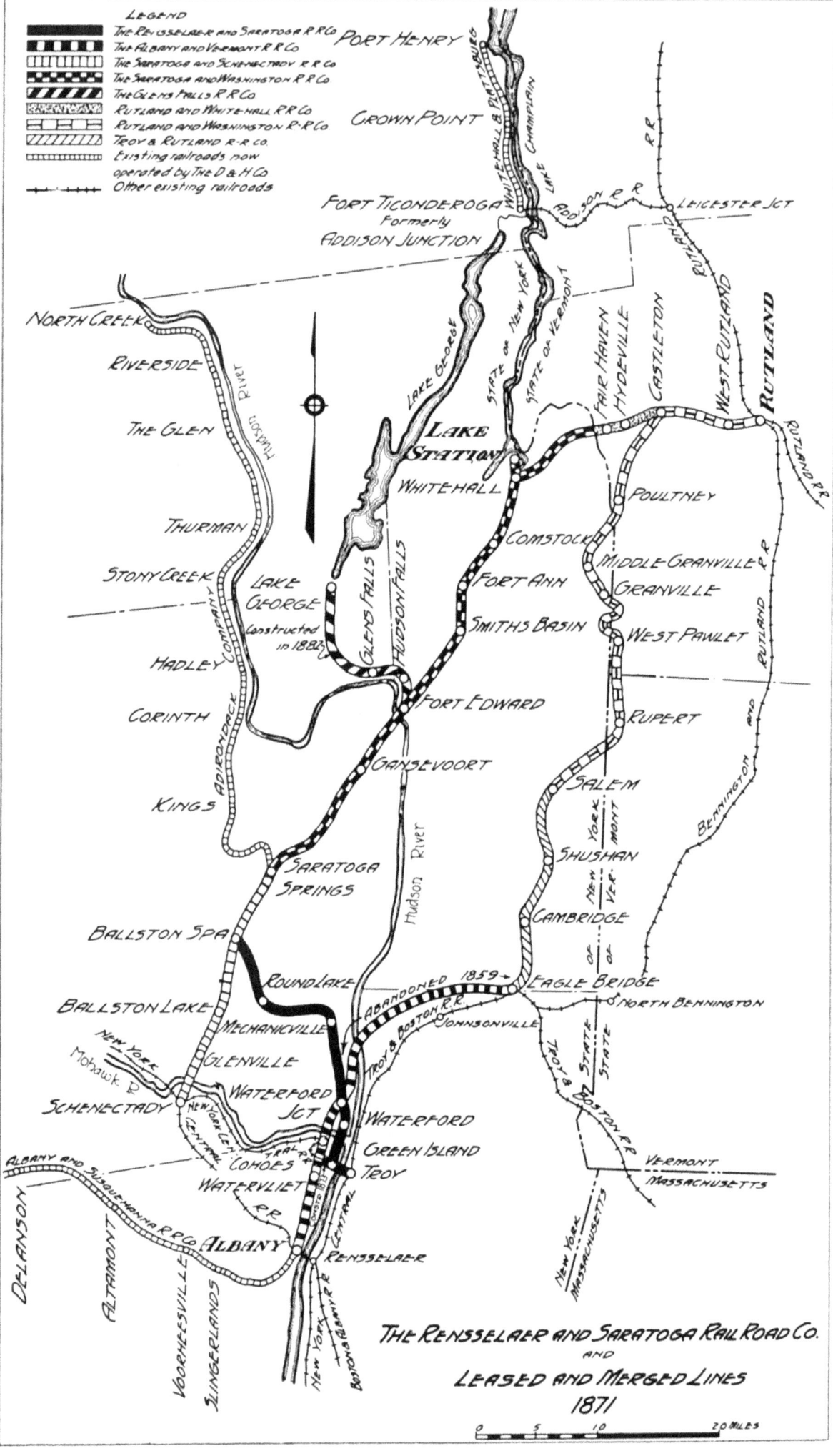

5. AN EMPIRE IN THE NORTH

It was October 25, 1825. News of the official opening of the Erie Canal boomed down the valleys of the Mohawk and Hudson rivers to New York City, relayed by a series of blasts from cannon placed strategically along the entire distance. Ten days later, November 4th, when the first flotilla of boats from Buffalo had arrived in Gotham, Governor DeWitt Clinton performed the famous wedding of the waters from Lake Erie with those of the Atlantic. The Mohawk and Hudson valleys would never be the same again!

The echoes of the cannons' roar faded beyond the distant hills, and communities along the great new inland waterway settled down to a period of change, as a flood of business surged down the valley of the Mohawk from the west. Schenectady, for example, had prospered for more than a century and a half as the principal port of the lower Mohawk River. It was a cargo transfer point for merchandise carried on the river and hauled overland to and from Albany. With completion of the Erie Canal this traffic went by boat all the way and commerce dwindled in Schenectady. Merchants there were anxious to secure new markets.

About 17 miles to the east was Albany, one of the nation's very oldest cities, and since 1797 capital of New York State. The two cities were a two-hour stage ride apart, over a rough road that was dust or mud, hot or cold, depending on the weather. With the opening of the canal, a more comfortable alternative presented itself—if one didn't mind being cooped up on a canal boat for from 24 to 48 hours as it negotiated 21 locks. Shortly after the canal was placed in service, it was evident that this particular situation had to change. On the Hudson River, Albany had been enjoying an ever-growing steamboat trade with New York City, about 145 miles to the south, but Albany merchants were well aware of the potent competition offered by a much newer city across the river and some six miles upstream.

Troy was located at the head of navigation on the Hudson and at the terminus of both the Erie and the Champlain canals, the latter serving the lake region to the north. Since its incorporation in 1816 it had grown greatly in population and had come to dominate the commerce of much of the upper Hudson and Champlain valleys. Boats traversing the Erie Canal from the west reached Troy before they came to Albany, which gave the good burghers of Troy an advantage over the Albanians in the keen rivalry that had developed between them.

The merchants of Albany were always looking for a way to skin their Trojan rivals and had an idea, the exuberance and daring of which matched that of the Delaware & Hudson Canal Co. managers when they faced the necessity of transporting coal from the Carbondale mines, across the Moosic Mountains to the canal boats at Honesdale. They decided to build a railroad! A line to Schenectady would connect Albany much more easily with the Mohawk valley and the west than did the rough road or the circuitous canal route. It would nicely bypass the boys in Troy and possibly even capture some of their trade to the north. Now that railroads were becoming feasible, this seemed to be an answer to their problem.

Accordingly, the Mohawk & Hudson was chartered and built, the first train from Albany reaching Schenectady on August 9, 1831. This had the distinction of being the first train pulled by a locomotive to run on the first railroad built in New York State. It ran through the flat country to the crest of its namesake river valleys at each end; there the cars were let down or pulled up an in-

89

cline to get baggage and passengers to and from the docks. This business brought some prosperity to Schenectady in passenger traffic, but freight continued to go all the way by canal.

The little Mohawk & Hudson was the first unit of what has become the great New York Central System. Before it was completed, however, Schenectady merchants, backed by others in Albany, sought to incorporate a company to build a railroad from Schenectady to Saratoga Springs.

The Saratoga & Schenectady. Indians are said to have introduced the virtues of waters found at the springs we now know as Saratoga to Sir William Johnson, patroon of the Mohawk valley, as early as 1767, and to have even taken him there when he was in poor health. The spa developed as a watering place and resort for the affluent people; the merchants of Schenectady could see this increasing influx as not only a transportation market but also as an opportunity for other forms of commerce.

On February 16, 1831 the Saratoga & Schenectady Rail Road was incorporated with a capital of $150,000 and authorized to carry property and people "by the power and force of steam, of animals, or any mechanical or other power." This certainly left the motive power situation open for any eventuality, and when the company's subscription books were opened in both Albany and New York on April 24, they were substantially over-subscribed. Albany alone provided investors for $124,000 worth of shares, and New York speculators went for it enthusiastically enough to meet the entire cost of building the road, including all the extras that inevitably crept in as construction progressed.

On August 20, the Honorable C. C. Cambreleng, president of the new line broke ground at Saratoga Springs, and construction was quickly started under the direction of engineer John B. Jervis, of D&H Canal fame. By October 25, the available supply of laborers was exhausted and a call went out for an additional 500 men at "liberal wages." During the winter Mr. Jervis suggested improvements that would substantially increase the road's capacity; additional funds were willingly advanced, and the entire line, except for a small gap, was opened to traffic July 12, 1832. A bridge across Kayderosseras Creek at Ballston Spa was not yet finished and passengers were transferred across the half-mile gap in post coaches. Considering construction methods and equipment in 1831, 11 months was not a bad building time for a 21½-mile railroad.

The trip from Schenectady to Saratoga took two hours, or 4½ hours from Albany including breakfast in Schenectady. Horsepower, in its literal sense, was the form of locomotion used on the line at the beginning.

During the winter of 1832-33 two major problems confronted the S&S management. It was necessary, of course, to complete the unfinished portion of the road at Ballston Spa, and work was pressed to accomplish this. They also needed some sort of locomotive for tractive power and in 1833 the technology of locomotive-making was still in the formative stage. The S&S's approach to the solution of this problem had historic implications.

John B. Jervis had observed the problems encountered with the solid wheel-base, when early locomotives were required to negotiate curves in the track. His experience with the STOURBRIDGE LION of the D&H and the DEWITT CLINTON of the Mohawk & Hudson led him to the concept of the bogie design. The principle of the bogie engine was simple: nothing more, in fact, than to connect the frame of the forward wheels with the crosspiece by a kingbolt at the center only, thus enabling this wheel assembly to turn freely on curves. He had built such an engine in 1832 for the Mohawk & Hudson, but due to a poor boiler it proved less than satisfactory.

On Mr. Jervis' advice, the S&S ordered a locomotive of his design from Robert Stephenson &

The English-built DAVY CROCKETT weighed six tons and had 1100 pounds tractive effort. She worked so well that a sister, the FIRE FLY, was ordered the following year.

Co. and the DAVY CROCKETT departed the shores of merrie olde England for the New World on April 6, 1833, with the distinction of being the first bogie engine this already-famous builder ever made.

While the engine was at sea, on April 15, the bridge over Kayderosseras Creek was completed and the two sections of the line were connected. On arrival the DAVY CROCKETT was set up in the shops of the Mohawk & Hudson, and it made its first trip from Schenectady to Saratoga Springs on July 2, 1833. The test train consisted of "freight wagons," but at Ballston Spa it overtook a horse-drawn passenger train there at the station and soon showed old Dobbin what the future held for him by pulling the whole shebang, passengers and all, the rest of the way into Saratoga Springs.

An article in the *American Railroad Journal* declared that with five bushels of coke, at a total cost of $15 a day, this locomotive could do the work of fifty horses, costing a dollar a day each for feed—$50 for a stable full of nags.

The traveling public quickly took advantage of the new facilities and in the month of July, 3,550 passengers were carried between Schenectady and the Springs. On many occasions a train of eight coaches and three baggage wagons, with over 175 patrons, made the trip. As a result of this passenger boom the first 5% dividend was paid in August. Freight began to appear in the road's 18 small freight wagons, and on November 21, a quantity of anthracite was hauled from Albany on the Mohawk & Hudson to Schenectady, then up to Ballston Spa for manufacturing purposes—the vanguard of a traffic that would loom large in the road's future. A financial report of November 30, 1833 showed total receipts of $42,266.79, with expenditures of only $16,990.92—not bad for a start.

The road's management was so pleased by this business and with the performance of the DAVY CROCKETT that late in 1833 it decided to obtain another engine. John Hampson, the road's engine driver, sailed on December 1 for Liverpool to work out the details with Robert Stephenson & Co. He was free to make the trip, because the company decided not to use the engine on the line in the winter—a practice it followed for many years; what winter business there was at first could be handled by a horse and cutter. At that time the company's motive power roster consisted of one locomotive, 24 horses and 33 sets of harness, so Mr. Hampson's mission seemed to be a step in the right direction. On July 5, 1834 the second engine, the FIRE FLY arrived in New York and joined the CROCKETT ten days later.

The track was standard for the day: wood stringers capped with iron strap rails, imported from England, laid on longitudinal sills of wood or, in some places, stone. The original station in Schenectady was at the corner of Railroad and Water Streets. From there the track extended north, passing under State Street, across Union at grade, under Front Street and then to the Mohawk River, which it crossed on a highway bridge to the town of Glenville near the present site of Scotia. This portion of the line was operated by horses, the locomotive being hooked on at the north end of the bridge. In 1838 this route into the city was abandoned after the S&S made arrangements with the Utica & Schenectady Railroad, now part of the New York Central, to use its tracks and bridge from the north side of the river into its station in the city. This route continued until 1871 when a new and independent line was built into Schenectady.

The early years of operation on the Saratoga & Schenectady were picturesque and prosperous, perhaps even including an element of sport. The road was crowded with pleasure seekers in summer and a ride in a horse-drawn cutter the length of the line in the winter must have been exhilarating, to say the least.

The Rensselaer & Saratoga. In the meantime, back in Troy, the merchants were not at all pleased by the potential flurry of business activity surging from Albany to Schenectady and on to the north. The obvious answer was a railroad of their own. Prime movers for the Trojans were Richard P. Hart and Stephen Warren. Hart had amassed a large fortune in stage lines between Troy and Lake Champlain, but he had been forced out of the picture with the opening of the Champlain Canal. Warren was a leading merchant and stove manufacturer. In February they petitioned the Legislature for the incorporation of a rail line and on April 14, 1832 the Rensselaer & Saratoga Rail Road was chartered. It provided for capital of $300,000 and authority to construct a railroad from Troy, via Waterford, to Ballston Spa, to carry persons and property for a 50-year term.

Richard P. Hart, first president, Rensselaer & Saratoga Rail Road.

The Albanians were apparently so engrossed in their Schenectady-Saratoga route to the north and so smug at having finally done in their Trojan rivals that they failed to notice, or realize the importance of, the provision granting the R&S the right to build a bridge over the Hudson. A bridge over the river had been the bone of long and bitter contention between the two cities and had resulted in the denial of the authority to each. It now appeared that Troy had finally gained a distinct advantage over her old rival.

The entire stock issue was promptly sold and Richard P. Hart was elected president. Location surveys were made in 1833 and on August 1, the City of Troy granted the company the right to lay rails through its streets and run carriages thereon.

The line would run from River and First Streets north on River Street to Federal and across the controversial bridge over the Hudson to Green Island. It would continue along the west shore of the Hudson to Waterford, crossing three sprouts of the Mohawk, proceeding to Mechanicville (then called the Borough) and finally on to Ballston Spa and into Saratoga Springs over the Saratoga & Schenectady rails. Work on the section from Waterford to Ballston Spa began immediately, but the section from Troy to Waterford, with its four bridges, was placed under contract in the following year, the summer of 1834.

Early in January of 1835 orders went out to M. W. Baldwin of Philadelphia for two locomotives, to be named the ERIE and CHAMPLAIN and to Gilbert, Veazie & Eaton of Troy for 18 passenger cars and 20 baggage and freight cars.

The completion of the line from Waterford to Ballston Spa was celebrated on August 18, 1835, by a large group of officials and stockholders who assembled on the east bank of the Hudson opposite Waterford and, escorted by two military bands, triumphantly marched across the covered bridge spanning the river at the upper end of Lansingburgh, now North Troy, to the new station. After the usual round of speeches extolling the great accomplishments and future prospects of great wealth and success, they all climbed aboard a special train and were off to Ballston Spa for another blast. The blast at Ballston was both figurative and literal, for as the triumphant special rolled into town the village militia fired a series of cannons welcoming the conquering Trojans, before all retired to the Sans Souci Hotel for food, drink and more speeches.

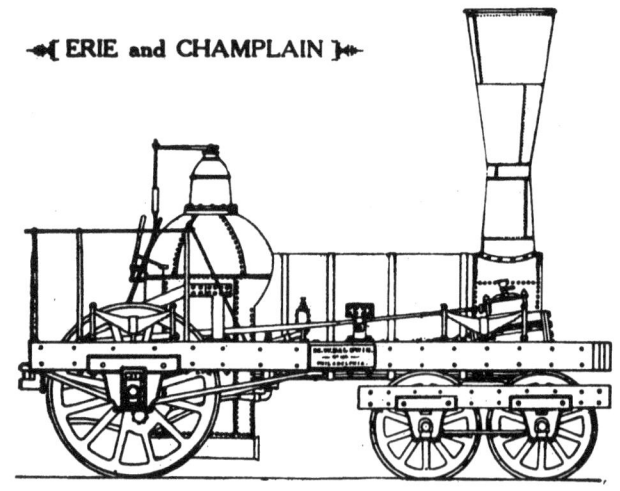

The R&S carried commerce north from the busy inland port of Troy at the head of Hudson River navigation. The 1838 scene above was made from Watervliet Arsenal. The first R&S engines were the ERIE and the CHAMPLAIN, weighing ten tons each. They operated with 100 pounds of steam to produce 2750 pounds of tractive force.

The return trip was marred by a minor derailment; no one was hurt and after a day of revelry no one much cared or perhaps even knew the difference. The next day the line was opened to the public with two trains each way and a stage connection was provided from Waterford to Troy. It would even pick up passengers at their homes. The fare from Troy to Ballston Spa was $1.00 and to Saratoga $1.25.

The most difficult section to build from Troy to Waterford, containing four bridges including the large one over the Hudson at Troy, was opened October 6, 1835, and the cars that rolled over the bridge at Troy that day were the first ever to cross the Hudson. The trains were pulled by horses through the Troy streets from the depot at 10 First Street to the bridge and across to Green Island where the locomotive was hooked on.

Troy's first railroad station was the Troy House on River Street, shown in this old engraving with a coach, before tracks were laid on the cobblestone street. The 1841 notice on the opposite page sets forth details of R&S accommodations to Saratoga and points north. *(Rensselaer County Historical Society, above)*

The passenger cars were 24 feet long and eight feet wide, high enough to walk in and divided into three compartments surrounded by movable panels allowing the passenger to choose his degree of comfort. The seats were cushioned with black and crimson morocco and trimmed with coach lace. Outside, the cars were painted a fawn color with buff shading and in each of the many panels in the woodwork copies of paintings were reproduced surrounded by gold borders trimmed with rose, pink, vermilion and black scroll work. There were more than 200 different scenes such as Napoleon crossing the Alps, great men of the country, popular steamboats and many more on the 24-car roster. It was more like a movable art gallery than a train.

Some comments from the diary of Philip Hone, one-time Mayor of New York and first president of D&H Canal Co., compare the routes to Saratoga via the competing lines during a June 25, 1836 trip he made over the road: "We came to Troy in two hours and a quarter, through fine country, without interruption, and faster than I have ever traveled on the Mohawk & Hudson road. The enterprise of the Trojans has raised up a powerful rival to the other two lines." He noted, "The Troy Railroad has a great advantage over the Mohawk & Hudson, in its having no inclined plane, a most serious difficulty, and one which travelers always look upon with apprehension." He went on to say that on that very day one of the trains from Schenectady was waiting at the foot of a plane and a balance car full of stone used on the opposite end of a line to pull the train up the hill as gravity pulled it down, broke loose and came thundering down the incline. It was switched out in time to avoid hitting the waiting cars but one workman was killed in the process. Hone summed it up by saying, "The truth is, the modern Trojans are the most enterprising, persevering, go-ahead set of fellows in the world." You would almost think he was about to run for mayor of Troy, and after such comments would probably have been elected for sure.

As patronage on the line increased, efforts of the R&S to conclude a definite arrangement with the Saratoga & Schenectady for handling its freight and passenger traffic from Saratoga Springs to Ballston Spa failed completely. In the fall of 1835 Richard P. Hart and other Troy merchants had the financial backing to take prompt advantage of an unexpected opportunity to buy enough stock in the S&S to secure control. With the differences settled in this manner and trackage rights gained, through service to Saratoga Springs was imme-

diately established and in October a nine-hour route from Troy to Whitehall was formed by a stage connection between Saratoga and the head of Lake Champlain. With the inauguration of this service, in connection with the Hudson River and Lake Champlain steamboats, the Rensselaer & Saratoga became a key link in the New York-to-Montreal route. The early success of the passenger business was, without doubt, largely due to the great popularity of Ballston Spa and Saratoga Springs as resorts for the wealthy and fashionable of the country. This prominent position was retained for almost a century after 1835 and exercised a marked influence on the operations of the R&S.

The Saratoga & Schenectady station at Marvin Square in Saratoga Springs was in later years also used by the R&S and the Adirondack Railway. When the GOVERNOR PAGE, R&S No. 34, was photographed outside the station, just about everybody in the area crowded into the picture with the Schenectady-built 4-4-0.

As traffic increased, especially the freight volume which was practically nil at the outset, it became necessary to replace the strap rail in use since the line's opening with a more substantial arrangement. In 1848 the entire track superstructure was replaced, substituting crossties for the longitudinal stringers and 58-pound rolled "T" rails. After the reconstruction was completed the following year, it was possible to acquire new and heavier equipment and the first eight-wheel locomotives were obtained and put into service.

To accommodate the increased traffic, the tracks had been extended south along Troy's River Street so freight and passengers could be transferred directly to and from the wharves used by the New York steamboats. As early as 1837 railroad traffic on River Street caused considerable congestion there in the center of the business district. The problem was compounded as other railroads came into town: the Troy & Schenectady in 1842, the Troy & Greenbush in 1845 and in 1853 the Troy & Boston.

In 1851 the Legislature authorized the formation of a stock company to build a railroad within the city limits. Under this authority the Troy Union Railroad Co. was chartered and a quarter of its stock was purchased by each of the roads then entering the city. Construction of the new line through the city began in 1853, using 65-pound pear-headed rail. On February 22, 1854, it was formally opened and steam locomotives crossed the Hudson into Troy for the first time as they headed for the newly-built Union Station between Broadway and Fulton Street on 6th Avenue, then at the eastern end of the business district. The horses that for over 18 years had hauled the cars across the bridge and through the streets of Troy were now technologically unemployed.

At noon on May 10, 1862, a sudden and drastic fire broke out on the R&S's bridge into Troy, and the burning embers were driven by a brisk northwest wind into the heart of the city. It was thought that a spark from a passing locomotive was probably the cause, but the result was beyond question or even belief.

When the station pictured on the opposite page burned, this one was built to replace it in 1871. *(D&H collection, three pictures)*

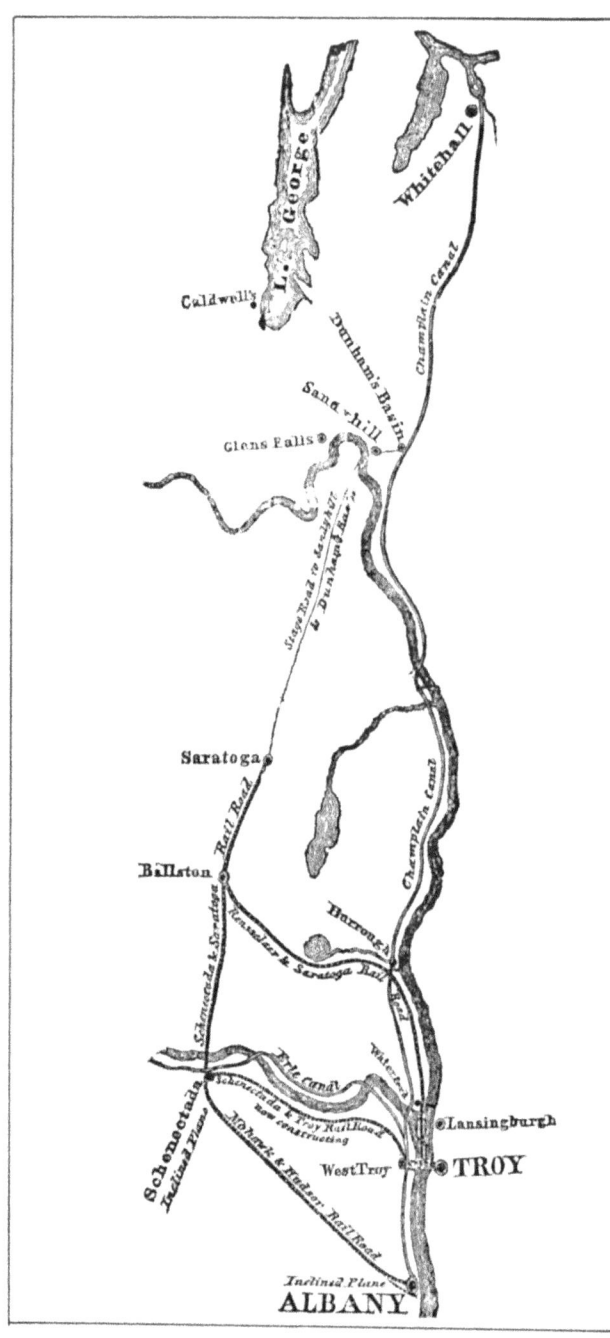

1841 map showing three railroads, a stage road and the canal to the head of Lake Champlain at Whitehall.

Firemen were promptly on the scene, but were immediately driven back as the flames surged out of control across Troy in a great cloud of smoke, heat and destruction. People were overcome and burned to death in the streets. By 6 p.m. that night the wind and flames subsided and 75 acres, including 507 buildings, lay in smoking ruin. Actually there was little left to burn. A contemporary account states that the tally of 507 buildings did not include barns or outhouses, and had these little structures been included in the count, the number would no doubt have been double the figure. Numbered among the lost was Troy's Union Station. The wooden bridge across the Hudson, where it all started, was partly destroyed as well.

The Albany Northern. The Rensselaer & Saratoga was doing pretty well in the north and the ever-watchful Albany merchants sought to build a line north from Albany and across the Hudson to connect with Rutland, Vermont, a New England gateway and an era from which large and profitable shipments of marble originated. The Rutland & Washington Railroad was interested in an outlet to the south and access to the traffic potential of the Hudson valley, so it was willing to co-operate in the venture.

On February 20, 1851, the Albany Northern Rail Road was chartered to build from Albany, through West Troy (now Watervliet), Cohoes, Waterford, Schaghticoke, Pittstown, Johnsonville and Buskirk to Eagle Bridge, New York. At this little village, about twenty miles northeast of Troy and near the Vermont state line, the road would connect with the Troy & Rutland, which was to operate jointly with the Rutland & Washington on the route.

The Albany Northern was quickly built and opened from Albany to Cohoes on April 11, 1853, including a branch down 16th Street in West Troy to a ferry connection to Troy. A month later the line was finished to Waterford. Planned but never built was an 18-mile branch to Saratoga from Waterford Junction, where the A.N. crossed the R&S, several miles north of Waterford proper. The first train over the entire line puffed into Eagle Bridge on July 1, 1853, and the first through train, via the Rutland & Washington, reached Rutland the following November. From the beginning a shaky affair both financially and physically, the Albany Northern went from crisis to crisis with machine-gun rapidity during eight years of unbelievable financial chaos.

The tale of woe started immediately when several Albanians advanced extra money to pay for completing the line, and then took over operations until they had reimbursed themselves for these advances. By January, 1854, the management was knocking on the front door of the Albany City Hall

Troy's second station was built by the newly-formed Troy Union Railroad in 1854 as a result of increased traffic on the four railroads then entering the city. It lasted only eight years until it was destroyed on May 10, 1862, by a fire which consumed much of the heart of Troy. Ruins of the train shed are at the right, below, looking southeast over Federal Street and Fifth Avenue. On the hill are the original buildings of Rensselaer Polytechnic Institute, left, and, with the six spires, Troy Monastery, later St. Joseph's Seminary. *(D&H collection, above; H. Irving Moore collection, below)*

The original towered Union Station, probably the biggest victim of Troy's great fire of 1862, was soon replaced by this simpler structure which survived until 1900, when it gave way to a new station with no train shed. The massive depot at West Rutland, Vermont, originally property of the Rutland & Washington, became part of the R&S when leased by that line and later by similar means found itself in the D&H empire. *(D&H collection, below)*

for a loan. No doubt at the urging of Albany investors in the line, a committee of Councilmen reported favorably and the City of Albany went out on the financial limb to the tune of $300,000. Next, interest payments on the second mortgage bonds could not be paid and the line was plunged into receivership. After purchasing the majority of the stock in the Troy & Rutland—itself in a court battle with its lessee, the Rutland & Washington—as a protective measure against unfavorable outside influences, the whole works crashed into bankruptcy.

At a public auction October 16, 1856, in Albany, the Albany Northern was sold to one Christopher Binder for $250,000 and reorganized as the Albany, Vermont & Canada Rail Road, articles of association being filed November 7. Soon it too was bankrupt and up for auction. There simply was not enough traffic for any operator to survive. It was foreclosed again in 1859 for only $25,000 and organized as the Albany & Vermont Rail Road, which soon abandoned service to Eagle Bridge. More money went down the drain and on April 5, 1860, a majority of the stock was purchased by agents of the Rensselaer & Saratoga and the Troy & Boston.

The R&S quickly leased the section from Albany to Waterford Junction and agreed not to use the portion of the line beyond that point. From there to Eagle Bridge the rails were removed. Although the Troy & Boston acquired the abandoned roadbed as a protective measure, it never did anything else about it.

With this lease, the Rensselaer & Saratoga increased its total operated mileage to 60. At last the Trojans had gained access to the front doors of their old rivals in Albany.

The Rutland & Washington and the Troy & Rutland. The story of the railroads that served the marble quarries of Rutland County, Vermont, began in the 1840s. At this time commercial quarrying of the great deposits of beautiful white rock there began in earnest, but the industry's growth was seriously hampered by the difficulty and high cost of getting the tremendously heavy blocks over to Whitehall, New York, for shipment via the Champlain Canal to New York City and other markets. A railroad would provide a means of handling this job effectively, and when large deposits of commercially usable slate were discovered in the area straddling the border between Vermont and New York, impetus was added to the proposals already made for such a line.

The Vermont Legislature granted a charter to the Rutland & Washington Rail-Road Co. on November 13, 1847, enabling it to build a line from Rutland to the New York border, there to connect with those lines projected or in operation in the Empire State.

The directors, however, decided to have the line go southwest through the town of Poultney, Vermont, rather than directly west through Castleton and the village of Fair Haven, Vermont, as originally proposed. This brought a storm of protests from the public at large and from the Saratoga & Washington interests, whose story will be told later. The directors, nevertheless, were determined to push forward with their plans. As a result, the Saratoga & Washington people formed a company, the Rutland & Whitehall, to complete the stretch of track from their branch at the state line, through Fair Haven to a connection with the Rutland & Washington at Castleton, Vermont.

The Rutland & Washington then sought a southerly outlet through New York, the object being Troy where both rail and water connections could be secured. Interest now grew in the New York villages of Granville, Salem and Cambridge, resulting in numerous petitions seeking a charter for a railroad to run from the state line, down through the heartland of Washington County, to Troy. On July 2, 1849, a charter was granted by the New York Legislature to the Troy & Rutland to build such a road from Troy to or near the town of Poultney, and there to connect with the Rutland & Washington.

As the survey for the R&W was being made, it was apparent that the most feasible route would necessitate crossing and recrossing the state line at several points. The charter was amended to allow the extension of the line south of Poultney to make connection with the Troy & Rutland.

In June 1849 a contract for construction of the road from Rutland to Poultney, at a cost of $25,000 per mile, was let. The first ten miles, from Rutland to Castleton, were opened in October of 1850, allowing through travel from Rutland to Whitehall and the south, via the Rutland & Whitehall in Vermont and the Saratoga & Washington's branch from Whitehall to the state line.

101

This is the sad result, September 23, 1865, of the inexperience of an engineer who, with his locomotive, the JAY GOULD, had just come over to the R&S with the lease of the Rutland & Washington. Bringing his engine and the consist for the 8 p.m. sleeper to Rutland, over to Troy from the Green Island yards, he failed to notice that the bridge was open to pass a steamboat. He and his fireman jumped to safety and there were no fatalities, but coach and engine caught fire, causing fear that the bridge might again catch fire as it had three years before with disastrous results. Only the coach was destroyed and the GOULD was hauled out to run another day. (*G. M. Best collection*)

In 1850, the Troy & Boston was about to build a line north out of Troy to Eagle Bridge, then east to the Massachusetts state line. It would have been a duplication for the Troy & Rutland to construct its own line paralleling this one, so on February 22, 1850, an agreement was made with the T&B allowing the T&R trains to continue on into Troy over the rails of the Troy & Boston.

The following June the Troy & Rutland, in an effort to achieve smooth and harmonious operations, conveyed its rights and franchises from Eagle Bridge to the Vermont state line to the Rutland & Washington, making it essentially one railroad all the way to Rutland. Contracts were then let for the sections from Salem, New York, to Poultney and from Eagle Bridge to Salem at the same price as the northern portion, $25,000 a mile.

On November 29, a scant six months after making its agreement with the Troy & Rutland, the Troy & Boston—a company with a rather checkered reputation for integrity—abandoned the arrangement in favor of an alliance with the Western Vermont Railroad. The T&B would build a connection to the Vermont road at North Bennington, providing an alternative through route to Rutland that would prove to be a serious threat to the financial stability of the Rutland & Washington. This sudden and unforeseen move required that line's management to seek another southern outlet, one on which it could depend. Negotiations were begun with some prominent Albany businessmen which ultimately led to the incorporation of the Albany Northern Rail Road. Since this road was not ready when the R&W-T&R line from Rutland to Eagle Bridge was completed and opened for its entire length, March 9, 1852, there was no connection to the south and no records were set for through business.

It was not until the next year that the Albany Northern provided this connection, when it opened to Eagle Bridge, July 1, 1853. With an independent, jointly-operated through line from Albany to Rutland, business improved a bit, but it was not to last. There were now three different routes to Rutland. In addition to the Troy & Boston-Western Vermont connection, this line had to meet the competition of a route involving the Rensselaer & Saratoga in conjunction with the Saratoga & Washington. The available traffic simply could not support this many routes.

Jay Gould was president of the Troy, Salem & Rutland Railroad before he became involved in the "Erie War" with the A&S.

On October 20, 1859, when the Albany Northern, by then called the Albany & Vermont, finally threw in the towel, the Rutland & Washington was once more dangling with a loose end at Eagle Bridge. This line was now in a receivership, following a dispute over the lease of the Troy & Rutland in 1855. In 1863 the Troy & Rutland was sold in foreclosure to none other than Jay Gould, the very gentleman who would soon be infamous for his manipulations and robbery of the Erie Railroad. In 1865 the Rutland & Washington was bought by William T. Hart, associated with the Rensselaer & Saratoga interests. The new owners incorporated the Troy, Salem & Rutland Rail Road on June 3, 1865, with a charter allowing them to operate the line in New York State and lease the section in Vermont.

A more important provision of the charter authorized the owners to lease the property and to

The JAMES M. MARVIN, No. 36, built for the R&S by the Schenectady Locomotive Works in 1867, awaits departure from the north end of the Troy Union Station at Fulton Street, probably with the afternoon run to Whitehall and Rutland, while some of the gang from the Ward Saloon gather by the big wooden cowcatcher. Baldwin-built No. 151, originally named the CANADA, stands on the turntable at Green Island Roundhouse, while 4-4-0 No. 13 is eased out of her stall in the background. This roundhouse, with the great shops just out of the picture to the right, was the center of R&S operations and after that line was leased to the D&H continued to serve in that capacity until 1912. S. M. Craver himself, master mechanic of the R&S, stands at the left with top hat and hand on the brass stanchion at the front of his newly delivered namesake, No. 25. The bicycle-type 4-2-4 was built by Danforth & Cook in 1863 with a 62-inch driver. Only in good weather could she pull three cars, so she was soon rebuilt into a 4-4-0. (*D&H collection, two lower pictures*)

consolidate the stock with that of the lessee, and that is just what they did. Twelve days later, on June 15, 1865, they consolidated their line with the Rensselaer & Saratoga.

The Saratoga & Whitehall. To trace the story of the other route from Troy to Rutland, further to the west, it is necessary once more to go back in time, to the 1830s. Even before the Saratoga & Schenectady was completed, in 1832, Gideon M. Davison, a prominent citizen of Saratoga Springs, envisioned the future potential of transportation over the gap that separated the Hudson from Lake Champlain and Canada. With a rail line now coming to the Springs, a connection north to the head of the lake was the next logical step. He petitioned the Legislature and received on April 17, 1832, the charter for the Saratoga & Fort Edward Rail Road. He then engaged John B. Jervis, chief engineer of the Mohawk & Hudson and the Saratoga & Schenectady, to look over the proposed route. Jervis reported favorably, but somehow the project fell into abeyance.

Davison's faith in the project continued and he succeeded in interesting the projectors of the Rensselaer & Saratoga along with some influential people in the area counties in 1834. A new charter was obtained, this time for the Saratoga & Washington Rail-Road Co., to build a line from Saratoga Springs to Whitehall. The Legislature, however, in its desire to retain for the State-owned Champlain Canal the traffic to the north and Canada, gave the new company the right to carry persons and their baggage "only" and strictly prohibited the transportation of "freight of every description."

Stephen Warren, one of the officials of the R&S, was elected president and Mr. Davison the vice-president. In 1835 paper money was abundant, speculation in land was at an all-time high and with the prospects of this new line carrying nearly all the travel between New York and Canada, it was fully and promptly supported.

In 1836 the surveys were completed and two routes proposed across the Hudson. One through Fort Edward and thence north to Whitehall on a level route followed the valley occupied by the Champlain Canal; the other through Sandy Hill, now Hudson Falls, over high undulating ground involved an 80-foot-high bridge across the Hudson. Both routes joined again at Fort Ann and continued up the valley to Whitehall.

Unfortunately for the company, two of its directors lived in Sandy Hill but none in Fort Edward and they demanded that the line follow the more difficult, and therefore more expensive, route through their town. Work began late in 1836, but the boom era came to an abrupt and crashing end in the severe panic of 1837, and with it the end of Mr. Davison's dream.

Ten years passed while the grass grew on the partially-graded roadbed, the weather deteriorated the half-completed bridge piers over the Hudson at Sandy Hill and appeal after appeal went out to the State Legislature for financial aid.

In 1845 a new location leaving the original line near Gansevoort, then following one of the original routes through Fort Edward, was surveyed and the Legislature authorized an increase of $250,000 in the capital of the company. In addition, the lawmakers allowed the route to be extended to the western boundary of Vermont. All this revived interest and in February of 1847, under a new administration, the old line through Sandy Hill was abandoned and contracts let for building the road from Saratoga to Fort Ann over the more practical valley route.

In April, 56-pound iron "T" rails were placed on the new roadbed and four locomotives, the BENNINGTON, MONTREAL, TICONDEROGA and NEW YORK, were ordered for delivery later in the year. Additional funds allowed the remainder of the line to Whitehall to be placed under contract and the section from Saratoga to Gansevoort was opened on August 15, 1848. The entire line to Whitehall was placed in service by December 10th of the same year.

This ended the career of the packet boats on the canal and the several stage lines that had served for years as the connection between Lake Champlain and the Hudson. In March of 1848, the Legislature allowed the railroad to carry freight if it would pay the State the full tolls that would have resulted if shipment were made by canal. In December of 1851 this requirement was waived by the Legislature in an act applicable to all railroads in the state.

Of the two branches authorized to the state line, the only one built was a 6.63-mile line east from Whitehall to a connection with the Rutland & Whitehall Railroad. It was opened in the fall of

105

Railroads and Expresses.

Saratoga & Washington, Rensselaer & Saratoga and Saratoga & Schenectay, Rail Road Line,

From Castleton & Whitehall to Saratoga Springs, Troy, Schenecatdy & Albany.

TRAINS RUN AS FOLLOWS:—

Leave	1st Mail.	2d Freight,	3d Express.
" Castleton at	5.00 a.m.		3.30 p. m.
" W. Hall "	6.20 "	10.30 a. m.	4.10 "
Arrive Sar.Sps.	8.00 "	1.00 "	5.50 "
" Troy	9.45 "	4.00 "	7.45
" Schenectady	9.33 "		7.00 "

On Sundays leave Whitehall at 6 o'clock a. m. arrive at Saratoga Springs at 8 a.m. leave at 3½ p.m. arrive in Troy at 4.00 p.m. leave Troy at 8 a.m. arrive at Saratoga Springs at 9,45 a.m. leave at 3 p.m. arrive at Whitehall at 5 p.m.

Through fare from Burlington to New York $4,00.

Tickets to be had on board of Lake Champlain Steam Boats. Steam Boats leave Troy on arrival of evening Train.

J. VAN RENSSELAER,
Supt. Sar. & Wash. R. R.
L. R. SARGANT,
Supt. Rens. & Sar. & Sch. R. R.
d&wtf

A CARD.

THE CHAMPLAIN STEAMBOAT COMPANY hereby give *particular* notice that the price of passage through Lake Champlain, will be *One Dollar*, as soon as their New Boat is completed and ready to run.

T. D. CHAPMAN,
d&wtf   Agent for the People.

90 DOZ Feesh **Eggs** Just received by I. D. BIXBY & Co.
Burlington, May 1, 1851   d&wtf

Advertisements from the Burlington *Free Press*.

1850. Upon completion of the Rutland & Whitehall on November 1, a Vermont company running about seven miles from the state line to Castleton, the Saratoga & Washington leased it, affording access to New England. By building a short extension, involving a 682-foot tunnel through the village of Whitehall to a point on the shore of Lake Champlain, called Lake Station, direct connection could be made with the lake steamers.

Now, working in harmony with the Rensselaer & Saratoga, a through rail connection was established between the Hudson River and Lake Champlain. The line from Whitehall to Castleton connected with the Rutland & Washington, thus opening a route through Rutland to northern and western Vermont, including an all-weather route to Montreal, via the Rutland & Burlington Railroad.

Things went fairly well until late 1854, when the S&W was unable to pay the principal or interest on its second mortgage bonds, amounting to a quarter million dollars. At foreclosure proceedings, it was sold to a group including E. Thompson Gale, a director of the R&S. They, in turn, sold it to a new firm which was formed in June of 1855, the Saratoga & Whitehall Rail Road Co., headed by John M. Davison, son of the original founder of the whole business.

The road was operated by the new management until March 14, 1865, when it was leased with all its property, rights and franchises, in perpetuity, to the Rensselaer & Saratoga.

Rensselaer & Saratoga Expansion. Having traced the ups and downs of the various railroads that became part of the R&S system, it is now possible logically to trace its history from the beginning of its period of expansion, in 1851, with the lease of the Saratoga & Schenectady. Men in the R&S management had held a controlling interest in the S&S since 1835, but the most noticeable effect of this was joint use of S&S trackage between Ballston Spa and Saratoga Springs. Incorporation of the S&S into the R&S added 22 miles, to make a total of 47 route miles in the system.

In 1860 the R&S purchased the stock of the Albany & Vermont, last incarnation of the unfortunate Albany Northern, and leased the tracks from Albany to Waterford Junction, thus gaining for the first time a foothold in the capital city, stronghold of the bitter Albanian rivals of the Trojan business community. This also added another 11 miles to its tracks.

The day after this transaction was consummated, on April 13, 1860 the lease of the Saratoga & Schenectady by the R&S was made perpetual.

Members of the R&S management had been gradually acquiring interests in the Saratoga &

When the railroad was opened into Glens Falls, the R&S provided a special train with 11 cars in its consist on July 4, 1869, making 11 round trips to Fort Edward with free rides for all who cared to ride the cars. Here the decorated but unidentified 4-4-0 is pictured by photographer S. R. Stoddard at the Glens Falls depot on that festive day. (*Glens Falls Historical Society*)

Headquarters of the Rutland & Washington was at Salem, New York. The railroad shops and roundhouse, with its covered turntable, quite dominate the village, as these nostalgic views demonstrate. The roundhouse burned in 1876, five years after it was taken over by the D&H, but the shops were used as car repair and erecting facilities for that railroad for years. The view above, taken in a quiet moment, is an impressive scene of old-time railroading. *(D&H collection, above)*

Whitehall since that line was foreclosed in 1854. By December of 1864 the R&S had stock control of that line and by the following April had leased it in perpetuity, including the little Rutland & Whitehall which met it at the Vermont state line and connected with the Saratoga & Whitehall. This brought the R&S empire into contact with New England and added 53 more miles to its tracks, bringing the total to 113.

A big boost in revenue resulted in 1865 from an agreement with the Champlain Transportation Co., providing for exclusive rights through Lake Champlain from Whitehall. This was later expanded to include the Rutland & Burlington Railroad with its northern and eastern connections. The next year the line made a traffic agreement with the Lake George Transportation Co.

The last major step in the building of the Rensselaer & Saratoga empire occurred on June 15, 1865, when the Troy, Salem & Rutland, itself the result of a combination of the Rutland & Washington and the Troy & Rutland only two weeks previously, was gathered into the family. The R&S now consisted of a 175-mile railroad with control of the entire upper Hudson and Champlain valleys, forming "The North & South Through Line" between the Hudson River and Montreal.

In June, 1868, the company secured stock control of the Champlain Transportation Co., with which the traffic agreement had been concluded three years before. The following October, all these recently-acquired companies were merged into the Rensselaer & Saratoga Railroad. In December of that year, the company purchased 21 acres of land in Green Island, where extensive modern locomotive and car shops were built. They were completed in 1872.

The six-mile Glens Falls Rail Road, connecting its namesake community with Fort Edward via Hudson Falls, was incorporated in 1867. Before the line was completed, the Rensselaer & Saratoga acquired its stock and on June 24, 1869 leased the partially-built line in perpetuity. It was completed by the R&S and opened on July 4, bringing the line's total mileage to 181. Four years later extension of this line to Lake George was authorized, but nine years passed before it finally was open for the entire 16-mile distance from Fort Edward to Lake George.

Coal was first used as a locomotive fuel beginning in 1868, its economy and value having been clearly proven in extensive tests. Eight wood-burning locomotives were then converted and two new coal-burning engines ordered. The 23 wood-burners remaining in service were soon converted to coal.

To meet the mushrooming traffic needs of this growing transportation empire, 50 new freight cars were ordered and three more were built each week in the company's Salem shops.

American steel rails were first used by the R&S in 1869, when 300 tons were installed. Only two years earlier, 2100 tons of new iron rails had been placed.

Many improvements were made all over the line in 1870, and the construction of a connection with the Albany Division between Green Island and West Troy was authorized. This would afford better connections with the north and east, and provide a direct line between Albany and Troy. Now plans were made to provide hourly passenger service between the rival cities. This link would also permit the abandonment of one of the two relatively parallel lines to Waterford Junction, eliminating the five-mile line along the Hudson with its three bridges over the sprouts of the Mohawk, but this has never come about, even to the present.

Waterford Junction was where Albany and Troy sections of northbound trains came together. On the northbound runs, the joining of the sections was accomplished in a normal operation, involving a stop, but with the down trains, the procedure was quite different. Approaching the junction, from the north, the engineer would give the crew slack, so the pins could be pulled, splitting the train in three sections. The first part, the engine and baggage car, would race ahead and be switched to the Troy line. The center section, usually five or six coaches, continued at the same rate, to be switched onto the Albany branch where a moving locomotive would meet it; the coupling was made on the fly. To give the Albany cars a chance to get in the clear, the last portion of the original train was slightly braked, and then would catch up with the first part on the Troy line, where the coupling was also made on the fly, and the whole works continued on to the Trojan city.

RENSSELAER & SARATOGA RAILWAY.

(Comprising Rensselaer & Saratoga, Albany Northern, Saratoga & Schenectady, Saratoga & Whitehall, and Rutland & Washington Railways.

Geo. H. Cramer, President, Troy, N. Y. | Otis N. Crandall, Gen. Ticket Agent, Troy, N. Y.
I. V. Baker, Gen. Supt., " | H. S. Marcy, Gen. Freight Agent, "

Trains Leave. (June 28, 1871.) Trains Arrive.

Exp.	Mail.	Spec	Exp	Ac.	Exp	Mail	Mls.	STATIONS.	Mls.	Acc.	Exp	Exp	Mail	Acc.	Exp	Mail
P.M.	P.M.	P.M.	P.M.	P.M.	P.M.	A.M.		LEAVE ARRIVE		A.M.	A.M.	P.M.	P.M.	P.M.	A.M.	P.M.
		7 50	4 45	1 10		7 00		.....Albany [1].....	102	9 35		5 05	8 35	11 20		
			5 00			6 15		...Schenectady....	85	8 40			8 00			
10 00	1 30	8 25	5 00	1 35		7 15	0	.......Troy [2].....	95	9 25	10 10	4 50	8 25		5 10	4 45
			5 05	1 40		7 20	1	...Green Island....	94	9 20		4 45	8 20			
			5 18	1 52		7 34	4	.....Waterford.....	91	9 05		4 33	8 06			
			5 28	1 57		7 42	6	..Albany Junction..	89	8 57		4 28	7 59	10 42		
			5 44	2 11		7 57	12	..Mechanicsville...	83	8 42		4 15	7 42	10 27		
		9 01	9 26	6 15	2 39	8 28	25	..... Ballston [3]	70	8 12		3 45	7 12	9 57		
		9 15	9 40	6 35	2 55	8 45	32	ar } Saratoga { lv	63	7 55	9 00	3 30	6 55	9 40		
		P.M.	P.M.	6 45	3 15	8 50		lv ar		7 45	A.M.	3 15	6 45	P.M.		
				7 10	3 40	9 17	43	..Gansevoorts.....	52	7 20		2 50	6 20			
			A.M.	7 25	3 55	9 33	49	..Fort Edward [4].	46	7 05		2 35	6 05	P.M.		
			7 10	7 30	3 55	9 35		lv..Fort Edward..ar		7 00		2 30	6 00	7 25		
			7 20	7 40	4 05	9 45		..Sandy Hill..		6 50		2 20	5 50	7 15		
			7 30	7 50	4 15	9 55	54	ar..Glens Falls..lv		6 40		2 10	5 40	7 05		
			A.M.	7 34	4 04	9 43	52	..Dunham's Basin..	43			2 25		P.M.		
				7 44	4 14	9 53	57	..Smith's Basin....	38	6 46		2 16	5 46			
				7 54	4 24	10 03	61	.....Fort Ann.....	34	6 36		2 06	5 36			
				8 04	4 34	10 13	65	.....Comstock's....	30	6 26		1 56	5 26			
				8 20	4 50	10 30	71	..Junction..	24	6 10		1 40	5 10			
				8 30	P.M.	10 45	73	W'hall }L. Cham.[5]{ W'hall	26	6 00		P.M.	5 00			
				8 25		10 40	71	..Junction ..	24	6 04			5 06			
				8 48		11 03	79	....Fairhaven.....	16	5 42			4 44			
				8 54		11 09	81	.....Hydeville.....	14	5 36			4 38			
10 50	2 20						23	..Eagle Bridge [6].	62						4 20	3 50
11 05	2 35						29	..Cambridge..	56						4 03	3 35
11 17	2 47						34	.....Shushan......	51						3 45	3 22
11 34	3 04						41	.....Salem.....	44						3 27	3 04
11 57	3 27						49	.....Rupert......	36						3 03	2 41
12 14	3 44						56	.....Pawlet.....	29						2 44	2 24
12 22	3 52						59	.....Granville....	26						2 34	2 15
12 27	3 57						61	..Middle Granville..	24						2 29	2 10
12 42	4 12						67	.....Poultney.....	18						2 12	1 54
12 59	4 29			9 03		11 18	84	....Castleton	11	5 27			4 29		1 54	1 37
1 15	4 45			9 20		11 35	91	W. Rut. & Clar. Spr.[7]	4	5 11			4 05		1 36	1 20
1 20	4 50			9 25		11 40	93	...Center Rutland...	2	5 05			3 57		1 30	1 15
1 25	4 55			9 30		11 45	95	.....Rutland [8].....	0	5 00			3 50		1 25	1 10
A.M.	P.M.			P.M.		A.M.		ARRIVE LEAVE		A.M.			P.M.		A.M.	P.M.

ALBANY DIVISION.

P.M.	P.M.	P.M.	P.M.	A.M.	A.M.	L'VE ARR.	A.M.	A.M.	P.M.	P.M.	P.M.
7 50	4 45	2 00	1 10	7 50	7 00	..Albany..	8 35	9 35	3 00	5 05	8 35
	4 55	2 25	1 26	8 05		..Cemetery..	8 23		2 45	4 55	
		2 35		8 15		.West Troy.	8 15		2 35		
8 10	5 12	2 50	1 42	8 27	7 25	...Cohoes..	8 03	9 10	2 18	4 40	8 10
	5 20	3 05	1 50	8 35	7 33	.Waterford.	7 55	9 02	2 10	4 33	
8 19	5 25	3 15	1 55	8 40	7 40	.Junction.	7 50	8 57	2 05	4 28	7 59
P.M.	P.M.	P.M.	P.M.	A.M.	A.M.	ARR. L'VE	A.M.	A.M.	P.M.	P.M.	P.M.

SCHENECTADY DIVISION.

P.M.	A.M.	A.M.	Mls.	L'VE ARR.	A.M.	P.M.	P.M.
5 00	9 10	6 15	0	.Schenectady.	8 40	1 40	8 00
5 20	9 30	6 35	8	....Branch....	8 15	1 20	7 40
5 40	9 50	6 55	15	....Ballston....	8 00	1 00	7 20
6 00	10 10	7 15	22	...Saratoga...	7 45	12 40	7 00
P.M.	A.M.	A.M.		ARR. L'VE	A.M.	P.M.	P.M.

CONNECTIONS.

[1] With New York Central & Hudson River, Albany & Susquehanna, and Boston & Albany Railways.
[1] With Steamboats to New York.
[2] With railways diverging from Troy.
[3] Junction of Schenectady Division.
[4] Branch Railway to Glens Falls.
[5] Steamboats to Burlington, Plattsburgh and Montreal.
[6] With Troy & Boston Railway.
[7] With Stages for Clarendon Springs.
[8] With Rutland & Vern. Val. R'way.
[8] With N. Y. & Harlem and Harlem Extension Railways.

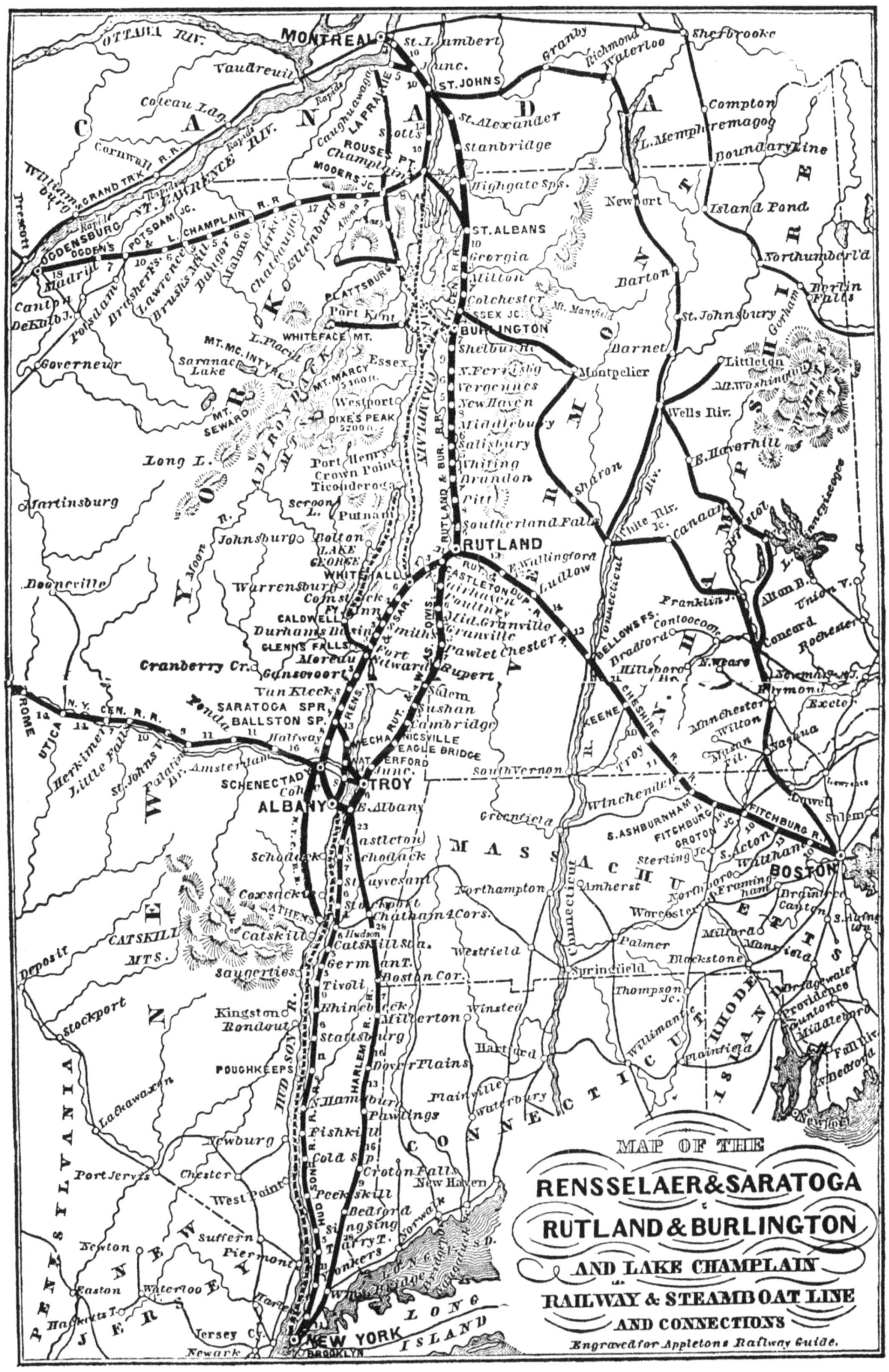

This whole operation was accomplished with link-and-pin couplings and, needless to say, required a degree of agility and concentration beyond that exhibited on railroads today—to say nothing of the rules! Although the records apparently show no mishaps, logic would seem to suggest otherwise.

In the meantime, the Delaware & Hudson Canal Co. had been expanding into the railroad business in an effort to secure a wider year-round market for its coal. Its sphere of influence had already reached Albany with the lease of the Albany & Susquehanna Rail Road in 1870, and in that same year the managers of the D&H made a proposal to the directors of the Rensselaer & Saratoga to lease their road as well.

It may have seemed surprising that the R&S should give up an apparently good thing in its booming business, but the D&H offer must have been most attractive. After all, $750,000 a year rental, with none of the responsibilities or headaches of operation was a good deal, especially in 1871, so on May 1, 1871, the lease in perpetuity was executed and the empire built by the Rensselaer & Saratoga—steamboats and all—became part of an even bigger empire: that of the fast-moving Delaware & Hudson.

The heavy gold leaf decoration on these three Schenectady-built locomotives of the R&S matched the pride of the men who ran them. Oldest of the three was the GEORGE H. CRAMER, No. 35, built in 1868, with 66-inch drivers, shown in two views by the Green Island shops. The gentleman in the cab with the gray derby hat was probably the master mechanic. She was numbered 130 by the D&H, which later sold her to the Poughkeepsie & Eastern, where she became No. 6. A year younger was the E. THOMPSON GALE, No. 36, with 60-inch drivers. The D&H rebuilt her, after leasing the R&S, and renumbered her 131. She was scrapped in 1894. A classic American-type locomotive of all time was the COMMODORE VANDERBILT, No. 37, built in 1870. Her namesake sat on the R&S Board of Directors; his name appeared in flowing script along her tender and his portrait rode proudly on her great headlamp, but this engine never ran on Vanderbilt rails. Above, she is shown on the Fulton Street crossing at the north end of the Troy Union Station. *(D&H collection, lower pictures; G. M. Best collection, upper left)*

Various officials and employees assume an assortment of poses to share the picture with the trim 4-4-0, GEORGE LEAVITT, outside the company's office in Saratoga Springs, in this post-Civil War scene. *(D&H collection)*

6. THROUGH THE MOUNTAINS—NOT AROUND THEM
The Adirondac Company

The year was 1826. A half dozen men stood at the site of the faltering North Elba Iron Works which was suffering from a poor quality ore. This was a remnant of a tiny Revolutionary forge in the mountain wilderness west of Lake Champlain. Their attention was focused, not on the shabby iron works beside them, but on a sample of ore in the hands of an Indian named Lewis Elija who had appeared from the surrounding forest. They examined the dark-colored rock carefully, their questions growing more pointed and excited as they questioned the bearer.

No more time was wasted at North Elba. The party quickly broke camp and followed the Indian in a southerly direction through the almost trackless mountain forest. For two days they traveled, and finally walked out on the shore of a small, clear lake a few miles southwest of a mountain called Tahawas, "The Cloud-Splitter"—the peak known in this more prosaic century as Mount Marcy.

Without speaking, the Indian pointed to the foot of the lake, where a little rivulet cascaded over a natural dam. It was a pretty sight, but the astonished party of prospectors had little appreciation for its natural beauty; the dam was a solid ledge of rich iron ore!

This was a find beyond their wildest dreams, and more careful prospecting of the area indicated an almost limitless deposit of the ore. Moreover, the dense woods pressing in on all sides offered a ready source of charcoal for processing on the spot, and the ore dam itself offered water power! The Indian forgotten, the five men in the prospecting party drew plans for an operating company around the campfire that night. David Henderson was the guiding genius of the group which comprised two brothers, Duncan and Malcolm McMartin, Dyer Thompson, and John MacIntyre, whose name was later to grace an Adirondack mountain range.

MacIntyre, Henderson and Duncan McMartin set off immediately for Albany where, within the next few days, they arranged with the State of New York for the purchase of a vast tract of land surrounding the ore deposit. The others remained on the site, laying preliminary plans for the development of the deposit.

Within days the Adirondac Iron Works was organized with the five prospectors as partners. It soon became evident, however, that one great problem would have to be overcome: transportation, a phase of the operation that was to prove troublesome for more than a century to come. In order to obtain additional working capital, the firm reorganized into the Adirondac Iron & Steel Co. in 1829 with Archibald MacIntyre, a brother of John, as president.

A railroad to the "outside" may have been considered at that time, but railroads were yet in their infancy and the rugged country surrounding the working on every side presented an awesome barrier to the rudimentary motive power of the period. The mere construction of a usable wagon road was a staggering undertaking to the little company, but without it the rich deposit was virtually useless.

The Adirondac Iron & Steel Co. could not afford the luxury of a big-city board of directors. The officers, between desperate trips to New York to raise more money, labored along with their men on the construction of the works and the vital road that wound eastward through the peaks to Lake Champlain, fifty miles away, and the boats that

115

David Henderson, founder of the Adirondac Iron Works. (*Adirondack Museum, two pictures*)

could transport the mine's products to the mountains of the lower Hudson valley via the Champlain Canal.

While the road was building, work progressed rapidly at the mine. In 1837 and 1838 Henderson had managed to construct a small puddling furnace and a primitive blast furnace. Hauling raw, unprocessed ore by wagon 50 mountain miles to the boats was unthinkable. Despite its isolation, the project prospered, and a village of some four hundred people grew up around the works. Adirondac was a big and important town by mountain standards of the day, but proved to be a short-lived one.

David Henderson was the man who held the enterprise together, often by sheer tenacity. His untimely and unfortunate death from an accidental gunshot wound in 1845 doomed both the little village of Adirondac and the Adirondac Iron & Steel Co.

The company was languishing when in 1852 the Sackets Harbor & Saratoga Railroad was incorporated to build a line from Saratoga Springs through the upper Hudson valley, and then westward to Lake Ontario, beyond Watertown. Its route passed through what was then largely virgin wilderness. The proprietors of the iron works at Adirondac rubbed their hands in anticipation of seeing their iron bars roll out of the little landlocked industrial empire on the rails of the SH&S to the markets of the world.

But this was not to be! The project lagged and within a decade of the death of David Henderson, the forest had begun to reclaim the tiny industrial plant, the mine, and the ghost town of Adirondac. The Champlain road, laboriously carved from the wilderness, became for the most part a barely passable trail.

The remaining officers of the Adirondac Iron & Steel Co. succeeded in interesting a group of British speculators in the possibilities of the iron mines in the Sanford Lake country. The combine, which included a famous railroad contractor of international repute, Thomas Brassey, sent a survey crew in 1857 to study the ore deposits and lay out a railroad line—called the Lake Ontario & Hudson River to move the mine's products to market. When the Civil War began to darken the horizon, the cautious British investors became a bit nervous and nothing further was done.

The idea of building a railroad to the Great Lakes was revived as the Adirondack Estate & Railroad Co. in 1860, this time with a proposed branch to Ogdensburg as well. Beyond a few survey reports, prospectuses and a mile or so of disconnected grading at the end of nowhere, the only tangible results were a torrent of fanciful oratory and indigestion from the innumerable banquets held for the purpose of discussing and promoting the project.

The idea had some merit. The proposed route was not too difficult; it would unlock tremendous reserves of resources in the mountains, and would tap the considerable traffic of the Lakes at one of the finest natural harbors on our northern water border. At Carthage it would touch the rich Black River valley. In some ways, the proposition could have been considered more sound than similar proposals in the growing West at the time.

Giants of Finance. The iron of the Sanford Lake country was not entirely forgotten, however.

Giants of finance were growing to full stature and in this era before the Civil War they had not yet turned their eyes exclusively to the West. These were the men to take the center of the stage in the next episode of the drama of the Adirondacks. These were the men toward whom the remaining owners of the defunct Adirondac Iron & Steel Co. turned—and to whom they promptly lost control of the lagging enterprise.

Dr. Thomas C. Durant was born in Lee, Massachusetts, in the Berkshires, and graduated from the Albany Medical College, about 35 miles from his native town. From his own personal contacts with the Adirondack region he had more than a casual knowledge of it, but he went to New York and turned from medicine to business. In 1862, at the age of 42, he had already attained considerable stature in New York financial circles and was gaining wide experience in the lucrative field of railroad finance. He had been associated in the construction of the Peoria & Bureau Valley, the Rock Island and other roads. This year, while the Civil War was raging, he was elected vice-president of the newly-chartered Union Pacific, with responsibility for management and finance. It was at about this time that he awoke to the possibilities and resources of the Adirondacks.

Certain extremely liberal provisions for the purchase of vast tracts of state-owned lands had been obtained by the organizers of the earlier companies. Durant and his associates were quick to realize the possibilities of an economic empire and encountered no difficulty at all in obtaining transfer of these concessions from the previous corporation when the Adirondac Co. was finally chartered on October 24, 1863. It was an opportune time, with the pressures of war forcing greater and greater demands on the natural resources of both the North and the South.

The company was incorporated primarily as a land and development organization, the charter authorizing it to acquire over a million acres of Adirondack real estate. The company promptly purchased over 250,000 acres, which had been acquired by the defunct Sackets Harbor & Saratoga, at an average price of six cents an acre. Other lands were grabbed, often with more speed than judgment, until the company held a total of more than 700,000 acres, including some ore-laden tracts.

Dr. Thomas C. Durant, first president of the Adirondack Co. and one of the promoters of the Union Pacific.

Railroading was not the primary purpose of the Adirondac Co. It was merely an instrument to strip the Adirondack Mountains of their latent riches, yet ironically, the railroad was the only part of the whole plan ever to take shape and substance.

The promise was sufficiently enticing to attract, with Dr. Durant's persuasive arguments, an imposing array of investors. Daniel Drew, of Erie fame, C. S. Bushnell, who was affiliated with Durant in the Union Pacific venture, Chauncey Vibbard and others appeared as directors, along with some lesser fry, including Orange Ferris and Albert N. Cheney, local lumber barons from Glens Falls. These two already controlled timber tracts along the upper Hudson and conducted yearly drives down the river to their mills, and had already established respectable fortunes from the Adirondacks.

These men were opportunists and expansionists. Some have called them men of vision and enterprise, others have cursed them as robber barons.

More likely, these men and their methods were products of their times. It was an age of rapid growth and development, a time of great business risk and for the fortunate, a time of great reward. Codes of business ethics, like the politics of the day, were somewhat nebulous and always flexible. In their eyes, the proposed exploitation of the Adirondacks was legal, logical and an eminently respectable undertaking. Whatever opposition may have developed was submerged in the urgencies of the war and its insatiable appetite for the materials the mountains could yield. The promoters of the Adirondac Company could conveniently wrap their motives in the flag of the Union.

The charter authorization to "convert and prepare for market the iron ores and minerals upon its lands and to transport, sell and dispose of same," coupled with the privilege of purchasing a million acres of state lands at token prices gave the company a practically unlimited license to do as it pleased in a territory as large as some European kingdoms. It is perhaps due to the fact that the charter provided for company control of nearly a fifth of the Adirondack area that the firm finally added the "k" to its corporate title, as more fitting to its ambitions.

Operations began in the spring of 1865, with another of Durant's Union Pacific associates, George T. M. Davis of New York, in the president's chair. The grade pushed rapidly north out of Saratoga, with over 200 men and 54 teams slicing through the rolling, sandy terrain. Their number swelled as woodsmen and farmers, their plowing and seeding out of the way, joined them. Track gangs followed close behind the graders, spiking 56-pound iron on the native hemlock ties. A neat general office building and a two-stall engine house went up in Saratoga Springs. Here no station was needed as the company had arranged for the joint use of the Rensselaer & Saratoga depot.

The company's franchise contained only one major stipulation—that the road be built a distance of 60 miles from Saratoga Springs into the upper Hudson valley, and this provision Durant intended to meet without delay.

The first motive power was an ancient diamond-stacked American type locomotive, leased from the Rensselaer & Saratoga, and a scant half dozen battered old flatcars—hardly an imposing roster but sufficient to push the line 25 miles to Wolf Creek, where masons were putting the finishing touches on the abutments for the Howe truss bridge that was to span the stream.

Engine No. 1 arrived at Saratoga from the Schenectady works, and was ceremoniously named the MAJOR GENERAL HANCOCK, in honor of the hero of the great battle of Gettysburg which in 1864 was still fresh in the minds of everyone. The balloon-stacked monster was a thing of beauty, with its handsome brass-filigreed headlight bracket and gleaming steam dome atop the boiler above the brilliant red drivers. It was a fitting locomotive to highball the three bright yellow coaches that rolled in over the Fitchburg and the R&S from the Bradley works in Worcester. The first train, up through Greenfield, South Corinth, Jessup's Landing and Hadley on its first run December 1, 1865, was loaded to capacity.

Crisis, however, preceded the first train. Now that the little railroad was at last in a position to earn revenue, the company's credit ran out its slack with a bang. The masons at Wolf Creek put down their trowels, the farmers stabled their teams when the winter's work that was promised had not materialized. Paydays had been postponed through the autumn; now they stopped entirely.

Financial Troubles. The company had vast resources on paper, but no cash. Dr. Durant and his associates had always treated the Adirondack line as a side bet, while concentrating on the bigger and richer game west of the Mississippi, where they were profiting hugely at the time from a construction company named Crédit Mobilier, organized by Durant along with Oakes Ames and a few other Union Pacific insiders. As directors of the railroad, they made construction contracts with themselves, as Crédit Mobilier, and garnered profits estimated as high as $23,000,000, at the expense of run-of-the-mill UP stockholders. Members of Congress were implicated by the time the scandal came to light in 1872, after some five years of manipulations. In the Adirondacks there was no cash subsidy from a hard-pressed government in the aftermath of disastrous war, no handsome bonus for every mile of track laid. The resources of the combine naturally went into the bigger and more rewarding game, while the Adirondack's bills went unpaid.

The Adirondack Company's original authorized capitalization had been set at $5,000,000 and, in-

The MAJOR GENERAL HANCOCK NO. 1, is pictured with a northbound train, just north of the company's office at Saratoga Springs in 1877, the first full year of the Adirondack Railway's operations. There was plenty of time to pose for pictures as the line was completed only part of the way, and in the yellow coaches were few patrons to become impatient. (*G. M. Best collection*)

cluding the land holdings of the defunct Sackets Harbor & Saratoga Railroad Co., $4,000,000 had been paid in. Unfortunately over half of this capital had been expended in the rapid acquisition of forest and mineral lands, and not always judiciously expended. Much of the land was far removed from the proposed line of the railroad and much was of doubtful value for purposes of exploitation. In any case, very little of the property was directly associated with the proposed 60 miles of track the company was, by charter, required to build, and there was little prospect of immediate revenue from it.

Construction costs rocketed far above the preliminary estimates, although there is no evidence that Durant and his friends applied the same ethics to the Adirondack that characterized their manipulations with Crédit Mobilier and the Union Pacific. Construction of the first 25 miles of track was easy, but debts mounted with every mile, and payments became slower with each passing month. The one item that was apparently paid promptly, according to the road's 1866 report to the New York State Engineer, was a matter of $125,000 for "agencies and commissions."

At the end of 1865, the company's debts totaled $1,333,000 at seven percent interest, and the treasury was empty. The men who met in the company's offices at 20 Nassau Street in New York had cautiously put few of their own blue chips into the game at the beginning and now they were reluctant to advance more. The inevitable happened.

In the words of H. C. Crane, the hapless treasurer of the Adirondack Co. "the railroad of the said company was entered upon, seized and taken on the first day of November, 1865, by James C. Kennedy and Charles Tuttle, trustees, under and by virtue of a mortgage or trust deed made by the said company to them, as trustees for the holders

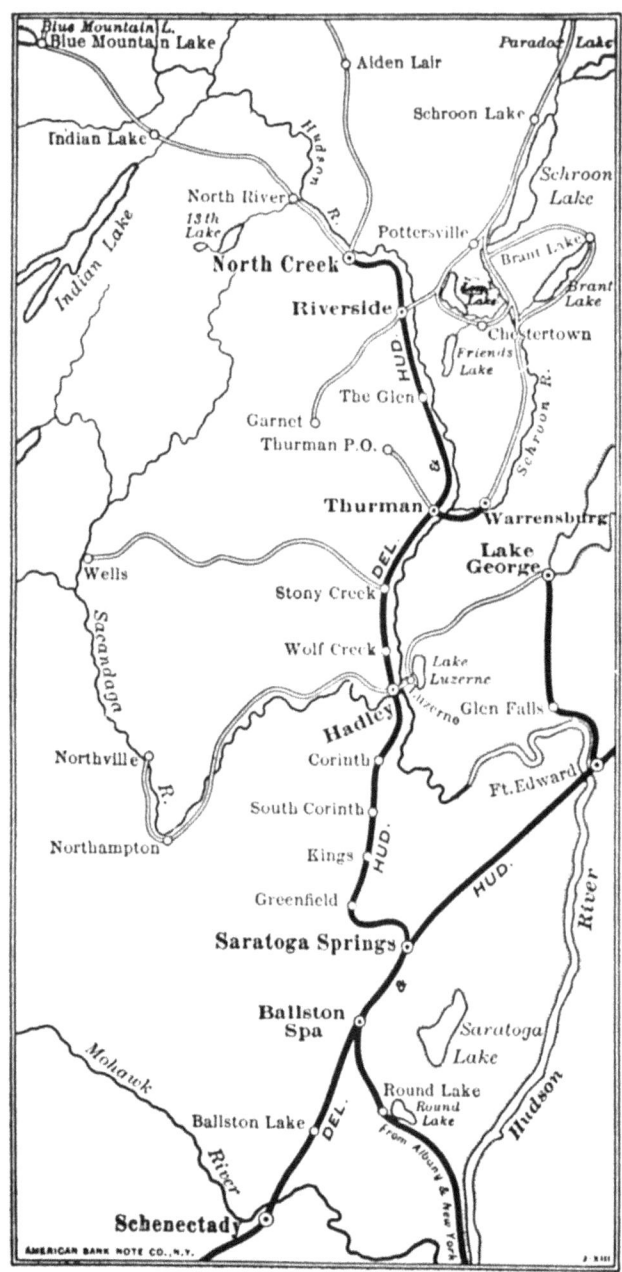

of the mortgage bonds, and thence hitherto the said railroad has been held and used by the said trustees and that the said company has not run or operated the railroad at any time since September 30, 1865, and the said company has not had and now has not any superintendent of operations." In short, it was bankrupt!

Even the start of scheduled operations on December 1 of that year produced little revenue. Beyond the junction at Saratoga Springs, the only town of any size was Corinth, while the other four stations on the portion of the line completed could hardly qualify as more than crossroads hamlets. After the first passenger train made its run, passenger service settled down to the operation of two mixed trains each way daily, the brilliant coaches trailing ignominiously at the tail of all-too-short freight manifests. In the first year of operation the operating department returned only $10,973.67.

Low as the revenues were, operating costs were even lower. This may have been of some small solace to the trustees. Taxes for the year amounted to only $101.79.

The road faltered through the winter of 1865-1866, the formidable combination of a bitter Adirondack winter and an uncertain future precluding any further work on extension of the line beyond Wolf Creek. Trackage beyond Hadley rusted beneath the drifting snows, while in New York City the trustees and the board of directors, now headed by doughty old Daniel Drew, struggled with the problems of reorganization. A half-million dollars of the company's stock was placed in the hands of the trustees to satisfy the company's most pressing debts. New faces appeared on the board of directors, along with new money to bolster its sagging financial structure.

A significant step forward was taken in the appointment of C. W. Ballard, a thoroughly experienced railroad operating man, as superintendent of the road. Also, the directors somehow found another $400,000 in credit and late in the spring of 1866 track gangs again began spiking down iron along the west bank of the Hudson, pushing the right-of-way toward the potential traffic-producing towns of Warrensburg and North Creek.

The roster had grown to three locomotives which, with "snow-plows and other appurtenances" were reported as costing $46,000. Another $17,000 was invested in the fleet of three passenger and three mail, express and baggage cars, and the original roster of six flats had grown to include 56 freight cars of all types.

Earnings improved steadily. Paper and lumber mills at Corinth originated growing streams of revenue traffic and hordes of tanbark gatherers ripped the bark from every hemlock in the territory along the line for use in leather tanning, almost decimating the species from local forests, but contributing substantially to the flow of outbound traffic.

In spite of the increased earnings, the line still labored under the handicap of financial trouble

North Creek was a wilderness outpost consisting of a few austere buildings and a hotel, when this view was taken soon after the Adirondack's line reached the mountain hamlet. In the distance, up by the station, No. 1 was switching boxcars while S. R. Stoddard was taking this picture. *(D&H collection)*

and work on extension of the trackage progressed slowly and sporadically. Money was tight after the war, and treasurer Crane, deeply involved with his contemporaries in the affairs of the Union Pacific, gave scant attention to the needs of the combine's eastern stepchild. An occasional crumb — a bridge here, a mile or so of track there — was thrown to the Adirondack.

With the return of postwar prosperity, Cyrus H. McCormick, the reaper king of the Midwest, appeared on the scene with his millions and concurrently with his appearance on the board of directors the line spurted forward. Early in 1871 the first train rolled into the mountain hamlet of North Creek amid much jubilation.

North Creek, the last town of any consequence in the upper Hudson valley, was still somewhat short of the sixty miles mandated in the company's charter and the track gangs pushed on through the village, laying iron along the very edge of the river up the narrow valley for another three miles. The line ended, literally, nowhere. Graders slashed their way to the middle of a pine grove on a narrow shelf between the slopes of Gore mountain and the rushing river and laid down their shovels. Trackmen spiked worn-out iron rail down on discarded ties and then drew their pay to head south out of this beautiful but rugged country.

Once a year a locomotive and a single coach chugged cautiously over the shaky track beyond North Creek, set the birds twittering in the pines with its whistle blast, and reversed to creep back to the yellow station. After a few years even this "service" was discontinued and the useless track ripped up after a long-hoped-for washout did not materialize.

The spring of 1871 also brought with it the road's first major wreck. The April log drive down from the headwaters to the mills along the lower stretches of the Adirondack region was always a big event, and its conclusion invariably marked the occasion for unrestrained celebration for those social circles which had spent the winter in the isolated camps of the north woods. The soirée usually lasted as long as the winter's wages, and in the case of one group of celebrants in Corinth that April, the party came to a conclusion on a cold and rainy afternoon.

It had been raining steadily for several days, rendering the roads back upriver a totally uninviting prospect, even for men accustomed to rough going in bad weather, especially since most of the

Engine No. 2, piloted by carousing lumberjacks, fortunately lurched to the left and into the soft mud rather than the boiling river when the unscheduled special hit a soft spot in the soggy roadbed. *(Don Wallworth)*

party was by now boasting colossal hangovers in various degrees of intensity. The noon train for North Creek had pulled out before the last of the spirits ran out, and these rugged individualists, now that the party was over, decided that it was time to head back to the upper country.

The same rains that made the trail a quagmire had also sent the Hudson roaring high and fast, the white water boiling along the riverside grade of the railroad as it paralleled the stream toward North Creek. A construction train, headed by Engine No. 2, had been working along the line, making emergency repairs to the soft roadbed and dropping additional riprap along the threatened banks for protection from the raging waters. As dusk fell, the little train dropped back into Corinth to go into the hole for the southbound mixed drag, which whistled out at 4:55. The crew of the repair train, leaving a brakeman in charge, had gone down into the village for a little warmth and a bite of supper before heading on up the line again.

The sight of the train idling on the siding, engine headed north, was an extremely inviting one to the inebriated lumberjacks. They waited in the rain for a time on the platform of the now-closed station. It was getting colder, and the wind shifted to whistle down the valley, driving the rain which was now changing to sleet seemingly into the very marrow of their bones. Over a dozen were in the group now, and they milled around uncomfortably. It seemed to them that the Adirondack was, indeed, rendering very poor service to such a gathering of potential passengers, with the crew so tardy in getting back to the waiting train, whose yellow headlight now gleamed unmoving in the darkness.

Almost as one man the small mob moved down the track and into the comparative shelter and warmth of the cab. Two of the husky woodsmen pitched the unfortunate brakeman, after a short but decisive struggle, out onto the right of way. Picking himself up out of the mire, he promptly set off at speed in search of the remainder of the crew and the town marshal.

Someone pulled the pin connecting the train; willing but unsteady hands, pitched wood in the general direction of the firebox, and one lumberjack, apparently aware of some of the rudiments of locomotive operation, cracked the throttle. Unfortunately, the waiting brakeman had lined the switch out onto the main. If he had not, probably the worst that could have occurred would be that No. 2 would derail and come to a stop on the ties. As it was, the little American locomotive slid her drivers on the slick rails, recovered and roared out of town to a madly tooting whistle and a clanging bell, with a dozen lusty voices roaring a ribald ditty to add to the jubilance of the occasion.

Slow orders might be the rule for regularly scheduled trains on the Adirondack that night, but this was one special over which the line's brass had no control. With sparks shooting from the big stack into the black night and yellow headlight etching the silent spruces crowding the right of way, No. 2 rocked with throttle wide open up the quiet valley.

Up through Jessup's Landing, on through Hadley, roaring over the bridge at Stony Creek, past lonely Thurman station and over the switch points of the Warrensburg branch, the old locomotive miraculously held the rails. People at The Glen rushed to their windows as the unscheduled special blasted over the crossing to disappear along the roaring river. Someone in the cab retained enough sober sense to ease her off as she entered a stretch of crooked track above The Glen, an act that probably saved the lives of all the non-paying passengers aboard.

No. 2 apparently entered the dangerous stretch of track at relatively slow speed, rocking precariously enough where the fill had settled along the river boiling a scant five feet below the track. Every lurch became more pronounced, and a suddenly stone-sober crew of impromptu railroaders joined the birds. With a final lurch, the locomotive eased over on her left side, fortunately away from the surging river, and plowed into the sodden mountainside. The lumberjacks trudged up the track to North Creek and melted into the woods where the matter became a subject of only the most guarded conversation for some time to come. The escapade was largely responsible for a reference in the road's report for the year. Item: Repairs to locomotives, $3,477.21.

Now that the line had reached North Creek, a crude village that provided the last oasis of any sort of civilization in the north country, business activity on the railroad picked up considerably. Durant had never lost sight of the possible extension of the line through the rugged terrain of the upper Hudson valley to the iron mines and beyond to the shores of Lake Ontario. It now seemed to be within reach again and he entered into negotiations with the MacIntyre mine interests to purchase the entire property, but again fate intervened. The money panic of 1873 took a staggering blow at Durant's fortune and with it went the hopes of building the railroad beyond North Creek. Within a few months the Adirondack Co. was insolvent once again.

ADIRONDACK CO'S RAILROAD.
Saratoga County AGRICULTURAL FAIR
AT SARATOGA SPRINGS,
September 3d, 4th, 5th, 6th & 7th, 1872.
Reduction in Fare!

Tickets will be sold for FARE ONE WAY, good for Return Passage above dates, if stamped on Grounds of SARATOGA AGRICULTURAL SOCIETY.

Full Fare will be charged all who do not procure tickets, except from Stations where there are no Ticket Offices.

C. E. DURKEE, Gen. Ticket Agent. C. H. BALLARD, Superintendent.

Saratoga Springs, Sept. 3d, 1872.

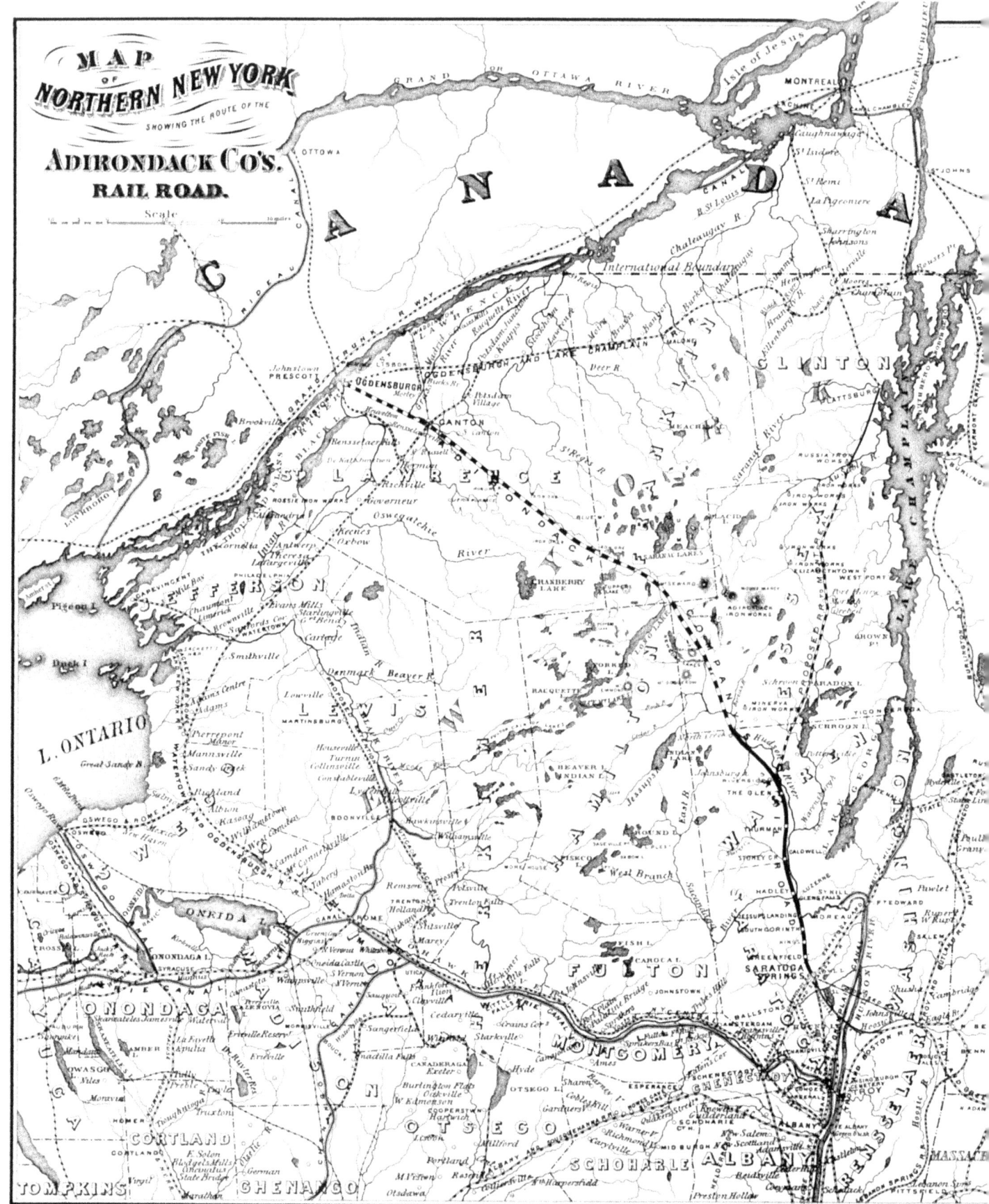

The young lady at the left is apparently composing a picture of the team while well-dressed travelers on the Concord coach and steamer watch both photographers in action. The stage linked the Schroon Lake landing at Pottersville with the Adirondack station at Riverside. Stage lines for Blue Mountain Lake and other points in the central Adirondack region met the train at North Creek. The Adirondack Co.'s railroad map of 1872 (at left) shows one of the proposed routes beyond North Creek and the connection from Saratoga Springs to the Boston lines, the overall plan contemplated by the financial boys of the Hub. *(Charles Clingman collection, above)*

As in past tradition, it struggled on and Dr. Durant was appointed receiver on February 13, 1875. In the meantime the Doctor, a never-give-up promoter, looked to other areas to justify the existence of his dead-end line, and discovered the American tourist.

As early as 1837, ill-fated David Henderson had foreseen that "were a railroad to be built," the scenery and restful life of the mountains had the makings of a fashionable summer resort. The lovely cool climate of the great north woods was attractive in the summer and the hunting and fishing were unequaled. As court-appointed guardian of the company the Doctor turned all his efforts toward promoting the summer vacation trade, particularly out of New York City. He improved the stage road up to Blue Mountain Lake and bought into the company which operated the small steamers on it and nearby Raquette Lake.

Wagner Palace Cars were run directly from New York over the Hudson River Railroad and the D&H to Saratoga, then on the Adirondack to North Creek, arriving there early in the morning. Most of the remainder of the day was spent on the stagecoach, jolting over the steep, rough roads to the many resort hotels nestled in the mountains. At the round trip excursion fare of $18.25, thousands of city dwellers made the combined rail-stage-steamboat trip to Raquette Lake and its surroundings each summer. In addition to the hotels, hundreds of summer cottages and children's camps in the mountains developed a passenger trade for the line that lasted 85 seasons. The winters were not lean either; lumber, paper, tanned hides and tanbark, mineral products, local passengers and coal kept the trains rolling.

The trip itself was a pleasure to experience. From the interchange with the D&H at Saratoga

125

A southbound D&H train at Riverside in the early 1880s is headed by No. 138, originally the MONTREAL of the R&S. Freight cars are tied to her last coach. The MAJOR GENERAL HANCOCK, under a lonesome telegraph line by a river spotted with stray logs from the spring drive inspired photographer Stoddard to take this wistful scene of the upper Hudson near The Glen. (*Al Gayer collection, above; De Sormo collection, below*)

126

Engine No. 5 was named in honor of the doctor-financier who put the Adirondack Railway on the map. She was built by Schenectady in 1884 and held down the varnish runs of the last years of the Adirondack's independent operation, and for a number more years after the D&H took over. *(D&H collection)*

Springs an eight-wheeler, more than likely the T. C. DURANT, rolled the train along Walworth Street to the edge of town, where it started the long, winding pull up the grade to the height of land south of Jessup's Landing (now Corinth). Beyond, the enchanting valley of the Upper Hudson opened up as the little train hugged the west bank of the river for the remainder of the trip. Sawmills, paper mills and tanneries were operating full blast along the river and its tributaries. An excellent hotel was located at The Glen, while the next station, Riverside, was the jumping-off place for all the summer delights of Schroon Lake. A long bend to the west brought the traveler rolling into the terminus at North Creek, where a captivating dinner at Eldridge's North River Hotel was waiting.

Passenger traffic was heavy during the summer, with as many as four full road trips on the timecard. Along with the many special excursion movements there frequently would be the gilded private car of some bigwig bringing up the rear of trains to join others parked on the siding next to the station at North Creek.

For several years after 1874, rumors appeared that Boston investors would refinance the company and complete the route to Ogdensburg or Sackets Harbor. The Great Lakes always had a special magnetism for the boys from the Hub and the vision of "a grand independent line" to bring Canadian and Great Lakes traffic pouring into Boston with the tunnel for a funnel would suit

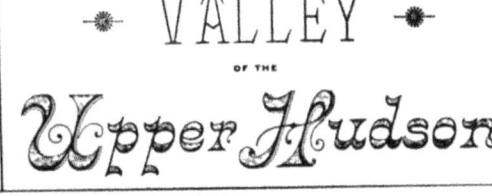

The Adirondack Railway Co.

SEASON 1887.

FROM SARATOGA SPRINGS

To Luzerne, Hadley, Thurman, The Glen, Riverside, North Creek, and Blue Mountain Lake,

— FORMING THE —

Most Direct Railroad Route TO THE

VALLEY OF THE Upper Hudson

AND THE ADIRONDACK WILDERNESS.

A New and Completely Equipped Line of Stages between NORTH CREEK and BLUE MOUNTAIN LAKE. Line of Steamboats on BLUE MOUNTAIN, EAGLE and UTOWANA LAKES; also on RAQUETTE LAKE.

THROUGH TICKETS SOLD FROM NEW YORK, PHILADELPHIA & BOSTON, and BAGGAGE CHECKED THROUGH.

A ROUTE OF PICTURESQUE AND DELIGHTFUL SCENERY.

At *RIVERSIDE STATION* stages connect, running to SCHROON LAKE, CHESTER, POTTERSVILLE and the NORTH WOODS.

The Blue Mountain Lake Stage and Transportation Company, carrying United States Mails between North Creek and Blue Mountain Lake, run first-class four and six-horse Concord Coaches, and supply comfortable covered spring buckboards to those who wish, at a slight additional charge over stage fare. The road between North Creek and Blue Mountain Lake has been put in first-class order at a large expenditure of money.

Express Trains leave Saratoga Springs in the morning and afternoon, making close connections with Night Boats from New York, and also the night train and morning trains from New York.

Enclose 4 cent stamp to C. E. DURKEE, Supt. Saratoga Springs, N.Y., for copy of "Birch Bark from the Adirondacks," which gives much valuable information relating to Adirondack Region—List of Hotels, Boarding Houses, &c., &c.

W. W. DURANT,　　　　　　　　　　C. E. DURKEE,
GEN'L MANAGER.　　　　　　　　　　SUPERINTENDENT.

Train crew, station agents and telegraph runner assume self-conscious postures at Stony Creek station in August of 1900. Although the D&H had not entirely taken over the Adirondack, its influence had been felt since the 1889 purchase, as illustrated by the gleaming new Mogul No.

75. The old covered bridge over the Sacandaga River near Hadley had seen better days, but the high Howe truss span dwarfs the little engine upon it, the MAJOR GENERAL HANCOCK which seems to serve as a signature for photographer Stoddard's pictures. *(D&H collection, both)*

them to a tee. This would involve a hookup between the Boston, Hoosac Tunnel & Western Railroad, which had already penetrated the state as far as Saratoga Springs, and the now infamous 120 miles of hardrock construction beyond North Creek. After a few weeks of discussion in the Boson tea houses, the *Railroad Gazette*, and the New York papers, the proposal would fade away as perennially as the apple blossoms of the upper Hudson valley, only to reappear the next season.

By July 1, 1881, the unpaid interest charges and bonds had mounted to a staggering $9,763,666, more than proof that no one from Boston, or anywhere else, had come to the rescue. As Dr. Durant was the principal bondholder, he himself had become insolvent. In foreclosure proceedings at Saratoga Springs on September 29, 1881, the road was sold for $350,000 to William West Durant, the Doctor's son, and an associate. It could be assumed that the Doctor himself had, in the best traditions of his past genius, called the shots in the deal.

The reorganized property, now the Adirondack Railway Co., with W. W. Durant as president, had acquired its predecessors' land holdings in Essex, Franklin, St. Lawrence and Hamilton Counties, then variously reported at between 500,000 and 700,000 acres.

During the remaining four years of his life, after the sale of the line to his son, Dr. Durant guided the young man in the rather routine operation of the line. This must have been somewhat of a letdown for the old man who had envisioned an empire in the mountains with this railroad, now barely able to keep its financial head above water, as the gateway to it all.

Probably the most spirited run ever made on the Adirondack took place October 5, 1885. It was on the rather sad occasion of the Doctor's approaching demise. A special train brought his son, then owner of the road officially, to the dying financier's bedside in North Creek. William Durant told engineer Frank Myers that he must be in North Creek, 57 miles up the winding line, by 9 p.m. It was 8:03 when the engine backed away from the station at Saratoga and the Doctor's son, followed by a pale, shaking crew, stepped off the car in front of the gate of the big mansion in North Creek, at exactly 8:57. The 54-minute trip, at an average of 63.52 mph, was the fastest ever recorded on the length of the Adirondack Railroad. Needless to say after looking at the map, it has never been equaled.

The Delaware & Hudson Canal Co., wary of interlopers grabbing the little line, sent out feelers to William West Durant, the Doctor's son and heir. The younger Durant had seen enough tries at a line across the forbidding mountain wilderness and he willingly sold his $6,000,000 road to the D&H on June 11, 1889 for somewhat less than $690,000. The purchase did not include the wild lands and operation was retained by home management for a while. The equipment and engines retained their Adirondack lettering until complete merger of the company with the D&H in 1902.

And so, the little company disappeared into the great D&H system without ever achieving its intended purpose—the hauling of iron ore out of the vast mountain deposits. The Adirondack's finest hour, however, had yet to come!

129

Seneca Ray Stoddard, born in 1844 at Wilton, between Saratoga Springs and Glens Falls, was a sensitive pioneer of American photography who left a priceless heritage of scenes of the Adirondacks. His more famous contemporaries, Mathew Brady, renowned lensman of the Civil War, and William Henry Jackson, photographer of the great American West, were also from the Adirondack region, Brady from near Glens Falls, Jackson from Keesville, south of Plattsburgh. Stoddard took his equipment through the woods and up the mountains, and had a special fondness for the railroads. On these pages the MAJOR GENERAL HANCOCK, which hauled his rolling "photo studio" to photogenic spots on the Adirondack, is featured on the Sacandaga bridge at Hadley, below, on the Howe truss over Stony Creek, opposite, and below that at Hadley station. The ghostly images at the right are of small boys who walked into the picture while the wet plate was being exposed. (D&H collection, opposite; De Sormo collection, this page)

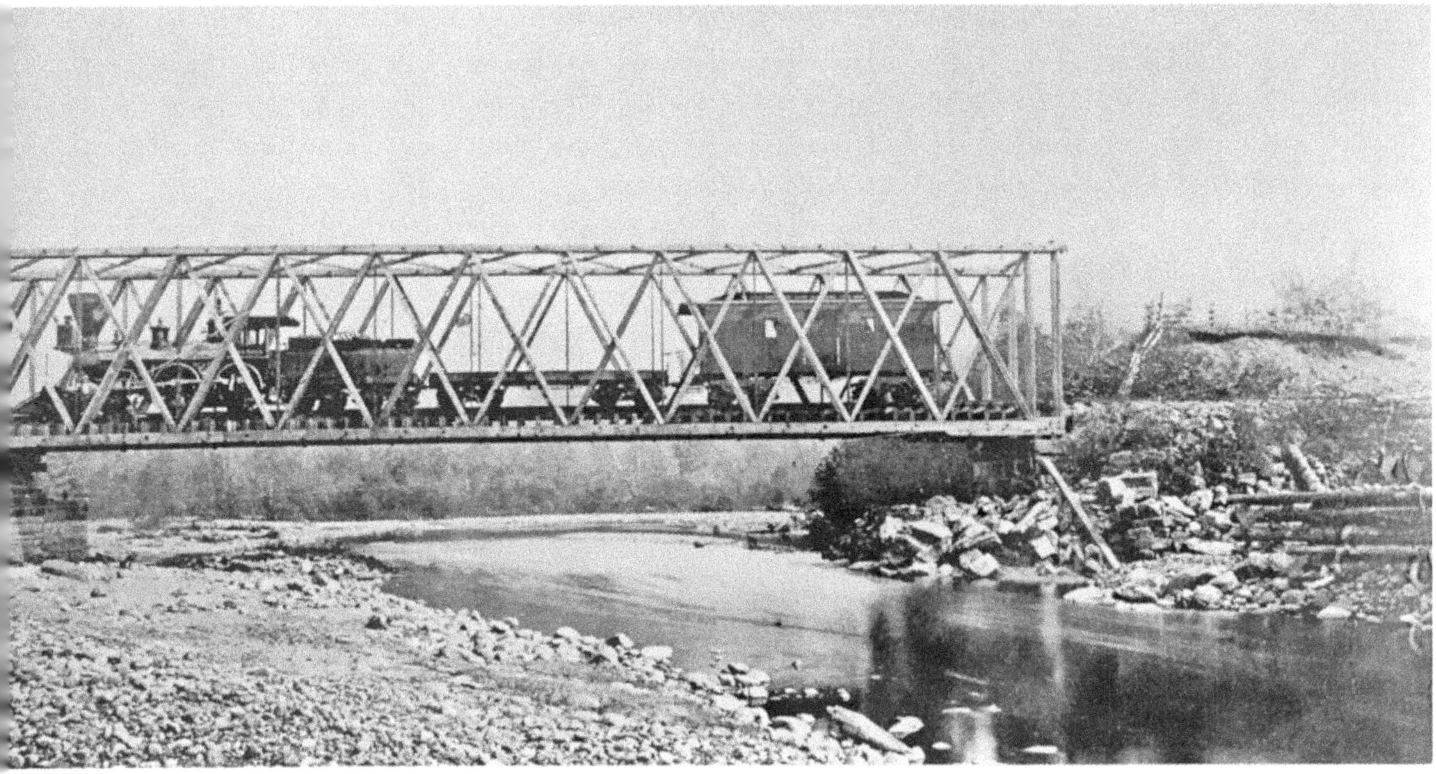

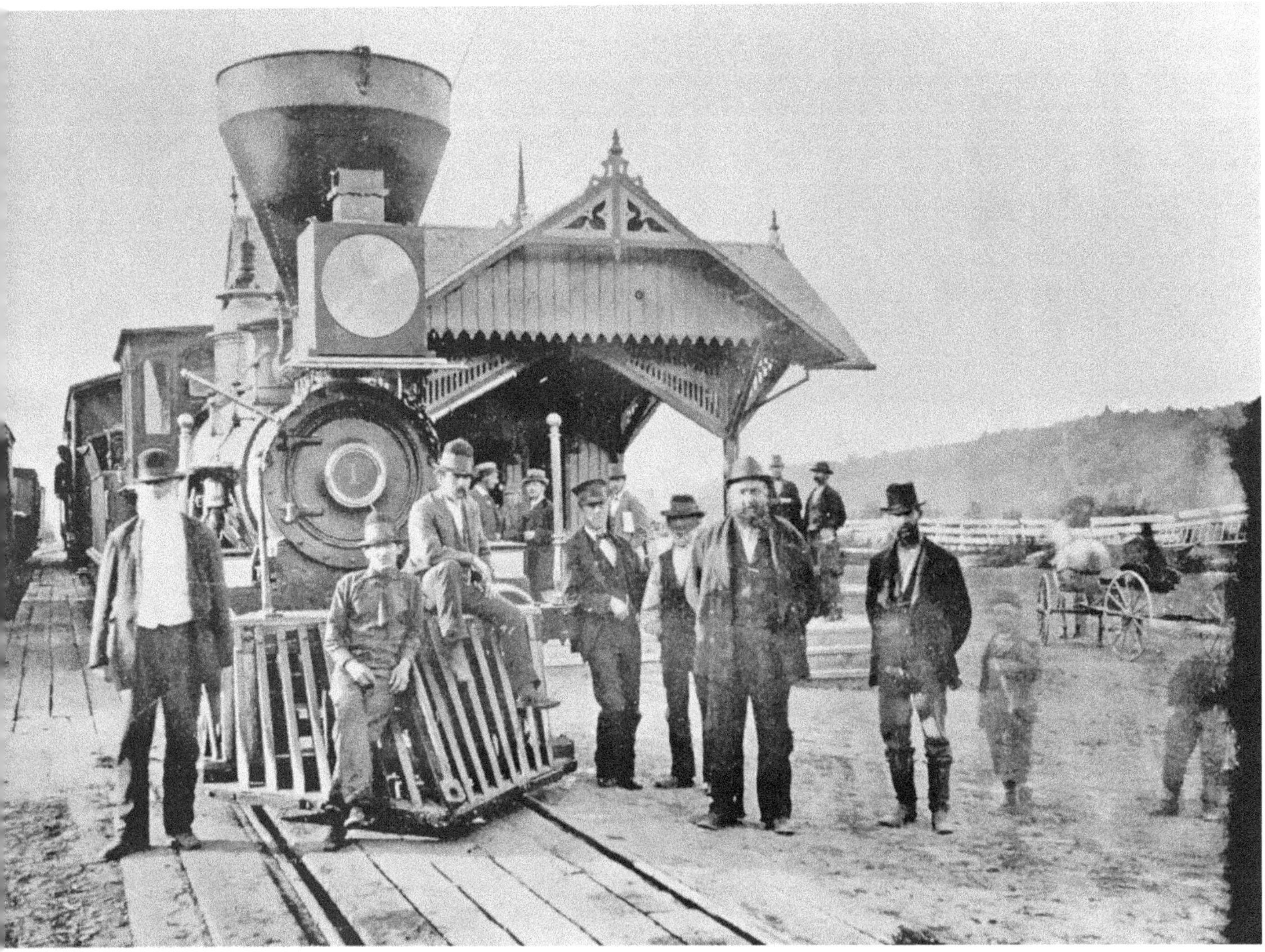

Three of the four Stoddard photographs on these pages show the familiar engine No. 1. It is depicted above at The Glen, below with a southbound passenger train at Thurman and at the lower right beside the upper Hudson River between The Glen and Riverside. In the picture above that, for a change, he features a Concord coach ready to leave North Creek station to take its capacity load of well dressed passengers up the rough road to Blue Mountain Lake. *(D&H collection, this page; Adirondack Museum, upper right)*

Cut through sparkling quartz, the south portal to Red Rocks tunnel, above Willsboro Bay, forms a dramatic frame for 4-4-0 No. 130 which, before the lease by the D&H had been No. 35 on the R&S, the GEORGE H. CRAMER. On the occasion of this picture she was hauling Stoddard's photographic special. (*De Sormo collection*)

7. NORTH TO CANADA
The New York & Canada

Bob Ferguson, the rural mail carrier was delayed, slogging through the spring mud on his trip up from Port Henry with the evening mail. His arrival at Zebadiah Sartwell's grist mill, also the Whallonsburgh post office, was the daily signal for the townspeople to gather and pick up their mail. It was Thursday and the best day of the week for socializing and gossiping around the office because the Elizabethtown *Post*, the Essex County weekly, was due.

The headlines this particular day arrived with the impact of a bolt out of the blue in the sleepy little farm community. Essex County was to have a railroad!

A railroad through the quiet, peaceful Boquet Valley was something unheard of, and would be opposed by some to the bitter and gruesome end. Everyone was well satisfied with the steamboats that plied up and down Lake Champlain. They could haul their produce, or themselves, down to the dock at Essex and get anywhere they wanted to go, which for most wasn't very far afield. The idea of a steam locomotive screaming like a banshee through their pastures, scattering the stock and causing pandemonium in the chicken house, was something they could well do without.

Zebadiah's role as postmaster and miller cast him as one of the community leaders, and the lot seemed to fall to him to arrange a meeting that everyone now felt was necessary to protest this ominous threat to the very life and solidarity of the valley. Zeb said "I saw some fellers surveyin' down on the flats a few days ago but they said somethin' 'bout a telegraph line bein' put through. Humbug! Telegraph line indeed! There's lots of things built on paper that never gits a foothold on the ground."

So, a meeting was called and on the following Monday night the little brick schoolhouse on the brow of the hill overlooking the village of Whallonsburgh was filled with a motley gathering. Zebadiah Sartwell was unanimously appointed chairman and, one by one, everyone who cared to took his cracks at the proposed project.

Mike Doolin, an irate little Irishman, was the first to speak. He raved on about the horrors of the railroad, ending with the statement ". . . and that I'll shpill me lasht drop of me blood to protect me rights"—ending this sentence, like all the others, with a hearty *Begorra!*

Others dwelt on the death and destruction brought to children and livestock by the terrible and terrifying iron horse. Some, probably a more intelligent and realistic lot, including Zeb, thought there might be some good that might come with a railroad, pointing out how other similar areas had achieved considerable prosperity soon after the arrival of the first train.

The arguments raged on, but as midnight neared it was clear to all that nothing other than more talk would be forthcoming. Zeb suggested that a delegation be formed to go across the lake to Vermont and query the farmers there, whose property the Rutland Railroad was already running through, as to how it had affected them.

When a call for volunteers went out, Mike Doolin was the first to jump up—"Begorra!!" Poor Mike's heart was broken when Zeb assured him that the committee was only going over to talk, not to tear up the railroad.

*   *   *   *

It was quite clear to President Dickson that the D&H would be running solid trainloads of coal to Canada to feed the hungry furnaces of our north-

The track gang of the Crown Point Iron Co.'s three-foot gauge railroad demonstrates the tools of its trade, including a sort of notched track gauge and the push car with brake lever. The engine is an 1883 Dickson-built Mogul, No. 5, the CROWN POINT. The station is Hammondville, where in 1821 Timothy Hunter, seeking bees, discovered an iron ore deposit. The railroad was built in 1872 between here and Crown Point, where there was a blast furnace. The little trains brought ore down the hill until 1893. Photographer Stoddard went to Hammondville to take the lower picture of the GEN. PUTNAM, No. 3, an 1873 Mogul from the Dickson works, with Knob Mountain in the background. On a flatcar is his wheeled portable darkroom. *(Penfield Foundation, Crown Point, above; D&H collection)*

ern neighbors during their long and dismal winters, with or without the blessing of the Essex County farmers. Just as the lease of the Rensselaer & Saratoga was the result of their earlier acquisition of the Albany & Susquehanna, now an interest in reaching northern New York and Canada beyond was generated by the D&H's lease of the R&S—each step led to the next.

The Champlain valley had always been an avenue of north-south communication for the white man from the time of its discovery in 1609 by Samuel de Champlain and for decades before by the Indians. Water transportation was adequate but at best only seasonal until the Rutland & Burlington Railroad completed its line up the east side of the lake to Burlington, Vermont, in 1849. With a connection there north to the Canadian border via the Vermont Central, an all-rail north-south route existed on the east side of the lake. The west side, however, remained barren of tracks, other than for a few isolated stretches.

In 1850, the Plattsburgh & Montreal Rail Road Co. was incorporated to build a line from Plattsburgh north to the New York-Canada line in the town of Mooers. Here it was to connect with the Lake St. Louis & Province Line Railway and the Montreal & Lachine, two lines projected down from Montreal by Canadian interests. In 1851 an agreement was made between the companies providing that construction on all three lines should be commenced simultaneously and ground was eagerly broken July 16. Tracklaying began in May 1852 and the line was opened to Mooers Junction, on the Northern Railroad of New York, July 26 and all the way to the border by September 20. In the summer of 1853, the steamboat *Francis Saltus* was purchased for the common interest of the Plattsburgh & Montreal and its Canadian associates and was put into service across Lake Champlain from Plattsburgh to Burlington. This provided a through route—that is, in the summer at least—from Boston to Montreal via the railroads down to Plattsburgh, the steamboat to Burlington, the Rutland & Burlington Railroad to Bellows Falls and connections from there on to Boston. Strangely enough the first president of the Plattsburgh & Montreal was John B. Page, who was also deeply interested in the Rutland & Burlington and a member of its board. Despite the fact that this line was only 23 miles long, its importance in the Champlain valley transportation picture was considerable, for in addition to providing a portion of the route between Montreal, Albany and New York—by virtue of its access to a connection with the Rensselaer & Saratoga at Rutland, via the Rutland & Burlington's line—the steamboat plying between Plattsburgh and Burlington connected the line with all the existing railroads in Vermont.

Despite all the traffic advantages the P&M seemed to have, it passed into the receivership of Moss Kent Platt in February, 1857, after having been deserted by its Canadian friends and virtually murdered by its American rivals. After a period of uncertain financial status, it emerged in the summer of 1868 as a reorganized company, the Montreal & Plattsburgh.

The Whitehall & Plattsburgh Rail Road was chartered in February, 1866. Its object was to join Whitehall and Plattsburgh by a rail line along the west side of Lake Champlain. The proposed route was to skirt the lake north to Port Henry where—to avoid the extremely rugged terrain along the lake, especially in the vicinity of Willsboro Bay—the line would swing west to the Ausable River valley near Ausable Forks, and then continue down the valley toward Plattsburgh. The difficulties of the enterprise were considerable, both technically and financially, and construction proceeded slowly.

Isaac V. Baker and James Forsythe were elected directors of the Whitehall & Plattsburgh in March, 1868, obviously to represent the interests of the Rensselaer & Saratoga. The R&S was still independently operated at the time and Baker had been superintendent of that company for many years. The selection of these two directors was well calculated to advance the interests of both companies on the west side of Lake Champlain. Naturally, it implied that the R&S would support the W&P project to the extent, if necessary, of financial assistance, expecting thereby to obtain the benefit of the through route to Canada that the completed road could furnish.

Twenty miles of the line were completed that year in Clinton County, from Plattsburgh southwest to Rogers, then called Point of Rocks, a dozen miles west of the lake in the Ausable Valley. The weakness of the Whitehall & Plattsburgh was emphasized in May of 1869, when this Clinton County

The Crown Point Iron Co.'s lakeside blast furnaces were enlarged in 1879 to a capacity of 170 tons a day. The high-quality iron they produced was shipped out by rail and water until they fell victim to the 1893 depression and competition from the Mesabi Range. No vestiges of them now remain. Since she was photographed as the GEN. PUTNAM for the picture on page 136, the No. 3 had been noticeably modified and her name was changed to the HAMMONDVILLE.

This view looking west toward the lower part of Crown Point was made from the upper works of the blast furnace facility shown on the opposite page. The trestle in the foreground is for delivery of coal and limestone; the little station was built in 1868 by the Whitehall & Plattsburgh. The 0-4-0 tank engine switching by the station is a standard gauge Baldwin of the Crown Point Iron Co., No. 4. *(Penfield Foundation, Crown Point, three pictures)*

section of its line was leased to the Montreal & Plattsburgh, successor of the now-bankrupt Plattsburgh & Montreal which had originally built the line up to the Canadian border.

Despite this lease, the directors of the W&P didn't despair of effecting, through their own company, the completion of the line along the west side of the lake. Negotiations were opened with John B. Page and Levi Underwood on June 23, 1869, for building the middle section of the line between Port Henry and the Ausable River. This effort proved fruitless and was abandoned in June of 1870. Page was now president of the Rutland Railroad, and had some plans of his own for the tracks on the western side of the like.

In 1870 a section along the lake shore from Addison Junction, near Fort Ticonderoga, 17 miles north to Port Henry was finished. Iron ore had been discovered in the mountains west of both Crown Point and Port Henry and the new section of the Whitehall & Plattsburgh found some traffic by handling this ore. With the completion in 1870 of the Addison Railroad in Vermont, across the lake from Fort Ticonderoga, and the building of a bridge to the southern end of the W&P at Addison Junction, an all-rail route to New England and even the Hudson Valley was thus formed. Two small railroads fed the iron ore to the W&P, the three-foot gauge railroad of the Crown Point Iron Co., completed in 1873, connected at Crown Point from Hammondville; and the Lake Champlain & Moriah ran up to Mineville, six miles northwest of Port Henry.

A new factor now entered the picture: John B. Page's Rutland Railroad was a Vermont corporation, and the negotiations it started in August, 1870, had as their object nothing less than actually preventing further construction of a rail line along

The *Oakes Ames* was built at Marks Bay, Burlington, Vermont, in 1868. She was 285 feet long, 35 feet wide, displaced 1145 tons and her two engines generated 270 horsepower. She could carry 13 cars on her deck. She came to the D&H with acquisition of the Montreal & Plattsburgh and was sold in 1873 to the Champlain Transportation Co.

the west side of the lake. At the same time, it sought to insure that the widely separated portions of the W&P, already built, would be operated in the Rutland's interest. It leased the southern section of the W&P, between Ticonderoga and Port Henry, on September 26, 1870, for a 20-year term. The following January Page secured control of the Montreal & Plattsburgh, including the right to operate the northern section of the Whitehall & Plattsburgh by virtue of the M&P's lease of this section two years earlier.

Finally, with the opening of the Addison Railroad on December 1, 1871, a Vermont line the Rutland had leased for some time, even before its completion, a physical connection was achieved with the isolated stretch of the W&P on the west side of the lake. This gave Page and the Rutland access to the iron industry of Port Henry and Crown Point, and enabled them to monopolize the traffic via the Addison's bridge across the lake from Addison Junction, near Fort Ticonderoga, New York, to Larabee's Point on the Vermont shore. This connected with the Rutland's main line at Leicester Junction, 14 miles to the east.

In the north, the Rutland had a connection from Burlington across the lake to Plattsburgh via the big new car-carrying steamer *Oakes Ames*, and on to Canada and the west over their leased Montreal & Plattsburgh line. This enabled the Rutland people to create a through line independent of their Boston-Great Lakes competitor and archrival, the Vermont Central, and its ruthless master, J. Gregory Smith of St. Albans. Admittedly, it was only a seasonal route, but it served Page's twofold purpose to have an independent route from Boston to the west via the Great Lakes and to make J. Gregory Smith squirm on his corporate throne up in St. Albans. Both of these objectives were nicely obtained without even turning a shovelful of earth on new construction over on the west side of the lake.

In fact it did even more, and John Page pursued it to the fullest. By periodically sending survey parties over to New York on the proposed stretch between Port Henry and Ausable Forks — or at least word that they were there — he succeeded in making J. Gregory Smith nervous enough to make a move, and a rash one at that, as he would soon realize. If Page did complete the missing link over on the west side of the lake it would give the Rutland an all-weather route from Boston to Canada and the west that would pose a serious threat to the Vermont Central's monopoly. The steamer *Oakes Ames* was already nuisance enough, churning between Burlington and Plattsburgh at 19 knots carrying 1100 cars a month.

Smith made an offer to Page to lease his whole operation.

It wasn't enough. More surveyors went into the brush over in New York.

Putt's Creek trestle was the perch for the Crown Point Iron Co.'s GEN. PUTNAM in this picture by photographer Stoddard. *(New York collection, State University College at Plattsburgh)*

STATION HOUSE, HOTEL AND STEAMBOAT LANDING, AT ROUSE'S POINT, NEW YORK.

Finally, Smith offered $387,200 a year rental for 20 years and Page grabbed it. J. Gregory had himself the whole Rutland Railroad including a steamboat he didn't know what to do with.

This ended all the hopes for completion of the line on the west side of the lake to the chagrin of the area residents including the Honorable Smith M. Weed of Plattsburgh, prominent citizen of the community and member of the State Legislature. Under his persistent leadership the original concept of a through rail route along the western shore of Lake Champlain began to develop. His was one of the voices raised in opposition to the Northern Railroad of New York building a bridge across the foot of Lake Champlain at Rouses Point to connect the North Country with Boston rather than the Champlain valley and New York via Plattsburgh. He did succeed in getting legislation enacted restricting the span length of the bridge, but this was finally overcome by installing a floating center section, the first of its kind ever built.

Early in 1872, Weed journeyed to New York in an effort to interest the Delaware & Hudson Canal Co. in building north from Whitehall, a point they had recently reached by their lease of the Rensselaer & Saratoga's road. At a meeting with some of its officers and managers, at which I. V. Baker who shared his aspirations was present, Mr. Weed readily convinced George Talbot Olyphant, acting as president in the absence of Thomas Dickson, that such a line would be of great advantage to the D&H. He thereupon drew from his pocket articles of association of the New York & Canada Railroad Co., already signed by several prominent residents of Plattsburgh and Clinton County. The remaining signatures necessary to effect its incorporation were quickly and willingly supplied.

Some construction work was completed by the new company in 1872, and in January 1873 attention was given to negotiations with the Whitehall & Plattsburgh. The W&P management, now actually a part of the Vermont Central System, offered to lease the operational sections of their line to the New York & Canada, an offer no doubt prompted by the realization that the new company with the financial power of the D&H behind it could build parallel to the existing W&P tracks and leave them high and dry with a railroad and no trains on it. Accordingly, a lease was taken on January 14 which was immediately followed by a proposal for consolidation. The following day the D&H authorized, in behalf of the NY&C, the purchase from the Vermont interests of the control and leaseholds of the Whitehall & Plattsburgh, the

The two Stoddard photos on this page show a northbound train approaching the 682-foot tunnel at Whitehall on the New York & Canada, above, and the GEN. PUTNAM watering up halfway between Crown Point and Hammondville. Rouses Point, opposite, was the hub of transportation on Lake Champlain from the advent of the first steamboat in 1809. The Station House was a hotel at the end of the pier where trains met the steamers to transfer passengers and freight. (D&H collection, above; Howell collection, Witherill Hotel, opposite)

This construction train is in a borrow pit north of Whitehall during construction of the New York & Canada line along the west shore of Lake Champlain in 1873. (D&H collection)

Montreal & Plattsburgh and the steamer *Oakes Ames*, thereby paving the way for a consolidation of the rights, franchises and properties of all the roads on the west side of Lake Champlain. The *Oakes Ames* was subsequently sold to the Champlain Transportation Company who renamed her *Champlain*.

Under an agreement dated February 25, 1873, the Whitehall & Plattsburgh, the Montreal & Plattsburgh and the New York and Canada of 1872 were merged and consolidated into a second New York & Canada Railroad Co. with Isaac V. Baker as its president. The southern section continued for awhile to be operated for the new company by the Vermont Central, lessee of the Rutland, but according to the records that company was willing "to vacate at any time."

It was obvious that the goal of the Delaware & Hudson managers was nothing less than to reach Montreal with the company's anthracite, while both stimulating and profiting from the iron industry that was then in the process of development in the Champlain Valley.

Construction on the section north from Whitehall to Ticonderoga and Addison Junction was most difficult indeed. At Whitehall there existed a 682-foot tunnel built by the Rensselaer & Saratoga in 1851, piercing a ledge of rock right in the village, to reach a point on the lake at the north edge of town, called Lake Station. Here the R&S trains connected with the Champlain steamboats and both passengers and cargoes were transferred at this lakeside interchange for destinations down the lake such as Burlington, Plattsburgh, Rouses Point and even St. Johns, Quebec.

Almost insurmountable difficulties of an engineering nature had to be overcome on the section north of Whitehall where the track skirted the marshy reaches at the head of the lake. The road was carried across South Bay, just beyond

When the New York & Canada line was opened, the distinguished photographer S. R. Stoddard of Glens Falls was there to capture the scenery and atmosphere. He was provided with a special train consisting of a combination car to be used as a darkroom and engine No. 130, formerly the R&S's GEORGE H. CRAMER. These two scenes show the train on the pier at Montcalm Landing, on Lake Champlain near Fort Ticonderoga. (G. M. Best collection, above; Al Gayer collection)

The section of the New York & Canada north of Whitehall had stretches of trestlework to cross marshy areas like the one above. The lake is very narrow at this point and across it from Stoddard's photographic special are the rocky cliffs of the Vermont shore. Below is a latter-day view, made in the mid-1930s, of a southbound milk train, pulled by a 500 class Ten Wheeler through the Red Rocks section of the road above Willsboro Bay. The track was built on a narrow shelf blasted out of rock 100 feet above the water. *(De Sormo collection, above; D&H collection)*

the village, by means of a long trestle to the marsh on the north side which in many places seemed bottomless. Here ancient canal boats, trees, timbers, old railroad cars and great quantities of rock and earth were dumped in to make a solid roadbed.

Further north, five ranges of the Adirondacks were encountered, involving vast rock cuts and adding greatly to the construction difficulties. These ranges terminate abruptly in rocky headlands or mountains rising almost perpendicularly out of the lake. In order to reach and connect with the existing track at Addison Junction, a 439-foot tunnel had to be driven under the rocky finger of land, jutting out into the lake, upon which historic Fort Ticonderoga is built.

The road was opened from Whitehall to Port Henry, 39¾ miles, on November 30, 1874, including the difficult new 24-mile stretch up along the lake from Whitehall to Addison Junction. From the Junction to Port Henry, the track of the Whitehall & Plattsburgh was utilized, except for several relocations and grade modifications. The opening would probably have taken place during the preceding spring, but on April 18 a strong north wind swept down the length of the lake and threw a mountain of ice floes against the trestle across the mouth of Bulwagga Bay, stretching from a point near the ruins of Fort St. Frederick to Port Henry, completely demolishing the spindly structure. It was then decided to relocate five miles of track along the head of the bay to preclude another similar disaster.

As work progressed, the existing track between Addison Junction and Port Henry remained in use, but original plans, for a route north from there running inland to Ausable Forks and thence down the Ausable valley to Plattsburgh, were abandoned in favor of a bolder, more direct and costlier line adjacent to the shore of Lake Champlain most of the way. Construction was pushed north through Essex County toward Plattsburgh, by way of the Boquet valley and the village of Whallonsburgh.

* * * *

It was at this time that the local farmers of the Boquet valley, disturbed at the prospect of the railroad intruding on their lives and their farms, sent a delegation across to see how Vermonters had fared after the arrival of the Rutland Railroad. The Vermont farmers, from the vicinity of Vergennes, told the Essex County delegation that they had fought against the railroad at first, but soon came to depend on it and now wouldn't know what to do without it. Their York State contemporaries may have been doubtful at the time, but they would soon find out for themselves.

When the railroad construction crews were at last working feverishly in the Boquet Valley, both north and south of Whallonsburgh, the people there were already beginning to reap some economic benefits, and not a single train had yet to run. Zebadiah Sartwell's mill was running two shifts to keep up with the appetite for feed worked up by the army of contractors' mules and horses during the course of a day's work on the fill. Many of the teams were rented from the local farmers, and their once-irate owners followed behind, eager to collect the handsome going rate construction work brought, even then. It wasn't long before the farmers had raised the price of grain and hay and were practically running their hens through the clothes wringer to get eggs out of them faster. The lure of the extra income from the appetites of the construction men and their trusty steeds was more than these sturdy Whallonburghers could turn their backs on, in principle or in fact. They were coming around to the same conclusion reached by their Vermont contemporaries on the Rutland line, whether they cared to admit it or not.

* * * *

North of Port Henry, heavy rock excavation was largely avoided by keeping back from the lake on a location that took the line through the Boquet River valley, past the fields of the once-irate farmers, to Willsboro. Beyond there the most spectacular and difficult section, high up on the face of the cliffs above Willsboro Bay, was encountered. The Boquet range meets the lake with high bluffs extending along the bay for seven miles. Here the drillers had to be let down 100 feet on ropes from the top of the ledge to prepare the blasts. When the charges were fired, tons of rock would cascade another hundred feet down into the black depths of Willsboro Bay. A narrow shelf was carved out for the track and involved a 606-foot tunnel, several high bridges and many deep rock cuts. Despite the difficulties encountered, this section is one of the most beautiful and thrilling bits of railroad in the Northeast.

Here are four spectacular views of Stoddard's photographic special on scenic portions of the New York & Canada; opposite are views just north of Port Henry, above, and of the Red Rocks stretch three miles north of Willsboro. Above is another Red Rocks view, just north of the 606-foot curving tunnel. Below the train stands on the iron bridge across Higby Gulf, Willsboro Bay. *(Howard Warren collection, upper pictures; De Sormo collection, lower pictures)*

Construction materials, including ties and rails for much of the line above Port Henry were transported down the lake in boats from Whitehall and unloaded at convenient points. A locomotive was needed during construction on this isolated portion and it too was barged down the lake and after unloading was hauled up the bank to the right-of-way over a temporary track laid down to the shore.

The complete line was opened a year after the section from Whitehall to Port Henry, and the first regular train rolled into a jubilant Plattsburgh on November 29, 1875. By using the tracks of the former Montreal & Plattsburgh to Mooers Junction and then 12 miles of the Ogdensburgh & Lake Champlain's line east from that point, through service was opened on the same day to Rouses Point. There a connection was made with the Grand Trunk Railway for Montreal. Thus was realized the vision entertained by many as early as 1832 when the first train rolled into Saratoga Springs from the south.

The problems in building such a line were primarily of an engineering nature, but they were augmented by the financial and commercial conditions of the years from 1873 to 1879. The commercial depression following the panic of 1873 continued for a longer period than any other the country had experienced and it impeded railroad building to such an extent that few new enterprises were undertaken and many of those already in progress were interrupted. It is therefore remarkable that the D&H, through its agent the New York & Canada, was able to continue at all, much less complete the sizeable job in two years.

So it was with justifiable pride that the managers stepped back to view their achievement. They had looked forward to the day on which, for the first time, it would be possible to travel wholly by train from New York City via Albany and Plattsburgh to Montreal, eliminating the water portion of the trip on Lake Champlain, and decided to signalize the event with a gala excursion. President Dickson sent invitations to the most prominent railroad officials and other important individuals in the northeastern section of the country, requesting them to join with the managers in a commemorative excursion on Tuesday, November 16, 1875 to precede the opening of the route to the public. Among those invited were John Jacob Astor, J.

CHAMPLAIN DIVISION.

LEAVE.	GOING NORTH.				LEAVE.	GOING SOUTH.			
	Mail.	Mon'l Ex	Mixed.	Mixed.		Mail.	N.Y. Exp	Mixed.	Mixed.
	1	7	23	31		6	8	24	32
Albany	8.00 AM	11.45 PM			Montreal	9.05 AM	8.00 PM		
					Rouse's Point	11.15	5.10	4.00 AM	
Troy	8.10	11.50			Champlain	11.25	5.20	4.18	
					Mooers Junction	11.40	5.35	5.00	
Schenectady	8.00				Sciota	11.54	5.47	5.25	
					Chazy	12.10 PM	6.00	5.50	
Whitehall	11.05 AM	2.30 AM	5.00 AM	2.50 PM	Beekmantown	12.20	6.12	6.10	
Chubb's Dock	11.26		5 35	3.25	Plattsburg...Ar	12.30	6.22	6.30	
Dresden	11.32		5.50	3.40					
Putnam	11.43		6.15	4.20	Plattsburg...Lv			7.30 AM	
Patterson	‡11.52		6.40	4.40	Salmon River			7.55	
Ft. Ticonderoga Ar					Lapham's Mills			8.10	
Ft. Ticonderoga Lv					Peru			8.22	
Ticonderoga					Harkness			8.41	
Baldwin......Ar					Ferrona			9 00	
Baldwin......Lv					Ausable......Ar			9.15 AM	
Ticonderoga									
Ft. Ticonderoga Ar					Ausable......Lv	10.00 AM			
Ft. Ticonderoga Lv					Ferrona	10.17			
Addison Junction	12.10 PM	3.28	7.00	5.10	Harkness	10.32			
Crown Point	12.30		7.40	5.50	Peru	10.53			
Port Henry	12.50	4.04	9.00	6.30 PM	Lapham's Mills	11.03			
Westport	1.20		10.10		Salmon River	11.20			
Wadham's Mills	‡1.27		10.30		Plattsburg...Ar	11.45 AM			
Whallonsburg	1.36		10.20						
Willsborough	1.55		11.35		Plattsburg...Lv	12.50 PM	6.42 PM	9.00 AM	
Port Kent	2.25	5.38	1 20 PM		Valcour	1.05	6.57	9.35	
Valcour	2.40		1.50		Port Kent	1.20	7.12	10.25	
Plattsburg...Ar	2.55	6.10	2.30		Willsborough	1.55	7.48	11.35	
					Whallonsburg	2.16	8.04	12.20 PM	
Plattsburg...Lv		7 30			Wadham's Mills	‡2.28	‡8.12	12.40	
Salmon River		7.55			Westport	2.40	8.19	1.20	
Lapham's Mills		8.10			Port Henry	3.15	8.45	8.15	5.20 AM
Peru		8.22			Crown Point	3.35	9.08	4.20	6 20
Harkness		8.44			Addison Junction	3.55	9.20	5.10	7.00
Ferrona		9.00			Ft. Ticonderoga Ar				
Ausable......Ar		9.15			Ft. Ticonder'ga Lv				
					Ticonderoga				
Ausable......Lv	10.00 AM				Baldwin......Ar				
Ferrona	10.17				Baldwin......Lv				
Harkness	10.32				Ticonderoga				
Peru	10.53				Ft. Ticonderoga Ar				
Lapham's Mills	11.08				Ft. Ticonder'ga Lv				
Salmon River	11.20				Patterson	‡4.08		5.32	7.21
Plattsburg...Ar	11.45 AM				Putnam	4.20		5.55	7.45
					Dresden	4.31		6.29	8.12
Plattsburg......Lv	3.15 PM	6.30	4.00 PM		Chubb's Dock	4.39		6.38	8.35
Beekmantown	3.28	6.40	4 20		Whitehall...Ar	5.00	10.15 PM	7.10 PM	9.00 AM
Chazy	3.38	6.52	4.40						
Sciota	3.45	7.04	5.00		Schenectady...Ar	7.40			
Mooers Junction	3.55	7.15	5.85						
Champlain	4.20	7.35	6.22		Troy......Ar	8.10	1.00 AM		
Rouse's Point	4.80	7.45	6 40 PM						
Montreal......Ar	7.00 PM	10.00 AM			Albany......Ar	8.25 PM	1.10 AM		

‡ Trains stop to leave or take Passengers on signal.

CONNECTIONS.—At Whitehall with Saratoga Division. At Port Kent with Ferry to and from Burlington. At Mooers Junction with Central Vermont R. R. At Rouse's Point with Grand Trunk and Central Vermont R. R.'s. At Montreal with diverging Railroad and Steamboat Lines.

S. E. MAYO, Gen'l Passenger Agent, Albany.

C. F. YOUNG, Gen'l Manager, Honesdale, Pa.

Map and timetable of the D&H as of November, 1875.

Pierpont Morgan, Cornelius Vanderbilt, Chester A. Arthur, William H. Vanderbilt and many more. President Grant received an invitation, but was unable to accept.

The party left Albany at 9 a.m. and stopped at various points along the line to entrain more dignitaries. The train consisted of a baggage car, hotel car, seven Wagner Palace Cars, a directors' coach and at the rear, an open "Baldwin" coach. The locomotive used was the SARATOGA, a splendid new coal-burning 4-4-0 of classic proportions. The outstanding features of the trip were two festive banquets, the first at Plattsburgh that night tendered by the area citizens, and the second, a "collation" in Montreal, the next afternoon, provided by the city.

The train rolled into Plattsburgh at 4:30 p.m. having made the trip up from Albany in seven and a half hours—the shortest trip on record. At the Fouquet House, across the street from the station

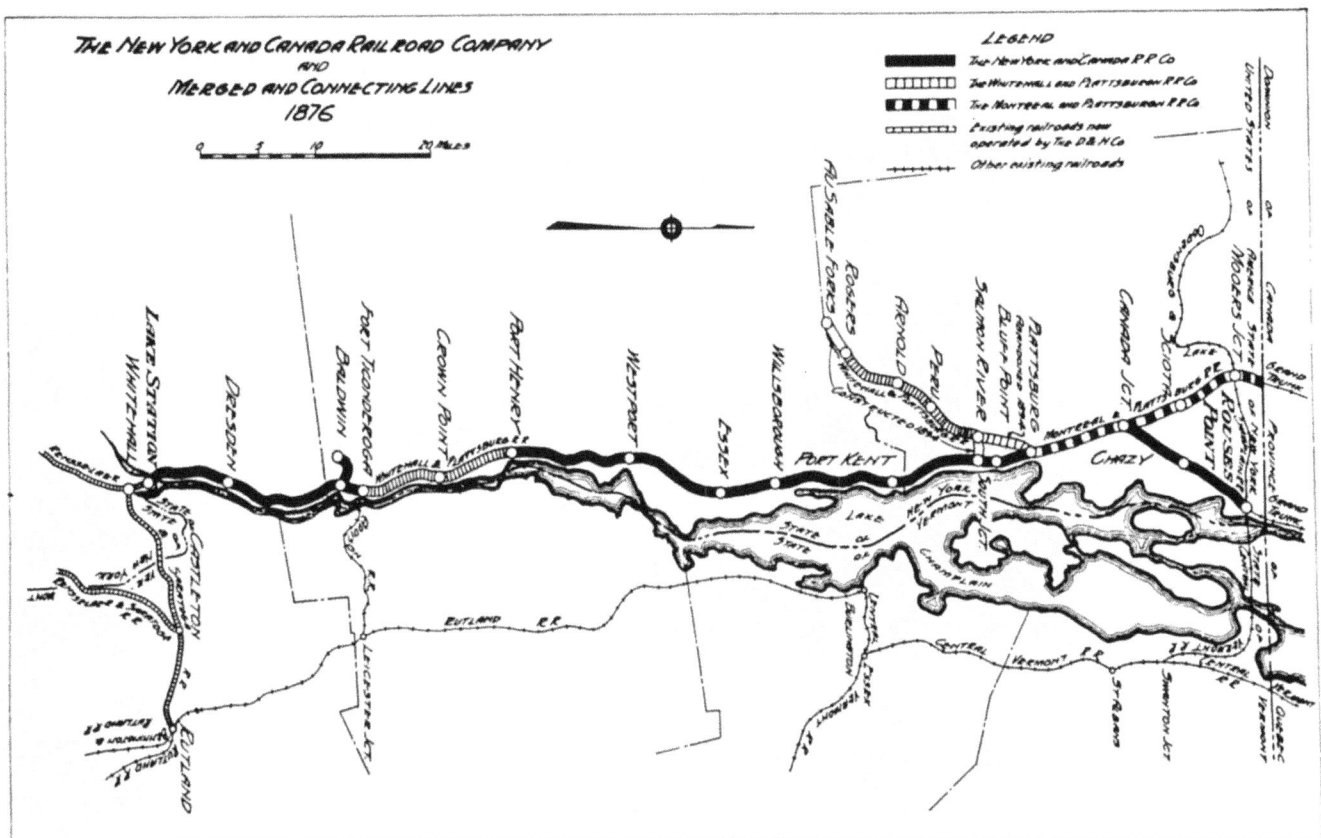

The detail, opposite, of the 1877 engraving of Plattsburgh that appears on page 155, clearly shows the railroad facilities of the old Plattsburgh & Montreal which were taken over by the D&H when its New York & Canada project pushed tracks all the way up the west side of Lake Champlain from Whitehall. The Fouquet House hotel is shown as the three story building across Bridge Street from the station. *(D&H collection)*

---

where the banquet was to be held later, the Plattsburgh Cornet Band was already out in force, playing its best aires for the entertainment of the principals as they left the train. Later, the speeches at the banquet ranged from the humorous to the serious and were similar to those to be heard at any good political rally. The Honorable Smith M. Weed acted as toastmaster, and President Dickson responded to the first toast with an address sketching briefly the early history of the company. After him others went on and on.

At 8:30 the next morning they all piled back on the train and were off to Rouses Point, this time behind the locomotive I. V. BAKER, named for the president of the New York & Canada, himself. At Rouses Point there was a huge crowd and after "a grand salute," the train headed across the boundary behind a Grand Trunk engine decorated with both the Stars and Stripes and a Union Jack. After another reception in St. Johns the train moved on into Montreal along the route of the old St. Johns & Montreal line opened in 1836, reaching the Canadian metropolis by one in the afternoon.

At three o'clock the city authorities entertained their American visitors with a déjeuner reception at the Corn Exchange, followed by the collation set for 300 guests. A toast to the Queen, more speeches, and the great commemorative trip was about over. All were back in Albany by 5:30 p.m. the next afternoon, their hearts warmed considerably more by the refreshments served in the hotel car on the return trip than by the ginger-pop recorded as flowing freely the day before in Montreal.

The Delaware & Hudson managers had wisely promised a free ride to all the people along the new line, upon its completion, and a few weeks after the official trip carrying all the dignitaries came this "fun" excursion, a much less pompous and publicized affair, from Port Henry to Plattsburgh and return.

As the 1 p.m. arrival time drew near at the new Whallonsburgh depot, an apprehensive crowd of curious country folk surrounded the platform and little station. People from the remote corners of the township had driven in, but had cautiously

The I. V. Baker, D&H 4-4-0 No. 126, was built by Schenectady in 1867 for the R&S as its No. 31. She pulled the commemorative special from Plattsburgh to Rouses Point on November 17, 1875. *(G. M. Best collection)*

hitched their teams to trees and fences a good half mile back from the scene of commotion, fearing that the first screech of the engine would send their normally docile plugs into a wild stampede. Some of the onlookers were 50 or 60 years old, had been born and reared in the county but had never crossed its boundary line nor even ridden on the lake steamers. This event was truly the coming of the future and they came from far and wide to see the new "thing," which they would talk about for the rest of their lives.

A stentorian blast on the whistle announced the approach of the iron monster as it plunged through the deep cut on the opposite side of the river from the station. As it neared the platfrom it began spitting spiteful jets of steam in a seemingly maddened charge toward the crowd. Its appearance was so alarming that all reserve was broken and there was a general scramble for safety.

When the smoke and steam lifted after the normal but seemingly spectacular arrival, and the onlookers saw that the whole lash-up was still on the track, they gingerly boarded the cars and sat nervously on the edge of their seats. All were ready for a hasty exit at the first sign of imminent disaster. A few were so badly shaken by the events thus far they could not be induced to venture further and the train pulled away without them. Zebadiah Sartwell, the miller of Whallonsburgh, and his wife were the first to ascend the train.

The shout of "All aboard!" boomed down the platform and with the clang of the bell, a jerk and the crash of coupler links, the train moved out while some fifty hearts beat like trip hammers within their respective bosoms.

Everyone was just beginning to relax and fully enjoy their new dimension in travel when one of the fears the early opponents of the railroad so vigorously voiced was literally thrust before them. There was a sudden and jolting stop, which sent passengers crashing into one another and down between the seats. Upon investigation it was found they had hit a cow, and needless to say, killed her. Her mangled remains lay scattered about under the engine. It wasn't necessary to feel her pulse. She passed away right in the prime of life without

The grand old Fouquet House had a dozen chimneys to serve the fireplaces in all its rooms. Its long verandas commanded a view over the new Plattsburgh station, built in 1886, and the steamer landing at the foot of Bridge Street, to the left. Its grand ballroom was the scene of the banquet celebrating the opening of the NY&C. The extent of Plattsburgh in 1887 can be seen in the engraving below of which a portion is enlarged on page 152. *(New York collection, State University College at Plattsburgh, above; D&H collection)*

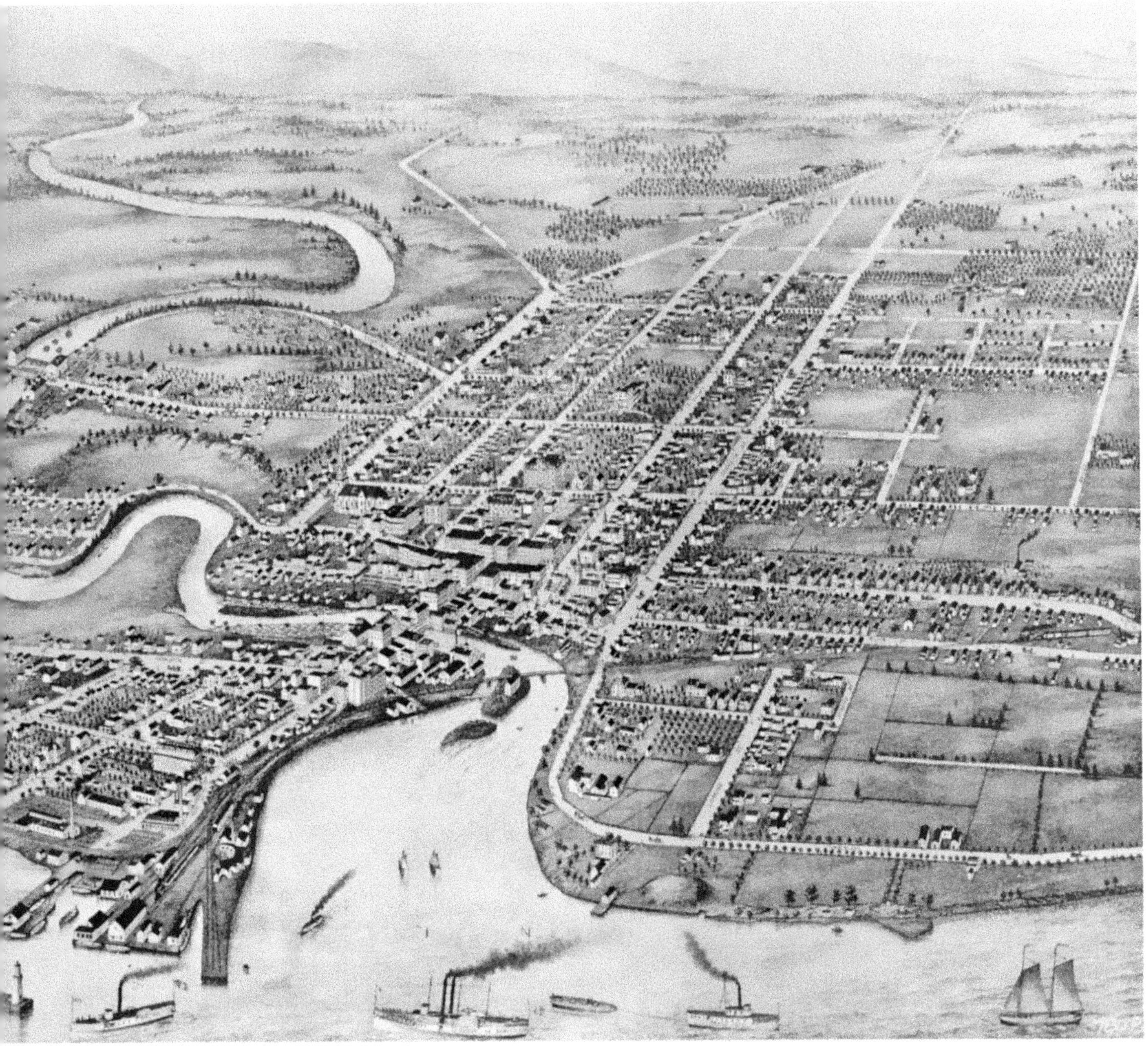

156   D&H 4-4-0 No. 130 on the shelf of rock, blasted out of the Red Rocks cliffs above Willsboro Bay was photographed in 1882 by S. R. Stoddard. *(Howard Warren collection)*

bidding any of her relatives good-bye. Mrs. Sartwell had just known something awful would happen before they got back. Zeb assured her that it wasn't all in vain. The cow had given her life in sacrifice as an object lesson to those aboard that it was useless to try and obstruct the wheels of progress. Zeb's wife wasn't convinced, saying that they would probably all be killed before they learned to stay off these murderous contraptions.

This was almost proven within minutes. All were enthralled by the scenery along the steep bluffs overlooking Willsboro Bay, the view past the Four Brothers Islands to Burlington and even to the Green Mountains beyond. The sordid accident involving Bossy was all but forgotten.

Mrs. Sartwell gave a sudden screech and yelled: "Zebadiah, ketch me quick! I'm struck blind!! I knew somethin' would happen afore we got home!"

As suddenly as the darkness came, it went, and the car was again flooded with light. It was, of course, the Willsboro tunnel, a modern phenomenon Mrs. Sartwell and the other fledgling gadabouts would have to get acquainted with in this modern world they were venturing into from the sleepy solitude of the Boquet Valley.

By the time they reached Plattsburgh, all had experienced the fastest and most action-packed ninety minutes of their lives. They would all have to get accustomed to this, for their lives would never again be quite the same.

It was plain to see, whether you were in the car with Zebadiah Sartwell or the one with Thomas Dickson, that the New York & Canada was truly an engineering marvel and a masterpiece of construction—but even more, it was the fulfillment of a dream and a step into the future for those on board each of the trains.

*   *   *   *

The Chateaugay & Lake Placid. New York State's maximum-security penitentiary at Dannemora has the nickname of "Siberia." This is especially appropriate to both the underworld and the weather world. When a convict is sent up to Dannemora he might just as well be in Siberia, as far as his contact with society is concerned, or as far as the climate is concerned, when the place is in the grip of the severe winters that are the rule there.

Clinton Prison, as the state's establishment at Dannemora is known, was opened in 1845, and for many years it was necessary to transport all supplies, fuel and men—both convicts and attendants—by teams over a crude road twenty miles from Plattsburgh. The State of New York decided to construct a railroad to provide access to the facility and authorized the venture in 1878.

Louis D. Pilsbury was superintendent of State prisons at the time and he immediately arranged for surveys and, after the line was located, a contract for its construction. The job was awarded to John O'Brien, and part of the agreement provided for convict labor to do the grading on the two miles of line nearest the prison.

The line was built with a gauge of three feet, the slim gauge being considered advisable in view of its lower cost and projected light traffic. To keep costs to a minimum the existing contour of the ground was frequently followed; this resulted in many curves and a rise of over 150 feet per mile in the last five miles of the line to Dannemora. The little road was completed in December 1878 and equipped with rolling stock during the following year. The line was never formally incorporated but was known as the Plattsburgh & Dannemora Railroad.

Extensive iron deposits had earlier been discovered at Lyon Mountain, about 18 miles west of Dannemora. This property was owned by the Chateaugay Ore Co. which was affiliated with an iron company of the same name. The ore was sorted by hand and a sizeable quantity had already been moved in wagons to furnaces that had been erected at various locations in the Saranac valley between Lyon Mountain and Plattsburgh. Here it was made into bloom iron and hauled to Plattsburgh by wagon for shipment. This operation was excessively costly and if it hadn't been for the high quality of the product, it would have been prohibitive.

Late in the 1870s the developers realized that in order to develop the rich resources of their property to the best advantage, they had to secure rail connections with the great ironmaking centers of the country. The question was in which direction they should strike out from the mine, lying there in the heart of the wilderness. Two routes were open to them: one went down the Chateaugay valley, northwest to Chateaugay, New York,

Dickson-built, 1879 model 2-6-0 No. 4 of the Chateaugay Railroad, the THOMAS DICKSON, stands before the hotel and general store in Standish, headed toward Lyon Mountain and Plattsburgh. *(Charles Clingman collection)*

on the Ogdensburg & Lake Champlain Railroad; the other went east to Dannemora for a connection with the new state-owned Plattsburgh & Dannemora line.

In February, 1879, while the snow lay four feet deep in the woods, the work of making a preliminary survey was undertaken and by spring the results were at hand. The Chateaugay route ran 17 miles in almost a straight line on an easy grade. Half of the line would go through the company's own lands, passing the Catalan forge at Belmont, with the remainder going through fine farming country from which considerable local traffic could be expected. The line to Dannemora was also 17 miles long, but ten miles of this lay through solid wilderness, a crooked line running around two mountains, going toward every point of the compass. It would be a hard line to grade and had little promise of local traffic. Everything seemed to indicate the Chateaugay route as the most logical choice.

Thomas Dickson, however, president of the Delaware & Hudson and close friend of Smith M. Weed, one of the promoters, concluded that the proper route for this ore was east, via Dannemora to Plattsburgh, where it could go to market over the New York & Canada and D&H-controlled rails. Accordingly, on May 15, 1879, the Chateaugay Railroad was organized with Thomas Dickson as its president. Five days later this new company secured a lease of the Plattsburgh & Dannemora from the State of New York for a term of 100 years, taking over operation of that property. Grading work began immediately on the new line, which was narrow gauge to match the rails of the P&D; it was completed and opened to Lyon Mountain on March 30, 1880.

The Chateaugay Ore & Iron Co. was incorporated on May 2, 1881, and purchased the properties of the ore company, the iron company and the railroad of the same name, as well as a furnace at Plattsburgh. The D&H was closely identified

Two Dickson-built locomotives of the Chateaugay Railroad appear on this page. Mogul No. 8, the DANNEMORA, looks none too secure roosting on the 72-foot-high trestle across the Saranac River at Cadyville, just west of Plattsburgh on the original P&D line in 1884. The line had been extended to Loon Lake so recently, when the lower picture was made, that the horse-drawn scrapers and plows, used in the construction, were still on the site. 4-4-0 No. 11, the ST. REGIS, is lettered for the Ore & Iron Co. (*G. M. Best collection, above; D&H collection*)

NEW YORK
TO
SARANAC LAKE,
Through Sleeping Cars to Plattsburgh.

LEAVE NEW YORK FROM GRAND CENTRAL STATION, FORTY-SECOND ST.

IN EFFECT MONDAY, JUNE 29th, 1891.

Lv. NEW YORK	*7 00 pm	11 59 pm	9 20 am
Lv. Albany	11 20 pm	6 50 am	1 00 pm
" Troy	12 00 n't	6 50 "	1 30 "
" Saratoga	1 40 am	8 00 "	2 35 "
" Whitehall	3 00 "	9 10 "	3 40 "
Ar. PLATTSBURGH	6 35 am	12 30 pm	6 30 pm
Lv. PLATTSBURGH	7 25 am	1 25 am	7 25 am
" Morrisonville	7 42 "	1 42 "	7 42 "
" Cadyville	7 52 "	1 52 "	7 52 "
" Dannemora	8 12 "	2 12 "	8 12 "
" Chazy Lake	8 40 "	2 40 "	8 40 "
" Lyon Mountain	9 00 "	3 00 "	9 00 "
" Loon Lake	9 55 "	3 55 "	9 55 "
" Rainbow	10 14 "	4 14 "	10 14 "
" Bloomingdale (Paul Smith's)	10 28 "	4 28 "	10 28 "
" SARANAC LAKE	10 45 am	4 45 pm	10 45 am
Ar. Chateaugay Lake	10 00 "	4 00 pm	10 00 "
" Loon Lake House	10 30 "	4 30 "	10 30 "
" Paul Smith's	11 30 "	5 30 "	11 30 "
" Ray Brook House	11 30 "	5 30 "	11 30 "
" Lake Placid	12 45 pm	6 30 pm	12 45 pm
Ar. Saranac Inn	12 45 "	....	12 45 pm

* Daily, including Sundays.

The Sleeping Cars leaving New York 7.00 p.m. from Grand Central Station arrive at Plattsburgh 6.35 a.m. Fifty minutes are allowed at Plattsburgh for Breakfast before leaving by Chateaugay Railroad at 7.25.

Or, leaving New York 9.20 a.m. (Through Wagner Drawing-Room Car), reach Plattsburgh 6.30 p.m., lodge, and proceed next morning as above.

SARANAC LAKE
TO
NEW YORK,
Through Sleeping Cars Plattsburgh to New York.

ARRIVE GRAND CENTRAL DEPOT, FORTY-SECOND STREET.

IN EFFECT MONDAY, JUNE 29th, 1891.

Lv. Saranac Inn	*1 30 pm	....	
" Lake Placid	1 25 "	6 35 am	
" Ray Brook House	2 25 "	7 30 "	
" Paul Smith's	2 25 "	7 15 "	
" Loon Lake House	3 45 "	8 30 "	
" Chateaugay Lake	4 30 pm	9 20 am	
Lv. SARANAC LAKE	3 35 pm	8 25 am	
" Bloomingdale (Paul Smith's)	3 55 "	8 43 "	
" Rainbow	4 09 "	8 57 "	
" Loon Lake	4 29 "	9 18 "	
" Lyon Mountain	5 22 "	10 13 "	6 40 am
" Chazy Lake	5 39 "	....	7 13 "
" Dannemora	6 07 "	10 52 am	8 12 "
" Cadyville	6 20 "	....	8 55 "
" Morrisonville	6 29 "	....	9 15 "
Ar. PLATTSBURGH	6 50 pm	11 30 am	9 45 "
Lv. PLATTSBURGH	7 25 pm	12 00 n'n	10 05 am
" Whitehall	11 10 "	3 00 pm	2 25 pm
" Saratoga	12 35 am	4 05 "	4 05 "
Lv. Troy	2 15 am	4 55 pm	4 55 pm
" Albany	2 15 "	5 25 "	5 25 "
Ar. NEW YORK	6 45 am	9 20 pm	9 20 "

* Daily, including Sundays.

TICKETS,
SLEEPING and DRAWING-ROOM CAR ACCOMMODATIONS

Can be obtained at either of the following Offices:

Lake Placid, Paul Smith's, Saranac Lake, Bloomingdale, Loon Lake and Lyon Mountain.

—*William Howell collection, Witherill Hotel, Plattsburgh.*

with this new company from its inception. In 1885 it built a blast furnace on its lands at Standish, about four miles to the southwest. The tracks were immediately extended to the new facility, and soon afterward to Loon Lake, 14 more miles to the south. This segment of the line opened November 15, 1886.

The next year it was decided to extend the line another 19 miles south to Saranac Lake, there to tap the rapidly growing passenger business attracted to the Adirondack resort area; this was completed and open to traffic on December 5, 1887, thus providing a narrow gauge line 73 miles long between Plattsburgh and Saranac Lake.

The Chateaugay Railway Co. was incorporated July 13, 1887, and purchased the railroad that had been built by the Ore & Iron Co., emerging with Smith M. Weed as its president. The property of the Chateaugay Railway Co. was leased to the Chateaugay Railroad Co. in perpetuity on July 1, 1888, and was operated by the lessee from that date.

The Saranac & Lake Placid Rail Road Co. was organized in June, 1890, to build a line from Saranac Lake to Lake Placid. The ten-mile road was opened August 1, 1893, and although it was built to standard gauge, a third rail was provided to accommodate the narrow gauge equipment of the Chateaugay Railroad Co. After several changes in management the line was leased to the Chateaugay Co. in December of 1896, thus placing the entire 83 miles between Plattsburgh to Lake Placid under one control.

The D&H had a substantial financial interest in the Chateaugay Ore & Iron Co. and the Chateaugay Railroad Co., although the properties were separately operated. When it became necessary to refinance these companies in 1901, the D&H assumed control of the railroad, acquired the stock of the Saranac & Lake Placid, and arranged a consolidation of the railroad properties under one ownership. This culminated two years later.

Meanwhile, in order to meet more fully the needs of traffic and to avoid the transfer of loads arriving at Plattsburgh for movement beyond that point, it was deemed advisable to change this narrow gauge line to standard. The rebuilding was undertaken in 1902 and completed in 1903, under the supervision of the D&H. The entire line was virtually rebuilt, with many sharp curves and heavy grades, that were unsuited to standard gauge operation, eliminated. It was decided to relocate the junction of this line with the D&H's New York & Canada from Plattsburgh to a point called South Junction, three miles south of town, for the original route passed through the center of a military reservation.

In 1903 the Chateaugay Railroad, the Chateaugay Railway and the Saranac & Lake Placid Railway were consolidated and incorporated as the Chateaugay & Lake Placid Railway Co., which immediately took over the lease of the Plattsburgh & Dannemora from the state, which had first been negotiated in 1879 by the Chateaugay Railroad. The consolidated line, now in first class condition, was on July 29, 1903, leased for a period of 500 years to the Delaware & Hudson, thus becoming an integral part of that expanding system that had started as a canal.

The MIRROR LAKE, 4-4-0 No. 12, was built by Dickson in 1889 for the Chateaugay. The little three-foot gauge engine had 45½-inch drivers and 15-by-20-inch cylinders. (D&H collection)

A stage connects with the Chateaugay train at the Loon Lake station to take passengers to the Loon Lake House. At the same station, Chateaugay engine No. 12, the MIRROR LAKE, takes water after a run up from Plattsburgh. The 1891 map, opposite, shows not only the Chateaugay, but also the Crown Point Iron Co.'s railroad and its projection to Schroon Lake, and the Keesville, Au Sable Chasm & Lake Champlain line out of Port Kent. Out of Port Henry, west and north to Mineville, is the line of the Lake Champlain & Moriah. *(G. M. Best collection, two pictures; William Howell collection, Witherill Hotel, Plattsburgh, map)*

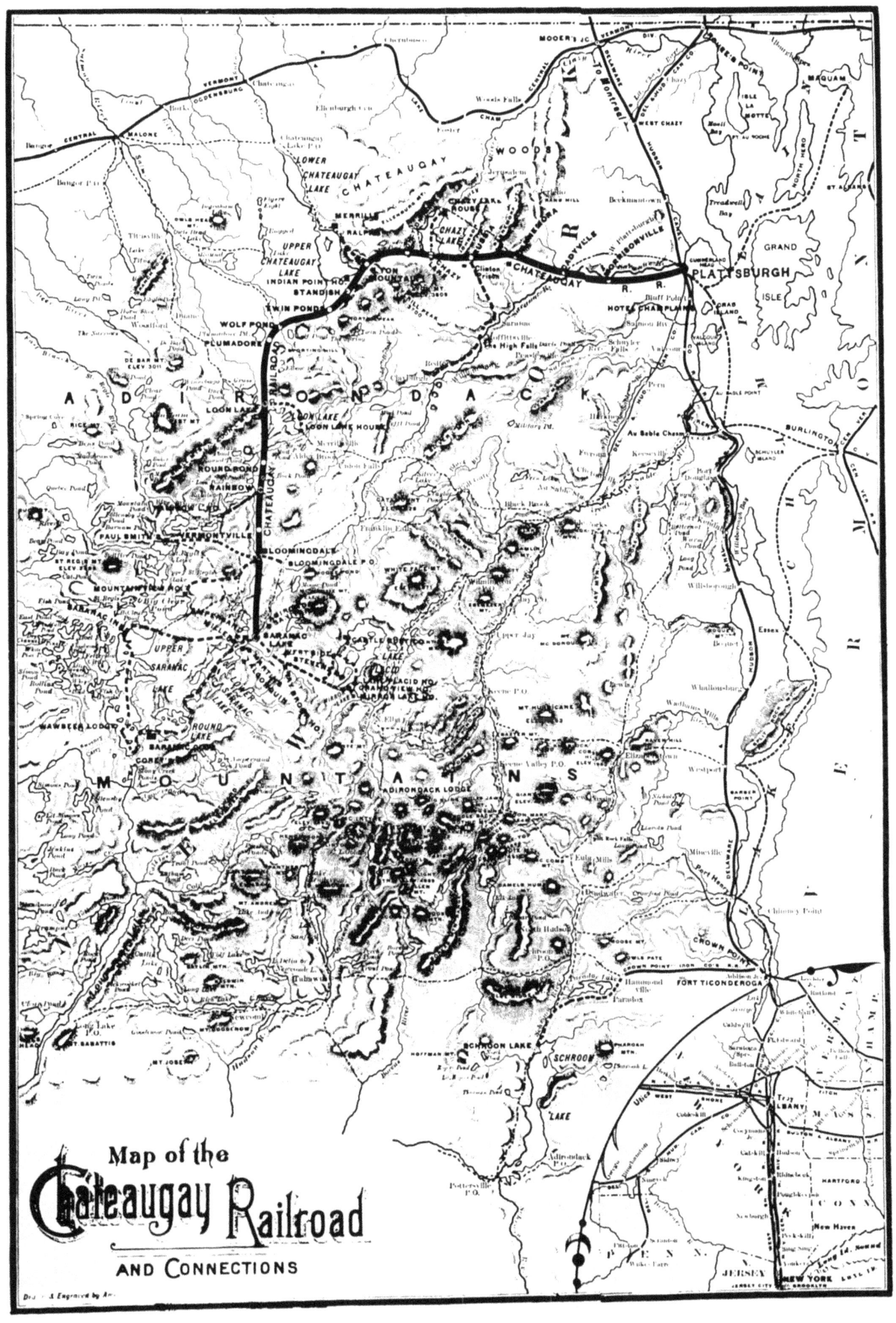

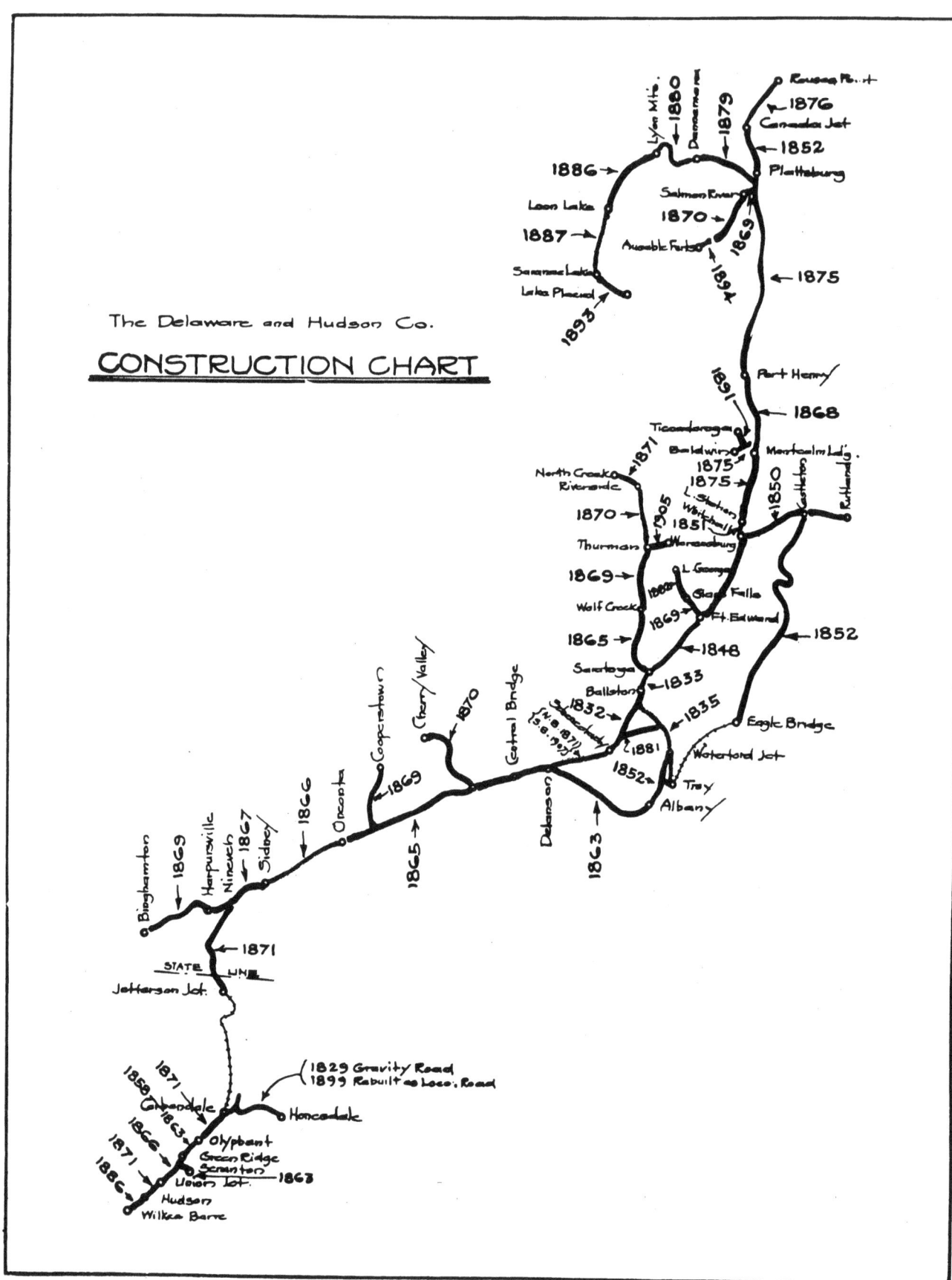

Two-year-old 4-4-0 No. 10, the LOON LAKE, with 44½-inch drivers and 15-by-20-inch cylinders was photographed near her namesake in the 1889 picture, above. At the Lyon Mountain station in the 1880 picture below, the MIRROR LAKE, No. 12, displays her unusual pilot beam with three link-and-pin coupler pockets for switching standard gauge cars in the yards down at Plattsburgh. (D&H collection, both)

S. & L. P. R. R.

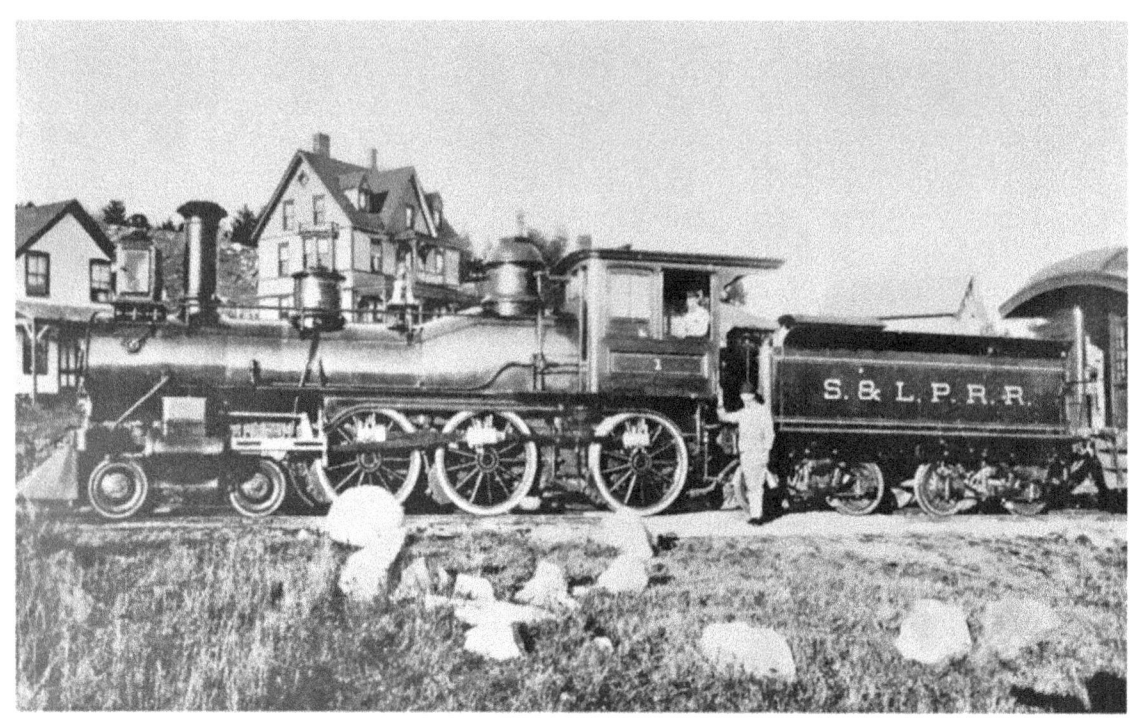

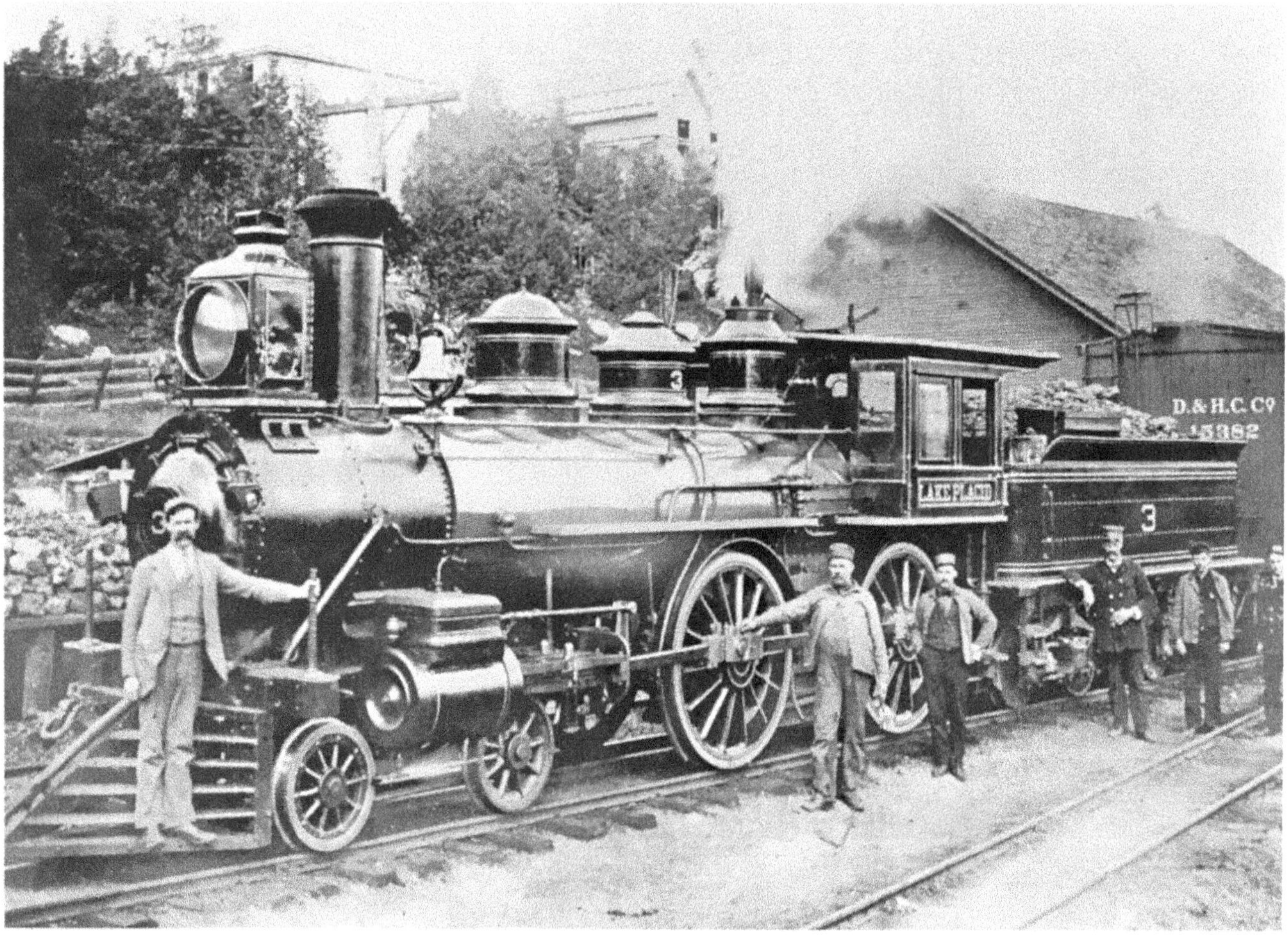
LAKE PLACID
D.&H.C.Co
3

The winter snow of the Adirondacks was the environment in which No. 11, the little St. Regis, above, had to work for at least half the year. She was built for the Chateaugay, along with her sister, No. 10, the Loon Lake, by the Dickson Manufacturing Co. in 1887. On the other page, a grand old Lake Placid summer home rises above the sand dome of No. 1 of the Saranac & Lake Placid, a standard gauge line opened in 1893 between its namesake villages. By means of a third rail, the narrow gauge Chateaugay trains could run the entire 83 miles from Plattsburgh to Lake Placid. In the lower picture, the Lake Placid stands on three-rail track at Saranac Lake, with a narrow gauge Chateaugay track in the foreground. (*D&H collection, above; G. M. Best collection, two pictures*)

The local between Caldwell, at the south end of Lake George, and the main line connections at Fort Edward was on this occasion hauled by the racy and spotlessly clean 4-4-0 No. 376. Justifiable pride is evident in the stance of the crew, lined up by it at the shore end of the Lake George pier at Caldwell. *(Fred Thatcher, from original glass plate in author's collection)*

8. A TIME TO BREAK DOWN AND A TIME TO BUILD UP*

*Ecclesiastes 3:3

With the completion of the New York & Canada, a new and prosperous era opened up for the Delaware & Hudson. While the cost of the project was substantial, its purpose was realized in that the outlet for the company's coal was considerably expanded, with access to Canada and the additional towns, as well as to the blossoming iron industry along the line itself. The managers assumed that income from the leased lines would, for a while at least, be less than the rental fees paid, and this was the case. Nevertheless, the added volume of coal marketed along these newly-acquired lines was in itself enough to make up the difference.

Several improvements in the form of additional construction were required on the NY&C in 1876, the year following its opening. Upon reaching Mooers Junction north of Plattsburgh on the Ogdensburgh & Lake Champlain, the D&H trains had to run 12 miles directly east over that company's line to Rouses Point in order to connect with the Grand Trunk Railway and Montreal. To eliminate this situation and somewhat to shorten the route, a line was built leaving the original Montreal & Plattsburgh's location at a point called Canada Junction north of West Chazy and running directly northeast to Rouses Point. The grading was started in February and the line was opened for traffic by the end of November.

Another short line, known as the Baldwin branch and stretching between the boat landing at Fort Ticonderoga and the north end of Lake George, was put into service in May of 1875. This little line afforded an important connection between the boat lines on the two lakes and would prove to be a key link in the D&H's future tourist business.

During 1873 the D&H had loaned $200,000 to the New York & Oswego Midland Railroad to acquire a line from Norwich into Utica and Rome. It was hoped that the lease of the Rome & Clinton Railroad and the Utica, Clinton & Binghamton Railroad by the NY&OM, would bolster the coal traffic up out of Carbondale for the D&H. Financial problems, a menace that would haunt the "Old and Weary" for the rest of its life, overtook the NY&OM shortly after the panic of 1873 and as a result operation of these branches fell back on the D&H for three months in order to guarantee their investment. On January 18, 1876, arrangements were made for the Delaware, Lackawanna & Western to take over the leases. Thus for a time during the slow years of business depression, the D&H's rail operations were enlarged in a manner which it did not seek.

The New England market was brought to the attention of the managers early in 1877 by the incorporation of the Boston, Hoosac Tunnel & Western Railway Co. The new organization, financed by Boston capital, proposed to open a new route between Boston and the west via Schenectady and Binghamton. This was to be accomplished by building track from the state line west to Mechanicville and on November 1, 1877 an agreement was made between the BHT&W and the D&H providing for joint operation and maintenance of the necessary facilities at Mechanicville and Eagle Bridge. The Bostonians would build the line east of Mechanicville while the D&H would handle construction from there to Schenectady. Early in 1879 the BHT&W finished its part of the line, making it possible for east-west traffic through the Hoosac Tunnel to move in almost a direct route, avoiding the delays, confusion and extra mileage involved in using junctions either north or south of Mechanicville. The D&H completed its part of the line over to Schenectady late in 1881 and this

169

Port Henry on the Lake Champlain shore was a center that handled ores from iron mines a few miles west in the Adirondacks. Above is a blast furnace of Witherbee, Sherman & Co., later part of Republic Steel Co. On the right is a two-stall roundhouse, while to the left is the D&H freight shed. The same structure appears in the distant right of the lower view. A Dickson-built 2-8-0 is at work nearby, while in the center a 2-8-0 Camelback steams under the great traveling crane that moves ore to and from the stockpile at the left. *(Sherman Free Library, Port Henry, above)*

direct route has existed ever since as one of the major rail gateways to New England.

Another project that interested the managers, and particularly President Dickson, as early as 1872 was the construction of a railroad from Albany to New York along the west bank of the Hudson. The New York & Albany Railroad Co. had been chartered in 1866 and about $40,000 was spent in setting up its organization and securing property between Albany and Rondout but beyond this, no progress had been made. During the interim, some construction had been completed on a railroad following the southern section of the proposed route under the auspices of a company called the New Jersey Midland. In this state of affairs, President Dickson presented the question to his Board in the fall of 1880: should the D&H become involved or not? This interest was prompted by an inquiry from the Erie, expressing the desire for joint control of such a line and offering its facilities in Jersey City as a terminal.

Dickson was for it, but he contented himself with summarizing the advantages and disadvantages that would follow the completion of such a line. Having guided the D&H through its period of railroad expansion, he was now ready for new conquests, pushing forward with all the persistence and vigor of his nature. Such a railroad, he urged, would put the D&H in contact with New York and Philadelphia, as well as connecting the Albany & Susquehanna division of the D&H the year around with all the towns on the west side of the Hudson. A completely independent New York-Montreal through route would be produced but he thought such a move might "provoke the hostility of the New York Central, which might culminate in an extension by them to Saratoga." A committee was appointed to confer with the Erie but nothing further came of the idea. The so-called West Shore railroad was completed by outside interests and was opened to Albany in July 1883, entering Albany over the D&H tracks from Kenwood Junction at the south end of the city.

Another communication, of far reaching significance for the D&H, was submitted to the managers a few weeks later. Dickson proposed the idea of abandoning the canal and substituting a railroad along the towpath in its place. He said, "This change I would have advocated long ago had I not been aware that there was a traditional prejudice among the members of the Board in favor of canal navigation." Arrangements had been made back in 1867 when Dickson had first become interested in the management of the company, to increase the canal's capacity by doubling all the locks at a cost of over a million dollars. Work had even begun at Honesdale, where a double lock was actually completed and put into service, but further work was postponed after he convinced then President Olyphant to study the project further.

Each year it was becoming more difficult to obtain sufficient water for the canal and compared to railroads, canals were more expensive to maintain, more liable to damage, usable during only a portion of the year, and under the most favorable conditions could not move traffic as rapidly or as cheaply as by rail. He cited facts in support of these contentions and urged "the placing of rails upon the banks of the canal, or in brief, the abandonment of water and the substitution of steel, a proposition that may be startling to those who have regarded the canal as the sheet anchor of our prosperity." He estimated that this substitution could be effected without injuring the credit pic-

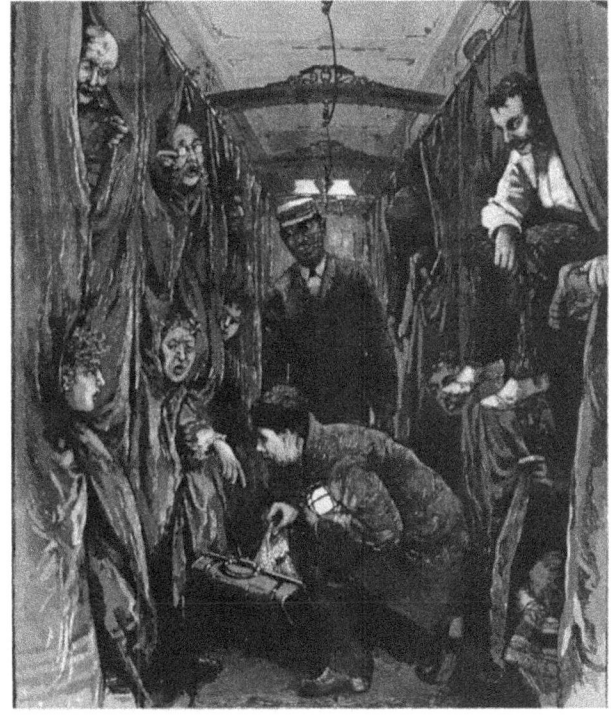

An 1883 cover picture on *Frank Leslie's Illustrated* depicted the rather dubious joys of night customs inspection in the sleeping cars at Rouses Point.

Port Henry's castle-like limestone station was built by the D&H in 1888 and is still used today, little changed. Below, the morning local up from Albany rolls north out of the station. On the hill in the background is the village, with an appearance of repose that contrasts with the industrial muscle evident in the views on page 170. *(Jean Banta collection, below)*

ture and would result in a transportation saving of $750,000 a year.

The manager considered this as well as the West Shore Railroad proposal but Dickson seems to have been somewhat in advance of the opinion of his Board and nothing definite was accomplished during his term of office. Ill winds, however, were beginning to ripple the calm waters of the old canal.

By 1881 marked improvements in the general business picture had taken place and were pleasantly reflected in the company's balance sheets. The operations of the leased lines also showed that they were comfortably self-sustaining and furnished an outlet for 750,000 tons of anthracite annually, an amount in excess of that forwarded by the Erie to western points. The increased development of the iron industry along the west side of Lake Champlain began to add to the receipts of the New York & Canada and the Rensselaer & Saratoga, and each year considerable quantities of steel rails were substituted for the rapidly wearing iron ones on these lines. In January 1880, $495,000 was appropriated for railroad improvements and within a period of about two years 35 miles of the Albany & Susquehanna line were double-tracked including the heaviest grades and the most difficult areas of operation. In addition, the standard gauging of the remaining equipment had been completed and the now-necessary third rail was removed except for about four miles at Binghamton for the convenience of Erie yard movements.

In the following year, an additional $525,000 was slated for more double track on the A&S and during the year some double-tracking took place on the railroad in Pennsylvania, between Scranton and Pittston. During 1882 additional mileage south of Carbondale and 14 miles on the A&S between Central Bridge and Richmondville was double tracked. The prosperity of the company also allowed the purchase of 12 new locomotives from the Dickson Manufacturing Co., a Scranton organization founded in 1856 by Thomas Dickson (before he was in the D&H high command) and several others. That year the company laid 3916 tons of steel rail and nearly half a million new ties.

Prosperity probably had its hand in another development that occurred in a little four-wheeled caboose one night in Oneonta. Labor organizations were beginning to spring up, mostly isolated groups with good intentions but little power; they were easily beaten into the cinders by management. Quite by chance on September 23, 1883, eight trainmen met in caboose No. 10, assigned to conductor Charles J. Woodworth, and among other current topics, discussed the formation of a better and larger association to look out for their interests. An earlier organization, a Brakeman's Brotherhood, failed to survive a strike in 1877. A short time later the Capital City Aid Association was formed in Albany by local employees as a benefit association and the trainmen and yardmen at Oneonta joined them. The Oneonta gathering that night decided to form an organization under the name of the Brotherhood of Railroad Brakemen and soon absorbed the Albany group. The Brotherhood idea spread rapidly and from this small beginning blossomed into a national organization called the Brotherhood of Railroad Trainmen on October 23, 1889.

The only new railroad construction that took place for some time, aside from extensive double-tracking, was the extension of the line north of Glens Falls to the head of Lake George at Caldwell. Just prior to the time the D&H leased the R&S, the stretch up from Fort Edward to Glens Falls was completed and opened. The D&H was currently in the process of bettering its establishment and rounding out the system, rather than embarking on any grand new plans, and informed its lessor that construction of this extension should be undertaken before the time limit expired under the existing charter of the Glens Falls Rail Road Co., which orginally obtained the rights. Accordingly, on January 8, 1881, the executive committee recommended the building of the extension, provided the rights of way could be obtained at a cost not to exceed $10,000. Although only nine miles in length, the completion of the line was not rapid and regular trains did not begin to use the new track until May 29, 1882, just in time for the summer tourist season. The line was formerly leased by the R&S and on the same day the lease was assigned to the D&H. This opened up a spectacular new tourist route whereby vacationers could leave Plattsburgh on the steamboat, sail down through Lake Champlain to Fort Ticonderoga, transfer via the previously built Baldwin branch from there to the north end of Lake

The far-flung double-tracking projects of the 1880s and succeeding years kept members of the D&H engineering department busy and on the move. For their use the Schenectady works in 1889 built the graceful inspection engine, TRANSIT. In 1922 she was rebuilt; her boiler pressure was increased from 150 to 200 pounds, her drivers from 54 to 56 inches. In depression-wracked 1933, regrettably, she was scrapped. One of the double-tracking projects on the A&S at Delanson is shown in the 1889 scene, below, with 25 short-handled shovels and an equal number of bearded operators on the flatcar; a goodly throng of other men, perhaps supervisors, stand about or perch on the tender of Dickson-built Mogul No. 274. Three more Dicksons on the opposite page are topped by the 1886 pioneer Mother Hubbard No. 61, featuring a canopy for the rear-end fireman, mounted on the tank rather than on the firebox as on subsequent Camelbacks. The pyramidal Wooton firebox was designed to burn large chunks of anthracite from the D&H's own mines. In the middle, on the armstrong turntable at Delanson roundhouse, where pusher engines were kept to help heavy trains over Richmondville Hill, is Mogul No. 177, an 1882 model named the C. N. KENDRICK. At the bottom, with a venerable hogger in her cab, a sort of midsummer Santa Claus, and guarded by an aggressive young brakeman armed with a link, is the old 1880 0-6-0T switcher No. 161, originally the THUNDERER, No. 1. She and half a dozen similar engines, served many more years, with and without tenders, until well after the turn of the century. (*G. M. Best collection, above; D&H collection*)

The Dickson Manufacturing Co. of Scranton built 1387 wonderful little locomotives from 1862 until the company was purchased by the American Locomotive Co. in 1902. One of the earlier products was D&H 4-4-0 No. 143, originally the JOHN RAYMOND, built in 1873. The engineer salutes the unknown photographer who caught this outstanding action shot sometime in the 1880s. Below, the crew of Mogul No. 80, built by Dickson in 1888, stands with the engine in the dual-gauged Carbondale yard, unperturbed by the roar and spray of her popping safety valve. On the opposite page is the caboose enshrined in Oneonta City Park. Two large placques list the founders of the Brotherhood; the middle plate's text appears below the picture. *(D&H collection, below; Jim Shaughnessy, opposite)*

BENEVOLENCE - SOBRIETY - INDUSTRY

IN THIS CABOOSE, AT ONEONTA, NEW YORK, SEPTEMBER 23, 1883, EIGHT TRAIN AND YARD EMPLOYES OF THE D. & H. C. CO. ARRANGED TO ORGANIZE THE B. OF R. R. B. THE TITLE WAS CHANGED OCTOBER 23, 1889, TO THE B. OF R. T.

PERSUADED THAT IT IS FOR THE INTERESTS BOTH OF OUR MEMBERS AND THEIR EMPLOYERS THAT A GOOD UNDERSTANDING SHOULD AT ALL TIMES EXIST BETWEEN THE TWO, IT WILL BE THE CONSTANT ENDEAVOR OF THIS ORGANIZATION TO ESTABLISH MUTUAL CONFIDENCE AND CREATE AND MAINTAIN HARMONIOUS RELATIONS.

George, steam 32 miles down through that lake—even more spectacular than Champlain—to the dock at Caldwell, board a waiting train there to roll out over the new extension and down the R&S to Albany where a connection could be made with the Hudson River Night Line for a morning arrival in Gotham. This routing soon became one of the most enchanting and sought-after trips in North America.

Early in 1884 President Dickson fell ill but nevertheless was re-elected president on May 14, only to die on July 31. Robert M. Olyphant, the younger brother of former president George Talbot Olyphant, one of the managers and the vice-president since May 1882 was immediately appointed acting president and was formally elected to that post on October 24.

The passing of Thomas Dickson was an especially sad occurrence for the D&H as he, more than any other man in the past or future history of the company, was responsible for shaping both the map and the destiny of the organization. It was through his efforts and with his untiring guidance that the D&H embarked on its railroad career. Then, after building some lines and leasing others, he sewed the parts together with interconnecting stretches of track to form a unified, efficient and smooth-working network stretching out from the mines in Pennsylvania to wide areas of the northeast and New England.

In the fall of 1884, General Ulysses S. Grant, national hero and former President of the United States, was stricken with cancer and lay suffering in the oppressive heat of New York City. The General's physician, Dr. J. H. Douglas, had a friend named Joseph Drexel who owned a cottage near the Balmoral Hotel on Mount McGregor in the hills a few miles north of Saratoga. Mr. Drexel offered the house to the doctor for the use of his distinguished patient so the General might be somewhat more comfortable away from the heat and humidity of the city. This offer was quickly and graciously accepted and the General, along with his doctor and several members of his family,

The free stage which carried people from the boat pier and the green D&H station up to the Crown Point House was for many years drawn by Philo and Lib, above, who with Driver Hayes await the arrival of the morning train up from Albany. The ornate William Henry Hotel, overlooking the south end of Lake George, was built in 1858 and soon turned out to be a means of developing and promoting tourist traffic on D&H trains and steamboats. Until completion of the nine-mile extension from Glens Falls to the lake in 1882, access to the lake was by stage. Photographer S. R. Stoddard has here pictured the stage heavily loaded with well-dressed passengers, about to leave the hotel to connect with the cars at Glens Falls. *(Ned Spaulding collection, above)*

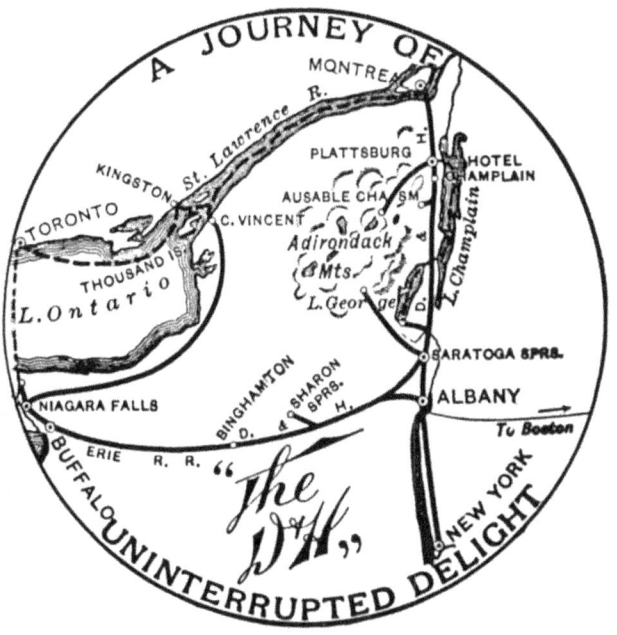

THE SARATOGA LINE.

Delaware and Hudson Canal Co.'s R.R.

THE ONLY COMFORTABLE ROUTE TO

THE ADIRONDACKS,

AND THE ONLY LINE TO

Saratoga, Lake George, Sharon Springs, Howe's Cave, and Cooperstown.

THE SHORTEST ROUTE TO MONTREAL AND THE PROVINCES.

TO THE WHITE MOUNTAINS,

VIA SARATOGA, LAKE GEORGE, LAKE CHAMPLAIN, AND BURLINGTON.

No other route can offer as great attraction, for, by special arrangement, all-rail tickets reading via DELAWARE AND HUDSON CANAL CO.'S R. R. are accepted on the Lake Champlain Steamers. *See that your tickets read via this route.*

Tickets and Time-Tables at all the principal Railroad Ticket Offices in the United States. For information, apply to

J. W. BURDICK, *Gen. Pass. Agent,* ALBANY, N.Y.

Soon after expansion of the line from Glens Falls to Lake George in 1882, No. 218 and her passenger train hit a soft spot in the roadbed at Glen Lake with the unpleasant result shown below. If it weren't for the long exposures required by the slow early photographic plates, the blurred image of an approaching train would suggest imminent disaster. Fortunately this was not the case. *(Jean Banta collection)*

The elegant ornamentation of the Wagner Palace Car and the clothing of the people on the Lake George pier, above, display the tastes of affluent Americans in the 1890s. The ladies' hats reflect varied styles, with the fedora evidently favored by the younger set. Another sample of the elegance of the 1890s is the steam yacht *Ellide*, below, riding a flatcar down the makeshift launching track by the steamboat dock at Baldwin, near the northern end of Lake George. The winch on the first flatcar will allow the boat to roll gently down the ramp into the water. The fireman on Dickson-built Mogul No. 313 had cramped quarters in the cab, but he perhaps didn't mind, as he was usually down in the gangway, shoveling. *(Fred Thatcher, from original plates in author's collection)*

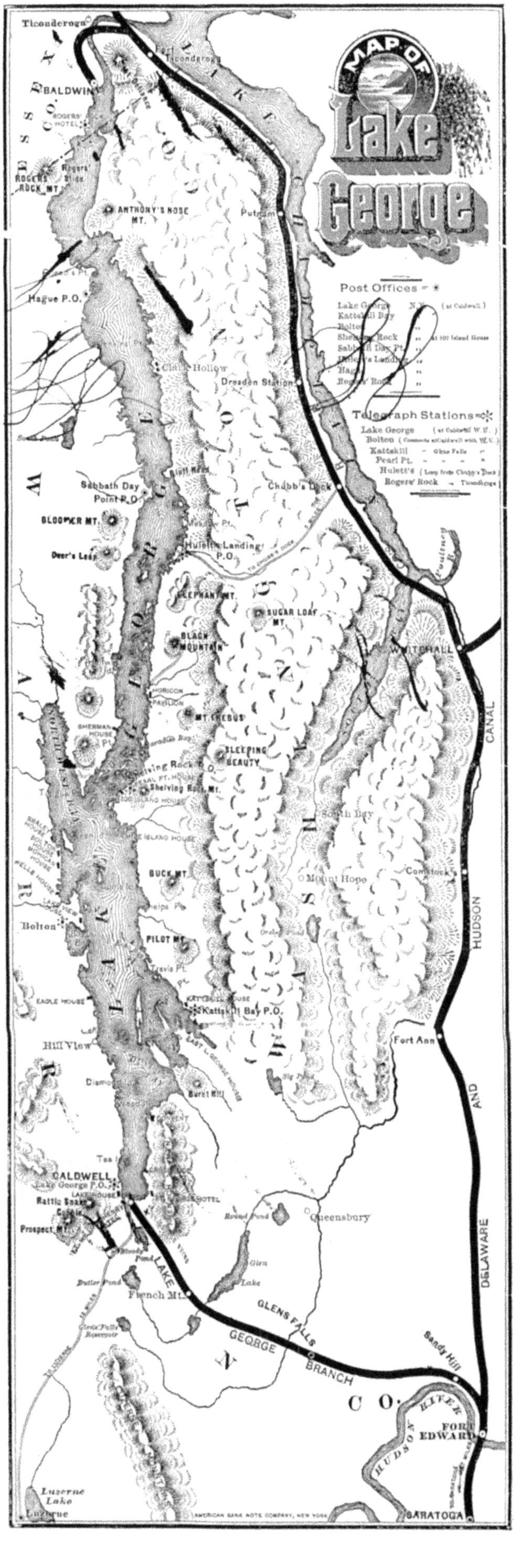

Robert M. Olyphant was sixth president of the D&H from 1884 to 1903. The map of Lake George is from an 1885 D&H timetable. *(Carl Wooley collection, map)*

arrived in Saratoga Springs on June 16. There a large group of local residents and summer people eagerly greeted the old soldier when he transferred from the D&H train to the little three-foot gauge Saratoga, Mount McGregor & Lake George Railroad for the 11-mile trip up to the mountain.

Although the General was pleased with the place and its surroundings, his throat cancer became increasingly painful and prevented him from enjoying it, as well as interrupting work on the completion of his memoirs, an effort he was desperately trying to complete with what little strength he had left. Old friends and sometimes dignitaries junketed up the mountain on the little train to see the failing hero, but he wasn't always able to meet them and when he could, it would only be briefly. He had to converse with them via pad and pencil as he could only speak in a whisper and even then with difficulty. His family and the nation eagerly looked for improvement but the old soldier must have known his battle with this unseen enemy—his last—was being lost. Five weeks after his arrival on the mountain, at 8:08 a.m. July 23, 1885, Ulysses Simpson "Unconditional Surrender" Grant, hero of the Civil War who forced Lee to surrender at Appomattox, 18th

Hundreds of mourners watch silently as the remains of General Grant are brought into Saratoga Springs station behind tank engine No. 1 of the Saratoga, Mount McGregor & Lake George. On the adjacent track is the D&H funeral train which appears below, behind heavily-creped 4-4-0 No. 210, with a baggage car, the bunting-draped funeral car *Woodlawn,* Wagner drawing room cars *Excelsior, Highland* and *Catskill* and four New York Central & Hudson River coaches. (*Al Gayer collection, above; D&H collection*)

President of the United States and a legend in his own time—slipped away to the ages.

Plans immediately were made for returning the old soldier's body to New York. The funeral car *Woodlawn* was brought up from New York and the D&H began draping a new passenger engine, 4-4-0 No. 210, with 350 yards of black crepe in the Green Island shops.

Early in the afternoon of August 4, the little Mount McGregor train eased down off the mountain with the body and the mourners aboard. At Saratoga Springs the cortege transferred to the waiting D&H train for the run to Albany. There the body was transported in a solemn procession up to the State Capitol where it lay in state overnight. The following day it was returned to the station and moved to New York on the New York Central & Hudson River Railroad.

General Ulysses Simpson Grant, 1822-1885. (*Grant Cottage Museum, Mount McGregor, New York*)

DELAWARE & HUDSON CANAL CO.

NORTHERN R. R. DEPARTMENT.

SARATOGA DIVISION.

SPECIAL TIME SCHEDULE
— FOR —
FUNERAL TRAIN
GEN. U. S. GRANT,
TUESDAY, AUGUST 4TH, 1885.

Leave SARATOGA,	2.20 P. M.
" BALLSTON,	2.35 "
" HIGH STREET,	2.37 "
" EAST LINE,	2.41 "
" ROUND LAKE,	2.48 "
" COONS,	2.55 "
" MECHANICVILLE,	3.00 "
" WATERFORD JUNCTION,	3.14 "
" WEST WATERFORD,	3.17 "
" COHOES,	3.22 "
" WEST TROY,	3.28 "
" CEMETERY,	3.32 "
" ALBANY (N. Y. C. & H. R. R. R. Depot),	3.40 "

This train will make no stops and will have the right of way over all other trains. Employees will be governed accordingly.

H. G. YOUNG,   THEODORE VOORHEES,
Ass't Gen'l Manager,   Superintendent,
ALBANY, N. Y.   ALBANY, N. Y.

It was Robert M. Olyphant's policy to improve and upgrade the railroad and he pursued this goal with the same enthusiasm and vigor during the latter half of the 1880s as his predecessor Thomas Dickson had demonstrated during the railroad expansion period several years earlier. During 1886 many improvements were made on the Pennsylvania division including the double-tracking of all but one short stretch of the line south of Carbondale. Passenger revenues on the gravity road were considerably bolstered by a picnic ground built on the summit of the Moosic Mountains at Farview. Quite a large quantity of new equipment was acquired during the period including 18 locomotives and 1200 freight cars in 1888 alone.

Saratoga's popularity as a watering place and summer resort grew steadily and achieved even new heights in the late 1880s and early 1890s. Business on the D&H reached such volumes that double-tracking of the line up from Troy was nec-

The Saratoga, Mount McGregor & Lake George Railway was built in 1882, 10.5 miles of three-foot gauge from the spa to the mountain, but it never reached the lake. It had two of these 0-4-2T engines, with a tall spark arrester that, in the upper picture, can be seen folded down onto a semicircular holder atop the dome. The train here is at Saratoga Springs station, adjacent to the standard gauge tracks. Below, the little train has stopped on one of the many wooden trestles on the 7% grade between Wilton and the mountain. In 1883 the company built the Balmoral Hotel which generated enough traffic to keep the trains running summers. After 1888 the company was beset by financial troubles and changed hands several times before the hotel burned down in 1898. The roadbed from Saratoga to Wilton was later used by an electric interurban, the Hudson Valley Railway. *(Ed Bond collection, above)*

essary to handle the density of trains moving over that stretch; special trains of Wagners rolled up from New York and on to the Springs. During the August thoroughbred races, solid trains of horse cars would burnish the rails into the spa, followed by more specials filled with Kentucky bluegrass and other special feeds for the elite of the barnyard set. The spa was the "in" place to be and Vanderbilts, Rockefellers, Morgans and the like flocked in, followed by hundreds of steamer trunks and champagne cases. The court of the United States Hotel was the center of activity in the Edith Wharton years and displayed a fashion and splendor unequalled anywhere short of Bond Street in London or the Champs Élysées in Paris. The Grand Union and the Grand Hotels were ranked equally with or perhaps a close second to the United States, but all reflected the spaciousness, tranquility and ease of Saratoga's great days in a world of cold bottles, fast horses and blue chips.

The D&H's business, both coal and rail, had been blessed with large receipts in the late 1880s and considerable earnings were accumulated. Late in April of 1889, the railroad committee recommended the purchase of about 80% of the stock in the Adirondack Railway from W. W. Durant, son of Thomas C. Durant, the original builder of the line. This little line ran northwest out of Saratoga Springs into the heart of the Adirondacks. It was the elder Durant's dream to build on through the mountains to the Great Lakes, tapping the rich resources of iron and lumber en route. Alas, it never came about, but the line did provide access to a great vacation wonderland that was becoming more and more interesting to the D&H and its passenger sales representatives. The tourist business to Saratoga and the Champlain valley was already booming and this would add handsomely to the areas accessible over D&H rails, and the purchase was made.

In a further effort to develop the passenger business later in the year, especially the summer earnings of the New York & Canada, President Olyphant was authorized to acquire an interest in the projected Hotel Champlain, on Bluff Point overlooking Lake Champlain several miles south of Plattsburgh. This expenditure, $250,000 in bonds and $75,000 in stock of the hotel corporation, although not an investment directly in the betterment of the railroad plant itself, did improve

1876 ARRANGEMENTS 1876
FOR
Saratoga Springs!
COMMENCING JUNE 27
VIA
Boston & Albany and Delaware & Hudson Canal Co. Line.

Drawing Room Cars Through without Change Daily (Except Sundays.)

LEAVE		LEAVE	
Boston,	8.30 A. M.	Springfield,	11.45 A. M.
S. Framingham,	9.07 "	Westfield,	12.03 P. M.
Worcester,	9.55 "	Pittsfield,	1.30 "
Palmer,	11.07 "	Chatham,	2.19 "

Arriving at SARATOGA SPRINGS 4.45 P. M.

PASSENGERS FOR BOSTON and Principal Points on B. & A. R. R., LEAVE SARATOGA at 8.30 A. M., arriving in Boston 4.45 P. M.

Office Boston & Albany R. R.
Springfield, June 21, 1876.

Weaver, Shipman & Co., Printers, Springfield, Mass.

The charms and attractions of Saratoga Springs were so famous by 1876 that they needed no mention in this advertisement directed to New Englanders.

patronage of the railroad and therefore served its purpose. The Champlain Hotel became a pet project of the president and he devoted a notable share of his personal attention to the development and improvement of both the hotel itself and the passenger service throughout the area covered by the leased lines. In June of 1893 dining car service was inaugurated between Whitehall and Montreal as just one more facet of the program. The Champlain Hotel became the finest and most picturesque hotel in the Champlain valley and as a crowning achievement, served President McKinley as the summer White House for several weeks during the season of 1897.

The snow-draped Dickson-built Mogul, left, with another behind it, battled its way through heavy drifts to Bath Street crossing in Ballston Spa following a March 1888 blizzard that left 46.7 inches of snow on the landscape. That frigid scene contrasts with three sunny views of Saratoga Springs in the glory days of the spa. The gateway, of course, was the D&H station, above; the railroad yards were very near the United States Hotel, below. Grandest, perhaps, of all the great Saratoga hotels was the Grand Union, opposite below, where W. H. Vanderbilt sat on the porch during racing season, barking betting instructions to his commissioners. *(J. S. Wooley, left)*

187

Every September during the 1890s and the early 1900s, Saratoga Springs held a Floral Festival not unlike Pasadena's Tournament of Roses. The D&H was twice represented in 1896. Its inspection engine TRANSIT was modeled half size in flowers and given a crew of costumed children. Below are the results of artistic efforts by engineer Jack Howe, near the pilot, and fireman Augustus Bradley, who adorned their Dickson-built Mogul No. 107 with garlands, deer heads and floral lettering on the tank. She had the run between Saratoga and Lake George and was the hit of the day when she rolled into the Springs that morning. *(Art Bibb collection, above; D&H collection)*

The Champlain Hotel at Bluff Point was built in 1890, with D&H aid, as President Olyphant hoped to promote passenger traffic on the New York & Canada. It became the finest establishment in the Champlain Valley. An army of waiters manned the great dining room and music of the masters pervaded the lobby. President McKinley used the hotel as his summer White House during 1897. This building burned on May 25, 1910, but by then the D&H owned it outright and quickly replaced the old structure with a new one that was ready for the 1911 guests. *(S. R. Stoddard, N. Y. collection, Feinberg Library, State University College at Plattsburgh, two pictures; J. S. Wooley from original negative in author's collection, below)*

In August, 1897, President McKinley rode the three-foot gauge Chateaugay Railroad from the summer White House at Champlain Hotel to Saranac Lake, where we see him holding his top hat on the rear platform of the coach at Saranac Lake. Below him on the step is portly Vice President Garret A. Hobart; Mrs. Hobart, with the flowers, and Mrs. McKinley stand behind the President and behind them is the tall railroad president, Smith M. Weed. Other company officials and their children are in the picture, but no guards for the President. *(D&H collection)*

A similar interest was soon acquired in the Fort William Henry Hotel overlooking the south end of Lake George at the village of Caldwell, later renamed Lake George Village in 1903. The D&H could provide the traveler with the best and most splendid accommodations, whether it was in one of these fine hotels, aboard its fleet of lake steamers or on the high iron and President Olyphant's plan to increase passenger business flourished. How could it be otherwise?

During the winter of 1889 the great "ice rush" occurred on the D&H. Ordinarily Capital District ice houses were usually stocked with ice for the summer from local bodies of water but in that year, due to a particularly mild winter, none of the local area ice pounds froze over and ice had to be brought south from Ballston Lake and Lake Champlain. For several weeks every available car and locomotive was kept running the 77 miles between Whitehall and Albany with 350-ton trainloads of ice to stock the empty ice houses of Albany, Troy and Schenectady so that father's beer would be cool and mother's butter wouldn't turn rancid during the following summer.

As it became available, the D&H had gradually bought up stock in the Rutland Railroad and by 1887 had enough to control the line. The Central Vermont had leased this Vermont railroad since

1871, a move which in fact cleared the way for the building of the New York & Canada on the west side of the lake.

The CV's 20-year lease of the Rutland expired at the end of 1890 and the D&H, now the majority stockholder, authorized a renewal of the lease. The D&H had taken an interest in the Rutland as a means of possible expansion into New England but was satisfied for the time being to collect the regular rental fee sent down by the CV.

Adding to the general problems President Olyphant faced on his own line following the panic of 1893, he received notice from the CV not to expect any more rental checks for their lease of the Rutland after March. As a result, the now-orphaned Rutland undoubtedly would not be able to meet its obligations and in order to protect its stock interest in the company, the D&H would have to come to the rescue. Only two weeks prior to this disagreeable development Mr. Olyphant had to borrow $450,000 for his own company as a part of the year's financing. There was no escaping this outlay if the Rutland were to survive, and the cash was reluctantly sent forthwith.

In 1898, after several years of nursing the Rutland along, the D&H became disenchanted with the idea of expansion into New England and seized the opportunity on October 22 to unload its Rutland stock to Rutland banker Percival W. Clement. Clement was seeking to control the line and fell into 30,000 shares of preferred and 10,000 shares of common stock at a most attractive price, as the D&H was now anxious to get out from under the burden and uncertainties connected with that shaky Vermont line.

Probably the most significant move of the decade—and one of the saddest, if you consider the heritage involved and the contribution made to the overall prosperity and development of the company down through the years since its inception by the Wurtz brothers—was the move to abandon the canal. Only a small amount of coal

A passenger train from Rutland to Troy, via the Salem-Cambridge-Eagle Bridge route of the old Rutland & Washington, crosses the high bridge over Otter Creek in Center Rutland, Vermont, behind 4-4-0 No. 397.

Abandonment of the canal was soon followed by standard-gauging of the gravity, and a couple of new sections were built to change the line into a regular steam road, the Honesdale branch. Here the little Dickson-built Mogul No. 45 pulls out of the terminal and across the now-abandoned canal basin on a bridge strengthened by driving piles into the canal bed. The old gravity cars were first used on the new steam road, with standard gauge trucks, but were soon replaced by regular equipment. The track gang working beyond the bridge indicates that this view was made soon after the gauge change in 1899.

moved through the old waterway in 1897, so little in fact that on November 24 Mr. Olyphant recommended that $6795 be distributed to the boatmen to help relieve their impoverished families. This was nothing new; several previous years were as bad. With the network of railroads, including the D&H's own lines, now available to market the coal both more cheaply and to a vastly wider market, the old canal was left literally in the dust and smoke of progress.

The year of decision was 1898 indeed.

On October 26 the powerful railroad committee reported to the managers that great economies would result by transporting the company's anthracite directly from the mines to the Hudson River at Weehawken by means of existing railroads, namely the Erie, rather than the present routing over the Gravity line and the Canal. The whole idea was nothing new — Thomas Dickson had proposed the idea back in the fall of 1880 — but nothing had come of the proposal despite a continuing decline in volume, at least not until now.

The question had been on the horizon for many years but now things fell into place with almost terrifying rapidity. Ten days later, on November 5 boat No. 1107 was loaded and cleared Honesdale for tidewater with the last lumps of coal ever to move down the Canal.

The Gravity road continued to operate, but only for the movement of passengers. January 3rd of the following year was the last day of operation for the Gravity when several loads of coal that had accumulated at various points were run off and more than 4600 cars were moved to convenient locations for disposal. On the following day the fires in the stationary boilers at the head of the planes were dropped and they cooled off forever.

Work began immediately and moved along rapidly on converting portions of the gravity line into a locomotive road. This involved moving each rail out 2¾" from its original position making the 4'3" gauge into standard. This job was finished by January 22 and 23.74 miles of the old road were opened for regular locomotive operation.

Naturally, the steep inclined planes could not be negotiated by any regular locomotive so the route was altered to comply with a more conventional railroad. From Carbondale the loaded car track was used south to the junction of both lines near Bushwick. Here the light car track down from the summit was picked up and used as the main line up the mountain to the head of Plane No. 20. From this point, a new stretch of track was built south to the town of South Canaan where a wide horseshoe curve swung the route back up to Waymart. The new line required 6.16 miles on an 80 feet per mile grade to cover the same distance, accomplished in only 1.25 miles up the incline via cable. From Waymart on into Honesdale, the old loaded car track served as the rebuilt stretch of line.

The standard gauge trains operated around the famous Shepherd's Crook curve for a time but the short radius proved to be an excessive strain on the equipment and a switchback replaced the familiar landmark. The switchback was called Panther Bluffs and its existence required all passenger trains leaving Carbondale to run with the engine operating tender-first, at the head end of the train as far as the switchback. There the engine was run around the train allowing a normal-looking arrival at Honesdale. On freight movements, the helper engine at the rear of the train ran backwards out of Carbondale so that no time was lost at the switchback, where the helper became the road engine for the remainder of the trip.

The old gravity passenger cars were equipped with standard gauge trucks and used in the passenger service provided on what was now called the Honesdale branch, but after about a year vanished from the line as regular equipment from other parts of the system replaced them. The old

Last boat to be loaded with coal at Honesdale was No. 1107, Captain Hensberger. She started her six-day 108-mile trip to Rondout on November 5, 1898 and ended an era that would never be forgotten. *(Manville B. Wakefield collection, two pictures)*

Honesdale was hardly recognizable after the boat basin was filled in and the new station and a yard were built where legions of canal boats once gathered. The new standard gauge steam line entered the city from the left distance over what had been the loaded gravity line. The embarrassing 1900 "service interruption," below, occurred right in front of Putnam station on the shore of Lake Champlain. The relatively new Alco 4-4-0 was working a northbound passenger run, while the venerable Dickson 4-6-0 had a southbound freight. *(D&H collection, above; G. M. Best collection)*

gravity passenger cars along with the open excursion cars were sold off to become chicken coops and summer camps and dotted the countryside of Wayne County for many years as a reminder of the glory days of the Gravity.

After Captain Hensberger guided boat No. 1107 down through the canal in November the old waterway lay unused, its future uncertain beyond the fact the D&H was finished with it as a means of moving coal to market. It was hoped that the New York, Ontario & Western Railway, the Pennsylvania Coal Co., or the Erie Railroad might be interested in buying it, and although negotiations were initiated, nothing developed. Finally, on June 13, 1899, the entire canal with all its franchises, rights and privileges was sold for a mere $10,000 to S. D. Coykendall, President of the Cornell Steamboat Co. of Rondout.

The new owners just operated the section from Ellenville to Rondout, and then for only two seasons. Finally, just a few boatloads of cement occasionally moved down from Rosendale, and five years after the D&H sold the canal, all operations ceased.

At their February 1899 meeting, the D&H managers had given official sanction for the canal's abandonment and adopted a resolution that the company cease to operate its canal and the officers be authorized to take such action as may be necessary to accomplish this end. It was further resolved to take the necessary steps to change its corporate title from the President, Managers and Company of the Delaware and Hudson Canal Co. to simply the Delaware & Hudson Co.

By a special act in April, the New York Legislature confirmed this change in the corporate name, and by so doing formally started the heritage of the old canal on its long journey down through the corridors of history. It was with a keen sense of sadness that this link with the past was broken but the canal and the glory days of its existence would live on forever.

The 36 summer passenger cars used on the gravity railroad since 1877 became surplus and were scrapped when the canal was closed and the gravity railroad was standard gauged and converted to steam. (G. M. Best collection)

195

Theodore Roosevelt did not know it at the moment pictured above, but he had become 26th President of the United States the previous night, while he was in a lurching buckboard, riding forty miles down from the Tahawas Club, near Mount Marcy, to North Creek station. There D&H Superintendent C. D. Hammond gave him the telegram notifying him of the death of President McKinley and signaled the waiting crew to get the special train going on its twisting 98-mile dash to Albany. *(Don Walworth, above; Adirondack Museum, diorama below)*

9. BRANCHING OUT

Short line railroads have often had lives in some ways like those of highly independent men. Born rugged individualists, they frequently died young or were wedded into oblivion, but while they lasted they plodded back and forth, doing their best to earn an honest living through the performance of routine chores. It has been said that in each humdrum life there comes a moment of glory. This happened to the old Adirondack Railway—now almost completely lost in the D&H's corporate structure and physical system—on the night of September 13, 1901.

Teddy Roosevelt had long been a lover of the Adirondack country, and was a principal figure in the setting aside of vast areas of the mountains to be retained as "forever wild" country. On this fateful night, the young Vice-President of the United States could thank Providence that he was again in his beloved mountains, and earlier that day had climbed Mount Marcy. He was a marked man. The killer whose gun struck down President William McKinley in Buffalo had also marked the President's second in command for death. Believing the President to be recovering, five days after the attack of September 5, Roosevelt had quietly detrained at North Creek. From here, he traveled the 40 miles to the upper clubhouse of the Tahawus Club, ten miles from the nearest telephone, in a buckboard wagon. And from the Tahawus Club he pushed even deeper into the woods, setting up camp at Lake Colden. That same night in Washington, the President suffered a relapse.

An urgent message clicked over the wires to North Creek, to be delivered by any means possible. A rudimentary telephone line got it part way; a galloping horseman the rest.

Roosevelt's secretary, Will Loeb, had been left in Albany, and he immediately notified Delaware & Hudson officials of the emergency. A special train was made up and rushed to Saratoga Springs and on to North Creek, under the personal charge of Superintendent C. D. Hammond, to be placed at the Vice-President's disposal. Everything was cleared, and the special rolled into North Creek before noon—two hours and fifteen minutes out of Albany over ninety-eight miles, most of it wavy, crooked single track. The crew hurriedly turned, coaled and watered . . . and waited.

Steam feathered from the pop valves, the engineer oiled and checked around a dozen times while the tallowpot skipped innumerable stones on the river across from the station. The regular afternoon train pulled in, shifted around and chuffed off again, down the valley for Saratoga Springs.

The shadow of Gore Mountain lengthened across the valley, and finally night settled down over the upper Hudson.

Roosevelt had received the message high on the slopes of Mount Marcy shortly after lunch, and made a leisurely descent to the Tahawus clubhouse, arriving at dusk. Since no further news was waiting there, he decided to spend the night and leave for the railroad in the morning.

In the North Creek station, the crew idled away the hours while the Super dozed fitfully with one ear open for the sounder. The operator sharpened his pencils and laid them beside a fresh pad. Wisps of fog rose up over the dark, panting hulk of the waiting Mogul. At ten o'clock the sounder chattered into life and the op's flashing pencil spelled out the message, "The President is dying!"

Early in the 1900s the D&H lines were modernized in many ways. High speed was possible on the section between Ballston Spa and Saratoga Springs, along which the *Saratoga Limited* roars, above, paralleled by the electric line used by the Hudson Valley and Schenectady interurbans. High speed was less feasible in the spectacular vicinity of Willsboro Bay, but safe travel was expedited by block signals there. (*J. S. Wooley, both; Industrial Photo Service, above*)

The telephone repeated the message at the end of the wire, and once again the horseman galloped his lonely way through the blackness of the night.

At eleven o'clock Roosevelt climbed into the buckboard and his host, swinging the team into the woods road, lashed the horses into a reckless run. The mountain roads, never good, were soft and treacherous from the fall rains. The 40-mile drive, lighted up by a flickering lantern, was made in three relays that had been arranged by a local stage company.

Dawn was tinging the eastern sky when at 5:30 the mud-caked buckboard lurched into North Creek's main street. Word had passed, and an anxious knot of citizens had gathered at the station. With the first rattle of the speeding wagon, the weary train crew, that had been called nearly 24 hours earlier, climbed to its position. Engineer George Hydorn checked his pressure and leaned out for the signal.

Roosevelt went from wagon to car steps in almost one leap; Hammond handed him a telegram and waved the highball in almost a single motion. Hydorn cracked the throttle and got a wheel under the Mogul; fast-moving exhausts echoed up and down the valley along with the two sharp whistle blasts.

In the coach Roosevelt ripped open the telegram. President McKinley was dead! Somewhere on the side of the Boreas River, in the dark of the Adirondack night, clinging to a careening wagon, Theodore Roosevelt had become the 26th President of the United States.

The Saratoga Limited. With the turn of the century, new heights of luxury and elegance were brought to the passenger accommodations on American railroads and in 1900 the Delaware & Hudson joined with the New York Central & Hudson River Railroad to bring out the most important passenger innovation of the season, the *Saratoga Limited*. It began running in July, leaving Grand Central Station every afternoon except Sunday, and after being turned over to the D&H at Troy, arrived at Saratoga in time for dinner. It returned from the Spa after an early breakfast and arrived in the City in time for the financiers on board to have a full afternoon of trading before the Exchange closed.

All the cars were built especially for the service by the Wagner Palace Car Co. at its Buffalo

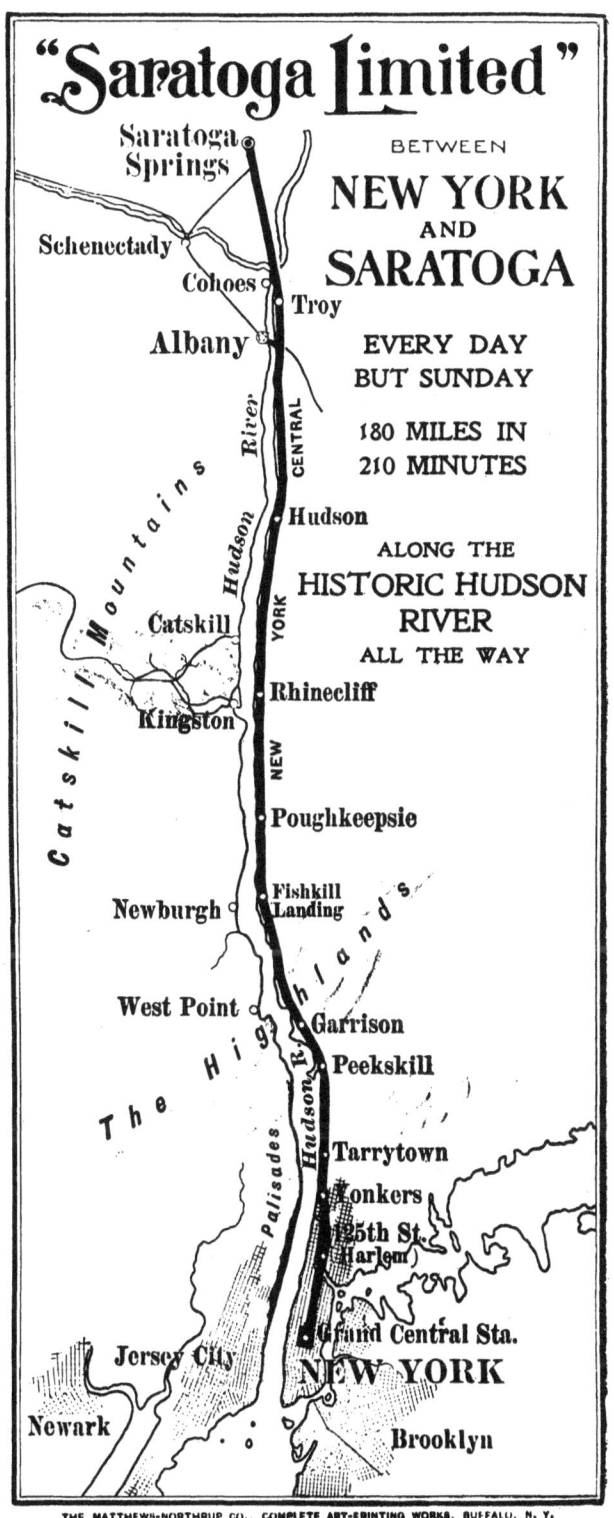

The *Saratoga Limited*, inaugurated in 1901, was the favorite means of reaching the spa by those who invariably demanded the finest of accommodations. It left Grand Central in the afternoon and reached Saratoga in time for dinner.

199

Spectators at the scene of this North Albany mishap seem more interested in the photographer than in the still-steaming 0-6-0. The Cooperstown & Charlotte Valley Railroad, which the D&H purchased in 1903, crossed the D&H tracks at Cooperstown Junction, by the bridge, below, on which the venerable 4-4-0 stands with a short train. The dirt road passing under the trestle in front of the engine is now State Highway 7. *(Ed Van Wormer collection, above; G. M. Best collection)*

works, and they made one of the handsomest and most superb trains in the world. In the consist were a combination buffet, a smoking and library car that provided all the comforts and conveniences of a first class club, four large parlor cars which were unusually roomy and attractive, and a combined parlor and observation car with large plate glass windows from which the traveler could view and enjoy the beautiful panorama of the Palisades and the majestic Hudson River to the utmost. The interior arrangements were complete, and especially rich and harmonious. It compared favorably in artistic effects, good taste and luxurious comfort with the New York Central's *Lake Shore Limited*, and in running time with the *Empire State Express*, itself the world-wide hallmark of speed in those days. This train inaugurated a new era of pleasure for the many travelers between the metropolis and America's greatest watering-place. Many New Yorkers made regular trips during the summer season, and invariably demanded the very best.

Railroading, as an art, progressed so rapidly after the turn of the century that the D&H was hard-pressed to keep up with the times.

Automatic signaling had come of age and a great new generation of motive power and equipment rolled out of the erecting halls of Dickson and Schenectady. The coal business was especially good in 1901, with 4,667,387 tons produced by D&H mines and over 7,500,000 tons carried over its rail network. A good part of the earnings from this activity were allocated for the installation of block signals on the Saratoga Division—to help maintain the safety and fast schedule of the *Saratoga Limited*—and for the acquisition of new rolling stock and motive power.

Despite the general prosperity that prevailed all over the country at the turn of the century, the Chateaugay Ore & Iron Co. found itself in a stormy state of affairs, financially. The D&H held one-fifth interest in the outfit and the situation early in 1901 gave the managers some degree of concern over the future prospects of their Adirondack Mountain stepchild. By November it was clear that the interest on its mortgage bonds could not be paid and a reorganization was necessary.

The D&H was enjoying a sizeable volume of traffic generated by the ore company, coming to it via the Chateaugay Railroad; this business

David Willcox was seventh president of the D&H, from 1903 to 1907.

would be completely lost should mine operations be discontinued. A plan was worked out whereby the D&H would guarantee a million and a half dollars worth of ore company bonds at an additional expenditure by the D&H of a mere $24,000, and this would be necessary only if the ore company was unsuccessful. This gave the D&H full stock control of the ore company, as well as the Chateaugay Railroad, and the additional lines operated under lease, extending all the way to Lake Placid.

On October 30, 1902, the Adirondack Railway Co. conveyed all its property to the D&H and by November 5 it was formally merged, thereby losing even its paper identity. D&H power and equipment had been used on the line since 1890.

Robert M. Olyphant, who had been president since 1884, was advancing in years, and his health

201

was precarious. Following the stockholders' meeting of May 13, 1903, he declined re-election to the D&H presidency. David Willcox, who had been general counsel and vice-president since 1889, was elected in his place and Mr. Olyphant became chairman of the executive committee, where he provided invaluable service and advice for several more years. The administration of David Willcox can be characterized by improvement and modernization of the physical plant, simplification of the corporate structure—to which his training as a lawyer no doubt contributed, and by broader new financing and diversification.

Soon after Mr. Willcox became president, the D&H purchased stock control of the Cooperstown & Charlotte Valley Railroad for $112,500 in June of 1903. This line connected with the D&H just north of Oneonta, New York, and the main reason for acquiring it was to block any extension of the New York & Mohawk Valley Railroad, which had recently been incorporated and might pick up this road and encroach on D&H territory. The C&CV was completely self-sustaining and the traffic from it supplied over $43,000 of earnings to the Susquehanna Division of the D&H, a condition that would be quite different if the little road fell into other hands.

Closer relations were established with the Champlain Transportation Co. in the summer of 1903. This company had been chartered in 1826 and operated extensive steamboat services on both Lake George and Lake Champlain. It had just built two new boats costing about $350,000, and the D&H had assisted in the project to the tune of $45,000, for which it received stock adding to what was already a majority interest. On July 16, President Willcox arranged for the business of the steamboat company to be carried on as a department of the Delaware & Hudson Co., to be managed as a part of the parent company's business, under the jurisdiction of the passenger and freight departments. This would result in a substantial saving and create cooperation and efficiency with respect to the whole passenger-handling and tourist-development operations. This aspect of the railroad business was a large one, actively sought and greatly appreciated in the early decades of the century.

This same month, as a means of saving $40,000 a year, the D&H leased the Chateaugay Ore & Iron Co. By concentrating the office work of the ore company under the D&H's supervision, and by substituting birdseye anthracite in place of the bituminous fuel formerly used in the operations, greater efficiency and therefore lower costs resulted. The lease included all the railroad operations, of course, and now gave the D&H access to Lake Placid in the central Adirondacks. The only real problem here was the line's narrow gauge which prevented any through operation from either direction. This was inconvenient enough for passengers who had to change trains at Plattsburgh, but it was grossly inefficient for handling freight, especially such bulky commodities as iron ore and coal.

As soon as the lease was executed, the D&H began the job of widening the line to standard gauge, a task that required some changes in alignment and grade, especially, on the route up the hill to Dannemora. Despite the improvements, several stretches of 5% grade had to remain, and down through the years have provided some interesting operations.

When the widening job was finished in 1903, a new connection with the main line was established several miles south of the original terminus in Plattsburgh, at a place called South Junction. The Ausable Forks branch joined the main line here. The purpose of the change was to allow room for the building of additional yard and storage tracks, not possible in the cramped yard area in downtown Plattsburgh, and also to remove the line from the grounds of a military reservation. The quaint little engines of the old Chateaugay Railway, that used to charge the grades with a vengeance to surmount the heights west of Plattsburgh, disappeared from the scene to be replaced by regular D&H power and equipment.

The Schenectady & Duanesburgh Railroad Co. was merged into the D&H corporate structure in August of 1903. The D&H had owned all the stock of this subsidiary and operated it since its construction back in 1873, to connect the Albany & Susquehanna's line with that of the Rensselaer & Saratoga after both were leased. The merger was completed at this time as a means of saving the separate organizational expense and simplifying taxation and other legal problems connected with a paper corporation. President Willcox's background in the law probably prompted him to

Mother Hubbard No. 536 was a year old in 1906, when she was photographed at the head of the five-car Albany local at Lake George station. Here passengers transferred from the *Sagamore* and such up-lake points as Baldwin, Silver Bay, Pilot Knob or Bolton Landing. The station house at the left had been built in 1882 when the line was completed from Glens Falls to the lake; six years later it was to be replaced by a grand new structure. Keesville, Ausable Chasm & Lake Champlain Mogul No. 1 was obtained by Trustee-owner Thomas B. Cotter in 1911, when electric operation ceased after a stockholders' squabble in 1911. Occasionally she came to the D&H Colonie shops for repairs, as at the time of the 1913 picture below. After the KAC&LC was abandoned in 1924, she went to the Schoharie Valley and finally to the Hoosac Tunnel & Western, where she served out the rest of the age of steam. (*J. S. Wooley, Jean Banta collection, above; D&H collection*)

The crew of a northbound coal drag, just arrived at Oneonta from Carbondale, clings to its four-wheel bobber. With no grabiron to hold, the young man in the middle seems rather unhappy. The conductor's self-assured bearing, his uniform with tie and collar and his generous lunch basket all suggest his dignity and status as captain of the train. The Cherry Valley branch local rounds the bend into Hyndsville, below, behind Camelback Mogul No. 117, on one of its three daily round trips between Cobleskill and Cherry Valley. *(Jean Banta collection, both)*

realize the complexities involved in such an arrangement. He recommended the same course as had been taken the year before in the case of the Adirondack Railway.

The Erie Railroad had always been most cooperative in its dealings with the D&H, from the building of the Jefferson Railroad up out of Carbondale to the present-day interchange agreements. They in turn did rather nicely too, hauling millions of tons of D&H coal to New York City and the West. One such manifestation of this spirit was presented to Mr. Willcox in the fall of 1903 when the Erie suggested a willingness to provide the D&H with trackage rights over its line from Binghamton west to Owego. There a direct interchange could be made with the Lehigh Valley Railroad and the operation that has continued to the present time went into effect December 1.

The output of coal reached an all-time record in 1903—5,979,311 tons—and provided enough profit through its sale and movement to buy 32 locomotives, a dozen passenger cars, 52 service cars and over 500 freight cars.

The new year of 1904 dawned literally in a blaze of glory when, on January 23, the huge paint shop portion of the shops at Green Island burned to the ground. The hair was singed on one side of the horses pulling the McGowan hose wagon, as driver Henry Barndart galloped them past the flaming building while laying a line of hose.

Trolley Lines. President Willcox's policy of diversification took the form of bringing in new operations that were in line with the transportation mission of the D&H itself; it was an extension and continuation of the policy that had characterized the company through the years. There were the coal mines, which of course were more of a starting point than a diversion. Of late there were the new interests in the hotels, steamboat lines and the iron business. Now, the development of urban and interurban trolley lines in the Capital District area both intrigued and worried the managers. They saw in the growing network of electric railways a definite threat to the steam railroad passenger business, and at the same time a possible area of expansion that could net a handsome return on the required investment—in short, joining 'em rather than trying to beat 'em.

In the fall of 1903 President Willcox suggested to the managers the desirability of acquiring the

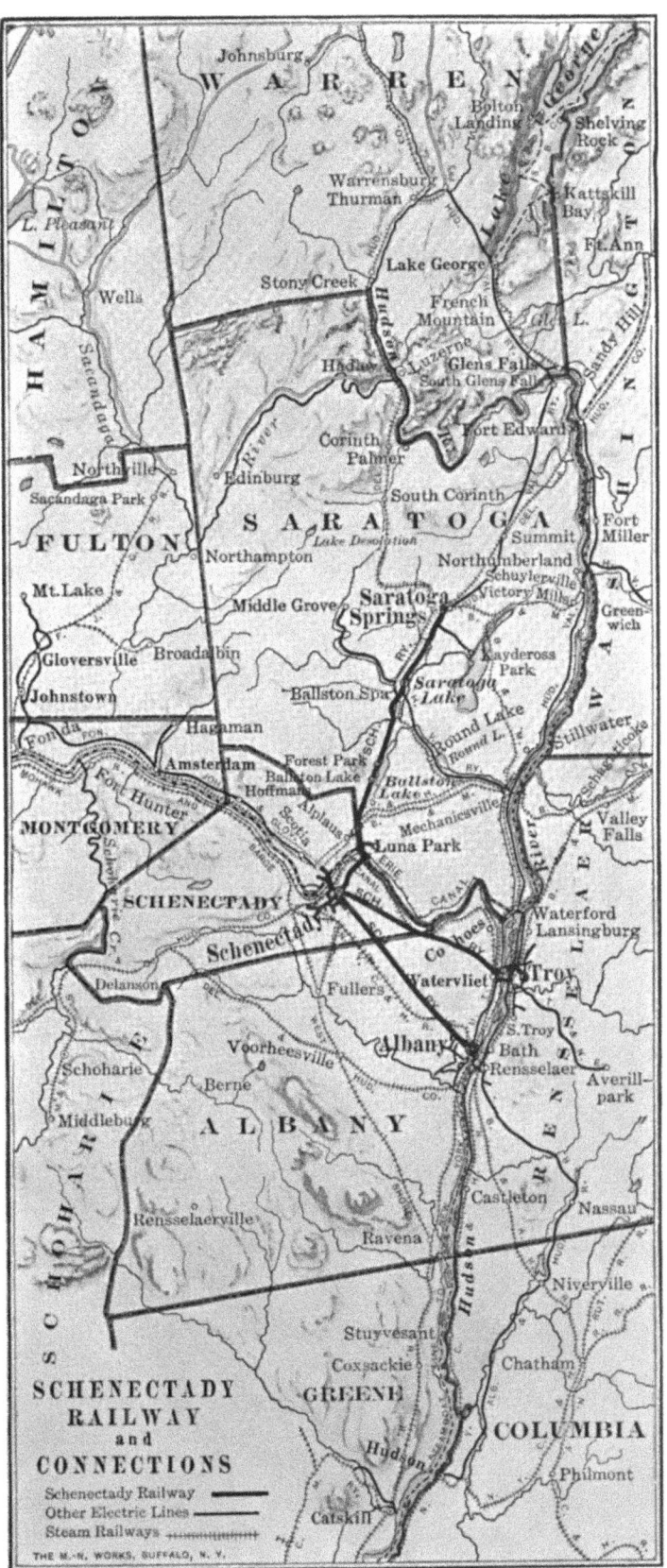

Map from collection of Manville B. Wakefield.

The Schenectady Railway's extension to Saratoga Springs was finished in 1907 and an impressive party of dignitaries was on hand at the new terminal below for the opening. Car No. 505 was built by the St. Louis Car Co. and featured wicker seats; the other two dark green cars were the product of Jones Car Co. in nearby Watervliet. A similar car, No. 510, is pictured in the 1914 night scene, above, following a winter storm, headed west on Schenectady's State Street. *(Ed Bond collection, both)*

United Traction Co. of Albany and Troy and the Schenectady Railway Co. as a means of broadening the company's transportation services in the area, and at the same time effectively eliminating any possible competition that might arise.

The Schenectady Railway had been organized and developed a few years earlier by the General Electric Co. as a means of providing its employees with access to the big GE works from the various parts of the city and its suburbs. It also served as an ideal proving ground for the company's traction motors and control equipment, principal products of the big plant. In addition to all the streetcar lines in Schenectady, the company owned the gas and electric works, a 17-mile interurban line to Troy, another of the same length to Albany and a 22-mile line north through Ballston Spa to Saratoga Springs. The last 7 miles of the line into Saratoga were over the tracks of the Hudson Valley Railway, where the Schenectady company had trackage rights. In all, the Schenectady Railway consisted of 116 miles of double-tracked line laid with 80-pound rail, and was considered to be, along with its equipment, in excellent condition.

The United Traction Co. was organized in 1899 by an amalgamation, for 1000 years, of the Albany Railway Co., the Troy City Railway Co., the Watervliet Turnpike & Railway Co., and the lease of the Capitol Railway of Albany. Lines extended from Albany to Waterford and included numerous local lines in Albany, Rensselaer, Watervliet, Green Island, Troy, Cohoes and Waterford—85.67 miles in all. This company had important connections with other electric lines in the area: To the west with the Schenectady Railway, to the north with the Hudson Valley interurban line, to the east with the Troy & New England Railway and to the south with the Albany & Hudson Railway. The central location of the United Traction Co., serving as a sort of hub out of which, and through which these other electric lines could be reached, made it especially interesting to the D&H.

Clearly President Willcox was in favor of the purchase of these lines, despite the fact that the latter months of 1903 were not an auspicious time for the acquisition of new property, because of a general slowdown in the overall economy of the nation. The Schenectady system could probably be obtained by guaranteeing the bonds and stock

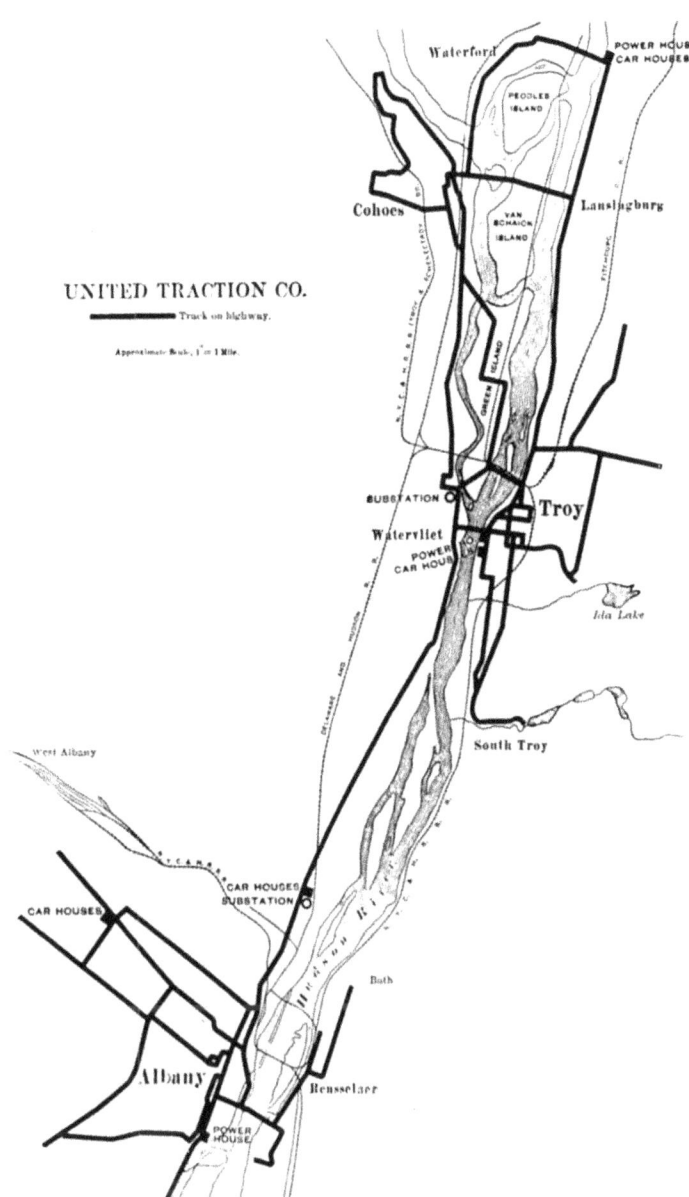

of the trolley company and at the current rate of earnings would result in a profit of over $100,000 to the D&H. Willcox was more cautious about the United Traction Co. and nothing was done immediately about the purchase of either operation but the report was clearly an effort to place the study of trolley expansion before the managers.

Expenditures required for various purposes and acquisitions in 1903 had drawn heavily on earnings and reduced the cash balance in the treasury. Besides this, $5,000,000 of the New York & Canada bonds would fall due on May 1, 1904, along with other accounts that would need attention. At the annual meeting in March, the stockholders authorized the issuance of $10,000,000 in

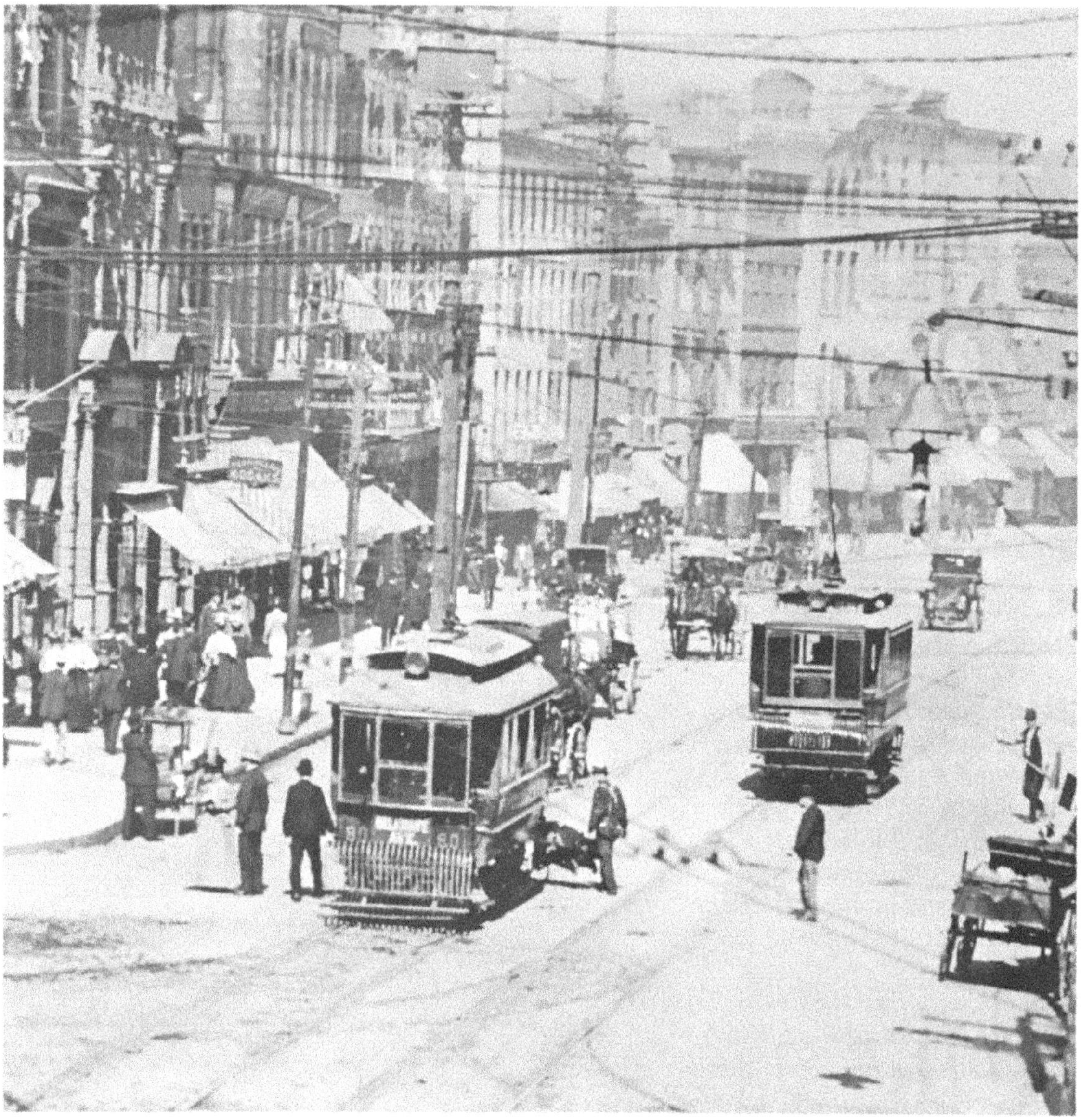

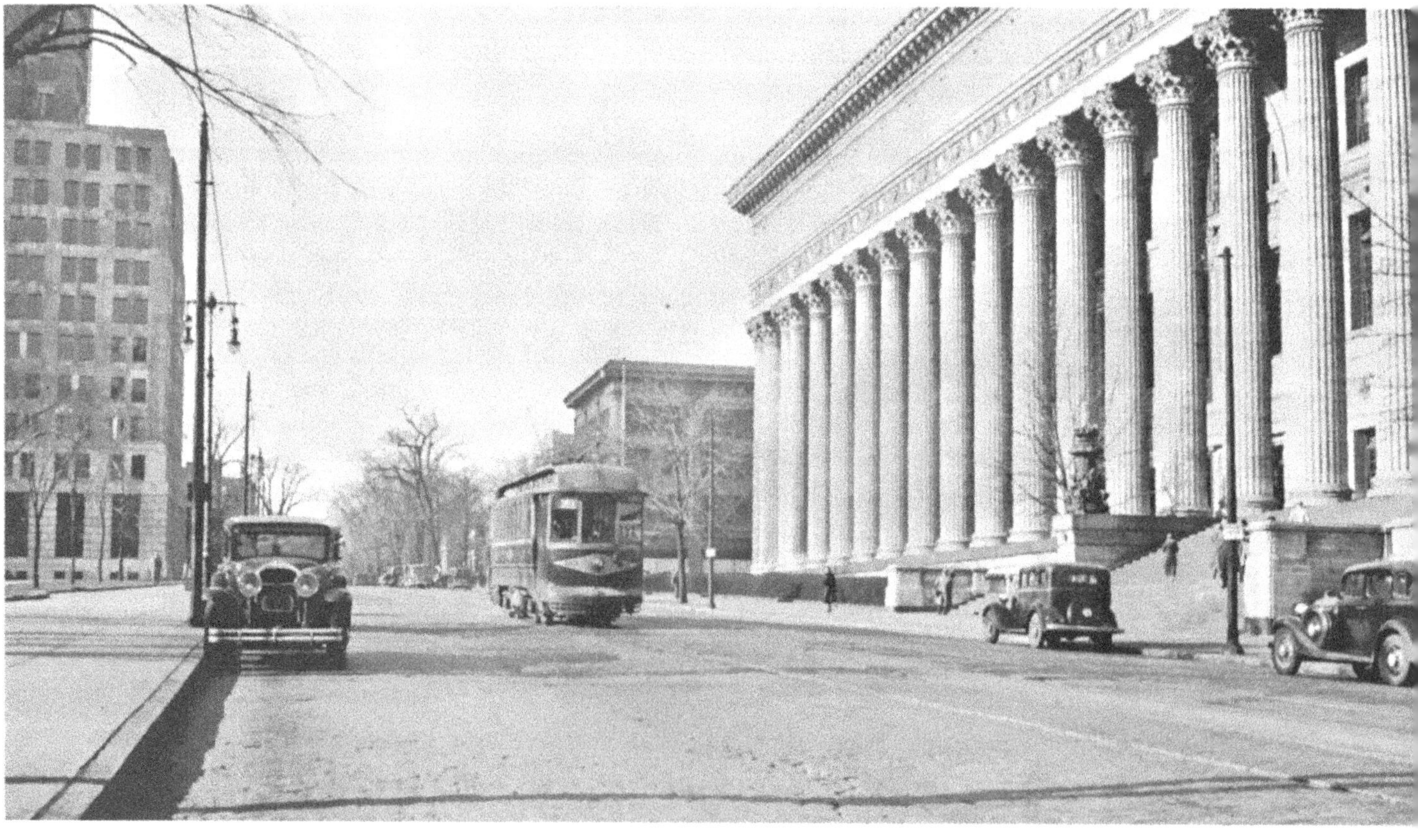

These four views of the United Traction Co. span 37 years and illustrate the changes both in the street scene and the cars during that time. Albany's wire-draped Broadway is shown in the upper picture, opposite, looking north from State Street. Only one horseless carriage is in view and a peanut vender does business at the left. Newer types of the dark green cars clogged Troy's Franklin Square in 1904, below. The "Saratoga Through Car" in the foreground is the Hudson Valley Railway's No. 124, which ran on United Traction Co. trackage as far as Waterford. By 1926 the cars were painted red and cream. The handsome structure above is the North Albany barn, built by the Albany Railway in 1892. It was the company's main facility for many years, well into the era of busses. Growing automobile traffic required that the streetcars be more visible, and to this end a cream-colored diamond was added to the painting, giving a smile to the face of the 623, lower left, as it trundles down Albany's cobbled Washington Avenue past the colonnade of the State Library and Museum. The car was 33 years old by 1937 when the picture was made. (*Ed Bond collection, three pictures; Roger Borrup, left below*)

Inspection engine SARATOGA may have lacked the TRANSIT's grace and refinement (page 174), but her four drivers must have given better traction. She was built as a single-cab Baldwin, No. 4 for the Cooperstown & Charlotte Valley. After lease of that line to the D&H, she was rebuilt at Green Island first as No. 148 and then 397, emerging as the SARATOGA in 1904. Below is a 1915 view of the Averill Park terminal of the Troy & New England, a popular outing line. Open car No. 2 is ready to depart for Troy. (*D&H collection, above; Ed Bond collection*)

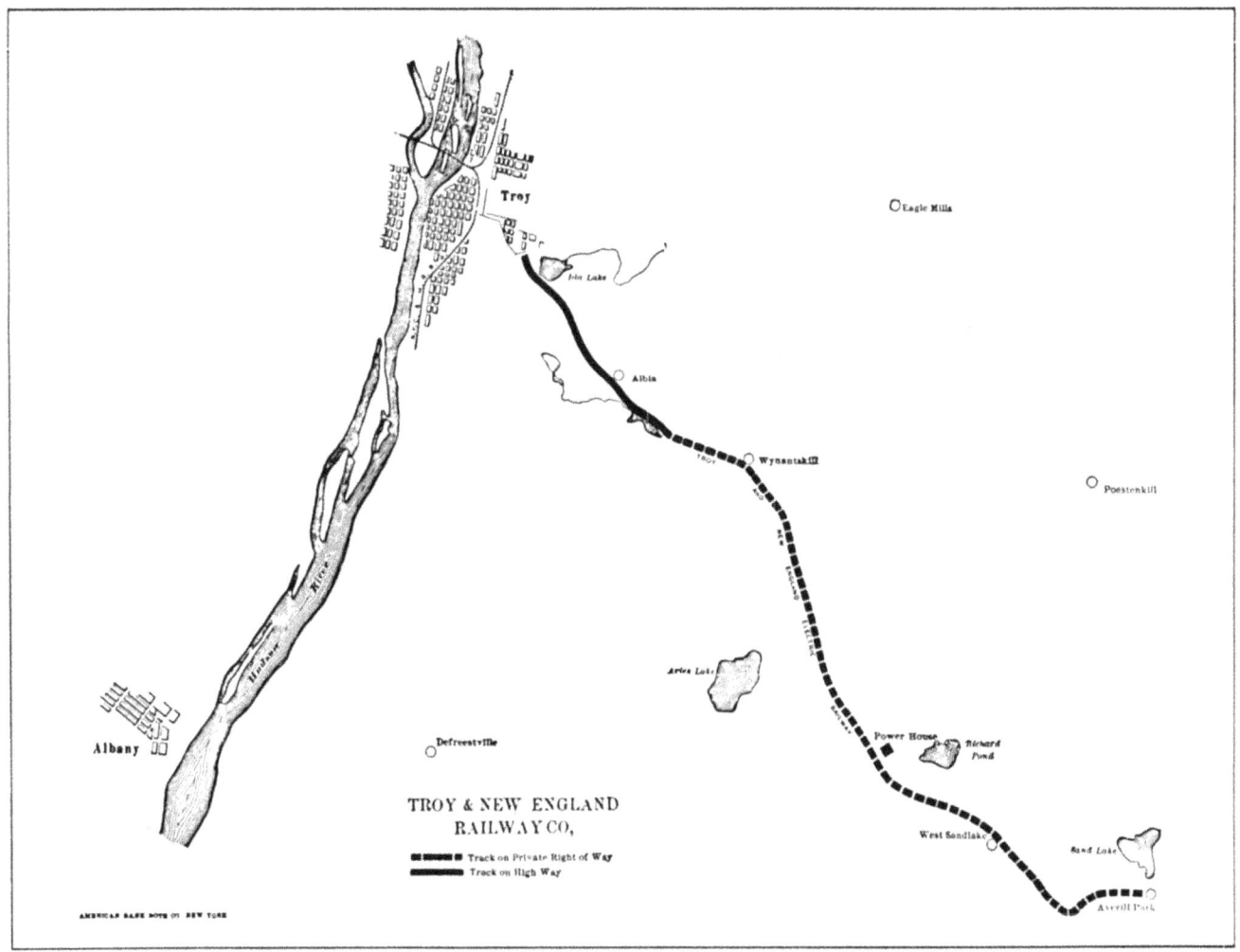

additional stock. The $100 face value stock was selling for $165 on the open market and $7,000,000 was released to the current stockholders at $135, thus producing $9,450,000 for only $7,000,000 additional capital liability.

In October, 1904, a year after the trolley issue first came up, the D&H in partnership with the New York Central & Hudson River Railroad each bought a half interest in the Schenectady Railway at a cost of $2,500,000.

The D&H then built a high-speed double-tracked trolley line adjacent to its steam line from Ballston Spa to Saratoga Springs for the new addition to the family.

Additional funds obtained from the 1904 stock issue allowed the purchase of new engines and other equipment for the steam lines. In January, 1895, 15 class E3a Consolidations were acquired, and before the year had passed, 7 more locomotives, 151 coal cars, 6 baggage cars, a dozen milk cars, 4 combination cars and a locomotive crane were brought into the fold. More automatic block signaling was installed and along with that put into service the previous year, a total of 91.4 miles of single track and 64.6 miles of double track had been equipped by the close of the year.

In October 1905 the entire stock of the Troy & New England Railway was purchased. This outfit had a small electric line running nine miles southeast from Troy to the little town of Averill Park. As it existed this road was nothing to rave over but the charter held by the company was something else again. The franchise allowed the line to be extended on to the state line in the town of Canaan in Columbia County, some 40 miles away. Here a connection could be made with the New York, New Haven & Hartford and if a steam line were built over this route by the D&H it could offer many new destinations for coal and merchandise.

General Electric's first gas-electric car, below, entered service between Schenectady and Saratoga, February 3, 1906. It seated forty passengers, had a smoking compartment and toilets. This 160 hp V-6 engine with 9" bore and 10" stroke was started by firing a black-powder shell. It turned a 120 kw generator at 480 r.p.m., powering regular streetcar motors on the front truck at a comfortable 50 m.p.h., with a 75 m.p.h. maximum. As it used a gallon of fuel a mile, officials hoped such cars could replace steam on short runs, but the No. 1000 could not pull a trailer on branch lines and its engine became troublesome, so it was sold in 1908. The No. 2000, bottom, appeared in 1911 on the same run, one of 120 such cars built by GE after the trials on the 1000. Steel bodies were fitted at Schenectady with General Electric's own V-8 engine and electrical equipment.

Camelback No. 523 rolls D&H train No. 7 up from Binghamton and Oneonta into Delmar, just outside Albany. Her combine and two arch-windowed coaches are all-wood and painted Brewster green. (*Abram Le Galley, Ed Van Wormer collection, above; Al Gayer collection, opposite bottom; Industrial Photo Service, two pictures*)

After much negotiation, on November 17, 1905, President Willcox made a final report to the managers on the proposed acquisition of the United Traction Company. The central location of this line made not only the D&H, but its current owners as well, aware of its strategic and monetary value. Back in 1903 this property had not commended itself strongly to the president or the managers because of the high price asked for its stock. As time passed and the D&H interest in Capital District electric lines broadened, the acquisition of the United Traction Co. seemed to be more and more essential. Soon after the President's report, the managers authorized the purchase of all the stock in the United Traction Co., at $150 a share—in all, a whopping $7,000,000 shot. Electric railways were riding high on the crest of a huge wave of success at the moment and only time would tell how long the ride would last.

Large additions were made to the steam roster in 1906 including 57 locomotives, 2014 coal cars and 18 milk cars. The freight yard at Oneonta was enlarged and remodeled, involving the erection of a new 52-stall roundhouse with a 75-foot turntable and associated service facilities.

Considerable progress on the installation of block signals had also been accomplished by the middle of 1906; over 152 miles of completed trackage had been put into service for slightly more than $353,000. The president noted that several important segments of the main line were still without block signals and that the number of trains from Saratoga Springs north made it especially necessary to have this equipment installed as far as Westport. The job, he said, was being completed as soon as possible. By the following year block signals would be completed and operational on all of the main line and two principal branches. He noted with pride, that in the 12 preceding years the company had carried over 75 million passengers with but three fatalities, and although he did not elaborate on the subject, it had been accomplished with a maximum of luxury and a minimum of mishaps.

Notwithstanding this record and the new electronic marvels of block signals, the elegant *Saratoga Limited*, advertised as the fastest train on the Delaware & Hudson running between New York and Saratoga Springs, was derailed near Ballston Spa on July 3, 1906. The locomotive and four cars left the track, several persons were injured, but none seriously.

Still another facet of the program of branching out into the electric railway field was shown on March 27, 1906 when all the stock in the Plattsburgh Traction Co. was purchased for $25,000. This outfit owned and operated a 7½-mile electric line in the city of Plattsburgh with an extension southward through the military reservation to the Champlain Hotel.

Gathering of this little line into the fold was minor compared to the simultaneous acquisition, through the United Traction Co., of the Hudson Valley Railway Co. This was a full-fledged 130-

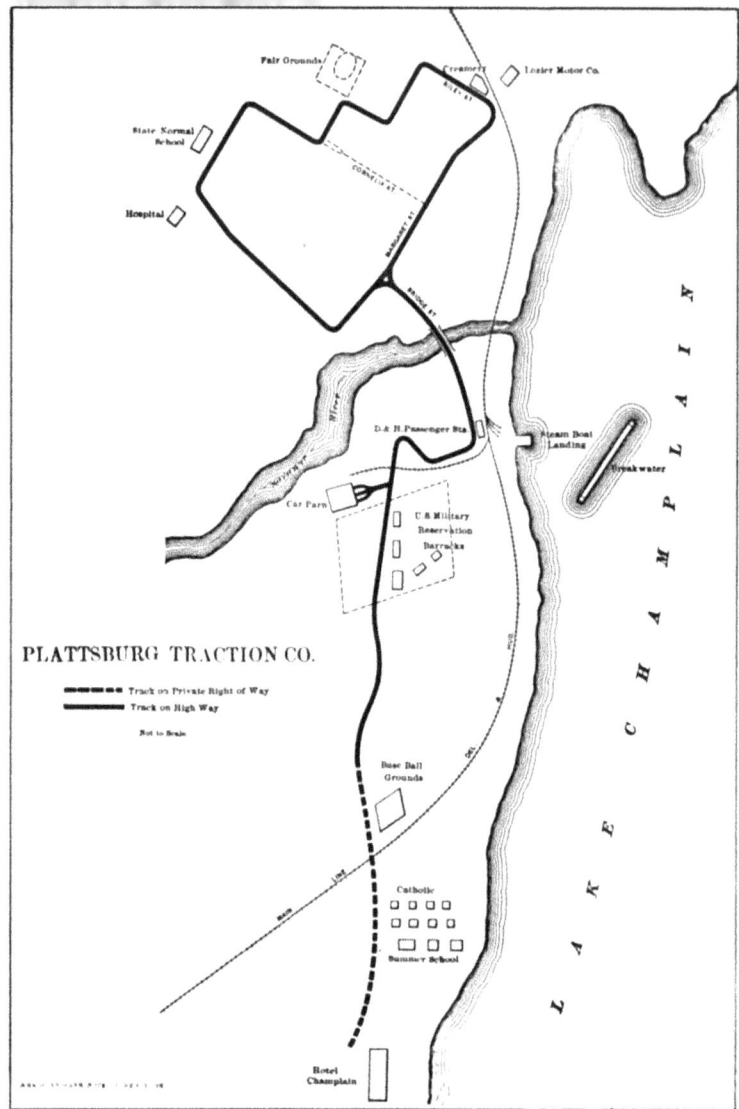

PLATTSBURGH TRACTION COMPANY
SUMMER TIME-TABLE

Bridge and Margaret Sts. to Cliff Haven and Bluff Point

SOUTH BOUND Minutes Past the Hour				NORTH BOUND Minutes Past the Hour		
00	20	40	Bridge and Margaret	20	40	00
02	22	42	D. & H. Station	18	38	58
04	24	44	Peru and Hamilton Sts.	16	36	56
05	25	45	Car Barn	15	35	55
08	28	48	Elizabeth St.	12	32	52
10	30	50	Drill Hall (at Barracks)	10	30	50
12	32	52	City Line	08	28	48
15	35	55	Clinton Park	05	25	45
17	37	57	Champlain Club	03	23	43
18	38	58	Cliff Haven	02	22	42
20	40	00	Bluff Point	00	20	40
8.00 a. m. to 11.00 p. m.				8.00 a. m. to 11.20 p. m.		

READ DOWN / READ UP

Additional Trips:—Leave Bridge and Margaret Sts. for Bluff Point at ‡6.30 a. m., ‡6.55 a. m., D7.25 a. m. and D11.40 p. m., and Bluff Point for the City at ‡6.55 a. m., ‡7.25 a. m., and D12.00 midnight. Cars leave Bridge and Margaret Sts. at 11.20 p. m. and 12 midnight, carrying passengers to Barracks only.

— ‡ Runs one hour later on Sundays.
† Daily except Sunday.
D Daily

Two open cars of the Plattsburgh Traction Co. are packed with children from the Catholic Summer School of America at Cliff Haven, south of town just above the Champlain Hotel. A straw-hatted priest stands by the second car which is decorated with bunting, probably for the 1910 celebrations of the 300th anniversary of Champlain's discovery of the lake named for him. *(James R. McFarlane collection, timetable; N. Y. collection, Feinberg Library, State University College at Plattsburgh, below)*

Plattsburgh station, built in 1886 is seen from the street side, above, with two elecrtic cars of the Plattsburgh Traction Co. The First National Bank of Glens Falls looked the same in 1917 as it did in 1967, and made a handsome backdrop for the company portrait of the No. 81, bright with new paint and polished windows and freshly rebuilt from an open car. *(James R. McFarlane collection, above; Ed Bond collection, below)*

The 1909 scene above, with two dark green interurban cars, looks north on Ballston Spa's shady Milton Avenue. At the left a Schenectady Railway car stands on Washington Street, beyond the awning of the shop of photographer J. S. Wooley whose pictures on this page, and many others in this book, depict life in Ballston Spa and the Lake George region with the sensitivity of a true camera artist. This car, and the Hudson Valley's No. 34, right, were built by Jones Car Co. Milton Avenue, is decorated for centennial of Ballston's incorporation as a village.

The views on this page look west along Front Street in Ballston Spa, with open Hudson Valley cars on the track from Milton Avenue on the right. The historic Eagle Hotel is at the left. Electric lines of the Schenectady Railway and, from Troy, the Hudson Valley met at Ballston, going the remaining seven miles to Saratoga Springs on the same high-speed trackage. Both were under D&H control when these pictures were taken. *(Ed Bond collection, four pictures)*

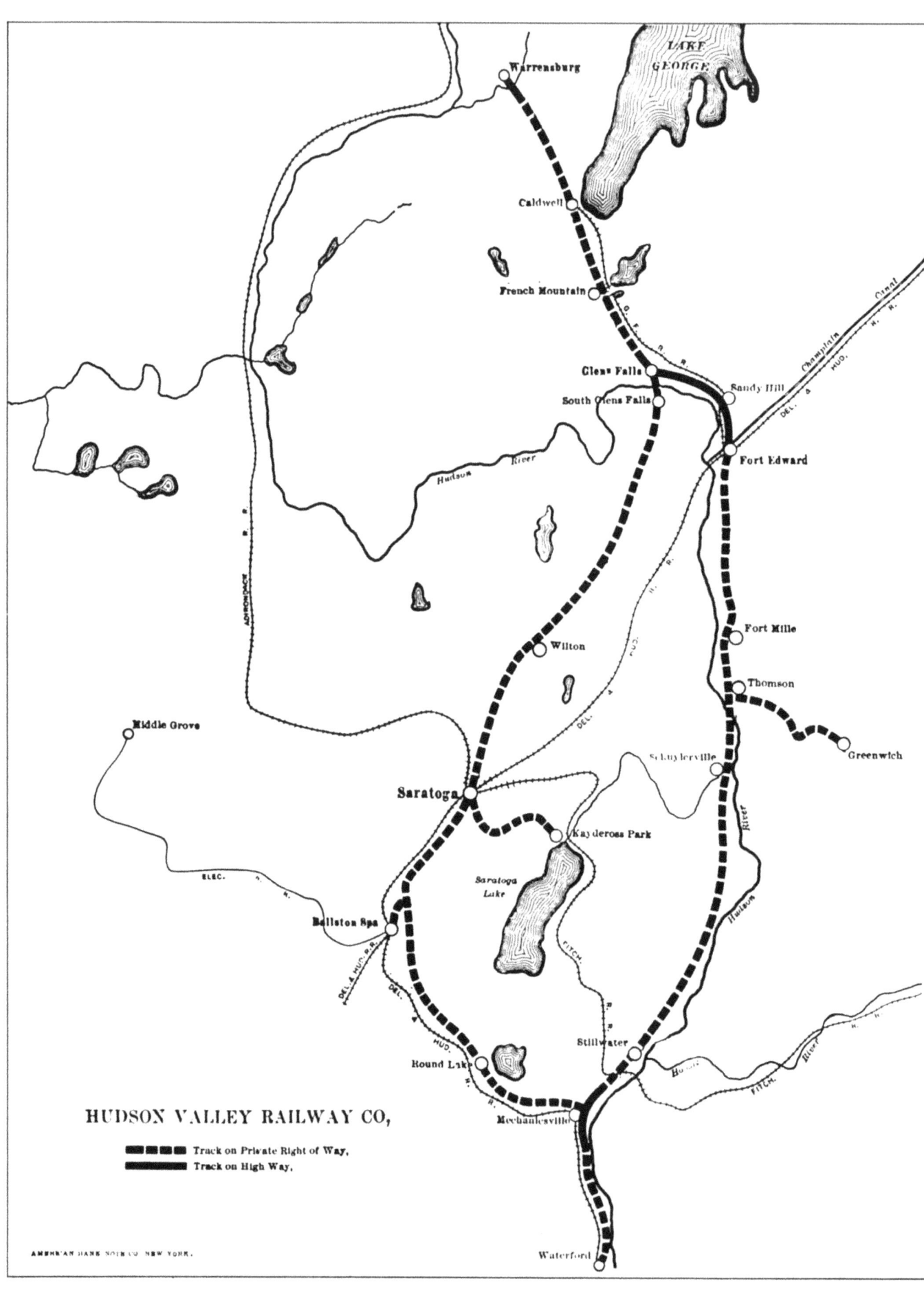

The Greenwich branch joined the Hudson Valley at Thomson. The passengers waiting on the steps of the little lunchroom are well dressed, in contrast with the drabness of the dusty car and the shabby surroundings. Morning papers are piled in the doorway of the car at the right. *(Industrial Photo Service)*

mile interurban railroad built to high speed standards extending from Waterford through Mechanicville, Saratoga Springs, Glens Falls, and Lake George to Warrensburg. Two alternate lines existed between Mechanicville and Glens Falls, one through Saratoga closely paralleling the steam lines of the D&H and the other followed the Hudson north from Mechanicville to Fort Edward and Glens Falls with a branch from Thompson east to Greenwich. This relatively large line was quickly snapped up as it was apparent that the price of the property would be increasing with each passing day because it served a rapidly growing territory that originated a large volume of passenger and express traffic. Local service was provided in the heavily populated section from Glens Falls through Hudson Falls to Fort Edward.

The remaining months of 1906 were not particularly quiet, either, when it came to spending money and branching out. In quick succession: The Glens Falls Railroad was merged into the R&S corporate structure; the majority of the stock in the Greenwich & Johnsonville was bought; all of the stock in the little Schoharie Valley Railway was obtained, and in Canada complete ownership was acquired of the Quebec, Montreal & Southern Railway Co., a 143-mile railroad extending almost to Quebec City.

The Greenwich & Johnsonville line was started in 1866 by the Union Village & Johnsonville Railroad Co. but before the 14-mile line was finished and opened on August 31, 1870, financial problems were encountered and a reorganization of the company, now called the G&J was required. In 1903 by some additional construction and by absorbing a little line called the Battenkill Railroad, the G&J was extended westward to Thompson and across the Hudson to Schuylerville where a connection was made with the Saratoga branch of the Boston & Maine that ran up from Mechanicville. This line ran through a rich farming area but, more important, about 20 paper mills, knitting mills and other industries flourished along its route.

Industrial growth and the possibilities of future development were encouraging enough that the D&H initiated the building of a branch line by the G&J running east from Greenwich 10.12

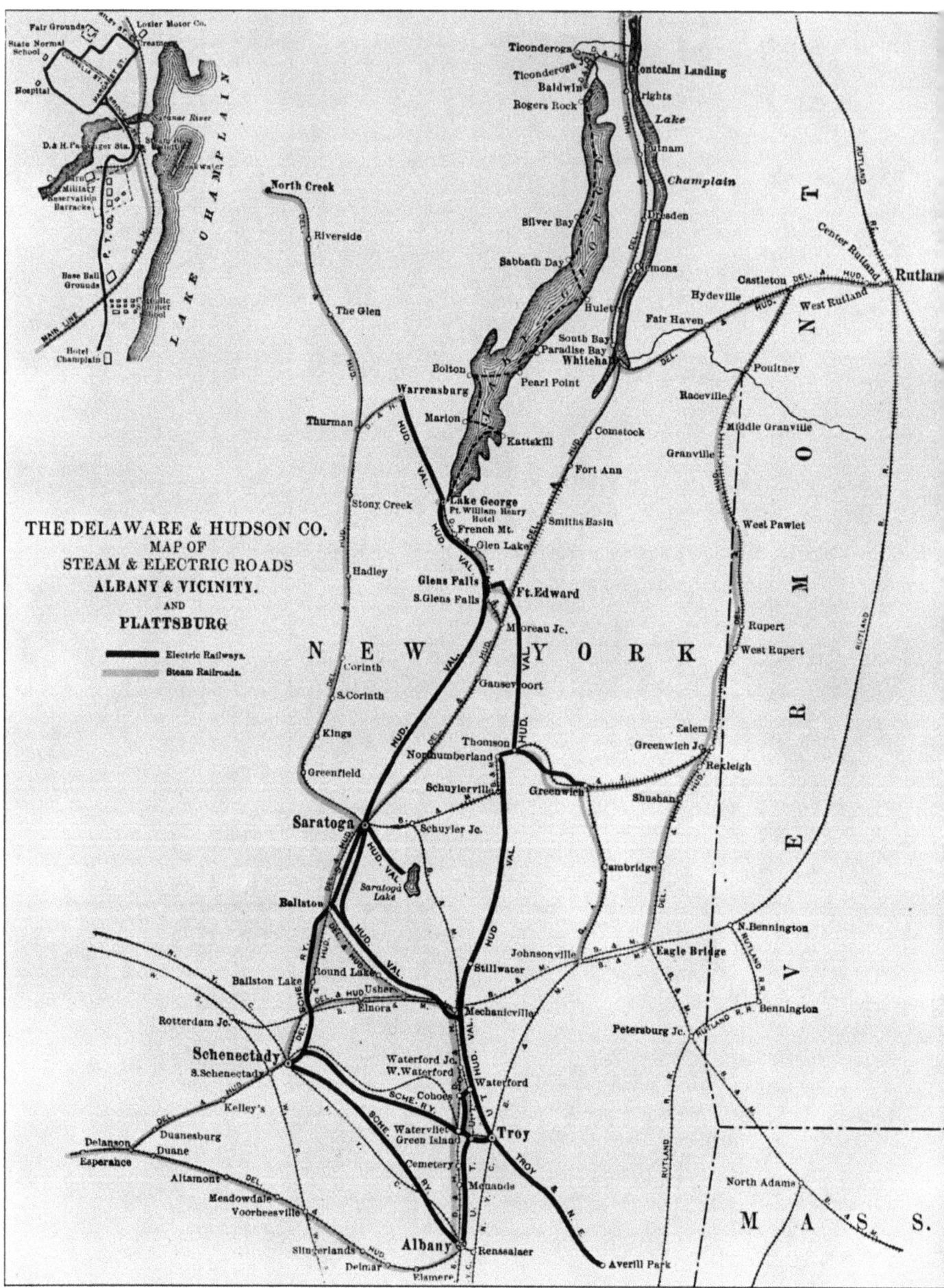

Greenwich & Johnsonville 4-4-0 No. 2 wheels a combination and a coach through a cut on the line from Greenwich down to Thomson in about 1910.

miles to Salem where a connection with the D&H's Rutland & Washington branch would be made. It was expected that a large portion of the pulpwood used in paper mills of the area would be routed over the newly-acquired Quebec, Montreal & Southern Railway and the D&H, finally rolling into the beaters over the G&J.

The Salem branch was completed during the following year, enabling traffic off the R&W branch to be routed over the G&J, cross the Hudson to the B&M and move on to Mechanicville, a 30-mile trip compared to a 68-mile run north through Castleton and Whitehall. The G&J handled a large volume of traffic, and still does, but little if any was given to the B&M at Schuylerville; instead it made the entire trip over D&H rails north to Whitehall. In later years the bridge over the Hudson between Thompson and Schuylerville was washed out and not replaced.

The Schoharie Valley Railway was a short line running from Schoharie Junction on the Albany & Susquehanna line southward toward the village of the same name, some 4.3 miles distant. Another little railroad called the Middleburgh & Schoharie ran a bit more than five miles farther down the valley from Schoharie to Middleburgh, but remained in local hands.

Expansion in Canada. By far the most spectacular addition in the way of steam roads was the Quebec, Montreal & Southern Railway north of the border. This line had a rather chequered past, being the result of several mergers between small weak lines in the eastern townships section of Quebec just north of the U. S. border.

The road formed a sort of wishbone shape on the map, with one leg extending from St. Lambert, just across the Victoria Bridge from Montreal, down along the south shore of the St. Lawrence to Sorel. This stretch had started out as the Montreal & Sorel and the Great Eastern Railway but after 10 years of floundering was bought out from under the junkmen in 1894 by Montreal interests

The train from Troy to Rutland, over the former Rutland & Washington line, now the D&H's R&W branch, rolls into Salem, New York, behind a 400-class 4-4-0 Mother Hubbard above. A sizeable revenue crowd waits on the platform in this early spring scene. The old R&W shops were located in the right distance and the D&H used them for car building and repair until 1912. In October, 1908, below, the local freight from Whitehall to Rutland had a mishap at Fair Haven, Vermont. The Whitehall wrecking gang is cleaning up the mess while townsfolk look on. *(Al Gayer collection, above; Jean Banta collection)*

who formed the South Shore Railway. They poured new money into the project and the line was finished to Sorel and continued on down the shore of the river toward Quebec City. By 1900 trains were running from St. Lambert to Pierreville at the St. Francis river, 62 miles in all.

The other leg of the wishbone was the result of work by the United Counties Railway, chartered in 1883 to build a line south from Sorel to Iberville through St. Hyacinthe. Nothing was done immediately due to a lack of funds and time ran out on the charter. When the charter was renewed things got off to a flying start with $100,000 from investors and 600,000 acres of land from the provincial government and construction was begun in both directions from St. Hyacinthe; trains were running over the 60-mile line by September 1895.

Meanwhile, in December 1890, the East Richelieu Valley Railway was organized to run a line from St. Hyacinthe to Lacolle where it would join the Grand Trunk and Canada Atlantic lines near the international boundary. This track would almost parallel the United Counties line for about half the distance so the logical and obvious agreement was made; the United Counties would be given trackage rights over the lower half of the ERV and in turn, the East Richelieu would use UC tracks from Iberville to St. Hyacinthe. The southern terminus of the ERV was changed from Lacolle to Noyan Junction to avoid bridging the Richelieu River and a connection was made there with a spur of the Rutland Railroad built up from Alburg, Vermont. The United Counties assisted financially in building its partner's 22-mile line but when all the bills were paid neither outfit had a nickel to its name and the sheriff immediately moved in and took everything over.

On July 7, 1900 the Quebec Southern Railway was formed by agents working behind the scene for the D&H. It absorbed the East Richelieu Valley, which was already purchased on May 30, and the United Counties, acquired on August 7, forming an 82.8-mile line from Noyan Junction to St. Robert with trackage rights into Sorel from the latter point over the South Shore Railway.

In the meantime the South Shore line wasn't doing so well itself and its owners began to look around for a sugar daddy; independent operation on their part was proving to be a losing game.

They approached the Quebec Southern, in reality interests actually working for the D&H, and received an offer they wanted to grab but couldn't. Due to some legal complexities over the transfer of titles and control of the government subsidies they couldn't actually prove they had the right to sell the line at all and the usual court battle ensued for clear control. By the end of 1903 the court appointed a receiver who immediately sold the line to the Quebec Southern. This added 62 miles of track and 22 more miles of partially-completed roadbed from the St. Francis River at Pierreville easterly across the Nicolet River to the Grand Trunk Railway at St. Gregoire. In all, the Quebec Southern now comprised 144 miles of mediocre railroad.

After the QS was reorganized into the Quebec, Montreal & Southern, the D&H formally bought all the outstanding stock for $1,212,929.04 in the spring of 1906. Contracts totaling $2,067,237.85 were immediately let for completion of the line from Pierreville to St. Philomène, a town on the Lotbinière & Mégantic Railway seven miles south of St. Jean des Chaillons, 48.5 miles down the St. Lawrence toward Quebec City. Eventually it was planned to push the line all the way down to Chaudière Junction where a connection would be made with the great Quebec bridge then under construction.

The whole idea of getting involved in these Canadian lines was to have the entire haul on the pulpwood and paper moving to southerly points on the D&H, and to protect the supply of pulpwood necessary for the continued operation and enlargement of the paper industry already located along their lines. Likewise, the ever-present thought of new markets for the company's coal in eastern Canada, moving to market entirely over their own lines must also have been consoling indeed.

Upon reaching Quebec City, the Quebec & Lake St. John Railway would afford access to the vast forest lands located in the area 245 miles north and east of the old walled city. From Bécancour, a branch to the St. Lawrence would allow vast numbers of cars to be ferried across the river on car floats from the mills of Three Rivers and Batiscan to the QM&S tracks on the south side thus avoiding the longer haul over foreign roads through Montreal to the D&H at Rouses Point.

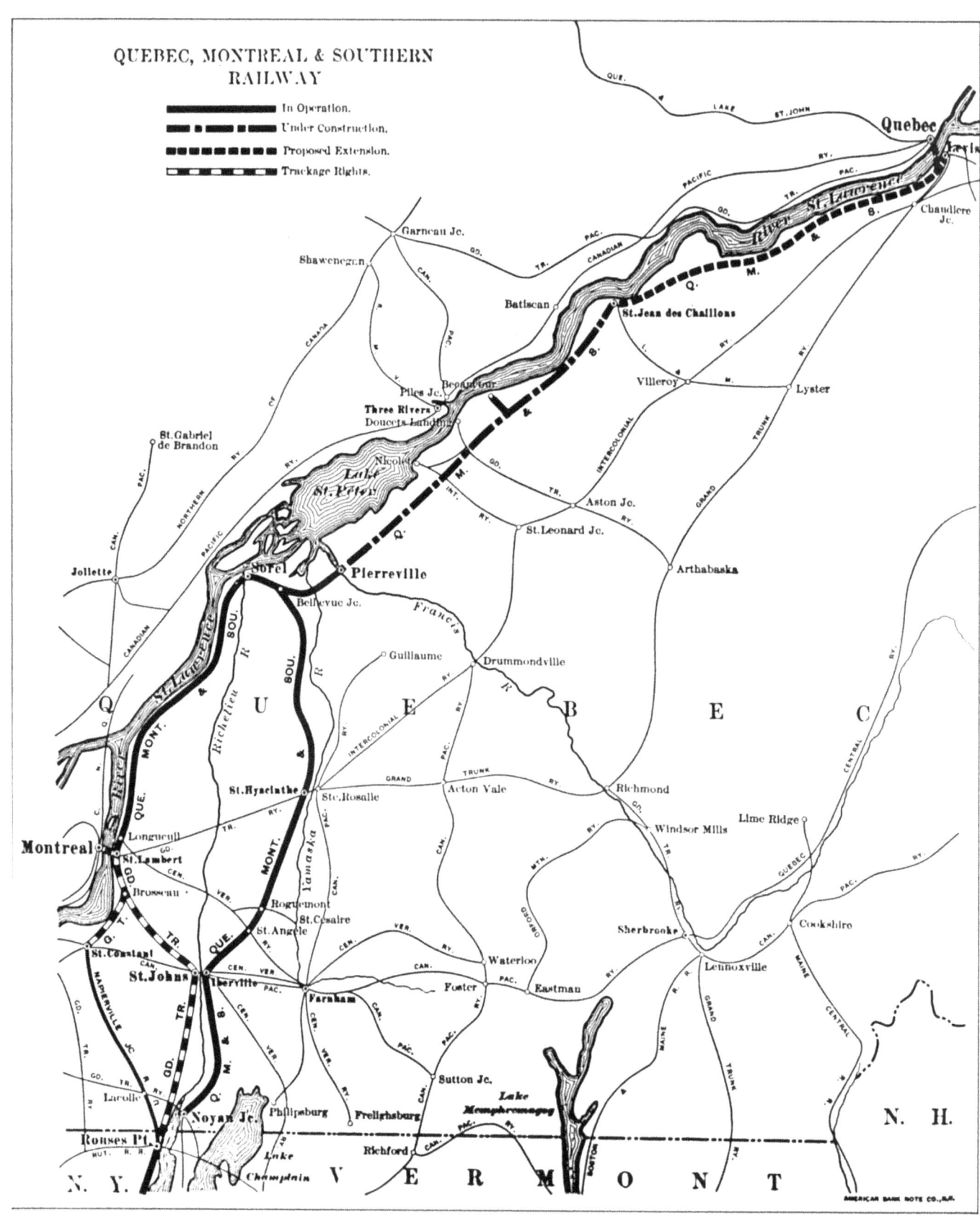

225

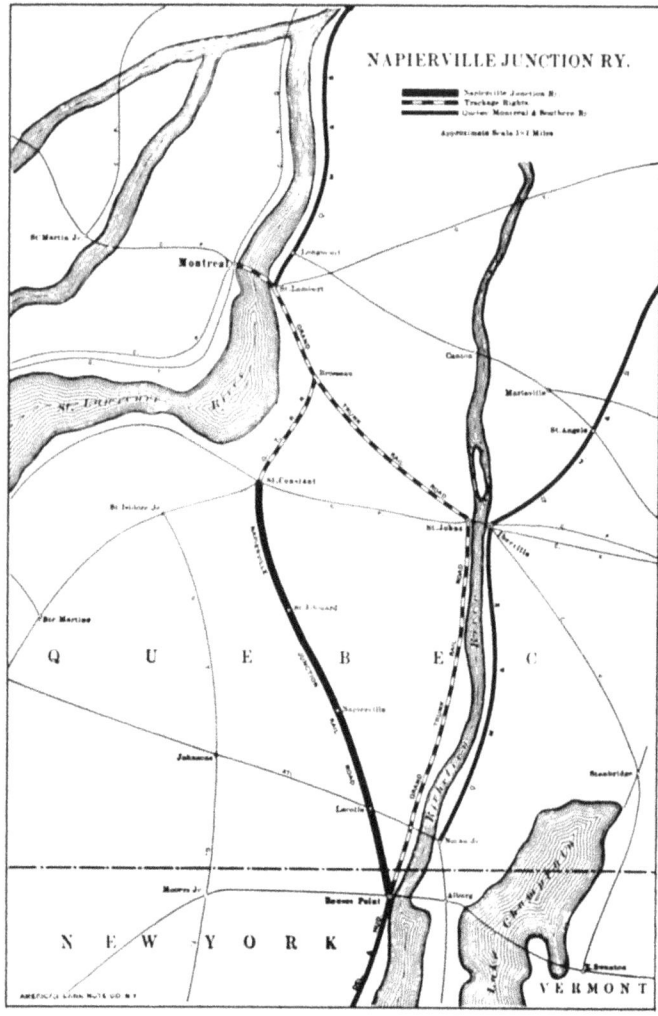

The line to St. Philomène was completed early in 1908, with the exception of the bridge over the Nicolet River and the whole extension was opened by May of 1909.

As if this QM&S deal weren't enough to cope with, the D&H bought still another Canadian railroad in the spring of 1907. This time it was the Napierville Junction Railway extending from Rouses Point north 29 miles to the Canadian Pacific and the Massena Springs branch of the Grand Trunk Railway at St. Constant, 20 miles southwest of Montreal and 14 miles west of St. Lambert and the Victoria Bridge.

This railway was originally undertaken by the Pacific Construction Co. and was turned over to the Napierville Junction Railway. The entire line, with all rights, franchises and privileges, was bought outright by the D&H on April 9, 1907, for $615,680.56. By securing trackage rights over the Grand Trunk between St. Constant and St. Lambert, direct access was gained to both Montreal and the QM&S, allowing a direct connection for the anticipated large volume of traffic funneled south over the other D&H stepchild in Canada when completed to Quebec City. This new line reduced by seven miles the distance between Rouses Point and Montreal as compared to the existing route over the Grand Trunk via St. Johns as well as providing the D&H with an independent route of its own. The new line also gave the D&H a direct connection with the Canadian Pacific at St. Constant that would provide still another outlet for the company's coal to the territory served by that road. A 1.1-mile piece of track had to be built by the D&H from Rouses Point up to meet the Napierville Junction tracks at the international border.

There was very little new construction on the D&H lines themselves after the abandonment of the canal and the turn of the century. Down in the mine area of Pennsylvania the Northern Coal & Iron Co. built the Buttonwood branch, extending from Buttonwood north to the Plymouth branch at South Wilkes-Barre in 1906 and the Plymouth "No. 5" branch in 1907. In 1901 a line was built from Moreau Junction, just south of Fort Edward on the Saratoga division, to South Glens Falls, primarily to serve several large paper mills there. A 3.5-mile branch was built in 1905 from Thurman on the old Adirondack Railway to Warrensburg and in 1906 an extension of the New York & Canada was pushed one mile from Rouses Point to the Canadian boundary. The third and fourth track being built between Ballston and Saratoga Springs and its electrification for use jointly by the Hudson Valley Railway and the Schenectady Railway was completed and put into service early in 1907.

All the shopping that had taken place in the field of electric lines and Canadian railroads, not to mention the double-tracking, block signal installations, new equipment and other improvements on its own lines, had cost the D&H a pretty penny. The financial structure of the company had always been exceptionally good but this buying spree stretched its solvency to new limits.

In February 1907, the health of President Willcox became seriously impaired. The trouble was deep-seated and had its origin in the unspar-

Camelbacks No. 521, southbound, above, and 537, with the northbound *Montreal Limited*, roar along the multiple track with long trains of turn-of-the-century passenger cars. Beneath the catenaries east of the D&H main line is the electric line that was used by Hudson Valley and Schenectady interurbans. *(Industrial Photo Service, below)*

ing dedication with which he had devoted himself to the legal and official duties of the company for years past. Anxiety over the corporate finances no doubt was a secondary cause. The considerable expansion under his guidance had been only temporarily financed, largely by short-term loans, and more permanent arrangements were becoming imminently necessary. In an effort to induce the President to relax from the strain, Edward H. Harriman, who had been a member of the board since 1903 and was then at the apex of his brilliant career as a railroad organizer, operator and financier, assured Mr. Willcox that he would place securities worth more than 25 million dollars at the company's disposal if necessary to allow it to meet its obligations until, with health restored, he could work out more permanent arrangements for the financing. Willcox respectfully rejected the offer and remained at his post.

In March of 1907, however, his physical condition worsened and he was forced to obtain relief from the responsibilities of the presidency and accepted a leave of absence. Before sailing for Europe, with the hope that the ocean voyage in a milder climate would be of benefit, he left his formal resignation with the instructions that it was to be presented to the managers at their April 10th meeting.

His resignation was sadly and reluctantly accepted and a man who would loom large in the history of the Delaware & Hudson, Leonor F. Loree, was elected president and a member of the Board. Word of Mr. Willcox's unexpected death was received with profound sorrow on April 24th.

The new president, therefore, commenced his work with much of the new property and stock holdings acquired during the preceding administration, not permanently financed. Preliminary indications showed those who were able to read the signs of the times that a financial panic was developing. Government regulation in the form of the Interstate Commerce Commission, as well as State regulation through the Public Service Commission, was becoming more and more prevalent, and unions were gaining considerable strength and pressing for higher wages and shorter hours, which resulted in a 7% overall increase during the early part of 1907 alone. In addition, local and corporate taxes were rising, prices of materials and supplies were skyrocketing, Henry Ford had perfected his horseless carriage and even the hemline of women's skirts was on the rise. The simplicity and tranquility of the 19th century had been gone now for seven years—things would never be quite the same again.

At left, Mother Hubbard 4-4-0 No. 445 rolls a local along the raceway between Ballston Spa and Saratoga Springs. The banjo-type signal beyond the lead baggage car is located on the new electric right-of-way built by the D&H in 1907. The fireman leans out of his cab for a breath of air now that he has bailed enough coal into the firebox to take the train on into the Springs. *(J. S. Wooley, Industrial Photo Service collection)*

The trolley terminal at Saratoga Springs was a busy place during the glory years of the electric interurban railway, for it served both the Schenectady and the Hudson Valley Railways in that popular resort city. Built in 1916 to serve the rapidly growing traffic, it is shown here several years later with three big wooden 600-class Schenectady cars at the left, two Hudson Valley open cars for the local and lake runs in the center and a big road car, No. 66 of the Hudson Valley, coming into the terminal off of Broadway at the right. It has come down the main line through Wilton from Glens Falls; its final destination is Troy via Ballston and Mechanicville. *(Ed Bond collection)*

From a 1926 company timetable.

10. A SIDEWHEEL SAGA

Early in the morning of July 4, 1609 a birchbark canoe carrying Samuel de Champlain and two companions glided out from among the overhanging cedars and maples at the head of the Richelieu River and entered the broad waters of the lake that now bears his name. Champlain was the last of a long line of intrepid navigators and explorers who sought the coveted Northwest Passage; he missed it as did his illustrious predecessors but discovered instead an inland sea that would be a great battleground and artery of commerce in years to come.

The Algonquin Indians had told him about the great body of water to the south and he set out in April from Quebec City in his *chaloupe,* a large boat with two masts. He sailed up the St. Lawrence with a party of Indians and turned south up the Richelieu but was stopped by the falls of Chambly. There a war party of sixty more Algonquins joined them and portaged 24 canoes along with their baggage and arms around the falls and continued south to the lake.

After entering the lake at what is now Rouses Point, they pushed south with great caution, traveling mostly at night and camping by day in order to avoid a surprise ambush by unfriendly Indians, the Iroquois. They paddled around and made a thorough exploration of the shores and islands of the lake, including the mouth of the Winooski River, which the Indians said led to a rich and abounding valley beyond. He arrived on the 29th at the promontory on which Fort Ticonderoga would be built, and here he was persuaded by his Algonquin allies to fight a successful but ill-advised battle with a group of Iroquois. This encounter, probably more than any other single factor, aligned the powerful Indian confederation of the Iroquois against the French, determining that the language, customs and government of the vast region surrounding the Champlain Valley were to be English rather than French.

Thirty-three years after Champlain's escapade, a string of Indian canoes carrying 36 Hurons and three Frenchmen paddled up the St. Lawrence from Quebec City. The leader of the group was Father Isaac Jogues, a Jesuit priest, who was returning to Sault Sainte Marie where he had established a mission the year before. As they neared the outlet of the Richelieu, several Iroquois canoes pushed out from the shadows and bore down on the peaceful party. Some of the Hurons and the three Frenchmen were seized, and the white men were immediately put to torture. The Iroquois evidently had not forgotten their defeat at the hands of Champlain and his Algonquin allies in 1609.

The Indians loaded the captives into their canoes and started up the Richelieu, continuing south through Lake Champlain to an inlet near the site of Champlain's unfortunate victory, the present location of Ticonderoga. From there they carried their canoes around the falls and rapids and re-embarked on the beautiful body of water now known as Lake George. From the south end of that lake, the party traveled overland to the Indians' village in the Mohawk Valley. It was under these rather unpleasant circumstances, certainly not those that would greet millions of tourists three centuries later, that the white man first laid his eyes on the crystal waters of this majestic lake.

Father Jogues had to endure frightful tortures under which his two companions succumbed, and he was held captive for two years until he was

231

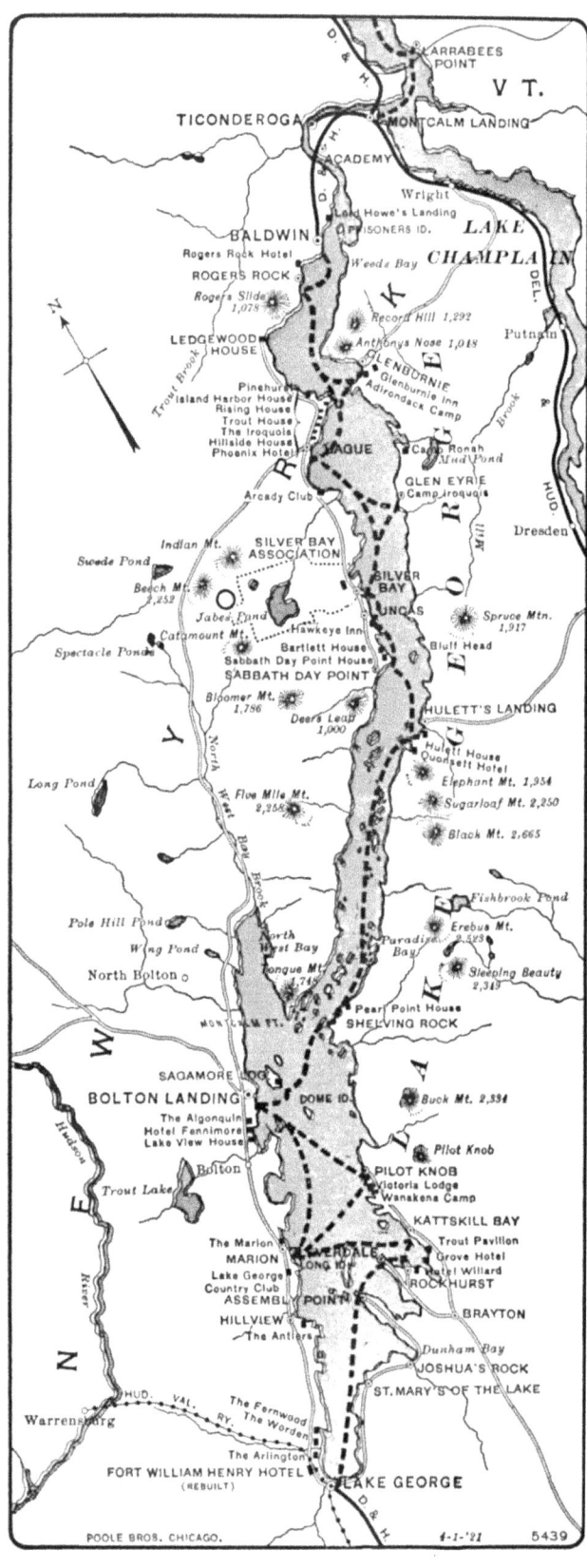

ransomed by some Dutch traders in Fort Orange, now Albany, where he had accompanied some braves on a trading trip. He then returned to France.

A tireless missionary, Jogues returned in two years to establish a mission in the Mohawk Valley. In 1646 he left Quebec and voluntarily returned over his "Via Dolorosa." On the eve of the festival of Corpus Christi, he once again arrived at the shore of the beautiful lake. In commemoration of the ecclesiastical significance of the date, he proclaimed it "Lac du Saint Sacrament." For a few months things went well between him and the Indians, but in 1646 some Mohawks turned on him and put him to death.

The two lakes gradually assumed increasing importance as the natural route for military expeditions between Canada and the British possessions. In a day when overland movements were practically impossible due to the dense forests, rugged mountains, impassable streams, imminent danger from savage and beast, and when there were certainly no roads, the strategic importance of these waterways could hardly be overemphasized. Northern New York and the Mohawk Valley formed a line of contact between two traditional and bitter rivals, England and France. The English controlled the Atlantic seaboard from Maine to Florida, while the French held Canada and great areas of the Ohio and Mississippi valleys. War parties connected with one side or the other moved back and forth through this area from 1666 up through the French and Indian War, continuing through the Revolutionary War and even the War of 1812, ending with the famous Battle of Plattsburgh in 1814.

The most spectacular of these expeditions was in 1758 when 15,000 men and over 100 boats, under the command of the British General James Abercromby, sailed the length of Lake George (as the British had three years previously renamed Lac du Saint Sacrament) to storm Carillon, the most southerly French outpost. The fleet almost literally obscured the surface of the water from view as it moved down the lake — to meet disaster. It was in this battle that the famous 42nd Royal Highlanders, the "Black Watch," won their reputation as fierce fighters, for they were just that in this encounter, but the French remained in victorious possession of Fort Carillon. In 1759, under Baron

Jeffrey Amherst, the British finally succeeded in dislodging the French from the fort, which was then renamed Ticonderoga.

✓ ✓ ✓

The first vessel to engage in regular commercial traffic on Lake Champlain was the small sloop launched in 1770 by Major Philip Skene of Skenesborough, now the village of Whitehall. This vessel had the monopoly on what little traffic there was on the lake until the outbreak of the Revolutionary War, whereupon she was commandeered by General Benedict Arnold, was fitted out as a warship called the *Liberty* and took part in the battle of Valcour.

Trade between Whitehall and the settlements on Lake Champlain flourished after the war and the subsequent admission of Vermont into the Union as the 14th state. Between 1790 and 1815 thirty ships of various sizes were launched to accommodate this business. Most of this water-borne traffic was controlled by Gideon King, who rejoiced in the title of "Admiral of Lake Champlain." His fleet plied between all the ports on the lake from Whitehall to St. Johns, Quebec, until, and for some time after, a new propulsion force appeared on the lake—steam.

The first commercially successful steam-powered boat service in America was inaugurated by Robert Fulton, whose pioneer steamboat, now remembered as the *Clermont*, steamed up the Hudson River from New York to Albany, arriving at the capital city on August 19, 1807, after 32 hours of running time. Following this major breakthrough, the Winans brothers, John and James of Burlington, Vermont, set out to build a similar but larger vessel on the shore of Lake Champlain at their home town, and launched her in the summer of 1808. Appropriately christened the *Vermont*, their ship began puffing around the lake in June, 1809, just 22 months after the *Clermont's* historic run, and 200 years after Champlain entered the same waters in his birchbark canoe. The *Vermont* had the distinction of being the first steamboat to be regularly operated in commercial service on Lake Champlain.

She was 120 feet long, 20 feet wide, displaced 167 tons and cost $20,000. Her 20-horsepower engine had a single horizontal cylinder with a 20-inch bore and a 3-foot stroke. This equipment was poor but probably the best obtainable at the time,

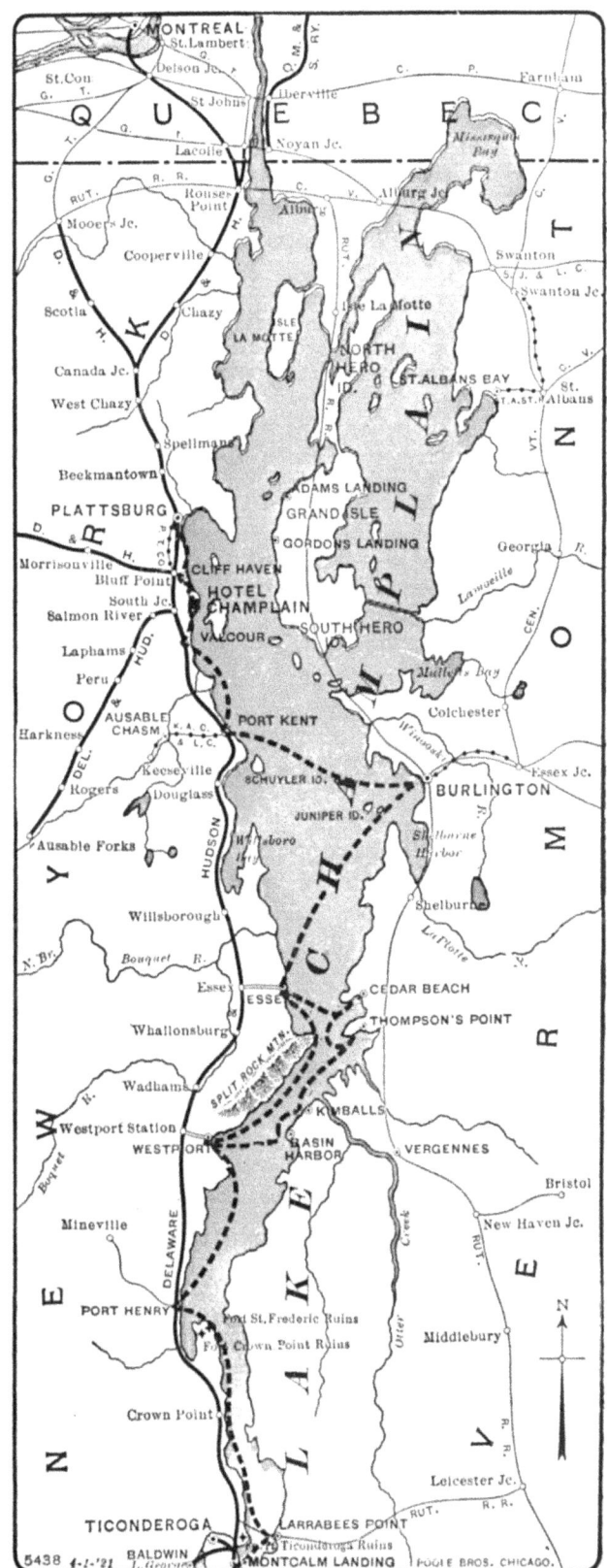

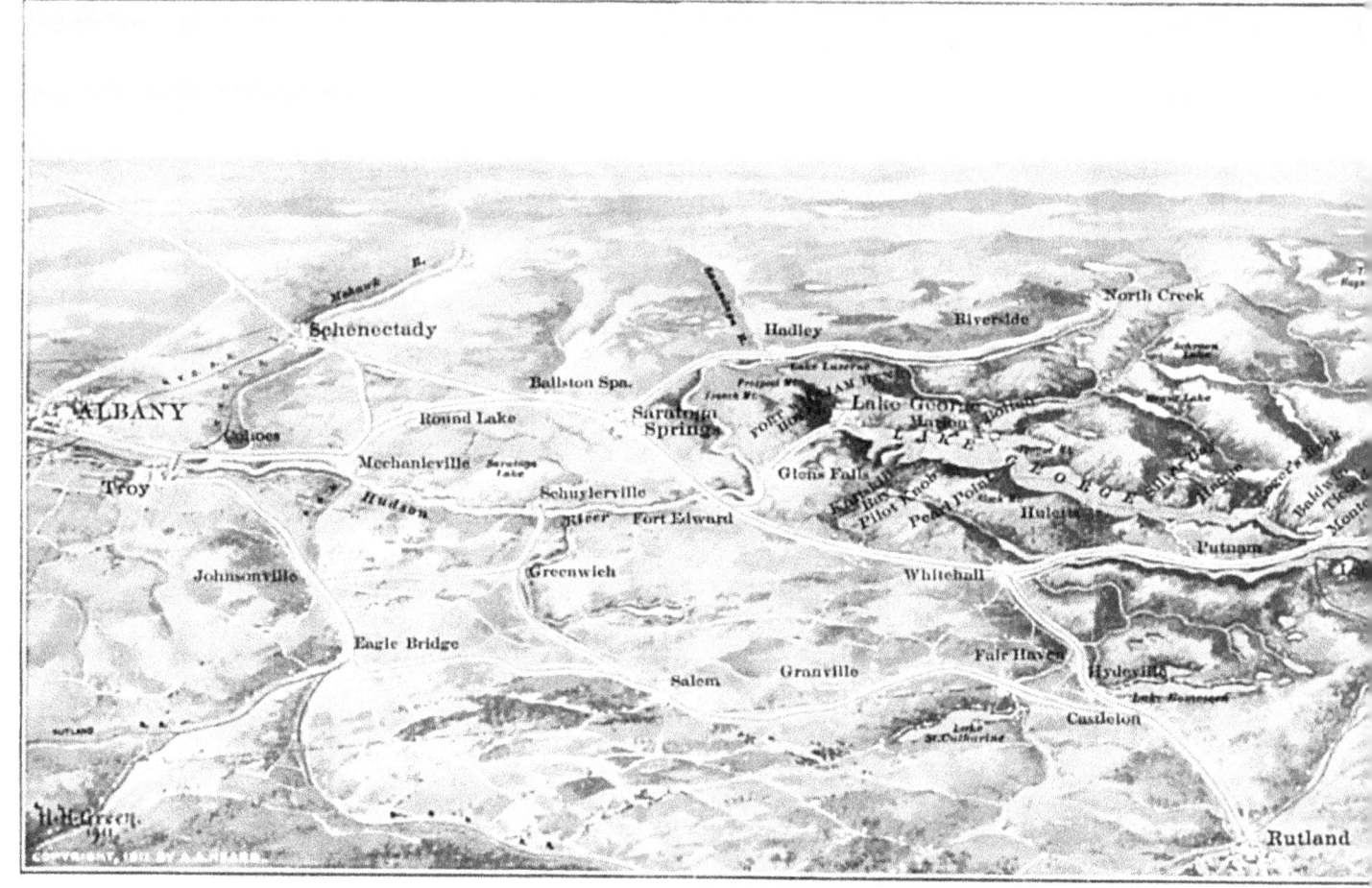

as American-built engines of the day were neither dependable nor properly machined for smooth and efficient operations, and breakdowns and delays were expected and encountered. Her overall appearance resembled a canalboat with a single smokestack in the center; her deck was clear, having no pilothouse and only a small room below for both sleeping and dining. In fair weather she made four to six miles per hour on her one round trip a week between St. Johns and Whitehall, and served as a part of the 150-mile water link between New York and Montreal. The crew and passengers on "Admiral" King's sloops would jeer as they swept past her—especially so upon overtaking her while going in the same direction.

In spite of frequent breakdowns and the keen competition from the sailing craft, the *Vermont* continued to perform her schedule with a commendable degree of regularity for six years. During the War of 1812, communication with St. Johns was interrupted and she ran only to Plattsburgh and transported troops and supplies for the government.

After the war she resumed her run to the Canadian city but on October 15, 1815, while steaming up the Richelieu River on her way south from St. Johns, she suffered her most severe and final breakdown. The connecting rod became detached from the crank pin and before the engine could be stopped it stove a hole through her hull. She sank in a matter of minutes near Ile-aux-Noix, about three miles north of the international boundary.

The loss of the *Vermont* did not end steam navigation on the lake; rather her operation by the Winans brothers only served to prove to businessmen on the lake and as far away as Troy that steam was a practical power source and was here to stay. Between the launching of the *Vermont* in 1808 and 1835 there were five distinct organizations formed to run steamboats of one type or another and over different routes on Lake Champlain.

⚓ ⚓ ⚓

The success of steamboating on Lake Champlain naturally spread to nearby Lake George and in 1817 construction of a steamboat named the *James Caldwell* was completed by Captain Jahaziel Sherman, with the aid of James and John

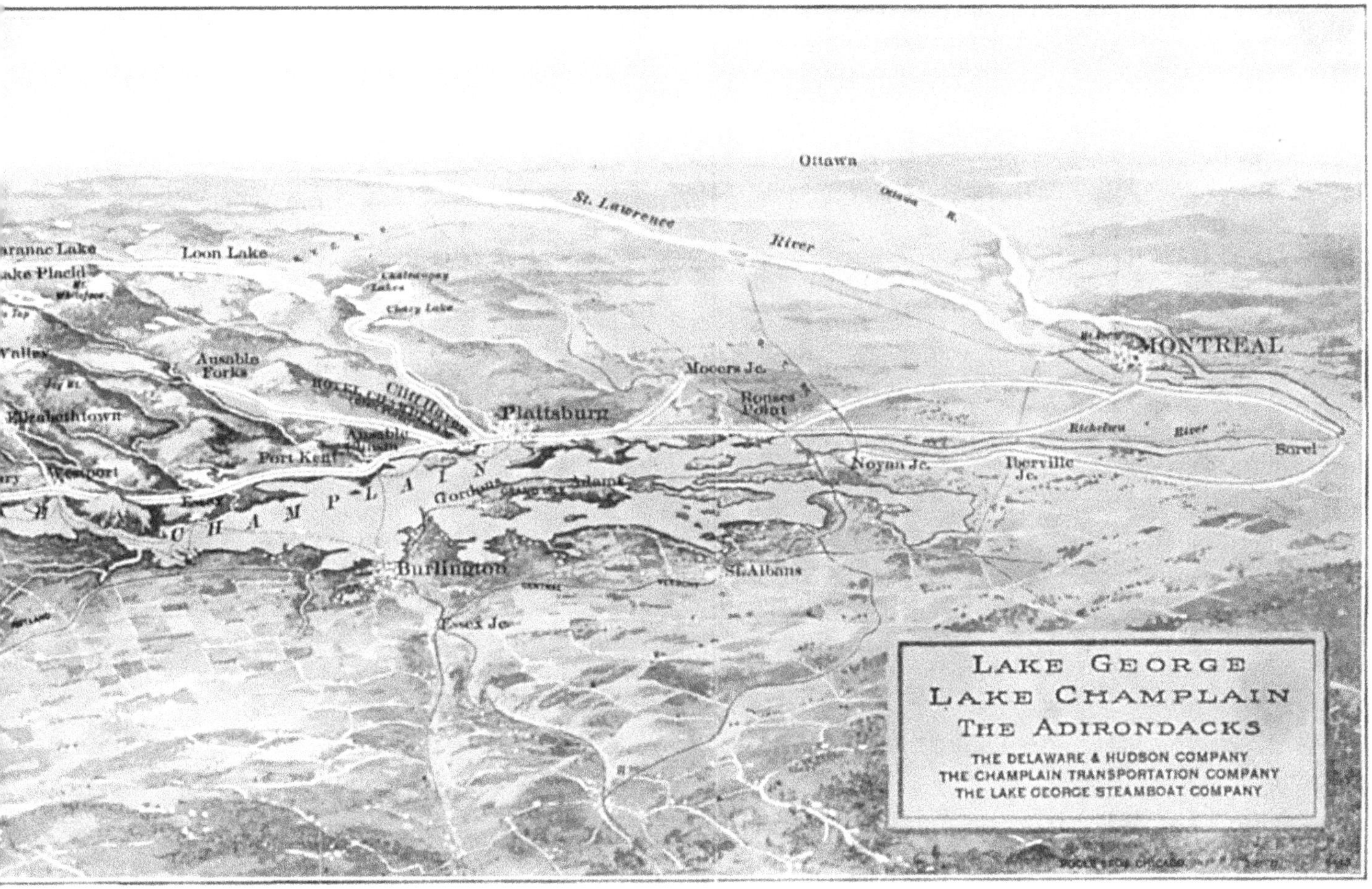

Winans. The boilers and engine were salvaged from the sunken *Vermont* and placed in the new boat during the winter of 1816, after first being used in a Lake Champlain boat for the previous summer. The $12,000, 80-foot vessel had the unusual distinction of a brick smokestack, and steamed the length of the lake at four miles per hour until 1821 when she burned while lying at her dock at Caldwell Village at the southern end of Lake George.

↑ ↑ ↑

In October of 1826, a group of Burlington businessmen formed and chartered the Champlain Transportation Co., with Luther Loomis as its president. By this time steam had fought its way to supremacy on the lake and in the 15 years that had elapsed since the opening of the Champlain Canal the volume of traffic on the lake resulting from this connection with the Hudson River and New York City had greatly increased. Fleets of canalboats were towed by steamers through the lake en route from Canada to New York and the commercial sailing vessels slowly began to disappear.

This perspective of the country from Albany to Montreal, together with the maps on pages 232 and 233, is reproduced from a 1921 company brochure describing the attractions of this "Summer Paradise" and listing its accommodations for tourists. The old advertisements on pages 236 and 237 are from the D&H collection.

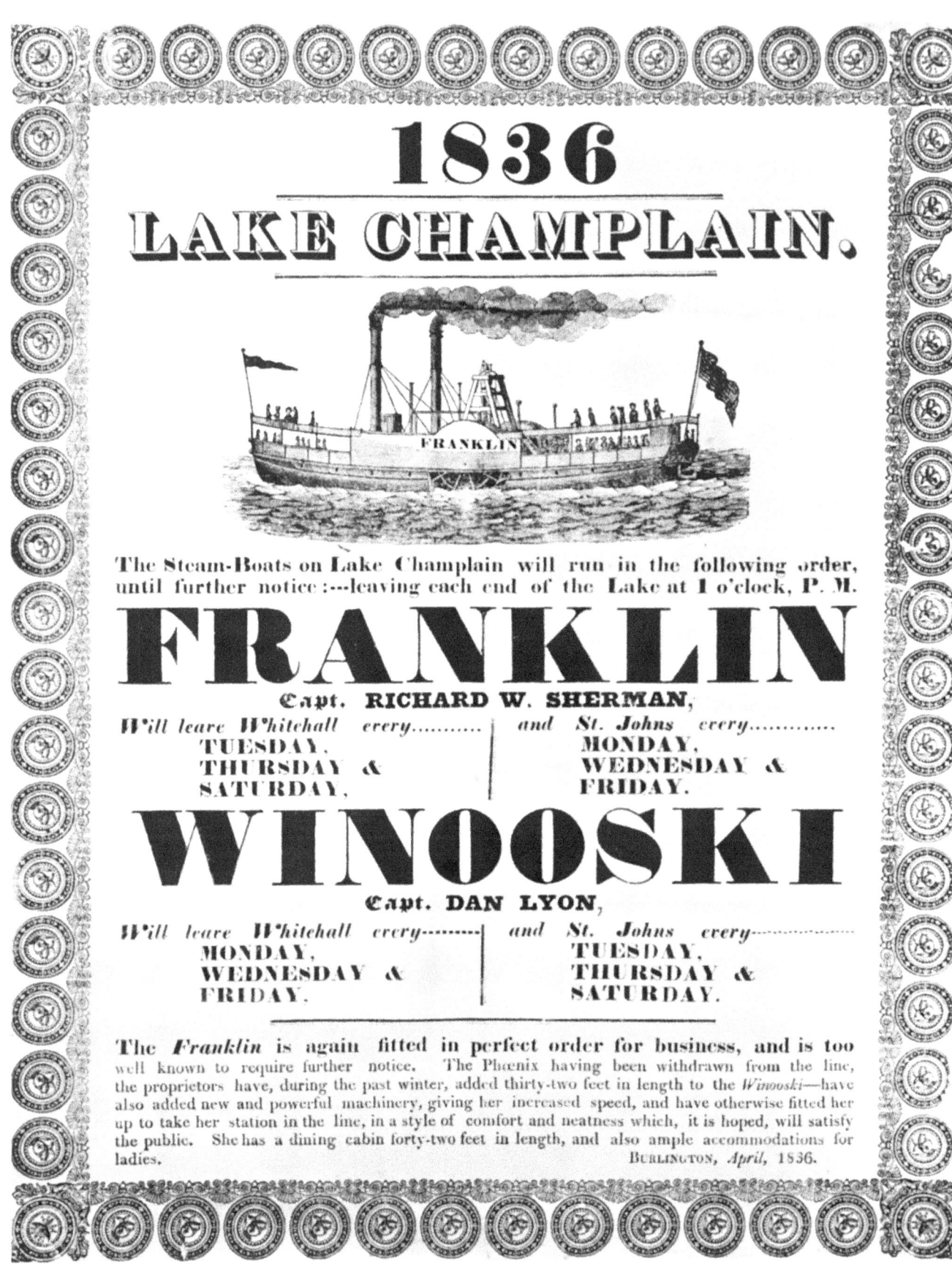

The new company wanted to have the best and most powerful boat on the lake and commissioned a $50,000 vessel, the *Franklin,* to be built at St. Albans Bay and launched for the 1827 season. The *Franklin* was the largest steamer built thus far on the lake, and her nearest rival, the *Phoenix* of the Lake Champlain Steamboat Co. was outstripped in every respect. Her 75 horsepower engine allowed her 10 miles per hour and soon won for her a steady and profitable patronage. Her boilers were located on the guards instead of in the hold and diminished the hazards of fire and explosion within the hull of the vessel. This placement set a standard that would be used on practically all subsequent boats. Her passenger accommodations were vastly improved over the other boats running on the lake, featuring a covered promenade deck, a ladies' cabin on the main deck and 48 berths provided in larger and more numerous cabins than on her predecessors.

The new Champlain Transportation Co. went after the business with vigor, enthusiasm and the superior boat. Soon it became apparent there were more steamboats and more companies operating them than the traffic would bear. In 1830 the lesser lines began to capitulate and by 1835 the C.T. Co. reigned supreme on the lake, having bought out all the competition, and owning all seven of the boats then on the lake. It retained the three best boats for the Whitehall-St. Johns and the Burlington-Port Kent-Plattsburgh runs and disposed of the others or assigned them to towboat service.

The company was expanding and business was growing rapidly; competition appeared at intervals, but in one way or another was always overcome. It was soon apparent that a larger, more sumptuous and more powerful boat was needed to accommodate the ever-increasing volume of customers lining up at the ticket windows. In 1836 the keel of the *Burlington* was laid at Shelburne Harbor, near the boat's namesake city, and Captain R. W. Sherman, who was to be her master, was put in charge of the job. He was the son of Jahaziel Sherman, a well-known captain in the early days of steamboating. No expense was spared to produce a vessel superior to any then in existence on the lake. She was 200 feet long, displaced over 400 tons and had a 200-horsepower engine, a tremendous advance over the 45-horsepower in the *Phoe-*

Lake Champlain Steam Boats.

THE PHŒNIX,

GEORGE BURNHAM, Master,

WILL leave *Whitehall* every *Tuesday* and *Saturday,* at 2 o'clock. P. M., and St. Johns every *Monday* and *Friday,* at 8 o'clock in the morning.— The price of passage is reduced to the following rates:

From Whitehall to St. Johns, and from St. Johns to Whitehall, $8,00.

From Whitehall		From St. Johns	
To Ticonderoga	$1,50	To Champlain	$1,50
" Chimney Point	2,50	" Chazy	2,00
" Basin Harbour	3,00	" Plattsburgh	3,00
" M'Neil's, (Charlotte)	3,50	" Port Kent	3,50
" Burlington	4,00	" Burlington	4,00
" Port Kent	4,00	" M'Neils (Charlotte)	5,00
" Plattsburgh	5,00	" Basin Harbour	5,50
" Chazy	6,00	" Chimney Point	6,00
" Champlain	6,50	" Ticonderoga	6,50
" St. Johns	8,00	" Whitehall	8,00

Children from two to ten years of age, half price; under two years. quarter price. For each dog or other animal, not exceeding the size of a sheep, one dollar; they are to be tied on deck foward of the capstan.

For the particular accommodation of passengers and travellers, crossing the Lake, the prices are reduced to the following rates:

From *Burlington* to *Port Kent* and from *Port Kent* to *Burlington,*

For Each Passenger,	$0,50
" Each Horse,	0,75
" Each Horse, Gig, and Driver,	1,50
" Each Waggon, with 2 Horses and Driver,	2,00

From *Burlington* to *Plattsburgh* and from *Plattsburgh* to *Burlington,*

For Each Passenger,	$1,00
" Each Horse,	1,00
" Each Horse, Gig and Driver,	2,00
" Each Waggon, with 2 Horses and Driver.	3,00

Deck Passengers will be required to remain forward of the Shafts.

The proprietors have determined to reduce the price of Freight—which they hope will be satisfactory to the publick. They will be responsible for damage sustained on merchandize by the mismanagement of their Captains, and for no other loss or damage whatever.

THE CONGRESS,

E. L. HURLBURT, Master,

Will commence towing rafts at the opening of the navigation, and previous to her completing that business. the publick will be notified of her future destination.

Vergennes. 23d *March* 1824.

I, Elijah Root, *of Shelburn, in the District of Vermont, having been appointed by the* Hon. Elijah Paine, *District Judge for said District of Vermont, to inspect the boilers and machinery of all vessels propelled in whole or in part by steam, on Lake Champlain, under an act of Congress approved on the* 7th *day of July, A. D.* 1838, *do hereby certify, that I have made an examination of the boilers and machinery on board the Steam Boat* Burlington Commanded by Capt Wm Anderson *and find them sound and fit for use. That the said boat is owned by* The Champlain Transportation Co *and that said* boilers and machinery *of said Boat were built in the year* 1838 *and that said boilers and machinery are* 12 *years old.*

Burlington, Sept 30 1850 E Root

The engraving of the *Burlington* is from an 1837 advertisement of a tone calculated to appeal to the "best people" and to reflect the distinction of the brand new steamer and the elegance of her famous commander. Elijah Root, the man who inspected her boilers and machinery and signed her 1850 certificate, was chief engineer of the Champlain Transportation Co. from 1827 to 1883. He was in charge of building all the line's boats from the *Franklin* to the *Chateaugay*. (D&H collection, three documents)

nix and 75-horsepower in the *Franklin*, the mainstays of the company's fleet at the moment.

Amid the general satisfaction the managers of the company felt with the *Burlington*, about to be commissioned, and which they were sure would soon be regarded as the "Mistress of the Lake," news arrived of a disconcerting nature. A rival boat was being built at Whitehall by Peter Comstock, a shipper and freight forwarder there. The managers knew him to be a formidable competitor and realized that he would pose a serious threat to the $75,000 they had already sunk into the *Burlington*.

In an effort to protect their investment, the C.T. Co. directors approached Mr. Comstock to work out some sort of a deal that would be mutually agreeable. They generously offered Comstock $20,000 for his unfinished boat still on the ways, a salary of $1000 a year as agent for the company in Whitehall and a seat on the Board. Probably the most important part of the deal was that Comstock would agree in writing not to involve himself in any other sort of steamboat activity or to patronize any other steamboat line, should one crop up, for a period of eight years, a rather odd figure, but perhaps a compromise. Comstock accepted the deal and, since they now owned it anyway, the C.T. Co. managers decided to complete his boat and, in the process, to have it lengthened and provided with power equal to that of the *Burlington*. The decor of the *Whitehall*, as she was to be christened, was to be plain, substantial and respectable, not in the elegant and expensive manner of the "Mistress of the Lake."

The *Burlington* was completed and put into service under the command of Captain Richard W. Sherman in the spring of 1837; the *Whitehall* was ready for the following season. The two steamers were placed on opposite sides of the through line from St. Johns to Whitehall and began a service that was to last for 17 seasons.

Although in many respects the equal of her sister ship, the *Whitehall* never quite attained the noteworthy fame and popularity of the *Burlington*. This was due in some measure to the latter vessel herself, but more likely to her famous commander, Captain Sherman. Steamboating had gradually become America's "Grand Passion" and for it, and the man engaged in it, the public readily prepared a pedestal. Trained by his father, the veteran lake

This poster, advertising the day line service provided by the Champlain Transportation Co., was issued six years before the stormy "Comstock War" on the lake.

boatman and now a director of the company, young Sherman saw the advantages of system and order in every phase of steamboat operation and created on the *Burlington* an atmosphere of discipline and order equal to that on a man-of-war. The combination of man and boat allowed the *Burlington* to be celebrated as the "paragon of steamers" both in America and Europe.

There is no doubt that Sherman was a bit of an autocrat and that he catered largely to the "best people." In 1840, President Martin Van Buren was a passenger on the *Burlington* and upon boarding the steamer one of his staff asked if he would like to meet the famous captain. The President replied, "No. I know Sherman. He thinks the world is a steamboat and he is the Captain."

Two years later, Charles Dickens traveled the length of the lake on the *Burlington* and when he returned to England and wrote his volume "Amer-

The *Francis Saltus*, above, was Peter Comstock's challenge to the Champlain Transportation Co. and as such was one of the most famous steamboats ever to sail the lake. It was not until the spring of 1837 that the 19 m.p.h. speed of the *United States*, below, finally "beat the *Saltus*." Both views are at Whitehall in the upper narrows of the lake. The huge coal pile dates the lower picture as after 1858, the year the black fuel was first used on the *United States*, and later on the other steamers. (*D&H collection, three illustrations*)

ican Notes," he lauded the vessel and its captain. Dickens was generally accused of a strong antipathy to most things American, so he surely must have been impressed by the *Burlington*.

In 1842, the company seemed satisfied with its two principal steamers and the acclaim they were both winning from the public. The agreement with Comstock had two years to run and the managers thought it a good time to replace the aging steamer *Winooski*. She had been built in 1832, was acquired when the Champlain Ferry Co. was bought out in 1835, and was used on the cross-lake operation between Burlington and Plattsburgh. To replace her, a medium-sized boat, the *Saranac*, was built for $25,000 at Shelburne Harbor and launched for the 1842 season. She had a 100-horsepower engine in her 166-foot, 375-ton hull.

With predetermined conniving, Peter Comstock resigned his seat on the C.T. Co.'s board just before the expiration of the "armistice" arranged eight years earlier when the company bought him off and took over his steamer *Whitehall* to eliminate his possible competition. Now he resumed hostilities and announced plans to build another steamer in competition with the Transportation Company. Obviously, Comstock was maneuvering to be bought out again as he and the others had been before. Precedent would certainly suggest such a move and he was sure it was in the bag. To the surprise of everybody—and no one more than Comstock—the usually ultra-conservative managers of the C.T. decided to meet the situation head-on and fight.

After Comstock recovered from his shock, he found himself out on a limb, and realized that it would be sawed off behind him if he didn't go ahead with his scheme. His new steamer slid down the ways at Whitehall basin in the spring of 1844 and he christened her the *Francis Saltus*. This boat was slightly smaller than the *Whitehall* or the *Burlington*, but was able to make as good a speed as the bigger boats—15 miles per hour—and had plenty of power—160 horsepower—for her 185-foot length. She entered service, and what would soon be called a war, for the season of 1845 under command of Captain H. G. Tisdale, an old sloop skipper.

The Champlain Transportation Co. snapped into action and put the *Burlington* on the same

PASSAGE REDUCED.

MORNING LINE FOR
ST. JOHNS,
AND INTERMEDIATE LANDINGS

CABIN PASSAGE THROUGH, 50 Cents.
DECK PASSAGE   25   "

Breakfast on Board.

The Fast Running Steamer
SARANAC,
CAPT. P. T. DAVIS,
Will leave Whitehall on

 Saturdays, on the arrival of the ... and ... St. Johns in time for the Cars ... the same evening.

Returning, leaves St. Johns
... and Fridays, at 4 1-2 o'clock, A. M., and arrives at Whitehall in the afternoon, ... Packet ... be in readiness to run to the Morning Boat for New York, and to the Great Western ... in time to take the Cars for Boston.

WM. S. SOUTHMAYD, Printer. Whitehall, N. Y.

The bargain fare of 25¢ for the 150-mile trip on the competitive route between Whitehall and St. Johns took some patronage away from the *Saltus*, but not enough to put her out of business.

schedule as the *Saltus*, cut the fare and planned to run the competition off the lake, now that "war" had been declared. Much to the surprise of the C.T. Co., the *Burlington* made but little if any headway against the *Saltus*. A fair percentage of the clientele on the lake were the "plain people" who had long looked askance at Captain Sherman

1844.
STEAM PACKET
Wm. Caldwell,

LAKE GEORGE,
L. C. Larabee, Master,

WILL commence her regular Trips on *TUESDAY*, the fourth day of June next—Leaving J. F. SHERRIL'S *Spacious Lake House* at Caldwell, every Morning, (except Sundays,) at 8 o'clock. The Boat will remain at the foot of the Lake 3 1-2 hours, giving Passengers time to visit

THE RUINS OF FORT TICONDEROGA,

and Dine and return to Caldwell the same Day, leaving Ticonderoga at 3 o'clock, P. M. Should any alteration be made in the Steam Boat Arrangement on Lake Champlain, the above arrangement will be altered so as to conform thereto. And thus

Form a regular Communication between

SARATOGA SPRINGS AND LAKE CHAMPLAIN THROUGH LAKE GEORGE.

☞ Passengers taking or leaving the Champlain Steamers at the Hotel near the Fort, now kept by Mrs. ATHERTON, formerly of the Hotel on the Outlet of Lake George, will find Carriages to convey them from one Lake to the other.

May 1st, 1844.

as an aristocrat and the *Burlington* as a steamboat designed only for the "swells." The public always seems to support the underdog anyway, and Captain Tisdale had many friends among shippers and schooner operators who did everything they could to help their old comrade. These land-locked seamen sang songs of opposition on every wharf from Whitehall to St. Johns.

One of the few doggerel compositions that can be printed about the gallant commander of the *Burlington* went like this:

> Dick Sherman is so very slick
> The fops all swarm around him thick
> As humbugs 'round a pot of honey;
> So Dick's cologne brings him the money
>   Ha, Ha, Ha. That's the fun
>   For Dandy Dick of the *Burlington*
> Oh! Dicky is a gallant lad,
> He makes the ladies very glad;
> He smiles and flirts with great parade,
> And then makes love to the cabin maid.
>   Ha, Ha, Ha. That's the fun
>   For Dandy Dick of the *Burlington*
> His decks are scrubbed with so much care
> That cowhide boots can't come there;
> If you can't make your money rattle
> You must go forward with the cattle.
>   Ha, Ha, Ha. That's the fun
>   For Dandy Dick of the *Burlington*
> The *Saltus* and the *Montreal*
> Will drive him from the lake next fall.
>   Ha, Ha, Ha. That's the fun
>   For Dandy Dick of the *Burlington*

After several months of conflict it was soon apparent that more drastic action would have to be taken or the crisis would deepen. Accordingly, a night line was established between Whitehall and St. Johns and the *Burlington* and *Whitehall* were placed in that service with a continuation of the $3.00 fare. Now, the new *Saranac* was pulled off the Plattsburgh ferry run and replaced there again by the old *Winooski*, thoroughly overhauled, lengthened and refitted at Shelburne Harbor to

Captain Richard W. Sherman's aristocratic manner inspired the nickname "Dandy Dick" and the doggerel printed to the left.

take on the *Saltus* on a day run through the lake. The fare was reduced on the *Saranac* to a flat 50 cents between any and all the wharves from Whitehall to St. Johns.

Now the real fun began when Captain Tisdale of the *Saltus* met a foeman worthy of his steel in Captain P. T. Davis, the master of the *Saranac* and one of the most popular and experienced boatmen of the lake. The two steamers tied up on opposite sides of the same dock at terminals, left together and steamed through the lake side by side, each making the same landings. Coming south into Whitehall, sometimes one would lead the way up through the narrows of the lake and on the next trip it would probably be the other. The *Saltus* was slightly the faster of the two, but this by no means prevented the *Saranac* from leading her rival. Frequently the trailing steamer would skip a landing to take the lead, much to the dismay of those waiting on the shore, to say nothing of those on board who might want to disembark at that particular landing. In those days before steamboat inspection laws, the engineers

The *William Caldwell*, opposite, was the first steamer on Lake George to provide through service between Lake Champlain and Saratoga Springs, via stagecoaches from Montcalm Landing on the north and Caldwell on the south. The 32-mile trip took her about 3½ hours. (*D&H collection, opposite, also advertisement reproduced on page 244*)

243

1849 LAKE CHAMPLAIN. 1849

EVENING LINE.

THE STEAMER BURLINGTON
CAPT. WM. ANDERSON,

Leaves Whitehall, MONDAY, WEDNESDAY and FRIDAY, at 12 M.

and Saint Johns, TUESDAY, THURSDAY and SATURDAY, at 2½ P. M.

THE STEAMER WHITEHALL,
CAPT. GIDEON LATHROP,

Leaves Whitehall, TUESDAY, THURSDAY and SATURDAY, at 12 M.

and Saint Johns, MONDAY, WEDNESDAY and FRIDAY, at ½ P. M.

MORNING LINE.

THE STEAMER UNITED STATES,
CAPT. J. T. DAVIS.

Leaves Whitehall, TUESDAY, THURSDAY and SATURDAY, at 4 A. M.

and Saint Johns, MONDAY, WEDNESDAY and FRIDAY, at 2½ A. M.

THE STEAMER FRANCIS SALTUS
CAPT. T. D. CHAPMAN,

Leaves Whitehall, MONDAY, WEDNESDAY and FRIDAY, at 4 A. M.

and Saint Johns, TUESDAY, THURSDAY and SATURDAY, at 2½ A. M.

The Boats of the Day Line will leave St. Johns either in the evening (after the arrival of the last train of Cars from Montreal) or as early as 2½ o'clock, A. M. of the above mentioned days, as their convenience may require or weather permit. Passengers intending to take the Day Boats at either end of the Lake can lodge on board,—at St. Johns it will be necessary for them to do so.

The Day Boats will arrive at St. Johns in time for the Cars to Montreal same evening, and at Whitehall at half past 2 o'clock. P. M., in time to arrive at Troy by the Rail Road Cars for the evening boat to New York. Every attention will be paid to the comfort and convenience of Passengers.

PASSAGE THROUGH $2. MEALS EXTRA.

No charge for berths in the Cabin on the Night Boats. When Passengers lodge on board the Day Boats and the Passage does not amount to 50 cents, 25 cents will be charged for berths. Berths in State Rooms 50 cents each in all cases. ☞ *This arrangement to continue until further notice.*

The Captains and Officers of the Boats are strictly prohibited from taking in charge in any manner whatever, any letters containing Money or any Bank Bills, Jewelry or other light and valuable articles. The Champlain Transportation Company will not undertake to transport any of the above named articles, nor will they hold themselves responsible therefor. Neither will they hold themselves responsible for letters containing Money, or any Bank Bills, Bills of Exchange, Jewelry, or any other light and valuable articles which may be put in charge of any Express man, or the Agent of any Express line, who may be on board; nor for any other goods or property in such charge unless specifically reported to the Captain.

Merchandise deemed extra hazardous on account of fire, and green Hides, will not be taken on board nor transported at any price.

BURLINGTON, APRIL, 1849.

J. C. KNEELAND & CO'S STEAM PRESS, TROY.

would bail pitch pine and kegs of tar into the boilers to increase the steam pressure, and thereby the speed, to gain the advantage.

As early as 1845, the year after the *Saltus* was launched, the company had discussed the possibility of a new boat and they had gradually been accumulating a supply of timber and iron at Shelburne Harbor toward the building of this vessel. In the fall of 1846 the Board passed a resolution to build the proposed steamer with the express words—"to beat the *Saltus*." The following spring they decided to name the boat the *United States*.

Captain Sherman had been at odds with the directors over the invention of a steam cutoff device which he patented and wished to have installed on the company's steamers; he resigned from the board some months before the 1847 annual meeting. Nevertheless, he was offered reappointment as master of the *Burlington* for her 11th season. Apparently feeling himself aggrieved, he declined and thus concluded his association with the Champlain Transportation Co.

Peter Comstock's answer to the plans for construction of the *United States* was to lay down in Whitehall the timbers of a new 224-foot, 417-ton steamer to be called the *Montreal*. Nevertheless, he was beginning to feel the sting of the rate aspect of the "war," which became more acute when the fare on the *Saranac* was dropped to a quarter for deck passage; the cabin fare remained at a half dollar.

The contest now became epic in its character to all the communities in the Champlain Valley and not only the crews but even the passengers entered into the spirit of the struggle with ardor. Favoritism ran high; bets were made on various runs and fist fights often ensued. The bars on the boats had to be closed, first at stops, and when enthusiasm still remained unsuppressed, they were closed entirely.

With the *Burlington* and the *Whitehall* running at the regular $3.00 fare, the C.T. Co. was able to earn enough to keep the 25-cent fare in effect on the *Saranac*, but try as he would, Comstock could not cut his rate under a dollar and have anything left to buy pitch pine for fuel. The good will of the people toward Comstock was helpful at first, but the lower fare was most attractive, and gradually the *Saranac's* decks became as crowded as those of the *Saltus*.

Comstock finally had to give up, but the war wasn't over. Control of the *Saltus* passed to a group of Troy businessmen and they continued the battle, refusing all offers of the olive branch held out by the C.T. Co.

The trial run of the *United States* in the spring of 1847 more than demonstrated that the company had succeeded in its purpose, for she logged a speed of 19 miles per hour, four miles faster than any other boat on the lake. She was definitely a step forward, with a 250-horsepower engine to propel her 250-foot hull. Expectations were aroused to a high pitch when the season opened.

The new skipper, Captain William Anderson, had every confidence in the new steamboat and determined to make the first runoff with the *Saltus* as public as possible. The *United States* lay at her dock in Burlington with steam up and her rails lined with eager passengers and gentlemen of the press, as the *Saltus* smugly steamed out into the lake. She was well out past the breakwater when Captain Anderson cast off his lines and signaled, "Full speed ahead." Gradually the *United States* closed the distance, came alongside and finally, amid a pandemonium of wild cheering and whistle blowing, roared past the *Saltus* and disappeared up the lake in the direction of Whitehall in a smoke trail of glory.

The superior speed of the *United States* broke the back of the competition and on February 10, 1848, the *Saltus'* owners eagerly arranged the details for transferring the *Francis Saltus* and the *Montreal*, then partially completed on the ways, to the Champlain Transportation Co. for $37,000. The company now owned the *Saltus* outright and the celebrated "Comstock War" was over.

⸻

On Lake George, in the meantime, steamboat activities had progressed, although not in the grand manner of events on the larger lake. There was much less business on Lake George than on Champlain, and development was correspondingly slower.

Two years after the *James Caldwell* burned in 1821, a 100-foot, 20-horsepower steamer, the *Mountaineer*, was built at the south end of Lake George. She began service in the spring of 1824, but her skipper, Captain L. C. Larabee, apparently did not have the knack of developing

245

DINNER.
Bill of Fare.

STEAMER UNITED STATES.

Captain GEORGE RUSHLOW.

FISH IN THEIR SEASON.

ROAST.

Sirloin Beef,	Turkey.
Rib of Beef,	Goose.
Lamb, *Mint Sauce,*	Duck,
Veal,	Chickens.

BOILED.

Leg Mutton, *Caper Sauce,* Fowls,
Ham, Corned Beef.

PASTRY.

Steam Boat Pudding,	Apple Pie,
Plum "	Lemon Pie,
Rice "	Custard Pie,
Custard "	Cocoa Pie,
Bread "	Berry Pie.
Cracker "	
Tapioca "	

DESSERT.

FRUITS IN THEIR SEASON.

Ice Cream, Jelly, Pecans,
Almonds, Raisins, Eng. Walnuts.
Filberts.

TEA AND COFFEE.

DINNER $1.00.
WINE LIST NEXT PAGE.

Wine List.

CHAMPAGNE.

MARCEAUX,	(quarts)	$3 00
"	(pints)	1 75
VERZENAY,	(quarts)	3 00
"	(pints)	1 75
VERZENAY, (Dry)	(quarts)	3 50
" (do.)	(pints)	2 00
VERZENAY, Green Seal,	(quarts)	3 50
"	(pints)	2 00
ROEDERER, (Carte Blanche,)	(quarts)	3 50
"	(pints)	2 00
" (Dry Sillery,)	(quarts)	3 00
"	(pints)	1 75
HEIDSEICK,	(quarts)	3 50
"	(pints)	2 00

CLARET.

PAUILLAC,	(quarts)	1 50
"	(pints)	75

SHERRYS, &c.

SHERRY WINE, (Harmony,)	2 50
PORT WINE, (London Dock,)	3 00
HOCK,	2 50
JOSEPH'S HOFFER, (Rhine Wine,)	2 50

ALE & PORTER.

MUIR'S Scotch Ale	50
YOUNGER & SONS' Ale	50
PHILADELPHIA "	25
DOW'S PALE INDIA, "	30
GUINNESS' Dublin Porter,	30
CARPENTER'S Champagne Cider,	30

Waiters are supplied with Cards.

Cruising down the lake on a bright summer day, how could the hungry traveler go wrong for a dollar, with a rib of beef, steam boat pudding and ice cream; and, for $1.75 a pint of Marceaux? *(D&H collection)*

patronage that his Champlain counterparts demonstrated. He seemed reluctant to stop his vessel, once she was under way, and although chivalrous enough to slow up for a lady to board, he evidently considered it a waste of time to make a landing for a lone male. It developed that a passenger boarding in the middle of the run would be rowed out from shore in a small boat and transferred, while in motion, to the steamer's yawl which was always towed astern; whereupon the yawl was drawn alongside the steamer and the determined traveler pulled aboard.

The *Mountaineer* ran for 13 seasons and was finally condemned and dismantled near the northern outlet of the lake in 1837. The year after the demise of the *Mountaineer*, the charter of the first Lake George Steamboat Co., formed in 1817, expired and there is no record of it being renewed, nor was there any new boat built or even proposed. The population, and therefore the business it generated, did not exist on Lake George to the extent that it did on Champlain, and it is remarkable that the steamboats that did exist on the smaller lake could survive at all.

In the following year, Captain Jahaziel Sherman, builder in 1817 of Lake George's first steamer, the *James Caldwell*, built a more modern boat at the northern end of Lake George, near Ticonderoga, and named it the *William Caldwell*. He incorporated improvements in design he had observed while on Lake Champlain, and his 140-foot, 40-horsepower vessel was a real step forward for Lake George. Resembling somewhat the *Franklin*, of the Champlain Transportation Co., she was equipped with the old-fashioned Fulton type of "steeple" engine, operating a horizontal crosshead up and down, and could make 12 miles per hour, three times the speed of her predecessors on Lake George. She ran successfully from the spring of 1838, under the command of Captain Larabee until she was retired ten years later. A through service was provided in 1844 when it was advertised that the *William Caldwell* would wait 3½ hours at the foot of the lake for passengers to stage to the ruins of Fort Ticonderoga, or make connections with the Champlain boats.

* * *

After the Champlain Transportation Co. had "beat the *Saltus*," things quieted down on the larger lake and the *Burlington* and *Whitehall* continued on the night run. The *United States* and the newly-acquired *Francis Saltus* were assigned to the day service, while the *Saranac* went back on the cross-lake ferry run, now extended to St. Albans. The company had been locally owned by essentially the same group of men since its beginning in 1826, and despite doing business in a quiet, old-fashioned way it had attained a position of real importance in the transportation world. During the summer of 1849 several of the local directors sold their holdings to a group of investors headed by Daniel Drew and Nelson Robinson, the well-known Hudson River steamboat magnates, giving them control of the company. The quiet atmosphere of business that prevailed in the company's Burlington offices was due for a rude awakening.

The new owners installed one of their own men as president, Oscar Burton, and through their connection with various railroads and other steamboat lines, they inaugurated policies that proved quite progressive. They established a through route to New York via the company's steamers, the Saratoga & Washington Railroad (which had been completed to Whitehall the previous year), the Rensselaer & Saratoga, and the Citizens' Line steamers from Troy down the Hudson to Manhattan. This system became known as the "North and South Through Line" and enabled passengers to buy tickets and check their baggage direct from Montreal to New York.

On completion of the Champlain & St. Lawrence Railway's extension south to Rouses Point from St. Johns, the northern terminus of the steamboat line was moved up the Richelieu River to Rouses Point for the opening of the 1852 season. This left St. Johns without Champlain steamer service for the first time since the maiden voyage of the *Vermont* in 1809.

Apparently the absentee majority of directors were not interested in the company either traditionally nor sentimentally, but rather viewed it strictly as an investment, for when the chance presented itself for a quick turnover and division of the profits, they seized it. The Rutland & Burlington Railroad, not entirely satisfied with northern connections out of Burlington via its archrival, the Vermont Central, offered to buy everything

The *Minne-Ha-Ha* was built near Caldwell on Lake George in 1857. Her 75 hp engine could drive her 144-foot hull at 13 m.p.h. Ten years later, at Shelburne Harbor on Lake Champlain, the *Adirondack* was built with a 250 hp engine that could drive her 251-foot hull at 18 m.p.h. She is pictured below at Whitehall. *(D&H collection, both)*

the steamboat company owned except its charter, to form a water link north to the railway connections north and west from Rouses Point. The company agreed to the sale, for $125,000, in September 1852, turning over to the railroad the steamers *United States, Francis Saltus, Burlington, Whitehall* and the *Montreal*, which was still in frame, and the *Boston*, which the company had built in 1851, but had not yet placed in service.

A large modern boat named the *R. W. Sherman* had also been launched in 1851 at Whitehall, and in the following year another, the *Canada* slid into the lake. These vessels were sponsored by private interests and were larger and more modern than those the C.T. Co. had sold in 1852 to the Rutland & Burlington Railroad. That same year the *R. W. Sherman* established a record for the fastest run ever made between Port Kent and Burlington, 27 minutes. This time has never been surpassed by any other steamboat on the lake.

Since the Champlain Transportation Co. had divested itself of its older steamers, but not of its charter to operate boats on the lake, President Burton negotiated the purchase of these two new ones for $225,000 in 1853. The *R. W. Sherman* was renamed *America* and with the *Canada* she gave the company a fleet that far surpassed any of the boats it had recently sold, with the exception of the *United States*. Now it was in a better position than ever to command its traditional supremacy on Lake Champlain.

The ferry operation between Burlington and the Grand Trunk and Ogdensburg railways at Rouses Point did not pan out quite the way the Rutland & Burlington wanted and in 1854, after two seasons of operation, that line offered to resell most of the boats back to the Champlain Transportation Co. With its two new boats, that company was anxious to regain possession of the shipyard at Shelburne Harbor and to take over the old steamers, including the *Montreal*, still unfinished and in frame, to prevent possible competition from cropping up. Only the *Boston*, which the C.T. Co. had built but never used, was retained by the railroad to continue the transfer operation to Rouses Point.

The *United States* was put in service with the new *America* and *Canada*, but the *Whitehall, Saranac* and the famous *Burlington* were all retired and dismantled by 1855.

The Champlain Transportation Co.'s old nemesis, the *Francis Saltus,* was not included in the deal, because the railroad had sold her to the Plattsburgh & Montreal, which had just opened its line from Plattsburgh to the Canadian border. There was as yet no railroad south of Plattsburgh on the west side of the lake and the P&M hoped to build up a good passenger business to New York via Burlington. The *Saltus* was scheduled to perform the connection across the lake between the P&M and Rutland & Burlington trains at Burlington. This, of course, was in direct competition with the C.T. Co.'s vessels and the *Saltus* thereby resumed her old status as an opposition steamboat.

She ran for the P&M during 1853 and 1854, and in the spring of 1855 she was sold to Edward V. Price, one of the directors of the railroad. The competition was proving injurious to both the C.T. Co. and the *Saltus* and a meeting was called with all parties concerned to work out some sort of compromise. The result amounted to a split in the revenue from the cross-lake traffic, using only C.T. Co. boats, and the *Saltus* was brought to Plattsburgh and tied to the breakwater with a watchman aboard.

Several weeks later Captain Lot Chamberlin, her skipper, boarded the *Saltus*, put the watchman ashore and fired up the boilers. As a free agent he put her back in service, actually with the approval of her owners despite the agreement, by virtue of a lien he held on her for some repairs he had made. This led to lawsuits, fistfights, sheriffs' writs, midnight raids, and finally to piracy. The whole affair, called the "Lot Chamberlin Piracy," did not end until 1858, when the C.T. Co. once again had to buy the *Saltus*. Before any more problems cropped up in connection with this vessel, the company decided to take no chances and turned her over to the wreckers at Shelburne Harbor. Thus ended the bizarre career of the *Francis Saltus*, probably the most controversial and spirited vessel ever to leave a wake in the waters of Lake Champlain.

In the fall of 1855, the directors decided at last to complete the *Montreal*. Although only a bare hull still in frame, she had changed hands five times since Peter Comstock had originally laid her timbers at Whitehall, eight years before, and she came to the company along with the renowned *Francis Saltus*. The engine of the scrapped *Sara-*

The Fort William Henry Hotel, opened in 1855, stood on a slope near Lake George at Caldwell. In the 1880 scene, above, the grand old structure is reflected in the calm water while the steamer *Ganouskie* and, behind her, the *Minne-Ha-Ha* ride quietly at the dock. The *Vermont II*, one of the best loved and longest lived of all the Champlain boats, steams through the lake near Montcalm Landing. (*S. R. Stoddard, De Sormo collection, above; D&H collection*)

nac was installed in her 224-foot, 417-ton hull and she entered service for the 1856 season.

The Robinson-Drew faction sold its interest in the Champlain Transportation Co. in 1858 to Colonel LeGrand B. Cannon and Captain L. H. Tupper, both big shareholders in the Renesselaer & Saratoga Railroad. These men at once began to improve the physical and financial condition of the steamboat line. One immediate result of their efforts was the introduction of coal. All the steamers on the lake thus far had been wood-burners, but in 1858 the *United States* was converted to coal.

The period of the Civil War brought no momentous changes in either policy or operation of the steamboats on Lake Champlain. Although far removed from the action, they did carry large numbers of troops at various times during the four years of conflict.

⁋   ⁋   ⁋

After the *William Caldwell* was withdrawn from service in 1848, there were two years when no steamboats operated on Lake George. Finally in 1850 a new vessel was built by one John Harris and called the *John Jay*. She represented a substantial advance over the canalboat-like vessels thus far built on the smaller lake, for she was 145 feet long and her 75-horsepower engine could move her at 13 miles per hour. In 1854 she was purchased by a newly-organized Lake George Steamboat Co., replacing the similarly-named firm whose charter ran from 1817 to 1838. The *John Jay* came to a tragic end on July 29, 1856, while on a southbound run. She took fire and burned to the water's edge with the loss of six lives, the only such loss during the entire history of steamboating on Lake George.

The loss of the *Jay* was a severe blow to the new company, which was then not particularly strong, financially. Nevertheless, only 12 days after the disaster, at a meeting in the Fort William Henry Hotel, the directors decided to replace the lost vessel with a new one. The boiler and engine would be salvaged from the *Jay*. The Board set a $20,000 limit on the cost of the new boat and she was completed in the spring of 1857.

The *Minne-Ha-Ha*, as she was named, had about the same dimensions as the *Jay*, but was the first on Lake George to resemble a more modern steamboat in appearance. She had two decks, the upper one covered aft and open forward, and could carry 400 people. She required six cords of firewood on a round trip, but would be the last wood-burner on Lake George.

The Civil War was especially serious, financially, for the Lake George Steamboat Co. and receipts dropped to but half of their usual amount in 1862. The Board resolved to reduce expenses by dispensing with the services of any officers not absolutely necessary. They thereupon took the unusual step of abolishing the position of captain. This demonstrated what they thought of that esteemed position, and for the next season the engineer ran the engine while the pilot steered.

⁋   ⁋   ⁋

The reconstruction era following the war applied to the Champlain Transportation Co. as well as to the country as a whole. The war and its aftermath brought such a volume of traffic to the steamboats that peace had not yet been declared before plans had been laid for a new vessel.

She was launched in the spring of 1867 and christened the *Adirondack*. She would replace the *America*, originally built as the *R. W. Sherman*, a newer boat by four years than the *United States*, but not as well preserved. A 250-horsepower engine in her 251-foot hull, gave the *Adirondack* a speed of 18 miles per hour.

Material was immediately ordered for another steamer, the *Vermont II*, named after the pioneer steamer on Lake Champlain, but construction dragged and she wasn't ready for four years.

While the two new boats were abuilding, the Champlain Transportation Co. began to expand in another direction—toward Lake George. Traffic relations between the two steamboat companies had been steadily growing closer during the war and in 1867 the Champlain Transportation Co. loaned the Lake George Steamboat Co. $20,000, receiving stock as collateral.

Just before the Civil War, George H. Cramer had been elected president of the Rensselaer & Saratoga Railroad. He was brother-in-law to Colonel LeGrand B. Cannon of Burlington, who had secured control of the C.T. Co. from the Drew faction. Cramer's connection with the R&S and

The *Vermont II* was built in 1871 and ran on Lake Champlain for 32 seasons. Her 1500 hp engine drove her 262-foot hull at 19 m.p.h. Below is what happened when the pilot fell asleep at the wheel while running the *Champlain* at full speed. Each of the boat's two separate engines had its own walking beam. *(D&H collection, below)*

Cannon's interest in the C.T. Co. led to the purchase in June, 1868, of $350,000 worth of stock in the steamboat operation by the railroad until it held 1909 shares, a majority amount, thereby gaining complete control. Mr. Cannon decided that conditions on Lake George warranted expansion. The $20,000 loan was followed by an agreement for exclusive traffic rights on the two lakes and adjacent rail connections. Finally in 1868, after a change in its charter to allow the move, the Champlain Transportation Co. bought all the stock in the Lake George Steamboat Co. and thus secured full control of the organization.

Backed by the experience of years of successful steamboat operation on the larger lake, and by the resources of the Rensselaer & Saratoga Railroad that owned the Champlain operation—and through it that on Lake George—Colonel Cannon and his associates injected new life and money into the once-struggling smaller line. By 1869 it showed a profit of $14,000, over three times that of 1867.

Almost immediately after taking over, the C.T. Co. decided that one steamer was not sufficient to furnish the service planned for Lake George and authorized the building of a new boat. A contract was let early in 1869, under the supervision of the C.T. Co.'s master mechanic, Elijah Root, and by late spring the *Ganouskie* was launched and put into service. She was not as large as the *Minne-Ha-Ha*, but was the first vessel on either lake to be driven by a propeller rather than paddle wheels. The odd-looking craft was designed to supplement the service of the larger steamer and was only 72 feet long, with a little pepperbox pilothouse forward and an observation cabin aft on her second deck. Like the *Minne-Ha-Ha*, she burned wood at first but, unlike the larger vessel, she was converted to coal in 1877. With the appearance of the *Ganouskie*, two steamers now operated simultaneously on Lake George for the first time, and a pattern of operation was established that would last as long as steamboats themselves plied the lake. The *Minne-Ha-Ha* left the south end of the lake in the morning and made the midday connection, via stage line, with the Champlain boats from the north end of that lake, returning south in the afternoon. The *Ganouskie* ran the opposite directions.

*   *   *

On December 7, 1870, the Rensselaer & Saratoga Railroad, which owned the Lake Champlain Transportation Co., and through it the Lake George Steamboat Co., accepted an offer from the Delaware & Hudson Canal Co. for a permanent lease of all its property and holdings. Thus it was that the two steamboat operations became part of the D&H system.

On Lake Champlain, the steamer *Vermont II* was finally completed and put into service in 1871, replacing the old *Canada*, and was destined to become one of the finest vessels ever to run on the lake. In size, cost, displacement and horsepower she was without peer and exceeded in every respect the *Burlington*, considered to be a giant in her day, 35 years before. The new *Vermont II* was 262 feet long, weighed 1124 tons, cost $200,000 and had 1500 horsepower to crowd her through the water at 19 miles per hour. All things considered, she was one of the most satisfactory vessels ever owned by the C.T. Co. Her dignity and richness in decor contributed greatly to her popularity with passengers, and her seaworthiness and ease of handling endeared her to the crew.

The *Adirondack* having replaced the *America*, and the *Vermont II* the *Canada*, it was decided in the spring of 1873 to retire the last of the Civil War fleet—the *United States*. She was completing her 26th year, and maintenance costs were mounting, but rather than building another vessel, the company undertook negotiations to buy one.

At the time there was a car ferry named *Oakes Ames* operating on the lake which had been built in Marks Bay at Burlington five years earlier to transport railroad cars across the lake between the Montreal & Plattsburgh and the Rutland railroads. The D&H had acquired this steamer in the process of preparing the way for the consolidation of all the railroads on the west side of the lake. These railroads owned the *Oakes Ames* and the D&H bought these railroads from the Vermont Central which was leasing all these lines including the Rutland at the time. The boat was of no value to the D&H itself so they sold her to the C.T. Co. for $85,000 and $24,000 more was spent converting her from a car ferry to a passenger vessel.

The name *Oakes Ames* carried with it at the time the stigma of the recent Crédit Mobilier congressional scandal and so the vessel's name was changed in 1874 to the *Champlain II*. She was 258

Gibson girl fashions were the mode of the day when the *Horicon I* docked at Ripley's Point on Lake George's eastern shore, above. The same boat backs away from the Lake George steamer dock after boarding passengers from the train on the pier in the 1907 scene below. In the distance the *Sagamore* approaches on her afternoon return trip from Baldwin and passengers will board the waiting train to continue on to Albany and perhaps take the night boat to New York. *(D&H collection, above; Detroit Photographic Co. collection, Library of Congress)*

254

feet long, could make 19 miles per hour and had two 270-horsepower engines, each with its own walking beam and connected separately to each sidewheel. This was required when she was a car ferry as the two tracks on her main deck would not allow an engine in the center of the boat or a shaft to run between the two sidewheels across the main deck.

The $109,000 wasn't a high price to pay for a boat of her caliber and potential but it turned out to be an expensive year and a half of service for the *Champlain II*. While running on the night line service opposite the *Adirondack* in the spring of 1875, her pilot, who was taking drugs while suffering from the gout, fell asleep at the wheel on the night of July 16 and ran her at full speed up on the rocks at Steam Mill Point, just north of Westport, N. Y. Miraculously, no one was even seriously injured, although many people including Captain Rushlow were thrown from their bunks. Later her boilers and engines were removed and her broken hull was sunk off the point in deep water.

In 1874 the Delaware & Hudson built the Baldwin Branch between Montcalm Landing, on Lake Champlain near Ticonderoga, and Baldwin at the north end of Lake George. This afforded a shuttle service between the boat lines on the two lakes, a great improvement over the stage coaches that had previously made the connection.

The gradual extension of the railroads around the valley, particularly the opening of the New York & Canada by the D&H on the west side of Lake Champlain, cut seriously into the traffic using the steamers. Accordingly the route was shortened on Lake Champlain. The southern terminus was changed from Whitehall to Montcalm Landing in 1875, when the lower portion of the railroad was opened, and the following year, when the line was completed, the northern terminus was moved from Rouses Point to Plattsburgh. These changes reduced the steamers' route mileage from 125 to 81. For the first time since its inception, the steamer line ceased to be a necessary link in the direct Montreal service, and the results were immediate and serious.

The management had realized it would be suicidal to continue two line steamers the size of the present vessels after the through railroad was finished, and that one must be sacrificed. The lot fell to the *Adirondack*, only eight years old, but nevertheless older than the *Vermont II*, and she was sent to Shelburne Harbor where her fires were dropped and the wreckers went aboard. Her upper works, the cabin, fixtures and furnishings were sold, together with the engine of the *United States*, and placed in a steamer under construction on the Great Lakes, the *City of Cleveland*, later renamed the *State of Ohio*. The *Adirondack's* own engine, formerly that of the *America*, was sold to a Hudson River boat operator.

Now, in order to save money the managers had to spend some in spite of falling revenues and a first-class steamer being demolished right under their noses, and they authorized the purchase of a smaller boat. The *A. Williams*, built by two men at Marks Bay, Burlington, in 1870, was purchased for $16,500 in February of 1874. She was only 132 feet long; expenses of operating her were considerably smaller too, and she was put on the crosslake ferry service while the *Vermont II* remained on the shrinking through line run.

*   *   *

The steamboat business on Lake George had progressed smoothly since 1868, when the Champlain Transportation Co. had taken over the Lake George line, and traffic increased after the advent of the *Ganouski* in 1869. By 1875 the *Minne-Ha-Ha* was growing old and a new boat was planned. In the spring of 1877, at the north end of the lake, the *Horicon* was launched with the boilers and an engine from the *Champlain II*, which had been wrecked on Lake Champlain the previous summer. Because of a continuing lack of funds, the Lake George boats had never been decorated very lavishly, but when the *Horicon* came out she was handsomely furnished in the best of taste for her time. She was 195 feet long, could make 20 miles per hour, and her main saloon on the promenade deck was 108 feet long, 27 feet wide and finished in several varieties of native wood.

As there was no further use for the old *Minne-Ha-Ha*, she was sold in 1878 to a Cyrus Butler, who removed the engine and moored her remains in a little bay on the north side of Black Mountain Point, where she remained for several years as a floating hotel, before finally sinking.

The Delaware & Hudson extended its track up from Glens Falls to the south end of the lake in

As the sun sets behind Prospect Mountain, to the left, on a summer Sunday in 1912, the new steamer *Horicon* has arrived at Lake George station with a load of tourists returning from a pleasant day's cruise on the majestic lake. Soon they will board the waiting train with three engines which will return them to Troy, Albany or Schenectady and the reality of life in an era of iceboxes and the ten-hour workday. *(Fred Thatcher, from original plate)*

The *Minne-Ha-Ha's* active years on Lake George ended in 1876. In 1878 she was sold to Cyrus Butler, a hotelman who moored her in a little cove north of Black Mountain Point. There she was a floating hotel for several years. In time she sank; her upper works were dismantled and her hull was dynamited. On a clear day her old timbers can still be seen on the bottom of the bay. The *Vermont II* is at her winter berth at Shelburne Harbor in the 1890 era scene below. The *Chateaugay* is up on the ways in the distance. The old hull in the foreground is probably the remains of the *Canada*. (S. R. Stoddard, De Sormo collection, above; D&H collection)

1882, and with the trains came a flood of tourists. The through rail route up along Lake Champlain that hurt the business of the Champlain boats actually helped things on Lake George. Thousands of tourists now made the side trip through the beautiful, island-studded lake, or came to it for a day's outing. All this was quite different from the hand-to-mouth existence that had been the lot of steamers on the smaller lake since the days of the *James Caldwell*. The idea of replacing the *Ganouskie* with a much larger boat had been considered and when this new surge of business showed up on the books at the end of 1882, plans were quickly made and executed. Materials had been gradually accumulated at Cooks Landing, where most of the other recent boats had been built, and the *Ticonderoga* was in the lake and ready to go by the spring of 1883.

She was 172 feet long, displaced 500 tons, could run at 20 miles per hour and accommodated slightly less than the 1000 passengers the *Horicon* could handle. She was placed on the line to run opposite the *Horicon*, and the *Ganouskie* was sold and used as a floating barroom near Big Burnt Island near the Narrows for several years.

*   *   *

Since the railroad was now handling the through traffic on the western shore of Lake Champlain, the steamers could no longer compete in this business and the Champlain Transportation Co. began to solicit the summer tourists by advertising the historical and scenic features of the lake and its surroundings. Revenues were down, but so were expenses and between 1880 and 1887 the *A. Williams* and the *Vermont II* earned enough to pay several dividends and at last to justify the company in providing itself with a new steamer. The *A. Williams* had built up a very tidy business and the demand for pleasure excursions was growing rapidly.

The Board decided at its January 1887 meeting to build a new boat and to depart from previous practice on the lake by using iron for the hull. The boat was built at Shelburne Harbor and upon launching in the spring of 1888 was christened the *Chateaugay*. Designed as a passenger and excursion boat, she was the last word in marine construction and boatmen came from far and wide to see her. A 1000-horsepower Fletcher beam engine powered her 205-foot, 724-ton bulk at 20 miles per hour. Old Andrew Fletcher came up from New Jersey to operate the engine on her first trip. When the gong sounded he opened the throttle wide and the engine seemed almost to rise right out of the hull as it hurtled into life. "By God!" he said as the paddles churned the lake to a white froth on either side. "If anything was going to go, I wanted to be here when it went!" Nothing went but the boat, and the *Chateaugay* started on a career that even the most optimistic souls there at the time would never have believed.

With the advent of the *Chateaugay*, the *A. Williams* was sent to Shelburne Harbor and held in reserve for excursions and special parties until 1893 when she was broken up. Four years later, the C.T. Co. purchased a vessel slightly larger than the *A. Williams*, named the *Maquam*, for the Burlington-St. Albans service and also for excursions. She had been built in 1881 by the St. Johnsbury & Lake Champlain Railroad in Maquam Bay, near Swanton, Vermont, for excursions in connection with that railroad.

*   *   *

In 1895 the Lake George Steamboat Co. purchased the *Mohican*, a small vessel only 93 feet long that was already in operation on Lake George. She was to be used for local service and to open up a route into scenic Paradise Bay, an area inaccessible to the larger boats.

The Lake George Steamboat Co. was hard hit on August 28, 1901, when the *Ticonderoga* was destroyed by fire just after leaving Baldwin. Captain F. G. White got her to Rogers Rock landing and everyone got off, but the wooden vessel was doomed. The *Ticonderoga* had served the company well for 17 years and her destruction left it with but one ship for the line service, the 24-year-old *Horicon*. The *Mohican* could not fill the gap, so a new boat was immediately authorized.

The Lake George line had not built a boat since steel hulls came into use, and with the experience gained by the parent company in building the *Chateaugay* for service on the other lake, the Board decided to make the new boat of steel. With an 850-horsepower Fletcher in her 203-foot hull, she was launched at Caldwell in April, 1902, and christened the *Sagamore*. She cost $150,000 and could carry 1500 people at 20 miles per hour.

The *Vermont II* drifts into the company dock at Burlington, above; near the Burlington Yacht Club in the background can be seen the bow of the little *Maquam*. Below, the *Chateaugay* approaches the dock at Port Kent, where a hack waits and another comes in, probably from the railroad station. (*Lake George Park Commission, above and opposite below; Detroit Photographic Co. collection, Library of Congress, the others*)

The *Chateaugay* nears the landing of the Champlain Hotel; across the lake, in the view from Bluff Point, above, South Hero Island appears and beyond it, dimly visible through the haze, are Mount Mansfield and the hills of Vermont. The beautiful S. R. Stoddard photograph, below, features the *Maquam* at Burlington dock, with the *Vermont II* at the right. In front, old canallers relax outside their boat's living quarters.

The *Sagamore* has just been lengthened by twenty feet, above, and is sliding back into Lake George, while the *Mohican I* steams about Heart Bay, with the Rogers Rock Hotel in the background. Silver Bay, below, was a particularly busy spot in the summer with several hundred people coming and going each weekend. The *Sagamore* is stopping there. *(Fred Thatcher, from original glass plate, above; J. S. Wooley)*

Although the builders followed the general dimensions of the *Chateaugay*, more headroom was allowed and as a result the *Sagamore* was somewhat topheavy. She was run up the Baldwin yard where she was cut in half and a 20-foot section was added amidship; she came out for the 1903 season measuring 223 feet over all. This increase in length, along with the addition of ballast tanks just forward of the paddle boxes, solved the problem and she turned out to be one of the best handling boats ever built by the company.

The village of Caldwell changed its name to Lake George Village on April 1, 1903, and for the next three years the *Sagamore*, *Horicon* and *Mohican* provided an ever-growing service through the lake from the pier at the village.

⸎ ⸎ ⸎

By 1902 the *Vermont II* had completed 31 years of service on Lake Champlain and was getting a bit shaggy, both in appearance and mechanically. Plans were now made for the biggest and best steamer ever to sail on the lake. The *Vermont III* was launched from Shelburne Harbor in the spring of 1903. She was 262 feet long, 62 feet wide, weighed 1195 tons, had 50 staterooms each with running water, and was licensed to carry 900 passengers. Her 1800-horsepower Fletcher beam engine allowed her a speed of 23 miles per hour. The stateroom hall was furnished in gold and white; her furniture was mahogany with red carpeting throughout. She cost the company slightly over $200,000. She was placed on the 162-mile round trip line run formerly served by her namesake and predecessor, the old *Vermont II*, to the satisfaction and pleasure of all who rode.

The *Maquam* was retired in 1905 after 24 years service, the last eight with the Champlain Transportation Co. She was the company's chief excursion boat at the time the Board once again sought bids for a new vessel. The T. S. Marvel Shipbuilding Co. of Newburgh, New York, was chosen to build the new steamer, which was to be powered by the usual reliable Fletcher beam engine, this one of 1500 horsepower, with a 52-inch cylinder and a nine-foot stroke. The steel plates were fabricated in Newburgh and brought to Shelburne Harbor for assembly. On a bright April day in 1906, the 29th steamboat, and unfortunately the last on Lake Champlain, stood on the ways ready for her first trip. The *Chateaugay* had brought 1200 people over from Burlington for the launching and as the blocks were knocked out from behind her cradle, a young girl smashed a bottle of champagne across the bow of her 200-foot hull and said, "I christen thee *Ticonderoga!*" Like her ill-fated namesake on Lake George, this new Champlain steamer was named for the famous historic fort that stood between the two lakes.

The "*Ti*", as she would be best known, was similar in construction to the *Vermont III*, but smaller in all her dimensions, for she was designed primarily for excursion and local service, and had only a few staterooms. Her deck area, on the other hand, was much larger and she was allowed to carry 1037 passengers. She was heated by steam and lighted by electricity, as was the *Vermont III*. She could also make 23 miles per hour and cost her owners $170,000. She was assigned to the Burlington-Westport-Plattsburgh run while the *Chateaugay* was reserved for excursions and special parties.

⸎ ⸎ ⸎

By 1905 the *Mohican* on Lake George needed considerable work and the company decided to replace her with a vessel of similar size. The *Mohican II* was fabricated of steel by the Fletcher company, and was launched from the Baldwin yard in time for the summer of 1908. She was 115 feet long, had twin propellers driven by two triple-expansion engines totaling 550 horsepower. She carried 500 people and cost $64,372.

The old wooden *Horicon* was now in her 32nd year, still doing the local work south from Baldwin. An inspection of her hull and machinery in the fall of 1908 found her to be in need of extensive work. The old girl hardly justified the cost and a letter went off to the reliable old Fletcher company in Hoboken for what would be the last of a long line of vessels built by that firm for the upstate lakes, the *Horicon II*.

The hull was built in Newburgh at the Marvel Shipyard and then disassembled for shipment to Baldwin. There she was put together again, the 1280-horsepower Fletcher beam engine was installed and she was launched late in November, 1910. The biggest of all the Lake George boats, she was 230 feet long, displaced 1175 tons, cost $210,000 and could carry 1700 passengers.

DOCK AT LAKE GEORGE
ON THE DELAWARE AND HUDSON RAILROAD

"The D&H"

Eastern and Central New York
Retail Coal Merchants' Association

DINNER

Cream of Tomato Soup

Sliced Tomatoes   Radishes   Olives

Boiled Kennebec Salmon
Cucumbers   Saratoga Chips

Sweet Bread Croquettes, French Peas   Queen Fritter, Wine Sauce

Prime Ribs of Beef
Roast Turkey, Cranberry Sauce

Potatoes in Cream   Green Corn   Mashed Potatoes

Waldorf Salad

Tapioca Pudding, Wine Sauce

Apple Pie   Ice Cream   Berry Pie   Assorted Cake   Lemon Pie
Fruit in Season

Edam Cheese   American Cheese
Bent's Water Crackers
Tea   Coffee   Milk

J. T. McKEE, Superintendent of Dining Service, Albany, N.Y.
A. A. HEARD, General Passenger Agent, Albany, N.Y.

Steamer Horicon
September Ninth
Nineteen Hundred and Six

It was then with this steel fleet of six steamers that the two steamboat companies faced the growing threat of the internal-combustion engine in the private automobile. Without even knowing it, the gleaming white steamboats, with a rainbow of colored flags flapping in the breeze, were steaming proudly but inevitably into their twilight years.

*   *   *

A strange passenger boarded the *Ticonderoga* in Burlington on September 23, 1913, for the trip across the lake to Plattsburgh. The lady, called Minnie, was a huge elephant and the star of a small circus touring the area. She was pretty cramped on the forward main deck and if she were to stand erect would be taller than the deck above. Her feelings regarding the accommodations were not made known as were those of Charles Dickens and other distinguished travelers but upon reaching the Plattsburgh dock she reared up on her hind feet almost as high as the pilothouse and trumpeted a sigh of relief. There was no tariff published for elephants and the bewildered purser charged the rate listed for two horses — not a bad deal in all.

The operation of the boats, as well as all the railroads in the country, was taken over and run by the Federal government during World War I. Revenues fell off sharply but the *Vermont III* and *Ticonderoga* were frequently used in 1917 and 1918 to acquaint soldiers training at Fort Ethan Allen and Plattsburgh with historic battle sites of the Revolutionary and 1812 wars throughout the valley. The *Chateaugay* was withdrawn from service and laid up at Shelburne Harbor but the Lake George steamers continued their usual service with exceptionally light patronage.

Traffic returned after the war and reached a peak in 1921, but after that it was downhill all the way. In an effort to recoup some of the revenue lost to the automobile the *Chateaugay* was pulled out of storage in 1925 and converted into an automobile ferry — if you can't beat 'em, join 'em! She was 37 years old at the time and a thorough inspection proved her to be as sound as the day she

---

At the top of the menu, opposite, the *Sagamore* approaches the pier at which the old *Mohican I* is tied. (Jean Banta collection)

was launched, much to the surprise of the steamboat inspector who figured he was on a fool's errand. Her superstructure was cut down fore and aft and her deck was strengthened throughout to accommodate the new traffic. In July 1925, with many hundreds of thousands of miles behind her, she steamed out of Burlington with a load of automobiles bound for Port Kent across the lake and embarked on a whole new career.

In November 1927 a disastrous flood ravaged Vermont, knocking out all highways and railroads, effectively isolating the state from the outside world. The *Chateaugay* was fired up, proudly paddled out of Shelburne Harbor and for two weeks, night and day, carried thousands of tons of food, medical supplies, building materials, clothing and other essentials across the lake from the New York side. She plowed almost guard deep through waters littered with floating trees, dead cows and even whole barns, and luckily never hit a thing.

The depression year of 1933 was the straw that broke the camel's back. The boats on both lakes were plowing through seas of red ink during the previous season of 1932 to the tune of a $200,000 deficit and now all operations were suspended completely on Lake George. The *Sagamore* was laid up for good and the *Horicon II* was fitted out as a night club for the Saratoga crowd, called the *Showboat*, and was leased to a private operator who brought in big name bands for several seasons.

In 1937 the Champlain Transportation Co., with its shipyard, docks and three great sidewheelers was sold to Horace W. Corbin of Burlington for a round $100,000. At the time the *Vermont III* had been laid up for some time, the *Chateaugay* was still in ferry service, the *Ticonderoga* was occasionally used for excursions and the D&H wanted out. The engines of the two older boats were scrapped and the hull of the *Vermont III* was stripped and sold for a Diesel freight boat, being moved down the canal to New York, after World War II. The hull of the *Chateaugay* was cut into sections and shipped on flatcars to Lake Winnipesaukee, New Hampshire, where she was welded back together and operates today as the Diesel powered *M. V. Mount Washington*, almost 80 years after her iron plates were first riveted together at Shelburne Harbor.

Hundreds of people attended one- and two-week YMCA and YWCA summer conferences at Silver Bay; between conferences there was a great turnover of guests and a huge amount of luggage to be handled in those days before drip-dry clothing. College boys at Silver Bay, above, form a human chain to expedite loading luggage on the *Sagamore*. Below, the boat has docked at the Sagamore Hotel on Green Island. *(Silver Bay Association, above; Detroit Photographic Co. collection, Library of Congress)*

On Lake George the *Sagamore* was scrapped in the fall of 1937. The *Horicon II* ran a few more times as the *Showboat* but after an extended period of idleness was pushed out from her dock at Baldwin one day in 1939 and set afire. This was the quickest and cheapest way to separate the joiner work from the valuable metal but without a doubt probably the cruelest to a proud ship of her heritage. The *Mohican II* was kicked about from one owner to another and somehow has survived to the present, rebuilt and Diesel powered.

This left the *Ticonderoga* on Lake Champlain, the last sidewheel steamboat on the lakes. Captain Alanson Fisher, who had mastered the *Sagamore* and both *Horicons* on Lake George purchased the *Ti* and formed the Fisher Steamboat Co. He was able to hold on for a while but by 1950 was about to throw in the towel. Just as all hope for survival was about to fade a grass-roots movement called "Save the *Ti*" sprung up under the leadership of the Junior Chamber of Commerce and Ralph Nading Hill, both of Burlington. The area residents rose to the occasion and the *Ti* sailed again.

After only one season of grand operation the old nemesis returned—a lack of money. At this juncture Mrs. Watson Webb, a multi-millionaire descendant of William H. Vanderbilt and backer of the Shelburne Museum then abuilding on a site at Shelburne, Vermont, overlooking the lake, stepped in and bought the *Ti* during the last week of December in 1950—a nicer Christmas present for future generations could not have been acquired.

After three more years of operation in an effort to have the *Ti* pay her own way it was decided to move the 892-ton vessel two miles overland to the museum—not a small project by any stretch of the imagination or budget. The bizarre scheme was undertaken in the fall of 1954 by the renowned contractors Merritt-Chaplin & Scott. A cradle mounted on 16 freight car trucks riding two parallel tracks did the trick and she arrived in her permanent berth, her last harbor, high on the Vermont hillside overlooking Shelburne Bay —out of which she and her forebears steamed proudly for so many past seasons—at 5:22 p.m. April 6, 1955, a 65-day trip in all.

As she entered the newly-excavated basin where she would be floated onto the cradle on November 6, 1954 for her overland journey, a deep-throated blast from her great whistle echoed and re-echoed across Shelburne Bay for the last time ever. The last sidewheel steamboat on the lakes of America was beginning her voyage to posterity.

The *Horicon II* slices through Lake George at 21 m.p.h., past Tongue Mountain, on her regular morning run, connecting the train at Lake George Village with the Champlain boat at Montcalm Landing, via the shuttle train from Baldwin. The *Sagamore* was on the opposite side of the run. (*Francis L. Bayle*)

Running in a dense fog on July 1, 1927, the *Sagamore* missed Blair's Bay by 75 yards and hit the base of Anthony's Nose Mountain. Mattresses were stuffed into the holes in her crumpled plates and the boat made it to the Glenburnie dock where passengers, mail and express were unloaded. The captain then headed her for the beach at full steam so she would not sink in deep water, but she finally went down at a depth of about 18 feet. It took three weeks to raise her and months to make repairs. She returned to service in the spring of 1928.

The spectacular 1910 view of Lake George, left, is from Shelving Rock Mountain on the east side, north of Bolton Landing. Here in The Narrows, the *Sagamore* threads her way through the islands in the shadow of Tongue Mountain, to the left. The 1915 picture, below, from the lawn of the Fort William Henry Hotel shows the gasoline launch *Mountaineer*, the propeller steamer *Mohican II* and the *Sagamore*, all at Lake George Village dock. *(Two J. S. Wooley photos, D&H collection, below, and Carl Wooley collection, opposite top; Morton MacDonald collection, opposite bottom)*

The *Ticonderoga's* 1500 hp engine of gleaming brass and polished steel ran like a watch. Her dining room, aft on the main deck, provided a panoramic view of the lake. Her feathering paddle wheels, below, could pull her at 23 m.p.h. Opposite are two views of the *Ti* at Shelburne Museum, where she stands near the old Colchester Lighthouse, which she had passed daily when both were on the lake. (*D&H collection, above; Edward O. Clark, left and below; Jim Shaughnessy, two pictures, opposite*)

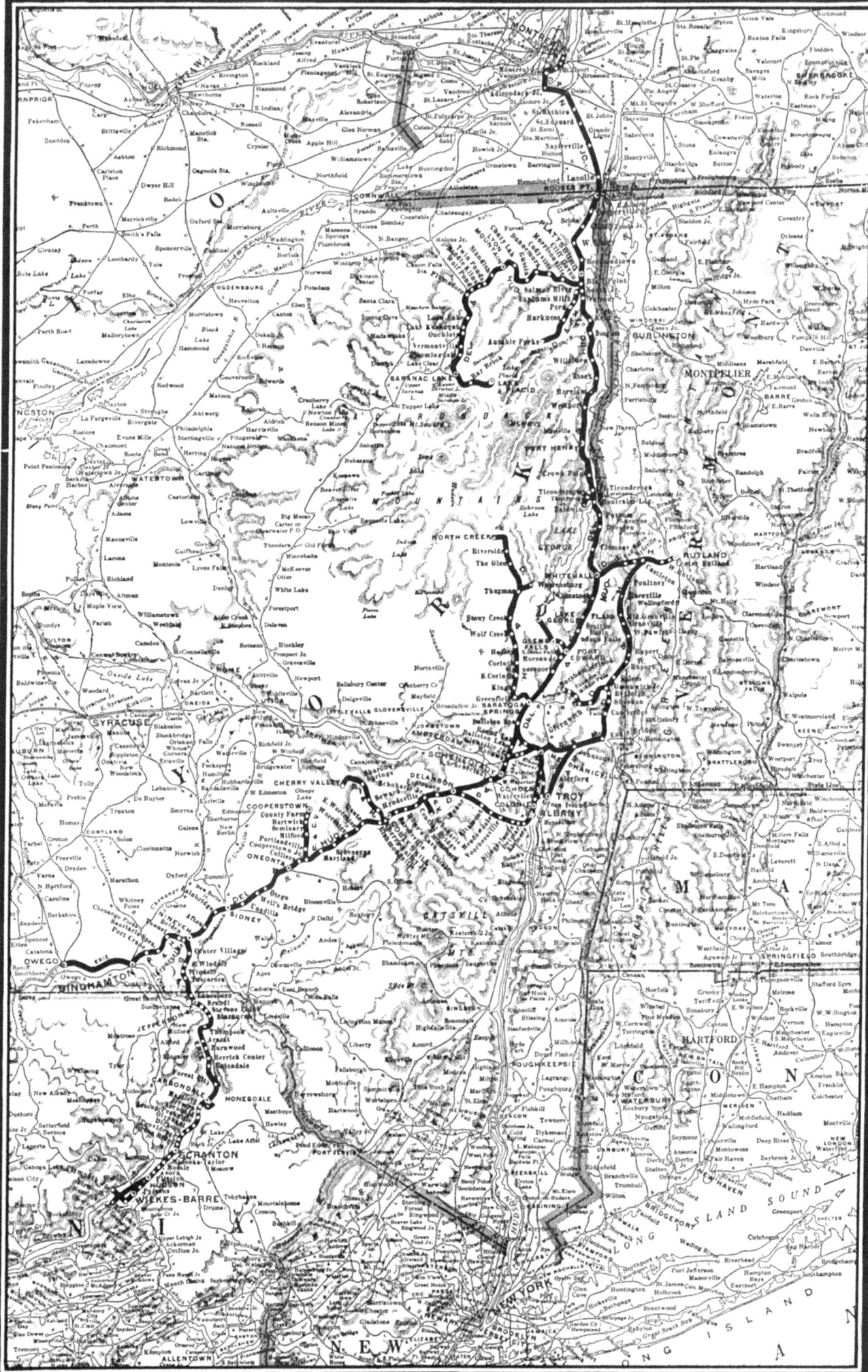

11. THE REIGN OF L. F. LOREE

Leonor F. Loree moved into the Delaware & Hudson like Grant into Richmond. He was a formidable figure in appearance, background, energy and capacity Educated as a civil engineer at Rutgers, he entered the service of the Pennsylvania Railroad as a rodman in the engineering department in 1877. After two years in the Army Corps of Engineers he went with the Mexican National Railway in 1881 as an instrument man, topographer and preliminary layout man on the proposed route between the Rio Grande and Saltillo.

After returning to the PRR, and while still but a junior official, he made a critical evaluation of some plans for a new yard sent down from the chief engineer's office. Instead of being fired because he dared question them, the yard was built along the lines of his suggestions and gained for him close attention and blessing from above. His career was immediately switched to the main line with a high green and clear track ahead. He quickly rose to assistant engineer in the Chicago division in 1883, and engineer, maintenance of way, on various divisions. He waded into flood-ravaged Ohio in 1886 to rebuild 26 bridges, three stone-arch culverts, two trestles and seven miles of track, all in six days. When the dam at Johnstown, Pennsylvania broke at 3 p.m. on May 31, 1889 and swept 2500 people to their death, Loree was called and with 1500 men brought order out of chaos and in two weeks traffic was resumed. For performances like these he was made superintendent of the Cleveland and Pittsburgh divisions in 1889, general manager of the whole system at the age of 38 in 1896 and fourth vice-president in 1901.

In June of the same year he resigned to become the president of the Baltimore & Ohio and took over that road when much-needed rehabilitation work was just beginning, installed a complete system of interchange freight yards, reduced many grades, built a fleet of freight cars that were "huge" for their time, and introduced the first Mallet articulated type of locomotive ever built and operated in the United States.

In 1904, he moved to the presidency of the Chicago, Rock Island & Pacific where he was faced with the task of consolidating the varied geographical interests of the newly-combined Rock Island and the St. Louis & San Francisco, covering a wide territory in the Mid- and Southwest. Discontent and troubles in the financial circles dominating the roads irked him, and in nine months he left.

At the urging of E. H. Harriman, a close friend and a member of the D&H board of managers, Loree came to the small but prosperous D&H on April 10, 1907, to succeed the ailing David Willcox. At the same time, he became chairman of the board of managers, thus becoming responsible for financial as well as operating matters.

The first and most pressing problem to confront Loree was the extraordinary indebtedness, largely in the form of floating debt, that had been recently incurred through the purchase of railways in Canada, electric railways and additional coal reserves. Payment had also become necessary for a large quantity of equipment that had been ordered, as well as for an extensive construction program too far along to be suspended. The financial market wasn't in the best of condition for the flotation of new securities, no matter how soundly they were backed, in the middle and latter part of 1907, but nevertheless, Loree was able to peddle

An Old English "S" adorns the smokebox of the inspection engine SARATOGA, which was rebuilt in 1892 from an old Baldwin. It is pictured above in 1913 at Sidney, New York, together with business car No. 199, which was built at the D&H's Oneonta shops in 1903. Camelback Ten-Wheeler No. 504, below, stands on the bridge across the New York State Barge Canal at Waterford. *(David Herbert collection, above; D&H collection, opposite)*

$10,000,000 in first-lien equipment gold bonds by July 1.

At the beginning of the year, President Willcox had raised the dividend rate from 7% to 9% where it would remain until the depression years of the 1930s. Despite this increase, Loree was able to arrange for the long-term financing of all the loans and floating debts within a relatively short time and the D&H started down the road to financial integrity unparalleled in eastern railroading circles.

With the financial problem generally provided for, Loree dove into the task of upgrading the property physically and technically as well as financially with the vigor and flair that made him a legend in his own time.

Fortunately, unlike earlier financial crises, the panic of 1907 was short-lived and the activities of the company continued during that year without significant interruption. Over 6,500,000 tons of anthracite was produced by company mines, much double-tracking was completed and block signals were in operation on the entire main line with the exception of the stretch from Plattsburgh to Rouses Point, 480 miles in all.

In 1908, a steam-powered generating plant to produce power for the company's electric railways was completed and put into operation at Mechanicville. In Canada, the extension of the Quebec, Montreal & Southern's line was completed down along the south shore of the St. Lawrence toward Quebec City, as far as Fortierville, with the exception of the bridge across the Nicolet River. Operations began in June 1909 on the whole line but plans made to complete the remaining stretch down the valley to the Quebec Bridge, then under construction, had been suspended by its complete collapse on August 29, 1907 with the loss of 75 of the 83 men on it at the time. As it turned out, the bridge wasn't completed for another ten years and by that time the great hopes for developing the QM&S had proven unattainable and the extension was never completed. In New York, the 10.2-mile Salem branch of the Greenwich & Johnsonville, connecting with the D&H's Rutland & Washington branch, was completed and put into service.

Loree was always an advocate of bigger and better motive power and began to upgrade the D&H's roster as soon as he arrived in 1907. Larger

Eighth President of the D&H, 1907-1938.

and heavier engines sparked a long series of alterations and improvements on the D&H. The new locomotives were capable of improving the speed and tonnage of trains and, to operate to their best advantage, required stronger bridges, longer roundhouses, better roadbed, longer turntables, easier grades, larger capacity cars, more water and better service at terminals and shops. Each improvement was followed closely by another, for larger locomotives brought about longer trains which demanded longer passing tracks, larger and more efficient yards, and eventually the cycle returned to even bigger locomotives again. In 1908 the yard at Binghamton was enlarged and in the following year new yards were built at Bluff Point, near Plattsburgh, and Jermyn, near Carbondale. The larger locomotives anticipated in the spiral of improvements and increase in freight train tonnage and efficiency came as early as 1909, in the

275

Mother Hubbard No. 500, with the Albany train for Binghamton didn't quite make it to the Susquehanna River bridge just outside Sidney, New York, on September 3, 1908. Running on the northbound track, probably to pass a slow drag freight, it nosed off the rails and down the embankment, followed by three of her four cars. Wrecking cranes came from Oneonta and Binghamton to drag the battered engine back up the embankment. Enterprising local photographer C. H. Phelps was there to record the scene. *(Jean Banta collection, below)*

Rouses Point terminal, above, is the northernmost point of D&H activity, where tonnage is turned over to the Canadian railways and subsidiaries of D&H. In 1911, when the picture was made, these were the Quebec, Montreal & Southern and the Napierville Junction. Below are two samples of new motive power of the early Loree years. A Mallet articulated is shown being tested with the dynamometer car near Carbondale in 1911. At the bottom is a dazzlingly new Alco Ten-Wheeler with its equally gleaming varnish train and the proud crew at Saratoga Springs in 1908. *(D&H collection, bottom; Warren Hamm, two pictures)*

Consolidation 999, at Saranac Lake, above, was a rarity on the D&H in that she did not have the wide Wooten firebox. She was designed to burn oil in the summer, reducing fire hazard in the Adirondack woods on the Chateaugay branch, and to convert to soft coal in the winter. Stopping by the flower bed at Oneonta station at 4 p.m. one day in 1908, engine No. 500, at the head of the Binghamton train, looks far better than she did after the wreck pictured on page 276. Oneonta's great 52-stall roundhouse, bottom, was center of D&H operations, with engines running north and south in round-the-clock activity. *(H. F. Haight, above)*

A vast new shop and servicing complex was opened in 1912 at Colonie, some seven miles north of Albany, near Watervliet. Older facilities at Carbondale, Oneonta and Green Island were inadequate to the size of the engines and the volume of work required to keep equipment in the top shape demanded by President Loree. After Colonie was opened, the others were used for car building and repair, and other lighter work. An 800 class E-3 Consolidation drifts downgrade from Ararat Summit over the high bridge near Starrucca, Pennsylvania, with northbound tonnage including several reefers in the 1907 scene, below. *(D&H collection, above; Warren Hamm)*

The new Fort William Henry Hotel overlooking the south end of Lake George, above, was opened in the summer of 1911. This hotel provided a splendid stopover on the famous rail-steamboat combination trip from New York through the mountains to Montreal. It ranked among the finest resort hotels in the Adirondacks, along with the Champlain Hotel, below, which was located high above the picturesque shore of the big lake, just south of Plattsburgh. A couple in the attire of the period enjoy the putting green in front of the new fireproof structure. It was the scene of many conventions. *(Fred Thatcher, from two original glass plates)*

form of six Mallet articulated compound 0-8-8-0 behemoths from the erecting halls of Alco.

In 1907 the New York Legislature enacted the law setting up the Public Service Commission, which along with the already-established Interstate Commerce Commission would prove to be a gigantic burr under Loree's saddle for the rest of his life, even more than organized labor. The ICC's jurisdiction was extended by the Hepburn Act of 1906, and a restriction followed on shipment across state lines of, among other things, coal that had been produced in railroad-owned mines. This of course was the very purpose for which the D&H got into the railroad business in the first place. In 1909 the Supreme Court finally decided that it would be acceptable if the coal was first sold to another company, even if this company was in part or totally owned by the railroad. So the D&H met this requirement by contracting with its subsidiary, the Hudson Coal Co., to buy outright all the coal produced at the pit mouth.

More locomotives were obtained in 1910, including four more Mallets, six Ten-Wheelers for passenger service and an oil-burning Consolidation for the Chateaugay branch, where the fire hazard from sparks was high in the summer. In his annual report for 1910 Loree said, "During the past four years the freight car equipment of the company has about doubled in numbers and 79 locomotives have been purchased or contracted for."

It was soon apparent that the existing shop facilities in Carbondale, Oneonta and Green Island were becoming obsolete in both capacity, location and size. Accordingly, during 1911 an 1100-acre tract of land was purchased in Colonie, a few miles north of Albany near the city of Watervliet, for vast new shops and a terminal. When it was completed and opened in 1912, the $2,500,000, centrally-located complex boasted 10 acres of floor space and featured many new concepts in shop design and economy. A bay was provided to transfer complete engines by a huge overhead crane between overhaul positions within the building, eliminating the cumbersome and space-wasting transfer table. A large roundhouse and servicing area, a freight yard, a coal storage area and car shops, were built and along with the new back-shop provided one of the most advanced and complete establishments of its kind in the country.

Lake Champlain and Lake George

HOTEL CHAMPLAIN
Bluff Point-on-Lake Champlain, N. Y.

HOTEL CHAMPLAIN is commandingly situated on the summit of Bluff Point, the highest promontory of Lake Champlain. The house is luxuriously furnished throughout in the style of Louis XVI and rivals the great metropolitan hostelries for its modern conveniences.

The vast Hotel Park, consisting of over 800 acres, provides every facility for rest and recreation. The famous Hotel Champlain Golf Course of 18 holes is a delight to the most exacting player. The first half of the course winds gracefully along the shore of the lake, the second half is carved in the woodlands. Boating, swimming, riding and all other outdoor sports are splendidly provided for. Dancing and musicales feature the indoor entertainment.

THE FORT WILLIAM HENRY HOTEL
Lake George, N. Y.

AT the head of Lake George, on a site immeasurably rich in historic value and remarkable natural beauty, stands the magnificent FORT WILLIAM HENRY HOTEL, a monument to the early days of our country and an acknowledged leader among the resort hotels of the Empire State. The house is furnished in the American-Colonial style, and has every modern convenience and attraction, including a handsome Italian Pergola-Casino on the lake-shore with a sunken garden dancing court, and open air restaurants. Guests are privileged to a choice of golf links. Well kept tennis courts are provided and the "Queen of American Waters" imposes no limitations on aquatic sports, for which there are splendid facilities at the Hotel.

The two great D&H hotels, dating back to the 1850s, were both destroyed by fire within a year, the Fort William Henry on June 24, 1909, and the Champlain on May 25, 1910. Both were rebuilt at once and the new structures opened on June 17, 1911.

281

The pastoral 1911 view, above, finds the afternoon train north from Binghamton curving through the shadows of tall elm trees along the mirror-surfaced Susquehanna River north of Unadilla. This train's consist usually amounted to three coaches and two head-end cars pulled by Camelback Ten-Wheelers of the 500 series. The highway is now part of New York State Route 7. Below, while Mother Hubbard No. 455 awaits a connection at Nineveh, the crew passes time in conversation, perhaps about the increasing tension between their brotherhoods and the D&H's bearded baron, Leonor F. Loree. The young fireman sitting on the pilot is taking a breather between sessions with the short-handled scoop in the tiny rear cab all alone. In the background is a Pennsylvania division local that will soon leave for Carbondale and Scranton. *(Warren Hamm, above; Jean Banta collection)*

A 40-stall roundhouse in Carbondale and a 10-stall house and new engine terminal in Binghamton were completed in 1911, while a long-range plan for the enlargement of the classification yard at Carbondale was launched. On Lake George, the last of the fleet of great sidewheel steamboats, the *Horicon*, was launched that same year and two new and fireproof hotels were opened.

The D&H had owned the Champlain Hotel at Bluff Point for several years and in 1909 purchased the remaining stock in the Fort William Henry at Lake George. Within a year both of the old wooden structures burned to the ground, the William Henry on June 24, 1909 and the Champlain on May 25, 1910. Plans were immediately made to rebuild each with fireproof materials, private bathrooms and steam heat and both opened on June 17, 1911 for a successful summer season.

Loree's theory on efficient railroading was to have the road as flat as possible and to pull as many cars as you could with one engine and crew. This, of course, couldn't be accomplished on the D&H or many other roads but in an effort to approach this end, a grade-reduction project was undertaken on the stretch between Nineveh and Oneonta, a distance of 37 miles in 1911. This $250,000 project was designed to allow one locomotive to move the same tonnage the remaining distance to Oneonta that it could haul up the 1.2% grade of Belden Hill out of Binghamton, or over Ararat out of Carbondale with the aid of one of the Mallet pushers, and involved reducing the grade from 36 to 15 feet per mile north of Nineveh.

Organized labor, Loree's old antagonist, increased its pressure for higher wages and better hours during 1912. The idea of a day's pay for a day's work was one of the old man's battle cries and any deviation from his interpretation of it came unwillingly, to say the least. He met the situation head-on, his usual way, but found his case beat down when the government stepped in, and he reluctantly had to capitulate. The enginemen on 52 eastern roads were after a general wage hike and modifications in the rules governing employment. The situation was presented to a federal arbitration committee and resulted in fixing minimum rates for engineers in freight and passenger service, overtime and layover payments. A 4.34% increase was obtained and along with similar increases won by the firemen, trainmen and conductors, cost the D&H over a million dollars more than the same service did in 1910.

＊   ＊   ＊

Traditionally the company's headquarters had always been in New York City. From the time the D&H was organized in 1823 at the Tontine Coffee House they occupied various spaces in the financial district and in 1876 the company built an impressive edifice at 21 Courtland Street called the Coal & Iron Exchange. In 1906 this building was sold and space was rented at 32 Nassau Street. It was here that Loree spent most of his time, convenient to his dabblings in the Stock Market; he commuted from his country estate "Bowood" near West Orange, New Jersey.

As the rail operations moved north with the lease of the Albany & Susquehanna and the Rensselaer & Saratoga, offices were established first in the old A&S station at Steamboat Square, Albany, New York, now known as the Plaza, and in 1892 were moved to a building purchased at 58 North Pearl Street. With the broadening of interests during the administration of David Willcox and the ever-increasing volume of paper work required by general business practice and in particular governmental control, more space was desperately needed.

In 1912 the City of Albany undertook a redevelopment of the Steamboat Square area and the D&H was one of the major participants. A new office building was proposed on the site and $750,000 was authorized to purchase the land and relocate the maze of tracks dating from the days of the A&S.

By 1913 the project was well under way and Marcus T. Reynolds, an Albany architect, originator of the whole project idea, and a grandson of the first president of the Albany Northern Railway, was commisioned to design the Flemish-Gothic castle-like structure that would be the new home of the D&H general offices, although the office of the president and high-level officers of the corporation remained in New York City where they had been since the founding of the company in 1823. The new headquarters involved a 12-story tower in line with State Street and two five-story wings, extending at an angle in each direction with a frontage of 664 feet along the Plaza. A wing containing a freight house ran north along

WALKER & GIBSO
WHOLESALE
DRUGGISTS

Coca-Cola
HUDSON RIVER DAY LINE

Albany's State Street appears in 1907, opposite above, before motor cars took much business from the D&H-owned streetcars. Below that a switcher backs a cut of cars toward the Hudson River dock of the *Berkshire*, largest steamer on the river. This 1916 scene is behind the new D&H Building which appears here in views from the 1920s. It was a part of Albany's water-front redevelopment. The tower weather vane depicts Henry Hudson's *Half Moon* and is supposed to be directly above her 1609 anchorage. The Albany *Evening Journal* owned the matching building to the right. (*D&H collection, this page; Detroit Photographic collection, Library of Congress, opposite above*)

The automobile was definitely here to stay when the picture above was taken on Albany's lower State Street. A 1920 Packard turns off Green Street in front of a downbound United Traction car heading toward the Plaza and the still-new D&H Building. In the distance an Albany Southern car awaits departure for Hudson, thirty miles downstream. The mercury was well below zero on February 17, 1914, when the view of Albany station, below, was taken from the New York Central bridge. D&H trains from the north and south used the lower level, while New York Central platforms are on the upper level to the left. *(Industrial Photo Service collection, above)*

Dean Street for 435 feet. By 1915 all but the south wing was completed and occupied. In the following year the remaining section was begun in co-operation with the Albany *Evening Journal* newspaper publishing company which built almost a matching structure. Upon completion in 1918 the new headquarters building presented a most imposing impression and even to the present is often mistaken for the State Capitol by strangers. High atop the tower a weather vane in the form of a bronze replica of Henry Hudson's ship, the *Half Moon*, stands almost directly over the spot Hudson reputedly dropped anchor on his voyage of discovery in 1609.

*   *   *

Continuing the program of improved motive power, 15 E-5 class Consolidations were acquired in 1913 and in the following year ten Pacifics were turned out by Alco for the increasing demands of passenger business, primarily the New York-Montreal service. In September 1913 the New York State Legislature passed the full-crew law thus adding extra men to trains over a certain length. This only served further to aggravate Loree who continually felt that labor was getting more than it was entitled to anyway and was trying to take over management of the railroads. There may have been some justification for the size of the crew in those days when the air-brake retainers had to be turned up on each car coming down long grades. The D&H certainly had long grades and with the new and greater power the trains were getting longer and heavier.

The motive power program soon showed definite results. In 1910 the average load hauled on one train was 432.06 tons and by 1916 this figure had climbed to 747.55. In addition to almost doubling the load, the new power was able to move it over the road faster, thereby increasing overall productivity even more. With the constant increases in wages and other costs this new-found efficiency was not only welcome but necessary to maintain profitable operations and the 9% dividend rate to stockholders.

*   *   *

The operations on the electric railways were nowhere nearly as encouraging. The dividends received in 1914 from the United Traction Co. were only 2%, 2½% from the Troy & New England, 4% from the Plattsburgh Traction and 6% from the Schenectady Railway, all being down from previous years and none having any future prospects that looked brighter. In December of that year the Public Service Commission ordered sweeping changes in the facilities and services of the U.T. Co., involving an estimated $1,106,580. Among other things the company was ordered to buy 42 new cars, provide higher powered snow-fighting equipment and extend its lines. The management threw up its hands in despair and went to the courts for relief, claiming the demands were unreasonable and excessive considering the needs of the public and the pending financial conditions resulting from the growing conflict in Europe. The order was subsequently modified somewhat but the great empire of electric railways was already over its peak and suffering from the inroads of the private automobile and buses. The war years would help to some extent, but the great prospect seen for this form of transportation when David Willcox bought these properties was rapidly melting away into the morass of higher costs, governmental control and, most important of all, waning patronage.

Passenger business was down somewhat on the railroad in 1915, again the result of the automobile, but overall income was up owing to the increased industrial activity with the outbreak of the war in Europe. The boat lines suffered, however, as the bulk of their patronage was from pleasure travelers who were getting worried about the tense world conditions.

The Wilkes-Barre Connecting Railroad, last significant addition to the company's lines, was opened on March 29, 1915 at a cost of $2,200,000. This trackage was built by a company chartered in 1912, jointly owned by the D&H and Pennsylvania Railroad, to make a connection between the two roads running from Buttonwood north, 6.65 miles to Hudson, Pennsylvania. This new line avoided using the tracks of the Lehigh Valley Railroad through downtown Wilkes-Barre and gave the D&H a connection to its mine tracks in the Plymouth district as well as direct interchange with the PRR.

The grade revision introduced in 1912 south of Oneonta served to emphasize the need for extending the work to the grades between Oneonta

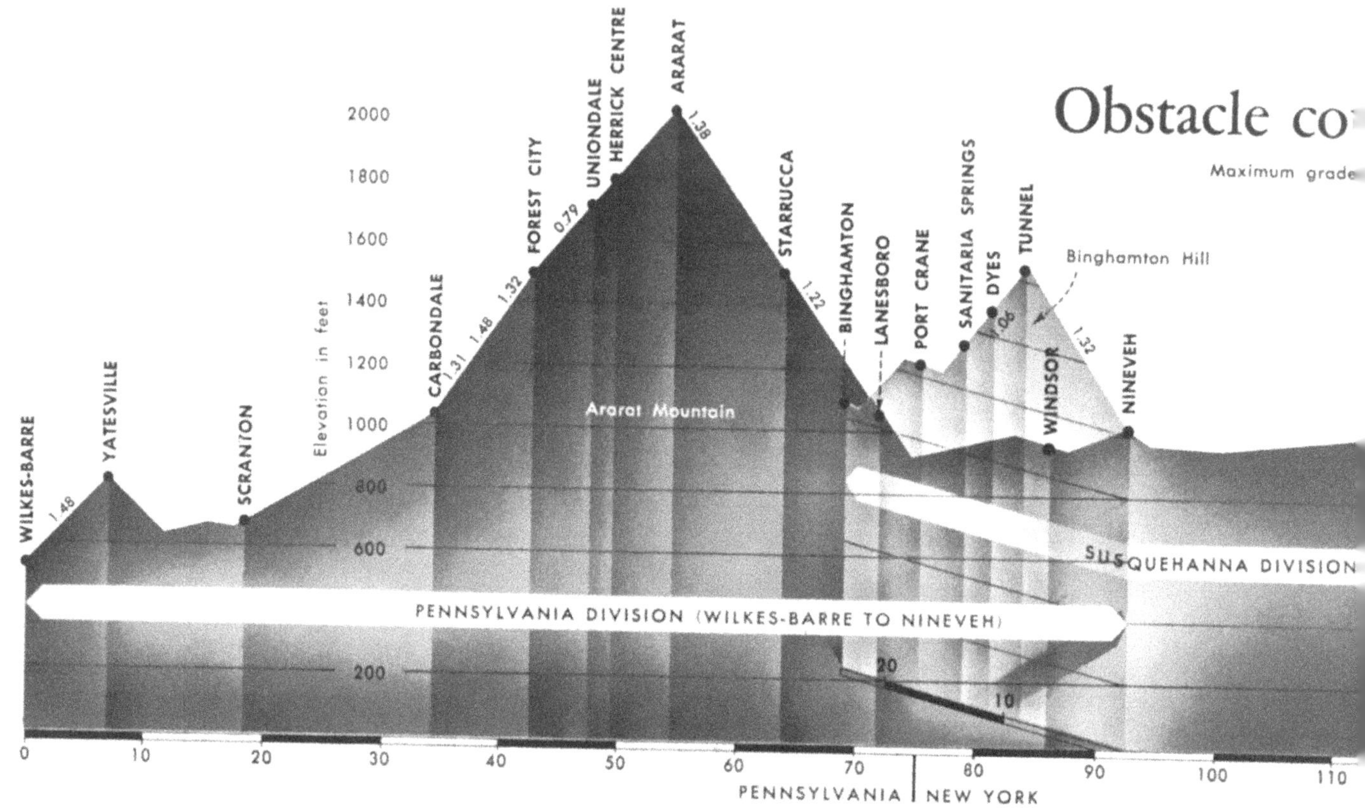
Obstacle co
Maximum grade
2000
1800
1600
1400
1200
1000
800
600
200
Elevation in feet
WILKES-BARRE
YATESVILLE
SCRANTON
CARBONDALE
FOREST CITY
UNIONDALE
HERRICK CENTRE
ARARAT
STARRUCCA
BINGHAMTON
LANESBORO
PORT CRANE
SANITARIA SPRINGS
DYES
TUNNEL
WINDSOR
NINEVEH
1.48
1.31
1.48
1.32
0.79
1.38
1.22
1.06
1.32
Binghamton Hill
Ararat Mountain
SUSQUEHANNA DIVISION
PENNSYLVANIA DIVISION (WILKES-BARRE TO NINEVEH)
20
10
0
10
20
30
40
50
60
70
80
90
100
110
PENNSYLVANIA
NEW YORK

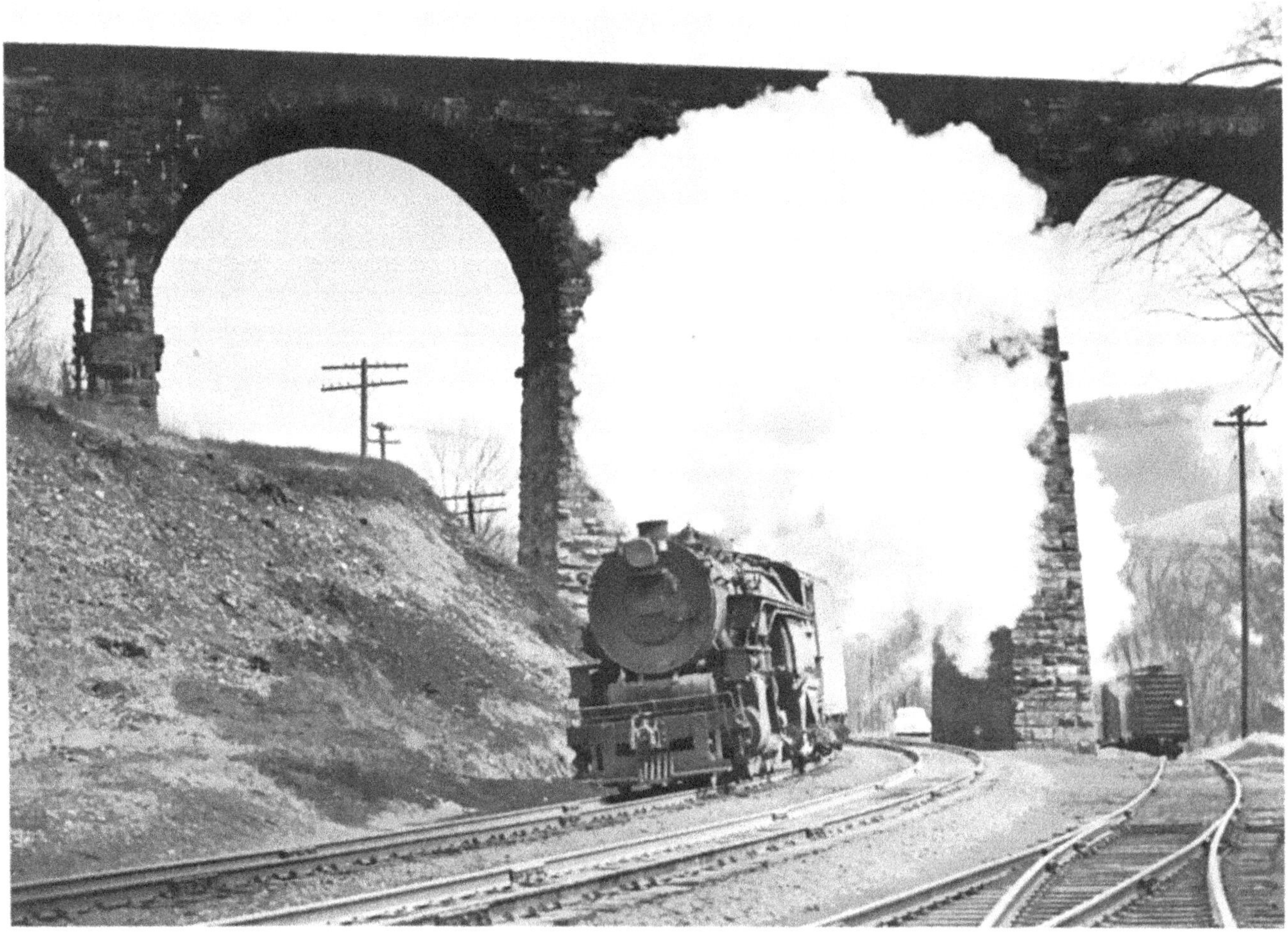

2-8-0's

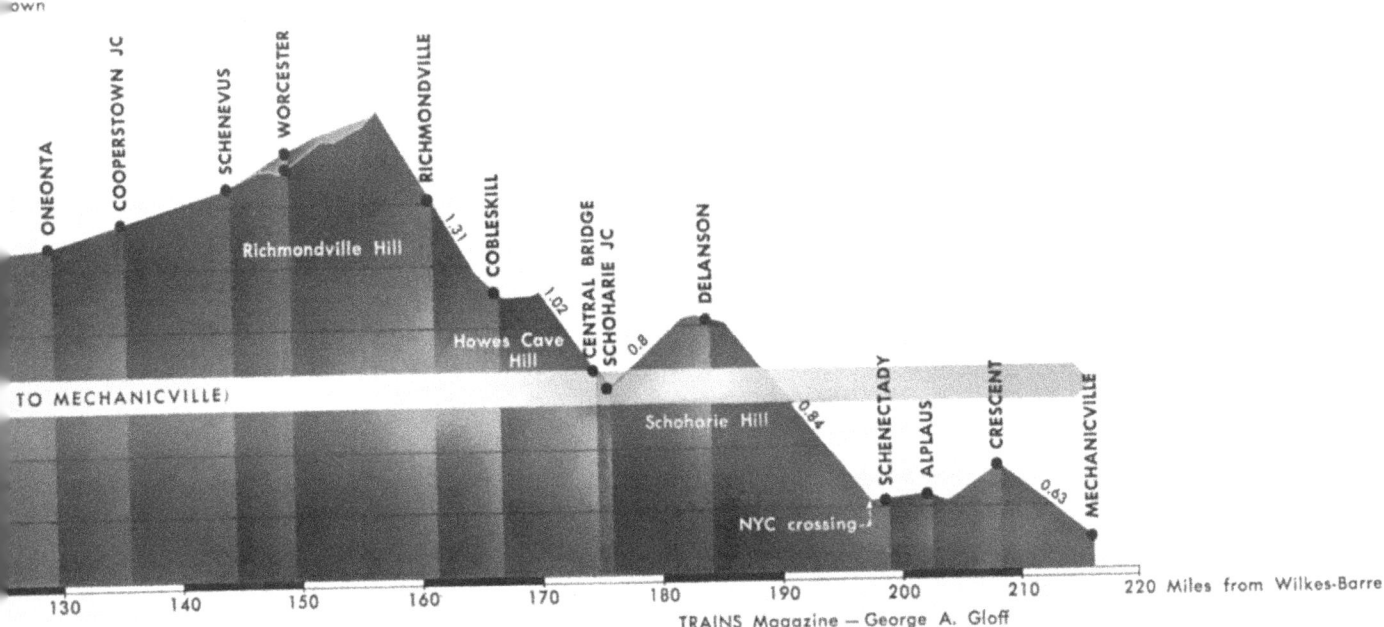

Consolidations 1208, 1213 and 1217, below, push 96 cars through Forest City, Pennsylvania, toward Ararrat Summit, with No. 1532 up front. A total of 36 driving wheels are biting into the sanded rails. The 1208 is at the head end of a similar train in 1951, down from Ararat Summit and rounding the curve under the Erie's Starrucca Viaduct. *(Profile, copyright 1967, Kalmbach Publishing Co.; Robert F. Collins, below; William P. Price, opposite)*

Pacific No. 602, built by Alco in 1914, was still new when the view at the top of the opposite page was made. Behind it is an extra string of new steel coaches and a wooden diner entering the north gate of the Colonie yards. The big oil headlight dates this view as before 1918; the 602 has yet to undergo any of the many changes that will completely change her looks during a long, proud career. The 1915 Maxwell touring car, fitted with flanged wheels, extra flags and engine markers, was used by supervisors in the engineering department for inspections and sundry purposes, probably with great pleasure. The spry little American, bottom opposite, pictured with her crew at the Altamont order board, after a run out from Albany on the local, was built in Scranton by the Dickson Manufacturing Co. in 1895 and, regretably, was scrapped in August, 1926, after a relatively short life span, by D&H standards. As the morning train from Binghamton to Albany rolls into Cobleskill, above, a score of baggagemen and clerks hustle into position as the big Mother Hubbard rushes past to spot the head-end cars in the days of oil headlights and straw hats prior to the "Great War." Below, American Camelback No. 433, built by the D&H in 1900 at Oneonta, waits with the midday train to Carbondale at the Honesdale station which, with its yard, was built on the site of the old canal basin, after the waterway was abandoned in 1899. *(Jean Banta collection, above and opposite below; D&H collection, below)*

A southbound milk train on the Susquehanna division works upgrade near Howe's Cave on April 10, 1929 behind Mother Hubbard passenger Ten-Wheeler No. 549, Alco-built in 1907. Originally the milk traffic went to New York City over the Erie from Binghamton, but by 1915 the loads came north out of the Susquehanna Valley to Albany, then down the Hudson on the New York Central. Below, the single-stage air pump of No. 422 sends out a puff of steam as she waits by the beautiful limestone station at Cooperstown which was built in 1916, not long before this scene was made. *(D&H collection, above; Beach collection, Oneonta Public Library)*

and Delanson. On this stretch some grades ran as high as 1.16% and it was hoped to reduce this to a possible .5%. In 1916 progress was made and the grades between Worcester and Richmondville summit, Cobleskill and Barnerville, and Schoharie Junction and Delanson were reduced to a maximum of .8%. A third track was installed on this most northerly section costing $318,400 and another new track built on a completely new location running along the east side of the valley between Schenevus and Richmondville summit was begun in 1917.

*   *   *

As the time approached when the United States would enter the World War, April 6, 1917, the business of railroad management in America was becoming more difficult each year owing to governmental controls and red tape, rising costs and the demands of organized labor. In the early months of the war the managers of the American railroads united in an effort to expedite all transportation functions and to help bring a successful termination to the conflict. The American Railway Association called a meeting in Washington on April 11, and organized a group that would be called the railroads' "War Board" in an effort to obtain maximum communication and efficiency on the nation's sprawling rail network. Mr. Fairfax Harrison, president of the Southern Railway was named chairman and L. F. Loree represented the eastern of the six overall districts.

For nine months the board administered a working cooperation among the railroads and effectively controlled the immense volume of material moving over the railroads. Due to the inflationary trends that had been imposed in the country during the years before it entered the war many railroads were in a dubious financial shape. An item that cost $1.00 in 1913 was $1.76 in 1917 and would go to $2.12 in 1919. Labor costs were on a wild spiral, especially with the war crisis, and as a result the federal government dictated to the railroads that wage rate demands would be met in almost every case to avoid any breakdown in the transportation system. At the same time, iron-clad restrictions were placed on freight rate increases thus bringing the profit margin rapidly toward zero.

As the end of 1917 approached, the government was becoming worried about the financial situation this created for many lines and directed the ICC to study alternative methods of railroad administration during the war period—operation by the carriers themselves or as a unit by the President. Finally Woodrow Wilson, by proclamation on December 26, 1917, took over each and every transportation system in the country as of noon December 28. Thereby, the United States Railroad Administration was created and William G. McAdoo, former Secretary of the Treasury, was appointed its Director General.

The Federal Control Act authorized the President to pay a just compensation to the railroads, a sum not exceeding the average annual operating income for the three previous years. For the D&H this amounted to $7,480,204.83 a year for the use and operation of all the facilities of the company including the steamboats and electric lines but excluding the Canadian properties. The Government assumed responsibility for all expenses of operation, including maintenance, and all taxes.

The less said about the two-year operation of this Governmental agency the better. It must be admitted that for the relatively short period of its existence, the Administration did manage to move an enormous amount of war materiel, but with great chaos and at a terrific cost to the seized lines. If Loree thought he had problems in management before, he hadn't seen anything yet! The Old Man must have worn a trench a foot deep in his office carpet, pacing back and forth in despair as he saw the tight management and high efficiency he had worked so hard to create, falling apart around him.

While the general policy was to suspend all but the transportation aspects of railroading in the country, most of the programs the D&H had started before the federal takeover were allowed to move ahead. These were primarily the installation of some double track and small grade revisions, along with expansion of the Carbondale yard. Work on the low-grade line from Schenevus to Richmondville summit, on the other hand, was suspended and lay partially completed for the duration of federal control.

The motive power of the D&H was in first-class shape at the time of the takeover, and it probably fared better than that of many other

Milk came over the Champlain division, too. In the upper picture, opposite, a milk train is picking up milk cans at Westport in 1925. The peaceful 1916 scene at Plattsburgh, below that, shows no hint of the war then raging in Europe. That same year, on a rainy day in June, Company K, Second Regiment, New York National Guard, left Glens Falls to pursue Pancho Villa in Mexico. Families and well-wishers huddled under umbrellas to bid them farewell. A happier errand drew the crowd of people to the pay train, below, near one of the many breakers of the Hudson Coal Co. (*George King collection, upper opposite; Francis Bayle, above; D&H collection, two pictures*)

This way to the ore
Adirondack Branch & Sanford Lake Extension
Proposed railroads (notes on map give dates)
Abandoned (notes on map give dates)
Other railroads
Stage line
Scale in miles
0 5 10 20
MT MARCY
Old McIntyre Iron Works
Original Adirondack Railroad 1839
MacIntyre Development
TAHAWUS
Proposed 1839
SANFORD LAKE
Sanford Lake reached 1944
To Ogdensburg 70 miles
Proposed 1882
Proposed 1897
NYC (Old Forge-Malone)
Long Lake
Champlain & Sanford
Boreas River
Right of way still held
Proposed 1908
Mineville
Port Henry
Burdick's Crossing
Crown Point
LAKE CHAMPLAIN
RUT
Ticonderoga
Ft Ticonderoga
RAQUETTE LAKE
Steam launch line
Blue Mountain Lake
Stillwater
Schroon Lake
SCHROON LAKE
Boreas River Canyon
Raquette Lake
Proposed 1852
75 miles to Sackets Harbor
Indian Lake
North River
Abandoned stub end reached 1871
NORTH CREEK
RIVERSIDE
Reached 1870
Schroon River
VT
LAKE GEORGE
D&H
The Glen
Whitehall
Map area
NEW YORK
Thurman
Reached 1869
WARRENSBURG
Stony Creek
Lake George
NY
Wolf Creek
Abandoned 1958
Reached 1865
HADLEY
Glens Falls
Hudson River
Ft Edward
CORINTH
Palmer
South Corinth
Kings
SACANDAGA RESERVOIR
SARATOGA SPRINGS
New bypass line around Saratoga Springs, under construction 1958
Old line through Ballston Spa
Ballston Spa

Sanford Lake
TAHAWUS
Stillwater
Hudson River
North River
NORTH CREEK
2.00 .30 .30 .30 1.00 1.50 1.00 .97 1.30 2.07 1.50 1.50 1.00 1.80 .60
Elev in feet
1800 1700 1600 1500 1400 1300 1200 1100 1000
30 28 26 24 22 20 18 16 14 12 10 8 6 4 2 0
Scale in miles
TRAINS Magazine — JRR

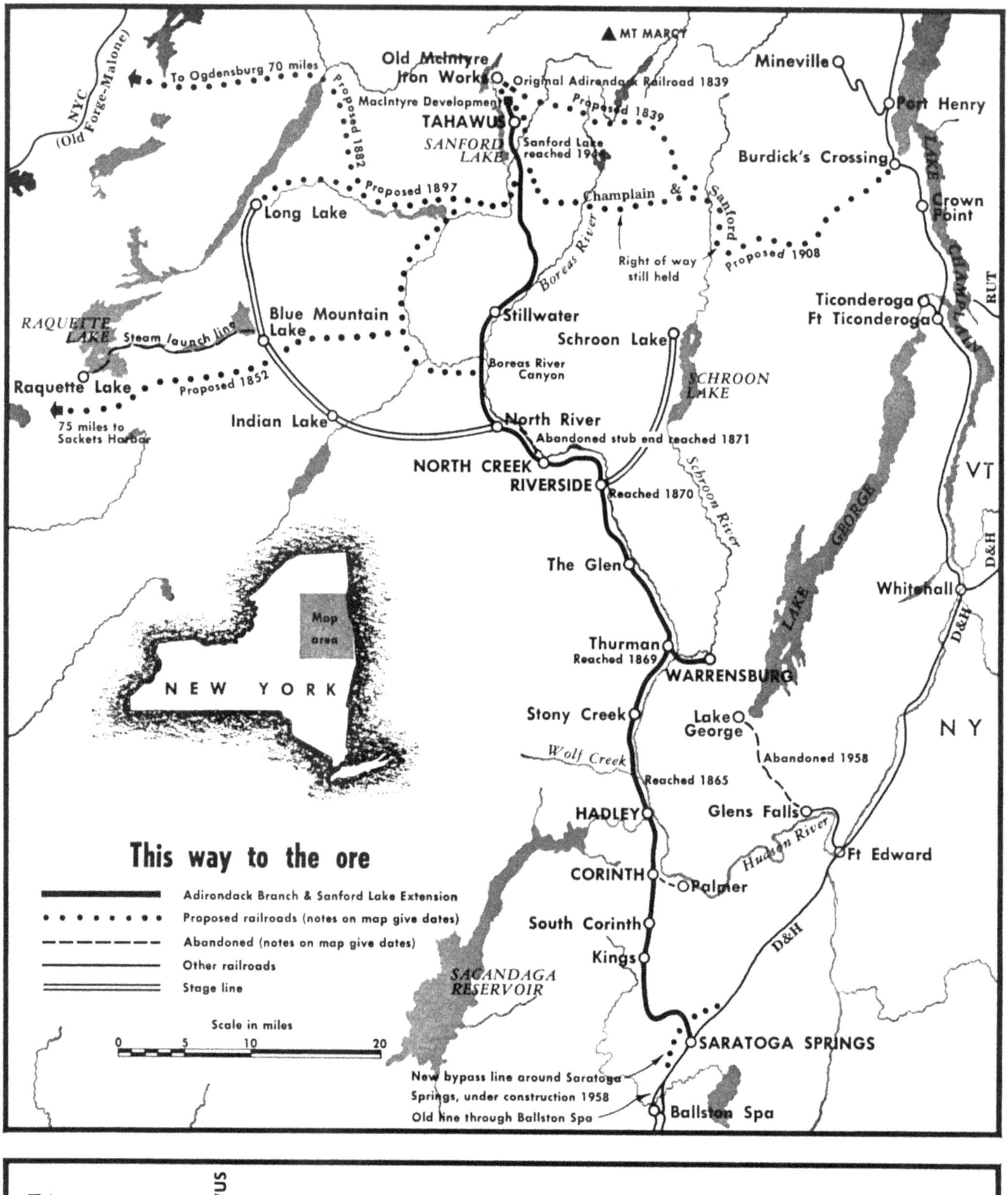

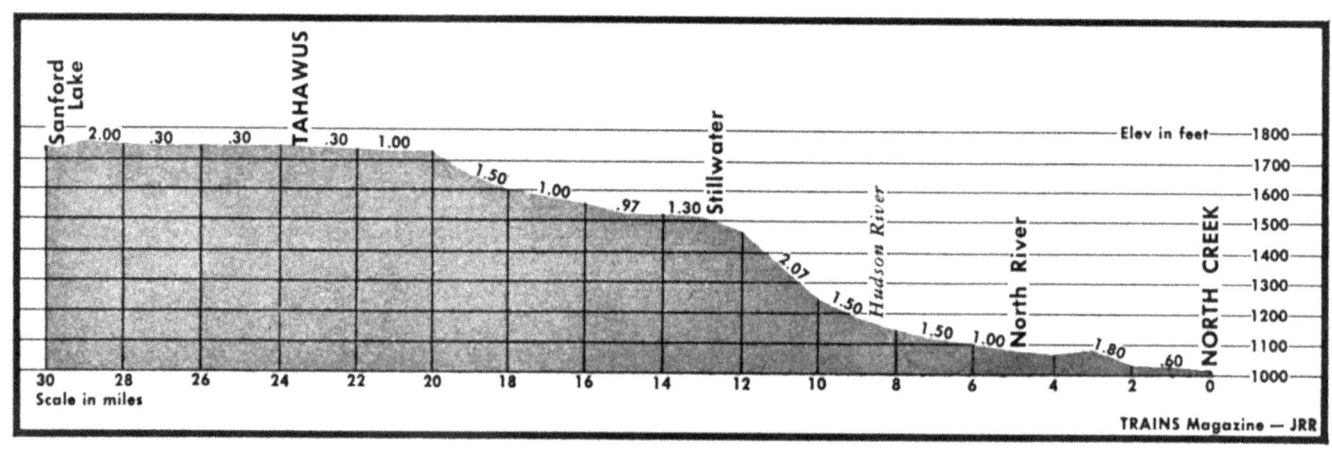

roads. Installation of superheater units, begun prior to federal control, continued, although higher wages and inexperienced help did contribute to large increases in costs, and to maintenance standards much lower than were formerly tolerated on the D&H. Some men previously employed as helpers had to be classified as mechanics under the government rule and were quickly dubbed "McAdoo mechanics" by their more experienced fellow workers. During 1918, twenty E-6-A class heavy Consolidations, that had been ordered earlier, were received from Alco and were a welcome addition to help the aging Mother Hubbards move the added wartime tonnage over Ararat and Belden hills. None of the standardized USRA models came to the D&H, because the fuel used on this road required a special wide Wooton firebox, not a part of the standard USRA design.

The Canadian subsidiaries enjoyed increased traffic, and therefore more pleasant operating results than the U.S. roads, because of the lack of governmental control and increased movements of war materials north of the border. The Napierville Junction Railway enjoyed a large increase in passenger receipts because of the beginning in October, 1917, of through operation of D&H trains over its line to the Canadian Pacific connection at Delson and then on into Montreal's Windsor Station. Since the initiation of this Montreal service in 1875, the trains from Rouses Point had used the Grand Trunk's line over Victoria Bridge to Bonaventure Station. The Quebec, Montreal & Southern also showed marked improvement as a result of increased shipments of coal moving north while hay and pulpwood came south, bolstered further by a 25% increase in rates allowed by the Canadian Railway War Board.

The cessation of hostilities in Europe by the Armistice of November 11, 1918 didn't bring federal control to an end; instead, an act of Congress, passed in March 1918 allowed governmental authority to continue as long as 21 months after a proclamation of peace, should it be required. It was bad enough before but this extension of governmental fumbling and "gerrymandering" nearly broke the proverbial camel's back. Among other things, the USRA placed an order early in the war for 100,000 freight cars. In an effort to get out from under this questionable bit of judgment after the Armistice, the commission arbitrarily assigned various numbers of these cars to the unsuspecting railroads and literally jammed a thousand 55-ton hopper cars and 500 boxcars down the D&H's throat to the tune of over $3,900,000.

Federal control finally ended at 12:01 on the morning of March 1, 1920, in accordance with a Congressional mandate contained in the Transportation Act. This legislation, in addition to returning the railroads to their owners, provided a six-month period of guaranteed earnings at the rate of one-half the annual compensation during federal control.

Twenty big Consolidations, like the 1218, were ordered from Alco by the D&H in 1918. Their 66,100-pound tractive effort was a welcome help in moving wartime tonnage. They weighed 296,000 pounds, had 63" drivers and carried 210 pounds of steam pressure in their fat boilers. Although the D&H was under USRA authority at the time, it received no standardized engines, because the wide Wooton combustion chambers were needed to burn the fuel then used on the D&H. *(Map, opposite, copyright 1959 Kalmbach Publishing Co.)*

A southbound double-headed manifest, led by No. 927, rolls into Oneonta from Cooperstown Junction, near Emmons, during the great traffic boom following World War I. In June, 1919, only 131 days after an old wooden breaker burned to the ground on the same site, the ultra-modern all-steel plant below was completed and put into operation. It could process 6000 tons of anthracite a day and during 1921 it prepared 1,502,180 long tons for market, a world's record for a single plant. (*D&H collection, both*)

As the battered fleet of D&H rolling stock found its way back to home rails the funds provided by the Transportation Act quickly disappeared in the form of pay checks and material bills required to patch up the sway-backed cars and the worn rails they rolled in on. In 1920 and '21, 7800 cars were extensively rebuilt but more than 900 were so badly beaten that they had to be scrapped.

In summary, the war period was one of increased traffic accompanied by mounting costs. Some betterments of a permanent nature were made at government expense but maintenance was severely lacking in both plant and equipment. After 26 months of chaos compounded, the government could not free itself from the responsibility for its enormous losses, nor could it endure the stigma of failure. Costly as it was to the American railroads, it was after all a small price to pay for proof positive that the often talked of nationalization of the industry was economic heresy. The USRA completely killed all roots of that movement for some time to come.

⸎ ⸎ ⸎

Work on the third track between Schenevus and Richmondville Summit was resumed in 1920, as soon as practicable after the end of federal control, and the low grade line was opened to traffic on December 7, 1921, at a total cost of $1,500,000. By July 1, 1920, in compliance with an ICC order issued several years earlier, 284 locomotives had been equipped with electric headlights and over 225 four-wheeled cabooses were converted to eight-wheelers and given steel underframes. A section of the roundhouse at Oneonta was remodeled and extended. Electric interlocking plants were installed at Schoharie Junction, in 1921 and at Mechanicville and Schenevus in the following year.

Improving postwar conditions and revenues were cut back sharply in all aspects by the short but sharp recession of 1921. Wage rates in all areas had been enormously increased by the government managers—some whom were actually former labor leaders sympathetic to the cause—and a day of reckoning was at hand. The government itself initiated a so-called "back to normalcy" program aimed at restoring prices and wages to somewhat near their prewar level. Needless to say, this idea didn't rest too comfortably with laborers who had come to enjoy their new-found wealth in the form of higher pay and shorter hours. Actually you couldn't blame them when you consider the average shop rate in 1920 was 70 cents an hour as compared to 33 cents in 1917, a 112% increase. On June 6, 1922 the United States Labor Board ordered reductions in the wages of shop employees of from five to ten cents an hour. The shop crafts refused to accept this action and walked out all over the nation to compel continuance of the previous rate.

All but about 260 of a normal force of 4000 employees of the motive power and car departments on the D&H left their jobs but old Loree stood firm. It was difficult to appreciate how he could pass judgment on hard-working men covered with grease and oil getting seventy cents an hour at a time he was receiving $100,000 a year from the D&H alone to say nothing of his other income as Chairman of the Board of the Kansas City Southern. He even convinced railroad officials on other lines who were considering a settlement to hold their ground. Outside help, mostly unskilled—strikebreakers in fact—were hired and somehow struggled along. In June the unions dropped their demands on the wage rates but insisted on restoration of full seniority rights. Loree said no! Reinstatement of strikers, except as new men would not be tolerated and few returned. By the middle of September the strike had totally failed and although Loree had his victory, the business had severely suffered through the busy summer tourist season.

In practically all cases the shopmen just went to work for other railroads in the area as new men even before the strike was over. The result was a reshuffling of shop forces between the New York Central at West Albany, the D&H at Colonie and the Boston & Maine at Mechanicville. The bitterness generated by the conflict, however, lasted up and down the D&H for many years.

A similar wage problem caused an even more severe difficulty on the United Traction Co. in 1921. Here motormen and conductors went out and the company imported "scabs" to run the cars. Much violence occurred when pickets stoned cars, derailed them, turned them over and tore down overhead wires by placing a length of pipe vertically on the rail and letting it fall against the trol-

Eight-man carbuilding teams from Oneonta, Colonie, Carbondale and Green Island are shown competing for a trophy and a $20 gold piece for each man, on the winning team, in the second annual car fabrication contest, at Oneonta, May 8, 1922. The home team was leading when the picture was taken, three hours after the contest began, and went on to win the day, completing the standard 40-foot, 30-ton capacity boxcar in 8½ hours. At Salem, New York, in the 1920 scene below, the crew of a Rutland-bound mixed train discusses the orders beside Camelback No. 713, while town gossips look over the newspaper brought up from Troy by the morning passenger train. The small boy playing with the station hand truck may be the son of the agent who looks on. *(D&H collection, three pictures; Washington County Historian's collection, below)*

All the passenger equipment of the Greenwich & Johnsonville is lined up beside Greenwich station in the June, 1924 scene, above. The Brill gas car used on the Salem branch and off-hour trips is dwarfed by 4-4-0 No. 4 and by the two wooden passenger cars of D&H origin but lettered G&J. The D&H gained control of this little Washington County line in 1906, built the Salem branch the following year, and still operates it as a separate organization without, of course, passenger service or the like of No. 4. Oneonta's big 52-stall roundhouse was built in 1906 and enlarged in 1921. The heavy Consolidation No. 1218, shown in detail on page 297, is being hosed down.

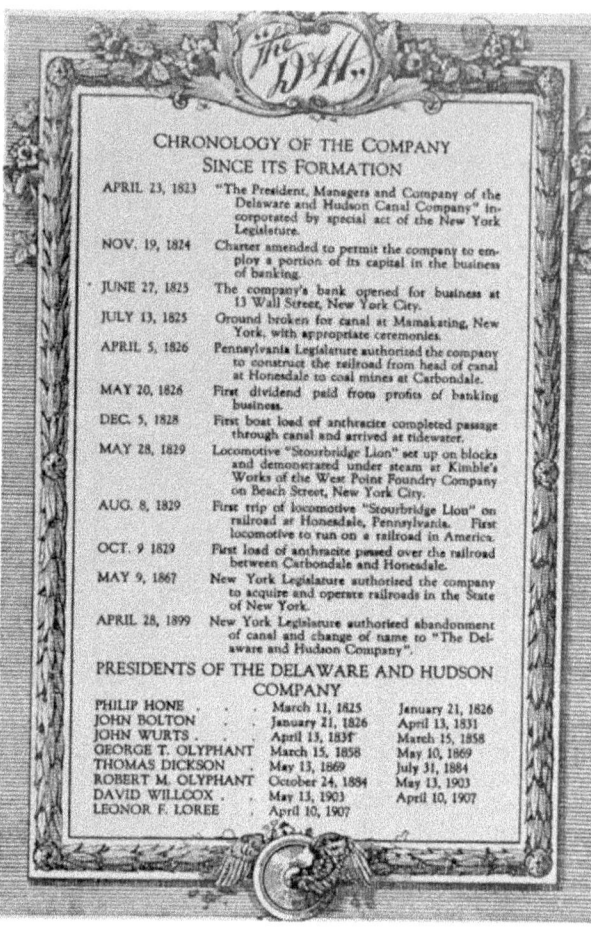

The fancy cake and commemorative program, a page of which appears above, were both prepared for the D&H's centennial banquet at the Hotel Astor, April 23, 1923, which also happened to be the birthday of President Loree. The cake was donated to a downtown hospital where it arrived after the banquet, a bit the worse for wear as it appeared when the picture was made. Hudson Valley Railway lines from four directions met at the intersection of Glen and Warren streets in Glens Falls. Fort Edward was on the line to the right, Lake George straight ahead, Saratoga to the left and the four-wheeled car comes off a local line. *(D&H collection, left above; Ed Bond collection)*

ley wire causing a short circuit and bringing it down in a shower of sparks. This strike extended beyond the U.T. Co. to the Hudson Valley Railway as well, and for eight months the HV crews refused to operate south of Waterford into Troy over the U.T. Co. trackage thereby considerably reducing operating revenues on that line as well.

Still another strike, this time in the coal mines, lasted for 163 days, cutting revenues in both sales and carloadings and making the year 1922 an expensive one for the D&H. As a result, the early days of 1923 were somewhat anxious times financially but on January 11 the stockholders were notified that despite the difficulties of the previous year, no change in the 9% dividend rate was contemplated and that the regular quarterly dividend would be paid out of the surplus accumulated prior to 1922.

* * * *

The year 1923 brought with it a flood of business, no strikes and the D&H's 100th birthday — all much more pleasant events indeed than those of the past five years. During the early months of the year a committee of managers consisting of Cornelius Vanderbilt, E. H. Outerbridge and C. S. Weston was appointed to formulate plans for an appropriate recognition of the hundredth anniversary on April 23. The principal event of the celebration would be a banquet at the Hotel Astor in New York City with President Loree as the toastmaster.

Nearly 600 guests representing delegates from public life, railroad officialdom, equipment suppliers, shippers and financiers gathered at the appointed hour in the grand ballroom of the Astor for the festive affair. As the dessert course approached the waiters marched in with small cakes each featuring the "D&H" monogram for the tables, followed by a single enormous confection, more than five feet high illuminated by 100 candles, and having sugar decorations representing various areas of company activity. Appropriately enough the cake celebrated Mr. Loree's 65th birthday as well as the 100th of the D&H.

In the barrage of speeches that followed, the development of the company was outlined, including the invention of steam propulsion. When Loree's turn came he took a swipe at one of his favorite subjects, the government controls placed on the industry, saying at one point, "Railroading is no longer a business, it has become a calamity." He compared extreme governmental influence here to the situation that was developing in Russia saying, "Has Russia no meaning for us?" and went on to call it a "nightmare of Utopian intoxication."

After the banquet that night a delegation traveled by special train over the Lehigh Valley Railroad to Scranton where more festivities were held on the following day. The *Centennial Special* consisted of a rider coach, six Pullmans, the president's private car No. 500 and an observation car on the rear. Breakfast was served to the group in three dining cars spotted at the Hudson Coal Co.'s Laflin breaker. A tour of the mines followed and a luncheon for 300 was given at the Hotel Casey where more speeches were endured. After lunch, at 2:40 p.m., the special eased over the Honesdale branch to the site of the first historic trip of the STOURBRIDGE LION. From Honesdale the special rolled over Erie tracks, paralleling the route of the company's old canal for much of the distance down the Lackawaxen and Delaware valleys and arrived back in Gotham at 8:30 that evening.

* * *

The rest of 1923 proved pleasant too; an all-time record year in traffic and income with 49,-814,970 loaded cars moving for a gross income of $47,320,452, 15% above 1922. The economy was beginning to get back on its feet after the effects of the war and the brief recession of 1921, as the furnaces of industry were hungry for the D&H's anthracite. Ninety-seven new industries were located along the D&H's line in 1923 alone. The passenger business on the New York-Montreal run was brisk as the swingers of the Roaring 20s excursioned to Canada for a weekend of bonded Scotch, a welcome change from the vile bathtub gin of the early prohibition years. The challenge of sneaking a bottle or two past the customs inspectors at Rouses Point enlivened the return trip.

Even in later years an indication of the demand for service to Montreal in 1928 was typified by the patronage on New Year's weekend. On December 29th the night train alone to Montreal was run in four sections with 38 Pullmans and 636 passengers. Returning on the night of January

The husky laborers above are standing on a 1200-class 2-8-0 buried in a drift just north of the Rouses Point station during the 1925 winter. Below, the *Laurentian* to Montreal rolls along the neat main line just north of Waterford with the immaculate Pacific No. 603 at the drawbar of six revenue cars. This stretch of track was originally the Albany Northern's route. *(Jean Banta collection, above; D&H collection, three pictures)*

Wrecking crane No. 30020, with a 160-ton capacity, was bought new in 1921 at a cost of $44,418.98. She appears above at Oneonta in 1924, with a riding car built from an old coach and containing kitchen, sleeping quarters, wreckmaster's office and cupola. The Centennial Special, shown below at Scranton, had left New York after the banquet the night before, bringing Loree and his guests over Lehigh Valley rails to Wilkes-Barre for a morning visit to the mines, and then to Scranton for a luncheon at the Hotel Casey. After the guests return, it will travel over the original D&H rail line to Honesdale and return to New York on the Erie.

As streetcar patronage waned and costs mounted, the D&H's newly formed subsidiary, the Capitol District Transportation Co. tried cutting costs during the 1920s by the use of trackless trolleys, like the one in Cohoes, above, and gas-electric-powered buses in Rensselaer. Below, the morning train up from Binghamton is greeted with a bit of activity at the Worcester station. This string of wooden coaches and two other trains a day was Worcester's contact with the outside world in 1925. (D&H collection, above; Jean Banta collection)

1st, six sections with a total of 60 Pullmans were required to carry 939 passengers.

In the summer of 1924 a dumpy old caboose body, serving as a switchman's shelter in the Oneonta yard at the time, was moved into the car shop there, rebuilt, repainted and presented to the Brotherhood of Railroad Trainmen for permanent display in Neahwa Park. It was back on September 23, 1883 that the Brotherhood was formed in this caboose, No. 10 of the A&S division, and 41 years later to the day, the little four-wheel veteran assumed its rightful place in history. Four of the original founders, including Charles J. Woodworth, to whom the caboose was assigned in train service at the time of the original gathering, were proudly in attendance.

⚹ ⚹ ⚹

Earnings on the electric lines became progressively more and more discouraging. As each new Ford, Maxwell, Star and Durant appeared in front of Capital District homes, and as each mile of macadam crept across the countryside the fare counters on the electric lines rang up smaller and smaller totals. Gas pumps sprang up on every street corner from Wilkes-Barre to Rouses Point and passengers abandoned the rails, both steam and electric. Labor trouble, lack of fare increases, sharply reduced patronage and street paving costs constantly plagued the trolley lines. One-man cars helped for a while, but other means of urban transit were sought. A new subsidiary corporation, the Capital District Transportation Co. was formed on April 14, 1924 in an effort to reduce costs, and some streetcar trackage in Rensselaer and Cohoes was abandoned. Gas-electric powered buses were introduced in Rensselaer while trackless trolleys went onto the streets of Cohoes.

The patronage, and therefore the operating results, on the Plattsburgh Traction Co. and the Troy & New England Railway had been so uniformly unsatisfactory and losses so high over the past several years, that it was deemed advisable to discontinue their operation. On March 31, 1925 the last car rolled into Troy over the Troy & New England from Averill Park and the Plattsburgh Traction Co. was sold to a local group on May 1 for a nominal amount, just about scrap value.

The first abandonment on the lines of the D&H itself took place in February of 1925 when service on 12.76 miles of the Mooers branch was discontinued. This line ran from Canada Junction through Mooers Junction to the Canadian border and was the original route of the Plattsburgh & Montreal Railway. This line was used for only a year after the opening of the trackage up along the shore of Lake Champlain in 1875 until the direct line to Rouses Point was completed. Over 75% of the traffic to Mooers was moved in over the Rutland through Rouses Point and traffic on the line itself didn't justify its existence.

⚹ ⚹ ⚹

As president of the small but well-heeled D&H, Loree departed from his former preoccupation with purely operating matters and entered the exciting game of railroad buying, selling and agglomeration. He had done his share of dealing while on the B&O by acquiring for that road a dominant interest in the Central of New Jersey and the Reading, but it was as president of a road with plenty of surplus cash for filling its securities portfolio with judicious buys that the Old Man really came into great prominence as a financier. He could make "Wall Street" buzz with gossip and admiration whenever he raised a bushy eyebrow or paused over a listing on the big board.

He opened fire with his so-called "Fifth Trunk Line" in 1925, when he submitted a plan to the ICC while it was still considering the general "four-system" plan of railroad consolidation in the East. His line would consist of the Buffalo, Rochester & Pittsburgh, the D&H, Lehigh Valley, Wheeling & Lake Erie and the Wabash together with a proposed low-grade line through central Pennsylvania to be called the New York, Pittsburgh & Chicago. The new line would be 50 miles shorter than any route from New York to Chicago and 30 miles closer to St. Louis. Stretching from the Canadian border to southern Pennsylvania and from the Atlantic Ocean to the Mississippi, the transportation empire thus created would encompass the whole tonnage-producing area of the industrial heartland of the nation. This proposal, needless to say, shook many an Eastern railroad official who knew the bearded baron of the D&H could do what he proposed, given the chance.

Loree's plan never jelled because of governmental opposition, one of his pet peeves, nor did the ICC's own plan. The Buffalo, Rochester &

By 1928 anthracite, originally the main commodity moved over D&H rails, had yielded 87% of the freight tonnage to interchange traffic. This amounted to about 1600 cars a day. Above, Camelback Consolidation No. 884 moves a cut of cars onto the New York Central interchange track out of the D&H's Mohawk yard at Schenectady. Even so, the anthracite haulage was massive indeed, with a total of 264,168 cars aggregating 12,288,926 tons that same year. Below, 2-8-0 No. 1212 drags a train loaded with anthracite-filled hoppers up the south side of Ararat Hill out of Carbondale while two big 0-8-8-0 Mallets push in the distance. (*D&H collection, both*)

Pittsburgh directors refused to extend a lease option negotiated by the D&H in 1924 and be completely Loree-ized while the NYC, B&O and Nickel Plate gained control of the W&LE, a key road in Loree's trunk line plan. His foray into the stock market, in an effort to bring off his amalgamation plan, obtained for him virtual control of the Lehigh Valley and the Wabash. When he sold these interests to the Pennsylvania in 1928 for $63,000,000, a tidy $22,000,000 profit was netted for the D&H. Money from this sale was invested in 595,000 shares of NYC stock in 1932 giving the 840-mile D&H over a 10% control and the largest single ownership in the 11,000-mile giant.

* * *

In 1922 the ICC ordered the D&H and 48 other roads to install automatic train control devices on one complete passenger-carrying division of their lines by January 1, 1925. The D&H's installation was slated for the Albany to Wilkes-Barre territory but was changed to the Champlain division between Whitehall and Rouses Point. This concept was quite new and it was felt that no equipment then on the market was sophisticated enough to meet the requirements of the order and some additional experimentation was needed, so a test section was installed between Albany and Colonie and the necessary hardware was installed on two locomotives. A year's testing showed that much additional development was required if a widescale application were to be undertaken, and the D&H went to the courts for an exemption from the ICC order on the grounds that in its unproven form it might in fact prove more dangerous to passengers than previous methods of protection should a malfunction occur and the high cost, considering its value, was unjustified. The Commission's order was upheld, however, and the D&H began installation of automatic train control on 60 locomotives and along the track north of Whitehall, and put the system into operation in the summer of 1925. A subsequent order in 1924 required another division to be equipped by February 1, 1926 and the Saratoga division between Albany and Whitehall was selected.

Revenues from the electric lines never regained their prewar levels and by 1924 began a wild downhill plunge. Even the newly-formed Capital District Transportation Co. lost money despite the economies projected through its trackless trolley and bus operations. America was always on wheels, but now everyone owned his own! The stretch of the Hudson Valley Railway from Mechanicville to Saratoga was cut in 1926 and the same year application was made to the Public Service Commission to abandon that railway's Greenwich branch and its northernmost line running from Lake George to Warrensburg. This was granted early in 1927, and right on the heels of that, in June of 1928, the Schuylerville to Fort Edward section and all the city lines in Glens Falls were cut away, with the commission's approval, leaving the HV a sad remnant of its former self. Now that the ball was rolling and patronage fell to practically nothing, the remaining sections of the original 130-mile system ceased operation on November 30, 1928. Several days later, over 50 wooden cars were put to the torch in the storage yard at the Glens Falls barn, and the Hudson Valley Railway literally went out in a blaze of glory.

The handwriting was more than on the wall for the future of electric lines, and while he had a chance, Loree unloaded the United Traction Co., the Capital District Transportation Co. and the half-interest in the Schenectady Railway Co. on December 31, 1928 to E. L. Philips and G. W. Olmsted for a marginal sum and considered himself lucky to find anyone even interested.

The Quebec, Montreal & Southern, another of David Willcox's stars, never rose much above a profitable horizon and fell deeper and deeper into the shadows of deficit after the war. The projected line continuing down the valley to a connection with the Quebec Bridge was never finished. This great span across the St. Lawrence had fallen down twice during its construction, which took nine years to complete, and as a result, by the time it was finally opened in 1917, the glitter of an independent rail line into rich northern Quebec was obscured. By 1926 the loss had mounted to a whopping $2,399,040. For some reason the local member of Parliament felt the Canadian government should shoulder the burden of keeping a railroad running along the south shore of the river and Loree by now was more than willing. On July 15, 1929, the Canadian National stepped in as the government's agent after much wheeling and dealing on Parliament Hill, and paid $6,000,000 for the

Newsprint from the Canadian mills moved through Rouses Point, 11,870 cars of it in 1928. Above, 2-8-0 No. 854, rebuilt from Camelback No. 869, rolls a paper train out of Whitehall on its daily 33-hour run from Rouses Point to Wilkes-Barre. Engine No. 1611 is shown below in the great Colonie shops where more than a hundred engines were upgraded during the reign of President L. F. Loree. In depression years, this activity served to keep the shopmen employed. Sometimes an engine with only 10,000 miles of service would be shopped. Keeping the men on the payroll during the hard times demonstrated that beneath his gruff, dictatorial manner the Old Man had a big heart. (D&H collection, three pictures; John Frisbee collection, below)

Ten-Wheeler No. 556 was an unusual product of Loree's upgrading and rebuilding program. Alco-built in 1907 as a Camelback with flat "D" valves and 21″ x 26″ cylinders, she emerged from Colonie in May 1927 with a rear cab, outside-journal lead truck, inch-larger cylinders and piston valves. Her chrome-plated boiler jacket, cylinder housing, steps, bell and whistle made her a thing of beauty as she clipped off the miles along Lake Champlain. The neat engine shown below near Barnerville, between Cobleskill and Howe's Cave, in 1928, is 2-8-0 No. 942, upgraded from old No. 838 in the mid-1920s. After the war operations were frequent and trains came like streetcars, as most of the Consolidations could handle only about 40 cars at a time.

The Adirondacks offered—and still offer—almost unlimited recreational opportunities to the sportsman, both summer and winter. On March 4, 1934 the D&H operated the first snow train from the Capital District to North Creek at the request of the Schenectady Winter Sports Club. Baggage car, diner and coaches provided a ski lodge on wheels for the day. Winter sports excursions became regular offerings during the winter ski season. On this page are two views at North Creek of the group that came February 10, 1935. *(Charles Clingman collection, both)*

marginal line, a windfall indeed for the D&H, no matter how you consider it.

The setbacks suffered by Loree at the hand of the ICC in railroad consolidations with the "Fifth Trunk Line" affair in 1925 didn't discourage or dissuade his belief in individual voluntary amalgamations. As chairman of the Kansas City Southern in 1926, he hatched a 5800-mile system in the Southwest involving the KCS, the Missouri-Kansas-Texas and the St. Louis Southwestern, but the ICC got that one too in 1927, with a 7 to 4 vote.

In 1929 he sprang a new plan in transportation circles, the North Atlantic Terminal System. This scheme provided that the D&H would obtain several roads having a combined length of more than 13,500 miles and would incorporate 17 Class 1 carriers into the D&H family, including the New Haven, the Delaware, Lackawanna & Western, the Western Maryland and the Boston & Maine. Alas, this time the great depression following Wall Street's "Black Friday" got to him before the ICC could.

In 1930 the Delaware & Hudson Railroad Corporation was set up to take over all the railroad properties formerly operated by the Delaware & Hudson Co. Thus the railroad became a wholly-owned subsidiary of the parent company, along with the Hudson Coal Co., the Greenwich & Johnsonville Railway, the Napierville Junction Railway, the steamboat companies, the Chateaugay Ore & Iron Co., the hotels and sundry other holdings. The officers of all were essentially the same.

Despite the great inroads the prolonged depression made, the D&H continued various capital improvements backed up by a century of frugality. A section of Centralized Traffic Control was installed on the Nineveh branch, the first on the D&H, with a single control board located at Windsor. One passenger Pacific and six freight locomotives including a third high-pressure Consolidation were built, all in 1930. The dividend, however, was reduced to a dollar a share, a comparatively modest figure compared with the almost-traditional 9%.

By 1929 the taxes paid by the D&H had increased 806% since 1900, while the actual property owned was only 148% more. This, no doubt, along with diminishing traffic, led to the unfortunate abandonment of 23.62 miles of the Honesdale branch on September 9, 1931. This line had a particularly special place in the history of the D&H as it was the original railroad property operated by the company, by gravity, and was the ground on which the first steam locomotive in America turned a wheel. Nevertheless traffic was gone now and the line had to go. Even the dollar-a-share dividend had to go in 1931 ending an uninterrupted run of spectacular returns to its owners that had lasted for over a century.

As the effects of the depression deepened in 1932, the fleet of steamboats on Lake George and Lake Champlain were laid up and their boilers drained. A 14-mile branch of the Greenwich & Johnsonville Railway running between its namesake towns was abandoned on July 28, resulting in a $43,000-a-year saving. In the throes of the great depression, Loree still had enough cash stowed away in the company vaults to make his judicious buy, while the price was down, of nearly half a million shares of New York Central stock for a cool $11,000,000.

A tunnel elimination and track relocation project under way in Whitehall was completed in 1933 and the ultimate locomotive—a 4-cylinder triple-expansion 500-pound-pressure poppet-valved 4-8-0 was delivered by Alco. The only locomotive built in the country that year, it was numbered 1403 and proudly, and appropriately, christened the L. F. LOREE.

* * *

No single phase of Loree's long career was more turbulent than his relations with labor. In 1931 he initiated a plan for paying the men in train service on a monthly basis instead of by the complicated mileage and hourly system which had been the case on railroads for some time. This "monthly plan" put men in regular service on the basis of 30 eight-hour days or a flat 240 hours a month; extra men would get 160 hours a month or 20 regular days' pay. An engineer would be paid $300 a month in regular service and $200 if on the extra board. Conductors and brakemen had a similar scale.

This, of course, threw the unions into a rage as the time-honored hours or miles system and the freight, passenger, yard and road scale differentials were cut to ribbons. The men were called in separately by the officials and offered a contract containing the terms of the "Monthly Plan" and it

When the first winter sports excursion arrived at North Creek, March 4, 1934, skiers were met by local residents who took them in their cars to the slope on Gore Mountain. The 1206, below, was built by Alco in 1918 at Loree's command. As she roared down the neatly-ballasted roadbed at Unadilla in the Susquehanna Valley in the spring of 1938, the Old Man was nearing his 80th birthday and retirement; the engine had still many years of useful service ahead of her. (*Charles Clingman collection, above Donald W. Furler*)

was quite apparent, although nothing directly was said, that those not signing would get their pink slips. This rather circumvented the Brotherhoods and their contract but times were pretty hard; the men knew it and so did Loree—they signed!

Loree's victory was short-lived. When conditions changed for the better several years later the Brotherhoods locked horns again with the Old Man and demanded abandonment of the Monthly Plan or a strike would be called. A fact-finding committee was formed by President Roosevelt and, after lengthy hearings in Albany it recommended that the former plan be reinstated and the decision was reluctantly accepted. The shopmen who were so badly beaten back in 1922 also won some representation once again.

D&H firemen were probably the group from which Loree most consistently got his cherished "day's work for a day's pay." There wasn't a single stoker-fired engine on the property and one of the big Mallet pushers would gobble up more than five tons of coal on a 16-mile, 90-minute trip up out of Carbondale and a muzzle-loading Consolidation consumed almost 20 tons on a trip in less than eight hours. When approached by the firemen's union during a round of negotiations to have stokers installed on some of the engines, Loree was almost speechless—a situation seldom seen. "Stokers!!", he roared, his whiskers virtually bristling. "You've got the best stokers that $1.25 can buy—Red Edges!" They were a popular brand of coal scoop on the market at the time. The "Red Edge" stoker remained standard equipment as long as Loree himself remained, although after more hearings the ICC made him put two firemen on some runs.

*   *   *

The depression eased somewhat under the "New Deal" and conditions improved a bit although dividends remained undeclared. After consistently poor results with automatic train control, the ICC allowed the abandonment of the D&H's installation on the Saratoga and Champlain divisions and all the equipment on 141 locomotives and along the road was removed in 1935. Smoke deflectors were installed on eight Pacifics giving them a distinctive appearance that was the hallmark of D&H locomotives for the remaining years of steam. Another CTC district was installed between Albany and Watervliet eliminating a dozen employees in 1937, and continuous welded rail was laid for the first time with the longest single rail stretching 6983 feet down the road.

The steamboats hadn't operated in the company service since 1933, although several had been leased by other operators from time to time. In February of 1937 a deal was made to sell all the vessels and property of the Champlain Transportation Co. On April 1st a check for $100,000 was received from Horace Corbin of Burlington and the familiar reference disappeared from the annual reports of the D&H forever.

Fire-eater though he was, the sands of time were finally running out for L. F. Loree, now approaching his 80th year. His son, James Tabor Loree, a chip off the old block and probably responsible for some of the things actually blamed on the Old Man, had been general manager since 1916, and the bearded elder was unable to be his active self in the years after 1935 due to failing health. On March 31, 1938 Leonor F. Loree submitted his resignation to the Board of Managers and it was reluctantly accepted. Thirty-one tumultuous years on the D&H had come to an end.

Many observers of the transportation scene considered Loree the last of the genius railroad leaders, one of the great and versatile railroad men of all time. With his retirement an epoch in American railroading ended. He truly earned the title *Patriarch of the Rails* given him some years later by Charles Penrose, president of the Newcomen Society in North America, an organization devoted to business history and development founded by Loree himself in 1923.

Leonor F. Loree was many things to many people; a dynamic leader, a genius of operation and management, a wizard of finance, a kind soft-spoken man, an inventor and experimenter, a firm capable businessman, a bearded Scotch tyrant, a man with a final and dogmatic tongue, a ruthless cold-hearted despot—hated by some, loved by others, but remembered by all.

The third of the experimental high-pressure locomotives was named in honor of the man whose passion for efficiency inspired the program. *(D&H collection)*

12. LOREE'S LOCOMOTIVES

The D&H had always been in a life and death battle with gravity. Newton's law prevailed on, and in fact actually operated, the old gravity railroad, judged the STOURBRIDGE LION too heavy for the tracks over which it ran on its first historic trip, and resisted the movement of anthracite up over Ararat and Belden hills like a giant invisible foot being dragged along the ground.

As soon as a new and bigger locomotive was built by Dickson or Schenectady it would be out on the hills of the D&H showing its stuff against the age-old enemy. By the mid-1880s, practically all the primitive American types obtained from the leased lines were replaced by a fleet of medium size Moguls that became the backbone of the motive power fleet until the late 1890s.

In the continuing quest for more tractive effort the D&H asked the Dickson people to come up with a larger locomotive and in 1882 they responded with a 2-8-0 Consolidation, the first of a long line to come on the D&H. It had 89,000 pounds on the drivers, almost as much as the entire weight of a typical Mogul. The 140-pound boiler pressure, 20"x 24" cylinders and 51-inch drivers gave a whopping 22,400-pound tractive effort, the largest enjoyed by the D&H operating department thus far. Three of these engines were built to push trains of almost 1000 tons up Belden Hill out of Binghamton.

It wasn't until 1896 that more 2-8-0s showed up on the D&H, and then only two. In the meantime more and larger Moguls were rolling out of the Dickson plant while others were being rebuilt and upgraded in the company shops at Green Island and Carbondale. The great stampede of Consolidations started in 1898 with the first order putting 36 in service by the turn of the century. The Consols grew steadily through the ever-increasing size ranges of Class E, E-1, E-2, E-2a, E-3, E-3a, E-4, and by the time Loree took over in 1907, over 200 2-8-0s had largely replaced all the Moguls in main-line service.

It didn't stop with Loree either. Long an advocate of big power, he continued buying now even larger 2-8-0s which fell into an E-5 classification. The first 18 of the new 1000s were double-cabbed but, with the arrival of No. 1025 in 1907, the throttle on D&H engines returned to the backhead once again. The double cab was introduced in 1886 with the advent of the wide Wooton firebox designed to use anthracite coal and was adopted by many of the eastern coal roads. It was felt visibility would be decreased appreciably by placing the engineer in a cab stuck behind the wide firebox so he was moved ahead. Although the center-cab gave the hogger a smooth ride and a better view, the safety hazard created in the event of failure for any reason on the part of the engineer curtailed the trend.

The E-5s had 222,000 pounds on the drivers, 210-pound boiler pressure, piston valves, Walschaert valve gear for the first time on the D&H and 57-inch drivers, giving them an impressive 49,650-pound tractive effort. The 48 new E-5s could easily handle 1230 tons up Belden Hill out of Binghamton where a hogger on an E-3 had his hands full with only 985 tons.

The advent of this heavier power, however, required the D&H to embark on an extensive program of rebuilding its roadbed, bridges and terminal facilities. When the last of 90 E-5s arrived in 1914 every main-line bridge had been strengthened to a Cooper E-60 loading, new roundhouses with longer turntables and improved servicing facilities had been built at Colonie, Binghamton, Oneonta and Carbondale, a new modern shop

317

facility erected at Colonie, several grade revisions completed and much track and roadbed improvement accomplished throughout the entire length of the line. These betterments, although naturally quite expensive, would prove to be an immeasurable asset to future locomotive developments as well as the general well-being of the line.

The first real motive power departure sired by Loree came in 1910 when he ordered six big 0-8-8-0 Mallet compounds from Alco for pusher service on the south end. While in Mexico before becoming president of the B&O Loree rode a double-ended Fairlie 0-6-6-0 up the 4% grades on the Mexican Central. He was quite impressed and began accumulating data on various valve gears and the Mallet type articulateds being operated in Russia and Switzerland. When he came to the B&O he proposed the idea of such an engine to his general motive power superintendent John E. Muhlfeld. A conference was held with the American Locomotive Co. and the first 0-6-6-0 compound, OLD MAUD, was introduced to this country. It thrilled the crowds at the St. Louis Exposition in 1904 and then went on to replace two husky Consol pushers on the rear of coal trains battling the grades on Sand Patch. A feature of the new engine, probably as important as its articulation, was its Walschaert valve gear. This linkage was invented by the Belgian engineer Egide Walschaert in 1844 and made its debut in this country on Loree's pusher. Its success was immediate and widespread.

It wasn't surprising then, that one day in the fall of 1909 a big Mother Hubbard 0-8-8-0 compound borrowed from the Erie lumbered into Carbondale for a try at the 19-mile, 1.3% ruling grade north out of the Lackawanna Valley. It took three of the D&H's best Consolidations to get 2600 tons up this hill to Ararat; from there a single engine could handle the train for the remaining 76 miles on into Oneonta. The big Erie brushed the double-headed 2-8-0 pushers aside and began to shove the train toward Ararat, easily accomplishing the job and proving Loree right once again.

The six D&H Mallets, the most powerful locomotives ever built at the time, with 144,100 pounds tractive effort working simple, replaced a dozen heavy Consols in the pusher pool. Their overwhelming success fostered the addition of seven more, these equipped with superheaters, to the roster in 1911 and 1912.

Aside from the 10 Pacifics obtained in 1914 for the Montreal passenger service, and of course the Mallets, the D&H staunchly continued its love affair with the 2-8-0. The primary endeavor of the road was to move anthracite in tonnage drags and speed was both unnecessary and uneconomical. Other roads of a less substantial nature were following the national trend toward engines with more drivers and trailing trucks to spread their greater weight as the size and power increased. The time and money spent to strengthen bridges and provide heavier rail allowed the further development of a good thing for the D&H—the Consolidation.

By 1915 over 8,000,000 tons of anthracite was being hauled up Ararat hill from the D&H mines alone. The E-5s were doing well, having taken over all the main-line work and pushed the operating ratio down to 62%, five points below the 1914 figure. This was primarily achieved through their greater power and the fact they used their fuel more efficiently by virtue of superheaters and a higher boiler pressure.

The pattern was well established now. If, with each successive class of Consolidation built, greater efficiency had been obtained by increasing the boiler capacity, piston size and engine weight, why stop now? The law of diminishing returns apparently hadn't been broken yet.

A gigantic machine, the class E-6 2-8-0, numbered 1200 emerged from the erecting halls at Alco in 1916. She had 267,800 pounds on her 63-inch drivers, 27"x32" cylinders, 105 square feet of grate area—a 17% increase over her predecessors—200-pound boiler pressure and exerted an amazing 63,950 pounds of tractive effort. She was designed to burn a pulverized form of coal and had covers over the coalbin in her tender to keep the fine material from blowing away at speed. This was an attempt at even further economies by utilizing a waste product obtained in the breaking and sizing operations at the mines. There were several flash-back fires in the cab from this form of fuel, among other difficulties, and she was soon placed on a regular diet of mixed hard and soft coal.

The 1200 proved herself so successfully that twenty similar engines classed as E-6a's were ordered from Alco in 1917 but with 210 pounds

Above are two of the six Mallet compounds ordered by Mr. Loree beginning in 1910, the 1600 as it first appeared and the 1610 following modernization in 1930. Aside from the obvious change in styling, boiler pressure and tractive effort were increased. Pacific No. 608 is typical of the ten engines received from Alco in 1914 that were used in passenger service to Canada. The 1200, Alco-built in 1916, was first of the E-6 class of Consolidations. The coalbin cover is apparent in the picture. Oil headlights were in 1920 changed to electricity by order of the Interstate Commerce Commission. *(D&H collection, 1600 and 1610)*

boiler pressure and delivering 67,150 pounds tractive effort, almost 5000 pounds more than the prototype. The results were indisputable; when all were placed in service the average tonnage in a northbound train out of Carbondale was 486 tons heavier than before. Efficient though these 1200s were, it took a fireman made practically of iron himself to bail enough coal into that gigantic roaring firebox to satisfy its huge appetite on a blasting run up out of Carbondale. Rather than succumb to the mechanical stoker, Loree doubleheaded the fireman on most of these runs and the long marriage to the Red Edge coal scoop was saved. He did concede the application of horizontal steam-activated coal pushers in the tender to keep the coal within reach of the foot plate for the two firemen, proving he did have a heart.

Federal control under the USRA had little impact on the D&H motive power situation other than to lower the maintenance standards previously demanded. The standard locomotive design, about the only positive thing the government administration could claim, was not allocated to the D&H since its motive power situation was in better shape than most roads, when the war began and the narrow firebox, standard on the USRA engines, was not suited for the D&H anthracite fuel.

When the railroads were finally returned to their private managements in 1920, Loree resumed his traditional aloofness on all matters including motive power. The salesmen peddling Lima's Super-Power, Alco's three cylinder concepts, ten-coupled locomotives, trailing trucks and other innovations of the dawning era of new power never even got past the front door of the motive power department.

Instead, a program of upgrading the older power was launched with a vengeance. In 1923, D&H began to modernize center-cab Mother Hubbards rather than replacing and supplementing its older power as was the case on most other roads. When an engine came due for its periodic overhaul they pulled out all the stops at Colonie. The cab was moved onto the backhead, saturated boilers received superheater units, Stephenson link motion and flat D-type slide valves were exchanged for new, enlarged piston-valved cast cylinder blocks with Walschaert valve gear, and boiler pressures were raised. The older E-2s retained their Stephenson gear but No. 754 got Baker valve gear — an incongruous modernity on a rather mundane old camelback.

All but three of the 900-class engines were the result of rebuilding 700s and 800s. In an effort to approach an assembly line production the boiler and frame of the older engines would be separated at the beginning of the rebuilding process. As soon as enough rebuilt parts were ready a new 900 would be assembled and as a result the lineage of the original locomotive was lost as the frame of one 800 was mated with the boiler from another. This was known as the swing-boiler method and considerably speeded the rebuilding process as work on the boiler usually required the most time.

This program lasted until the mid-1930s and over 100 locomotives were completely rebuilt while many others were upgraded to some degree in different ways. Many patented gadgets were tried. A big mechanically-actuated Dabeg feedwater pump on the No. 1076 was reminiscent of locomotives from the Civil War period. A different type of Dabeg feedwater heater was mounted behind the stack on top of the boiler of No. 1088. Lentz poppet valves were installed on the No. 925. Forced-feed lubrication, low-water alarms, flange oilers and many more were tried. The rebuilding program ranged from American Standards to the big Mallets and even included a sizeable number of light and heavy 2-8-0s that cashed in their lead trucks to become quite powerful 0-8-0 switchers. As an example of the improvement that resulted following modernizations, the tonnage rating for medium-sized 2-8-0s was increased from 2250 to 2600 tons on a northbound run out of Wilkes-Barre.

What was probably the ultimate Consolidation, of the traditional type anyway, came out of the D&H's own shops in 1926. Even bigger than the 1200s, the new engines, with their boilers built by Alco in Schenectady, were classed E-5a's, probably because their cylinders were the same diameter as the late 1000s but the similarity ended there. The 1111, first of a dozen to come, had 265-pound boiler pressure, 272,000 pounds on the drivers and exerted an incredible 72,700-pound tractive effort. The 63-inch drivers enabled it to run on manifest schedules while the great boiler with its 3377 square feet of heating surface and 775 square feet of superheater gave it the power

After No. 1200 showed the way, twenty similar engines were ordered from Alco in 1918, including the 1218, top. Classed as E-6a's, the new ones were a bit more powerful than the 1200. In 1926, boiler pressure was raised for the whole class, including the 1200. They worked on the Pennsylvania division until the 1950s. Double-cab Consolidation No. 1011 was built by Alco in 1906 and was one of the first of the flood of E-5s to come to the D&H. Her original cylinders were increased an inch in diameter in 1917. The right flank of E-5 Consolidation No. 1076, below, is decorated with a Dabeg feed-water heater, actuated by valve motion. *(D&H collection, all)*

The 1088's feed-water heater was mounted on top, behind the stack; its pump was operated by the eccentric crank on the last driver. Wear probably was excessive on all these joints, for the unit was removed in later years. Consolidation No. 925 was equipped with Austrian-made poppet valves in 1926. Operated by regular Walschaert linkage, they ran 142,000 miles in over 3½ years with but one failure, when a cotter pin worked loose and fell out. Biggest and best of the D&H Consolidations were the 1100 series, which could pull tonnage trains at passenger train speeds. The 1112 is pictured at the Colonie shops where she was built. *(D&H collection, six pictures)*

Consolidation No. 1111 was first of the dozen homemade D&H engines, the E-5a class, that were about as powerful and efficient as a 2-8-0 could be made. The last of the series was built in 1932, after which the Depression ended the need for new motive power. The 1114 had a different appearance from the others, because of the enclosure along the top; it also carried more boiler pressure and much more superheating surface. President Loree was always happy to show off his locomotives. Below, they are lined up at Colonie for a visit by the New York Central and Lehigh Valley presidents in 1927. A similar display was arranged each year for the annual inspection by the Board of Managers and usually showed the latest motive power developments of the year.

to lug on grades. By the depression year of 1930 the need for more power had decreased and the 1122 was the last to roll out of Colonie. The 1114 had a special boiler that carried 300 pounds pressure and contained twice the superheating surface provided in the others of the class. In the search for higher efficiencies, the 1100s brought the 2-8-0 type as close to perfection as it would ever come. They surely showed the way for Reading with its I-10s and Western Maryland's big H-9s. Few roads, however, were ever able even to approach the performance received from a mere lead axle and eight drivers that the D&H achieved in its mighty E-5a's.

The appearance of Loree's locomotives, especially the passenger engines, began to take on unique aspects after the Old Man returned from a post-war European trip. Recessed headlights, capped stacks, small rakish cabs, long low tenders, shrouded domes and clean-lined boilers free of external pipes and equipment began to emerge from the smoky depths of Colonie. The 556 sported chrome plating on its boiler jacket, cylinder housings, handrails, throttle lever and whistle, while the running boards, side rods and wheels were set off by white striping. The 10 Pacifics enjoyed the most drastic outward change, finally receiving the smoke deflectors that created the image of D&H power remembered most by all. All locomotives got a coat of black enamel that was usually kept so clean that you could shave in the reflection it cast back, even in the course of everyday road service. The stylized treatment was given to locomotives ranging from American Standards to the big Mallets.

In the constant quest for ever greater power and efficiency, much experimentation and development took place in the years following the war. Greater tractive effort was always the goal. A gadget called the tender booster was designed to give an extra stimulus to the tractive effort of the old Consols when all limits of boiler pressure and cylinder size was reached. Called an "auxiliary locomotive," this midget two-cylinder steam engine mounted on the rear tender truck and geared to one of its axles was devised by equipment superintendent J. A. McGrew and patented along with general manager J. T. Loree under the name M & L Tender Booster. Its two 10"x10" cylinders received superheated steam through a flexibly connected pipe attached to the feed for the left steam chest of the locomotive. The booster could only function when the locomotive throttle was open, and when it was cut in by a lever in the cab, the steam flowed back and actuated a piston which engaged the drive mechanism. The steam pressure held the gear engaged with the axle as well as feeding the cylinders while in operation, and when the booster was shut off or the throttle closed a spring disengaged the driving gear from the rear axle.

The device had a particular appeal for the D&H, as it had no freight engines with a rear engine truck, the more conventional location for boosters at the time. It served to convert the excess boiler capacity at low speed into additional tractive effort, changed the dead weight of the tender from a hindrance into an asset by using it as a source for adhesion and further tractive effort, smoothed out the power surges from the main cylinders and significantly increased the pulling power of a locomotive without appreciably increasing the overall weight. This last item enabled locomotives so equipped to pull bigger trains on branch lines without the expense entailed to strengthen bridges, as would be the case if larger engines were used. Finally, the exhaust steam passed through coils in the tender on the way out serving then as a junior feedwater heater.

The first model was installed on Mother Hubbard No. 901 in 1922 with outstanding success. The old Consol was able to haul 2477 tons over a grade on which she was previously rated for only 1650 tons, a 48% increase. A newer "B" model, with 2-inch larger pistons, was tested on 0.8% grade Schoharie Hill in June 1923 with a 35-car, 2476-adjusted-ton test train. Part way up the grade the train was stopped and couldn't be started again by the 901 itself, but with the booster's 14,400-pound added tractive effort she moved right out and attained a speed of seven miles per hour within 650 feet.

Performances on the Oneonta hump further proved the objectives were achieved and the D&H installed the units on a number of engines. Of all the steam locomotive developments pioneered by the D&H, the tender booster was the most widely accepted, and after the patent was bought by Bethlehem Steel Co. it became a familiar sight all across the nation.

Ten-Wheeler 556 had served the D&H faithfully for twenty years as a Camelback, top, when she arrived at the Colonie shops in 1927, a train control pickup shoe suspended from her tender. In the shops her usefulness and her beauty were enhanced and in May she emerged in the gleaming form shown above. Her cylinders were increased in diameter; boiler pressure was raised and tractive effort boosted by over 18%. With her outside-journaled lead truck, outside ash pans and nickel-plated boiler jacket she was an impressive looking machine indeed. The "elephant ear" smoke-lifters became the hallmark of D&H passenger power in the 1930s. *(D&H collection, all)*

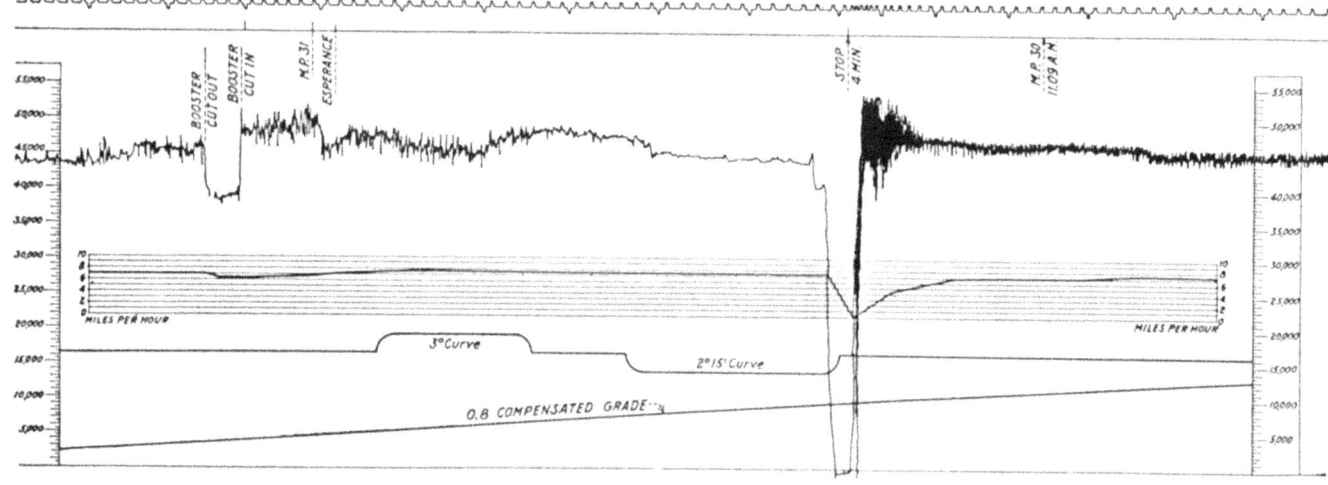

The ten passenger Pacifics were modified in various ways through the years until they had the distinctive look that set the D&H apart from all other railroads. At the left is the way Pacific No. 604 looked during the latter half of its 39 years of service. Next is evidence that even the lowly 4-4-0 got the treatment, too. At the right is an exposed view of the M&L tender booster, showing the two-cylinder steam engine, the driving gears that transmitted power to the axle and, center, the piston that threw an intermediate drive gear into mesh when steam was fed to the unit from the engine. The lower picture at the right shows the rods that transmitted power between the axles of the truck. The steam line from the locomotive can be seen at the right. Below is 2-8-0 No. 901 with tender booster installed. At the left the 901, still a Camelback before her 1925 rebuilding, is shown with the dynamometer car for tests of the operation of the booster. Springs in a housing attached to the drawbar transmitted the intensity of pull or push to a recording device, resulting in a tape such as that at the bottom of the other page, which shows the tractive pull on the 901's demonstration on the 0.8% grade of Schoharie Hill, June 5, 1923. The train was stopped and the 901 itself couldn't get it started again, but with the booster the train was moving at 7 mph within 650 feet. (*D&H collection, six pictures*)

327

Horatio Allen was the first locomotive engineer in America and important in the development of the D&H during the early years of the canal and gravity railway.

Another technological development originated on the D&H that gained wide acceptance was the application of roller bearings to locomotive driving wheels and side rods. Realizing the problem of proper lubrication of the driving wheel axles and the maintenance associated with this item a large bearing manufacturer was approached in January 1927 to offer a proposed design for the application of roller bearings. Three months later the reply was that such an application of roller bearings did not appear feasible at the time.

Naturally this didn't stop Loree and on September 13, 1930, 2-8-0 No. 1071 left the Colonie shops with roller bearings in all eight main driver journals. The results were gratifying and five of the Pacifics were equipped with them by 1936. The "Hiawatha" locomotives designed for high-speed service on the Milwaukee Road in 1935 had these bearings as original equipment and their value was immediately recognized.

Spurred on by this eminent success the motive power superintendent George Edmonds and his staff looked to the side rod bearings next. Here was a particularly troublesome spot as the pounding action on the brass bearings while in motion at high speeds and the exposed nature of the side rods to the abrasive elements of road dust and sand made the rate of wear high and replacements frequent. This time the roller bearing people didn't brush off the proposal lightly and on January 31, 1934 Pacific No. 609 emerged from Colonie with self-aligning SKF roller bearings on both the driving axle journals and side rod bearings—the first locomotive in the world to be so equipped. Aside from a minor grease seal problem that was soon corrected, they ran like a Swiss watch.

Other sophistications came too: the one-piece Commonwealth integrally cast frame and cylinder housing, alloy steel side rods, outside-bearing cast steel engine trucks, poppet valves and surely a dozen more. The D&H was more than a railroad, it was a test tube bubbling with progress as well.

✔   ✔   ✔

Loree was still possessed with the relentless ambition to raise the efficiency of his transportation hardware. He summoned his former associate while on the B&O, John Muhlfeld, the man who conquered Sand Patch with the first Mallet and was now a consulting engineer. They hashed over the seesaw problem of locomotive economics of higher tractive effort with less fuel. They agreed the answer was located in the locomotive's prime energy source—the boiler. Muhlfeld figured a high-pressure design developed along the lines of a marine unit should be substituted for the conventional firetube type. In addition, the engine should be a compound as it costs less to use most anything twice instead of once—including steam. Naturally the 2-8-0 was chosen to carry this boiler and cylinders—what else on the D&H! The blueprints were carefully prepared and a strange looking creature began taking shape in the shadows of Alco's great Schenectady plant.

In auspicious ceremonies at Colonie on December 4, 1924 No. 1400 was christened the HORATIO ALLEN in honor of the man who in 1829 first ran a D&H locomotive—the STOURBRIDGE LION. A bottle of champagne was broken over the pilot by Mrs. Russell Lewis, Horatio Allen's granddaughter.

Pacific No. 609 was twenty years old in 1924 when she emerged from the Colonie shops with roller bearings on her driving wheel and on the main side rod driving pins —the first such application anywhere in the world. The detailed pictures above show the alloy steel side rods and the SKF bearings. Below is experimental engine No. 1400, the HORATIO ALLEN. The remark of her designer, John Muhlfeld, that there was "nothing unusual" about her suggests that his engineering genius surpassed his eyesight! (D&H collection, all)

The front of the JOHN B. JERVIS peered out from a series of bulging shrouds. The top one was the front of the housing that covered plumbing around the throttle valve ahead of the boiler; the lower one was the receiver that carried steam from the high-pressure cylinder on the engineer's side to the larger low-pressure cylinder opposite it, which appears in the picture below. Walschaert linkage regulated the valves. Soon after arrival, her appearance was improved by extending the bulges on her water tube boiler to include the throttle box and associated piping, as well as the tall stack, as the bottom picture shows. (D&H collection, all)

Awed guests found that the 1400's smokebox peered out from beneath a freakish shroud of large pipes, that spoked pony wheels were set far out ahead of dissimilar cylinders, that an enormous firebox completely spanned the last two pairs of drivers, that a tiny typically-D&H cab was tucked behind all this plumbing and that the whole affair was concluded by a short boosterized tender.

In his speech for the occasion President Loree tried to explain the unique design by saying: "It takes about 1150 heat units to convert water into (one pound of) steam at no pressure. But to raise it to 200 pounds (per square inch) pressure—which is now the general locomotive practice—requires only about 49 additional heat units. To further raise it to 350 pounds (pressure), and thus secure 75% more power, requires less than 7½ additional heat units. It is this new pressure of 350 pounds that will be carried by the HORATIO ALLEN; and it is the economy of producing additional power by raising the pressure of the steam that this locomotive will realize. It is hoped that the HORATIO ALLEN will develop one-third more haulage capacity, with one-third less consumption of fuel and water, than the corresponding Consolidation locomotive."

The creator of this unique machine, Mr. Muhlfeld, noted in his remarks for the occasion that "there is nothing unusual in the HORATIO ALLEN." Needless to say, this observation raised a few skeptical eyebrows in the crowd gathered there, many of whom were seasoned mechanical men from other railroads. Muhlfeld went on to point out that the watertube boiler contained almost 1200 square feet of heating surface in the firebox alone compared to the 400 or so in both the firebox and combustion chamber of conventional boilers. The normal firebox heating surface generally represented about 5 to 10 per cent of the evaporating surface but in the 1400 the watertube firebox embraced almost 37%, 1187 square feet out of a total of 3200. This took advantage of the radiant heat of combustion for evaporating the water and provided for almost 75%—instead of 40% in regular boilers—of the steam-making capacity where it can be most efficiently generated. More water was circulated around the fire and even more was carried in the cylindrical drums directly exposed to the flame, eliminating the sluggish circulation of water found in more conventionally designed boilers. A square foot of heating surface in the firebox is five times more effective than an equal amount in the flues.

Further to exploit the steam produced in this boiler at 350 pounds pressure, along with a reasonable degree of superheating, the product was cross-compounded; first in a 23½-inch high-pressure cylinder on the right side and then after being exhausted into a receiver entered a 41-inch low-pressure cylinder on the opposite side. Steam from the boiler then was only admitted twice per revolution of the drivers rather than the four times in a more conventional locomotive, further adding to the efficiency. The steam was regulated by a Young valve gear, a motion connected to the crosshead rather than the crank pin, the more conventional place.

The starting tractive effort of this 298,500-pound, 57-inch drivered Consol was 85,800 pounds working simple and 71,600 pounds compound while the tender booster added another 19,700 pounds. Impressive figures indeed for a moderate-sized 2-8-0!

Out on the road she proved the slide rules to be correct by attaining a thermal efficiency of over 8%, considerably more than the other Consols on the D&H already noted for their high efficiency. She could handle the same train on eight tons of coal that it took two conventional 2-8-0s burning 12 tons to move. In brute lugging capacity she compared favorably to a 2-10-0. On Schoharie Hill she moved a 63-car 4509-ton test train with ease, at a steady four miles per hour exerting 86,000 pounds pull on the dynamometer car tape until a coupler knuckle broke. When the train was started again, with the ALLEN working simple and the booster cut in, the needle back in the dynamometer car rose to the unprecedented 111,000-pound mark. A big 1200 was only rated for about 3700 tons on this .8% grade.

Engine crews were a bit leary of her high steam pressure, especially older hoggers used to seeing the needle hovering around the 200-pound mark, but soon came to consider the 1400 more or less just another Consol in the pool. Maintenance was somewhat higher, but this—theoretically anyway—was offset by the other economies of fuel savings and heavier trains. After two years of in-service testing, the D&H seemed satisfied that the engine had accomplished its primary mis-

The 1400 is shown at Oneonta in July 1925, left, with dynamometer car and test train being readied for a northbound run to Mechanicville. An enclosure was built on the pilot to protect technicians from the wind while taking indicator cards and monitoring other aspects of steam pressure and consumption in high- and low-pressure cylinders. Despite her unconventional features, the JAMES ARCHBALD had the traditional clean-lined D&H look, as the middle picture to the left shows. The bottom view shows the huge low-pressure cylinder on the fireman's side, illuminated number board, mechanically actuated Dabeg feed water pump, Walschaert valve linkage, polished alloy steel side rods and the 63″ drivers. The 1402's cab was quite modern with quadrant throttle, speed recorder and power reverse lever, but featured 1000-pound steam gauges and a pyrometer at upper left to record high-pressure steam temperature. The water-tube boiler was built of nickel steel alloys to withstand the 500-pound pressure. It was designed to facilitate water circulation to the hottest parts of the boiler so its steam-making capacity was extremely lively and efficient. (D&H collection, all)

sion — to prove the feasibility of the basic concept. Much encouraged by this performance they moved ahead with even greater plans.

The HORATIO ALLEN was followed in 1927 by the JOHN B. JERVIS, No. 1401, having essentially the same dimensions, power and concepts but with slightly smaller cylinders compensated by the 400-pound pressure carried in her strange looking boiler. A larger tender holding 16,000 gallons of water and 20 tons of coal riding on 6-wheel trucks, the rear one with two of its three axles driven by a booster, was provided. She had Edmonds oil-lubricated driving wheel bearings, a German State Railways draft damper and the valves were operated by Walschaert linkage, a tradition now on the D&H. She achieved over 10% thermal efficiency and developed more than 2000 horsepower in exhaustive tests conducted with a 3500-ton train north of Oneonta on the new low grade line near Schenevus.

In April 1930 Alco built still another, the JAMES ARCHBALD; this 2-8-0 carried an incredible 500 pounds pressure in her nickel steel boiler. Her looks, however, were considerably improved by enclosing all the weird piping and bulges associated with her watertube boiler and cross-compound cylinders beneath a smooth outer jacket that extended from her smokebox to the cab. A long low tender, recessed headlight, small cab, illuminated number boards under her running board and outside-journaled pony truck gave her a more traditional D&H appearance. The tractive effort was exactly the same as her two predecessors, 102,300 pounds working simple, with the Bethlehem tender booster cut in. The increased efficiency expected from the 500 pounds boiler pressure, however, was reflected in the fact that her tender capacity was cut back to 17½ tons of coal despite the fact she was assigned to the same Mechanicville-Oneonta run with the other two experimentals.

✦ ✦ ✦

Always an avid student of steam propulsion, Loree knew the ins and outs of locomotives from Stephenson's ROCKET down to the most theoretical concepts of his day. He frequently looked to Europe, birthplace of the steam locomotive, where efficiency and technology had advanced further than in the New World. There, out of necessity, every last calorie was wrung out of the fuel. Coal and oil were at a premium and were used to best advantage through compounding, delicate valve gears and many other gadgets including poppet valves. These valves looked and functioned much like the valves in present-day internal combustion engines except they were considerably larger.

In an effort to overcome the difficulties of the flat side valves warping under the higher temperatures of superheated steam, a spool-shaped piston valve was developed. Although quite satisfactory and widely accepted they were far from perfect due to ring and valve-chamber-bushing wear. Power was lost when leakage did develop, and the overall maintenance associated with the whole assembly was costly.

There were four poppet valves on the cylinder, one for inlet and one for exhaust at each end. The valves were operated by a camshaft, just as in an automobile engine, and rotation — or in this case oscillation — was caused by the action of the normal valve gear. In addition to giving better steam distribution and finer cutoff settings it was claimed that the poppet valves remained absolutely tight over long periods of service, needed no lubrication and required very little power for their operation.

In 1926 an oscillating-type poppet valve, made in Austria by Lentz, actuated by a Walschaert gear, was installed on No. 925 to determine whether such an application was practical under the more severe and heavier duty American operating conditions. The superintendent of motive power was somewhat apprehensive of these new valves but was pleasantly surprised at the results observed on the old Consol. She was free-running and gave no appreciable trouble in 3½ years and 142,000 miles. In 1927 a visit by D&H officials to Mr. Caprotte in Florence, Italy, another builder of poppet valves, showed that poppet-valved engines, capable of a finer degree of cut-off settings, showed more than a 9% saving on coal over similar models equipped with piston valves.

It was decided that the D&H would build two new Pacifics in Colonie, almost identical in every way excepting their valves. One would have regular piston valves and the other Dabeg poppets. What better proving ground could be found than the rugged 250-mile Troy-Montreal passenger service? The motive power department got out its T-squares and in 1929 sleek stylized and powerful

Pacific No. 652 was an exceedingly sleek homemade product of D&H shops, with a beautiful blue-gray boiler jacket that set her off from the traditional black locomotives. After her completion in the spring of 1929 she was put on display behind the Flemish-Gothic towers of the general office building, where she was admired by railroad men and the general public. She was the first engine to display the Loree look that became the hallmark of D&H power. *(D&H collection, both)*

At first glance Pacific No. 651 was very similar to the 652 which had appeared a year earlier. They had the same clean-lined "European" look, from recessed headlight, capped stack and smooth pipeless boiler to the blue-gray enamel on the boiler jacket, polished steel side rods, white-lined drivers and yellow lettering and striping on cab and tender. The essential difference, embodying the concept the engine was designed to test, is shown on the opposite page: the Dabeg oscillating poppet valve actuated by the rod running to the right and connected with a conventional Walschaert valve gear. The whole assembly was covered by a jacket while in service. *(D&H collection, all)*

336

4-6-2 No. 652 emerged from the great shops at Colonie. A year later sister 651, with the poppet valves, joined her on *The Laurentian*, after being exhibited at the American Railway Association convention in Atlantic City.

These two Pacifics were unique in design having even more than the usual clean, racy D&H lines, with their recessed headlight, capped stack, smooth pipeless boiler, small cab and long, low tender. A single dome atop the bluish-gray boiler jacket housed the steam dome, safety valves and chime whistle. The sand boxes were placed beneath each running board just behind the cylinder. To clean up their lines further and give them a real British look the air compressor, turbo generator and power reverse units were suspended between the frames. This lowered the center of gravity considerably and gave them good stability but created a maintenance nightmare for shop crews. Both had 22"x28" cylinders and 73-inch drivers but the 651 was a bit heavier and with 275 pounds boiler pressure produced 44,000 pounds tractive effort compared with her sister's 260-pound, 41,600 tractive effort figures.

A third Pacific, completed in 1931, the 653, boasted 24"x32" modified uniflow cylinders, 64,000 pounds tractive effort, making it the most powerful 4-6-2 ever built, and carried an unprecedented 325 pounds steam pressure in her conventionally stay-bolted boiler. In this modified uniflow design a double piston valve operated to admit steam but a series of ports in the cylinder barrel controlled the exhaust steam when uncovered by the movement of the piston and valves in such a manner that the cylinders were maintained at a higher working temperature than in conventional designs thus reducing condensation losses in this area. The 325-pound steam exerted over 60 tons on the piston so the running gear had to be correspondingly beefed up with high-strength steels, and the piston rod was extended through the front cylinder head. This served to equalize the total force on the front and back of the piston, an inequality generally overlooked with the more conventional boiler pressures, and helped carry its weight more evenly, thus reducing packing and ring wear. Somewhat to offset the added weight of the heavier-than-usual parts, the cab, running boards, air reservoir and brake cylinders were made of aluminum. She had the same clean European appearance as the previous two Colonie creations and went on to join the other two Pacifics on the Montreal runs.

In 1934 the No. 653 received poppet valves and new cylinders, and the regular Walschaert valve gear was replaced by a rotary cam system to operate the valves. The modified uniflow design, mainly used on stationary and marine engines, proved to make little if any difference in operation or efficiency so a more advanced version of the Dabeg poppet valve was then installed. This rotary drive was accomplished by placing the free end of the eccentric crank on the main driving pin, exactly in line with the center of the axle. A bevel gear, attached to it, then transmitted the rotary motion through a shaft to the cam at the valves. The new cylinders were two inches smaller than the originals and reduced the tractive effort from the record figure down to 59,500 pounds.

In order to insure clear vision for the crew of this and other locomotives with a relatively low cylinder exhaust backpressure, various experiments had been made to carry the smoke up over the engine and train and keep it from swirling down around the boiler and cab. The most effective arrangement consisted of large rectangular plates fastened to the outside of the running boards at each side of the smokebox. This, along with a slope sheet rising on an angle from the pilot, together with doors covering the front steps leading to the running boards, created a scoop-like arrangement causing an upward current of air to rush between the plates and the smokebox, carrying the smoke well above the locomotive and train. These plates were dubbed "elephant ears" and were later applied to the earlier 600s giving the D&H passenger power the distinctive appearance it enjoyed right up until the end.

Surely the most unique and most far-reaching experiment tried by the D&H in its quest for higher efficiencies was No. 1403, appropriately christened the L. F. LOREE. As well as being the only locomotive built in the country during 1933, this was the world's first four-cylinder triple-expansion, non-articulated compound steam locomotive and carried 500 pounds pressure in the water-tube boiler. It had four cylinders, but unlike the well established articulated design, the 1403 had one at each corner of the machine's frame. Two on each side were connected through individual pistons, crossheads and driving rods to a single

Pacific No. 653 made its debut in 1931 with a number of new mechanical features. Three years later several changes were made and the engine was put on public display outside the general offices in Albany, below. Most noticeable, of course, are the "elephant ear" smoke lifters and the sloping plate running up from the pilot, which created an updraft of air when the engine was in motion, lifting the smoke higher than the force of the exhaust itself could push it, to keep it from obscuring the engineer's vision. The 653 pioneered this feature for the D&H and similar smoke lifters were later installed on other engines, such as those on pages 325 and 326. Another change is visible on the side view of the 653, the Dabeg rotary-cam poppet valve. *(D&H collection, both)*

340

"the D&H"

The highly unorthodox L. F. LOREE is shown at the top of the opposite page with the dynamometer car and a 92-car, 6103-ton test train running north out of Oneonta on the three-track stretch up to Cooperstown Junction in May, 1933. The head-on view discloses a clean-lined front end with recessed headlight, covered air tank on the pilot, enclosed piping around and behind the stack, two opposing cylinders on one side and the long, boosterized tender. The side view above clearly shows the three-truck tender booster and the driving wheels through which the maximum 108,000 pounds of tractive effort was exerted. The action of the driving rods is detailed in the middle picture to the right. They went to the same crank pin on the second 63" driver, with the eccentric crank set with the free end in exact alignment with the axle, so that the motion was circular. A bevel gear picked up this rotary motion and transmitted it through a shaft to the cams that lifted the poppet valves. The drive shown was on the fireman's side and operated the two low-pressure cylinders at the front. They are detailed in the bottom picture. The big casting that formed the cylinders, the boiler saddle and the low-pressure steam receiving chamber was so heavy that it required a four-wheel lead truck. *(D&H collection, all)*

main crankpin on the second driving wheel. The high pressure 20"x33" cylinder using the 500-pound steam was located under the engineer's feet beneath the cab at the rear of the engine, with the intermediate pressure 27½"x32" cylinder across from it on the fireman's side. Two low-pressure 33"x32" cylinders were up front in the conventional location. The two cylinder blocks were each cast integrally with the saddle and steam receiving chambers, and the forward assembly was so massive that a four-wheel lead truck was provided to carry the weight making the LOREE a 4-8-0, the first departure from the Consolidation type for freight service on the D&H in almost 40 years.

The complex problem of timing all these cylinders properly was solved by applying rotary-cam Dabeg poppet valves. The two low-pressure cylinders on the front were driven by a rotary motion obtained from the eccentric crank on the left side while the high and intermediate pressure cylinders took their motion from the other.

A system of bypass and bleed valves was provided to allow high-pressure steam to work all cylinders for high starting tractive effort and with the 18,000 pounds contributed by the tender booster, the No. 1403 could produce an amazing 108,000-pound pull, as much as a big Mallet and this with only eight driving wheels. During compound running the various pressures were properly maintained automatically in the intermediate receivers by make-up valves injecting just enough high-pressure steam to maintain a balance.

Out on the road she proved the theories of her creators to be correct; she was probably the most efficient steam locomotive ever built. The average thermal efficiency of a conventional locomotive of her time was around 6% but she attained the unprecedented figure of almost 13%, about 3% more than her closest rival the JAMES ARCHBALD. She surpassed the other high-pressure engines by virtue of using the steam three times rather than only two. The theoretical maximum for the perfect locomotive was only around 20%, so she did pretty well. On one test run made before going to the Century of Progress Exposition in Chicago for display, she pulled a 92-car, 6103-ton train up a .52% grade at 4½ miles per hour with the booster cut in and working compound, while the dynamometer car showed a drawbar pull of 74,000 pounds.

*   *   *

Despite all the impressive figures attributed to the high-pressure quartet, they were in fact failures. Oh, the concept and even the first two locomotives worked well, but other factors were against them.

Probably the biggest problem was their late arrival on the scene. Had they been built twenty years earlier, in the drag freight era, their breed would likely have become commonplace. In a time when high horsepower and high speed had become important their slow dragging power was no longer an asset. There was no question of their capability to keep a train, heavier than a conventional locomotive of the same size could handle, moving on a grade and on less fuel besides. Their tractive effort and constant torque, provided by the compound cylinders, was tremendous but the overall horsepower left much to be desired. They moved big trains all right but, at five miles per hour, certainly offering no competition to the growing trucking industry.

Their mechanical complexity was another strike against them. As time wore on, the savings they achieved in operation were nullified by higher maintenance costs in terminals and shops. The repairs on the boilers and parts increased with time; compounds were traditionally more costly to maintain anyway.

The LOREE, No. 1403, was particularly troublesome. The great force placed on the single crank pin produced bearing and stress problems. Roller bearings were on the axles, but hadn't been perfected for the side rods yet, at the time she was built. The long linkage driving the cams that operated the poppet valves was subject to wear and lost motion, which affected the synchronization of the opposed pistons, causing even more stress in the main pin and other parts. The high temperature and great pressure of the 500-pound steam kept breaking down the packing in pistons, valves and other plumbing. Regular lubricating oils would turn to carbon in the cylinders at the high temperature. When the LOREE was set out on a back track at Colonie after only a few years with little

---

An exact working replica of the STOURBRIDGE LION was built at Colonie, opposite, to accompany the L. F. LOREE to A Century of Progress at Chicago. (*D&H collection*)

The world's first fusion-welded locomotive boiler was built by Alco and installed by the D&H in 1937. The purpose was to reduce internal corrosion, ease maintenance and cleaning, and to reduce weight without loss of strength. The white placards on the compressor guards over the pilot were not part of the restyling treatment; they were ICC notification that she was equipped with an experi-

mental boiler. For six weeks after t[] was installed, she was tested outside temporary stack. After the work wa went into service, the ICC inspec months for several years until it wa her freedom from leaks and lifted the fabrication. *(D&H collection, both)*

fanfare compared to her debut, only 9845 miles of service showed on her record card.

The HORATIO ALLEN was the most successful of the experimental engines and ran the greatest number of miles for two reasons. She was around longer than the others and her pressures and stresses weren't pushed to the delicate limits approached on them. She rolled up 171,838 miles, most of these in regular everyday revenue service, while No. 1401, the JOHN B. JERVIS only made 83,021, and No. 1402, the JAMES ARCHBALD, only 54,108 miles. In summary Loree's high-pressure experiments were twenty years late operationally and twenty years early mechanically. The poppet valves were an example of the latter.

These valves were excellent in every respect, providing a quick snappy action, taking little power to operate, small and light in weight, and very efficient in their control of the steam. They were ahead of their time however in both material and workmanship. The slapping action of the valves upon seating caused the harder alloy steels to crack and the softer ones to hammer out of shape in time. The tolerances and workmanship required on these mechanisms wasn't the rule in other aspects of shop practice at the time so the poppets suffered as a result.

In 1938 the world's first fusion-welded boiler was installed on 2-8-0 No. 1219. This boiler was built by Alco and installed at the Colonie shop. It was not a high-pressure unit but embodied many advantages over the normal riveted type by virtue of eliminating joints and rivets where corrosion and pitting developed first, reducing weight and maintenance and producing a freer-breathing boiler. In the process, the World War I Consol got a face-lifting involving the traditional D&H look of recessed headlight, air pumps mounted behind guards on the pilot, rakish English cab and concealed piping leaving a relatively smooth boiler jacket.

After long and careful scrutiny by the ICC inspectors the welded boiler was approved for general use making this and roller bearings the most significant contributions made to the industry by Loree and his D&H.

*   *   *

"To assert that the steam locomotives of the Delaware & Hudson were daring in design and austere in appearance is to say they were cast after the character of the man who ruled the line for 31 tumultuous years." Thus does a respected railroad journalist characterize the man and his locomotives. "Like his engines, Loree was a stark model of efficiency—a great and proud figure of a man who believed in flat profiles and super locomotives, a day's work for a day's pay, discipline of organization and freedom of management.... Because of Loree the company achieved a rank out of all proportion to its modest mileage.

"The locomotives purchased or rebuilt throughout Loree's administration mirrored its trials and triumphs. Often experimental in concept, always disciplined in design, they ran the gamut from high-pressure 2-8-0s to Pacifics with rotary cam poppet valve gear and recessed headlights. They seldom agreed with contemporary U.S. engineering and yet they included the first driving-axle and side-rod roller bearing assemblies, tender booster and welded boiler. The industry learned to look when the D&H unwrapped a new engine because Leonor Loree was a man well versed in locomotives."*

Perhaps the whole experimental period on the D&H, with its trials and errors, successes and failures, might be summed up by the old proverb—it is better to have loved and lost than never to have loved at all.

---

*Morgan, David P. "Loree's Locomotives," *Trains Magazine*, July 1952, pages 20 and 22. Quoted by permission of the Kalmbach Publishing Co.

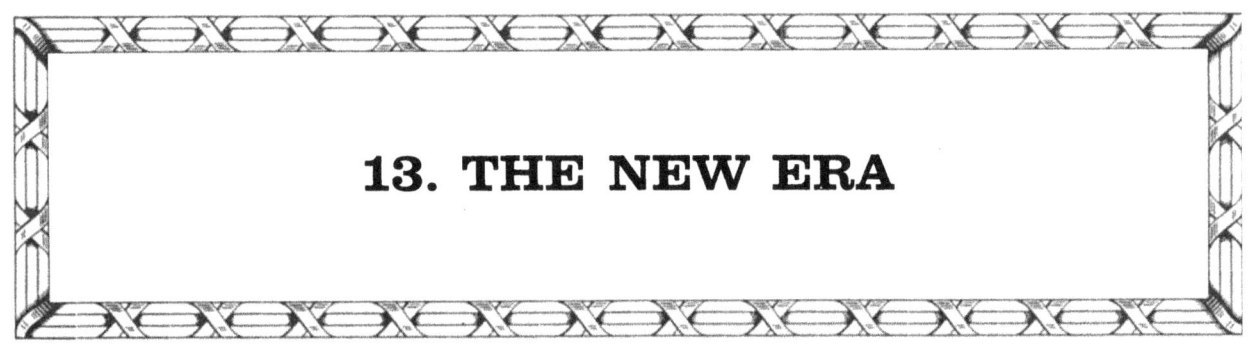

13. THE NEW ERA

When the Loree era ended on the D&H in 1938 the road was in first class shape—first class, that is, by 1925 standards! The era of the slow drag battling along at five miles per hour was over. The anthracite tonnage moved over the road had been constantly dropping as more and more homes and industries discarded the old coal scoop in favor of fingertip control with oil as a fuel. If the D&H was to maintain the strong financial position enjoyed down through the years, or indeed survive at all, the whole concept of its transportation mission had to be changed and updated.

Joseph H. Nuelle was the man chosen by the managers on May 16, 1938 to accomplish this transition. He was no stranger to the railroad or coal mining business, having been president of the Lehigh Coal & Navigation Co. and its Lehigh & New England Railroad when he was asked to come to the D&H. The two companies were quite similar in their overall endeavors and their corporate longevity. Prior to that, he had spent 31 years with the New York, Ontario & Western Railway, moving through the ranks in the engineering and operating departments to the presidency of that road for seven years beginning in 1930. That experience alone on the "Old Woman" surely taught him most of the problems encountered on an anthracite road and now with this experience, on a road with a reasonably good financial background and good traffic potential, he had the opportunity to make the progress he may have wanted but couldn't achieve on the weaker lines.

His first move was to get rid of the old guard, many of whom were old military cronies of "the Colonel," Vice-President and General Manager, James Tabor Loree, the old man's son. The official record shows the Colonel had declined to offer himself for re-election to his post on the Board, but it was quite clear a shake-up was in the offing and new blood was needed.

Next, the "bridge traffic" flowing between Canadian and New England gateways and the industrial heartland of the nation was eagerly sought. This type of business was already moving in considerable volume over the D&H but, as the coal traffic decreased, expenses rose and on-line industries moved, other sources of revenue had to be developed. To compete successfully in this bridge traffic movement it was necessary to get the cars over the road as quickly as possible and on time for their connections. The stable of 2-8-0s housed by the D&H was a fine group of engines, maintained in top condition but with the possible exception of the few 1100s, not one was capable of running the race with costs and time that would create a reputation for the high-speed service required in the new era.

To accomplish this, Nuelle made an about-face in motive power policy, probably one of the most radical on record. An order was soon placed with Alco for 20 Challenger-type 4-6-6-4 simple articulateds for delivery in 1940. These locomotives represented the very latest in high-horsepower, high-speed, superpower road engines and formed the nucleus of the new bridge line concept for the modernizing D&H. The 20 new locomotives cost $3,578,000 or $178,900 each. Although the basic motive power concepts went out when the old man left, the new power carried the Loree legacy of sleekness, good looks and discipline in design. The thin-barred pilots, recessed headlights, capped stacks, smooth boilers and white trim earned for

A pillar of cloud soars above Challenger No. 1523 on a crisp March day in 1950 near Starrucca, Pennsylvania, opposite. *(Donald W. Furler)*

347

The D&H's J class Challengers have been described as the most handsome articulated locomotives ever built. D&H engine designers had lost none of their flair for style after the retirement of President Loree. On this page are two views of these powerful engines working on the horseshoe curve at Thompson, Pennsylvania, bringing trainloads of Canadian newsprint over Ararat Summit. Challengers performed both at the head end and for pusher service at the rear of these trains. The great black embankment, below, was built of cinders and mine tailings in the 1860s. At the top of the opposite page is the first of the Challengers, No. 1500, in front of the great Alco erecting hall at Schenectady. Below it is a view of the 1501 on public display in Albany. At the bottom the 1500 is seen rolling through West Waterford on a winter's day at fifty miles an hour. *(This page: Rail Photo Service, S. K. Bolton, Jr., both; Jean Banta collection above. Opposite: Gene Baxter, bottom; D&H collection, two pictures)*

Old wooden coaches from the "splinter fleet" were beautifully reconditioned during World War II and still running in 1951. Here are four, behind Diesel No. 4018, on local No. 4 southbound at Comstock, New York. In the distance Northern No. 306, bound for Whitehall, sends forth clouds of steam. *(Philip R. Hastings)*

them the acclaim of being among the most handsome articulateds ever built. They arrived just in time to take the brunt of the traffic brought to the D&H by the growing European war off the shoulders of the aging fleet of E-5 and E-6 Consolidations. Day and night they raced between Binghamton and Mechanicville with trainloads of export goods and arms bound for the New England ports of Boston and Portland, with the deep-toned notes of their steamboat-type whistles echoing and re-echoing through the rolling confines of the Susquehanna valley en route.

In the meantime other changes were taking place. Surely the most significant, as far as the enginemen were concerned anyway, was the installation of mechanical stokers on 22 engines in 1939 alone, and more followed each year. Technology had finally overcome the Red Edge coal scoop on the D&H.

The Lake George Steamboat Co., the Fort William Henry Hotel and the Bluff Point Land Improvement Co., owner of the Hotel Champlain, were all sold to outside interests in 1939. The steamboats hadn't been operated in the company's service since the depression year of 1932 although one of the vessels had been on lease as a floating dance hall called "Showboat." The hotel patronage was likewise sparse during the lean years and with war clouds gathering over Europe future prospects for the resort business looked poor. The bonds of the Chateaugay Ore & Iron Co. that the D&H had guaranteed were retired early in 1942 and the company was subsequently sold to the Republic Steel Co. The 84-mile railroad to Lake Placid, however, was retained when the mine and blast furnaces were sold.

By the close of 1941 Nuelle's bridge traffic program showed amazing results. Tonnage interchanged with the Boston & Maine at Mechanicville for New England points had increased 43.7% over the previous year. The most impressive results, however, showed up at Rouses Point, where interchange traffic figures rose 263.8% over the previous year. This increase along with the impressive results obtained from the Challengers thus far prompted an order for 15 more of the big engines for delivery in 1942. The price of each was somewhat higher, at $213,500, reflecting the approaching wartime scarcity of men and materials.

Joseph H. Nuelle, ninth president of the D&H, 1938-1954.

The Utica, Clinton & Binghamton Railroad, a property held but sub-leased by the D&H since 1889, was sold to the New York, Ontario & Western in October, 1942, for $250,000 thus removing from the books this disconnected 32-mile stretch of track acquired by Robert Olyphant for purposes of possible expansion and further distribution of the company's coal. The other midstate railroad held under lease, the Rome & Clinton Railroad was similarly disposed of in 1944.

By 1942 the little Schoharie Valley Railroad, which had been purchased by David Willcox during his expansion program in 1906, no longer had enough traffic to justify continued operation. Application was filed with the ICC to abandon the 76-year-old, 4-mile rural line and on September 16, 1942 its infrequent operations ceased.

When the United States became involved in World War II in both the Atlantic and the Pacific

Prototype of the D&H's K class 4-8-4 Northerns was No. 300, above, parked outside the Alco erecting hall in Schenectady for its official portrait. They were stylish enough for the *Laurentian* and the *Montreal Limited*, rugged enough for the heavy tonnage runs. The 312, below, digs its 75″ drivers into the sanded rails on the 1.02% hill at Howe's Cave. Behind her tank is an export passenger locomotive from Alco and, on its own wheels, one of the big 2000 horsepower passenger units being delivered to the Rio Grande Railroad. *(D&H collection, above; John Pickett)*

regions, at the end of 1941, a flood of traffic was moving over the nation's railroads. It is without question that the railroads contributed immeasurably to the gigantic task of moving troops and supplies, hampered in many cases by shortages of men and equipment. One big factor in their favor, however, was the fact that the government elected to allow the individual managements to operate their own railroads, thus avoiding the miscarriage experienced during World War I under the United States Railroad Administration.

L. F. Loree would have been pleased with this but the old man didn't live to see it. He passed away at the grand old age of 82 on September 6, 1940, at his home "Bowood" near West Orange, New Jersey, after a short illness. As might be expected, however, the spectacular was commonplace with Loree right up to the end, even as it had been throughout his career. He was in his beloved Europe when war broke out there in 1939 and all regular accommodations were flooded by people fleeing the conflict. Unable to secure passage on any of the regularly scheduled vessels, he chartered an entire steamer himself, bringing 252 other stranded Americans back with him.

Gasoline rationing brought a surge of passengers back to the D&H too, especially on the locals. Six new semi-streamlined, air-conditioned, reclining-seat coaches were bought in 1939 but a number of wood truss-rod cars from the old splinter fleet were hauled out of retirement, repainted and placed in service on the Binghamton and North End locals. Their straight-backed green velvet seats and clean warm interiors were a welcome sight to many a weary traveler during the war years. Often distinguished patrons traveled on the D&H, including President Roosevelt, but none was more revered than Winston Churchill who in 1941 rode a special D&H train, pulled by one of the great "P" class Pacifics, en route to Canada after a visit to Washington seeking aid from Congress and the people of the United States against Hitler's air attacks.

In 1943, 15 big dual-service Alco-built 4-8-4s with 75-inch drivers, the largest ever to roll on D&H rails, joined the 35 Challengers and the famous fleet of Consolidations on the road. These engines cost $185,000 apiece and, although the latest in superpower design, they retained the unique Loree look. A recessed headlight peered out from between big elephant-ear smoke lifters and two bug-eyed engine marker lights atop the smokebox framed a capped stack. Their boilers and tenders were smooth, and illuminated number boards were built into the running boards above white-tired drivers. They performed equally well on a heavy string of Pullmans making up the *Montreal Limited* or on fast manifest freights.

Later in the year, all non-associated railroad stock holdings that Loree had judiciously tucked into the company portfolio over the years, except 304,600 shares of New York Central stock, were sold for $2,622,402, and half the money was put into a sinking fund while some no doubt was used to pay for the new engines.

✦ ✦ ✦

World War II finally brought to fruition the cherished plans of Thomas C. Durant for his Adirondack Railway, at least in part. The original aim of the project was to tap the rich iron ore deposits in the heart of the mountains at Sanford Lake, then continue on to the shores of Lake Ontario at Sackets Harbor west of Watertown. Financial problems and the difficult hard-rock construction required on the route only allowed the rails to reach North Creek—there they terminated for almost a century. World War II and titanium finally brought the railroad to the shores of Sanford Lake.

Actually, the titanium contained in iron ore, that gave the old ironmasters so much trouble, now became the primary reason for seeking out the ore deposit; the iron was only of secondary interest. Twentieth Century technology made titanium vital and the war threatened to cut off sources in Australia, Brazil and India. Before the conflict spread a domestic source had to be secured for ilmenite, an ore bearing the element.

This Adirondack deposit had been known for some time to the National Lead Co., a large chemical and metal products manufacturer, and it purchased the property in 1941, believing the deposit could be quickly developed into a large-scale producer of ilmenite. In 15 months a large plant rose beside Sanford Lake. Power shovels began digging ore out of a huge open pit and a sizable village grew up amidst the mountain wilderness. The first load of ilmenite ore concentrate rolled out by

The first Diesel power on the D&H operated on the line shown below, through the Boreas River gorge north of North Creek to the Sanford Lake mines. It took just nine years from the opening of this line for Diesel to replace the last D&H steam power. Above two units haul the ore train down from North Creek across the Sacandaga River bridge at Hadley just before sundown on a midsummer's day, 1966. The two boxcars behind the units contain merchandise, probably wood products from North Creek; they are followed by a long string of hopper cars loaded with titanium and iron ore, headed for Schenectady. *(Jim Shaughnessy, both)*

truck in July 1942 for rail loading at North Creek. In the first five months of operation, over 100,000 tons were trucked down the winding mountain roads to North Creek but it was frightfully clear that a railroad was needed if the full potential of the operation was to be realized. This very fact had doomed the ore body and frustrated those who had tried to develop it since its discovery.

Work had already started on such a line in the spring of 1942 when a right of way was secured through the Adirondack forest preserve by the Defense Plant Corporation, a United States government agency. If it hadn't been for the emergency brought about by the war, the conservationists would never have allowed the slashing encroachment of progress into the forest preserve that by law was to remain "forever wild"; even then, it was with much consternation and opposition. Under contract for the operation of the line on behalf of the government agency and the National Lead Co., the D&H began building the first new railroad seen in New York State in several decades.

The big bulldozers and power shovels of an experienced highway contractor, Steve Scullen of Cohoes, began carving their way up through the spectacular canyon of the Boreas River beyond its junction with the Hudson north of North Creek. It took two full years to complete the 33-mile line up through the difficult hard-rock mountain terrain. The first train of ore wound its way down to North Creek and the outside world on June 19, 1944 with little fanfare due to the hush-hush nature of the proceedings dictated by the war. David Henderson and Thomas Durant would have been pleased.

It was on this new line that a harbinger of the future appeared. The first ore train out of the so-called MacIntyre development rolled behind a 1000-horsepower switcher, No. 3000, built by Alco the previous month. This was the first Diesel on the D&H. Operation of steam locomotives in the tinder-dry forest was considered dangerous and the D&H bought two Diesel switchers in 1944 at a cost of $79,039 each, thus perhaps unknowingly making the Sanford Lake extension the first step toward total Dieselization of the road. The Diesel had been around for several years already and was turning in some impressive performances on various other roads. The D&H steam engines that ran on the Chateaugay branch burned oil in summer and were converted back to coal each fall at the Colonie shops to comply with the state regulations regarding forest fire prevention. By using the Diesels on this new branch this seasonal inconvenience could be eliminated along with providing an opportunity to judge the actual merits of this new locomotive concept in regular everyday service.

Apparently the Diesels proved themselves worthy of consideration, for the next year, 1945, saw ten more 1000-horsepower units arrive "for switching" at various points on the system. This didn't alter the D&H's position on the steam locomotive at all, not for a moment. Just to prove the point, a $1,125,000 order went out to Alco in 1946 for five more Challenger-type articulateds. The last of this batch, the 1539, was equipped with an all-welded boiler, a concept pioneered by the D&H in 1937 on Consolidation No. 1219. Also, five more stokers were installed during the year, a practice that had been continued yearly since Loree had left. Tempering this testimonial to steam however, was another order later in 1946 for five 1500-horsepower road switchers, costing $121,039 each. These units were acquired to provide a more economical power source for handling branch line traffic.

For several years increased expenses and dwindling revenues had made that portion of the Chateaugay branch in the Adirondacks between Lyon Mountain and Lake Placid a losing operation. In 1940 the 27-mile stretch of D&H trackage between Plumadore and Saranac Lake that paralleled the New York Central was abandoned and trackage rights were secured over the Central between the two points. Now in 1946, application was made to the ICC to abandon the whole 51 miles of line beyond Lyon Mountain and to sell the 10 miles of track between Saranac Lake and Lake Placid to the NYC. The request was granted and operations ceased on November 1, 1946. The scrap rails brought a good price and helped pay for the new Diesels.

The Albany & Susquehanna and the Rensselaer & Saratoga railroads, leased on a long-term basis in 1870 and 1871 respectively, had maintained their own organizations, with separate officers and shareholders, down through the years. The officers and principal stockholders would gather once a year for a short business meeting while throughout the rest of the year the rental payments quietly but steadily rolled in to the coffers of the railroad companies that themselves ran no trains. These two leased railroads made up the backbone, if not indeed the entire body of the D&H system. It had been the policy of the D&H managers for some time to acquire direct ownership and consolidation of all the principal properties constituting their overall enterprise. Early in 1944 negotiations began with the managements of the two leased lines to merge their companies into the D&H Railroad once and for all. An exchange of stock and the issuance of bonds were arranged and the R&S and A&S mergers were consummated in 1945, on January 30th, and July 2nd, respectively. The aggregate effect of these and earlier moves, involving the sale of non-productive subsidiaries and trackage was to simplify the capital structure of the Delaware & Hudson Co. and its subsidiary railroad corporation along with cutting down interest and operating expenses.

* * *

In 1947 Joseph Nuelle reflected back on his first 10 years with the D&H. On January 1, 1938 the road stabled 375 locomotives principally of the Consolidation type, many of which were too old, too slow, or too small to meet the new demands placed on them by the bridge traffic and the war. With the arrival of 40 articulateds, 15 4-8-4s and two dozen Diesels the roster showed only 300 locomotives in 1947. This change reflected the rapid increase in efficiency brought by the new power and the longer trains it could handle, particularly the 40 J class 4-6-6-4s.

Along with the motive-power revolution, practically the entire main line roadbed had been replaced with 131, 130 and 112-pound rail by 1947, 486 track miles in the previous decade alone. This in addition to new ties and tie plates, crushed-stone ballast, greater clearances, stronger bridges, longer passing tracks and Centralized Traffic Control gave the new locomotives an opportunity to utilize their inherent efficiencies and to produce the impressive ton-mile figures with bridge traffic that saved the D&H from the perils of red ink in the new era after the war. This rejuvenation took on many aspects of the similar program initiated in 1907 by Loree that upgraded the road and allowed the use of heavyweight Consolidations for so many years.

This improvement program necessitated the expenditure of an enormous amount of money and the strengthening of the company financially before it could be accomplished physically. The first step President Nuelle had taken in this program resulted in the disposition of the unprofitable and marginal holdings in the late 1930s and early 1940s. The second factor was the decision to postpone resumption of dividends until debt maturities facing the company had been disposed of satisfactorily. Heavy expenditures for the modernization of the railroad combined with rapidly rising operating costs and laggard freight rates necessarily reduced net earnings available for debt retirement. Offsetting factors which aided were the available portfolio of securities and the sharply increased freight traffic resulting from wartime activities and the continued heavy volume that followed. In 1945, after a lapse of more than ten years a dividend of one dollar per share was declared, to the delight of all concerned. Since then a similar amount was declared for each quarter and by the end of 1947 a total of 302 dividends had been declared since the company's formation aggregating $192,478,064.

* * *

It didn't take long for the Diesel to establish a foothold on the D&H, even though the company had coal mines of its own and had long been a showplace of the steam locomotive, which it had in fact introduced to America in the form of the STOURBRIDGE LION. Even more than its inherent power and effectiveness, it was the great efficiency of the Diesel that convinced other roads as well as the D&H of its value. The need for water and coal stops, ash pan cleaning, fire tenders during layovers, and all the associated equipment, installations and manpower required to administer this care to the steam engine was eliminated in the Diesel. Track maintenance costs, too, were reduced through elimination of the pounding effect of the side rods, to say nothing of the flexibility of multi-unit operation. More work could be accomplished by a single unit, because when one crew stepped off at the end of a trick, another could step on and go right back to work, without needing time to clean fires and load coal and

Steam engines had one advantage over the Diesels, as in the 1947 flood scene at Albany, above. A Diesel's traction motors would be hopelessly short-circuited, but the 556 slogs through with a minimum of trouble, while her hogger leans out into the rain to watch out for rowboats and floating debris, and to be sure the track is still there. At Windsor Station of the Canadian Pacific in October 1953, D&H Diesel No. 4001, arrived with the *Laurentian,* while nearby a maroon-and-gray Pacific of the CPR simmered after a run down from Ottawa. *(Philip R. Hastings, below)*

The first 1500-horsepower road switcher, No. 4000, came to the D&H from Alco in November, 1946. It is shown below at Saratoga Springs. These engines, originally for branch line runs, were soon running in quartets, rolling manifest from one end of the D&H to the other. They arrived painted regular engine black to which yellow stripes were soon added to improve visibility. In the early 1950s, it was not uncommon to see two or three Diesels leading a big Challenger up the Richmondville, Ararat or Belden hills. Diesels were always ahead of steam to keep smoke and cinders out of their air intakes. *(D&H collection, below; Rail Photo Service, G. C. Corey)*

water; the only requirement was fuel oil, once a day at the most. This constant availability in yard operations had already proven itself beyond any question.

The flexibility was even more apparent with the advent of the road switcher concept. It would be impractical, if not indeed impossible, to put one of the big articulateds out in the yard on a switching assignment after it arrived in a terminal from a manifest run. A three- or four-unit Diesel road locomotive could easily be split up and cover three switching or transfer assignments, where the big Challenger would have to lay idle — and be attended to, also. It was soon clear that to cut the spiraling costs of operation, the answer lay in total Dieselization as soon as possible.

In 1948 an order went out to Alco for 29 units, bringing the D&H Diesel roster up to 59 units. In 1950 a $5,063,715 order for 41 Diesels was placed followed the next year by another order for 65 more. President Nuelle announced in 1952 that with the acquisition of ten more units, the D&H could be 100 per cent Dieselized. The units were obtained and on July 17, 1953, in the form of 4-8-4 No. 302, steam made its last official run, down from Montreal, on the sleeper, train No. 10.

The rather sad but nostalgic honor of making the D&H's last actual run under steam fell four days later to Engine No. 300, a big elephant-eared Northern. During the line's twilight months of steam, one side of the overnight *Montreal Limited* run between Troy and Montreal, Trains 9 and 10, was handled by steam, K class 4-8-4 No. 302 being assigned to the job. To provide for any sudden failure of power in passenger service, either steam or Diesel, a standby engine was kept available and ready to go at each end of the run. Engine 308 lulled away her last days in this capacity at Colonie, while the 300 awaited the final hours at Rouses Point. After steam had made its last official run on the 17th, Diesels were regularly assigned to the job and it was necessary to bring the No. 300 back from Rouses Point. So, in the darkness of the sultry summer night of July 21, 1953, Engine No. 300 was coupled on to local No. 8 and engineer John J. Cullen and fireman J. Terrence Bowen brought the train from Rouses Point to Albany, making the last run forever by D&H steam. The Diesel regularly assigned to that local was cut in multiple with the units on Train No. 10 for the down trip later the same evening.

In midmorning of the next day, Engines No. 300 and 308 were moved to the ash pit at Colonie where their fires were dumped. Then, under their own dying boiler pressure, they were sadly moved into the almost-deserted Colonie roundhouse and left there to cool off slowly beside several already-dead sisters, a number of K's, the remnants of the faithful 600 class Pacifics, and a few assorted 2-8-0s and 0-8-0s. The wonderful age of steam was now history on the D&H.

Now there was nothing but the 179 Diesels, and somewhat like old Loree, himself, they were austere in appearance, stark models of efficiency. All remaining steam locomotives were scrapped later in the year; 79 had already gone to the torch back in 1951. Roundhouses, water tanks and coal pockets came tumbling down and a mass of shiny new machinery replaced the big wheel lathes, drop forges and riveting guns in the great Colonie shops.

In the meantime, another revolution was beginning out on the road — Centralized Traffic Control. The first installation of this remote-control switching and signaling equipment occurred down on the single track line below Nineveh for 12 miles between Center Village, New York and Lanesboro, Pennsylvania back in October, 1930. As early as 1923, remote control was installed on the Champlain division to operate the switches and signals at the entrance to the northbound running track at Valcour, 2½ miles south of South Junction station from which they were operated. Isolated stretches of this equipment had been installed at strategic points along the road in the ensuing years, and by 1954, 121 miles, or 28% of the line was operated by CTC.

On September 30, 1954 Joseph Nuelle moved up to the post of Chairman of the Board of the Delaware & Hudson Co. and William White succeeded him as president. White had been president of the New York Central until he lost the proxy fight to Robert R. Young. His long career and impressive record of accomplishment made him a prime candidate for the job and the managers were fortunate to secure his services at a time when Mr. Nuelle was required to ease off of his heavy responsibilities.

William White, tenth president of the D&H, 1954-1966.
(Fabian Bachrach)

The Erie's 34.6-mile Jefferson branch was purchased outright for $3,500,000 on January 1, 1955. This was the line built just after the Civil War, north out of the Lackawanna Valley at Carbondale, enabling the D&H to market its coal at northern and western points the year around. The D&H had enjoyed trackage rights on the branch since its opening and now felt it should have complete control of the trackage, since it was a key link in the overall system. As the Erie's traffic had dropped considerably in recent years, there was concern that the upkeep of the line might be neglected as a result. Now the D&H in turn granted trackage rights to the Erie until the year 2015.

In 1956, the 21-mile Cherry Valley branch, long a losing proposition was finally abandoned. Six 3000 class Diesel units were sold, four to the South Buffalo Railway and two to the Buffalo Creek. The previous year five others were disposed of, four to the Erie and one to the Buffalo Creek Railway, because the need for these switching units was supplanted by some of the larger road switchers. Two-way radios were installed in most of the locomotives, yard offices and cabooses during the year and greatly improved the efficiency and simplified all aspects of operation, both yard and road. Now, the coupling of cars far back from the engineer's view could be accomplished as easily as if he were right next to the brakeman. As the trains increased in length this communication aid in the form of portable units became almost mandatory to set out a load or a hot-box 100 cars back from the engine in the black of night in less than an hour. The dispatcher too, through strategically placed relay stations out along the road, could contact the crew of a train anywhere along the whole line. Many other uses were found and operations almost certainly could not proceed at all today without it.

A merger study was undertaken in 1957 to consider the possibilities of combining the D&H with the Erie and the Lackawanna railroads to form a single unified system. The possibilities apparently failed due to the fact the D&H was the most stable and financially secure organization of the three and a combination would only result in the excessive drain of reserve funds from the treasury of the D&H. The other lines, particularly the Erie, suffered from a long-time indebtedness sustained as far back as the time of Jay Gould that had held back financial progress ever since. The Erie-Lackawanna merger did finally materialize but without the D&H as a partner.

The Lake George branch was cut back as far as Glens Falls in 1958 as a result of a drastic decline in passenger fares and practically no freight movement to the end of the line on the shores of the lake. On a more positive side, a gigantic relocation project, which removed the trackage from downtown Saratoga Springs thus eliminating well over two dozen crossings and several restricting curves, was completed in 1959. This 13-mile project was undertaken by the State of New York as a part of its grade crossing elimination program and 85% of the cost was absorbed by the state. It involved moving the main line well to the west of town and building a new modern station capable of handling Pullman and private cars on a layover basis as well as regular passenger, baggage and freight movements. A complete yard and small engine facility was provided south of the station and a new connection with the North Creek

It was like the burning of Rome each time D&H steam left West Carbondale and headed up the 1.48% grade to Forest City. In 1948 this line was still the Erie Railroad's Jefferson branch, over which the D&H had trackage rights. The view of the *Laurentian*, headed by Diesel 4012, at the new, relocated Saratoga Springs station, a mile west of the center of town, is in great contrast to earlier pictures of elegant 19th century trains headed by gleaming steam engines at the ornate downtown predecessors of this sleek new building. *(Donald W. Furler, above; Jim Shaughnessy)*

Three Alco Century 2750-horsepower units make a run for Richmondville Hill at Warnerville, New York, just south of Cobleskill, with a southbound manifest for Binghamton, with 127 cars. In the days of steam this scene would have been much more spectacular, especially in winter, but not as many cars would have followed the iron horse up the hill. *(Jim Shaughnessy)*

branch was made somewhat to the north where the new route crossed the old Adirondack Railroad's right of way. This first class alignment allowed high speed movement of long heavy freights where severe restrictions through the curves and grade crossings of downtown Saratoga Springs had previously hampered movements and presented hazards to both the railroad and the public.

A similar project, involving construction of 2.2 miles of relocated double track on a huge fill and bridge over Kaydeross Creek and a new station at Ballston Spa, was completed on August 16, 1950, also under the Public Service Commission's grade crossing elimination program. This job eliminated 13 highway crossings and a severe curve in the railroad through the center of the village, remaining from the original alignment of the old Saratoga & Schenectady Railroad.

On the last day of 1959, Joseph H. Nuelle retired from active duty as chairman of the board of the Delaware & Hudson Co. and its subsidiaries after 21 years of service to the company. During his years with the D&H, first as president from May, 1938, until September, 1954, and thereafter as chairman, he accomplished the entire rebuilding of the railroad; an almost complete turnover in its freight car equipment; its complete Dieselization; a vast reduction in debt and a resumption of dividends. His accomplishments certainly placed him in a category with the great L. F. Loree and Thomas Dickson.

*   *   *

For several years prior to 1960, the D&H had attempted to discontinue the local passenger train service between Albany and Rouses Point but was rebuffed each time by the Public Service Commission. At one time, these trains provided a necessary link between the capital district and the Champlain valley carrying mail, express, milk and, of course, passengers. As the economy boomed after the war and more and more people obtained their own automobiles, patronage dwindled and on many trips the crew exceeded the customers. This was nothing peculiar to the D&H as railroads the country over were experiencing the same problem. In July 1960 the Commission finally conceded and the eight locals north of Albany came off leaving only the through day and night trains, the *Laurentian,* the *Montreal Limited,* and a commuter train operating between Saratoga Springs and Albany. The Binghamton local remained, but only for another two years before making its last run on January 24, 1963.

After mining and marketing anthracite for 135 years by its predecessors and itself, the Hudson Coal Co. was sold on November 21, 1960 along with all its assets, physical property, name and good will to the Blue Coal Corporation of Maine, a subsidiary of Glen Alden Corporation. Underground mining was suspended but the processing plants continued to prepare coal from other sources, thereby continuing to originate shipments for the D&H trains.

During the 20 previous years there were only seven in which the Hudson Coal Co. showed any profit at all. The aggregate loss in those years was $9,200,000 but since this was a wholly owned subsidiary and filed a consolidated income tax return with the overall D&H corporation, these losses served as somewhat of a cushion for the railroad earnings and resulted in a cash saving in the tax bill far more extensive than the advances made by the D&H Co. during this period. As long as the Hudson Coal Co. was able to generate sufficient cash and its operating losses resulted in a tax saving it was an asset to the parent company.

With the constant decline in the demand for coal, however, competition sharpened and prices fell. Furthermore, Hudson's coal production came primarily from expensive deep mine operations that were subject to flooding. To suspend operations even for a time would require constant pumping if the mines were to be saved at all. Competition from non-union operators hurt, and in general future prospects for the whole operation, at even the moderate loss, seemed dim. When Glen Alden showed an interest in the property for $2,500,000 the D&H was quick to seize the opportunity to get out.

The D&H, like most roads which had been operating Diesels for a decade already, found out the locomotives had a realistic service life of about 15 years rather than the 20 originally projected. Beyond that age they became increasingly expensive to maintain. Six new 1800-horsepower units were purchased and six of the older units were sent back to Alco to be remanufactured and equipped with new 1800-horsepower engines. This procedure was undertaken to help decide whether it was more economical to retire Diesel locomotives as they became older and purchase new ones in their place, or to have the older ones remanufactured. The six new units (numbered in the 5000 series) and the six rebuilt locomotives cost approximately $1,700,000 which was paid in cash rather than being financed — a way of doing business the D&H had been able to enjoy for most of its long existence.

In 1962 the shareholders approved the change of the D&H charter from New York to Delaware, a state noted for its favorable corporation laws. The original charter, that still existed at the time, was granted to the company by the legislature back in 1823 and authorized the company to engage only in the business of mining and selling coal, operating a canal and a railroad. It had many outmoded provisions and since it was granted by an act of the legislature it could only be changed in the same manner. For that reason a new Delaware & Hudson Co. was incorporated in the state of Delaware with a modern and broader charter capable of taking advantage of all the up-to-date business and tax procedures. The old company was then merged with the new — strictly a paper change.

Mr. John P. Hiltz, Jr., who had been vice president in charge of operations and maintenance, was elected president and general manager of the railroad corporation effective September 1, 1962. Mr. White retained his position as president and chairman of the board of the D&H Co. as well as chairman of the Board of Managers of the railroad thus remaining the chief executive officer. During the following June, however, Mr. White became president of the Erie-Lackawanna Railroad and relinquished his position with the D&H railroad corporation but with special permission from the ICC retained the presidency of the parent D&H company.

Since its beginning the Delaware & Hudson Co. had maintained a New York City headquarters while its railroad was administered from the Gothic castle in Albany. On September 1, 1962, the parent company's entire staff was moved to the Albany building.

By the end of 1963, 24 replacement Diesels of 1800 horsepower had been obtained, the majority of them by trading in old 1600-horsepower units on the upgraded ones. The so-called second generation Diesel had been developed by this time, and was much larger in size and horsepower. These new units could replace the older ones on a one-for-two basis thereby cutting down overall maintenance and expense by reducing the total number of units operated. In 1964 Alco delivered nine big six-wheel 2750-horsepower units, costing $1,975,000 after allowances for the units traded in. Their numbers would have logically been in the 6000 series but when the first unit emerged from the builder's Schenectady plant it carried the number 601. This brought back many fond memories to those who were privileged to have seen the P class passenger Pacifics run during the glory days of steam on the D&H. They were a splendid machine possessed of style and class; the new 600s had a lot to live up to if they were worthy to carry the honored numbers. The following year nine more were obtained replacing another 20 older units and bringing the total number of Diesels operated by the D&H down to 134 from a high of 179 in 1953. This last batch of locomotives brought the motive power pool, on a horsepower basis, to the point where 42.1% of the fleet was now less than five years old.

By building a 1.1-mile connection between the freight line to Mechanicville and the old S&S line near Ballston Lake in the fall of 1964, the 10.6-mile stretch of the original Rensselaer & Saratoga's line between Mechanicville and Ballston Spa was abandoned. The last train over the old line was the northbound *Laurentian* on October 18, 1965. This move made the route to Montreal 6.2 miles longer but when a proposed change in the location of the New York Central's passenger station to a point halfway between Albany and Schenectady materializes the extra mileage traveled over the D&H will be eliminated. The Montreal-bound passenger trains will move through Schenectady where they will join the direct D&H route north to Saratoga Springs as did the horse-drawn trains of the Saratoga & Schenectady Railroad back in 1833.

This link was one of the last moves in placing the entire 744-mile main line of the D&H from Wilkes-Barre to Rouses Point under Centralized Traffic Control, making it one of the first major railroads in the country to be so equipped. This highly sophisticated electronic signaling system

A roundhouse laborer fills the front sand box on the 5012 at Mechanicville after a run up from Binghamton, above. The low-nosed DL-701s were the result of trading in some of the older 1600-horsepower units to Alco to be remanufactured into these 1800-horsepower engines. In the lower picture, also at Mechanicville, are three such units combined with the older RS-3 engines awaiting southbound runs to Binghamton and Wilkes-Barre. *(Jim Shaughnessy)*

permits the complete control of extended territories of single track road from a central location. Under CTC rules trains can operate on signal indication without train orders and with all main track switches leading to and from passing sidings power-operated by remote control. Sections of the original double track remained in place at strategic locations to provide passing tracks, while a maintenance road for trucks was provided where the second main track was originally located. As a result of this installation five sets of dispatchers and many towermen out along the line who were formerly required to operate the railroad were replaced by two sets of dispatcher-operators running the entire road from an office in the D&H building in Albany.

At the close of 1954 the D&H system consisted of 1652 miles of track. Upon completion in 1965 of the CTC installation—now referred to as a Traffic Control System (TCS)—this trackage amounted to only 1328 miles, a reduction of 324 miles or 20%. The 9.5-mile low-grade line between Schenevus and Richmondville summit, built in 1921 to ease the strain of northbound coal drags, fell victim to high horsepower Diesels and CTC and was abandoned in 1964. The salvage from these retirements was effectively used in maintenance programs elsewhere on the line with appreciable economy. This reduction in physical plant was possible largely because of the improved efficiency in operation and greater productivity from each train and employee.

*   *   *

The whole story of the D&H in the latter years of the new era can be summed up by saying technology along with tight management were able to keep pace—or perhaps even keep one step ahead —of ever-rising costs. Since the day the D&H was organized back in 1823 costs have been rising. The costs of anything and everything have been on a spiralized increase from the price of oats fed to the early mules to the cost of locomotives— $2,914.90 for the STOURBRIDGE LION versus a quarter of a million dollars for the latest 3000-horsepower Diesel units—to say nothing of labor costs. In 1924, the average hourly wage of the employees was 72¢ or $1709 a year while 40 years later in 1964 it was up to $2.95 an hour or $6,793, a fourfold increase.

Those two years, 1924 and 1964, make a rather remarkable comparison as it happens that the D&H moved just about the same amount of traffic in each, 3,500,000,000-ton miles. The freight revenue in 1924 was $38,623,354 and in 1964 was $39,743,997 or on a revenue per ton mile basis, $.011 for each. Considering the vastly increased cost of labor, materials and taxes it is a wonder an industry could possibly survive at all with no increase in volume or revenue in 40 years.

The real story of increased productivity through all forms of technology is brought into focus by comparing the indices which reflect the actual efficiencies of getting the traffic over the road:

	1964	1924
Freight train miles	1,798,673	4,396,584
Revenue tons per train	1,944	796
Revenue ton-miles per employee hour	514	108
Locomotives operated	145	480
Average number of employees	2,836	13,516

A 144% increase in train load and a 59% decrease in train miles took care of the same tonnage in the new era. The increased efficiency, higher horsepower and multiple unit capability of the Diesel permitted the hauling of more cars per train, including cars of far greater capacity, resulting in the substantial reduction of freight train miles.

Additional technological improvements including CTC, new rolling stock, radio communication, mechanized track maintenance equipment, improved shop methods, electronic business machines to transfer waybills and hundreds of other innovations resulted in a 376% increase in employee productivity over the 40-year period.

Traffic too took on new forms in the new era. Less-than-carload shipments proved too expensive, with freight houses, dockmen, clerks, reams of paper work and constant shuffling and handling. A rate that would net even a reasonable loss on this sort of traffic would have to be prohibitively high; other forms of transportation could handle this type of business more economically. On the other side of the coin, railroads could really take

Dispatcher Don Viault sits before one of the two great CTC boards in the D&H building at Albany and controls the entire busy line from Schenectady to Carbondale and Binghamton. Except for two short congested stretches, Wilkes-Barre to Carbondale and Albany to Mechanicville, operated from other consoles at points out on the line, the entire D&H is controlled from Albany. Carbondale is at the right end of the board and the Binghamton line branches off at right center. Brand new from Alco, two Century 628, 2750-horsepower units stand outside the Colonie shops, below. These were the first of 18 to come within the next two years. *(Jim Shaughnessy, both)*

Since its very beginning, the D&H has continued to move coal in impressive quantities. Above, three General Electric U30-C units, totaling 9000 horsepower, roll into Mechanicville with a 10,000-ton unit coal train in 100 cars. Below, three more of the new 1967 engines strain against the 1.31% Richmondville Hill grade with a long freight. Through the great waves of rising heat and exhaust can be seen several cars of the piggyback vans. *(Jim Shaughnessy, both)*

the honors with large bulk shipments, and with none more graphically than the unit coal train. This was so easily accommodated on the rails that a special low rate was established for solid trainloads moving from mine to destination, usually big utility company power stations. Almost daily 10,000-ton coal trains rolled north to the Albany area and New England points over the D&H, recalling the old days when coal was king—the very reason for laying the first rail on Moosic Mountain or north out of Carbondale.

Probably one of the newest forms of freight traffic to appear on the railroads after the war was piggybacking. This had been used in isolated places and in limited quantities but really didn't arrive at its full potential until the 1950s. It provided shippers with customized door-to-door delivery with no extra handling other than loading and unloading the trailer from the flatcar. Many plans evolved, using railroad-owned, customer-owned, trucker-owned trailers, and combinations of each. It has even brought back what was once LCL traffic, in the form of a freight forwarder's trailer on the flatcar. The D&H did not become one of the big piggyback haulers, but this form of traffic loomed large on the "bridge line" none the less, moving to and from New England points as well as the company's Colonie facility serving the Capital District. During the first seven months of 1967 a total of 13,558 flatcars carrying 19,296 trailers rode D&H rails. In an average year about 22,000 piggyback flats were moved and the number could be substantially increased with a proposed extension of this service north to Canada by enlarging the Willsboro tunnel.

Early in 1967 occurred what might well be considered a motive power revolution of sorts, at least for the D&H. Six big General Electric U30-C 3000-horsepower units rolled onto the property and, numbered in the 700 series, had the distinction of being the first non-Alco-built locomotives on the D&H in well over half a century. Until the purchase of these units, the D&H was one of the few all-Alco-powered lines of any size in the country. They performed so well that six similar units were authorized for future acquisition.

John P. Hiltz, Jr., president and general manager of the railroad corporation since 1962, succeeded William White as president of the Delaware & Hudson Co. at the beginning of 1967.

Frederic C. Dumaine, Jr. became 12th president of the D&H on August 1, 1967. *(D&H collection)*

Having reached mandatory retirement at 70, with 53 years of service in the railroad industry and over 12 with the D&H, Mr. White retired on December 31, 1966. In July Mr. Hiltz resigned both his D&H positions to accept the chairmanship of the National Railway Labor Conference with headquarters in Chicago.

Mr. Hiltz's successor was Frederic C. Dumaine, Jr., who had been elected Chairman of the Board of both the D&H Co. and the railroad corporation at the Board meeting on December 28, 1966, to succeed Mr. White, and now became president and chief executive officer of both companies. He had been president of the New York, New Haven & Hartford during stormy years when that troubled railroad faced mounting deficits and stockholders' demands for dividends, and he was ousted by a hostile faction that won control of the Board.

As president of the Amoskeag Corporation, a Boston firm representing the Dumaine family fortune which held the largest single block of D&H stock, some of it since the early 1930s, it was only natural that he had the proxies and the interest in the enterprise to attain the post.

He took on the awesome job at no salary, which was pretty good for openers, and certainly was a substantial testimonial to his interest in the enterprise. Remarking that railroads should "run trains, not take them off," and that if the D&H was going to be in the railroad business, it should be in it all the way—whatever that meant—he quickly reversed the railroad's policy of trying to discontinue the *Laurentian,* which had been losing money for several years before his arrival on the scene. Expo-67 in Montreal had brought a boom in passenger business on this train. He quickly reinstated dining car service on the *Laurentian,* first leasing New Haven equipment and later leased two streamlined diners from the Chesapeake & Ohio. In October, twelve relatively new streamlined cars, including a tavern-lounge car, were purchased from the Denver & Rio Grande Western to replace the ailing equipment in the Montreal service. He even put hostesses aboard the new passenger accommodations.

The Pandora's box of Eastern railway mergers was opened up in the fall of 1961 with the proposed Pennsylvania-New York Central combination, the Penn-Central. Panic hit smaller roads such as the Erie-Lackawanna, the D&H and the Boston & Maine. They were alarmed about this proposal, for the giant Penn-Central would siphon off the bulk of the traffic, leaving the other lines to dry up on the vine. There were three possible solutions: to block the Penn-Central merger, to become part of it or to join a competitive system. Characteristically the D&H followed all three courses.

After some hard bargaining, mostly with the Interstate Commerce Commission, the Norfolk & Western merged with the Nickel Plate and Wabash railways on October 16, 1964. A condition of that marriage, imposed by the ICC, was that the D&H, along with the Erie-Lackawanna and the Boston & Maine be allowed to join the family within five years, if they should choose. This was better than being left out in the cold, but the D&H still objected to the Penn-Central concept unless it was allowed to join that system in the event the N&W offer fell through.

A great deal of haggling ensued between the N&W and the D&H over just what the terms of any amalgamation of them would be. Most of the problem revolved around $20,700,000 in excess capital held by the parent D&H Co. Then there was the question whether the N&W would merge the whole D&H enterprise into the corporate structure, including all the tax ramifications, or just acquire the physical assets of the railroad and allow the parent D&H Co. to remain in existence.

In an order dated June 12, 1967, the ICC directed that the N&W include the Erie-Lackawanna, the D&H Co. and the Boston & Maine Corporation in its system by July 17. Nobody liked this. The D&H petitioned the ICC for reconsideration, contending that it was being offered $23,000,000 less than the property was worth and the N&W immediately filed suit to stop the order, alleging that the ICC exceeded its power in dictating a settlement. While officials in Roanoke and Albany continued haggling over the price, the Penn-Central people stood by and saw their plans shelved once more, as the final consummation of their merger depended on what happened to the Erie-Lackawanna, the D&H and the B&M.

The ICC reconsidered its June order and about a month later issued revised terms for the inclusion of the D&H into the N&W system. If the E-L was to be included, the N&W was directed, at its option, to include the D&H on the basis of sale of all railroad assets of the D&H enterprise rather than control of the D&H corporate structure, which would retain cash or its equivalent in the amount of $20,700,000. With this development the D&H withdrew most of its objections to the ICC decision involving N&W's acquisition of the D&H. It now seemed that the D&H would not lose its identity.

Early in September of 1967, addressing the convention of the National Railway Historical Society in Albany, President Dumaine called on the ICC and the courts to approve the Penn-Central merger forthwith, saying, "The sooner they get on with the job, the better off the country will be." He charged that "the ICC had placed a value on the D&H of 50¢ on the dollar—and that's the scrap value." He went on to say, "We've got some fine young men on the D&H and we're not going to

Two big General Motors 3600-horsepower, 20-cylinder units went to work for the D&H on September 16, 1967 and performed so well on the Binghamton-Mechanicville run that the D&H decided by the end of October to buy these two units plus another. A motive power shortage along with an attractive price on the demonstrator units prompted the purchase. The big GMs will be numbered in the 800s. Thus, in less than a year, the D&H departed from its traditional Alco preference and now operates power from all three locomotive builders. Above, they are easing into the B&M receiving yard at Mechanicville; below they roll through Delanson. *(Jim Shaughnessy, both)*

These cars were among the group acquired from the Denver & Rio Grande Western as part of President Dumaine's new emphasis on passenger service. They arrived in D&RGW paint with a large D&H stencilled on the letterboard, above, and were immediately repainted in a brilliant new blue and yellow color scheme. The first car, a diner, went into service November 5, 1967, followed by a second the next day. The five coaches, three baggage cars, cafe-lounge, and a combination baggage-mail followed soon after. The equipment had been used on the *Prospector* and *Royal Gorge,* until abandonment of this service in Colorado and Utah. *(Jim Shaughnessy)*

372

let them be sold down the river for 50¢ on the dollar of junk value of the railroad."

He topped it all off by saying that he really didn't want the D&H to be part of the N&W or the Erie-Lackawanna anyway, and suggested that he had a new plan for an all-New England system comprising the D&H, B&M, Bangor & Aroostook, Maine Central and New Haven. If it accomplished nothing else, this would certainly start the people down in Roanoke on the N&W thinking and show them they were dealing with an old Yankee horse-trader in the person of one Frederic C. Dumaine, Jr.

⸲　　　⸲　　　⸲

Nothing remains static. Change is inevitable. The whole railroad business from its beginning has been one of merger, amalgamation, readjustment and change. The D&H itself can certainly be described in such terms. Obviously no one can see into the future. The Delaware & Hudson name may in time disappear from view — but it will never be forgotten.

An old gray donkey stands on the abandoned towpath embankment of the historic Champlain Canal, where scores of his ancestors labored during the past century, pulling boats laden with the fruits of a young nation's economy. Today he cocks his big ears to the organ-like tones of the horns as the Delaware & Hudson train rolls through the upper Hudson Valley north of Waterford, New York. The great Alco 628s and the other throbbing Diesels are the present-day counterparts of his own four-footed forebears. *(Jim Shaughnessy)*

DELAWARE & HUDSON ALBUM

Yardmaster Paul Mooney, on the night shift at Colonie yard, throws a switch in the process of making up the nightly Whitehall fast freight. At the left, Northern No. 301 bites into icy rails to get southbound RW-4 under way leaving Plattsburgh. It came from Rouses Point and will traverse the entire length of the D&H to Wilkes-Barre. *(Jim Shaughnessy, both)*

Running light to pick up southbound tonnage for its parent D&H, the Napierville Junction Railway's 2-8-0 No. 914 and caboose No. 33 are seen in the station at Delson, Quebec, above. Below, Mohawk Yard operator Ron De Forest passes orders to the conductor of northbound WR-1 as it rolls past the yard office in Glenville, across the Mohawk River from Schenectady. For many years the road crossing over the D&H tracks at the north end of Colonie yard was guarded by the watchman in the lofty perch, opposite, as many locals, manifests and switching moves passed between his hydraulically-operated gates. The little tower became only a memory after completion in 1961 of an overpass. *(Allen Toohey, CRHA collection, above; Jim Shaughnessy, two pictures)*

During the 1930s the D&H experimented with devices to lift engine smoke above the eyes of the enginemen. The scoop-like affair on the brow of the 608, at Albany station, above, was soon replaced by the "elephant ears" that became famous on D&H steam power. The fat-boilered 1030, below, a real workhorse on the D&H for many years, rolls north through Port Kent, on the shore of Lake Champlain. Yardmaster Paul Mooney, opposite, rides the rear platform of the Whitehall fast freight's caboose in Colonie yard and signals the engineer of the yard engine as he places the hack on the rear of the night's cut before the 10:30 p.m. departure. *(Rail Photo Service, H. W. Pontin, this page; Jim Shaughnessy, opposite)*

Southbound accommodation and milk train No. 18 pulls out of Port Kent, above. The Norman-style station at Lacolle, Quebec, behind Pacific No. 609, was built in 1930 to house Canadian customs offices and to give passengers entering Canada a taste of the French flavor of Province of Quebec. Opposite is a view of the mess caused by the explosion of 4-6-6-4 No. 1510 as it was starting to climb Richmondville Hill in July 1941. Low water exposed the crown sheet of the 9′ x 12′ firebox and it collapsed with a roar. All the water in the big boiler instantly turned to steam and tore the boiler from the frame, hurling it out over the pilot 196 feet down the track ahead. The train, still moving, crashed into the wrecked boiler and pushed it 235 feet further down the track. The three men in the engine were instantly killed in the blast and eleven cars were derailed in the impact. By the end of the year, the 1510 was back in service. Opposite below she crests Richmondville Hill with a southbound consist a few years later. *(Perry Storm, lower pictures; John Gardiner, above, D&H collection, opposite above)*

Challenger No. 1517 turned over at Central Bridge, New York, in February, 1945, spilling 20 tons of coal and 15,000 gallons of water on the state highway. The D&H had never had such a heavy lift before and the engine had to lie there for three months until Industrial Brownhoist could build a 250-ton capacity crane to pick her up. Finally, late in May, with the new crane at the front end, they were able to right her. On the opposite page, Consolidation No. 1084 has her ash pan flushed out at Rouses Point engine terminal, while Napierville Junction Railway's No. 914 awaits her turn in the background. *(D&H collection, this page; Philip R. Hastings, opposite)*

King George VI and Queen Elizabeth visited the United States in the summer of 1939, then boarded this special train in New York for the overnight trip to Canada. It appears, opposite, in the early morning light on D&H rails at Delson, Quebec, where it will be turned over to the Canadian Pacific and that road's celebrated Royal Hudson No. 2850. The early morning sun casts its long shadows across the interlocking plant at QS tower in Crescent, New York as Challenger No. 1502 brings WM-1 up the short grade from the connection with the Saratoga line at Burnt Hills. Towerman and photographer Don Robinson is seen on duty in the tower, which is owned by the D&H but operated by the Boston & Maine at the point where the tracks of the two roads join to enter Mechanicville terminal. *(Leonard A. Seton, opposite above; Donald S. Robinson, two pictures)*

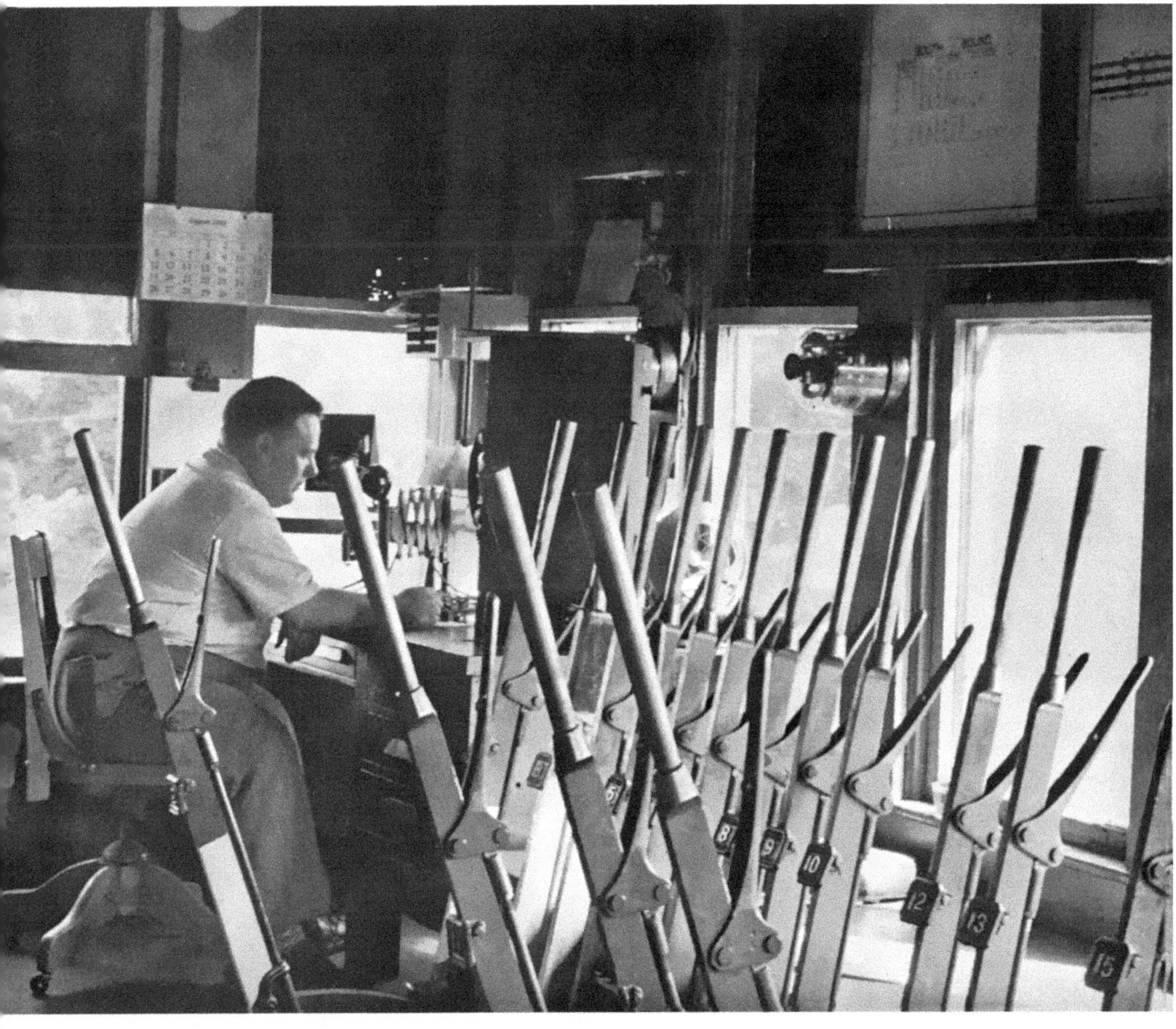

Challenger No. 1518, left, crests the summit of Richmondville Hill at Dante, south of West Richmondville, having fought her way southbound up the ten-mile 1.31% grade with Binghamton-bound manifest AB-4. Above is southbound local No. 4, a train that followed the *Laurentian* for local mail and express work, as well as local passenger traffic. It is shown here behind Pacific 652 at West Waterford. Below is the *Laurentian* itself, with Pacific No. 606, rolling over a neatly ballasted roadbed near Comstock, New York. *(John Pickett, left; William D. Middleton, above; Perry Storm, below)*

Pacific No. 607, with the southbound *Laurentian,* clears the south end of Rouses Point yard. *(Charles Clegg)*

389

Mohawk yard, just outside Schenectady, is a "balancing yard" where long trains from the north drop some tonnage in order to climb Richmondville Hill and other trains out of Mechanicville without full tonnage pick up a maximum or full train. There Challenger No. 1503, left, is working MB-4; underneath her is the 1504 pounding up the grade at South Schnectady with Binghamton-bound tonnage for the same manifest. At the right, northbound WM-1 glides down the grade toward Schenectady behind Challenger No. 1510 on its way to a connection at Mechanicville with the Boston & Maine for New England destinations. Below, 4-6-6-4 No. 1516 rolls OW-6 south out of Oneonta near Unadilla, New York, for a rendezvous with two pushers at Lanesboro for the climb over Ararat Summit and Wilkes-Barre. *(Perry Storm, left and below; William D. Middleton, two pictures)*

Here are three more pictures of the mighty Challengers in action and one of the cab from which they were operated. At the left the 1520 rolls manifest WR-1 into Nineveh on its daily northbound run from the Pennsy connection at Buttonwood yard to a CN connection at the border above Rouses Point. Below, the 1538 rumbles across the Mohawk River bridge at Cohoes, with Binghamton-bound AB-4. Opposite, below is an extra southbound out of Oneonta passing through the upper Susquehanna Valley at Sidney, New York, behind the 1533. The backhead of the great "J" class 4-6-6-4 was vast but simple, with plenty of room for the crew. A battery of valves and gauges on the fireman's side replaced the "Red Edge" coal shovels when the big articulateds arrived on the D&H, for they were equipped with mechanical stokers. *(Gene Baxter, below; D&H, right; Perry Storm, two pictures)*

Northern No. 300 emerges from the shadows of the Canadian Pacific's Windsor Station in Montreal with the southbound *Laurentian* on its daily run for Albany and the New York Central connection to Manhattan. The CPR's Glenn Engine Terminal in Montreal hosts engines with three versions of the "elephant ear" smoke deflector, below. Left to right are a CPR Pacific, D&H 4-8-4 No. 303 and Pacific No. 603. Opposite, below, is Pacific No. 652 with the Albany-Montreal overnight local No. 7, leaving Montreal West on the way to Windsor Station. Above her is a nostalgic view of Ten-Wheeler No. 536, pulling out of Cobleskill for Oneonta. *(This page: Allen Toohey, CRHA collection, above; S. S. Worthen. Opposite: John Pickett, above; Fred Sankoff)*

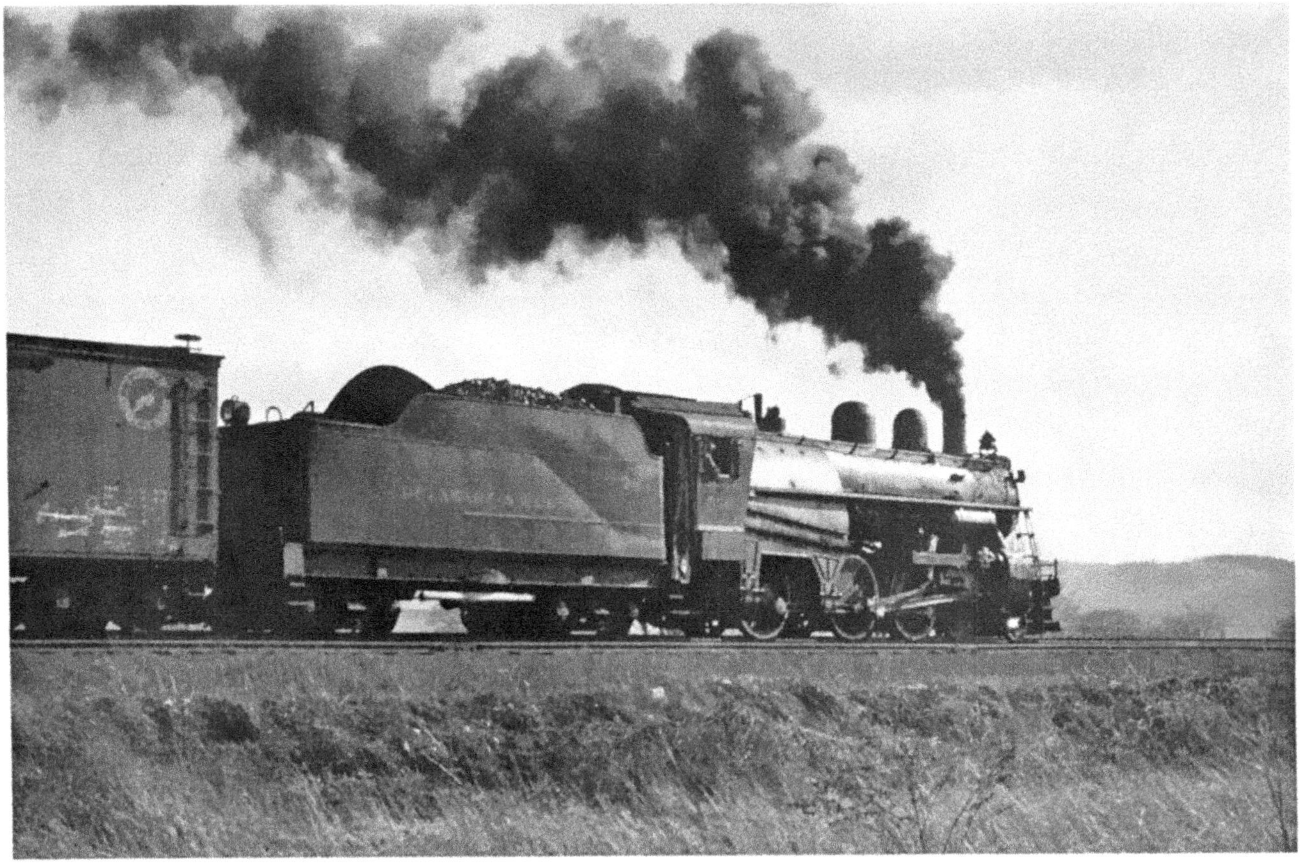

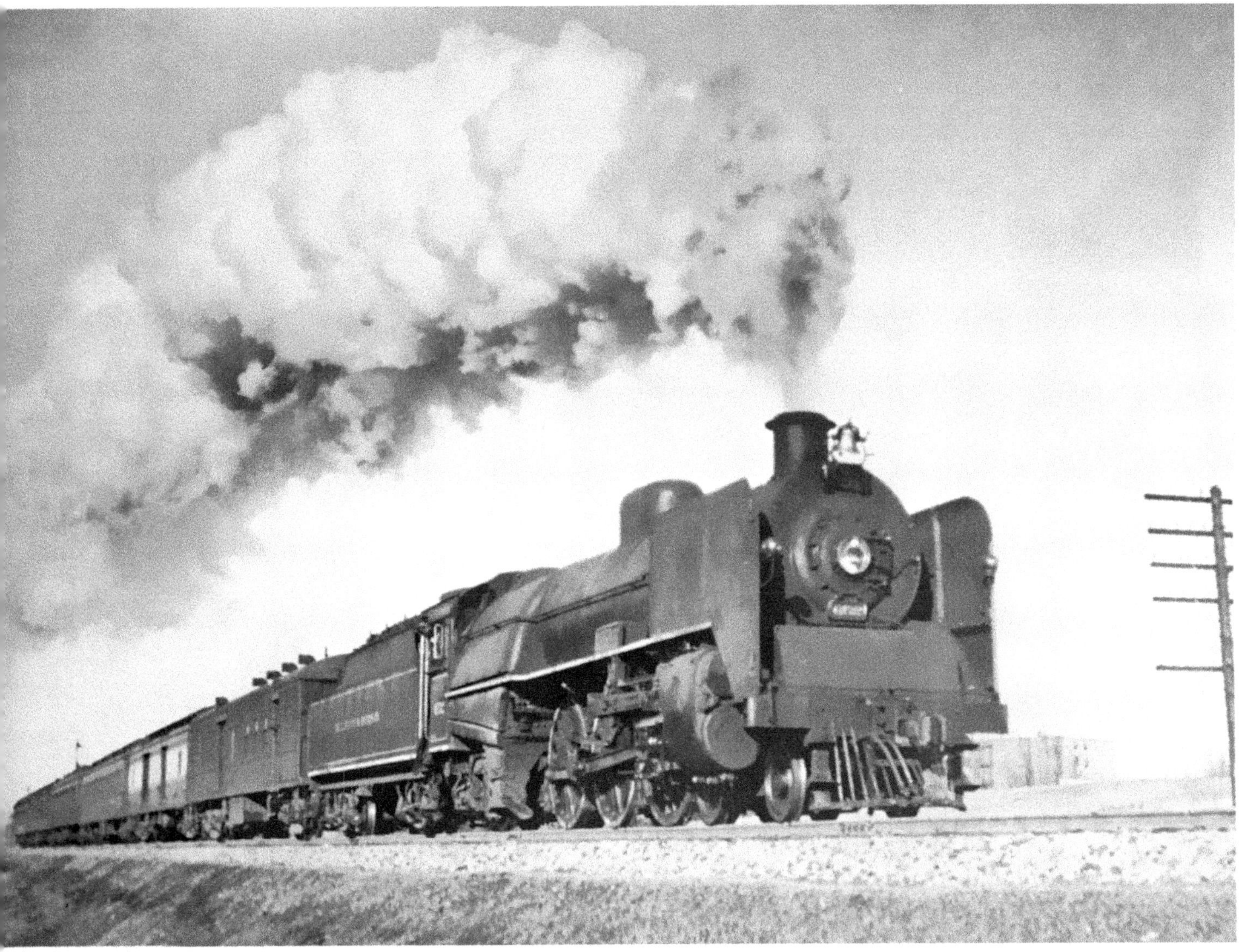

Dual-service Northern No. 306 eases the northbound *Laurentian* to a late afternoon stop at Port Kent, left, where Keesville passengers will detrain, along with Burlington-bound patrons who will take the ten-mile ferry voyage across Lake Champlain to Vermont's Queen City. Below that, behind 4-8-4 No. 305, the southbound *Laurentian* winds through the Red Rocks sector of the line high above Willsboro Bay. On this page, Ten-Wheeler No. 560 drifts downgrade into Corinth on the Adirondack branch, with the summer train from North Creek for Saratoga Springs and connection there to points south. *(John Gardiner, left; Perry Storm, left below; Ray E. Tobey, Rail Photo Service, below)*

The three-spired station house at Saratoga Springs, where Northern No. 307 waits with the southbound *Laurentian*, no longer stands. When the D&H tracks were relocated west of town in 1959, the honored old structure was replaced by a supermarket. The chill breeze of a November afternoon blows smoke across the yard at the Whitehall engine terminal, below, where Northerns 310 and 306 stand on the ready tracks. On the other page, after the car-knocker walking beside the cab of the 306 has finished looking over the consist, the southbound *Laurentian* will roll out of Rouses Point. (*John Pickett, opposite; Jim Shaughnessy, this page*)

Northern No. 307 rounds the curve into Port Kent on the Lake Champlain shore, above, with manifest WR-3 from Wilkes-Barre headed for Rouses Point. A few miles north of this point, below, the southbound version of the same train, RW-4, behind the 308, drags up the grade out of Plattsburgh, just south of the station and past the grounds of the old army barracks, the site of Champlain College at the time of this scene in 1952. On the other page, the No. 306 waits outside the engine house at Rouses Point. *(John Gardiner, above; Jim Shaughnessy, two pictures)*

Rolling into Whitehall station, above, Northern No. 310 eases up to the water plug where it will tank up for the rest of the run to Troy. There it will turn the *Laurentian* over to the New York Central for the fast trip to Grand Central Station. The two Northerns, below, are meeting at the south end of Mohawk yard near Schenectady. The lamp standard at West Waterford, opposite, frames the view of the northbound *Laurentian* crossing the Barge Canal bridge behind Northern No. 307 on a crisp December day. (Jim Shaughnessy, above; D. W. McLaughlin, below; Gene Baxter, opposite)

404

The prima donnas of the D&H fleet are lined up outside the great Colonie shops, above, for the 1934 inspection by President Loree and the Board of Managers. Each of the three—No. 609, left, the L. F. LOREE, in the distance, and the 653, right—was noted for its innovation in the technology of the steam locomotive. Opposite below, the Whitehall operator hoops up orders as Northern No. 306 brings northbound WR-5 past the station platform. Below, the 604 brings the *Laurentian* off the main line to Albany at Green Island, heading for Troy and the New York Central connection. (*D&H collection, above; Philip R. Hastings, left; William D. Middleton, right*)

Photographer Donald W. Furler has captured another memorable scene of a powerful Challenger articulated dragging a freight up the heavy grade toward Ararat Summit in Pennsylvania.

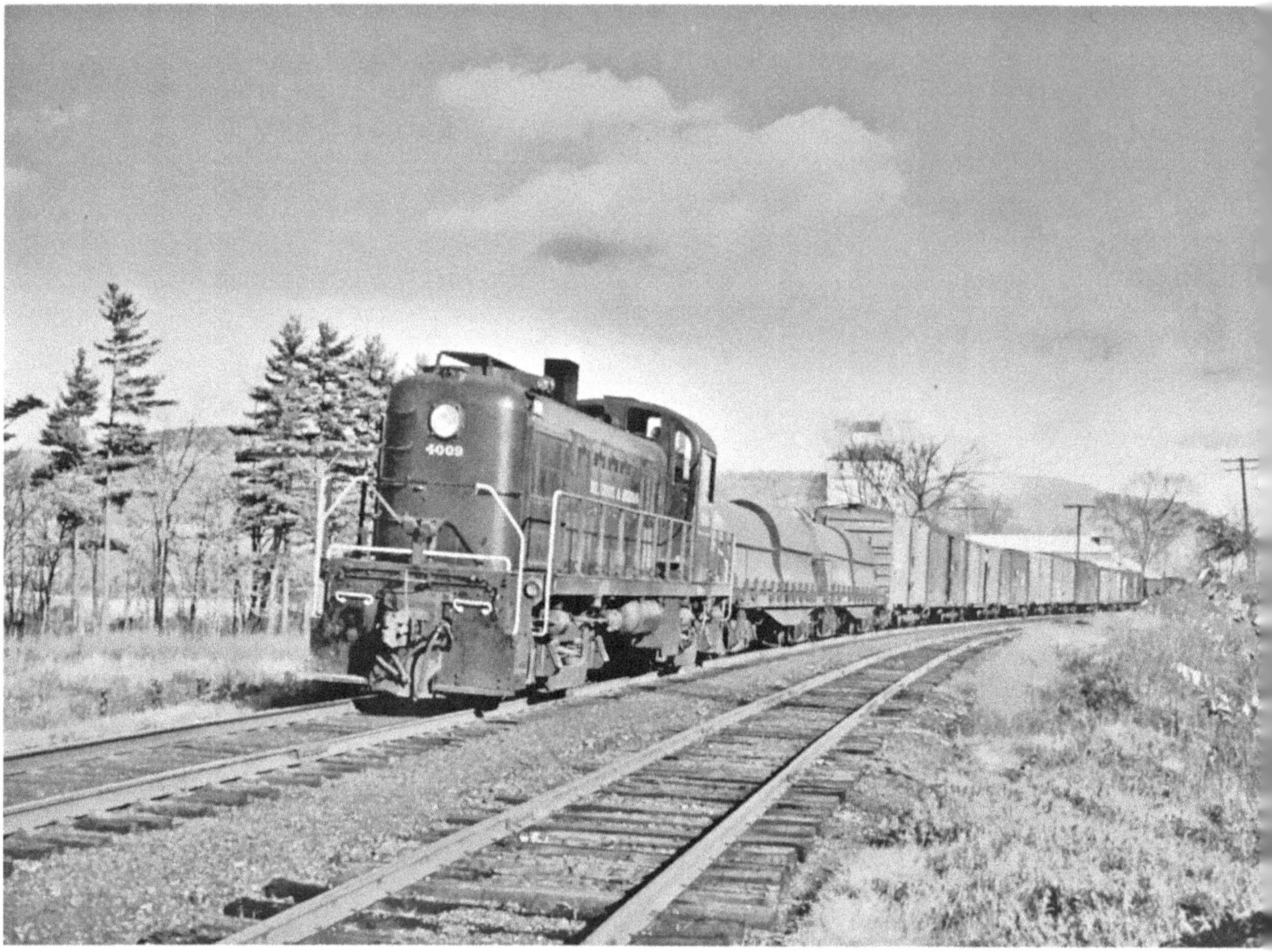
4009

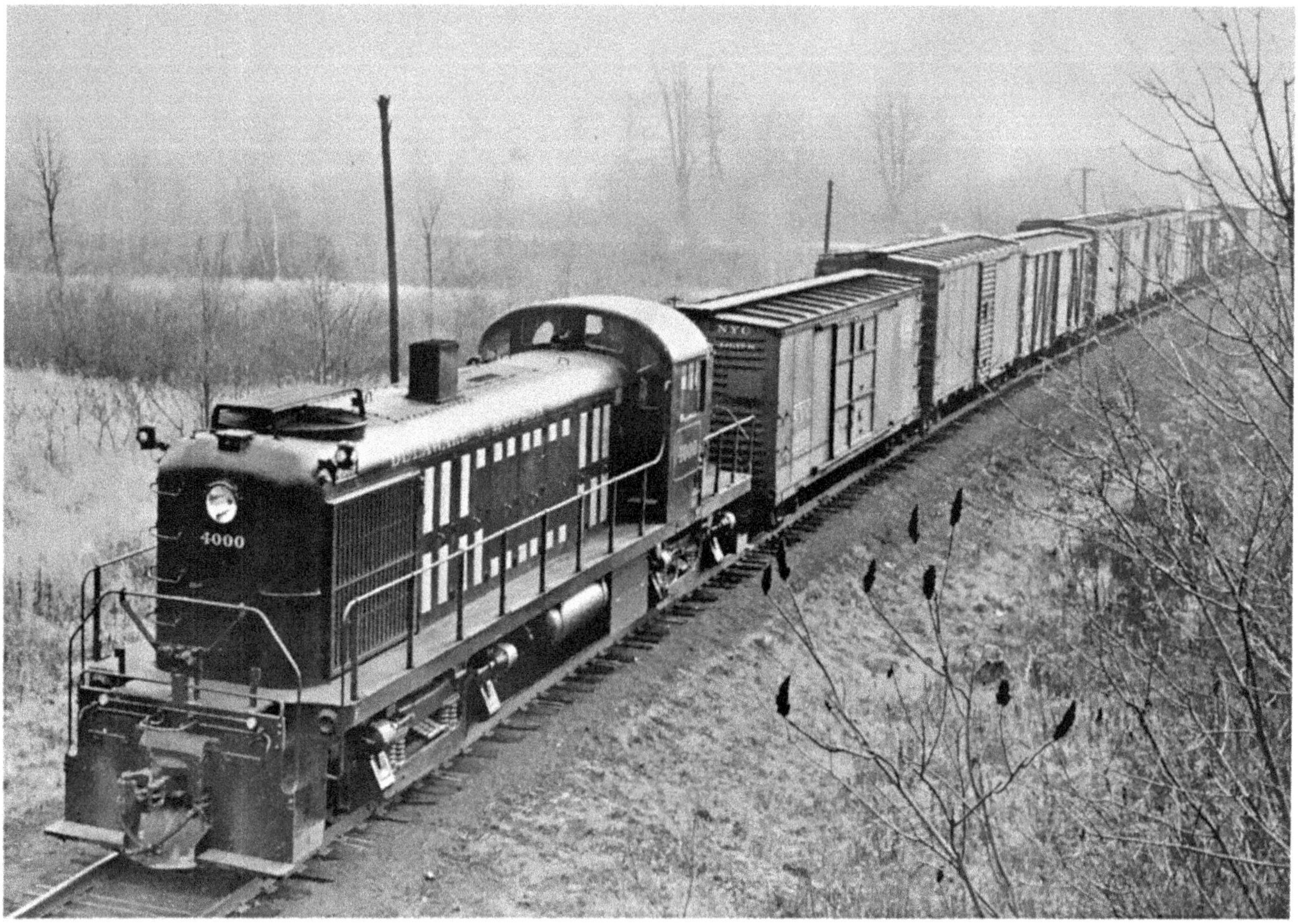
4000

The first of 130 1500-horsepower road switchers arrived on the D&H in November, 1946. The initial revenue trip of this power is shown in the lower picture, opposite, where No. 4000 hauls a freight up the Adirondack branch, just north of Saratoga Springs. Above it is RS-2, No. 4009 on the Rutland branch out of Whitehall, shortly after delivery. At the head end are two milk cars for the creamery at Fair Haven, Vermont. Shortly after they entered service, yellow stripes were painted on the ends of the Diesels for safety reasons. The year after the road switchers arrived, the old Mother Hubbard 2-8-0, above, was still on the job, shoving a work train through Center Rutland toward a washout of East Creek trestle on a spring day. Below, in a driving shower, road switcher No. 4006 adds a coach to the southbound *Laurentian* while in the distance Northern No. 305 backs a baggage car to the northbound section of the same fast train. *(Philip R. Hastings, this page and upper opposite; Rail Photo Service, upper opposite; D&H collection, opposite below)*

Some of the most colorful and spectacular steam action on the entire D&H system occurred on the 19-mile grade out of Carbondale to Ararat Summit. Here, near Forest City, Pennsylvania, a coal drag with a 4-6-6-4 up front, is pushed by another Challenger, No. 1526, with an Angus-type 0-8-8-0 Mallet behind it; behind the caboose a 1200-class 2-8-0 battles away. This last engine, called the Forest City Kicker, pushed on the very steepest part of the grade, a 1.48% stretch between West Carbondale and Forest City. Another 1600 0-8-8-0 Mallet drifts back down the hill after having helped a train up to Ararat Summit. *(Donald W. Furler)*

The Canadian Pacific's great bridge across Lachine Rapids of the St. Lawrence River is the gateway to Montreal for trains from the D&H. At the left, Pacific No. 607 is moving local No. 7 across the structure for an early morning arrival at Montreal after an all-night run from Albany. The end of the line is the CPR's Windsor Street station where Pacific 606 is seen through gate 2, right. Below are views of a southbound Northern entering and leaving the Red Rocks tunnel high above Lake Champlain's Willsboro Bay. At Whitehall, opposite below, mid-afternoon was a busy time when the north- and southbound *Laurentians* passed and a series of local, milk and accommodation trains converged on the place all at about the same time. In this view the northbound *Laurentian* has just arrived and passengers move toward it from the platform. At the left is train No. 3, an accommodation train that preceded the *Laurentian* to Whitehall. At the platform by the water plug in the right distance is milk train No. 18, while in the left distance another milk train is coming in off the Rutland branch. *(John Gardiner, two pictures below; Philip R. Hastings, three pictures)*

Two big Challengers ease along behind southbound MB-2 at Esperance, about halfway between Schenectady and Cobleskill, above. The steam won't be swirling lazily back over the long boilers as it is now when they encounter Howe's Cave Hill a few miles further south, or Richmondville Hill beyond Cobleskill. It is for those grades that the two pushers are on the train, almost 200 feet of locomotive, certainly dwarfing the little wooden buggy following them. The southbound *Laurentian* streaks out of Cantic, Quebec, on Napierville Junction rails behind 4-8-4 No. 304 on the bright snowy day, below. The Rouses Point switcher, 2-8-0 No. 1030, awaits the arrival of the southbound *Montreal Limited* on a cold January night, outside the warmly lighted station there, in the two pictures opposite. (*D. W. McLaughlin, above; Philip R. Hastings, three pictures*)

The Adirondack branch passenger train prepares to leave North Creek station for its run down to Saratoga Springs. In 1950 the service was cut back to summer season only and even that disappeared on September 9, 1956. During dry summer months in the Adirondacks it was necessary to have a fire watchman follow the steam-powered trains in the desolate section of the line between Port Kent and Willsboro. Below, he is shown on his motor car, in one of the many rocky cuts of that sector, following local No. 18 and the *Laurentian*. Opposite, the northbound *Laurentian* crosses the old Champlain Canal and swings onto the high fill at West Waterford with an eight-car consist. Oil marker lights provide an incongruous note on the bright streamlined observation car. (*Philip R. Hastings, both this page; Gene Baxter, opposite*)

The Rouses Point switcher, 2-8-0 No. 1030, moves out on Rutland trackage with four cars from the interchange track between the two railroads. In the foreground is the D&H main line crossing the Rutland's at grade. Below, an old arch-windowed wooden coach brings up the rear of northbound local No. 1, as Pacific No. 608 coals up at the South Junction coal tower, several miles south of Plattsburgh. This facility was built in 1922 to allow Montreal-bound trains to get enough fuel to go to the Canadian metropolis and back without refueling. Here, the line to Ausable Forks and the Chateaugay branch join the main line. *(Philip R. Hastings, both)*

The hostler at Whitehall stands alongside Consolidation No. 1111, making out the fuel slip after coaling the powerful home-built beauty. Below, Pacific No. 608 brings northbound local No. 1 into Plattsburgh station from Albany on a gray spring day. *(Allen Toohey, CRHA collection, above; Philip R. Hastings)*

Powerful Challengers were still moving heavy coal trains over Ararat Summit in 1950 when these pictures were made, but the end was near. Below a pair of pushers, assisted by the "Forest City Kicker," engine 1205, behind the caboose, are shoving loaded coal hoppers up the steepest part of the grade. Above, the grade is easier and the kicker has been dropped off. At the right, the 1530 crests the summit past the shanty where the operator controls the movement of pushers helping trains up the mountain. *(Robert F. Collins, below; Donald W. Furler, two pictures)*

Northbound at this point, Binghamton-bound freight AB-4 swings around a curve in northside Waterford and approaches the bridge over the present-day Erie Canal, below. This train originated in the Colonie yards near Albany and brought Capital District cars north to Mechanicville where usually a full tonnage was picked up from the Boston & Maine for the run down to Binghamton. At the right is a view repeated thousands of times during the glory days of steam on the D&H. A big "J" class articulated roars along the well-ballasted but cinder-covered roadbed, headed north toward Ararat Summit. *(Gene Baxter, below; Donald W. Furler, right)*

Northern No. 303 leans into the curve just north of Montcalm Landing (Ticonderoga) station with the northbound *Laurentian*, while a local freight awaits clearance off the Baldwin branch for a return trip to Whitehall. Past the water tank, at the Green Island end of the Hudson River bridge to Troy, rolls an extra train loaded with New York City children bound for the Police Athletic League summer camp in the Adirondacks. On the other page a big articulated crosses the fill at West Waterford, enveloped in a cloud of smoke and steam on a cold winter day. The Rorschach patterns in the sky below it are from the stacks of a pair of 4-6-6-4s hauling a freight over Ararat. *(This page: Philip R. Hastings, above; Donald S. Robinson, below. Opposite: Gene Baxter, above; Robert Collins, below)*

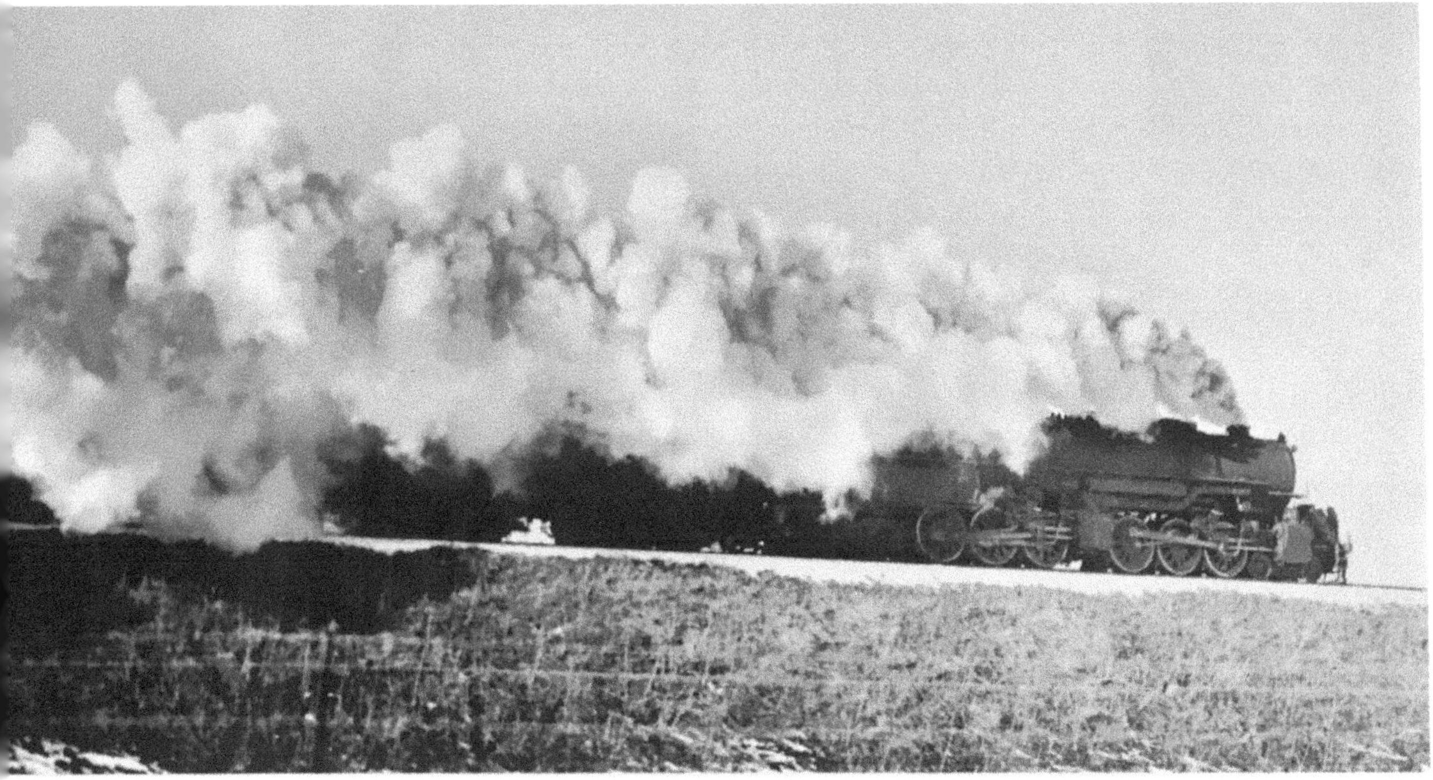

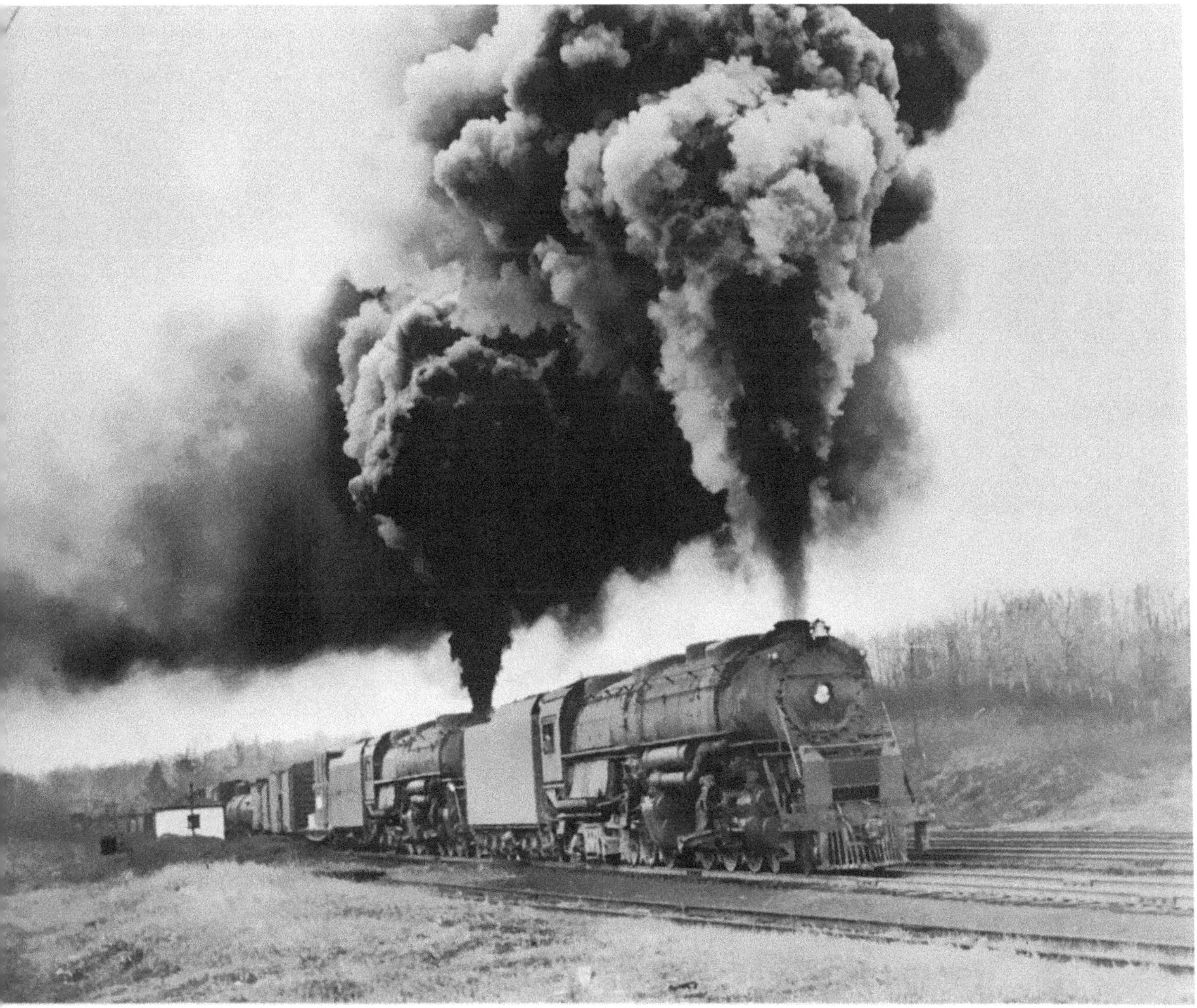

Over two miles of sharply curving track were relocated and 13 highway crossings were eliminated with completion in August 1950 of the Ballston Spa bypass. Southbound manifest RW-6 is shown crossing the big bridge over Kaydeross Creek just north of the new station, behind elephant-eared, grasshopper-eyed Northern No. 306. Local No. 1 between Albany and Rouses Point had a leisurely schedule that made it a rural institution in every way. Below it glides, northbound, under an overpass bridge near Crown Point. Opposite, milk train and local No. 18 works south out of Westport while the fireboy bails coal into the big Wooton firebox of Pacific No. 601. *(Perry Storm, above; Philip R. Hastings, below; Hal Carstens, opposite)*

The crew of local No. 3, a late-morning train from Albany to Whitehall ahead of the *Laurentian*, confers on the lower level of Albany station, left, before departing on the northbound run. On the right, at Round Lake, the old mail messenger prepares to put the afternoon dispatch aboard the southbound *Laurentian*. Now the station and even the tracks themselves, the original Rensselaer & Saratoga line, are all gone and the trains use an alternative route. Below that, a quartet of Diesels take symbol freight MB-4 south at East Worcester at the head of the 1.31% grade up Richmondville Hill. This point is on the divide between the Hudson and Susquehanna watersheds. The power line-up outside the Whitehall roundhouse on a Sunday afternoon, below, includes three Class E5 Consolidations and a heavy 0-8-0 rebuilt from a Consolidation. (*This page: Wallace W. Abbey, Trains Magazine, left; Hal Carstens, below. Opposite: Ladislav Dejnozska, above; Jim Shaughnessy, below*)

Luther Nunnally polishes the brass railings on D&H business car No. 300, left, in the Colonie coach yard prior to a trip over the road with the Board of Managers on their annual spring inspection trip. In the foreground is car No. 500, Pullman-built in 1917 for President Loree. Challenger No. 1535, right, awaits a southbound run in the Mechanicville roundhouse during the last few months of steam operations in 1952. The trim lines of the D&H Challengers blend nicely with the graceful lines of the Starrucca Viaduct, below. *(Robert F. Collins, below; Jim Shaughnessy, two pictures)*

At the top of these pages are two reminders of the old Rensselaer & Saratoga main line. The warehouse on the right was part of the old R&S Green Island shops, where many engines were built or rebuilt before completion of the Colonie shops in 1912. The Waterford local freight drifts past the stately old building that dates from 1871. At the left, on another day, the same local rumbles down Second Street in Waterford. This trackage on the R&S route between Troy and Ballston Spa opened in 1835 and is still used daily except Sunday. Below that picture is a moonlight view of the Mechanicville yard where symbol freight MW-4 is being made up for early morning departure. The hill in the background is silhouetted by the lights of the big paper mill of the West Virginia Pulp & Paper Co., by whom the paper for this book is made. Two early Diesels below, stir up dust at a Castleton, Vermont, grade crossing guarded by an old banjo-type signal. *(Hal Carstens, below; Jim Shaughnessy, three pictures)*

Alco Century No. 616 and two of the other 2750 hp road freight units have just brought symbol freight MB-2 from Mechanicville to Binghamton. Now, on the way to the engine house for servicing before their return trip, they cross the Erie-Lackawanna line north to Utica and Syracuse, formerly DL&W trackage. Below, other units from the series await assignment, along with assorted other Diesels, outside the Oneonta shops, still the original Albany & Susquehanna buildings. This facility now houses the D&H's principal car shops; light Diesel repairs are also performed there. At the right are three more of the powerful road freight units rounding a curve on the way up Ararat Hill at Thompson, Pennsylvania. A service road has replaced the former second track. *(Jim Shaughnessy, all)*

The Southern New York Railway, once known as the Oneonta & Mohawk Valley, is the remnant of a one-time interurban from Oneonta to Richfield Springs, with a branch to Cooperstown. It handles from thirty to forty cars a week and interchanges with the D&H a mile from its yard at West Oneonta, above. Its little GE locomotive is powered by big storage batteries in one hood, charged by a 150 hp Diesel and generator in the other hood. The century-old A&S station at Worcester, below, with a 154-car Mechanicville-bound freight passing it, appears in a sadder condition than in a picture taken forty years earlier on page 306. On the opposite page, the head brakeman of freight AB-4 swings onto the new Alco Century No. 618, the last locomotive in the second batch of these big road units received in the spring of 1965. The scene of this close-up is the Colonie yard. *(Jim Shaughnessy, all)*

Piggyback traffic did not become important on the D&H as early as on some other lines, but it has come to represent a considerable volume of business. A complete train is allotted to this purpose in each direction between Binghamton and Mechanicville, and the consist increases yearly. Above, a string of "pigs," Binghamton bound, rolls into the evening sun near East Worcester behind two of the new GE units. One of these 3000 hp brutes stands beside an old 1948 Alco 1600 hp road switcher in the Colonie shops below. Head-end brakeman O. K. Latimer rides the front platform of newly delivered GE Diesel 701 into Mohawk yard, Schenectady, opposite, as engineer Joe McNally eases symbol freight AB-4 for Binghamton to a stop. *(Jim Shaughnessy, all)*

The B-6 class 0-8-0s, represented by No. 94, above, were rebuilt E-3a 2-8-0s. The 349, built as a class E-4 2-8-0, was renumbered 342 then 1001 before being rebuilt in 1921 into B-5 class 0-8-0 No. 82. Low-drivered B-5 class 0-8-0s evolved from double-cabbed class E-4 2-8-0s; the 84 was one of this group. *(John Pickett, top and bottom; A. M. Payne, collection, below)*

ROSTER A
MOTIVE POWER OF DELAWARE & HUDSON R. R.
1915-1967
Compiled by Richard E. Cooper

You might expect the motive power roster of the railroad that ran the first steam locomotive in America to be not only long, but complex — and it is! The longevity of the operation alone would indicate this and with the D&H the unusual was commonplace. At times in the latter 19th century there would be only a few locomotives on the whole road that would be alike and this similarity usually didn't last for long.

The task of listing all the locomotives that descended from the STOURBRIDGE LION is virtually out of the question. The facts in many cases have faded into the ages and in this volume space alone precludes a coverage broader than what has been presented.

It took a man with a vast personal knowledge, who had access to accurate company records, a driving will to get the proper and complete facts and the patience of Job to do the job. Richard E. Cooper is a fireman on the D&H who has known most of the latter day engines well enough to throw coal into their roaring fireboxes and haul back on the shiny handles of their throttles.

Without Dick's tireless efforts in the dusty file room at Colonie, and his knowledge and dedication to the subject, this outstanding listing would not be available. The dean of steam locomotive historians, Gerald M. Best, provided valuable information to fill in the gaps and serve as a cross-reference check of these facts and his contribution can certainly not be overlooked.

The D&H, like many other roads, was the result of combining several smaller lines into a larger system, with the consequent integration and reclassification of the locomotives that came from the original companies. To compound this, the D&H was always rebuilding, upgrading, modifying and experimenting with its locomotives which doesn't make the locomotive genealogist's job any easier.

There were two major periods of turmoil in the specifications on the D&H: one in the late 1890s and the other in the late 1920s under the direction of the renowned L. F. Loree. In an effort to keep this roster to a reasonable size and avoid the geometric expansion of space and facts required to handle the details as they go back to the older engines with only a few in a class, the year of 1915 was chosen as a lower limit. This still includes many of the earlier engines but, more importantly, covers the last days of steam on the D&H, the period that most readers of this roster will best remember and be most interested in.

I am indeed indebted to Dick Cooper for his incredible undertaking and the outstanding results which are featured here.

JIM SHAUGHNESSY

⁋ ⁋ ⁋

When rosters such as this are prepared there is always the possibility of error in the facts dealing with the older power, due to the lack of complete documentation. The data used in compiling this material were obtained in the company's official motive power files and was quite complete in every respect. There are a few questions not fully answered but sufficient data exists that the information submitted here is as accurate as can be expected.

The D&H had quite extensive shops at Green Island, Oneonta and Carbondale. All three of these facilities participated in a major motive power rebuilding program during the 1890s. This was the era when the double-cabbed Wooten-fireboxed anthracite or culm burner became the vogue of several roads operating out of the Pennsylvania hard coal fields. Many of the old single cab, narrow fireboxed lump burners were converted by placing the wide Wooten fire boxes on the rear of the existing boilers in this rebuilding process. The Green Island shops also produced a number of completely new engines in the early 1900s. Most of the rebuilt engines were assigned a D&H shop builder's number and the original builder and number were dropped from the yearly folios. This made the tracing rather difficult but other records document many engines and indicate the rest were rebuilt as shown in this roster. When a 4-4-0 is rebuilt into a 2-8-0 as in one case, it takes some real imagination to determine—*How?* Perhaps they jacked up the bell, headlight and whistle and ran a new engine under them. Nevertheless, it was still classified as the same engine rebuilt rather than an entirely new one.

After the shop at Colonie was built in 1912, another and more spectacular era of rebuilding was launched and could probably be most effectively called an evolution. At first it was only slight, but in 1921 it began to take shape and gain momentum, reaching its peak activity during 1926 and 1927. After that it gradually diminished and came to an end in the depression years of the early 1930s. During this period, in round figures, 100 locomotives were rebuilt into totally new forms, another 50 were considerably upgraded and 15 completely new ones built. All this was accomplished along with routine shoppings of the other power and numerous experiments for which the D&H became famous.

During this period of evolution a new practice was devised to speed up the process known as the "swing boiler" system. During a major shopping, the boiler of a locomotive received an extensive "going over," the most time-consuming step of the overhaul. The "swing boiler" system was devised by setting up a schedule whereby there was usually a *spare* boiler in the shop for nearly every class of engine. This was accomplished in one of several ways; buying or building a *spare* boiler, scrapping an engine but saving the boiler, or just setting a locomotive aside (frame, etc. minus boiler) for a period of time, possibly even several years. By using the *spare* boiler, an engine could be turned out of the shop much quicker and the boiler it came in with then became the *spare*. This was overhauled separately and then used on some other engine at a later date.

This method was employed by some other roads also and has caused the "nuts and bolts" historians countless headaches, as will be seen.

When the class E-3a 900s evolved, many were made up from the frame and mechanism of one engine and the boiler from another. This was also true for some of the B-6 and B-7 classes. The confusion exists when you try to determine what old engine was rebuilt into what new engine. Actually it wasn't either, nor could you say it was renumbered. It would be logical to say when one locomotive is made from two—or likewise two locomotives made from one, depending on how you look at it—the resulting locomotives lose all identity with any particular original ones. It is purely a matter of personal opinion how a matter like this should be presented. The D&H had the habit of keeping the engine (road) number with the frame and chassis and the builder's number with the boiler. The builder's number was used in the federal boiler reports as a serial number to identify the boiler so it had to remain with the boiler no matter what engine it was mounted on and this roster is set up in that manner. This procedure was frequently followed in later years during regular shoppings and it was possible to see the same locomotive (or was it?) with up to three different builders' numbers over the years.

Space prohibits any attempt to trace out all the changes that occurred, but noted here is what became of each frame and boiler during the evolution, and the few "swings" made at that time. There are some dead ends as these missing parts sometimes did not show up again for several years during the progress of the program. In many cases the folio books dropped the builder's number after conversion. The majority of this data was double-checked through the federal boiler reports, which were also the source of most of the latter day "swings." The first boiler change noted was in July 1919 when engine 799 received a new boiler built in Colonie shops (No. 801) and boiler 25123 was scrapped.

RICHARD E. COOPER

In the presentation of the roster the following abbreviations will be used:

A&S	Albany & Susquehanna
Alco (D)	Alco—Dickson Works
Alco (M)	Alco—Montreal Works
Alco (S)	Alco—Schenectady Works
B	Boiler
CO&I	Chateaugay Ore & Iron Co.
Col	Colonie
Danf	Danforth
Dksn	Dickson
D&H (C)	D&H Carbondale Shops
D&H (GI)	D&H Green Island Shops
D&H (O)	D&H Oneonta Shops
F	Frame
NJ	Napierville Junction Ry.
NYO&W	New York, Ontario & Western Ry.
P&WV	Pittsburgh & West Virginia
QM&S	Quebec, Montreal & Southern
R&S	Rensselaer & Saratoga
rblt	Rebuilt
Schn	Schenectady
Scp	Scrapped
WSB	West Side Belt
Gone	No longer listed in folio; actual date and mode of disposition unknown.

Class B 0-6-0T or 0-6-0 (See Note)*

Cylinders	Drivers	Boiler Pressure	Weight on Drivers	Tot. Eng. Weight	Tractive Effort
17x22	47	150	85000	85000	17620

Last No.	Previous Nos. Orig 2nd etc.	Bldr.	Bldr. No.	Date	Disposition
3	163	Dksn	267	1880	rblt to
		D&H(GI)	44	1898	Scp 6/25
7	214	Dksn	509	1884	rblt to
		D&H(O)	20	1898	Scp 8/28

*Built as 0-6-0T, regular tanks applied about 1901. Engine 7 had tank removed again in 1914.

Class B-1a 0-6-0 (Single Cab)

Cylinders	Drivers	Boiler Pressure	Weight on Drivers	Tot. Eng. Weight	Tractive Effort
17x24	51	135	88700	88700	15918

Last No.	Previous Nos.	Bldr.	Bldr. No.	Date	Disposition
16	320	Dksn	827	1891	Gone 1/17

Class B-1b 0-6-0 (Double Cab)

Cylinders	Drivers	Boiler Pressure	Weight on Drivers	Tot. Eng. Weight	Tractive Effort
17x22	47	160	104000	104000	18800

Last No.	Previous Nos.	Bldr.	Bldr. No.	Date	Disposition
20	186	Dksn	386	1882	rblt to
		D&H(GI)	54	1899	Scp 7/29
21	215	Dksn	510	1884	rblt to
		D&H(GI)	32	1899	Scp 9/29
22		D&H(O)	34	1900	Scp 8/29

Engines 20 and 21 former 0-6-0T rebuilt and converted.

Camelback No. 21 was rebuilt at Green Island in 1899 from an 1884 Dickson-built tank engine. *(A. M. Payne, collection)*

Class B-2 0-6-0 (Singe Cab)

Cylinders	Drivers	Boiler Pressure	Weight on Drivers	Tot. Eng. Weight	Tractive Effort
18x24	51	135	97700	97700	17844

Last No.	Previous Nos. Orig 2nd etc.	Builder & No.	Date	Disposition
14	318	Schn 3316	1890	Gone 1/16

Class B-2e 0-6-0 (Single Cab)

Cylinders	Drivers	Boiler Pressure	Weight on Drivers	Tot. Eng. Weight	Tractive Effort
18x24	57	150	101800	101800	17709

Last No.	Previous Nos.	Builder & No.	Date	Disposition
101	313	Dksn 795	1890	Converted from class C-li in 1913 back to C-li in 1924

Class B-2f 0-6-0 (Single Cab)

Cylinders	Drivers	Boiler Pressure	Weight on Drivers	Tot. Eng. Weight	Tractive Effort
18x24	57	155	103700	103700	18293

Last No.	Previous Nos.	Builder & No.	Date	Disposition
139	102	Dksn 241	1880	Converted from class C-lj in 1913. Gone 1/16

Class B-2g 0-6-0 (Double Cab)

Cylinders	Drivers	Boiler Pressure	Weight on Drivers	Tot. Eng. Weight	Tractive Effort
18x24	57	130	95800	95800	15342

Last No.	Previous Nos.	Builder & No.	Date	Disposition
177	68 209	Dksn 586	1887	Converted from class C-lh in 1913. Gone 1/17

Class B-4 0-6-0 (Double Cab)

Cylinders	Drivers	Boiler Pressure	Weight on Drivers	Tot. Eng. Weight	Tractive Effort
19x24	51	180	137850	137850	26510

No.	Bldr.	Bldr. No.	Date	Disposition
23	D&H(O)	39	1902	Scp 5/42
24	D&H(O)	40	1902	Scp 10/45
25	Dksn	1297	1902	Scp 11/33
26	Dksn	1298	1902	Scp 12/29
27	Dksn	1299	1902	Scp 2/40
28	Dksn	1300	1902	Scp 4/35
29	D&H(GI)	65	1903	Scp 11/45

Engine 29 numbered 29 when built, renumbered 18, then back to 29.

Class B-4a 0-6-0 (Double Cab)

Cylinders	Drivers	Boiler Pressure	Weight on Drivers	Tot. Eng. Weight	Tractive Effort
(30-51) 19x24	51	180	139850	139850	26510
(52-56) 19x24	51	180	134800	134800	26510

No.	Bldr.	Bldr. No.	Date	Disposition
30	Alco(D)	27531	1903	Scp 12/45
31	Alco(D)	27532	1903	Scp 10/45
32	Alco(D)	27533	1903	Scp 11/45
33	Alco(D)	27534	1903	Scp 12/42
34	Alco(D)	27535	1903	Scp 10/45
35	Alco(D)	27536	1903	Scp 11/45
36	Alco(D)	27537	1903	Scp 11/45
37	Alco(D)	27538	1903	Scp 9/34
38	Alco(D)	27539	1903	Scp 10/37
39	Alco(D)	27540	1903	Scp 2/36
40	Alco(D)	27541	1903	Scp 2/31
41	Alco(D)	27542	1903	Scp 8/46
42	Alco(D)	27543	1903	Scp 11/47
43	Alco(D)	27544	1903	Luria 8/51
44	Alco(D)	28903	1904	Scp 10/45
45	Alco(D)	28904	1904	Scp 11/45
46	Alco(D)	28905	1904	Scp 11/49
47	Alco(D)	28906	1904	Scp 12/45
48	Alco(D)	29022	1904	Scp 7/34
49	Alco(D)	29023	1904	Scp 10/45
50	Alco(D)	29024	1904	Scp 5/30
51	Alco(D)	29021	1904	Scp 10/45
52	Alco(D)	42289	1907	Scp 10/45
53	Alco(D)	42290	1907	Scp 11/45
54	Alco(D)	42291	1907	Scp 12/45
55	Alco(D)	42292	1907	Scp 10/45
56	Alco(D)	42293	1907	to CO&I 7/37

Engine 51 originally numbered 29.

Bobtail 0-6-0 No. 44 was representative of the B-4a class.
(Philip Hayner collection)

Class B-5 0-8-0 (Single Cab except 82)

Cylinders	Drivers	Boiler Press.	Weight on Drivers	Tot. Eng. Weight	Tractive Effort
22x28	51	200	196750	196750	46050

No.	Bldr. & No.	No.	History and disposition
81	Schn 5089 from E-4	1899 2-8-0	rblt Col 2/24 1000 Luria 5/51
82	Schn 5090 from E-4	1899 2-8-0	rblt Col 9/21 1001 Luria 5/51
83	Schn 5091 from E-4	1899 2-8-0	rblt Col 4/22 1002 Luria 3/50
84	Schn 5092 from E-4	1899 2-8-0	rblt Col 7/24 1003 Scp 5/49
85	Schn 5111 from E-4	1899 2-8-0	rblt Col 12/24 1004 Scp 11/45
86	Schn 5088 from E-4	1899 2-8-0	rblt Col 11/25 1005 Luria 5/51
87	Schn 5868 from E-4a	1901 2-8-0	rblt Col 4/23 1006 Luria 8/51

Class B-6 0-8-0 (Single Cab)

Cylinders	Drivers	Boiler Pressure	Weight on Drivers	Tot. Eng. Weight	Tractive Effort
21½x30	57	215 (200) (205)	208000	208000	45350 (42100) (43250)

During various shoppings and modifications there were changes in boiler pressure and tractive effort made on some of these, as shown in parentheses, but it was not consistent with any one nor permanent with all.

No.	Bldr. & No.	Date	History and Disposition
91	Alco(S) 28824 from E-3a	1904 2-8-0	rblt Col 10/24 820 Scp 2/46
92	Alco(S) 25117 from E-3a	1902 2-8-0	rblt Col 8/24 793 Luria 2/53
93	Alco(D) 39804 from E-3a	1906 2-8-0	rblt Col 6/25 871 Luria 2/53
94	Alco(S) 30717 from E-3a	1905 2-8-0	rblt Col 7/25 806 Luria 5/51
95	Alco(D) 39810 from E-3a	1906 2-8-0	rblt Col 6/25 877 Luria 5/51
96	Alco(S) 25114 from E-3a	1902 2-8-0	rblt Col 8/25 790 Luria 3/50
97	Alco(S) 25122 from E-3a	1902 2-8-0	rblt Col 9/25 798 Luria 4/53
98	Alco(D) 27515 from E-3a	1903 2-8-0	rblt Col 11/25 843 Scp 10/49
99	Alco(S) 25116 from E-3a	1902 2-8-0	rblt Col 2/26 792 Scp 7/47
100	Alco(S) 28827 from E-3a	1904 2-8-0	rblt Col 4/30 Luria 8/53 (frame of 887, boiler of 2/884)

Class B-7 0-8-0 (Single Cab)

Cylinders	Drivers	Boiler Pressure	Weight on Drivers	Tot. Eng. Weight	Tractive Effort
25½x30	57	225	265000	265000	66650

No.	Bldr. & No.	Date	History and disposition
151	Alco(S) 40568 from E-5	1906 2-8-0	rblt Col 4/26 1009 Luria 5/52
152	Alco(S) 43281 from E-5	1907 2-8-0	rblt Col 11/26 1024 Luria 8/53
153	Alco(S) 43276 from E-5	1907 2-8-0	rblt Col 2/27 Luria 5/52 (frame of 1017, boiler of 1019)
154	Alco(S) 43277 from E-5	1907 2-8-0	rblt Col 4/27 1020 Luria 2/53
155	Alco(S) 43272 from E-5	1907 2-8-0	rblt Col 6/27 1015 Luria 5/52
156	Alco(S) 44724 from E-5	1908 2-8-0	rblt Col 10/27 Luria 8/53 (frame of 1022, boiler of 1039) (1039 received another boiler)
157	Alco(S) 43279 from E-5	1907 2-8-0	rblt Col 12/27 Luria 8/53 (frame of 1038, boiler of 1022)
158	Alco(S) 44723 from E-5	1908 2-8-0	rblt Col 2/28 Luria 5/52 (frame of 1040, boiler of 1038)
159	Alco(S) 44725 from E-5	1908 2-8-0	rblt Col 3/28 Luria 4/53 (frame of 1027, boiler of 1040)
160	Alco(S) 44712 from E-5	1907 2-8-0	rblt Col 9/28 Luria 5/52 (frame of 1044, boiler of 1027)
161	Alco(S) 44729 from E-5	1908 2-8-0	rblt Col 10/28 Luria 5/52 (frame of 1051, boiler of 1044)
162	Alco(S) 44736 from E-5	1908 2-8-0	rblt Col 10/28 Luria 8/51 (frame of 1033, boiler of 1051)
163	Alco(S) 44718 from E-5	1908 2-8-0	rblt Col 3/29 Luria 2/53 (frame of 1043, boiler of 1033)
164	Alco(S) 43278 from E-5	1907 2-8-0	rblt Col 10/30 1021 Luria 8/53

Class C-1e 2-6-0 (Single Cab)

Cylinders	Drivers	Boiler Pressure	Weight on Drivers	Tot. Eng. Weight	Tractive Effort
18x24	57	150	71200	83300	17700

Last No.	Previous Nos. Orig 2nd etc.		Bldr.	Bldr. No.	Date	Disposition
135	A&S 79	255 252	Dksn	157	1875	Gone 1/16

Class C-1i 2-6-0 (Single Cab)

Cylinders	Drivers	Boiler Pressure	Weight on Drivers	Tot. Eng. Weight	Tractive Effort
18x24	57	150	94300	108300	17709

Last No.	Previous Nos. Orig. 2nd etc.	Bldr.	Bldr. No.	Date	Disposition
61	289	Dksn	740	1890	to QM&S 1917 Gone 1/19
63	291	Dksn	742	1890	Scp 7/25
65	293	Dksn	744	1890	Scp 11/31
75	288	Dksn	693	1889	to QM&S 11/18
91	307	Dksn	789	1890	to QM&S 11/18
93	309	Dksn	791	1890	to QM&S 11/18
99	311	Dksn	793	1890	Gone 1/17
101	313	Dksn	795	1890	Scp 1/29 (See class B-2e)
110	330	Dksn	811	1891	to QM&S 1908 Gone 1/19
111	331	Dksn	812	1891	to QM&S 1917 Gone 1/19
112	332	Dksn	813	1891	Scp 10/29

Engines 63 and 65 converted to oil burners in 1912 and used on Chateaugay Branch through Adirondack Forest Preserve.

Class C-1j 2-6-0 (Single Cab)

18x24	57	155	94100	107400	18293
139	102	256	Dksn	241	1880	rblt 0-6-0 B-2f in 1913
142	105	259	Dksn	259	1880	Scp 4/24
145	167	262	Dksn	283	1881	Gone 1/17

Class C-1k 2-6-0 (Single Cab)

18x24	63	150	107700	123000	15991
58	323		Dksn	830	1891	Scp 6/25
59	324		Dksn	831	1891	to QM&S 11/18
60	334		Dksn	889	1893	Scp 7/26
66	335		Dksn	890	1893	Scp 9/26
67	336		Dksn	891	1893	Scp 10/26
70	116	55	Dksn	893	1893	to QM&S 11/18
71	321		Dksn	828	1891	Gone 1/17
72	322		Dksn	829	1891	Scp 8/25

Engines 60, 66 and 67 converted to oil burners in 1909 for Chateaugay services.

Class C-1m 2-6-0 (Double Cab)

18x24	57	165	95900	112600	19472
(119 & 179)		170			20070
119	8	270	Dksn	53	1870	rblt to
			D&H(C)	A119	1898	Scp 11/23
121	108	272	Dksn	262	1880	rblt to
			D&H(GI)	48	1898	Scp 8/26
122 A&S 38	241	273	Dksn	27	1867	rblt to
			D&H(O)	30	1898	Scp 6/26
123	234	274	Danf & Cooke		1864	rblt to
			D&H(GI)	43	1898	Scp 6/24
179	20	271	130 Dksn	136	1873	rblt to
			D&H(C)	A179	1898	Gone 1/17

This class is one of those almost completely built in the D&H shops from parts of old single-cab lump-burners during the upgrading of the 1890s.

Class C-2 2-6-0 (Double Cab)

	Cylinders	Drivers	Boiler Pressure	Weight on Drivers	Tot. Eng. Weight	Tractive Effort
(117)	19x24	57	200	126500	143500	26300
(118)	19x24	57	210	126500	143500	27700

Last No.	Previous Nos. Orig. 2nd etc.	Bldr.	Bldr. No.	Date	Disposition
117	299 268	Rogers	4228	1890	rblt to
		D&H(GI)	66	1904	Scp 10/39
118	301 269	Rogers	4234	1890	rblt to
		D&H(GI)	64	1904	Scp 8/35

Another old engine upgrading that produced the system's largest Moguls.

Class D-3 4-6-0 (Double Cab except 558 to 561)

Cylinders	Drivers	Boiler Pressure	Weight on Drivers	Tot. Eng. Weight	Tractive Effort
21x26	72	200	131500	175000	27540

No.	Bldr. & No.	Date	Single Cab	Disposition
500	Alco(S) 27651	1903	4/27	Luria 5/52
501	Alco(S) 27652	1903	1/29	Luria 5/51
502	Alco(S) 27653	1903	3/29	Luria 8/51
503	Alco(S) 27654	1903	5/31	Scp 9/46
504	D&H(GI) A504	1905		Scp 10/40
505	D&H(GI) A505	1905	1/25	Luria 5/51
506	D&H(GI) A506	1904	7/29	Luria 5/51
507	D&H(GI) A507	1904		Scp 11/39
508	D&H(GI) A508	1904	7/30	Luria 10/52
557	Alco(S) 42306	1907	3/26	Luria 5/51
558	Alco(S) 42307	1907		Luria 5/52
559	Alco(S) 42308	1907		Scp 3/49
560	Alco(M) 43703	1907		Luria 5/52
561	Alco(M) 43708	1907		Luria 5/51

Engines 557-558-559 rebuilt from class D-3b.

Engines 560-561 purchased 12/19 from Napierville Junction Ry. They were former QM&S engines and carried numbers 201 and 206 respectively on both roads.

As was characteristic of many D&H classes the D-3 underwent an evolution of gradual changes but once again with no definite pattern. Some engines were modified several times, others only once. The final forms shown below.

No.	Cyl.	Drivers	Boiler Press.	Weight on Drivers	Tot. Eng. Weight	Tractive Effort
500	22x26	72	200	156800	204800	30150
501	22x26	72	200	156800	204800	30150
502	22x26	72	210	156800	204800	31650
503	22x26	72	225	156800	204800	34000
504	22x26	72	215	149650	202300	32550
505	22x26	72	215	156800	204800	32550
506	22x26	72	200	156800	204800	30150
507	22x26	72	200	149650	202300	30150
508	22x26	72	225	156800	204800	34000
557	22x26	72	225	156800	204800	34000
558	22x26	72	200	156800	204800	30150
559	22x26	72	200	156800	204800	30150
560	22x26	72	225	156800	204800	34000
561	22x26	72	225	156800	204800	34000

Class D-3a 4-6-0 (Double Cab)

Cylinders	Drivers	Boiler Pressure	Weight on Drivers	Tot. Eng. Weight	Tractive Effort
21x26	69	200	131500	175000	28622 (as built)

Last No.	Orig. No.	Bldr. & No.		Date	Disposition
521	504	Alco(S)	28907	1904	Scp 11/40
522	505	Alco(S)	28908	1904	Luria 8/51
523	506	Alco(S)	28909	1904	Luria 5/51
524	507	Alco(S)	28910	1904	Luria 5/51

Rebuilt Single Cab: 522 — 12/28; 523 — 4/29; 524 — 11/28.

Again evolution to this end—

521-	21x26	69	200	136000	186000	28622
522-524	22x26	69	225	160000	208000	35300

Class D-3b 4-6-0 (Double Cab 535-557)
(Single Cab 534, 558, 559, 590-594, 599)

No.	Cyl.	Drivers	Boiler Pressure	Weight on Drivers	Tot. Eng. Weight	Tractive Effort
534-	21x26	63	200	143000	189000	31450
535-544	21x26	63	200	130000	173000	31440
545-557	21x26	63	200	134000	186500	31440
558-559	21x26	63	200	143000	189000	31440
590-594	21x26	63	200	146000	193000	31440
599-	23x26	63	170	147500	199000	32055

The 590 series were built in a way that they were readily convertible from soft coal to oil. They were used primarily on the Chateaugay, burning oil during the summer and soft coal winters.

No.	Bldr. & No.		Date	Disposition
534	Alco(M)	43704	1907	Scp 11/40
535	D&H(GI)	A535	1905	Scp 1/38
536	D&H(GI)	A536	1905	Luria 5/52
537	D&H(GI)	A537	1905	Scp 6/35
538	D&H(GI)	A538	1905	Scp 1935
539	D&H(GI)	A539	1905	Scp 2/40
540	D&H(GI)	A540	1906	Scp 2/39
541	D&H(GI)	A541	1906	Scp 2/39
542	D&H(GI)	A542	1906	Scp 6/35
543	D&H(GI)	A543	1906	Scp 9/37
544	D&H(GI)	A544	1906	Scp 2/35
545	Alco(S)	42294	1907	Scp 5/43
546	Alco(S)	42295	1907	Luria 10/52
547	Alco(S)	42296	1907	Scp 10/42
548	Alco(S)	42297	1907	Scp 4/42
549	Alco(S)	42298	1907	Luria 3/50
550	Alco(S)	42299	1907	Scp 4/30
551	Alco(S)	42300	1907	Scp 3/35
552	Alco(S)	42301	1907	Scp 10/42
553	Alco(S)	42302	1907	Scp 10/35
554	Alco(S)	42303	1907	Scp 11/47
555	Alco(S)	42304	1907	Scp 5/35
556	Alco(S)	42305	1907	Luria 6/51
557	Alco(S)	42306	1907	class D-3 3/26
558	Alco(S)	42307	1907	Rblt Class D-3
559	Alco(S)	42308	1907	Rblt Class D-3
590	Alco(S)	49656	1911	Scp 9/46
591	Alco(S)	49657	1911	Scp 11/46
592	Alco(S)	49658	1911	Scp 11/42
593	Alco(S)	49659	1911	Scp 11/42
594	Alco(S)	49660	1911	Scp 8/46
599	Alco(S)	49661	1911	Scp 11/46

Rebuilt Single Cab: 535 — 8/29; 536 — 7/28; 546 — 8/27; 556 — 5/27.

Engine 550 frame and chassis scrap — 4/30 — boiler to spare.

More evolution on engines shown only, only minor changes on others.

No.	Cyl.	Drivers	Boiler Pressure	Weight on Drivers	Tot. Eng. Weight	Tractive Effort
536 546 556						
	22x26	63	215	160000	208000	37200
549	22x26	63	200	143000	198500	34500
599	23x26	63	200	148000	200300	37700

Engine 534 purchased 12/19 from NJ, former QM&S, number 202 on both roads.

Engines 502, 506, 561 received new Alco(S) boilers GO-76687-1, GO-76687-3, and GO-76687-2 in June, October and July 1941 respectively.

Class E 2-8-0 (Double Cab)

Cylinders	Drivers	Boiler Pressure	Weight on Drivers	Tot. Eng. Weight	Tractive Effort
20x24	51	160	108000	123000	26110

Last No.	Previous Nos. Orig 2nd etc.	Bldr.	No.	Date	Disposition
700	93 348	Dksn	909	1893	Gone 1/27
701	94 349	Dksn	910	1893	Gone 1/27

Purchased secondhand from NYO&W in December 1896.

Class E-1 2-8-0 (Double Cab)

20x26	56 (57)	170	130000	150100	27330 (26836)

702	125	285	Schn	432	1867	rblt to
			D&H(GI)	51	1899	to QM&S 12/20
703	157	286	Dksn	279	1881	rblt to
			D&H(O)	33	1899	Scp 7/27
704	175	287	Dksn	294	1881	rblt to
			D&H(O)	31	1899	Scp 11/28

This is a remarkable and hard to believe set of conversions, a 4-4-0 and two 2-6-0s rebuilt to 2-8-0s but the records indicate that it was done!

Class E-1a 2-8-0 (Double Cab)

20x26	56 (57)	180	134500	151500	29000 (28410)

705	233	278	Danf & Cooke		1864	rblt to
			Dksn	993	1898	Scp 8/27
706	236	279	Danf & Cooke		1866	rblt to
			Dksn	998	1898	Scp 12/28
707	A&S 17	A&S 68				
	244	280	Dksn	30	1867	rblt to
			Dksn	999	1898	Scp 1928
709	343	281	Dksn	1000	1898	Scp 1928
	344	282	Dksn	1001	1898	Scp 9/27
710	345	283	Dksn	1002	1898	Scp 1928
711	346	284	Dksn	1003	1898	Scp 10/27

Again, the first three of this group represents a remarkable rebuild job as indicated by the records, this time at the Dickson Works in Scranton, Pa.

Class E-2 2-8-0 (Double Cab)

Cylinders	Drivers	Boiler Pressure	Weight on Drivers	Tot. Eng. Weight	Tractive Effort
21x26	56 (57)	180	133000	153000	31900 (31280)

Numbers Last	1st	2nd	Bldr. & No.		Date	Disposition	
712	353	300	Schn	5078	1899	Scp	6/37
713	354	301	Schn	5079	1899	Scp	10/46
714	355	302	Schn	5080	1899	Scp	4/45
715	356	303	Schn	5081	1899	Scp	8/47
716	357	304	Schn	5082	1899	Scp	1/35
717	358	305	Schn	5083	1899	Scp	2/34
718	359	306	Schn	5084	1899	Scp	9/44
719	360	307	Schn	5085	1899	Scp	12/36
720	361	308	Schn	5086	1899	Scp	3/30
721	362	309	Schn	5087	1899	Scp	7/36
722	363	310	Schn	5112	1899	Scp	2/39
723	364	311	Schn	5113	1899	Scp	9/31
724	365	312	Schn	5114	1899	Scp	12/40
725	366	313	Schn	5115	1899	Scp	9/36
726	367	314	Schn	5116	1899	Scp	1926
727	368	315	Schn	5117	1899	Scp	5/36
728	369	316	Dksn	1067	1899	Scp	12/33
729	370	317	Dksn	1068	1899	Scp	4/31
730	371	318	Dksn	1069	1899	Scp	8/36
731	372	318	Dksn	1070	1899	Gone	1/30
732	373	320	Dksn	1071	1899	Scp	11/27
733	374	321	Dksn	1072	1899	Gone	1/30
734	375	322	Dksn	1073	1899	Scp	9/36
735	376	323	Dksn	1074	1899	CO&I	4/25
736	377	324	Dksn	1075	1899	Scp	10/36
737	378	325	Dksn	1076	1899	Scp	3/36

Class E-2a 2-8-0 (Double Cab)

Cylinders	Drivers	Boiler Pressure	Weight on Drivers	Tot. Eng. Weight	Tractive Effort
21x26	56 (57)	180	137500	156000	31900 (31280)

Numbers Last	1st	2nd	Builder & No.		Date	Disposition	
738	326		Dksn	1128	1900	Luria	3/50
739	327		Dksn	1129	1900	Scp	4/35
740	328		Dksn	1130	1900	Scp	8/49
741	329		Dksn	1131	1900	Scp	6/44
742	330		Dksn	1132	1900	Scp	11/30
743	331		Dksn	1146	1900	Scp	2/36
744	332		Dksn	1147	1900	Scp	3/34
745	333		Dksn	1148	1900	Scp	10/36
746	334		Dksn	1149	1900	Scp	7/30
747	335		Dksn	1150	1900	Scp	1/39
748	336		Dksn	1151	1900	Scp	8/36
749	337		Dksn	1152	1900	Scp	1/37
750	338		Dksn	1153	1900	Scp	7/35
751	339		Dksn	1154	1900	Scp	3/31
752	346	340	Dksn	1155	1900	Gone	1/30
753	288		D&H(O)	A753	1901	Luria	5/51
754	289		D&H(O)	A754	1901	Scp	10/42
755	290		Schn	5377	1900	Scp	1/46
756	291		Schn	5378	1900	Scp	6/36
757	292		Schn	5379	1900	Scp	12/34
758	293		Schn	5380	1900	Scp	3/39
759	294		Schn	5381	1900	Scp	6/48
760	295		Schn	5382	1900	Scp	4/34
761	296		Schn	5383	1900	Scp	8/46
762	297		Schn	5384	1900	Scp	11/27
763	298		Schn	5385	1900	Scp	8/46
764	299		Schn	5386	1900	Scp	4/47

The 715 is shown here in her twilight years and reflects but little change over nearly half a century of service. The class E-2a and E-2b engines were essentially the same. *(G. M. Best)*

Class E-2b 2-8-0 (Double Cab)

Cylinders	Drivers	Boiler Pressure	Weight on Drivers	Tot. Eng. Weight	Tractive Effort
21x26	56 (57)	180	145000	166000	31900 (31280)

Numbers

Last	1st	Builder & No.		Date	Disposition
765	256	Alco(D)	1301	1902	Scp 7/36
766	257	Alco(D)	1302	1902	Scp 2/44
767	258	Alco(D)	1303	1902	Scp 2/44
768	259	Alco(D)	1304	1902	Scp 10/31
769	260	Alco(D)	1305	1902	Scp 7/37
770	261	Alco(D)	1306	1902	Gone 1/30
771	262	Alco(D)	1307	1902	Scp 7/47
772	263	Alco(D)	1308	1902	Scp 1/37
773	264	Alco(D)	1309	1902	Scp 1/34
774	265	Alco(D)	1310	1902	Gone 1/30
775	266	Alco(D)	1311	1902	Scp 6/36
776	267	Alco(D)	1312	1902	Scp 1/31
777	268	Schn	5864	1901	Scp 6/42
778	269	Schn	5865	1901	Scp 11/39
779	270	Schn	5866	1901	Scp 11/39
780	271	Schn	5867	1901	Scp 12/36
781	272	Dksn	1251	1901	Scp 3/42
782	273	Dksn	1252	1901	Scp 11/48
783	274	Dksn	1253	1901	Scp 2/37
784	275	Dksn	1254	1901	Luria 3/50
785	276	Dksn	1255	1901	Scp 6/34

There were no major changes in the class E engines thus far. From 1905 to 1908 all driving wheels were either replaced or, more likely, larger tires applied accounting for the change from 56" to 57" and corresponding reduction in tractive effort noted with each class in parentheses.

From 1915 to 1919 all E-2b engines except 781 and 785 were modified slightly to conform with and reclassed E-2a.

The above notes on driver diameter and modification also apply to E-3 engines shown below. They were reclassed E-3a after 1912 to 1916 modifications.

Class E-3 2-8-0 (Double Cab)

Cylinders	Drivers	Boiler Pressure	Weight on Drivers	Tot. Eng. Weight	Tractive Effort
21x30	56 (57)	190	164000	187000	38848 (38154)

The class E-3 and E-3a engines underwent the most extensive evolution of any D&H power plus considerable renumbering and for clarity they must be listed twice. In this initial listing, which will be before any major change, I will use the number assigned in the 1905-1906 renumbering or the original number for those built in 1906. Under "History and Disposition" will be given the renumberings and rebuildings of the late 1920s. The second listing will be regrouped under the final number and in the various sub-classes that evolved. Some were not renumbered or rebuilt so have no history in the first listing. All final dispositions are shown in second listing only.

Number 1906	Orig.	Bldr. & No.		Date	History and disposition		
786	238	Alco(S)	25110	1902			
787	239	Alco(S)	25111	1902	rblt single cab and renumbered	929	8/26
788	240	Alco(S)	25112	1902			
789	241	Alco(S)	25113	1902			
790	242	Alco(S)	25114	1902	rblt single cab B-6 0-8-0	96	8/25
791	243	Alco(S)	25115	1902	renumbered	801	11/26
					boiler to	957	8/30
					received boiler of	887	8/30
792	244	Alco(S)	25116	1902	rblt single cab B-6 0-8-0	99	2/26
793	245	Alco(S)	25117	1902	rblt single cab B-6 0-8-0	92	8/24
794	246	Alco(S)	25118	1902	frame to	952	1/28
					boiler to	897	6/28
795	247	Alco(S)	25119	1902			
796	248	Alco(S)	25120	1902	frame to	948	9/27
					boiler to	950	11/27
797	249	Alco(S)	25121	1902			
798	250	Alco(S)	25122	1902	rblt single cab B-6 0-8-0	97	9/25
799	251	Alco(S)	25123	1902	rblt and renumbered	803	11/26
		(D&H	801	1919	new boiler after explosion)		
800	252	Alco(S)	25124	1902			
801	253	Alco(S)	25125	1902	renumbered	883	10/26
					frame to	953	7/28
					boiler to	954	9/28
802	254	Alco(S)	25126	1902			
803	255	Alco(S)	25127	1902	renumbered	885	11/26

Class E-3a 2-8-0 (Double Cab)

Cylinders	Drivers	Boiler Pressure	Weight on Drivers	Tot. Eng. Weight	Tractive Effort	Numbers
21x30	57	200	170000	193000	40160	(804-818)
21x30	57	190	170000	193000	38154	(819-858)
21x30	57	200	178000	201000	40160	(859-902)

Number 1906	Orig.	Bldr. & No.		Date	History and disposition		
804	183	Alco(S)	30715	1905	rblt		
805	184	Alco(S)	30716	1905	renumbered	900	10/26
806	185	Alco(S)	30717	1905	rblt single cab B-6 0-8-0	94	7/25
807	186	Alco(S)	30718	1905	renumbered	833	10/26
					frame to	940	1/27
					boiler to	941	1/27
808	187	Alco(S)	30719	1905	renumbered	857	11/26
809	188	Alco(S)	30720	1905	rblt single cab and renumbered	919	4/26
810	189	Alco(S)	30721	1905	rblt single cab and renumbered	927	7/26
811	190	Alco(S)	30722	1905	rblt single cab and renumbered	937	12/26
812	191	Alco(S)	30723	1905	renumbered	858	11/26
					frame to	922	8/27
					boiler to	949	9/27
813	192	Alco(S)	30724	1905	rblt· Unique and infamous in that engine was victim of two boiler explosions. First at Schenevus 3/22/08, second at Maryland 8/14/42. Stations only three miles apart!		
814	193	Alco(S)	30725	1905	rblt single cab		5/25
					renumbered	909	4/26
815	194	Alco(S)	30726	1905	rblt		
816	195	Alco(S)	30727	1905	renumbered	864	11/26
817	196	Alco(S)	30728	1905	rblt single cab		1/26
					renumbered	910	3/26
818	197	Alco(S)	30729	1905	renumbered	865	11/26
819	198	Alco(S)	28823	1904	rblt single cab and renumbered	911	4/26
820	199	Alco(S)	28824	1904	rblt single cab B-6 0-8-0	91	10/24
821	200	Alco(S)	28825	1904	rblt		
822	201	Alco(S)	28826	1904	renumbered	873	10/26
823	202	Alco(S)	28827	1904	renumbered	884	11/26
					frame to	956	2/30
					boiler to	100	4/30
824	203	Alco(S)	28828	1904	renumbered	880	11/26
825	204	Alco(S)	28829	1904	rblt single cab and renumbered	935	10/26
826	205	Alco(S)	28830	1904	rblt		
827	206	Alco(S)	28831	1904	renumbered	898	11/26
828	207	Alco(S)	28832	1904	renumbered	899	11/26
					frame to	955	8/29
					boiler to SPARE		
829	208	Alco(S)	28833	1904	rblt		
830	209	Alco(S)	28834	1904	frame to	947	7/27
					boiler to	922	8/27
831	210	Alco(S)	28835	1904			
832	211	Alco(S)	28836	1904			
833	212	Alco(S)	28837	1904	rblt single cab and renumbered	912	4/26
834	213	Alco(S)	28838	1904	rblt and renumbered	806	11/26
835	214	Alco(S)	28839	1904	rblt and renumbered	809	10/26
836	215	Alco(S)	28840	1904	rblt single cab and renumbered	933	10/26
837	216	Alco(S)	28841	1904	rblt and renumbered	810	10/26
838	217	Alco(S)	28842	1904	frame to	942	2/27
					boiler to	943	3/27
839	218	Alco(S)	28843	1904	rblt single cab and renumbered	939	12/26
840	219	Alco(S)	28844	1904	frame to	951	12/27
					boiler to	952	1/28
841	220	Alco(S)	28845	1904	rblt and renumbered	811	11/26
842	221	Alco(S)	28846	1904	frame to	944	4/27
					boiler to	943	5/27

Number 1906	Orig.	Bldr. & No.		Date	History and disposition		
843	222	Alco(D)	27515	1903	rblt single cab B-6 0-8-0	98	11/25
844	223	Alco(D)	27516	1903	rblt and renumbered	805	11/26
845	224	Alco(D)	27517	1903	rblt single cab and renumbered	932	9/26
846	225	Alco(D)	27518	1903			
847	226	Alco(D)	27519	1903	rblt and renumbered	807	11/26
848	227	Alco(D)	27520	1903	rblt and renumbered	808	11/26
849	228	Alco(D)	27521	1903			
850	229	Alco(D)	27522	1903	rblt and renumbered	812	12/26
851	230	Alco(D)	27523	1903	rblt single cab and renumbered	920	5/26
852	231	Alco(D)	27524	1903	frame to	949	9/27
					boiler to	948	9/27
853	232	Alco(D)	27525	1903	rblt and renumbered	814	10/26
854	233	Alco(D)	27526	1903			
855	234	Alco(D)	27527	1903	rblt single cab and renumbered	938	12/26
856	235	Alco(D)	27528	1903	rblt single cab and renumbered	931	9/26
857	236	Alco(D)	27529	1903	rblt single cab		9/25
					renumbered	913	3/26
858	237	Alco(D)	27530	1903	rblt single cab		12/25
					renumbered	914	4/26
859		Alco(D)	39792	1906	frame to	950	11/27
					boiler to	951	12/27
860		Alco(D)	39793	1906	rblt and renumbered	816	11/26
861		Alco(D)	39794	1906	rblt single cab		?/25
					frame to	943	3/27
					boiler to	844	4/27
862		Alco(D)	39795	1906	rblt and renumbered	817	12/26
863		Alco(D)	39796	1906	rblt and renumbered	818	12/26
864		Alco(D)	39797	1906	rblt single cab	905	7/25
					renumbered	905	4/26
865		Alco(D)	39798	1906	rblt single cab		3/25
					renumbered	906	3/26
866		Alco(D)	39799	1906	rblt and renumbered	819	10/26
867		Alco(D)	39800	1906	rblt single cab and renumbered	934	10/26
868		Alco(D)	39801	1906			
869		Alco(D)	39802	1906	frame to	954	9/28
					boiler to	955	8/29
870		Alco(D)	39803	1906	rblt and renumbered	820	11/26
871		Alco(D)	39804	1906	rblt single cab B-6 0-8-0	93	6/25
872		Alco(D)	39805	1906	rblt single cab and renumbered	928	8/26
873		Alco(D)	39806	1906	rblt single cab		8/25
					renumbered	907	4/26
874		Alco(D)	39807	1906	frame to	946	6/27
					boiler to	947	7/27
875		Alco(D)	39808	1906	rblt and renumbered	822	11/26
876		Alco(D)	39809	1906			
877		Alco(D)	39810	1906	rblt single cab B-6 0-8-0	95	6/25
878		Alco(D)	39811	1906	rblt and renumbered	823	12/26
879		Alco(S)	40542	1906			
880		Alco(S)	40543	1906	rblt single cab (first conversion)		12/24
					renumbered	915	4/26
881		Alco(S)	40544	1906	rblt and renumbered	824	11/26
882		Alco(S)	40545	1906	rblt and renumbered	825	10/26
883		Alco(S)	40546	1906	rblt single cab		12/25
					renumbered	908	5/26
884		Alco(S)	40547	1906	rblt single cab and renumbered	921	7/26
885		Alco(S)	40548	1906	rblt single cab and renumbered	925	5/26
886		Alco(S)	40549	1906	frame to	941	1/27
					boiler to	942	2/27
887		Alco(S)	40550	1906	frame to	100	4/30
					boiler to	2/801	8/30
888		Alco(S)	40551	1906	rblt and renumbered	827	12/26
889		Alco(S)	40552	1906	frame to	957	8/30
					boiler to SPARE		
890		Alco(S)	40553	1906	frame to	945	5/27
					boiler to	946	6/27
891		Alco(S)	40554	1906	rblt single cab and renumbered	930	8/26
892		Alco(S)	40555	1906	rblt single cab and renumbered	923	11/27
893		Alco(S)	40556	1906	rblt renumbered	828	12/26
894		Alco(S)	40557	1906	rblt single cab		?/25
895		Alco(S)	40558	1906			
896		Alco(S)	40559	1906	rblt single cab and renumbered	936	11/26
897		Alco(S)	40560	1906	boiler to	953	7/28
					rec'd boiler of	794	6/28
898		Alco(S)	40561	1906	rblt single cab		2/25
					renumbered	916	3/26
899		Alco(S)	04562	1906	rblt single cab		10/25
					renumbered	917	4/26
900		Alco(S)	40563	1906	rblt single cab		4/25
					renumbered	918	4/27
901		Alco(S)	40564	1906	rblt single cab		?/25
902		Alco(S)	40565	1906	rblt single cab and renumbered	926	7/26

This ends the first listing of 117 locomotives that formed the backbone of the freight service from the time of their construction right up until 1940. True, they shared the honor of the soon-to-come E-5, and later the E-5a and E-6 power, but were not displaced. They worked side by side with these other classes, giving a performance record second to none. The 900 series and rebuilt 800s were crew favorites up until the arrival of the J and K classes, shown later. A good number remained in service, although displaced to minor roles, right up until the last fire was dumped making D&H steam a memory.

The second listing will be under the final number, regrouped in order by subclass. Like many roads, the D&H had a method of subclassing its engines by tractive effort. This was not too evident in the folio books, but was lettered on the engines themselves and in conductors' and dispatchers' tonnage rating sheets.

As to the upgrading and rebuilding of the 1920s this is roughly what happened: The class evolved into three major groups and five minor groups. The major groups were:
1. Those that had little or nothing changed—in general, the high 700s and the high 800s.
2. Those rebuilt with larger cylinders, superheaters, Walschaert valve gear, etc., but *remaining double-cab engines*—in general, the low 800s.
3. Those having all the refinements of group 2, above, plus a little more, and also *converted to single-cab engines*—in general, the 900s.

Class E-3a 2-8-0 (Second Listing)

Sub-Class E-38:

Cylinders	Drivers	Boiler Pressure	Weight on Drivers	Tot. Eng. Weight	Tractive Effort
21x30	57	190	166650	191150	38150 (Double cab)

Numbers Last	1st	2nd	Builder & No.	Date	Disposition
786	238		Alco(S) 25110	1902	Scp 4/39
788	240		Alco(S) 25112	1902	Scp 5/37
795	247		Alco(S) 25119	1902	Scp 6/42
885	255	803	Alco(S) 25127	1902	Scp 1/39

Sub-Class E-40:

21½x30	57	190	166650	191150	40150 (Double Cab)
789	241		Alco(S) 25113	1902	Scp 4/39
797	249		Alco(S) 25121	1902	Scp 11/46
21x30	57	200	175650	201150	40150 (Double Cab)
800	252		Alco(S) 25124	1902	Scp 5/41
831	210		Alco(S) 28835	1904	Scp 1/47
832	211		Alco(S) 28836	1904	Scp 1/40
846	225		Alco(D) 27518	1903	Scp 4/47
849	228		Alco(D) 27521	1903	Scp 10/47
854	233		Alco(D) 27526	1903	Scp 6/42
857	187	808	Alco(S) 30719	1905	Scp 9/46
864	195	816	Alco(S) 30727	1905	Scp 4/36
865	197	818	Alco(S) 30729	1905	Luria 3/50
868			Alco(D) 39801	1906	Scp 8/46
873	201	822	Alco(S) 28826	1904	Scp 6/42
876			Alco(S) 39809	1906	Some parts used in 652, rest Scp 4/29
879			Alco(S) 40542	1906	Scp 3/46
880	203	824	Alco(S) 28828	1904	Gone 1/43
895			Alco(S) 40558	1906	Scp 7/42
898	206	827	Alco(S) 28831	1904	Luria 5/51
900	184	805	Alco(S) 30716	1905	Scp 1/39

(Only double cab 900 series after evolution)

Sub-Class E-42:

Cylinders	Drivers	Boiler Pressure	Weight on Drivers	Tot. Eng. Weight	Tractive Effort
21½x30	57	200	183150	207150	42100 (Double Cab)

Numbers Last	1st	2nd	Builder & No.	Date	Disposition
897	(w/794B)		Alco(S) 25118	1902	Scp 3/47
21x30	57	210	200500	224500	42100 (Single Cab)
894			Alco(S) 40557	1906	Scp 9/49

(Only single cab 800 series after evolution)

| 901 | | | Alco(S) 40564 | 1906 | Scp 9/46 |

Sub-Class E-45:

23x30	57	190	180650	204050	45750 (Double Cab)
802	254		Alco(S) 25126	1902	Scp 5/47

Sub-Class E-48:

Cylinders	Drivers	Boiler Pressure	Weight on Drivers	Tot. Eng. Weight	Tractive Effort
23x30	57	200	184650	209050	48200 (Double Cab)

Numbers Last	1st	2nd	Builder & No.	Date	Disposition
801	(w/887B)		Alco(S) 40550	1906	Scp 7/43
803	251	799	Alco(S) 25123	1902	Gone 1/51
804	183		Alco(S) 30715	1905	Scp 1/45
805	223	844	Alco(D) 27516	1903	to NYO&W 9/47
806	213	834	Alco(S) 28838	1904	Luria 5/51
807	226	847	Alco(D) 27519	1903	Scp 9/45
808	227	848	Alco(D) 27520	1903	Scp 2/47
809	214	835	Alco(S) 28839	1904	Scp 10/47
810	216	837	Alco(S) 28841	1904	Scp 9/47
811	220	841	Alco(S) 28845	1904	Luria 5/51
812	229	850	Alco(D) 27522	1903	Luria 5/51
813	192		Alco(S) 30724	1905	Scp 9/42
814	232	853	Alco(D) 27525	1903	Scp 5/47
815	194		Alco(S) 30726	1905	Scp 9/44
816	860		Alco(D) 39793	1906	Luria 2/53
817	862		Alco(D) 39795	1906	Scp 3/49
818	863		Alco(D) 39796	1906	Scp 4/49
819	866		Alco(D) 39799	1906	Luria 5/51
820	870		Alco(D) 39803	1906	Scp 3/50
821	200		Alco(S) 28825	1904	Scp 3/47
822	875		Alco(D) 39808	1906	Scp 4/42
823	878		Alco(D) 39811	1906	Scp 1/48
824	881		Alco(S) 40544	1906	Luria 3/50
825	882		Alco(S) 40545	1906	Luria 3/50
826	205		Alco(S) 28830	1904	Scp 4/49
827	888		Alco(S) 40551	1906	Scp 2/47
828	893		Alco(S) 40556	1906	Scp 12/48
829	208		Alco(S) 28833	1904	Scp 11/46

Sub-Class E-51:

Cylinders	Drivers	Boiler Pressure	Weight on Drivers	Tot. Eng. Weight	Tractive Effort
23x30	57	210	204600	228600	50600 (Single Cab)

Numbers Last	1st	2nd	Builder & No.		Date	Disposition
905	864		Alco(D)	39797	1906	Luria 2/53
906	865		Alco(D)	39798	1906	Luria 5/51
907	873		Alco(D)	39806	1906	to Spokane Int 907 3/43
908	883		Alco(S)	40546	1906	to Spokane Int 908 3/43
909	193	814	Alco(S)	30725	1905	Luria 5/52
910	196	817	Alco(S)	30728	1905	Scp 12/47
911	198	819	Alco(S)	28823	1904	Luria 2/53
912	212	833	Alco(S)	28837	1904	Luria 5/52
913	236	857	Alco(D)	27529	1903	Scp 9/40
914	237	858	Alco(D)	27530	1903	to Nap. Jct. 914 1/30 Luria 11/51 (Disp in Canada)
915	880		Alco(S)	40543	1906	Luria 5/51
916	898		Alco(S)	40561	1906	to Spokane Int 916 3/43
917	899		Alco(S)	40562	1906	Scp 9/40
918	900		Alco(S)	40563	1906	Scp 2/47
919	188	809	Alco(S)	30720	1905	Luria 3/50
920	230	851	Alco(D)	27523	1903	Luria 5/51
921	884		Alco(S)	40547	1906	Luria 5/51
922	2/858 F 830		B Alco(S)	28834	1904	Scp 6/45
923	892		Alco(S)	40555	1906	Luria 5/51
924	Vacant Number					
925	885		Alco(S)	40548	1906	Luria 3/50
926	902		Alco(S)	40565	1906	Luria 5/51
927	189	810	Alco(S)	30721	1905	Luria 5/51
928	872		Alco(D)	39805	1906	Luria 5/51
929	239	787	Alco(S)	25111	1902	Luria 5/51
930	891		Alco(S)	40554	1906	Luria 4/53
931	235	856	Alco(D)	27528	1903	Luria 5/51
932	224	845	Alco(D)	27517	1903	Scp 3/46
933	215	836	Alco(S)	28840	1904	Luria 10/52
934	867		Alco(D)	39800	1906	Luria 5/51
935	204	825	Alco(S)	28829	1904	Luria 5/51
936	896		Alco(S)	40559	1906	to Spokane Int 936 4/43
937	190	811	Alco(S)	30722	1905	Scp 8/46
938	234	855	Alco(D)	27527	1903	Scp 7/48
939	218	239	Alco(S)	28843	1904	Scp 7/49
940	2/833 F New		B Alco GO-	18488	1927	Luria 5/51
941	886 F 2/833		B Alco(S)	30718	1905	Luria 5/52
942	838 F 886		B Alco(S)	40549	1906	Luria 5/52
943	861 F 838		B Alco(S)	28842	1904	Scp 8/45
944	842 F 861		B Alco(D)	39794	1906	Luria 5/51
945	890 F 842		B Alco(S)	28846	1904	Scp 10/46
946	874 F 890		B Alco(S)	40553	1906	Luria 2/53
947	830 F 874		B Alco(D)	39807	1906	Scp 3/49
948	796 F 852		B Alco(D)	27524	1903	Luria 5/51
949	852 F 2/858		B Alco(S)	30723	1905	Luria 5/51
950	859 F 796		B Alco(S)	25120	1902	Luria 5/51
951	840 F 859		B Alco(D)	39792	1906	Scp 12/46
952	794 F 840		B Alco(S)	28844	1904	Scp 4/48
953	2/883 F 897		B Alco(S)	40560	1906	Scp 3/47
954	869 F 2/833		B Alco(S)	25125	1902	Luria 5/52
955	2/899 F 869		B Alco(D)	39802	1906	Scp 5/50
956	2/884 F New		B Alco(S) GO-20065-I		1930	Luria 5/51
957	889 F 2/801		B Alco(S)	25115	1902	Luria 8/53

This ends the second listing of 107 locomotives in their final form, and the disposition of each. The remaining 10 were noted in the first listing as converted to B-6 0-8-0. See that class for their disposition. In this second listing, in cases where different frames and boilers were used to make a single engine, I used only the last number assigned before the engines were disassembled. Those who wish the complete set of previous numbers may trace it back to the first listing.

There remains one more E-3a engine, the 999, not previously listed because it did not figure in any of the evolution. It was somewhat of a special service engine, built to be readily converted back and forth from soft coal to oil and used primarily on the Chateaugay Branch with quite a bit of service on the Champlain Division.

Cylinders	Drivers	Boiler Pressure	Weight on Drivers	Tot. Eng. Weight	Tractive Effort
23x30	57	175	185500	211000	42155
boiler press. raised to		200			48200

No.	Bldr.	Builder No.	Date	Disposition
999	Alco(S)	49655	1911	Scp 12/47

Class E-4 2-8-0 (Double Cab)

Cylinders	Drivers	Boiler Pressure	Weight on Drivers	Tot. Eng. Weight	Tractive Effort
22x28	50	180	157500	176000	42310
	(51)				(41469)

Last No.	Previous Nos. Orig.	2nd	etc.	Bldr.	No.	Date	History	
1000	348	341		Schn	5089	1899		
				rblt single cab B-5 0-8-0			81	2/24
1001	349	342		Schn	5090	1899		
				rblt		B-5 0-8-0	82	9/21
1002	350	343		Schn	5091	1899		
				rblt single cab B-5 0-8-0			83	4/23
1003	351	344		Schn	5092	1899		
				rblt single cab B-5 0-8-0			84	7/24
1004	352	345		Schn	5111	1899		
				rblt single cab B-5 0-8-0			85	12/24
1005	347	340	346	Schn	5088	1899		
				rblt single cab B-5 0-8-0			86	11/25
1006	347			Schn	5868	1901		
				rblt single cab B-5 0-8-0			87	4/23

Engine 1006 designated as class E-4a. See class B-5 for dispositions.

Class E-5 2-8-0 (Double Cab 1007-1024)
(Single Cab 1025-1096)

as built					
23x30	57	210	217450	246500	50585
as built					(1007-1024)
23x30	57	210	222000	250000	50585
as built					(1025-1054)
25x30	57	185	228500	254000	52650
as built					(1055-1066)
25x30	57	185	230500	256000	52650
as built					(1067-1081)
25x30	57	200	236650	261850	56900
					(1082-1096)

There were no great changes in this class but the following may be of interest. All engines with 23x30 cylinders were given new 24x30 cylinders during 1917-18 resulting in 55100 tractive effort. These engines were again re-cylindered 25x30 during the period 1921-30 and at that time the boiler pressure was reduced to 200 on all engines but 1050. Also in 1921, those engines with 185 boiler pressure were raised to 200. Aside from weight variations this somewhat standardized the class.

Cyl.	Drivers	Boiler Pressure	Weight on Drivers	Tot. Eng. Weight	Tractive Effort
25x30	57	200			56900 (except 1050)
25x30	57	210	231800	261900	59850 (1050)

No.	Builder & No.	Date	History and disposition
1007	Alco(S) 40566	1906	Scp 2/42
1008	Alco(S) 40567	1906	
		rblt single cab 3/26	Scp 12/47
1009	Alco(S) 40568	1906	
		rblt single cab B-7 0-8-0 151	4/26
1010	Alco(S) 40569	1906	
		rblt single cab 6/26	Luria 5/52
1011	Alco(S) 40570	1906	
		rblt single cab 12/25	Scp 6/45
1012	Alco(S) 40571	1906	
		rblt single cab 6/26	Scp 2/46
1013	Alco(S) 43270	1907	
		rblt single cab 1/27	Luria 5/51
1014	Alco(S) 43271	1907	Luria 3/50
1015	Alco(S) 43272	1907	
		rblt single cab B-7 0-8-0 155	6/27
1016	Alco(S) 43273	1907	
		rblt single cab 9/26	Scp 8/47
1017	Alco(S) 43274	1907	
		frame to B-7 0-8-0 153	2/27
		boiler to 1045 3/27	
1018	Alco(S) 43275	1907	Luria 3/50
1019	Alco(S) 43276	1907	
		frame to 1111	
		boiler to B-7 0-8-0 153	2/27
1020	Alco(S) 43277	1907	
		rblt single cab B-7 0-8-0 154	4/27
1021	Alco(S) 43278	1907	
		rblt single cab B-7 0-8-0 164	10/30
1022	Alco(S) 43279	1907	
		frame to B-7 0-8-0 156	10/27
		boiler to B-7 0-8-0 157	12/27
1023	Alco(S) 43280	1907	Scp 6/43
1024	Alco(S) 43281	1907	
		rblt single cab B-7 0-8-0 152	11/26
1025	Alco(S) 44710	1907	Luria 3/50
1026	Alco(S) 44711	1907	Scp 4/47
1027	Alco(S) 44712	1907	
		frame to B-7 0-8-0 159	3/28
		boiler to B-7 0-8-0 160	8/28
1028	Alco(S) 44713	1907	
		boiler to 1036 8/27	
		received boiler from 1048 7/27	Luria 5/51
1029	Alco(S) 44714	1908	Luria 5/52
1030	Alco(S) 44715	1908	Luria 8/53
1031	Alco(S) 44716	1908	Luria 5/51
1032	Alco(S) 44717	1908	Scp 5/47
1033	Alco(S) 44718	1908	
		frame to B-7 0-8-0 162	11/28
		boiler to B-7 0-8-0 163	3/29
1034	Alco(S) 44719	1908	Luria 5/51
1035	Alco(S) 44720	1908	Scp 5/47
1036	Alco(S) 44721	1908	
		boiler to 1039 9/27	
		received boiler from 1028 8/27	Luria 5/51
1037	Alco(S) 44722	1908	Luria 10/52
1038	Alco(S) 44723	1908	
		frame to B-7 0-8-0 157	12/27
		boiler to B-7 0-8-0 158	2/28
1039	Alco(S) 44724	1908	
		boiler to B-7 0-8-0 156 10/27	
		received boiler from 1036 9/27	Luria 5/51
1040	Alco(S) 44725	1908	
		frame to B-7 0-8-0 158	2/28
		boiler to B-7 0-8-0 159	3/28
1041	Alco(S) 44726	1908	Luria 8/53
1042	Alco(S) 44727	1908	Luria 5/52
1043	Alco(S) 44728	1908	
		frame to B-7 0-8-0 163	3/29
		boiler to SPARE	
1044	Alco(S) 44729	1908	
		frame to B-7 0-8-0 160	8/28
		boiler to B-7 0-8-0 161	10/28
1045	Alco(S) 44730	1908	
		boiler to 1048 5/27	
		received boiler from 1017 3/27	Luria 3/50
1046	Alco(S) 44731	1908	Scp 10/46
1047	Alco(S) 44732	1908	Scp 4/47
1048	Alco(S) 44733	1908	
		boiler to 1028 7/27	
		received boiler from 1045 5/27	Scp 7/49
1049	Alco(S) 44734	1908	Luria 5/51
1050	Alco(S) 44735	1908	Luria 5/52
1051	Alco(S) 44736	1908	
		frame to B-7 0-8-0 161	10/28
		boiler to B-7 0-8-0 162	11/28

Industrial Photo Service

No.	Bldr. & No.		Date	Disposition
1052	Alco(S)	44737	1908	Luria 5/51
1053	Alco(S)	44738	1908	Scp 12/46
1054	Alco(S)	44739	1908	Luria 3/50
1055	Alco(S)	51084	1912	Luria 5/52
1056	Alco(S)	51085	1912	Luria 8/51
1057	Alco(S)	51086	1912	See Note
1058	Alco(S)	51087	1912	Scp 9/46
1059	Alco(S)	51088	1912	Luria 5/53
1060	Alco(S)	51089	1912	Luria 5/51
1061	Alco(S)	51090	1912	Luria 5/51
1062	Alco(S)	51091	1912	Luria 5/51
1063	Alco(S)	51092	1912	Luria 5/51
1064	Alco(S)	51093	1912	Luria 3/50
1065	Alco(S)	51094	1912	Luria 8/51
1066	Alco(S)	51095	1912	Luria 6/51
1067	Alco(S)	53294	1913	Luria 8/51
1068	Alco(S)	53295	1913	Luria 5/51
1069	Alco(S)	53296	1913	Scp 6/47
1070	Alco(S)	53297	1913	Luria 5/52
1071	Alco(S)	53298	1913	Luria 5/52
1072	Alco(S)	53299	1913	Luria 5/51
1073	Alco(S)	53300	1913	Luria 5/51
1074	Alco(S)	53301	1913	Luria 5/51
1075	Alco(S)	53302	1913	Luria 8/51
1076	Alco(S)	53303	1913	Luria 8/51
1077	Alco(S)	53304	1913	Luria 5/51
1078	Alco(S)	53305	1913	Scp 3/45
1079	Alco(S)	53306	1913	Luria 5/52
1080	Alco(S)	53307	1913	Luria 3/50
1081	Alco(S)	53308	1913	Luria 8/51
1082	Alco(S)	54808	1914	Luria 5/51
1083	Alco(S)	54809	1914	Scp 10/47
1084	Alco(S)	54810	1914	Luria 5/51
1085	Alco(S)	54811	1914	Scp 12/48
1086	Alco(S)	54812	1914	Scp 3/46
1087	Alco(S)	54813	1914	Luria 8/51
1088	Alco(S)	54814	1914	Luria 8/53
1089	Alco(S)	54815	1914	See Note
1090	Alco(S)	54816	1914	Luria 5/52
1091	Alco(S)	54817	1914	Luria 4/53
1092	Alco(S)	54818	1914	Scp 7/45
1093	Alco(S)	54819	1914	Luria 8/51
1094	Alco(S)	54820	1914	Luria 5/51
1095	Alco(S)	54821	1914	Luria 5/52
1096	Alco(S)	54822	1914	Luria 5/51

For dispositions of B-7 conversions, see that class.

Engine 1057 destroyed on CNR in Canada 7/47 "for records." (Engine blew up on ash pit of Turcott Engine Terminal, Montreal, 2/23/47 while on lease to CNR).

Engine 1089 sold to Napierville Junction Ry. 9/42, to Luria 11/51 to be disposed of in Canada.

Class E-5a 2-8-0 (Single Cab)

These engines were custom made in Colonie Shops with new boilers purchased from Alco(S). The records indicate that the 1111 received the frame and chassis of the 1019 but if so there must have been considerable changes made in it. The others were all new construction. There were some minor differences in some and most had boiler pressure raised in 1931 increasing the tractive effort as shown in parentheses. Some had slight weight variation from that shown.

No.	Cylinders	Drivers	Boiler Pres.	Weight on Drivers	Tot. Eng. Weight	Tractive Effort
1112	24½x32	63	275	272000	301500	70950
1114	24x32	63	300	270600	300400	71000
the rest	25x32	63	250 (265)	270000	298000	68500 (72700 in 1931)

No.	Builder & Boiler No.		Date	Disposition
1111 (1019 F)	D&H-Alco(S)	GO-18489	1926	Luria 8/53
1112	D&H-Alco(S)	GO-23604-1	1927	Luria 8/53
1113	D&H-Alco(S)	GO-27822-1	1927	Luria 8/53
1114	D&H-Alco(S)	GO-27821	1927	Luria 8/53
1115	D&H-Alco(S)	GO-27822-2	1927	Luria 8/53
1116	D&H-Alco(S)	GO-27822-3	1927	Luria 8/53
1117	D&H-Alco(S)	GO- 1380-1	1929	Luria 8/53
1118	D&H-Alco(S)	GO- 4896	1929	Luria 5/52
1119	D&H-Alco(S)	GO-17856-1	1929	Luria 8/53
1120	D&H-Alco(S)	GO-17856-2	1929	Luria 8/53
1121	D&H-Alco(S)	GO-20522-1	1930	Luria 10/52
1122	D&H-Alco(S)	GO-22511-1	1930	Luria 2/53

Class E-6a 2-8-0 (Single Cab)

1200	27x32	63	200	267800	293600	63950
the rest (1201-1220)	27x32	63	210 (215) (225)	265500	296000	67150 (68800) (72000)

Engine 1200 had boiler pressure raised to 210 in 1918. The entire class was raised to 215 in 1926. Engine 1219 received a new all welded boiler in 1937, Alco(S) GO-54290, which carried 225. Boiler 59913 held in *Spare*.

No.	Bldr. & No.		Date	Disposition
1200	Alco(S)	55555	1916	Luria 2/53
1201	Alco(S)	59895	1918	Luria 8/53
1202	Alco(S)	59896	1918	Scp 6/51
1203	Alco(S)	59897	1918	Scp 4/52
1204	Alco(S)	59898	1918	Luria 5/52
1205	Alco(S)	59899	1918	Luria 4/53
1206	Alco(S)	59900	1918	Luria 5/52
1207	Alco(S)	59901	1918	Luria 4/53
1208	Alco(S)	59902	1918	Luria 5/52
1209	Alco(S)	59903	1918	Luria 2/53
1210	Alco(S)	59904	1918	Luria 8/53
1211	Alco(S)	59905	1918	Luria 6/52
1212	Alco(S)	59906	1918	Luria 2/53
1213	Alco(S)	59907	1918	Luria 4/53
1214	Alco(S)	59908	1918	Luria 2/53
1215	Alco(S)	59909	1918	Luria 8/53
1216	Alco(S)	59910	1918	Luria 4/53
1217	Alco(S)	59911	1918	Luria 5/52
1218	Alco(S)	59912	1918	Luria 2/53
1219	Alco(S)	59913	1918	Luria 4/53
1220	Alco(S)	59914	1918	Luria 5/52

Class E-7 2-8-0 (Single Cab) (1400-1402)
4-8-0 (Single Cab) (1403)

Cylinders	Drivers	Blr. Press.	Wt. on Drivers	Tot. Eng. Weight	Tractive Effort°
23½&41x30	57	350	298500	348000	71600 c.
					85800 s.
					19700 b.

Number and Name	Builder & No.	Date	Disposition
1400 Horatio Allen	Alco(S) 62765	1924	Scp 4/42

Cylinders	Drivers	Blr. Press.	Wt. on Drivers	Tot. Eng. Weight	Tractive Effort
22¼&38½x30	57	400	295000	336500	71600 c.
					85800 s.
					19700 b.

Number and Name	Builder & No.	Date	Disposition
1401 John B. Jarvis	Alco(S) 67059	1927	Scp 5/42

Cylinders	Drivers	Blr. Press.	Wt. on Drivers	Tot. Eng. Weight	Tractive Effort
20½&35x32	63	500	300000	356000	71600 c.
					85800 s.
					19700 b.

Number and Name	Builder & No.	Date	Disposition
1402 James Archbald	Alco(S) 68222	1930	Scp 6/42

Cylinders	Drivers	Blr. Press.	Wt. on Drivers	Tot. Eng. Weight	Tractive Effort
20&27½&33(2)x32	63	500	313000	382000	76200 t.e.
					91500 s.
					18000 b.

Number and Name	Builder & No.	Date	Disposition
1403 L. F. Loree	Alco(S) 68606	1933	Scp 8/42

° Under "tractive effort" letters indicate:
  c.—compound   b.—booster
  s.—simple   t.e.—triple expansion

These four engines were the apex of the D&H experimentals. High-pressure marine-type boilers with water-tube fireboxes and cross compound steam distribution. The 1403 went even a step further, being a four cylinder triple expansion engine. It is doubtful if any could be called successful. They bore out numerous of the designer's theories but were full of bugs and the maintenance was terrific. The 1930 depression years ended the costly project. None of the four piled up any impressive amount of mileage and it is reasonably safe to say that the 1403 never made a successful trip.

The shop cards on these engines show repairs and mileage as follows:

1400 last classified repairs out of Colonie 7/25/32 at 168905 total engine miles to that date. 2933 miles added in pencil, with no date, indicating total engine mileage 171838.
1401 last classified repairs out of Colonie 3/27/31 at 83021 total engine miles to that date.
1402 last classified repairs out of Colonie 4/15/33 at 54108 total engine miles to that date.
1403 never received classified repairs. Card lists 9845 miles on "running" repairs.

They were all withdrawn from service around 1934 or 1935 and never ran again. The 1400 and 1401 were shoved "out in the weeds" behind Oneonta roundhouse and the 1402 and 1403 were stored in the Oneonta house until shortly before they were scrapped.

Class G-1c 4-4-0 (Single Cab)

Cylinders	Drivers	Boiler Pressure	Weight on Drivers	Tot. Eng. Weight	Tractive Effort
17x24	62	130	59100	89600	12563

Last No.	Orig. No.	Bldr.	Bldr. No.	Date	Disposition
397	148	Baldwin	3754	1875	rblt to
		D&H(GI)	18	1892	Scp 1/39

Rebuilt to Inspection Engine "Saratoga" in 1904
(17x24   63   165   67600   100600   15700)

Class G-3 4-4-0 (Double Cab)

Cylinders	Drivers	Boiler Pressure	Weight on Drivers	Tot. Eng. Weight	Tractive Effort
18x24	69	165	79400	116900	16050

Last No.	Previous Nos. Orig 2nd etc.		Bldr.	Bldr. No.	Date	Disposition
421	118		Smith & Jackson		1871	rblt to
			D&H(GI)	42	1898	Scp 7/24
422	237		Danforth & Cook		1876	rblt to
			D&H(O)	43	1898	Scp 5/24
423	A&S 238	11 A&S 62	Danforth & Cook		1866	rblt to
			D&H(GI)	45	1898	Scp 9/26
424	A&S 239	12 A&S 63	Dickson	19	1867	rblt to
			D&H(GI)	49	1899	Scp 7/35
425	A&S 243	16 A&S 67	Dickson	29	1867	rblt to
			D&H(GI)	50	1899	Scp 11/26
426	A&S 247	20 A&S 71	Dickson	38	1867	rblt to
			D&H(GI)	46	1898	Scp 8/24

Class G-4b 4-4-0 (Single Cab)

Cylinders	Drivers	Boiler Pressure	Weight on Drivers	Tot. Eng. Weight	Tractive Effort
19x24	69	165	79000	112200	17870

Last No.	Previous Nos. Orig. 2nd etc.	Bldr.	Bldr. No.	Date	Disposition
374	202	Dickson	426	1883	rblt to
		D&H(GI)	29	1896	Gone 1/17
375	205	Dickson	429	1883	rblt to
		D&H(GI)	A375	1896	to QM&S 11/18
376	210	Dickson	482	1884	rblt to
		D&H(GI)	A376	1896	Gone 1/17
377	211	Dickson	483	1884	rblt to
		D&H(GI)	A377	1896	Gone 1/17
378	219	Dickson	570	1887	rblt to
		D&H(GI)	37	1897	Gone 1/17
379	R&S 31 126	Schn	435	1867	rblt to
		D&H(GI)	A379	1897	Gone 1/17
380	182	Dickson	344	1882	rblt to
		D&H(O)	A380	1896	Scp 8/24
381	183	Dickson	345	1882	rblt to
		D&H(O)	A381	1897	Scp 4/24
384	229	Dickson		1875	rblt to
		D&H(O)	27	1897	Gone 1/17
386	235	Dickson	694	1889	rblt to
		D&H(O)	38	1897	Gone 1/17
387	246	Dickson	37	1868	rblt to
		D&H(GI)	A387	1897	Gone 1/17

Two more groups of quite extensive D&H Shops rebuilds.

Class G-4c 4-4-0 (Single Cab)

Cylinders	Drivers	Boiler Pressure	Weight on Drivers	Tot. Eng. Weight	Tractive Effort
19x24	69	170	80600	117000	18410

Last No.	Previous Nos. Orig 2nd etc.	Bldr.	Bldr. No.	Date	Disposition
391	339	Dksn	927	1895	Scp 5/24
392	340	Dksn	928	1895	Gone 1/25
393	341	Dksn	929	1895	Gone 1/17

Class G-4d 4-4-0 (Single Cab)

Cylinders	Drivers	Boiler Pressure	Weight on Drivers	Tot. Eng. Weight	Tractive Effort
19x24	69	170	89700	128490	18410

Last No.	Previous Nos.	Bldr.	Bldr. No.	Date	Disposition
388	121	Schn	4292	1895	Scp 5/24
389	131	Schn	4293	1895	Scp 6/24
390	338	Schn	4294	1895	Scp 7/26

Class G-4e 4-4-0 (Double Cab)

Cylinders	Drivers	Boiler Pressure	Weight on Drivers	Tot. Eng. Weight	Tractive Effort
19x24	69	175	90300	129100	18950

Last No.	Previous Nos. Orig. 2nd etc.	Bldr.	Bldr. No.	Date	Disposition
432	117	Schn D&H(GI)	52	1899	rblt to Scp 8/30
433		D&H(O)	A433	1900	Scp 11/26
434		D&H(C)	A434	1900	Scp 12/26
435	R&S 35 130	Schn D&H(GI)	504 53	1868 1899	rblt to Scp 1/30

Two more Green Island rebuilds and one each of new construction at Oneonta and Carbondale.

Class G-4f 4-4-0 (Double Cab)

Cylinders	Drivers	Boiler Pressure	Weight on Drivers	Tot. Eng. Weight	Tractive Effort
19x24	69	175	86650	128250	18950

No.	Bldr.	Bldr. No.	Date	Disposition
427	D&H(GI)	55	1900	Scp 6/27
428	D&H(GI)	56	1900	Scp 9/30
436	D&H(GI)	58	1901	Scp 2/30
437	D&H(GI)	437	1901	Scp 12/28

Class G-4g 4-4-0 (Double Cab)

Cylinders	Drivers	Boiler Pressure	Weight on Drivers	Tot. Eng. Weight	Tractive Effort
19x24	69	200	90000	134000	21660

Last No.	Previous Nos. Orig. 2nd etc.	Bldr.	Bldr. No.	Date	Disposition
438		D&H(GI)	60	1901	Scp 9/35
439		D&H(GI)	61	1901	Scp 9/26
440		D&H(GI)	62	1901	Scp 9/35
441*		D&H(GI)	60½	1901	Scp 12/28

*Boiler for engine 441 built by Franklin Boiler Works.

Class G-5 4-4-0 (Double Cab)

Cylinders	Drivers	Boiler Pressure	Weight on Drivers	Tot. Eng. Weight	Tractive Effort
20x24	69	190	93500	145500	22800

No.	Bldr. & No.	Date	Disposition
442	Alco(S) 27545	1903	Scp 11/40
443	Alco(S) 27546	1903	Scp 5/34
444	Alco(S) 27547	1903	Scp 10/29
445	Alco(S) 27548	1903	Scp 11/48
446	Alco(S) 27549	1903	Luria 3/50
447	Alco(S) 27550	1903	Scp 12/46
448	Alco(S) 28847	1904	Scp 3/37
449	Alco(S) 28848	1904	Scp 10/48
450	Alco(S) 28849	1904	Scp 11/44
451	Alco(S) 28850	1904	Scp 9/46
452	Alco(S) 28851	1904	Scp 10/40
453	Alco(S) 28852	1904	Scp 3/44
454	Alco(S) 28853	1904	Scp 3/35
455	Alco(S) 28854	1904	Scp 2/35
456	Alco(S) 28855	1904	Scp 8/34
457	Alco(S) 28856	1904	Scp 12/40

Rebuilt Single Cab: 442 – 12/29; 445 – 2/27; 446 – 5/28; 447 – 12/29; 449 – 12/28; 450 – 5/28; 451 – 6/29; 457 – 7/27.

Engine 444 frame and chassis scrap – 10/29 – boiler to spare.

All single cab rebuilds modified as below. Engines 445, 446, 449, 457 modified before conversion, the rest at time of conversion.

Cylinders	Drivers	Boiler Pressure	Weight on Drivers	Tot. Eng. Weight	Tractive Effort
20½x24	69	200	100600	157700	25200

Class H 0-8-8-0

Cylinders	Drivers	Boiler Pressure	Weight on Drivers	Tot. Eng. Weight	Tractive Effort
26&41x28	51	220	445000	445000	108000 (1600-1605)
26&41x28	51	220	457000	457000	108000 (1606-1609)
26&40x28	51	220	463000	463000	106500 (1610-1612)

No.	Bldr. & No.	Date	Disposition
1600	Alco(S) 46916	1910	Luria 10/52
1601	Alco(S) 46917	1910	Luria 5/51
1602	Alco(S) 46918	1910	Scp 6/44
1603	Alco(S) 46919	1910	Scp 2/43
1604	Alco(S) 46920	1910	Luria 5/52
1605	Alco(S) 46921	1910	Luria 5/52
1606	Alco(S) 49651	1911	Scp 3/44
1607	Alco(S) 49652	1911	Luria 12/51
1608	Alco(S) 49653	1911	Luria 8/51
1609	Alco(S) 49654	1911	Scp 7/43
1610	Alco(S) 50925	1912	Luria 12/51
1611	Alco(S) 50926	1912	Luria 12/51
1612	Alco(S) 50927	1912	Luria 12/51

In June 1930 engine 1610 received new Alco(S) boiler GO-20802. Boiler 50925 held in "Spare." At that time, beginning with engine 1610, and extending through 1937 engines 1600, 1601, 1604, 1605, 1607, 1608, 1610, 1611, 1612 were rebuilt to the below specifications.

Cylinders	Drivers	Boiler Pressure	Weight on Drivers	Tot. Eng. Weight	Tractive Effort
26&40x30	57	245	469400	469400	109200

Class H-1 2-6-6-0

Cylinders	Drivers	Boiler Pressure	Weight on Drivers	Tot. Eng. Weight	Tractive Effort
20½&33x30	55	235	330300	350900	78850

No.				Bldr. & No.	
1500	P&WV	20	WSB	1000	Alco(S) 47113
	Date	History and disposition			
	1910	Purchased 10/17 Scp 12/35			
1501	P&WV	21	WSB	1001	Alco(S) 47114
	1910	Purchased 10/17 Scp 12/35			

Converted to 0-6-6-0 shortly after purchase. Used extensively on Oneonta hump, at least near the end of their service, and stored there a number of years before scrapping.

Class J 4-6-6-4

No.	Cyl.	Drivers	Blr. Press.	Weight on Drivers*	Tot. Eng. Weight	Tractive Effort
1500 -1519	20½x32 (4)	69	285	205500 201000 406500	597000	95800
1520 -1534	20½x32 (4)	69	285	206000 200500 406500	600000	95800
1535 -1538	20½x32 (4)	69	285	207200 202300 409500	604500	95800
1539	20½x32 (4)	69	285	207100 202400 409500	599500	95800

*Front drivers, rear drivers, total weight on all drivers.

No.	Builder & No.	Date	Disposition
1500	Alco(S) 69297	1940	Luria 8/53
1501	Alco(S) 69298	1940	Luria 4/53
1502	Alco(S) 69299	1940	Luria 10/52
1503	Alco(S) 69300	1940	Luria 8/53
1504	Alco(S) 69301	1940	Luria 10/52
1505	Alco(S) 69302	1940	Luria 8/53
1506	Alco(S) 69303	1940	Luria 10/52
1507	Alco(S) 69304	1940	Luria 8/53
1508	Alco(S) 69305	1940	Luria 4/53
1509	Alco(S) 69306	1940	Luria 2/53
1510	Alco(S) 69307	1940	Luria 10/52
1511	Alco(S) 69308	1940	Luria 8/53
1512	Alco(S) 69309	1940	Luria 8/53
1513	Alco(S) 69310	1940	Luria 2/53
1514	Alco(S) 69311	1940	Luria 10/52
1515	Alco(S) 69312	1940	Luria 4/53
1516	Alco(S) 69313	1940	Luria 2/53
1517	Alco(S) 69314	1940	Luria 10/52
1518	Alco(S) 69315	1940	Luria 8/53
1519	Alco(S) 69316	1940	Luria 4/53
1520	Alco(S) 70006	1942	Luria 4/53
1521	Alco(S) 70007	1942	Luria 2/53
1522	Alco(S) 70008	1942	Luria 4/53
1523	Alco(S) 70009	1942	Luria 4/53
1524	Alco(S) 70010	1942	Luria 8/53
1525	Alco(S) 70011	1942	Luria 8/53
1526	Alco(S) 70012	1942	Luria 4/53
1527	Alco(S) 70013	1942	Luria 4/53
1528	Alco(S) 70014	1942	Luria 8/53
1529	Alco(S) 70015	1942	Luria 10/52
1530	Alco(S) 70016	1942	Luria 8/53
1531	Alco(S) 70017	1942	Luria 8/53
1532	Alco(S) 70018	1942	Luria 8/53
1533	Alco(S) 70019	1942	Luria 10/52
1534	Alco(S) 70020	1942	Luria 8/53
1535	Alco(S) 74666	1946	Luria 4/53
1536	Alco(S) 74667	1946	Luria 2/53
1537	Alco(S) 74668	1946	Luria 10/52
1538	Alco(S) 74669	1946	Luria 8/53
1539	Alco(S) 74670	1946	Luria 8/53

Engine 1510 blew up at Warnerville (about 2 miles south of Cobleskill) 7/15/41 while pulling symbol freight MB-2. Was rebuilt at Alco(S) with new boiler GO-81822-1 and returned to service 12/23/41. Engine 1539 built with all-welded boiler.

Class K 4-8-4

Cylinders	Drivers	Boiler Pressure	Weight on Drivers	Tot. Eng. Weight	Tractive Effort
24½x32	75	285	270000	470000	63000

No.	Builder & No.	Date	Disposition
300	Alco(S) 69975	1943	Luria 8/53
301	Alco(S) 69976	1943	Luria 10/52
302	Alco(S) 69977	1943	Luria 8/53
303	Alco(S) 69978	1943	Luria 8/53
304	Alco(S) 69979	1943	Luria 10/52
305	Alco(S) 70133	1943	Luria 8/53
306	Alco(S) 70134	1943	Luria 8/53
307	Alco(S) 70135	1943	Luria 8/53
308	Alco(S) 70136	1943	Luria 8/53
309	Alco(S) 70137	1943	Luria 10/52
310	Alco(S) 70138	1943	Luria 10/52
311	Alco(S) 70139	1943	Luria 8/53
312	Alco(S) 70140	1943	Luria 8/53
313	Alco(S) 70141	1943	Luria 8/53
314	Alco(S) 70142	1943	Luria 10/52

Class P 4-6-2

Cylinders	Drivers	Boiler Pressure	Weight on Drivers	Tot. Eng. Weight	Tractive Effort
24x28	69	205	191000	293500	41350

No.	Builder & No.	Date	Disposition
600	Alco(S) 54798	1914	Luria 5/52
601	Alco(S) 54799	1914	Luria 2/53
602	Alco(S) 54800	1914	Luria 4/53
603	Alco(S) 54801	1914	Luria 10/52
604	Alco(S) 54802	1914	Luria 8/53
605	Alco(S) 54803	1914	Luria 8/53
606	Alco(S) 54804	1914	Luria 2/53
607	Alco(S) 54805	1914	Luria 5/52
608	Alco(S) 54806	1914	Luria 8/53
609	Alco(S) 54807	1914	Luria 2/53

Engine 606 received new boiler No. 803 in 11/34 which was built in Colonie Shop. Boiler 54804 held in *Spare*.

The majority of the class received several modifications and rebuildings to this end on engines shown.

No.	Cyl.	Drivers	Boiler Pressure	Weight on Drivers	Tot. Eng. Weight	Tractive Effort
608	24x28	69	225	192500	295000	45450
603-607		73	225	192500	295000	42750
609	24x28	73	225	192500	295000	42750

Class P-1 4-6-2

No.	Cyl.	Drivers	Boiler Pressure	Weight on Drivers	Tot. Eng. Weight	Tractive Effort
651	22x28	73	275	191000	300000	44000

No.	Builder and No.		Date	Disposition
651	D&H (Colonie)	802	1930	Luria 4/53
652	22x28	73	260	185300	283300	41600
652	D&H (Colonie)	801	1929	Luria 8/53

The records state that some parts of the 876 were used in the 652.

653	24x32	73	325	191000	296500	64000
						1931
	(22x32)	73	325	191000	296500	(59500)
						1934
	(22x32)	73	(275)	191000	296500	(50300)
						1943
653	D&H-Alco(S)		GO-22906	1931	Luria 5/51

This engine re-cylindered in 1934 and equipped with poppet valves giving but moderate success. Boiler maintenance was considerable at 325 so in 1943 it was reduced to 275.

Inspection Engine "Transit" 2-2-4T

Cyl.	Drivers	Boiler Pressure	Weight on Drivers	Tot. Eng. Weight	Tractive Effort
9x16	54	150	26000	63000	3120 (as built)
9x16	56	200	32300	73700	4000 (rblt 1922)

Last No.			Bldr. & No.	Date	Disposition
350	300	Transit	Schn 2806	1889	Scp 9/33

Inspection Engine "Saratoga" 4-4-0

17x24	63	165	67600	1006000	15700
397	148	Saratoga	D&H(GI) 18	1892	Scp 1/39

(This engine rebuilt from class G-1c, refer to that class)

The D&H at one time owned two Gas-Electric cars.

No.	Type	Bldr. & No.	Date	Disposition
1000	Wood	General Electric	1906	sold in 1908
2000	Steel	General Electric 3721	1911	

Further data and disposition unknown at this time.

The new era of the Diesel which took over consisted of 181 units which, along with those to come later, were all built by Alco-GE or the successor Alco Products. In 1967, however, six units were obtained from GE, the first non-Alco power on the road in over a half century.

Diesel Yard Switchers

Type	Horsepower	Weight	Tractive Effort
B-B	1000	230000	69000

No.	Bldr. No.	Date	Disposition
3000	72035	5/44	Scp 10/62
3001	72749	9/44	Sold to Long Island RR 8/63 #444
3002	73358	5/45	Sold to Buffalo Creek RR 12/55 #48
3003	73359	5/45	Sold to Long Island RR 8/63 #445
3004	74329	9/45	Sold to South Buffalo Ry 2/56 #100
3005	74330	9/45	Sold to Buffalo Creek RR 8/56 #50
3006	74334	10/45	Sold to Buffalo Creek RR 1/56 #49
3007	74335	10/45	Sold to South Buffalo Ry 2/56 #101
3008	74344	11/45	Scp 1/63
3009	74345	11/45	Sold to South Buffalo Ry 2/56 #102
3010	74346	11/45	Sold to South Buffalo Ry 2/56 #103
3011	74347	11/45	Sold to Port of Albany 6/63 #5
3012	75550	12/47	Sold to Erie 11/55 #530
3013	75551	12/47	Sold to Long Island RR 1/64 #443
3014	75552	12/47	Sold to Erie 11/55 #531
3015	75553	12/47	Sold to Albany Port Dist. 1/7/68 #6
3016	75554	1/48	Sold to Erie 11/55 #522
3017	75649	1/48	Sold to Erie 11/55 #533
3018	76197	11/48	Sold to Birmingham Rail & Locomotive Co. 12/63 #481
3019	76198	11/48	Sold to Alpha Cement Co. 8/64
3020	76199	11/48	Sold to Long Island RR 1/64 #440
3021	76200	11/48	Sold to Manufacturers Equip. Co. 2/66
3022	76201	11/48	Sold to Birmingham Rail & Locomotive Co. 12/63 #482
3023	76512	12/48	Sold to Relco Eq. Co. 2/69 #1008
3024	76513	12/48	Sold to New York Central 6/65
3025	76514	12/48	Sold to Long Island RR 6/64 #439
3026	76515	12/48	Sold to Green Mt. Ry. 9/69 #302
3027	76516	1/49	Sold to Long Island RR 6/64 #441
3028	77816	11/49	Sold to Ky. & Tenn. RR 9/65 #104
3029	77817	11/49	Scp 1/64
3030	77818	11/49	Sold to Long Island RR 6/64 #442
3031	77819	11/49	Sold to New York Central 6/65
3932	77820	11/49	Sold to New York Central 6/65
3033	78029	9/50	Sold to Altoona Fgt. Car Parts Inc. 6/68
3034	78030	9/50	Sold to Relco Equipment Co. 2/66
3035	78031	9/50	Sold to Relco Eq. Co. 1/69 #1007; Lipsheet Steel Co., Peoria
3036	78032	9/50	Sold to Green Mountain Ry. 3/66 #303
3037	78231	9/50	Sold to Relco Eq. Co. 2/69 #1009
3038	78232	9/50	Sold to Altoona Fgt. Car Parts Inc. 6/68
3039	78233	9/50	Sold to Relco Equipment Co. 2/66
3040	78234	9/50	Scrapped Colonie 11/67
3041	78235	9/50	Sold to Portland Term. Ry. 8/67 #1061
3042	78236	9/50	Sold to Mfg. Eq. Co., Cleveland 12/70; to Solva Co
3043	78237	9/50	Sold to Schiabo Hudson Corp. 3/65
3044	78238	9/50	Sold to Texas & Northern Ry.; Lone Star, Texas 11/66
3045	78239	10/50	Sold to Portland Term. Ry. 8/67 #1062
3046	78240	10/50	Sold to Texas & Northern Ry.; Lone Star, Texas 11/66
3047	78406	10/50	Sold to Portland Term. Ry. 8/67 #1063
3048	78407	10/50	Sold to Odgensburgh Bridge & Port Authority 5/66
3049	78408	10/50	Sold to Relco Equipment Co. 2/66
3050	78409	10/50	Sold to Green Mt. Ry. 9/69 #305

Units 3018 to 3050 equipped to operate in multiple with other units of this group.

Diesel Road Switchers (RS-3)**

	Type	Horsepower	Weight	Tractive Effort
(4000-4069)	B-B	1500	See Notes	60000
(4070-4129)	B-B	1600	248100	60000

No.	Bldr. No.	Date	Disposition	No.	Bldr. No.	Date	Disposition
4000	74991	11/46	Scp 4/61	4052	78887	6/51	to Alco 5/64
4001	74997	12/46	Scp 7/61	4053	78888	6/51	to Alco 2/64
4002	74998	12/46	Scp 4/61	4054	78889	6/51	to Alco 8/65
4003	75131	12/46	Scp 5/61	4055	79652	2/52	to G.E. 11/68
4004	75132	12/46	Scp 6/61	4056	79653	2/52	to Alco 6/65
4005	75137	2/47	to Prec. Engr. 1/72	4057	79654	2/52	to G.E. 3/67
4006	75141	3/47	retired 5/65	4058	79655	2/52	to G.E. 11/68
4007	75566	1/48	Scp 4/61	4059	79656	2/52	to Alco 5/65
4008	75567	1/48	Scp 3/61	4060	79657	2/52	to Alco 5/65
4009	75568	1/48	to G.E. 5/68	4061	79658	2/52	to Prec. Engr. 1/72
4010	75569	1/48	Scp 5/61	4062	79659	2/52	to G.E. 5/67
4011	75570	1/48	Scp 4/61	4063	79660	2/52	to Alco 3/65
4012	76234	12/48	to G.E. 3/71	4064	79661	2/52	to Prec. Engr. 1/72
4013	76235	12/48	to G.E. 5/67	4065	79662	2/52	to Alco 5/65
4014	77541	10/49	Scp 5/61	4066	79663	2/52	to G.E. 3/67
4015	77542	10/49	Scp 7/61	4067	79664	2/52	to Alco 6/65
4016	77567	10/49	Scp 6/61	4068	79665	3/52	to J. T. Nestle 3/78 LVRR; #7801
4017	77568	11/49	Scp 10/62				
4018	77569	11/49	Scp 10/62	4069	79666	3/52	to Alco 5/65
4019	77570	11/49	to Long Island 8/62	4070	80160	8/52	to Alco 3/65
4020	77571	11/49	to Long Island 8/62	4071	80161	8/52	to J. T. Nestle 3/78 LVRR; #7803
4021	77572	11/49	to Prec. Engr. 1/72				
4022	77573	11/49	to C & CV 10/71 #100	4072	80162	8/52	to Alco 3/65
4023	77574	11/49	to G.E. 3/71	4073	80163	8/52	to St. J & LC 5/72
4024	77575	11/49	Wrecked beyond repair on #9 at Ballston 8/67	4074	80164	8/52	to Alco 7/65
4025	77576	11/49	Wrecked beyond repair on #9 at Ballston 8/67	†4075	80165	8/52	Swapped to B & M, 4BM, #1508
4026	78051	5/50	to Alco 5/64	4076	80166	8/52	to G.E. 9/68
4027	78052	6/50	to Alco 10/62	4077	80167	8/52	to G.E. 10/68
4028	78053	6/50	to Alco 5/64	4078	80168	8/52	to Prec. Nat. 4/78
4029	78054	6/50	to Alco 5/64	4079	80169	8/52	to G.E. 12/68
4030	78055	6/50	to Alco 5/64	4080	80170	8/52	to G.E. 7/71
4031	78056	6/50	to Alco 5/64	4081	80171	8/52	to Prec. Nat. 1/72
4032	78057	6/50	to Alco 2/64	4082	80172	8/52	to Prec. Nat. 4/78 (former B & M #1536)
4033	78356	10/50	to Alco 2/64				
4034	78357	10/50	to Alco 2/64	4083	80173	8/52	to G.E. 3/67
4035	78358	10/50	to Alco 2/64	4084	80174	8/52	to Prec. Nat. 4/78
4036	78359	10/50	to Alco 2/63	4085	80175	8/52	D. Beers 4/81 Ont. Eastern
4037	78336	10/50	to Alco 1/63	4086	80176	8/52	to Alco 5/65
4038	78337	10/50	to Alco 2/63	4087	80177	8/52	to G.E. 10/67
4039	78338	10/50	to Alco 1/63	4088	80178	8/52	Naparano Iron & Met. 3/72 (DO #101)
4040	78339	10/50	to Alco 1/63				
4041	78340	10/50	to PRR 1/58	4089	80179	8/52	tc G.E. 5/67
4042	78341	10/50	to PRR 1/58	4090	80180	8/52	to G.E. 5/68
4043	78342	10/50	to Alco 1/58	4091	80181	8/52	to VTR 3/72
4044	78343	10/50	to PRR 1/58	4092	80182	8/52	to G.E. 4/68
4045	78344	10/50	to Alco 2/63	4093	80183	8/52	to G.E. 10/68
4046	78353	10/50	to PRR 1/58	4094	80184	8/52	to J. T. Nestle 3/78 (LVRR #7804)
4047	78354	10/50	to PRR 1/58				
4048	78355	10/50	to PRR 1/58	4095	80185	9/52	to G.E. 6/68
4049	78886	6/51	to Alco 5/64	4096	80186	9/52	to Naparano Iron & Met. 3/7
4050*	76098	3/50	to MLW 12/78	4097	80187	9/52	to United Ry. Sup. Co. 4/72
4051*	76099	2/50	to MLW 12/78	4098	80188	9/52	to VTR 3/72; back 12/75; Prec. Nat. 4/78
				†4099	80299	9/52	
				4100	80300	9/52	to G.E. 4/68
				4101	80301	9/52	to G.E. 5/68
				4102	80302	9/52	to G.E. 9/68
				†4103	80303	9/52	
				4104	80304	9/52	to G.E. 6/68
				4105	80305	9/52	to Alco 5/65
				4106	80306	9/52	Rebuild, MK to D & H 12/75 #502
				4107	80307	9/52	Rebuild, MK to D & H 1/76 #503
				4108	80308	9/52	to G.E. 10/67
				4109	80309	9/52	to Alco 8/65

*Units 4050 and 4051 are assigned to and lettered Napierville Jct. Ry. They were built in Alco's Montreal Works.
**4000-4025, 4050-51 were RS-2s; all the others were RS-3s.

No.	Bldr. No.	Date	Disposition	No.	Bldr. No.	Date	Disposition
4110	80310	9/52	Prec. Nat. 4/78	4120	80522	8/53	to United Ry. Supply Co. 4/72
4111	80311	9/52	to G.E. 12/68	4121	80523	8/53	to Prec. Nat. 4/78
4112	80312	9/52	Rebuild MK to D & H 2/76 #506	4122	80524	8/53	Rebuild MK to D & H 2/76 #505
4113	80313	9/52	Rebuild MK to D & H 1/76 #504	4123	80525	8/53	to Prec. Nat. 3/72
4114	80314	9/52	to G.E. 11/68	4124	80526	8/53	to Prec. Nat. 4/78
4115	80315	9/52	Rebuild MK to D & H 12/75 #501	4125	80527	8/53	to J. T. Nestle 3/78 (LVRR #7802)
†4116	80316	9/52		†4126	80528	8/53	
4117	80317	9/52	to United Ry. Supply Co. 4/72	4127	80529	8/53	to Prec. Nat. 4/78
†4118	80318	10/52		4128	80530	8/53	Rebuild MK D & H 3/78 #508
4119	80319	10/52	Rebuild MK to D & H 3/78 #507	4129	80531	8/53	to United Ry. Supply Co. 4/72

All units equipped to be operated in multiple with other 4000, 5000, 600 and 700 series units.

As built units 4000-4006 had maximum continuous rating of 740 amperes load and 34000 lbs. tractive effort at 13.5 MPH.

Units 4007-4025, 4050 and 4051 had maximum continuous rating of 900 amperes load and 42500 lbs. tractive effort at 11.0 MPH.

All other units had maximum continuous rating of 1085 amperes load and 52500 lbs. tractive effort at 9.0 MPH.

In the mid 1950s all 4000 units were modified to conform with the later rating and those 1500 HP units were raised to 1600 HP.

Units with dagger are still in service as of 3/82.

The weights and various special equipment built with or later applied are as follows:

Numbers	Weight	Special equipment if any
4000 4002	229200	No special equipment.
4001 4003 - 4006 4009 4012 4013 4021 - 4025 4036	253500	Originally the same as above but Colonie Shops applied 1600 gal. water tanks and Clarkson OK-4725 steam generators for passenger service. These boilers produced 2500 lbs. of steam per hour. Unit 4036 only had 800 gal. water tank.
4007 4008	245000	Came with Clarkson DRK-4530 steam generators for passenger service.
4014 - 4020	245000	Came with Clarkson OK-4616 steam generators for passenger service. These two groups had 800 gal. water tanks and both type boilers had a steam capacity of 1600 lbs. per hour.
4010 4011	247000	Equipped with automatic train control. (Used on "Sayre Job" out of Binghamton via Erie and LV.) Unit 4054 also equipped and as these units were scrapped the equipment transferred to others. Currently 4120, 4125, 4129.
4050 4051	246400	No special equipment. Built at Montreal Locomotive Works.

All units above this note had 800 gal. fuel tanks, those below 1600 gal.

4026 - 4035 4049 4052 4069	247600	Roller bearing trucks and dynamic braking.
4037 - 4048	245400	No special equipment.
4070 - 4129	248100	Roller bearing trucks and dynamic braking.

The 4012, originally only 1500 horsepower, was upgraded with all the other earlier units and is one of those equipped with steam boilers for passenger service.
(Jim Shaughnessy)

Diesel Road Switchers (RS-11)

	Type	Horsepower	Weight	Tractive Effort
5000-5002	B-B	1800	244800	72000
5003-5005	B-B	1800	245600	72000
5006-5011	B-B	1800	249400	72000
5012-5023	B-B	1800	259800	72000

No.	Bldr. No.	Date	No.	Bldr. No.	Date
5000	83504	3/60	5012	84394	1/63
5001	83505	3/60	5013	84395	1/63
5002	83506	3/60	5014	84396	1/63
5003	83534	3/60	5015	84397	1/63
5004	83535	3/60	5016	84398	1/63
5005	83536	3/60	5017	84399	1/63
5006	83685	4/61	5018	84400	1/63
5007	83686	5/61	5019	84401	1/63
5008	83687	5/61	5020	84402	2/63
5009	83688	5/61	5021	84403	2/63
5010	83689	5/61	5022	84404	2/63
5011	83690	5/61	5023	84405	2/63

All units still in service. All equipped with roller bearing trucks and dynamic braking. Maximum continuous rating 1085 amperes and 53000 pounds tractive effort at 10 MPH.

Units 5000-5005 built as completely new units, the rest are rebuilt units under the Alco unit improvement and replacement plan. Originally built for New York Central as 8009-8014 but never were delivered.

Diesel Road Freight (Century 628)

Numbers	Type	Horsepower	Weight	Tractive Effort
601-609	C-C	2750	392000	103000
610-618	C-C	2750	388800	103000

No.	Bldr. No.	Date	No.	Bldr. No.	Date
601	3373-1	4/64	610	3407-1	5/65
602	3373-2	3/64	611	3407-2	5/65
603	3373-3	3/64	612	3407-3	5/65
604	3373-4	3/64	613	3407-4	5/65
605	3373-5	4/64	614	3407-5	5/65
606	3373-6	4/64	615	3407-6	5/65
607	3373-7	5/64	616	3407-7	5/65
608	3373-8	5/64	617	3407-8	5/65
609	3373-9	5/64	618	3407-9	5/65

Sold to Diesel Supplies Int.; Vienna, VA. Leased to M de M 10/78.

Diesel Road Freight (GE U 30-C)

Numbers	Type	Horsepower	Weight	Tractive Effort
701-706	C-C	3000	390438	120000 (7 MPH)

No.	Bldr. & No.	Date	No.	Bldr. & No.	Date
701	36232	3/67	704	36235	3/67
702	36233	3/67	705	36236	3/67
703	36234	3/67	706	36237	3/67

Sold to Diesel Supplies Int.; Vienna, VA. Leased to M de M 10/78.

The backbone of D&H Dieselization was the Alco road switchers. Early models were RS-2s with the fuel tank under the cab and 1500 horsepower. The 1600-horsepower RS-3s came later and in time all the others were upgraded to that power. In all, 130 of these rather utilitarian but efficient units displaced the grand stable of steam locomotives on the D&H in 1953 and served until the advent of more powerful second generation Diesels in 1964. *(Jim Shaughnessy)*

Roster B
LOCOMOTIVES OF THE D&H CANAL CO.'s GRAVITY RAILROAD

No.	Type	Name	Builder	Date	Remarks
1	0-4-0	Major Sykes	W. Cook & Co.	1860	Collided with #11 in 1871 and wrecked Rebuilt 1872 to 0-6-0. Scp 1/1889
2	4-4-0	C. P. Wurts	W. Cook & Co.	1860	Sold to Dickson Loco. Wks. 1874
3	0-4-0	Honesdale	W. Cook & Co.	1861	Also named "Terrapin" and "Fine Plume" Retired 1899
4	0-6-0	Lackawanna	Dickson #1	1862	Scrapped 1899
5	4-4-0	Isaac N. Seymour	New Jersey Loco. & Mach. Co.	1866	Exploded 3-10-1879 at Carbondale & sold to Dickson Loco. Works

Roster C
LOCOMOTIVES OF THE ALBANY & SUSQUEHANNA RAILROAD
(at the time of the lease to the D&H C. Co. in 1870)
All six-ft. Gauge

No.	Name	Builder	Bldr. No.	Date	Type	Cyls.	Drivers	Wgt.
1.	E. C. Delevan	McQueen & Co.		9/1862	4-4-0	13x22	60″	46000
2.	E. R. Ford	Norris & Co.		9/1862	4-4-0	15x22	60″	56000
3.	E. P. Prentice	Norris & Co.			4-4-0	15x22	60″	56000
4.	J. H. Ramsey	Danforth Cook		8/17/64	4-4-0	16x24	60″	60000
5.	Chas. Courter	Danforth Cook		8/17/64	4-4-0	16x24	60″	60000
6.	John Cook	Danforth Cook		5/ 1/65	4-4-0	16x20	54″	60000
7.	J. Goodyear	Danforth Cook		5/ 1/65	4-4-0	16x20	54″	60000
8.	A. B. Watson	Danforth Cook		10/25/65	4-4-0	16x24	60″	60000
9.	Jacob Leonard	Danforth Cook		10/25/65	4-4-0	16x24	60″	60000
10.	Peter Cagger	Danforth Cook		5/24/66	4-4-0	16x24	60″	60000
11.	John Westover	Danforth Cook		5/24/66	4-4-0	16x24	60″	60000
12.	Alonzo Everts	Dickson	19	1866	4-4-0	16x24	61″	66000
13.	Lewis Northrup	Dickson	20	1866	4-4-0	16x24	61″	66000
14.	Daniel Drew	Dickson	27	1867	4-4-0	16x24	61″	66000
15.	R. H. Pruyn	Dickson	28	1867	4-4-0	16x24	61″	66000
16.	J. J. Austin	Dickson	29	1867	4-4-0	16x24	61″	66000
17.	Samuel North	Dickson	30	1868	4-4-0	16x24	61″	66000
18.	C. W. Wentz	Dickson	36	1868	4-4-0	16x24	61″	66000
19.	Ira E. Shuman	Dickson	37	1868	4-4-0	16x24	61″	66000
20.	Azro Chase	Dickson	38	1869	4-4-0	16x24	61″	66000
21.	David Wilbur	Dickson	39	1869	4-4-0	16x24	61″	69900
22.	J. W. Van Valkenburgh	Dickson	50	1/31/70	2-6-0	18x24	56″	79000
23.	R. C. Blackall	Dickson	51	3/18/70	2-6-0	18x24	56″	79000
24.	Albany	Dickson	54	7/ 6/70	2-6-0	18x24	56″	79000
25.	Binghamton	Dickson	55	7/31/70	2-6-0	18x24	56″	79000

Roster D
LOCOMOTIVES OF THE RENSSELAER & SARATOGA
and preceding lines
Compiled by R. E. Cooper

Saratoga & Schenectady 1831-62

Name	Type	Builder & No.		Date	Cyl.	Dr.	Weight	TF	History
Davy Crockett	4-2-0	R. Stephenson		1833	9x14	53	12000	1100	Scp prior 1854
Firefly	4-2-0	R. Stephenson		1834	9x14	54	12000	1100	Scp prior 1854
L. G. Cannon	4-4-0			1851	16x	66	48000		to R&S 1862
G. L. Schuyler	4-4-0			1851	15x	60	40000		to R&S 1862

Rensselaer & Saratoga 1832-71

Name	Type	Builder & No.		Date	Cyl.	Dr.	Weight	TF	History
Champlain	4-2-0	Baldwin	12	1835	10½x16	54	20000	2750	Scp prior 1857
Erie	4-2-0	Baldwin	13	1835	10½x16	54	20000	2750	Scp prior 1857
Stephen Warren	4-4-0			1849	14x	60	40000		Unknown
Ballston	4-4-0	Seth Wilmarth		1852	16x	60	44000		Blew up 1861
Troy	4-4-0	Seth Wilmarth		1852	15x	60	44000		Blew up 1865 (Whitehall)
Farewell	4-4-0	RK&G	391	1853	14x	60	44000		to D&H #106
J. Knickerbocher	4-4-0	Schn	139	1856	15x22	55	55600		21, 27 D&H #116
Fort Edward	4-4-0	Smith & Jackson		1857	16x22	56	58340		22 D&H #117
Whitehall	4-4-0	Schn	219	1860	16x22	61	65500		26 D&H #121
L. H. Tupper	4-4-0	Smith & Jackson		1863	16x22	60			23 D&H #118
Ira Brownell	4-4-0			1863	12x20	60	51900		24 D&H #119
S. M. Craver	4-2-4T	Danforth Cook		1863		62	56000		25 D&H #120

Albany & Northern 1851-56
Albany, Vermont & Canada 1856-59
Albany & Vermont 1859-60

No.	Name	Type	Builder & No.		Date	Cyl.	Dr.	Weight	TF	History
1	Bleecker	4-4-0	Schn	16	1852	14x22	66			Unknown
2	Ten Eyck	4-4-0	Schn	17	1852	14x22	66			Unknown
3	White	4-4-0	Schn	39	1853	16x22	72			to D&H #107
4			Schn	40	1853					Unknown
5	Cohoes	4-4-0	Schn	41	1853	16x22	72			Unknown

Saratoga & Washington 1834-55
Saratoga & Whitehall 1855-65
Rutland & Whitehall 1850-65

Name	Type	Builder & No.		Date	Cyl.	Dr.	Weight	TF	History
Bennington	4-4-0				12½x20	60	46000		Unknown
Montreal	4-4-0				12½x20	60	44000		Unknown
Ticonderoga	4-4-0				12½x20	60	48000		Unknown
New York	4-4-0				12½x20	60	44000		Unknown
Saratoga	4-4-0	RK&G	213	1850	16x18	60	46000		to D&H #103
Whitehall	4-4-0				15x20	66	46000		Unknown
Alfred Bishop	4-4-0	RK&G	325	1852	14x20	66	46000		to D&H #104
Plattsburgh (alias Quickstep)	4-4-0	RK&G	340	1852	15x20	52	50000		to D&H #105

Troy & Rutland and successors 1849-65
including Rutland & Washington

Name	Type	Builder & No.		Date	Cyl.	Dr.	Weight	TF	History
E. Kirby	4-4-0	Taunton	86	1851	14x20	60			Renamed Bates to D&H #108
Col. Williams	4-4-0	Taunton	87	1851	14x20	60			to D&H #110
Gen. Clark	4-4-0	Portland	16	1850	15x20	66			to D&H #109
Moses Strong	4-4-0	Taunton	91	1852	15x20	54			Unknown
John Bradley	4-4-0	Taunton	92	1852	14x20	66			Unknown
Horace Clark	4-4-0	Taunton	95	1852	14x20	66			to D&H #111
Gov. Chittenden	4-4-0	Taunton	100	1852	15x20	54			to D&H #112
Timothy F. Strong	4-4-0	Amoskeag	54	1852	16x24	60	46000		to D&H #113
Jacob B. Eastman	4-4-0	Taunton	143	1853	16x22	54			Unknown
Chamberlain	4-4-0	Taunton	162	1854	16x22	54			Renamed Merritt Clark to D&H #114

All engines with history listed as "Unknown" are believed to have become R&S engines but direct identity has been lost in the void. Of these 15 engines it is believed that three of them became D&H numbers 101, 102 and 115 but cannot be positively traced as to which ones they were originally. It is also believed that there was a #100 coming also from this group but it cannot be definitely ascertained.

The following is a listing of R&S engines renumbered into the D&H system and includes all the above engines still in existence at that time plus all new power added since the merging of the several lines into the R&S.

D&H	R&S	Name	Type	Builder & No.		Date	Cyl.	Dr.	Weight		History
100											Retired 1876
101		Dan'l Southwick	4-4-0	Springfield		1848	14½x20	60	52200	XS&W	Scp 1880-1
102		Van-Schoonhaven	4-4-0	rblt R&S Shops		1868				XS&W	Scp 1880-1
103		Mohawk	4-4-0	RK&G	213	1850	16x18	66	46000	XS&W	Saratoga Scp 1880-1
104		H. C. Hall	4-4-0	RK&G	325	1852	14x20	66		XS&W	Alf Bishop Scp 1880-1
105		Judge Weller	4-4-0	RK&G	340	1852	15x20	54		XS&W	Plattsburgh Scp 1880-1
106		Wm. B. Gage	4-4-0	RK&G	391	1853	14x20	66	66000	XR&S	Farewell Scp 1880-1
				rblt after boiler explosion 3/67							
107		Thomas White	4-4-0	Schn	39	1853	14x22	60		XA&N	White Scp 1880-1
108		F. E. Woodbridge	4-4-0	Taunton	86	1851	14x20	66		XR&W	E. Kirby Scp 1880-1
109		Gen. Clark	4-4-0	Portland	16	1850	15x20	66		XR&W	Scp 1887
110		J. M. Williams	4-4-0	Taunton	87	1851	14x20	60		XR&W	Col. Williams Scp 1880-1
111		Horace Clark	4-4-0	Taunton	95	1852	14x20	60		XR&W	Scp 1880-1
112		Jay Gould	4-4-0	Taunton	100	1852	14x20	60		XR&W	Chittenden Scp 1880-1
113		Z. V. K. Wilson	4-4-0	Amoskeag	54	1852	16x20	60		XR&W	T. F. Strong Scp 1880-1
114		Merritt Clark	4-4-0	Taunton	162	1854	16x22	54		XR&W	Sold Lebanon Springs RR 1878
115	20	J. M. Cook	4-4-0	Schn			16x22	50	61000		Renumbered R&S 21 Scp 1887
116	21	J. Knickerbocker	4-4-0	Schn	139	1856	15x20	55	55600		Renumbered R&S 27 Scp 1892
117	22	Fort Edward	4-4-0	Smith & Jackson		1857	16x22	56	58340		Gone 1895
118	23	L. H. Tupper	4-4-0	Smith & Jackson		1863	16x22	60	70500		Gone 1895
119	24	Ira Brownell	4-4-0	Smith & Jackson		1863	12x20	60	51900		Scp 1880-1
120	25	S. M. Craver	4-2-4T	Danforth Cook		1863		62	56000		Rebuilt to 4-4-0 Scp 1880-1
121	26	Whitehall	4-4-0	Schn	219	1860	16x22	61	65500		Scp 1895
122	27	John A. Griswold	4-4-0	Schn	404	1865	16x24	60	63000		Renumbered 414 Gone 1902
		(If R&S 21 was renumbered R&S 27 this engine should have been renumbered also but no record is evident)									
123	28	Geo. M. Tibbetts	4-4-0	Schn	407	1865	16x24	60	63000		Scp 1887
124	29	Warren	4-4-0	Taunton	388	1866	16x24	60	56300		Renumbered 415 Gone 1902
125	30	J. M. Marvin	4-4-0	Schn	432	1867	15x24	60	64500		Rebuilt to 2-8-0
		Double Cab Green Island 6/1899		Renumbered 285, 702 to QM&S 150 12/14/20							
126	31	I. V. Baker	4-4-0	Schn	435	1867	15x24	60	64500		Renumbered 379 Gone 1917
127	32	Le Grand B. Cannon	4-4-0	Schn	439	1867	16x24	60	70300		Scp 1887
128	33	H. C. Lockwood	4-4-0	Schn	441	1867	16x24	60	70300		Scp 1892
129	34	Gov. Page	4-4-0	Schn	499	1868	16x24	60	70300		Sold A&St.L No. 1
130	35	G. H. Cramer	4-4-0	Schn	504	1868	15x24	66	64950		Sold Pough&E No. 6
131	36	E. Thompson Gale	4-4-0	Schn	577	1869	16x24	60	65500		Scp 1894
132	37	Com. Vanderbilt	4-4-0	Schn	629	1870	16x24	66	68400		Renumbered 416 Gone 1902
133	38	H. S. Marcy	4-4-0	Schn	637	1870	16x24	56	67600		Renumbered 417 Gone 1900
134	39	G. G. Maxon	4-4-0	Schn	693	1871	16x24	66	66500		Renumbered 418 Gone 1902
135	40	Major Cornell	4-4-0	Schn	725	1871	16x24	56	65300		Renumbered 419 Gone 1902
136	41	Rutland	4-6-0	Schn	791	1872	18x24	54	96500		Renumbered 234 Gone 1903
137	42	Ticonderoga	4-6-0	Schn	792	1872	18x24	54	96500		Renumbered 235 Gone 1903
138	43	Montreal	4-4-0	Schn	796	1872	16x24	60	78700		Renumbered 420 Gone 1902

Roster E

LOCOMOTIVES OF THE ADIRONDACK RAILROAD

Adirondack Number	Name	Builder	Bldr. No.	Year	Type	Cyl.	Drivers	Wgt.	Remarks
1	Maj. Gen. Hancock	Danforth Cook		1864	4-4-0	14x22	60"		Renumbered No. 3 (Same Name)
2	Luzerne	Danforth Cook		1868	4-4-0	16x24	60"		
3	George Leavitt	Schenectady	636	1870	4-4-0	16x24	60"		Renumbered 6
4	Utowana	Schenectady	1922	1884	4-4-0	17x24	64"	86200	D&H 411
5	T. C. Durant	Schenectady	1949	1884	4-4-0	15x24	63"	78700	
6	C. E. Durkee	(Was No. 3 George Leavitt)							
1 (2nd)		Dickson	755	1890	2-6-0	18x24	56¾"	104000	D&H 115
7		Dickson	756	1890	2-6-0	18x24	56¾"	104000	D&H 116
128		Dickson	895	1893	2-6-0	18x24	62"	123000	D&H 68
2 (2nd)		Dickson	896	1893	2-6-0	18x24	62"	123000	D&H 69

Roster F

LOCOMOTIVES OF THE CROWN POINT IRON CO.'S RAILROAD

No.	Name	Builder & No.		Date	Type	Cyls.	Drivers	Gauge
1.	Gen. Hammond	Dickson	126	7/24/1873	2-6-0	11x16	37"	3'
2.	Col. Chitty	Dickson	127	10/23/1873	2-6-0	11x16	37"	3'
3.	Gen. Putnam	Dickson	128	10/23/1873	2-6-0	11x16	37"	3'
	(Later named Hammondville)							
4.	Thomas Dickson	Baldwin		1875	0-4-0T	15x22	45"	4'8½"
	(Used as switcher at Crown Point Furnace, adjacent to D&H line)							
5.	Crown Point	Dickson	425	5/25/1883	2-6-0	15x18	36½"	3'

Locomotives No. 3 and 5 each cost $8000.

Data from G. M. Best (see Bibliography) and Penfield Foundation of Ironville, New York.

Roster G

LOCOMOTIVES OF THE CHATEAUGAY ORE & IRON CO.'S THREE-FOOT GAUGE RAILROAD

No.	Name	Builder	No.	Date	Type	Cyls.	Drivers	Wgt. on Drivers	Total Wgt.	
1.	Gov. Robinson	Dickson	184	8/78	4-4-0	11x16	42"	25000	36000	(Dannemora No. 1)
2.	Louis D. Pilsbury	Dickson	226	12/78	2-6-0	11x16	36½"	32500	36800	(Dannemora No. 2)
	(Renamed A. L. Inman)									
3.	Goo Goo	Dickson	204	4/79	0-4-0	9x12	29"	19000	19000	(Dannemora No. 3)
4.	Thomas Dickson	Dickson	244	11/79	2-6-0	15x18	36½"	46000	53100	
5.	Lyon Mountain	Dickson	273	10/80	2-6-0	15x18	36½"	46000	53100	
6.	Plattsburgh	Dickson	337	5/82	2-6-0	15x18	36½"	47000	56000	
7.	Chateaugay									
8.	Dannemora	Dickson	411	2/83	2-6-0	15x18	36½"	47000	56000	
9.	Saranac	Dickson	496	7/84	2-6-0	15x18	36½"	47000	56000	
10.	Loon Lake	Dickson	592	6/87	4-4-0	15x20	44½"	38000	55000	
11.	St. Regis	Dickson	593	6/87	4-4-0	15x20	44½"	38000	55000	
12.	Mirror Lake	Dickson	718	7/89	4-4-0	15x20	45½"	41228	60680	
13.	Crown Point				2-6-0					(Ordered for the Crown Point Iron Co.)
14.	(Vacant)									
15.		Baldwin	19210	1899	2-6-0	16x20	44"		74200	(Outside frame)
16.		Baldwin	19211	1899	2-6-0	16x20	44"		74200	(Outside frame)

(No. 15 and 16 sold when line was standard gauged in 1903 to Tonopah Railroad as its No. 2 and No. 3; sold by TRR to Sumpter Valley Railroad as its No. 2 and No. 1.)

BIBLIOGRAPHY

Publications of Delaware & Hudson Co., Albany, New York

Carpenter, W. S. *The Summer Paradise in History.* 1914.

A Century of Progress, 1823-1923. J. B. Lyon Co., 1925.

The Chateaugay Ore & Iron Co. 1934.

Motive Power on the D&H. 1926.

Motive Power, Passenger, Freight and Work Equipment. 1936.

Passenger and Freight Stations on the Delaware & Hudson Railroad. 1928.

Passenger, Freight and Work Equipment. 1927.

Ross, Ogden J. *The Steamboats of Lake Champlain, 1809-1930.* 1930.

——. *The Steamboats of Lake George, 1817-1932.* 1932.

A Summer Paradise. D&H guidebooks issued yearly from 1910 to 1925.

Transportation. 1929.

Other Books

Best, Gerald M. *Locomotives of Dickson Manufacturing Co.* San Marino, California: Golden West Books, 1966.

Dana, H. T. *Stray Poems and Early History of the Albany & Susquehanna Railroad.* York, Pennsylvania, 1903.

Excursion Opening the New York & Canada Railroad. New York: Baker & Godwin, 1876.

Hill, Ralph Nading. *Sidewheeler Saga.* New York: Rinehart, 1953.

——. *The Story of the TICONDEROGA.* Shelburne, Vermont: Shelburne Museum, 1957.

Johnson, Dr. S. Paige. *Zebadiah Sartwell (The Miller of Whallonsburgh).* New York: Broadway Publishing Co. 1903.

Pennypacker, Bert. *Eastern Steam Pictorial.* Riverdale, New Jersey: P. & D. Carlton, 1966.

Ringwald, Donald C. *Hudson River Day Line.* Berkeley, California: Howell-North Books, 1965.

Shaughnessy, Jim. *The Rutland Road.* Berkeley, California: Howell-North Books, 1964.

Stevens, G. R. *Canadian National Railways,* Volume 2. Toronto: Clarke, Irwin & Co., Ltd., 1962.

Van de Water, Frederic C. *Lake Champlain and Lake George.* New York: Bobbs-Merrill Co., 1946.

Wakefield, Manville B. *Coal Boats to Tidewater.* South Fallsburg, New York: Steingart Associates, 1965.

Weiss, A. J. *History of the City of Troy.* Troy, New York: William H. Young, 1876.

Periodicals

Allen, Richard S. "Better Late Than Never." *Trains,* 19:3, January 1959, pages 40-49.

Barker, E. E. "The Story of Crown Point Iron." *Bulletin,* New-York Historical Society, October 1942, pages 419-437.

Best, G. M. "The Gravity Railroad of the Delaware & Hudson Canal Co." *Bulletin 82,* Railway & Locomotive Historical Society, April 1951, pages 7-24.

"Booster for Tender Trucks Developed on D&H." *Railway Age,* July 22, 1922, pages 145-147.

Coniff, W. T. "The Delaware & Hudson." *Trains,* 5:3, January 1945, pages 24-35.

D&H Bulletin, 1:1, April 1, 1921 to 18:6, June 1, 1938. The company magazine, a source of much material in this book.

"D&H High Pressure Locomotive." *Railway Age,* February 7, 1925, pages 353-356.

"The D&H Receives a Second High Pressure Locomotive." *Railway Age,* March 12, 1927, pages 893-895.

"The Delaware & Hudson." *The Courier Magazine,* 3:2, February 1954, page 7.

"Delaware & Hudson Chartered 100 Years." *Coal Age,* 23:18, May 1923, pages 703-708.

"Delaware & Hudson Christens New Locomotive." *Railway Age,* December 4, 1924, pages 1071-1072.

"Delaware & Hudson Develops Fourth High Pressure Locomotive." *Railway Age,* June 17, 1933, pages 854-857.

Edmonds, G. S. "Locomotive Valves and Valve Gears." *Railway Age.* July 1, 1933, pages 27-28.

"J. H. Nuelle Elected D&H's President." *Railway Age,* May 14, 1939, pages 843-844.

"L. F. Loree Resigns D&H Presidency." *Railway Age,* April 9, 1938, page 659.

"L. F. Loree Dies at Age of 82." *Railway Age,* September 1940.

McLaughlin, D. W. "Consolidations, Incorporated." *Trains,* 27:6, April 1967, pages 38-47.

Morgan, David P. "Loree's Locomotives," *Trains,* 12:9, July 1952, pages 20-25.

"Pacific Locomotive Equipped with Poppet Valves." *Railway Age,* March 29, 1930, pages 767-768.

Pennypacker, Bert. "117 Years of Delaware & Hudson Steam Power." *Railroad,* 74:4, June 1963, pages 14-23.

Rhode, William L. "Delaware & Hudson." *Railroad,* 42:3, April 1947, pages 6-30.

Taylor, B. W. "Locomotive with Roller Bearings on Side Rods." *Railway Age,* July 7, 1934, pages 4-6.

"Tender Booster Increases Tonnage 31%." *Railway Age,* June 16, 1923, pages 1433-36.

"Third High Pressure Locomotive on Delaware & Hudson," *Railway Age,* July 26, 1930, pages 143-147.

INDEX

*Denotes picture reference

— A —

A. Williams, 255, 259
Abercromby, General James, 232
Addison Junction (N.Y.), 139-140, 142, 147
Addison Railroad, 139-140
Adirondac(k) Co. (Iron Works, Iron & Steel Co., Estate & Railroad Co., Railway), 69, 96, 114-133, 185, 197, 201, 205, 226, 353, 363, 397*, 408*, 418*
Adirondack, 248*, 251, 253, 255
Adirondacks (Mountains), 69, 115, 117-118, 125, 130, 147, 160, 167*, 185, 197, 199, 202, 278, 280, 312*, 353, 355
Afton (N.Y.), 80
Albany (N.Y.), 60-66*-74*-75*-76*-77*-83, 89-92, 98, 101, 103, 106, 109, 112, 115, 137, 151-153, 171-173, 177-178, 190, 196-197, 205-208*-209*, 213, 231, 233, 254, 276, 279, 281, 283-284*-285*-286*, 290, 292, 309, 315, 339*, 349*, 357*, 359, 363-370, 378*, 432*
Albany & Hudson Railway, 207
Albany & Susquehanna Railroad, 60-63*-64*-65*, 68-112, 137, 171, 202, 204, 221, 225, 283, 307, 355, 438*, 440*
Albany & Vermont Railroad, 101, 103, 106
Albany Common Council, 71
Albany *Evening Journal*, 285*, 287
Albany Medical College, 117
Albany Northern Railroad, 98-101, 103, 106, 283, 303*
Albany Railway Co., 207, 209
Albany Southern Railway, 286*
Albany, Vermont & Canada Railroad, 101
Algonquin Indians, 231
Allegheny River, 9
Allen, Horatio, 32*, 34-35, 328*
Altamont (N.Y.), 86*, 290*
America, 249, 251, 253, 255
American Locomotive Co., 318
American standard locomotives, 317, 320, 324, 326*
American Railroad Journal, 91
American Railway Association, 293, 338
Ames, Oakes, 118
Amherst, Baron Jeffrey, 232
Amoskeag Corporation, 370
Anderson, Captain William, 245
Anthony's Nose Mountain (N.Y.), 268*
Archbald (Pa.), 39, 41-42, 56
Archbald, James, 37, 69
Arnold, General Benedict, 233
Arthur, Chester A., 151
Astor, Hotel, 302-303
Astor, John Jacob, 151
Ausable (Forks, River, Valley, Branch), 137-140, 147, 202
Austin, 25*
Averill Park (N.Y.), 210*, 211, 307

— B —

Bailey, J. M., 81
Bainbridge, (N.Y.), 71, 75, 80
Baker, Isaac V., 137, 142, 144, 153
Baldwin (N.Y.), 169, 173, 180*, 203, 254-255, 259, 263, 267
"Baldwin" coach, 151
Baldwin, M. W., 92
Ballard, C. W., 120
Ballston Lake, 190, 364
Ballston Spa (N.Y.), 65, 69, 90-95, 106, 186*, 198, 207, 211, 213, 216*-217*, 226, 228-229, 363, 430*
Bangor & Aroostook, 373
Banks, Colonel Robert L., 83
Balmoral Hotel, 177, 184
Baltimore & Ohio, 273, 307, 309, 318
Barnard, Judge, 79
Barndart, Henry, 205
Barnerville (N.Y.), 293, 311*
Battenkill Railroad, 219
Beatysburg (N.Y.), 3
Bécancourt (Que.), 223
Belden Hill, 61-62, 65, 75, 283, 297, 317, 358
Belmont (N.Y.), 158
Berkshire, 284*
Berkshires (mountains), 117
Bethlehem Steel Co., 324
Big Burnt Island (N.Y.), 259
Binder, Christopher, 101
Binghamton (N.Y.), 17, 60-65, 71, 74-75, 79-81, 169, 173, 205, 213, 275-278, 282-283, 291-292, 306, 317, 351, 353, 362, 363, 365, 367, 371, 438*
Binghamton *Courier*, 71
Black Mountain Point (N.Y.), 255, 258*
Black River valley (N.Y.), 116
Black Watch, the, 232
Blackall, R. C., 80-83
Blair's Bay (N.Y.), 268
Blue Mountain Lake, 69, 125, 133
Bluff Point (N.Y.), 185, 261*, 275, 283
Bluff Point Land Improvement Co., 351
Bolton Basin, 22*-25
Bolton, John, 4*-6
Bolton Landing (N.Y.), 203, 269
Bonaventure Station, 297
Boquet Valley, 135, 147, 157
Blue Coal Corporation, 363
Boreas River (N.Y.), 199, 354*-355
Boston, 249
Boston & Maine Railroad, 219, 221, 299, 313, 351, 370-371*, 373, 384
Boston, Hartford & Erie Railroad, 62
Boston, Hoosac Tunnel & Western Railroad, 129, 169
Bowen, J. Terrence, 359
"Bowood" estate, 283, 353
Bradley, Augustus, 188*
Bradley works (car builder), 118
Brady, Mathew B., 130
Brassey, Thomas, 116
Brill gasoline car, 301*
Brookside Park (N.Y.), 210
Broome County (N.Y.), 71, 79, 82

Brotherhoods, railroad, 173, 177*, 307, 315
Browne, Sheriff, 79-81
Buffalo Creek Railway, 360
Buffalo, Rochester & Pittsburgh, Railroad, 307, 309
Bulwagga Bay (N.Y.), 147
Burlington (Vt.), 137, 140, 144, 157, 233-237, 241, 247-255, 259-260*-261*, 263, 265, 267, 315
Burlington, 237-238*-239*-244*-249, 253
Burlington *Free Press*, 106
Burlington Junior Chamber of Commerce, 267
Burlington Yacht Club, 260*
Burton, Oscar, 247, 249
Bushnell, C. S., 117
Bushwick, (Pa.), 42, 193
Buskirk (N.Y.), 98
Butler, Cyrus, 255, 258
Butler's Lock, 15, 27*
Buttonwood (Pa.), 226, 287

— C —

Cadyville (N.Y.), 159*
Caldwell (N.Y.), 168*, 173, 177, 190, 235, 248, 250, 263
Cambreleng, C. C., 90
Cambridge (N.Y.), 191
Canaan (N.Y.), 211
Canada, 249, 253, 258*
Canada Atlantic Railway, 223
Canadian National Railway, 309
Canadian Pacific Railway, 226, 297, 357*, 394*, 412*
Canadian Railway War Board, 297
Cannon, Col. LeGrand B., 251, 253
Cantic (Que.), 416*
Capital City Aid Association, 173
Capitol District Transportation Co., 306*, 309
Capitol Railway, 207
Caprotte, Mr. 334
Carbondale (Pa.), 1, 6, 17, 20, 31, 34-39, 42*, 45-48*-49*-50*-51, 54-56, 60-63, 68-69, 89, 169, 173, 176*, 193, 204, 275-283, 291, 293, 300, 308, 315-320, 360, 367, 369
Carillon (N.Y.), 232
Carpenter's Point (N.Y.), 2
Carthage (N.Y.), 116
Casey, Hotel, 303, 305
Casey, Mary, 29
Castleton (Vt.), 101, 106, 221, 437*
Catalan forge, 158
Catholic Summer School of America, 214*
Catskill, 182*
Catskills (mountains), 225
Center Rutland (Vt.), 191*, 409*
Center Village (N.Y.), 359
Central Bridge (N.Y.), 73-74, 173, 382*
Central of New Jersey, 307
Central Vermont Railroad, 190, 191
Centralized Traffic Control, 313, 315, 356, 359, 364-367*
Century of Progress Exposition, 33, 343

Challenger locomotives, endpapers*, iv, 346*-348*-349*-359, 380*, 382*, 384*, 386*, 390*-391*-392*-393*, 406*, 411*, 414*, 416*, 424*-427*, 429*, 435*
Chamberlin, Lot, 249
Chambly, falls of, 231
Champlain, (originally *Oakes Ames*), 144
Champlain II, 252*, 253, 255
Champlain & St. Lawrence Railway, 247
Champlain Canal, 89, 91, 101, 105, 116-117, 235, 373*, 419*
Champlain College, 400*
Champlain Division, 294-295, 309, 315, 359
Champlain Ferry Co., 241
Champlain Hotel, 185, 189*-190, 213, 261*, 280*-281*, 283, 351
Champlain, Samuel de, 137, 214, 231, 233
Champlain Transportation Co., 109, 140, 144, 202, 230, 235*-241, 245-249, 253, 255, 259, 263, 265, 313, 315
Champlain Valley, 89, 109, 137, 142, 144, 185, 231, 245, 363
Chateaugay (N.Y.), 157
Chateaugay, 230*, 258*, 259-260*-261*, 263, 265
Chateaugay (& Lake Placid Railroad, 157-167, 190*, 201-202, 278, 281, 355
Chateaugay Ore & Iron Co., 158-159, 201-202, 313, 351
Chateaugay Ore Co., 157-161
Chateaugay Valley, 157
Chaudière Junction (Que.), 223
Chenango County (N.Y.), 71
Cheney, Albert N., 117
Cherry Valley (N.Y.), 75, 86, 204
Cherry Valley branch, 75, 360
Cherry Valley & Mohawk Railroad, 75
Chesapeake & Ohio, 370
Chicago, Rock Island & Pacific, 273
Churchill, Winston, 353
Citizens Line steamers, 247
Clement, Percival W., 191
Clermont, 233
Cleveland (Ohio), 273
Cliff Haven (N.Y.), 214
Cornell, Ezra, 17
Cornell Steamboat Co., 195
Cornell, Thomas, 67
Clinton County (N.Y.), 137, 142
Clinton, De Witt, 5, 89
City of Cleveland, 255
Clinton Prison (Dannemora, New York), 157
Coal & Iron Exchange, 283
Cobleskill (N.Y.), 71, 74, 86, 204, 291*, 293, 311*, 362, 395*
Cohoes (N.Y.), 98, 207, 306-307, 355, 392*
Colchester Lighthouse, 270-271*
Colonie (N.Y., shops, yards), 33, 203*, 279, 281, 291, 299-300, 309-310*-311, 317-322*-325*-326*-329*, 334-335*-336-339*, 342*-345, 355, 359, 367*-369, 375*-376*, 379*, 404*, 434*, 441
Columbia, 34
Comstock (N.Y.), 350*, 387*
Comstock, Peter, 239-245, 240

472

Congress, 34
Consolidation locomotives, 317-319*-321*-322*-323*-326*-327* 328*, 331, 334, 343-344*-345, 353, 356, 383*, 417*, 422*-423*, 432*
Cook, W., & Co., 40-41, 59
Cooks Landing (N.Y.), 259
Cooperstown (N.Y., Junction), 200*, 292*, 298, 341
Cooperstown & Charlotte Valley Railroad, 200*, 202, 210
Corbin, Horace W., 265, 315
Corinth (N.Y.), 120-121, 127, 397*
Corn Exchange (Montreal), 153
Cotter, Thomas B., 203
Courter, Charles, 79-80, 82
Coykendall, S. D., 195
Cramer, George W., 251
Crane, H. C., 119, 121
Craven, S. M., 104*
Crédit Mobilier, 118-119. 253
Crescent (N.Y.), 384*-385*
Crown Point (N.Y.), 136, 139*-140, 143, 178, 430*
Crown Point House, 178*
Crown Point Iron Co., 136, 138*-141, 163
Crystal Lake Park (N.Y.), 210
Cuddebackville (N.Y.), 11
Cullen, John J., 359

— D —
Dabeg feed water pump and heater, 320-321*-322*, 332*
Dabeg poppet valves, 334-337*-339*,343
Daly, A. W., 45
Danforth & Cook locomotives, 104*
Dannemora (N.Y.), 157-158, 202
Dante (N.Y.), 386*
Davis, Capt. P. T., 241, 243
Davis, George T. M., 118
Davison, Gideon M., 105
Davison, John M., 106
DAVY CROCKETT, 90*-91
De Forest, Ron, 377*
Defense Plant Corporation, 355
Delanson (N.Y.), 84*, 175, 293, 371
DELAWARE, 34-35
Delaware & Hudson Building, Albany, 283, 285*-286*-287, 335*, 364, 366-367*
Delaware & Hudson Canal, 1-8*-14*-18*-21*-23*-25*-26*-27*-28*-30*-31, 59, 69, 171, 191-192*-193*-195
Delaware & Hudson Canal Co.: founded, 1; leases A&S, 83; leases R&S, 112; buys Adirondack, 129; decides to build NY&C, 142; opens NY&C, 153; leases Chateaugay, 161; abandons canal, 191, ff; changes name, 195; acquires steamboat companies, 253; changes name to D&H Co., 195
Delaware & Hudson Co.: formed, 195; controls Chateaugay R.R., 201; merges with Adirondack, 201; buys Cooperstown & Charlotte Valley R.R., 202; controls Champlain Transportation Co., 202; buys QM&S, 223; buys NJ, 226; general office building in

Albany, 283; sells hotels and steamboat companies, 351; merges with R&S and A&S, 356; last of steam, 359; reincorporates in Delaware, 364
Delaware & Hudson Railroad Co., 313
Delaware House, 10*
Delaware, Lackawanna & Western Railroad, 45, 169, 313, 360, 438*
Delaware River (Valley), 1-6, 8-9*-10*-12*-15*, 22*, 23*, 26*, 27*, 303
Delaware River Aqueduct, 8-9*-10*-12*-13
Delevan, Edward C., 71
Delmar (N.Y.), 213*
Delson (Que.), 297, 377*, 385*
Denver & Rio Grande Western, 352, 370, 372
Dickens, Charles, 239-241, 265
Dickson (Pa.), 102*
Dickson locomotives, 67, 86, 136*, 158*-159*, 167*, 170*, 173-174*-175*-176*, 180*, 186*, 188*, 192*, 194*, 201, 290*, 317
Dickson Machine Co., 41, 43
Dickson Manufacturing Co., 173
Dickson, Thomas, 47, 60-61*-69, 135, 142, 151, 153, 157, 158, 171-173, 177, 192, 363
Diven, Gen. Andrew S., 65
Doolin, Mike, 135
Douglas, Dr. J. H., 177
Drew, Daniel, 74, 76, 117, 120, 247, 251
Drexel, Joseph, 177
Dumaine, Frederic C., Jr., 369*-373
Durant, Dr. Thomas C., 117*-119, 123, 125, 129, 185, 353, 355
Durant, William West, 129, 185
Dynamometer car, 277*, 326*-327, 331-332*, 343

— E —
Eagle Bridge (N.Y.), 98, 101, 103, 169, 191
Eagle Hotel, 217*
East Richelieu Valley Railway, 223
East Worcester (N.Y.), 74, 433*, 442
Eddy's Factory (N.Y.), 3
Eddyville (N.Y.), 3-5, 17, 28
Edmonds, George, 328
Eldridge's North River Hotel, 127
Elija, Lewis, 115
Elizabeth, Queen, 384
Elizabethtown *Post*, 135
Ellenville (N.Y.), 3-4, 16, 20*, 195
Ellide, 180*
Emmons (N.Y.), 298
Empire State Express, 201
Engineers, Corps of, U. S. Army, 273
Erie Canal, 2-3, 89, 426*
Erie-Lackawanna Railroad, 360, 364, 370, 438*
Erie Railroad, 10*, 17, 22*, 25-27*, 60-62, 68-71, 75-82, 103, 117, 171, 195, 205, 288*-289*, 292, 305, 318, 360, 361, 373
"Erie War," 80-81*-83
Esperance (N.Y.), 416*
Essex (N.Y.), 135, 137

Essex County (N.Y.), 129, 135, 147, 154
Excelsior, 182*

— F —
Fair Haven (Vt.), 101, 222*
Farview (Pa.), 36, 41-42, 45-46*, 52*, 54*-55
Ferguson, Bob, 135
Ferris, Orange, 117
"Fifth Trunk Line," 307-309, 313
FIRE FLY, 90-91
First National Bank of Glens Falls, 215*
Fisher, Capt. Alanson, 267
Fisher Steamboat Co., 267
Fisk, Jim, 63, 76-83
Fitchburg Railroad, 118
Fletcher, Andrew, 259
Fletcher engines, 259, 263, 270*
Floral Festival, 188*
Florence (Italy), 334
Ford, Henry, 229
Forest City (Pa.), 289*, 361, 411*
Forsythe, James, 137
Fort Ann (N.Y.), 105
Fort Edward (N.Y.), 105-109, 168, 173, 219, 226, 302, 309, 421*
Fort Ethan Allen (Vt.), 265
Fort Orange (N.Y.), 231
Fort St. Frederick, 147
Fort William Henry Hotel, 178*, 190, 250*-251, 269*, 280*-281*, 283, 351
Fortierville (Que.), 275
Foster, Rastrick & Co. 34-35
Fouquet House, 151-152*-155*
Four Brothers Islands, 157
Francis Saltus, 137, 240*-249
Franklin, 236*, 239, 247
Fredonia (N.Y.), 17
Fulton, Robert, 233, 247

— G —
Gale, E. Thompson, 106
Ganouskie, 250*, 253, 255, 259
Gansevoort (N.Y.), 105
General Electric, 207, 212*, 368*, 440*, 442*
General Motors, 371*
GENERAL PUTNAM, 136*, 138, 141*-143*
GEORGE H. CRAMER, 66*, 112*, 134*, 145*
George VI, King, 384
German State Railways, 334
Gettysburg, battle of, 118
Gilbert, Veazie & Eaton, 92
Glen Alden Corporation, 363
Glen, The (N.Y.), 123, 126*-127, 132*-133*
Glen Lake (N.Y.), 179*
Glenburnie (N.Y.), 268
Glenn Engine Terminal, 394*
Glens Falls (N.Y.), 107, 117, 130, 145, 173, 178-179, 203, 215*, 219, 229, 255, 295*, 302, 309
Glens Falls Rail Road, 109, 173, 219, 360
Glenville (N.Y.), 91, 377*
Godefroid Lock, 15*
Gore Mountain, 121, 197, 314
Goshen (N.Y.), 3, 17
Gould, Jay, 63, 76-79, 83, 103*, 360
Grand Hotel, 185
Grand Trunk Railway, 151, 153, 169, 223, 226, 249, 297

Grand Union Hotel, 185-186*-187
Grant, Ulysses S., 151, 177, 181-183*
Gravity railroad, 5-6, 13-14, 17, 20, 30*-36*-38*-39*-40*-41*-42*-43*-44*-46*-48*-49*-50*-51*-52*-53*-54*-55*-56*-57*-58*-60, 69, 192*-195
Great Eastern Railway, 221
Green Island (N.Y.), 67*, 92-93, 102, 104*, 109, 112, 205, 207, 210, 222, 279, 281, 300, 317, 405*, 428*, 437*
Green Island (on Lake George), 266*
Green Ridge (Pa.), 69
Green Mountains, 157
Greenfield (N.Y.), 118
Greenwich (N.Y.), 219, 301*, 309
Greenwich & Johnsonville Railroad, 219, 221*, 275, 301*, 313
Grey, Zane, 10

— H —
Hadley (N.Y.), 118, 120, 130*, 354*
Half Moon, 285*, 287
Hammond, C. D., 196*-199
Hammondville (N.Y.), 136*, 139, 142
Hampson, John, 91
Harpursville (N.Y.), 75, 80-82
Harriman, E. H., 228, 273
Harris, John, 25
Harrison, Fairfax, 293
Hart Bay (N.Y.), 262*
Hart, Richard P., 91-92*, 95
Hart, William T., 103
Hawk's Nest cliffs, 15*, 27*
Hawley (Pa.), 10, 13, 17, 22, 59, 62
Henderson, David, 115-116*, 125, 355
Henry, Edward L., 17*
Hensberger, Captain, 193, 195
Hepburn Act of 1906, 281
Herrick, J. R., 79
"Hiawatha" locomotives, 328
Hickson, Captain, 5
Higby Gulf (Willsboro Bay), 149*
High Falls (N.Y.), 8, 11, 13
Highland, 182*
Hill, Ralph Nading, 267
Hiltz, John P. Jr., 364, 369
Hobart, Garret A., 190
Hoffman, Governor John T., 82-83
Hone, Philip, 3*-5, 94-95
Honesdale (Pa.), 5-7*, 13, 17-19*-20, 24, 28, 30*-31, 34-40*-42, 45, 48, 52*-53*, 60, 62, 89, 171, 192-194*, 291*, 303, 305, 313
Hoosac Tunnel, 169
Hoosac Tunnel & Western Railroad, 203
HORATIO ALLEN, 328-329*, 331, 332*, 334, 345
Horicon I, 254*, 255, 259, 263, 267
Horicon II, 230*, 257*, 263, 265, 267*, 283
Howard Coal & Iron Co., 60
Howe, Jack, 188*
Howe's Cave (N.Y.), 292, 311, 352*
Hudson (N.Y.), 286
Hudson (Pa.), 287

473

HUDSON, 34-35
Hudson Coal Co., 281, 295*, 303, 313, 363
Hudson Falls (N.Y.), 105, 109, 219
Hudson, Henry, 285, 287
Hudson River Day Line, 335*
Hudson River Night Line, 177
Hudson River Railroad, 69, 125
Hunter, Timothy, 136
Hudson Valley Railway, 184, 198*, 207, 209*, 213, 215*-216*-217*-219*, 226-227, 229*, 302*-303, 309
Huron Indians, 231
Hydorn, George, 199
Hyndsville (N.Y.), 204*

— I —
I. V. BAKER, 153-154*
Iberville (Que.), 223
Ile-aux-Noix (Que.), 234
Industrial Brownhoist, 382*
Interstate Commerce Commission, 229, 281, 293, 307, 309, 313, 315, 319, 344-345, 351, 355, 370
Iroquois Indians, 231
Inches, Martin B., 71

— J —
Jackson, William Henry, 130
JAMES ARCHBALD, 332*-333*, 334, 343, 345
James Caldwell, 234-235, 245, 247, 259
Jefferson Junction, 65
Jefferson Railroad, 60-63, 65, 68, 205, 360, 361*
Jermyn (Pa.), 45, 275
Jervis, John B., 3, 31-33, 36-37, 90, 105
Jessup's Landing (N.Y.), 118, 123, 127
Jogues, Father Isaac, 231-232
JOHN B. JERVIS, 330*, 334, 345
John Jay, 25
Johnson, Sir William, 90
Johnsonville (N.Y.), 98
Jones Car Co., 206*, 216*

— K —
Kansas City Southern Railroad, 299, 313
Kaydeross Creek, 363, 430*
Kayderosseras Creek, 90-91
Keen's Pond (Pa.), 31
Keesville (N.Y.), 130, 162
Keesville, Au Sable Chasm & Lake Champlain Railroad, 162-163, 203*
Kennedy, James C., 119
Kenwood Junction (N.Y.), 171
Kerhonkson (N.Y.), 13
Keyes, Mr., 71
King, "Admiral" Gideon, 233-234
Kingston (N.Y.), 1, 3, 5, 13, 67
Kingston (Pa.), 225
Knob Mountain (N.Y.), 136*

— L —
L. F. LOREE, 313, 316*, 338, 340*-341*, 343, 345, 404*
Lachine Rapids, 412*
LACKAWANNA, 41, 43*
Lackawanna & Susquehanna Railroad, 65

Lackawanna Valley, 39, 59-62, 318, 360
Lackawaxen (Pa.), 10*-11, 17, 22, 60
Lackawaxen Coal Mine & Navigation Co., 3
Lackawaxen River (and Aqueduct), 1-5, 8*-9*-10*-11*, 18*-19*, 34, 303
Lacolle (Que.), 223, 381*
Laflin (Pa), 303
Lake Champlain, 65-69, 91, 95, 98, 105-106, 109, 115, 135, 137, 140, 142*, 144-145*-146*-148*-149*-151, 154-155*, 170, 173, 177, 185, 190, 194, 198*, 202, 230-235, 245, 247-255, 259, 263-267, 270*, 280-281, 307, 311, 313, 400*
Lake Champlain & Moriah Railroad, 139, 163
Lake Champlain Steamboat Co., 237
Lake Colden (N.Y.), 197
Lake George, 65, 69, 109, 168-169, 173, 177-180*-181 (map), 188, 190, 202-203*, 216, 219, 230-234, 245-248, 250-251, 253-254*-255, 258*-259, 262*, 264*-267*-268*-269*, 280-281, 283, 302, 309, 313, 360, 421*
Lake George (Village, N.Y.), 190, 254*, 257*, 263, 267-269*
Lake George Steamboat Co., 247, 251, 253, 255, 259, 351
Lake George Trust Co., 109
Lake Ontario & Hudson River Railroad, 116
Lake Placid (N.Y.), 161, 167*, 201-202, 351, 355
Lake St. Louis & Province Line Railway, 137
Lake Shore Limited, 201
Lake Station (N.Y.), 106, 144
Lake Winnipesaukee (N.H.), 265
Lansingburgh (N.Y.), 92
Lanesboro (Pa., junction), endpapers*, iv, 60-62, 65, 359
Larabee, Capt. L. C., 242, 245-247
Larabee's Point (Vt.), 140
Latimer, O. K., 242
Laurentian, iv, 304*, 338, 352, 357, 361*-364, 370, 387*, 389*, 394*, 396*, 398*-399*, 402*-403*-404*, 409*, 412*, 416*, 419*, 421*, 428*, 433*
Lee, Robert E., 181
Lehigh & New England Railroad, 347
Lehigh Coal & Navigation Co., 347
Lehigh coal fields, 1
Lehigh Valley Railroad, 205, 287, 303, 305, 307, 309, 323
Leicester Junction (Vt.), 140
Lentz poppet valve, 320, 334
Lewis, Mrs. Russell, 328
Liberty, 233
Liverpool & Manchester Railway, 34-35
Locomotive & Machine Co. of Montreal, Ltd. engines, 225*
Loeb, Will, 197
Lookout Junction (Pa.), 42, 45
Loomis, Luther, 235
Loon Lake (N.Y.), 159*-160, 162*

Loon Lake House, 162
Lord, R. F., 5, 9, 69
Loree Breaker, 298*
Loree, James Tabor, 315, 324, 347
Loree, Leonor F., 228-229, 273, 275*-283, 293, 299, 302-348, 353, 356, 359, 363
Lotbinière & Mégantic Railway, 223
Lyon Mountain (N.Y.), 157-158, 165*, 355

— M —
MacIntyre, Archibald, 115, 123
MacIntyre development, 305
MacIntyre, John, 115, 123
Maine Central Railroad, 373
MAJOR GENERAL HANCOCK, 118-119*, 121*, 126*, 128*, 130*-131*-132*-133*
MAJOR SYKES, 38*, 41
Mallet articulated engines, 318-319*-320, 324, 328, 343, 411*
Maquam, 259-260*-261*, 263
Maquam Bay, 259
Marks Bay (Vt.), 140, 253, 255
Marvel, T. S., Shipbuilding Co., 263
Massachusetts, 103
Massena Springs (N.Y.), 226
McAdoo, William G., 293
McCormick, Cyrus H., 121
McGowan hose wagon, 205
McGrew, J. A., 324
McKinley, William, 185, 190*, 196-199
McMartin, Duncan, 115
McMartin, Malcolm, 115
McNally, Joe, 442
McQuade, General James, 82-83
Mechanicville (N.Y.), 92, 169, 219, 221, 229, 275, 299, 309, 332, 334, 351, 364-365*-368*, 371, 384*, 435*-436*
Merritt-Chapman & Scott, 267
Mesabi Range (Minn.), 138
Mexican Central Railroad, 318
Mexican National Railway, 273
Middle District Branch Bank, 3
Middleburgh (N.Y.), 221
Middleburgh & Schoharie Railroad, 221
Middleport (N.Y.), 13
Milwaukee Road, 328
Mineville (N.Y.), 139, 163
Minne-Ha-Ha, 248*, 250*-255
Minnie, 20*
Minnie, the elephant, 265
MIRROR LAKE, 162*, 165*
Mississippi River, 118, 307
Missouri-Kansas-Texas Railroad, 313
Mogul locomotives, 317
Mohawk & Hudson Railroad, 89-91, 94, 105
Mohawk River (Valley), 89-92, 109, 231-232, 392*
Mohawk Yard, 308*, 377*, 390*, 403*, 443*
Mohican I, 230*, 259, 262
Mohican II, 262-264*, 267, 269
Mongaup (N.Y.), 3-4
Mongaup Lock, 17*
Monongahela River, 9
Montcalm Landing (N.Y.), 145*, 250, 255, 267, 428*
Monthly Plan, 313, 315

Montreal (Que.), 95, 106, 137, 144, 151-153, 169, 171, 185, 221, 223, 226, 234, 247, 255, 280, 287, 297, 303, 304, 318, 334, 338, 359, 364, 370, 394*, 413*
MONTREAL, 105, 126*
Montreal, 243, 245, 249
Montreal & Lachine Railway, 137
Montreal & Plattsburgh Railroad, 137-140, 144, 151, 169, 253
Montreal & Sorel Railway, 224
Montreal Limited, 227*, 352, 353, 359, 363
Montreal West, 395*
Mooers (Junction, N.Y.), 137, 151, 169, 307
Mooney, Paul, 375*, 379*
Moosic Mountains, 1, 5, 31, 41, 45-46*, 54*, 89, 369
Moreau Junction (N.Y.), 226
Morgan, J. Pierpont, 151, 185
Morris, Miller, Baker & Co., 73
Mount Mansfield (Vt.), 261*
Mount Marcy (N.Y.), 115, 196-197
Mount McGregor (N.Y.), 177
Mount Washington, 265
Mountaineer, 245-247, 269*
Muhlfeld, John E., 318, 328, 329, 331
Myers, Frank, 129

— N —
Napierville Junction Railway, 225*, 226, 277, 297, 313, 377*, 383*, 416*
National Lead Co., 353, 355
National Railway Historical Society, 370
National Railway Labor Conference, 369
Neahwa Park, 307
Neponset River, 31
Neversink aqueduct, river, and valley, 1, 4-5, 11, 23
New Jersey Locomotive & Machine Co., 40
New Jersey Midland Railroad, 171
New York & Albany Railroad, 171
New York & Canada Railroad, 142-143-158, 161, 169, 185, 191, 207, 226, 255
New York & Mohawk Valley Railroad, 202
New York & Oswego Midland Railroad, 169
New York Barge Canal, 274*, 402*
New York Central, 67, 71, 76, 90-91, 171, 287, 292, 299, 308*-309, 313, 323, 353, 355, 359, 364, 370
New York Central & Hudson River Railroad, 182, 199, 211
New York, Lake Erie & Western Railway, 17
New York National Guard, 295*
New York, New Haven & Hartford Railroad, 211, 313, 369-370, 373
New York, Ontario & Western Railroad, 13, 195, 347, 351
New York, Pittsburgh & Chicago Railroad, 307
New York State Capitol, 284*, 287
New York State Legislature, 61, 71-73, 91, 97, 101, 105, 142, 281, 287

New York State Library & Museum, 208*
New York State Militia, 82
New York State Public Service Commission, 229, 281, 287, 309, 363
Newburgh (N.Y.), 17, 263
Newcomen Society of North America, 315
Nineveh (N.Y.), 61-62, 65*, 68, 80, 282*, 283, 313, 359, 392
Nickel Plate Railroad, 309, 370
Nicolet River, 223, 226, 275
Norfolk & Western, 370, 373
North Albany (N.Y.), 200*, 209*
North Atlantic Terminal System, 313
North Burlington, 103
North Creek (N.Y.), 69, 120-121*-129, 133*, 196*-199, 312*, 314*, 353-355, 360, 418*
North Elba (N.Y.), 115
North Troy (N.Y.), 92
Northern Coal & Iron Co., 60-62
Northern locomotives, 352*-353, 356, 359, 370*, 394*, 396*, 398*-399*-400*-401*-402*-403*-404*, 409*, 413*, 416*, 428*, 430*
Northern Railroad of New York, 137, 142
Norwich (N.Y.), 169
Noyan Junction (Que.), 223
Nuelle, Joseph H., 347, 351*, 356, 359, 363
Nunnally, Luther, 434*

— O —

Oakes Ames, 140*; (became *Champlain*), 144, 253
O'Brien, John, 157
Occidental Hotel, 17
Ogdensburg (N.Y.), 116, 127
Ogdensburg & Lake Champlain Railroad, 151, 158, 169, 249
Olmsted, G. W., 309
Olyphant (Pa.), 38*-39, 56, 68-69
Olyphant, George Talbot, 59-60*-63, 67, 69, 142, 171, 177
Olyphant, Robert M., 177, 181*, 185, 190-192, 201-202, 351
Oneonta (N.Y.), 64*-65, 71-72*-75, 84*-85*, 173, 177*, 202, 204*, 213, 274, 276, 278*, 279, 281, 283, 287, 291, 298*, 300*-301*, 305*, 307, 317-318, 324, 332*, 334, 341*, 438*
Oneonta & Mohawk Valley, 440*
Orange County Bank, 3
Orange Packet, 5
Otsego County (N.Y.), 71
Penn Central Railroad, 370
Otter Creek (Vt.), 191*
Outerbridge, E. H., 303
Owego (N.Y.), 17, 205

— P —

Pacific Construction Co., 226
Pacific locomotives, *ii, iv*, 318, 324, 325*-326*-329*, 334-335*-336*-337*-339*, 345, 353, 357*, 359, 364, 381*, 387*, 389*, 394*-395*, 404*-405*, 412*-413*, 422*, 431*, 432*
Page, John B., 137, 139-142
Panther Bluffs (Pa.), 193
Paradise Bay (N.Y.), 259

Paupack Eddy, 1
Peckham, Judge, 79-80
Peekskill (N.Y.), 17
Pennsylvania Coal Co., 13, 17, 22-23, 195
Pennsylvania Legislature, 2, 5-6, 59
Pennsylvania Northern Coal & Iron Co., 226
Pennsylvania Railroad, 273, 287, 307, 309, 370
Penrose, Charles, 315
Peoria & Bureau Valley Railroad, 117
Phelps, C. H., 276
Philips, E. L., 309
Phoenix, 237*, 239
Pierreville (Que.), 223
Piggyback freight, 368*-369, 442*
Pilot Knob (N.Y.), 203
Pilsbury, Louis D., 157
Pittston (Pa.), 173
Pittstown (N.Y.), 98
Platt, Moss Kent, 137
Plattsburgh (N.Y.), 130, 137, 140, 142, 144, 147, 151-152*-155*-159, 162, 165, 167, 169, 173, 185, 202, 213-215*, 232-237, 241, 243, 249, 255, 263, 265, 275, 280, 294*, 374*, 400*, 423*
Plattsburgh & Dannemora Railroad, 157-158, 161
Plattsburgh & Montreal Railroad, 137, 139, 153*, 249, 307
Plattsburgh Cornet Band, 153
Plattsburgh Traction Co., 213-214*-215*, 287, 307
Plaza, The (Albany), 283-284*-285*-286*-287
Plumadore (N.Y.), 355
Plymouth (Pa.), 60, 226, 287
Plymouth & Wilkes-Barre Railroad & Bridge Co., 60
Poppet valves, 328, 334, 336-337*-338, 341*, 343, 345
Port Griffith (Pa.), 13
Port Henry (N.Y.), 135, 137, 139-140, 147-151, 153, 163, 170*, 172*
Port Jervis (N.Y.), 1-2, 5, 11, 15, 22, 26
Port Kent (N.Y.), 163, 237, 249, 260*, 265, 378*, 381*, 396*, 400*, 418*
Point of Rocks (N.Y.), 137
Pottersville (N.Y.), 125
Poughkeepsie & Eastern Railroad, 113
Poultney (Vt.), 101, 103
Price, Edward V., 249
Princeton University, 6
Prompton (Pa.), 36
Prospect Mountain (N.Y.), 256*
Providence (Pa.), 39, 41
Pruyn, Robert H., 79-80
Putnam station (N.Y.), 194*
Putts Creek (N.Y.), 141*

— Q —

Quebec (Que.), 219, 223, 226, 231-232, 275
Quebec & Lake St. John Railway, 223
Quebec bridge, 223, 275, 309
Quebec, Montreal & Southern Railway, 219, 221, 223-225*, 226, 275, 277, 297, 309

Quebec Southern Railway, 223
Queen Victoria, 153
Quincy (Mass.), 31

— R —

Racket Brook Breaker, 50*-51*
Railroad Gazette, 129
Rainhill trials, 35
Ramsey, Joseph H., 63, 74-83
Raquette Lake (N.Y.), 125
Reading Railroad, 307, 324
"Red Edge" stokers, 315, 320, 351, 392
Red Rocks, 134*, 146*, 148*, 156*, 396*
Rensselaer (N.Y.), 207, 306-307
Rennselaer & Saratoga Railroad, 65-69, 88, 91-113, 118, 137, 142, 144, 173, 177, 202, 247, 251, 253, 283, 355, 364, 433*, 436*-437*
Republic Steel Co., 170, 351
Reynolds, Marcus T., 283
Richards, Abraham and wife, 45, 47
Richards, Catherine Hudson, 47*
Richards, Dinah Delaware, 47*
Richelieu River, 231, 234, 247
Richmondville (N.Y., hill, summit), 72*, 173-174, 293, 299, 358, 362*, 366, 368*, 380*, 386*, 433*
Rio Grande railroad, see Denver & Rio Grande Western
Ripley's Point (N.Y.), 254*
Riverside (N.Y.), 125-126*, 133*
Rix's Gap (Pa.), 5-6, 31, 46*, 54*
Roanoke (Va.), 370, 373
Robinson, Don, 385*
Robinson, Nelson, 247, 251
Rochester (N.Y.), 62, 83
Rock Island Railroad, 117
ROCKET, 34-35, 334
Rockefeller, John D., 185
Roebling, John, 9-13, 37
Rogers (N.Y.), 137
Rogers Rock (N.Y.), 259
Rogers Rock Hotel, 262
Roller bearings, 328-329*, 343, 345
Rome (N.Y.), 169
Rome & Clinton Railroad, 169, 351
Rondout (N.Y.), 5, 13, 28, 34-35, 65, 170, 193, 195
Rondout Creek, 1, 3-5, 8, 11, 24*-25*
Roosevelt, Franklin D., 315, 353
Roosevelt, Theodore, 196*-199
Root, Elijah, 238, 253
Rose, C. O., 7*
Rosendale (N.Y.), 24*, 195
Round Lake (N.Y.), 433*
Rouses Point (N.Y.), 142*, 144, 151, 153-154, 169, 171*, 223, 226, 231, 247, 249, 255, 275, 277*, 297, 303, 304*-307, 309-310*, 351, 359, 363, 364, 383*, 389*, 398*, 401*, 417*
Rushlow, Captain, 255
Rutgers University, 273
Rutland (Vt.), 98, 101-106, 191, 222, 300, 307
Rutland & Burlington Railroad, 106, 109, 137, 247, 249
Rutland & Washington (Railroad, branch), 68*, 98, 100-103, 106-108*-109, 222, 275, 408*

Rutland & Whitehall Railroad, 101, 105, 109
Rutland Railroad, 135, 139-140, 142, 190-191, 253, 422*
R. W. Sherman, 249, 251

— S —

Sacandaga River, 128*, 130*, 354*
Sackets Harbor (N.Y.), 116, 127, 353
Sackets Harbor & Saratoga Railroad, 116-119
Sagamore, 203*, 230*, 254*, 259*, 262*-264*-266*-268*-269*
Sagamore Hotel, 266*
St. Albans (Vt.), 140, 247, 259
St. Albans Bay, 237
St. Constant (Que.), 226
St. Francis River, 223
St. Gregoire (Que.), 223
St. Hyacinthe (Que.), 223
St. Jean des Chaillons (Que.), 223
St. Johns (Quebec), 144, 154, 226, 233-234, 237, 239, 241, 243, 247
St. Johns & Montreal Railway, 154
St. Johnsbury & Lake Champlain Railroad, 259
St. Lambert (Que.), 221, 223, 226
St. Lawrence River, 221, 223, 231, 275, 309, 412*
St. Louis & San Francisco, 273
St. Louis Car Co., 206*
St. Louis Exposition (1904), 318
St. Louis Southwestern, 313
St. Philomène (Que.), 223
ST. REGIS, 159*, 167*
St. Robert (Que.), 223
Salem (N.Y.), 101, 103, 108*, 191, 221, 222*, 275, 300*-301
Sand Patch, 318, 328
Sandy Hill (N.Y.), 105
Sanford Lake, 116, 353-355
Sans Souci Hotel, 92
Saranac, 241*, 243, 245, 247, 249
Saranac & Lake Placid Railway, 161, 167
Saranac Lake, 160*, 190*, 278*, 355
SARATOGA, 151, 210*
SARATOGA (inspection engine), 274*
Saratoga & Schenectady Railroad, 65, 69, 90-92, 95, 98, 105-106, 363-364
Saratoga Springs (N.Y.), 65, 68-69, 90-95*-96*-97*-98, 105-106, 114*-119*-120, 125, 129-130, 151, 171, 177, 181*-182*-184*-186*-187*-188, 197-201, 206*-207, 211-213, 219, 226, 228-229, 265, 277*, 302, 309, 315, 358*, 360-361*, 363, 364, 399*
Saranac River, Valley, 157, 159*
Saratoga & Fort Edward Railroad, 105
Saratoga & Washington Railroad, 101, 103, 105-106, 247
Saratoga & Whitehall Railroad, 105-106, 109
Saratoga Limited, 198*-201, 213
Saratoga, Mount McGregor & Lake George, 181*-182*
Sartwell, Zebadiah, 135, 147, 154, 157

475

Sault Sainte Marie (Ont., Mich.), 231
Schaghticoke (N.Y.), 98
Schenectady (N.Y.), 69, 89-91, 94-95, 169, 190, 206*-207, 212, 308, 320, 328, 349*, 352*, 354, 364, 391*, 443*
Schnectady & Duanesburgh Railroad, 202
Schenectady Railway, 198*, 205-206*-207, 216*-217*, 226-227, 229*, 287, 309
Schenevus (N.Y.), 293, 299, 334, 366
Schoharie (N.Y., junction), 221, 225, 293, 299, 324, 327, 331
Schoharie Valley Railroad, 203, 219, 221, 225*, 351
Schoonmaker, Horace B., 26*-27
Schroon Lake (N.Y.), 69, 125*, 127, 162
Schuylerville (N.Y.), 219, 309
Schuylkill Canal, 1
Scotia (N.Y.), 91
Scullen, Steve, 355
Seeleyville (Pa.), 34
Scranton (Pa.), 39-47, 55*, 60, 62, 69, 173, 176-177, 282, 290, 303, 305*
Severson House, 86*
Seward (N.Y.), 87*
Shawangunk Mountains, 2
Shelburne (Bay, Harbor) (Vt.), 237, 241, 243, 248-249, 255, 258*-259, 263, 265, 267
Shelburne Museum, 267, 270-271*
Shelving Rock Mountain (N.Y.), 268*
Shepherd's Crook, 41-43*-46*, 56*, 193
Sherman, Capt. Jahaziel, 234, 237
Sherman, Capt. Richard W., 236-237, 239, 241, 243, 245, 247
Shinglekill Creek, 25
Sidney (N.Y.), 274*, 276*, 393*
Silver Bay (N.Y.), 203, 262*, 266*
Skeels, Elliott, 45
Skene, Major Philip, 233
Skenesborough (N.Y.), 233
Smith, J. Gregory, 140-142
Slocum Hollow (Pa.), 45
Smith, Judge E. Darwin, 83
Smithsonian Institution, 34
Smoke lifters, 325*, 338-339*, 352*-353, 378*, 394*
Sorel (Que.), 221, 223
South Buffalo Railway, 360
South Canaan (Pa.), 193
South Corinth (N.Y.), 118
South Glens Falls (N.Y.), 226
South Hero Island (Vt.), 261*
South Shore Railway, 223
South Junction (N.Y.), 161, 202, 359, 422*
South Schenectady (N.Y.), 390*
South Wilkes-Barre (Pa.), 226
Southern New York Railway, 440*
Southern Railway, 293
Sparrow, Messrs, W. & I., 34
"Splinter fleet," 350*, 353
Standish (N.Y.), 158*, 160
Starrucca (Pa.), endpapers*, iv, 279*, 289*, 346*-347*, 414*, 435*
State of Ohio, 255
Station House Hotel, 142*
Steam Mill Point (N.Y.), 255

Stephenson, George, 34-35, 334
Stephenson, Robert, & Co., 34, 90-91
Stephenson link motion, 320
Stoddard, Seneca Ray, 107*, 121, 126-130*-136, 141-148, 157, 250
Stony Creek, 123, 128*, 131*
STOURBRIDGE LION, 32*-33*-35, 37, 59, 90, 303, 317, 328, 342*-343, 356, 366
Sullivan, Col. John L., 31
Summitville (N.Y.), 3
Superior, 5
Susquehanna (Pa.), 60-62, 65, 71-75
Susquehanna River (valley), 13, 60, 62, 276*, 282*, 292, 314*, 351, 393*
Swanton (Vt.), 259

— T —
Tahawas Club (N.Y.), 196-197
Tender booster, 324, 326*-327*, 331, 334, 341*, 343, 345
Ten-Wheeler locomotives, 325*, 395*, 397*, 421*
Thompson (Pa.), 348*, 439*
Thompson, Dyer, 115
Thomson (N.Y.), 219*, 221
Three Rivers (Que.), 223
Thurman (N.Y.), 123, 226
Ticonderoga (N.Y.), 139-140, 145, 147, 169, 173, 231-233, 247, 255, 263, 428*
Ticonderoga (Lake George, 1883), 259
Ticonderoga (Lake Champlain, 1906), 230*, 263, 265, 267, 270*-271*
Tisdale, Captain H. G., 241, 243
Titanium ore, 353, 354*-355
Toleration, 5
Tongue Mountain (N.Y.), 267*-268*-269
Tontine Coffee House, xii*, 1, 3, 283
TRANSIT, 174*, 188*, 210
Transportation Act, 297, 299
Tripler, 3
Troy (N.Y.), 65, 68-69, 89, 91-93*-97, 100-103, 106, 109, 190-191, 199, 205, 207, 209*-211, 217, 222, 234, 245, 247, 300, 303, 334, 359
Troy & Boston Railroad, 97, 101, 103, 109
Troy & Greenbush Railroad, 97
Troy & New England Railway, 207, 210*, 211, 287, 307
Troy & Rutland Railroad, 98, 101, 103
Troy & Schenectady Railroad, 97
Troy City Railway Co., 207
Troy fire, 97-99*, 100
Troy House, 94*
Troy, Salem & Rutland Railroad, 103, 109
Troy Union Railroad, 97-98
Troy Union Station, 97-99*-100*, 104*-105, 113*
Tunnels: Addison Junction, 147; Belden Hill, 81-83; Red Rocks (Willsboro Bay), 134*, 147, 149*, 157, 369, 413*; Whitehall, 144
Tupper, Capt. L. H., 251
Tuttle, Charles, 119

— U —
Unadilla (N.Y.), 61, 282, 314*, 391*
Underwood, Levi, 139
Uniflow cylinders, 338
Union Pacific Railroad, 117-119, 121
Union Coal Co., 60
Union Village & Johnsville Railroad, 219
United Counties Railway, 223
United States, 240*, 245-246*-255, 353, 355
United States Hotel, 69, 95*, 185, 187*.
United States Labor Board, 299
United States Railroad Administration, 293, 297, 299, 320, 353
United Traction Co., 205, 207 (map), 208*-209*, 213*, 286*-287, 299, 303, 309
Utica & Schenectady Railroad, 91
Utica, Clinton & Binghamton, 169, 351

— V —
Valcour (N.Y.), 233, 359
Valley Junction (Pa.), 38*-40*, 59-60, 69
Van Buren, Martin, 239
Van Inwegen, Moses, 29
Van Santvoord, Alfred, 74
Van Valkenburgh, J. W., 79-83
Van Wagner, S. R., Store, 20*
Vanderbilt, Cornelius, 67, 76, 151, 185, 303
Vanderbilt, William H., 151, 185, 186
Vergennes (Vt.), 147
Vermont I, 233-234, 247
Vermont II, 250*-252*-253, 255, 258*-260*-261*, 263
Vermont III, 230*, 263, 265
Vermont Central Railroad, 137, 140, 142, 144, 247, 253
Viault, Don, 367*
Vibbard, Chauncey, 117
Victoria Bridge, 221, 226, 297
Villa, Pancho, 295

— W —
Wabash Railroad, 307, 309, 370
Wagner Palace Cars, 69, 125, 151, 180*, 185, 199-201
Walschaert, Egide, 318
Walschaert valve gear, 317-320, 330*, 332*-336*-337*-338
Ward Saloon, 104*
Warnerville (N.Y.), 362*
Warren, Stephen, 91, 105
Warrensburg (N.Y.), 120, 123, 219, 226, 309
Water-tube boiler, 331, 333*
Waterford (N.Y., Junction), 91-93, 98, 101, 106, 109, 207, 209, 219, 274*, 303, 304, 373, 426*, 436*
Watervliet (N.Y., Arsenal), 93, 98, 206-207, 278, 281, 315
Watervliet Turnpike & Railway Co., 207
Waymart (Pa.), 36-37, 39, 41-42, 45, 193
Weed, Smith M., 142, 153, 158, 161, 190*
Weehauken (N.J.), 62, 192
Welded boiler, 344*-345, 355
Wells Bridge (N.Y.), 63*
West Albany (N.Y.), 299
West Carbondale, 361
West Chazy (N.Y.), 169

West Oneonta (N.Y.), 440*
West Orange (N.J.), 283, 353
West Rutland (Vt.), 68*, 100*
West Shore Railroad, 171
West Troy (N.Y.), 66*, 98, 109
West Virginia Pulp & Paper Co., 436*
West Waterford (N.Y.), ii, iv, 349*, 387*, 402*, 419*, 429*
Westbrookville, 29
Western Maryland Railroad, 313, 324
Western Union Telegraph Co., 17
Western Vermont Railroad, 103
Weston, C. S., 303
Westport (N.Y.), 213, 255, 263, 294*, 431*
Whallonsburgh (N.Y.), 135, 147, 153-154
Wharton, Edith, 185
Wheeling & Lake Erie Railroad, 307, 309
White, Capt. F. G., 259
White Oak Run (Pa.), 39
White, William, 359-360*, 364, 369
Whitehall (N.Y.), 65, 68-69, 95, 98, 101, 104-106, 109, 137, 142, 143*-147, 151, 185, 190, 221-222, 233-234, 237-240*-248*-249, 309-310, 313, 350, 399*, 403*-404*, 408*, 412*, 423*, 432*
Whitehall, 239-244*-249, 255
Whitehall & Plattsburgh Railroad, 137, 139-140, 142, 144, 147-148
Wilber, Mrs. William, 45
Wilkes-Barre (Pa.), 60-61, 287, 305-310, 364, 367
Wilkes-Barre Connecting Railroad, 287
Willcox, David, 201*-202, 205, 207, 213, 226-228, 273, 275, 283, 287, 309, 351
William Caldwell, 242*, 247, 251
William Henry Hotel, see Fort William Henry Hotel
Willsboro (N.Y.), 147, 418*
Willsboro Bay, 134, 137, 146*, 156*-157, 198*, 396*
Wilson, Woodrow, 293
Wilton (N.Y.), 130, 184, 229
Winans, John and James, 233-235
Windsor (N.Y.), 313
Windsor Station, 297, 357*, 394*, 413*
Winooski River, 231
Winooski, 241, 243
Witherbee, Sherman & Co., 170*
Wolf Creek (N.Y.), 118, 120
Wolverhampton (England), 34
Woodlawn (funeral car), 182*
Woodworth, Charles J. 173, 307
Wooley, J. S., 216*-217
Worcester (Mass.), 118
Worcester (N.Y.), 293, 306*, 441*
Wooton firebox, 317
Wright, Benjamin, 1-3, 31
Wurts, John, 6*, 59
Wurts, Maurice, 1-2*-3, 6, 29
Wurts, William, 1-2*-3, 6
Wurtsboro (N.Y.), 3, 26*
Wyoming Coal Association, 13
Wyoming Valley, 60

— Y —
Young, Coe. F., 7*
Young valve gear, 331
Young, Robert R., 359

www.ingramcontent.com/pod-product-compliance
Lightning Source LLC
Chambersburg PA
CBHW040749020526
44116CB00037B/2980